Princess Jellyfish 06

Akiko Higashimura

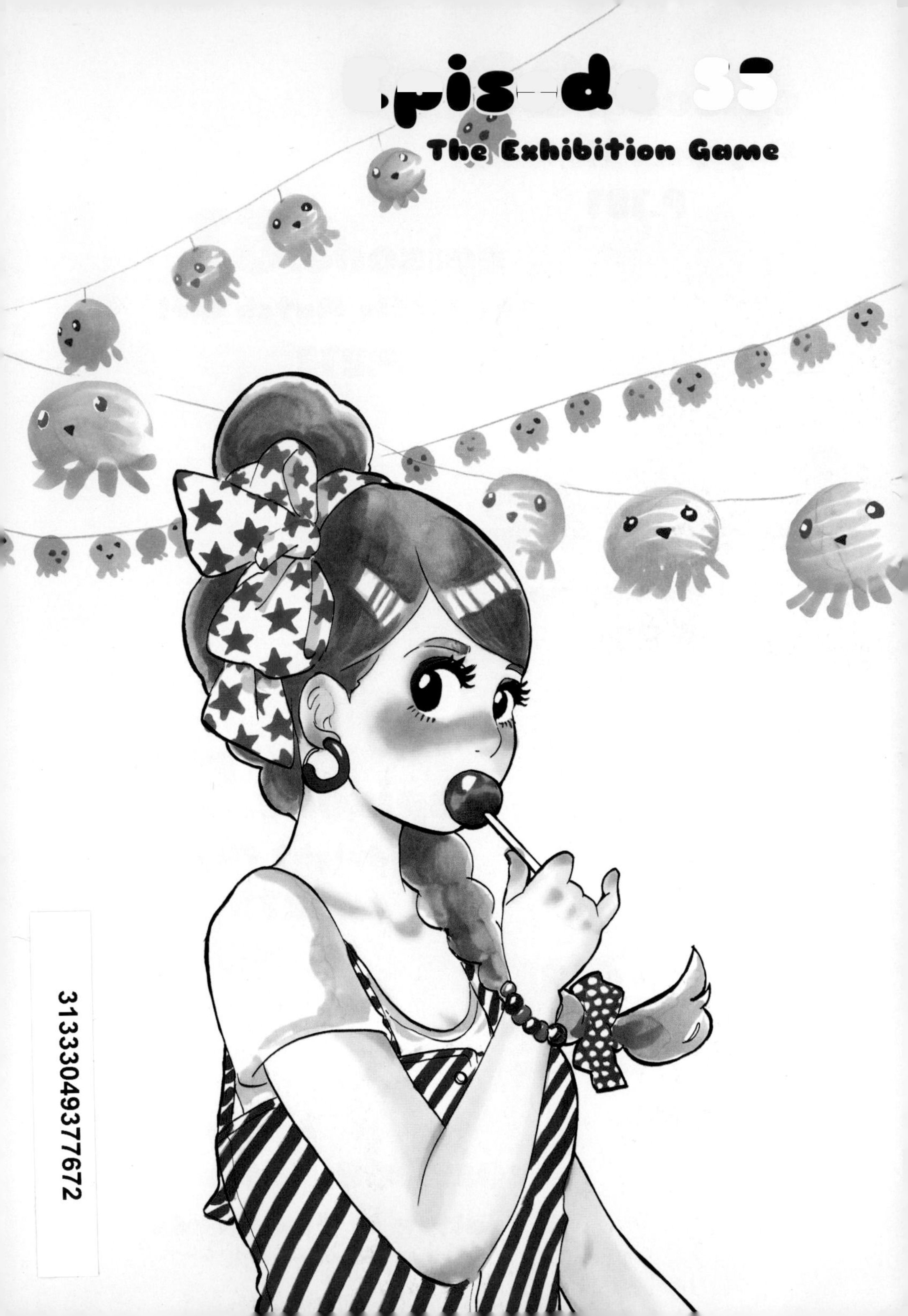
The Exhibition Game

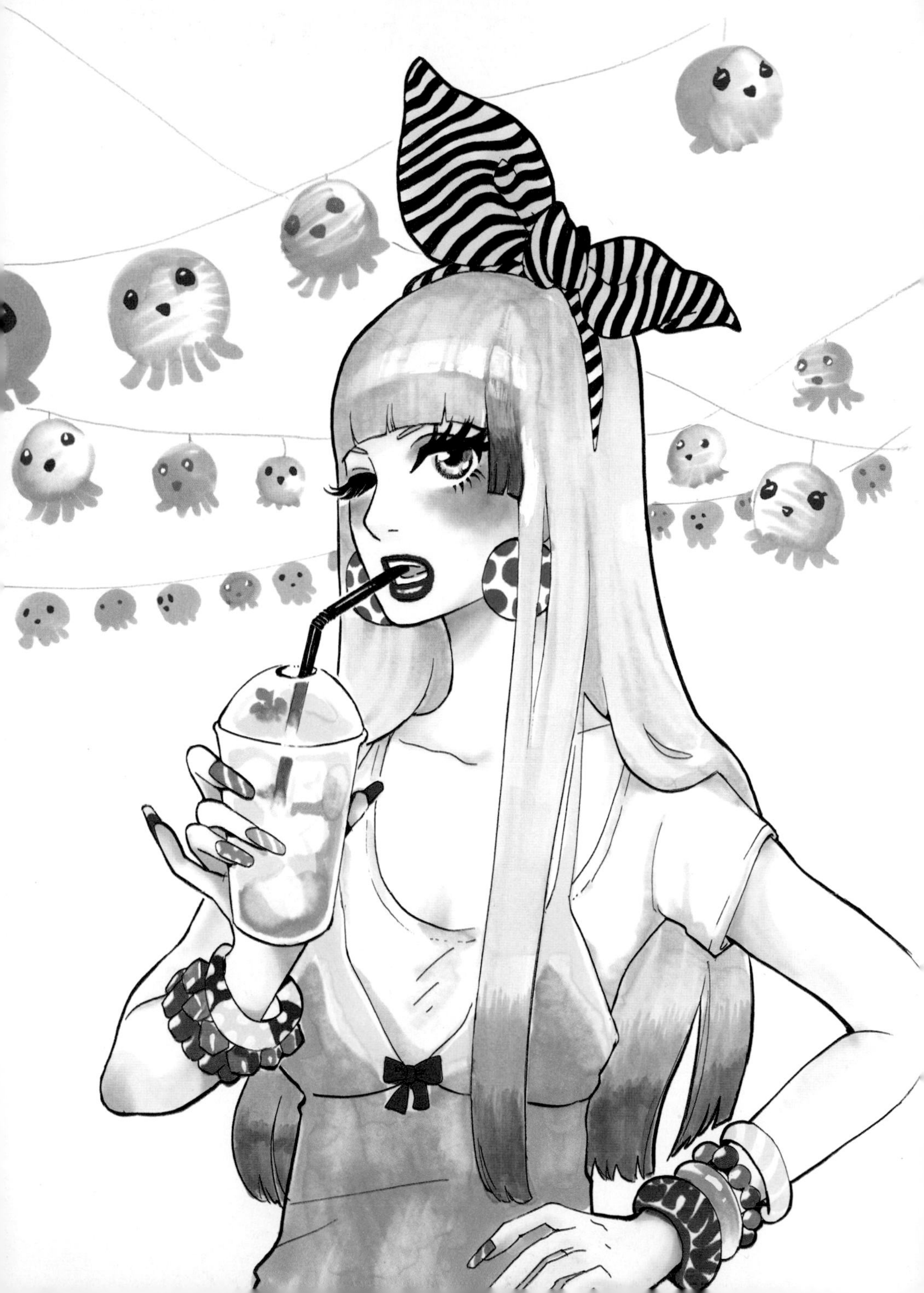

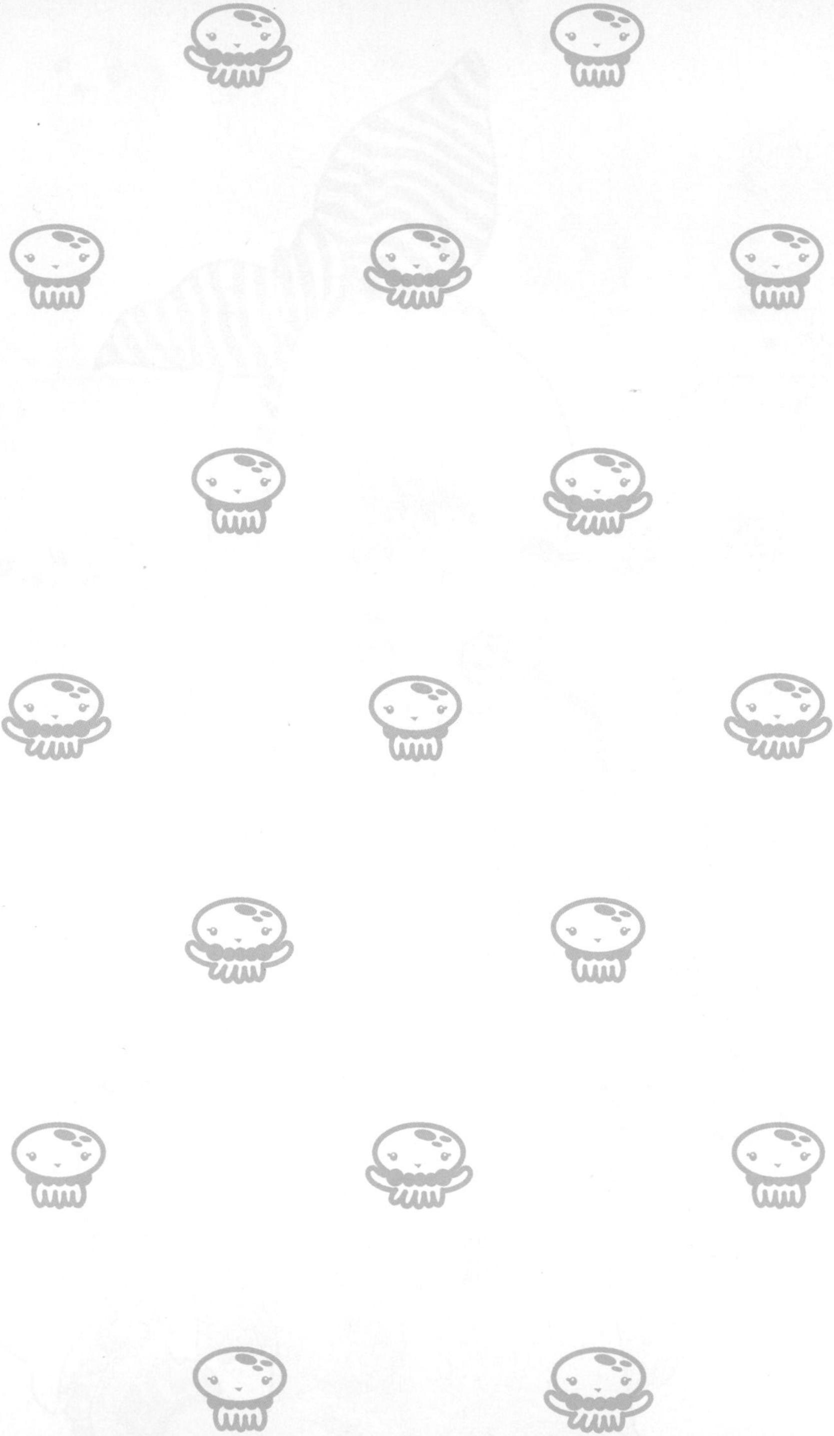

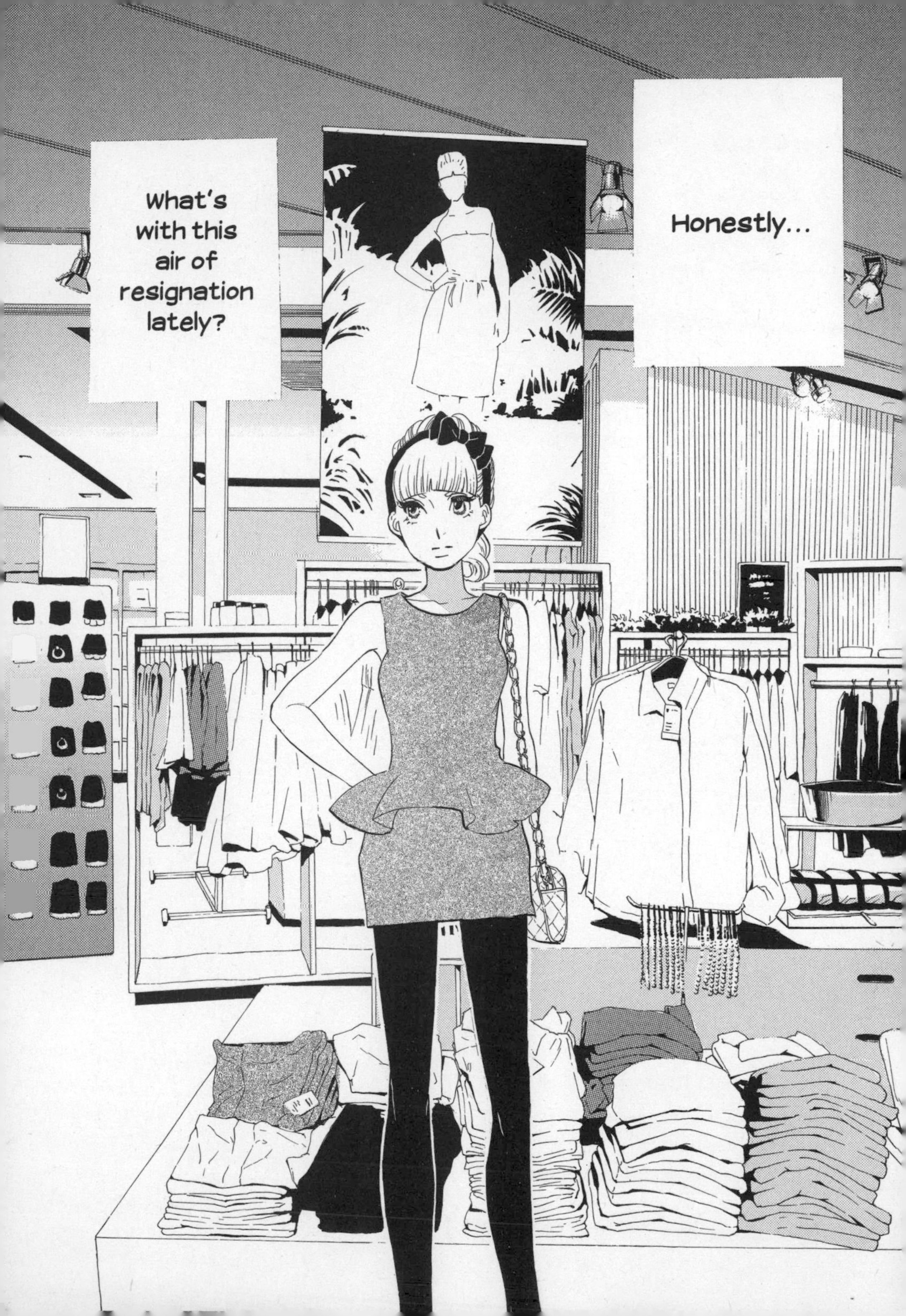
Honestly...
What's with this air of resignation lately?

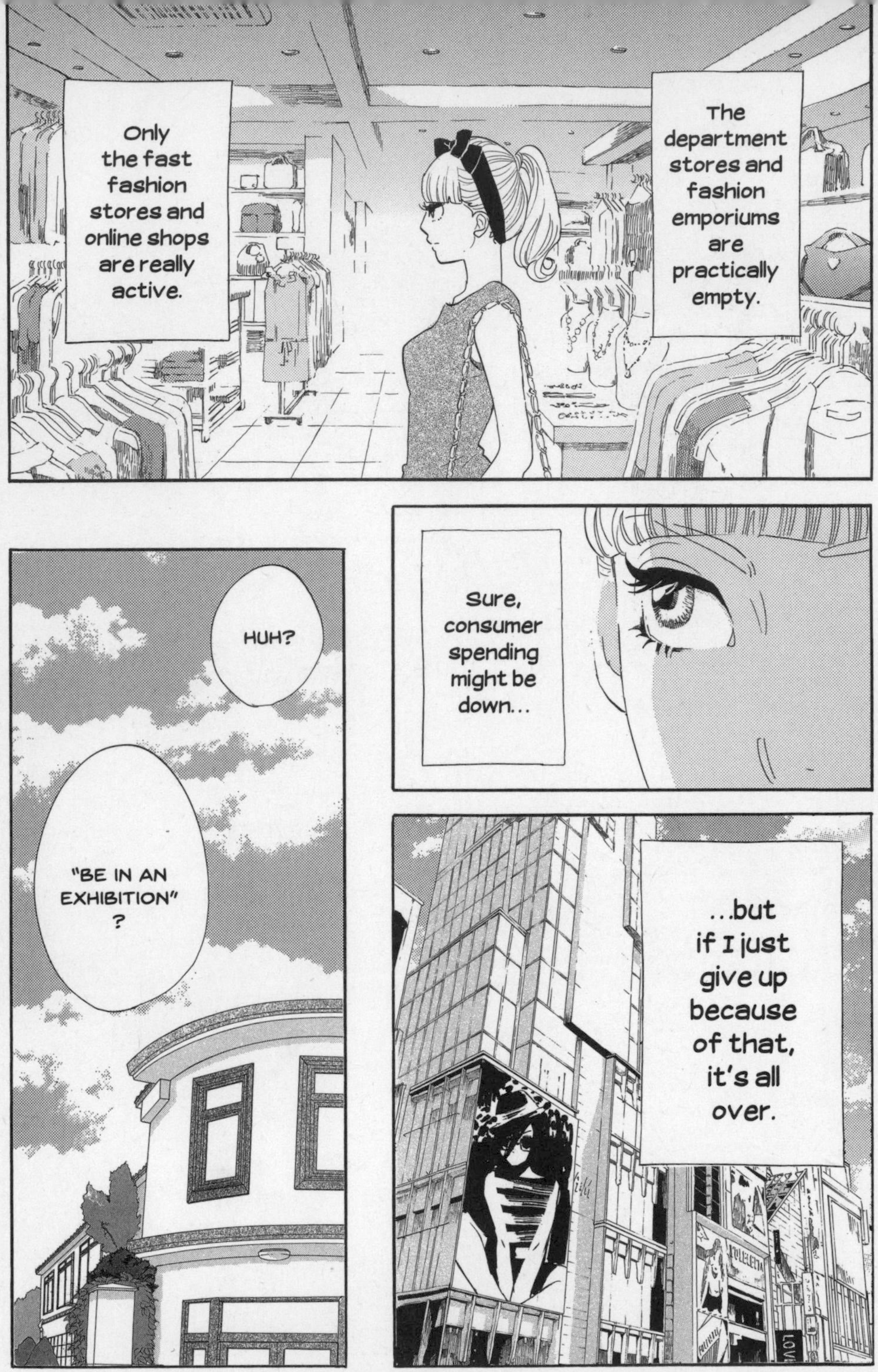
The department stores and fashion emporiums are practically empty.
Only the fast fashion stores and online shops are really active.
Sure, consumer spending might be down...
...but if I just give up because of that, it's all over.
HUH?
"BE IN AN EXHIBITION"?

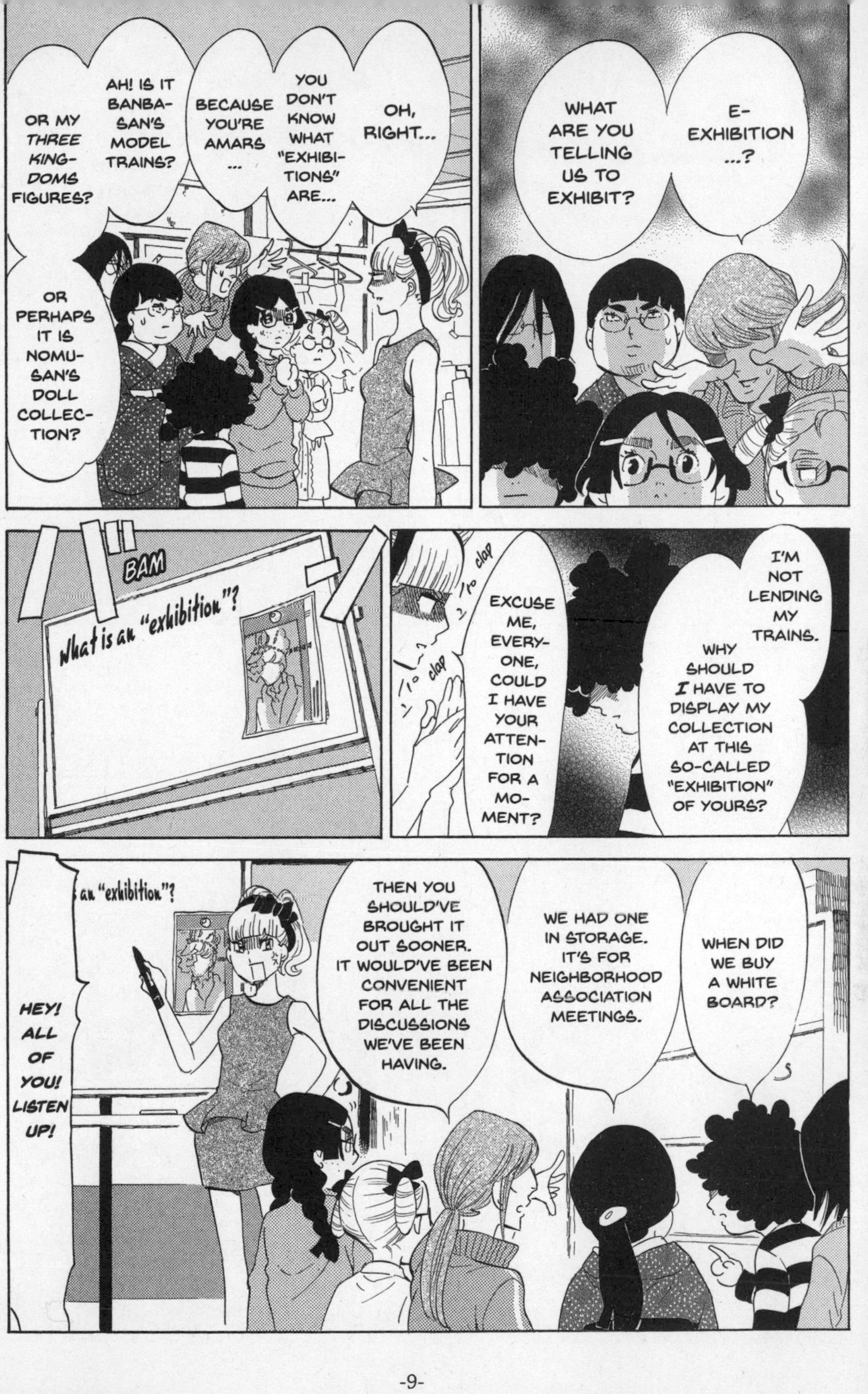
E-EXHIBITION ...?
WHAT ARE YOU TELLING US TO EXHIBIT?
OH, RIGHT...
YOU DON'T KNOW WHAT "EXHIBITIONS" ARE...
BECAUSE YOU'RE AMARS ...
AH! IS IT BANBA-SAN'S MODEL TRAINS?
OR MY *THREE KINGDOMS* FIGURES?
OR PERHAPS IT IS NOMU-SAN'S DOLL COLLECTION?
I'M NOT LENDING MY TRAINS.
WHY SHOULD *I* HAVE TO DISPLAY MY COLLECTION AT THIS SO-CALLED "EXHIBITION" OF YOURS?
clap
clap
EXCUSE ME, EVERYONE, COULD I HAVE YOUR ATTENTION FOR A MOMENT?
BAM
What is an "exhibition"?
WHEN DID WE BUY A WHITE BOARD?
WE HAD ONE IN STORAGE. IT'S FOR NEIGHBORHOOD ASSOCIATION MEETINGS.
THEN YOU SHOULD'VE BROUGHT IT OUT SOONER. IT WOULD'VE BEEN CONVENIENT FOR ALL THE DISCUSSIONS WE'VE BEEN HAVING.
an "exhibition"?
HEY! ALL OF YOU! LISTEN UP!

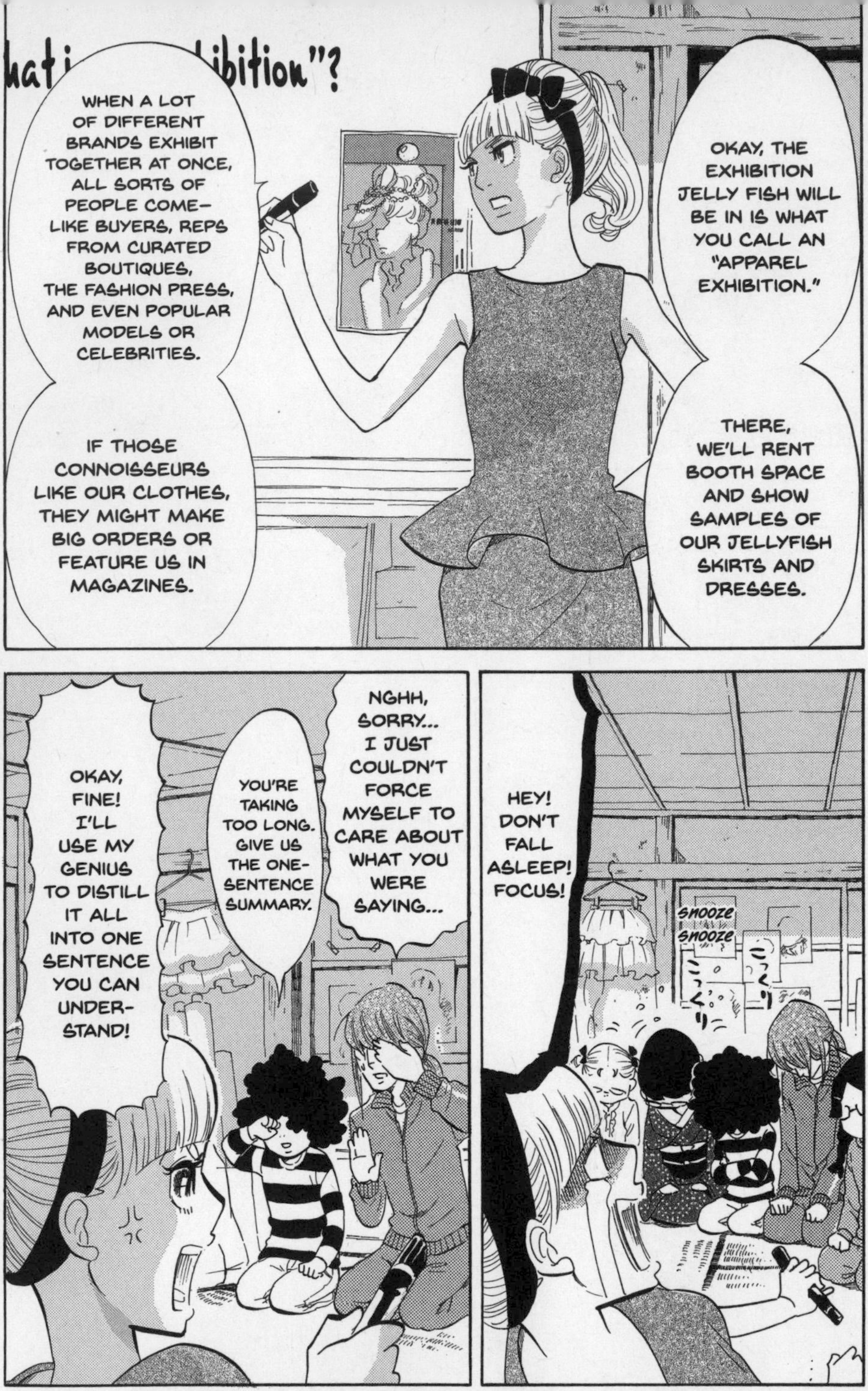
hat i ibition"?
OKAY, THE EXHIBITION JELLY FISH WILL BE IN IS WHAT YOU CALL AN "APPAREL EXHIBITION."
THERE, WE'LL RENT BOOTH SPACE AND SHOW SAMPLES OF OUR JELLYFISH SKIRTS AND DRESSES.
WHEN A LOT OF DIFFERENT BRANDS EXHIBIT TOGETHER AT ONCE, ALL SORTS OF PEOPLE COME– LIKE BUYERS, REPS FROM CURATED BOUTIQUES, THE FASHION PRESS, AND EVEN POPULAR MODELS OR CELEBRITIES.
IF THOSE CONNOISSEURS LIKE OUR CLOTHES, THEY MIGHT MAKE BIG ORDERS OR FEATURE US IN MAGAZINES.
HEY! DON'T FALL ASLEEP! FOCUS!
Snooze Snooze
NGHH, SORRY... I JUST COULDN'T FORCE MYSELF TO CARE ABOUT WHAT YOU WERE SAYING...
YOU'RE TAKING TOO LONG. GIVE US THE ONE-SENTENCE SUMMARY.
OKAY, FINE! I'LL USE MY GENIUS TO DISTILL IT ALL INTO ONE SENTENCE YOU CAN UNDER-STAND!

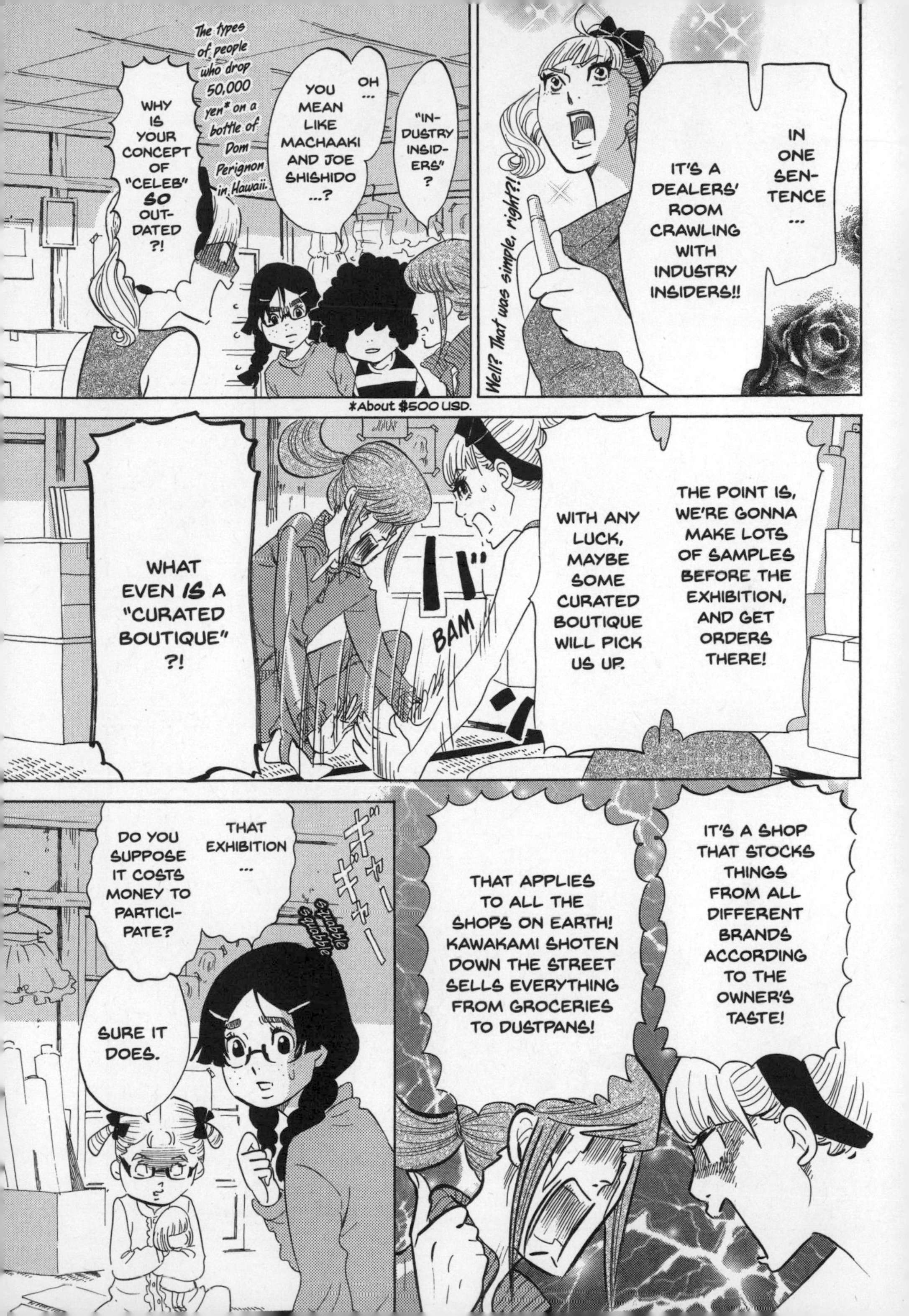
IN ONE SENTENCE...
IT'S A DEALERS' ROOM CRAWLING WITH INDUSTRY INSIDERS!!
Well? That was simple, right?!
"INDUSTRY INSIDERS"?
OH...
YOU MEAN LIKE MACHAAKI AND JOE SHISHIDO...?
The types of people who drop 50,000 yen* on a bottle of Dom Perignon in Hawaii.
WHY IS YOUR CONCEPT OF "CELEB" SO OUTDATED?!
*About $500 USD.
THE POINT IS, WE'RE GONNA MAKE LOTS OF SAMPLES BEFORE THE EXHIBITION, AND GET ORDERS THERE!
WITH ANY LUCK, MAYBE SOME CURATED BOUTIQUE WILL PICK US UP.
BAM
WHAT EVEN IS A "CURATED BOUTIQUE"?!
IT'S A SHOP THAT STOCKS THINGS FROM ALL DIFFERENT BRANDS ACCORDING TO THE OWNER'S TASTE!
THAT APPLIES TO ALL THE SHOPS ON EARTH! KAWAKAMI SHOTEN DOWN THE STREET SELLS EVERYTHING FROM GROCERIES TO DUSTPANS!
ギャーギャー
squabble squabble
THAT EXHIBITION...
DO YOU SUPPOSE IT COSTS MONEY TO PARTICIPATE?
SURE IT DOES.

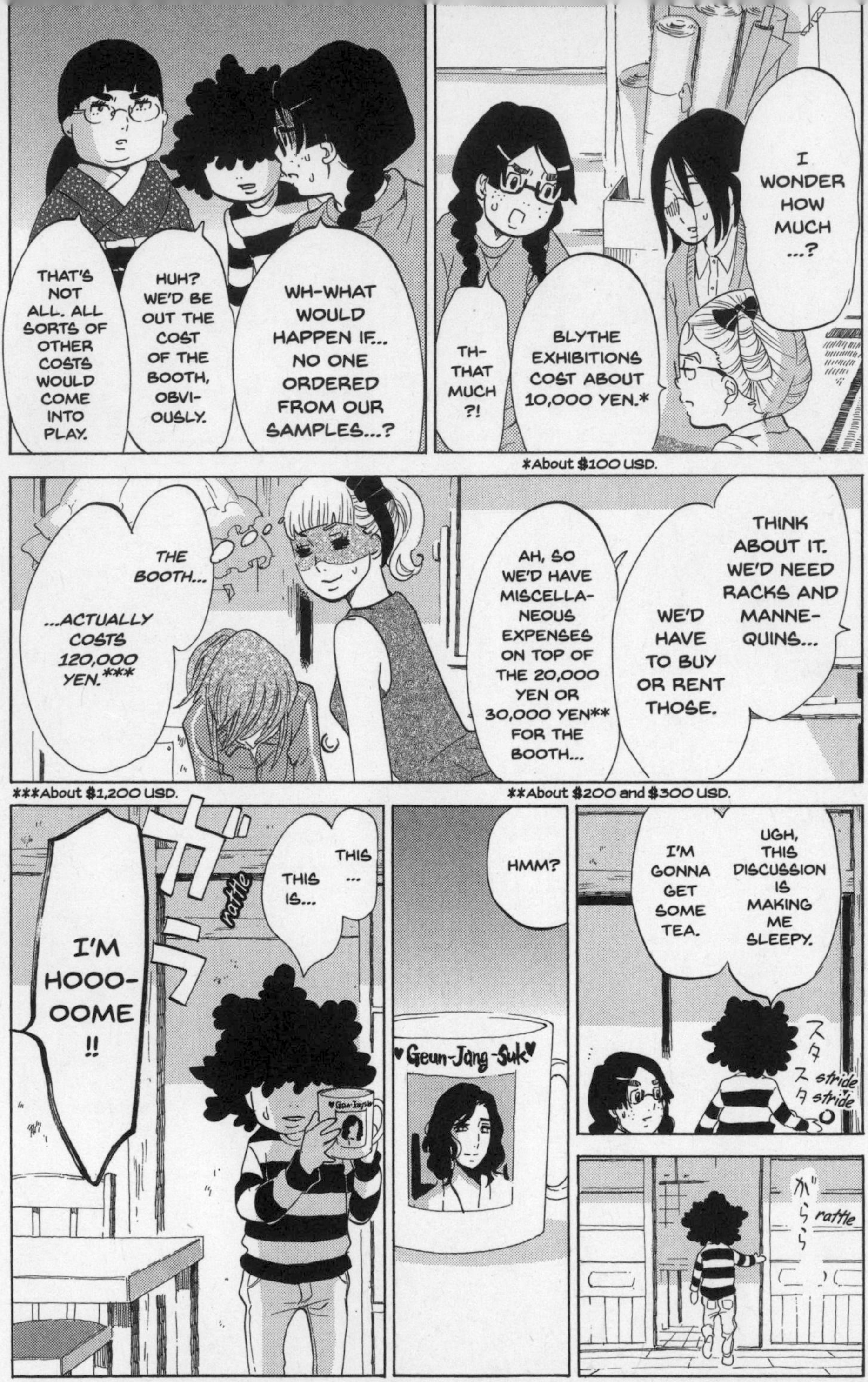
I WONDER HOW MUCH ...?
BLYTHE EXHIBITIONS COST ABOUT 10,000 YEN.*
TH-THAT MUCH ?!
WH-WHAT WOULD HAPPEN IF... NO ONE ORDERED FROM OUR SAMPLES...?
HUH? WE'D BE OUT THE COST OF THE BOOTH, OBVIOUSLY.
THAT'S NOT ALL. ALL SORTS OF OTHER COSTS WOULD COME INTO PLAY.
THINK ABOUT IT. WE'D NEED RACKS AND MANNEQUINS...
WE'D HAVE TO BUY OR RENT THOSE.
AH, SO WE'D HAVE MISCELLANEOUS EXPENSES ON TOP OF THE 20,000 YEN OR 30,000 YEN** FOR THE BOOTH...
THE BOOTH...
...ACTUALLY COSTS 120,000 YEN.***
UGH, THIS DISCUSSION IS MAKING ME SLEEPY.
I'M GONNA GET SOME TEA.
スタスタ stride stride
がらら rattle
HMM?
♥Geun-Jang-Suk♥
THIS ...
THIS IS...
rattle
I'M HOOOO-OOME !!

*About $100 USD.

**About $200 and $300 USD.

***About $1,200 USD.

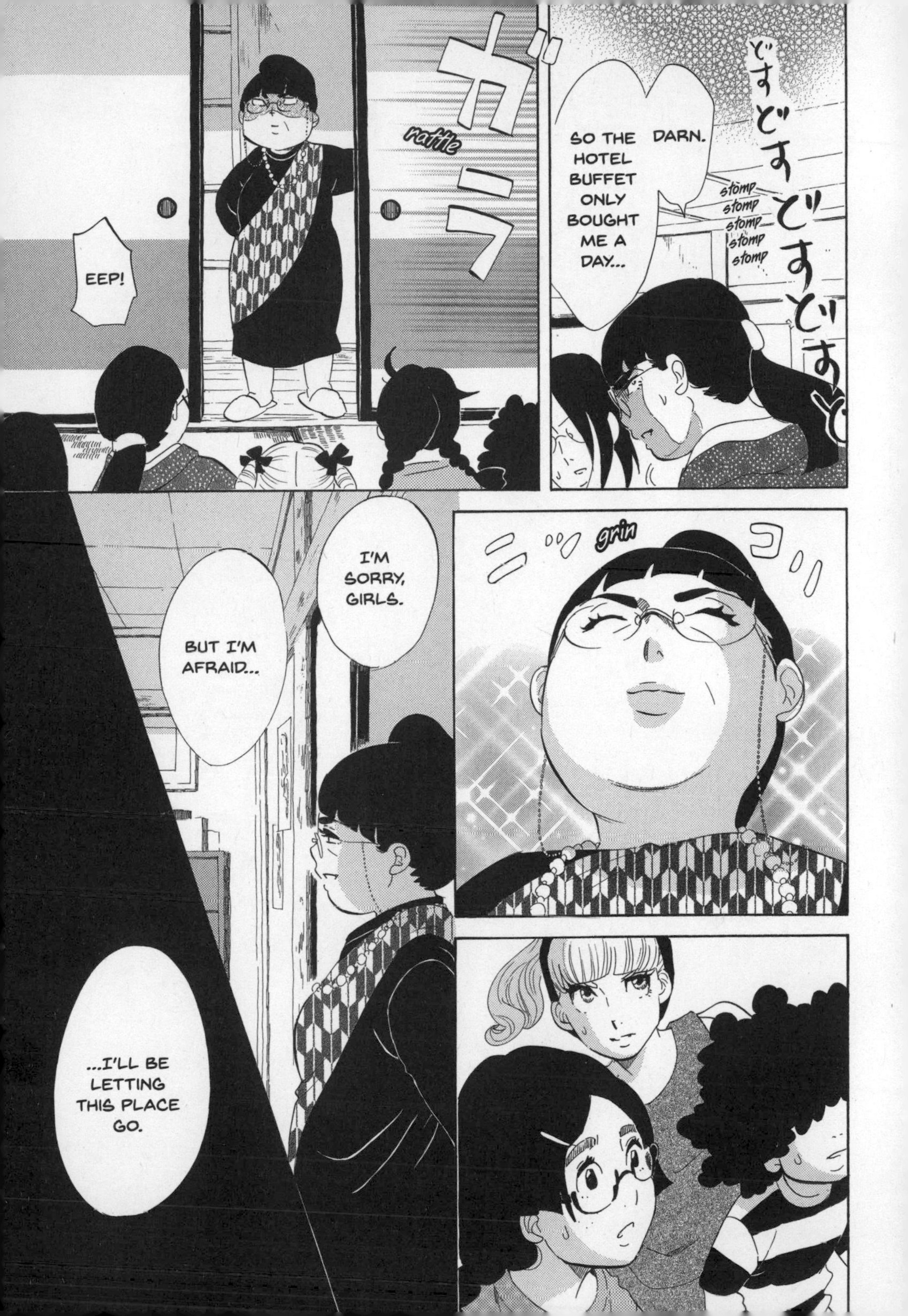

stomp stomp stomp stomp stomp
DARN.
SO THE HOTEL BUFFET ONLY BOUGHT ME A DAY...
rattle
EEP!
grin
I'M SORRY, GIRLS.
BUT I'M AFRAID...
...I'LL BE LETTING THIS PLACE GO.

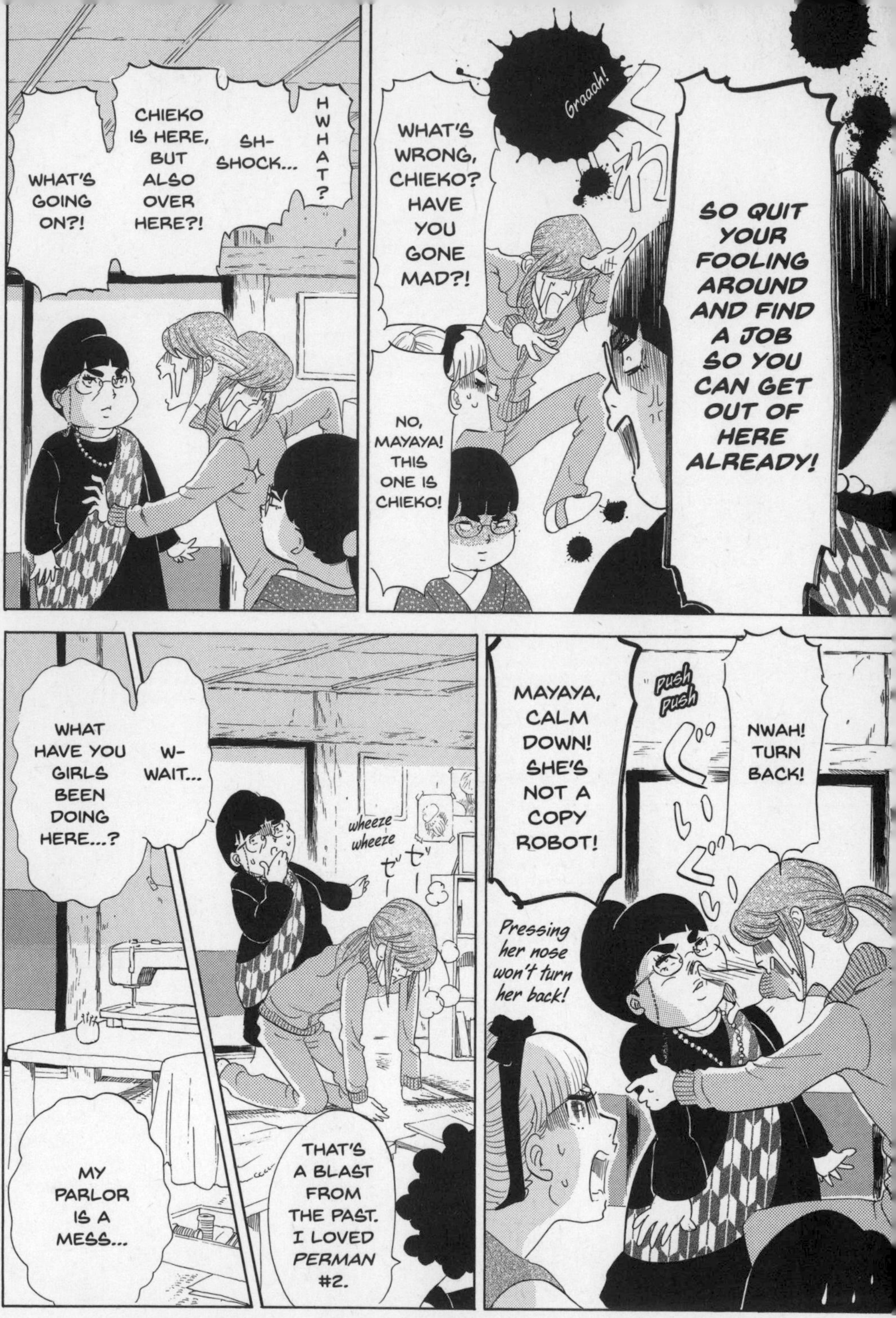
Graaah!
SO QUIT YOUR FOOLING AROUND AND FIND A JOB SO YOU CAN GET OUT OF HERE ALREADY!
WHAT'S WRONG, CHIEKO? HAVE YOU GONE MAD?!
NO, MAYAYA! THIS ONE IS CHIEKO!
HWHAT?
SH-SHOCK...
CHIEKO IS HERE, BUT ALSO OVER HERE?!
WHAT'S GOING ON?!
NWAH! TURN BACK!
push push
MAYAYA, CALM DOWN! SHE'S NOT A COPY ROBOT!
Pressing her nose won't turn her back!
W-WAIT...
WHAT HAVE YOU GIRLS BEEN DOING HERE...?
wheeze wheeze
THAT'S A BLAST FROM THE PAST. I LOVED PERMAN #2.
MY PARLOR IS A MESS...

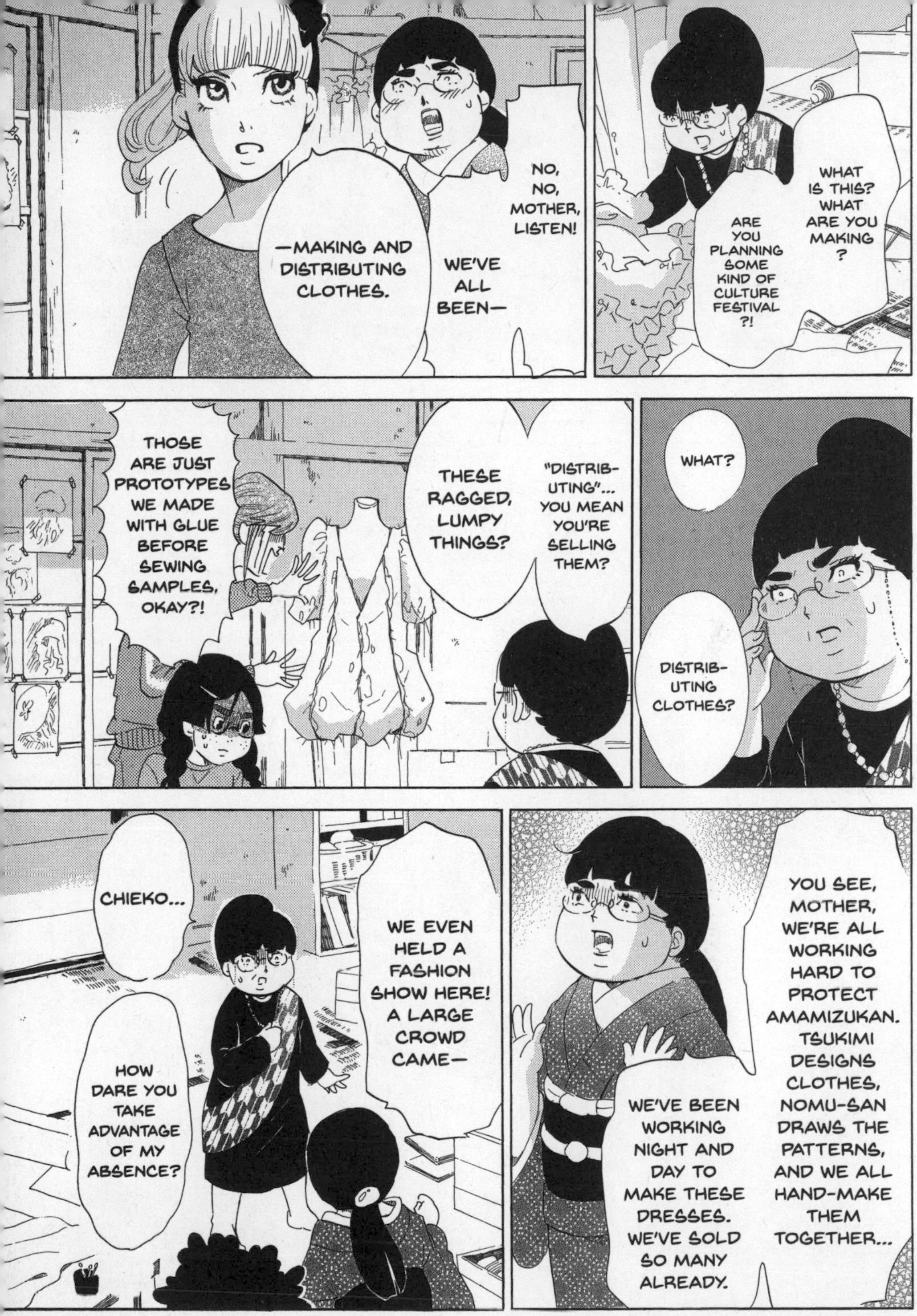
WHAT IS THIS? WHAT ARE YOU MAKING?
ARE YOU PLANNING SOME KIND OF CULTURE FESTIVAL?!
NO, NO, MOTHER, LISTEN!
WE'VE ALL BEEN—
—MAKING AND DISTRIBUTING CLOTHES.
WHAT?
DISTRIB-UTING CLOTHES?
"DISTRIB-UTING"... YOU MEAN YOU'RE SELLING THEM?
THESE RAGGED, LUMPY THINGS?
THOSE ARE JUST PROTOTYPES WE MADE WITH GLUE BEFORE SEWING SAMPLES, OKAY?!
YOU SEE, MOTHER, WE'RE ALL WORKING HARD TO PROTECT AMAMIZUKAN. TSUKIMI DESIGNS CLOTHES, NOMU-SAN DRAWS THE PATTERNS, AND WE ALL HAND-MAKE THEM TOGETHER...
WE'VE BEEN WORKING NIGHT AND DAY TO MAKE THESE DRESSES. WE'VE SOLD SO MANY ALREADY.
WE EVEN HELD A FASHION SHOW HERE! A LARGE CROWD CAME—
CHIEKO...
HOW DARE YOU TAKE ADVANTAGE OF MY ABSENCE?

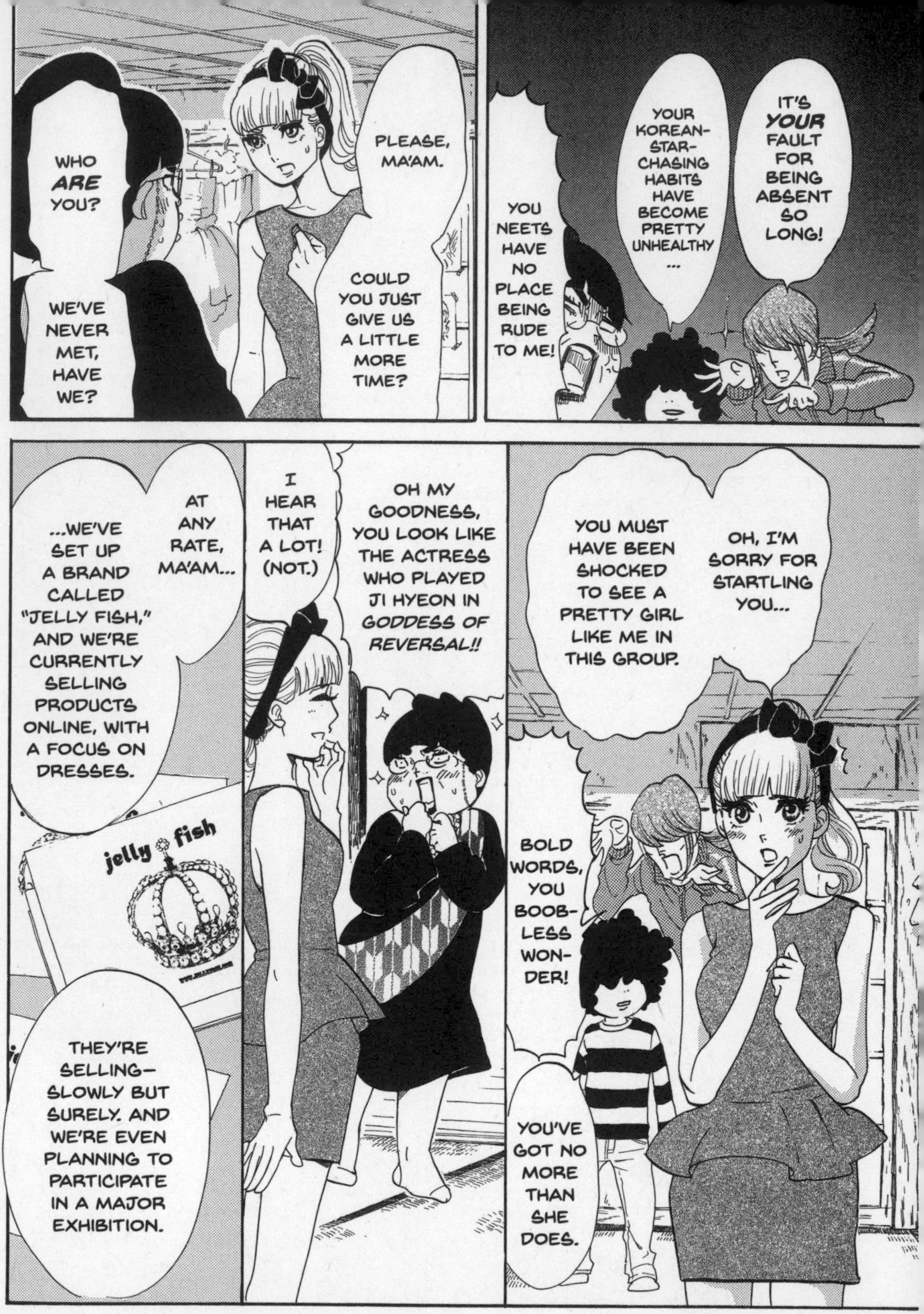
IT'S YOUR FAULT FOR BEING ABSENT SO LONG!
YOUR KOREAN-STAR-CHASING HABITS HAVE BECOME PRETTY UNHEALTHY...
YOU NEETS HAVE NO PLACE BEING RUDE TO ME!
PLEASE, MA'AM.
COULD YOU JUST GIVE US A LITTLE MORE TIME?
WHO ARE YOU?
WE'VE NEVER MET, HAVE WE?
OH, I'M SORRY FOR STARTLING YOU...
YOU MUST HAVE BEEN SHOCKED TO SEE A PRETTY GIRL LIKE ME IN THIS GROUP.
BOLD WORDS, YOU BOOB-LESS WON-DER!
YOU'VE GOT NO MORE THAN SHE DOES.
OH MY GOODNESS, YOU LOOK LIKE THE ACTRESS WHO PLAYED JI HYEON IN GODDESS OF REVERSAL!!
I HEAR THAT A LOT! (NOT.)
AT ANY RATE, MA'AM...
...WE'VE SET UP A BRAND CALLED "JELLY FISH," AND WE'RE CURRENTLY SELLING PRODUCTS ONLINE, WITH A FOCUS ON DRESSES.
jelly fish
THEY'RE SELLING—SLOWLY BUT SURELY. AND WE'RE EVEN PLANNING TO PARTICIPATE IN A MAJOR EXHIBITION.

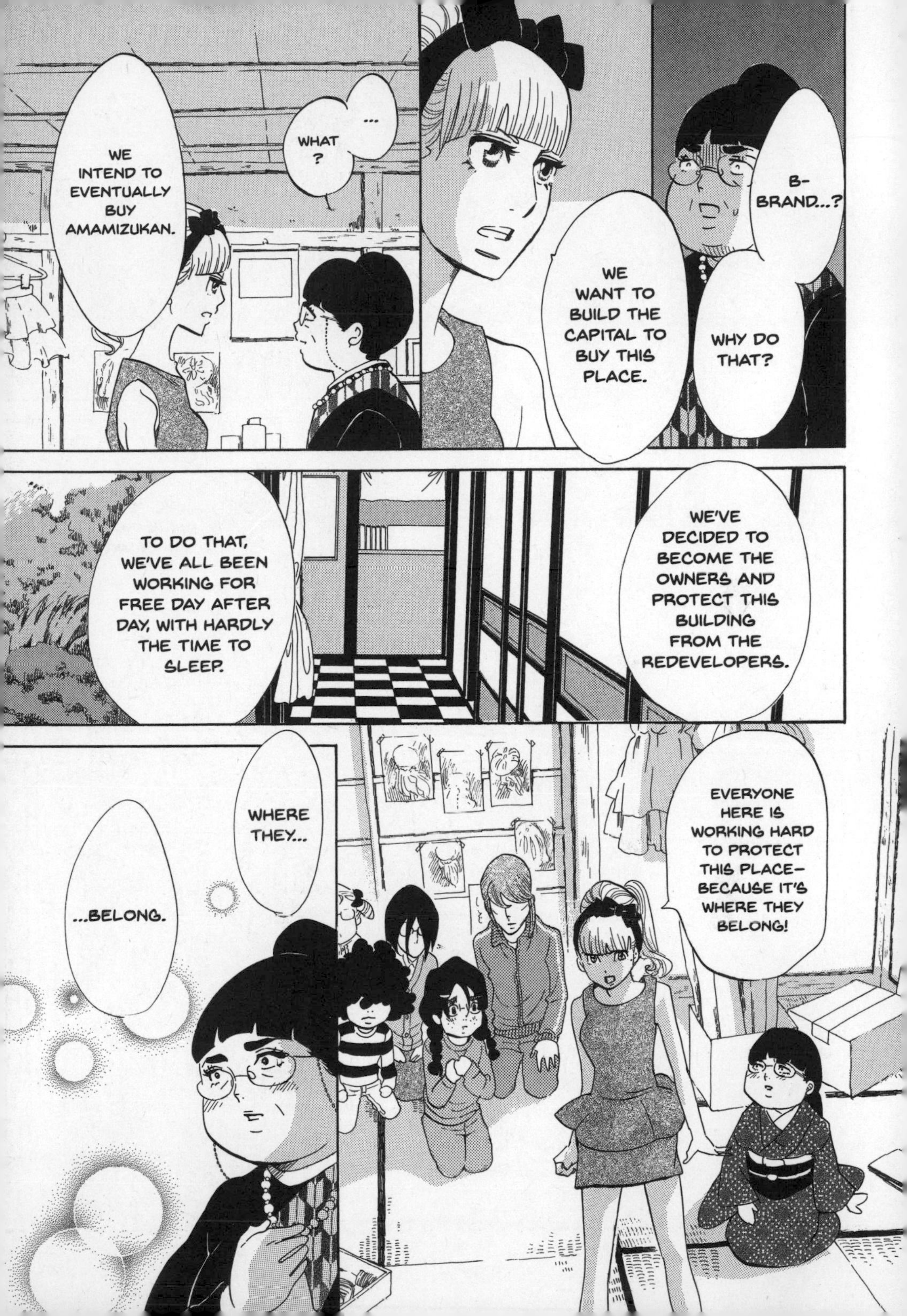
B-BRAND...?
WHY DO THAT?
WE WANT TO BUILD THE CAPITAL TO BUY THIS PLACE.
WE INTEND TO EVENTUALLY BUY AMAMIZUKAN.
... WHAT?
WE'VE DECIDED TO BECOME THE OWNERS AND PROTECT THIS BUILDING FROM THE REDEVELOPERS.
TO DO THAT, WE'VE ALL BEEN WORKING FOR FREE DAY AFTER DAY, WITH HARDLY THE TIME TO SLEEP.
EVERYONE HERE IS WORKING HARD TO PROTECT THIS PLACE—BECAUSE IT'S WHERE THEY BELONG!
WHERE THEY...
...BELONG.

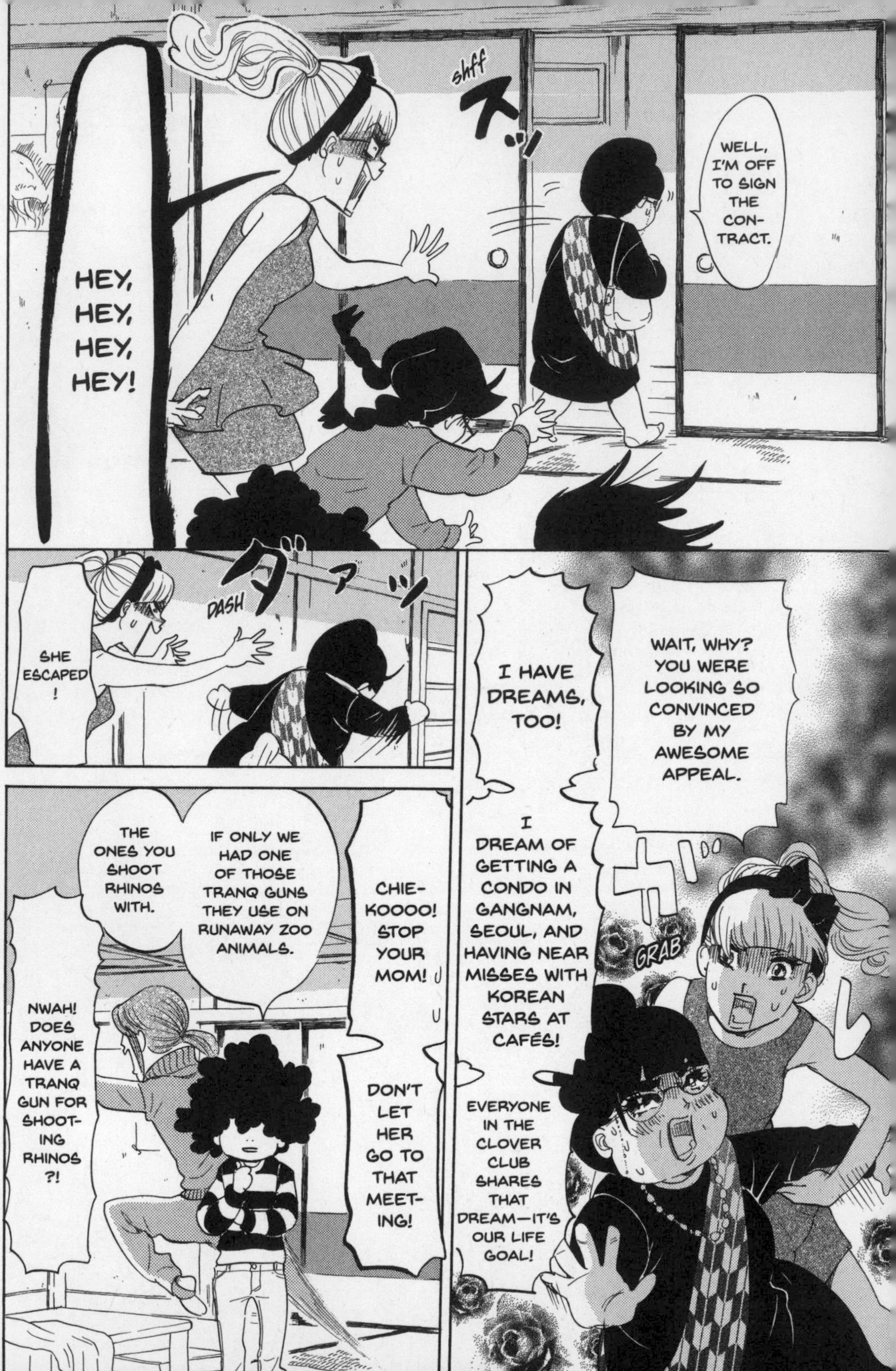
shff
WELL, I'M OFF TO SIGN THE CON-TRACT.
HEY, HEY, HEY, HEY!
WAIT, WHY? YOU WERE LOOKING SO CONVINCED BY MY AWESOME APPEAL.
I HAVE DREAMS, TOO!
I DREAM OF GETTING A CONDO IN GANGNAM, SEOUL, AND HAVING NEAR MISSES WITH KOREAN STARS AT CAFÉS!
GRAB
EVERYONE IN THE CLOVER CLUB SHARES THAT DREAM—IT'S OUR LIFE GOAL!
DASH
SHE ESCAPED!
CHIE-KOOOO! STOP YOUR MOM!
DON'T LET HER GO TO THAT MEET-ING!
IF ONLY WE HAD ONE OF THOSE TRANQ GUNS THEY USE ON RUNAWAY ZOO ANIMALS.
THE ONES YOU SHOOT RHINOS WITH.
NWAH! DOES ANYONE HAVE A TRANQ GUN FOR SHOOT-ING RHINOS?!

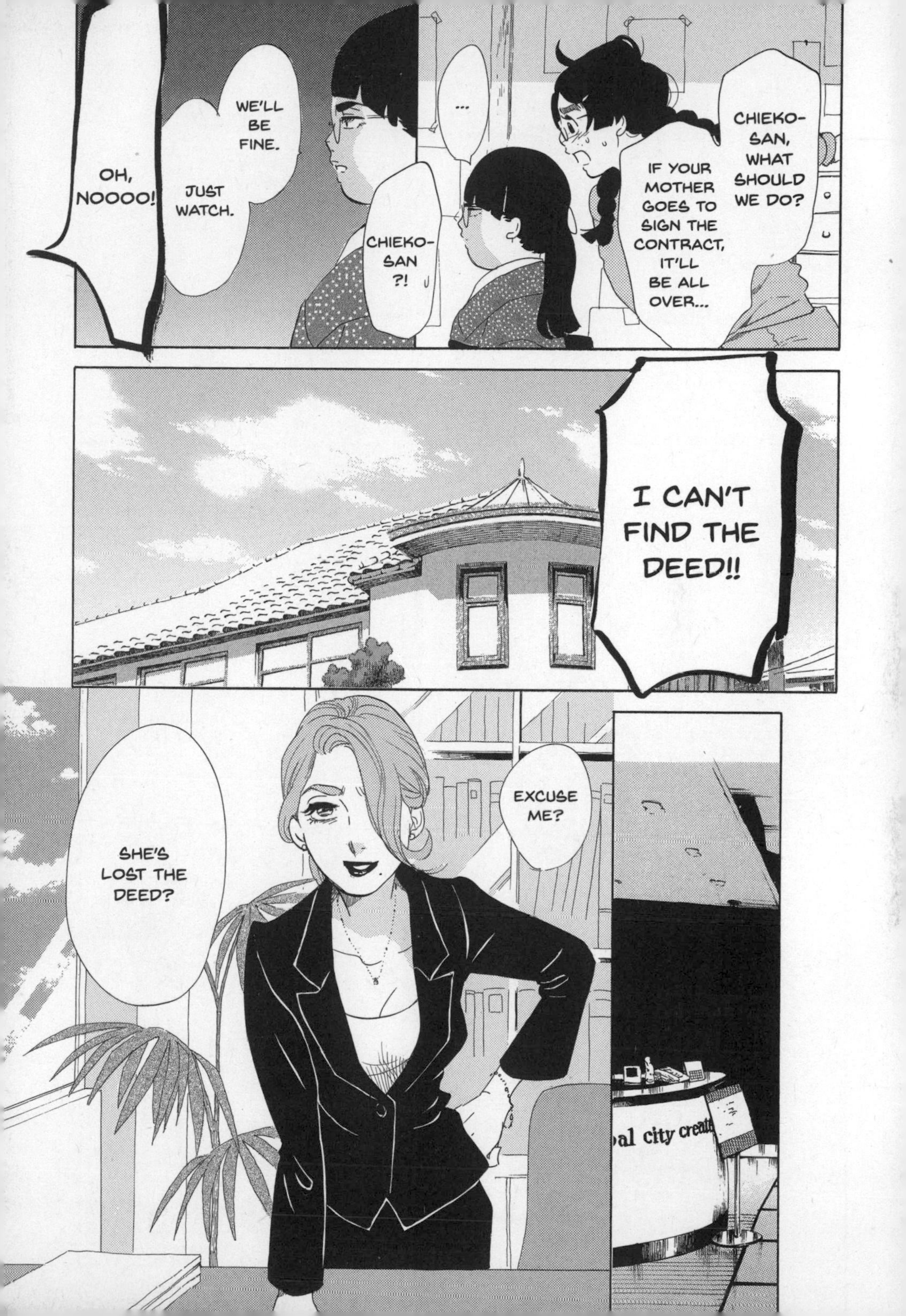
CHIEKO-SAN, WHAT SHOULD WE DO?
IF YOUR MOTHER GOES TO SIGN THE CONTRACT, IT'LL BE ALL OVER...
...
CHIEKO-SAN ?!
WE'LL BE FINE.
JUST WATCH.
OH, NOOOO!
I CAN'T FIND THE DEED!!
EXCUSE ME?
SHE'S LOST THE DEED?

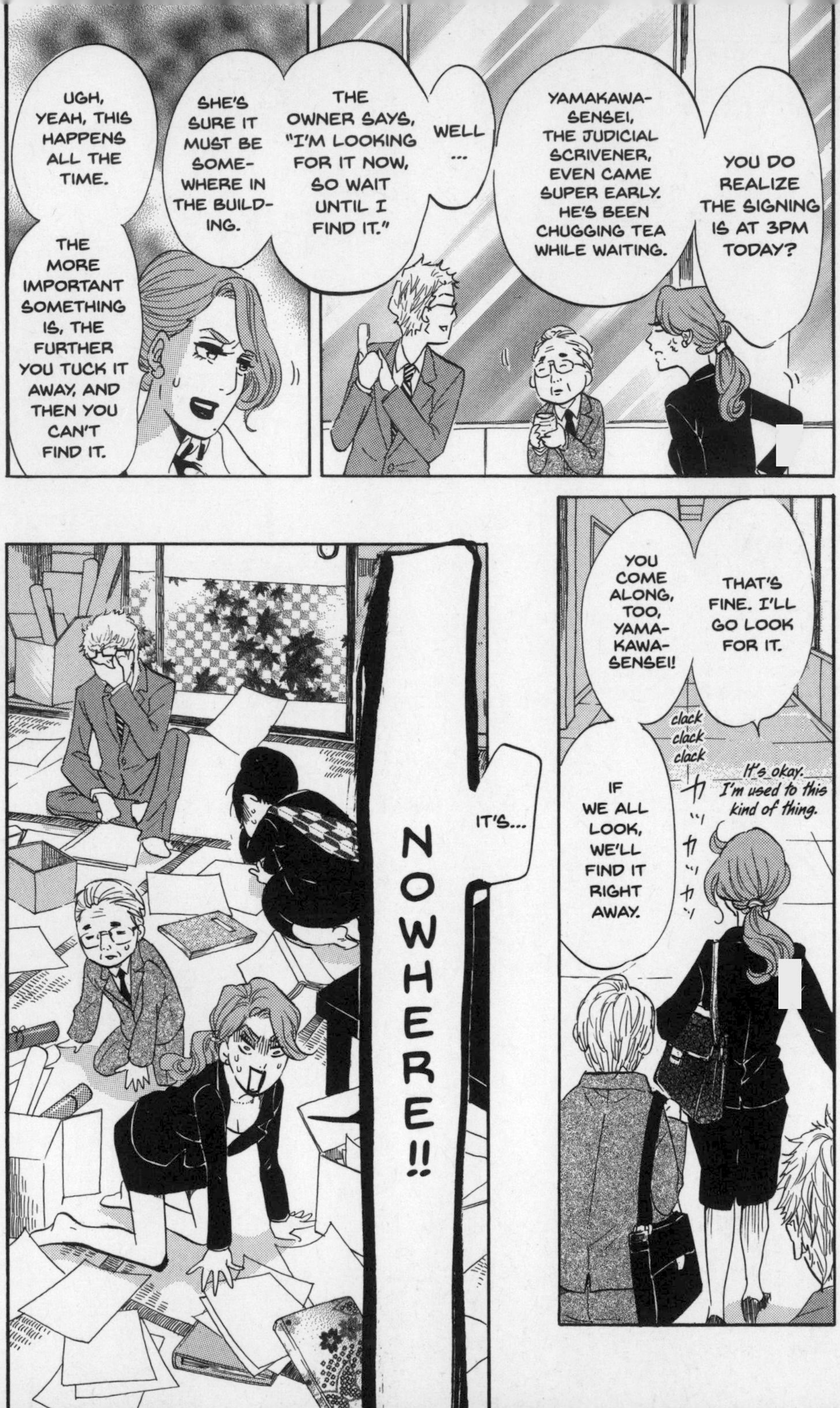
YOU DO REALIZE THE SIGNING IS AT 3PM TODAY?
YAMAKAWA-SENSEI, THE JUDICIAL SCRIVENER, EVEN CAME SUPER EARLY. HE'S BEEN CHUGGING TEA WHILE WAITING.
WELL ...
THE OWNER SAYS, "I'M LOOKING FOR IT NOW, SO WAIT UNTIL I FIND IT."
SHE'S SURE IT MUST BE SOMEWHERE IN THE BUILDING.
UGH, YEAH, THIS HAPPENS ALL THE TIME.
THE MORE IMPORTANT SOMETHING IS, THE FURTHER YOU TUCK IT AWAY, AND THEN YOU CAN'T FIND IT.
THAT'S FINE. I'LL GO LOOK FOR IT.
YOU COME ALONG, TOO, YAMAKAWA-SENSEI!
clack clack clack
It's okay. I'm used to this kind of thing.
IF WE ALL LOOK, WE'LL FIND IT RIGHT AWAY.
IT'S...
NOWHERE!!

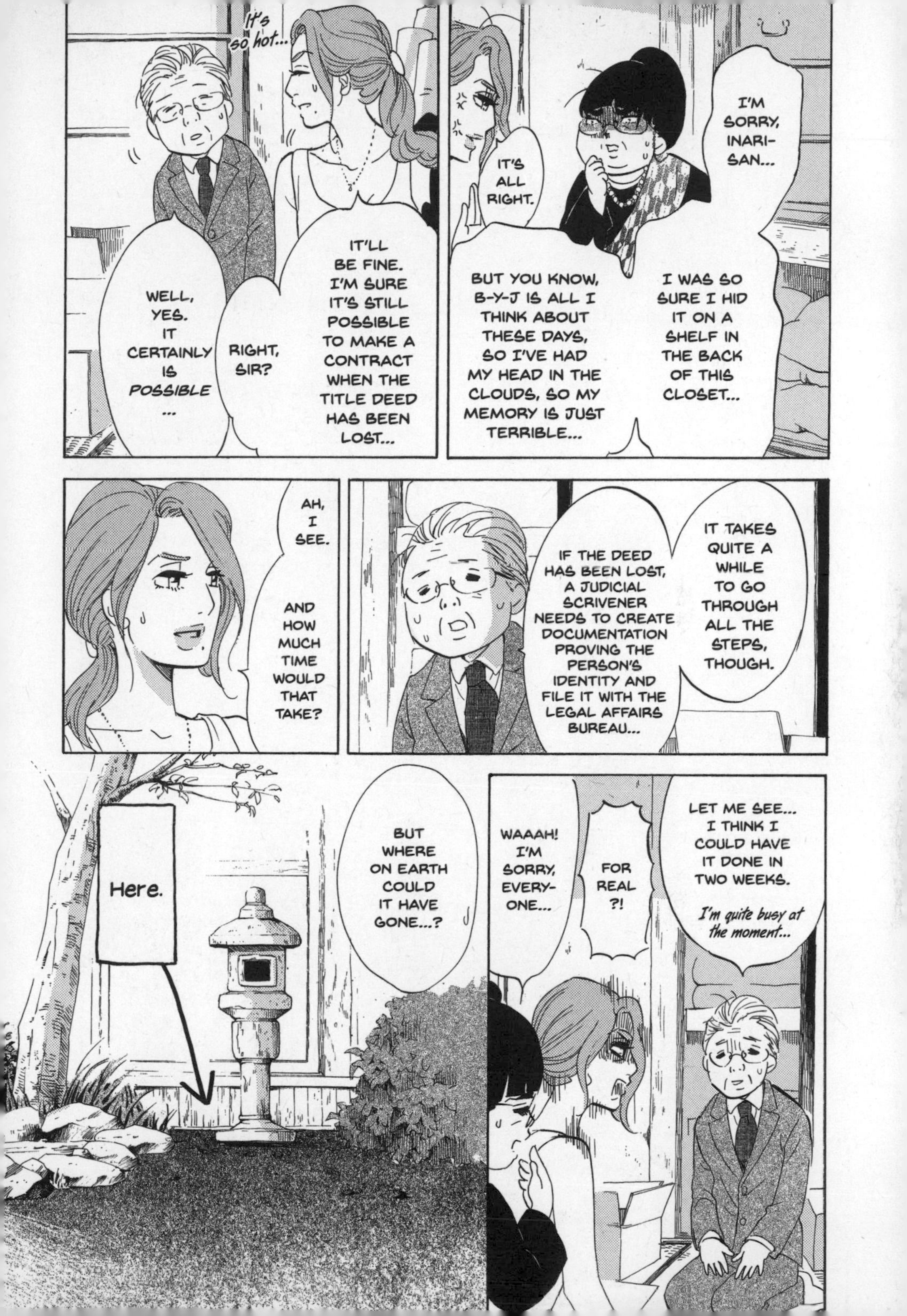
I'M SORRY, INARI-SAN...
IT'S ALL RIGHT.
I WAS SO SURE I HID IT ON A SHELF IN THE BACK OF THIS CLOSET...
BUT YOU KNOW, B-Y-J IS ALL I THINK ABOUT THESE DAYS, SO I'VE HAD MY HEAD IN THE CLOUDS, SO MY MEMORY IS JUST TERRIBLE...
It's so hot...
IT'LL BE FINE. I'M SURE IT'S STILL POSSIBLE TO MAKE A CONTRACT WHEN THE TITLE DEED HAS BEEN LOST...
RIGHT, SIR?
WELL, YES. IT CERTAINLY IS *POSSIBLE* ...
IT TAKES QUITE A WHILE TO GO THROUGH ALL THE STEPS, THOUGH.
IF THE DEED HAS BEEN LOST, A JUDICIAL SCRIVENER NEEDS TO CREATE DOCUMENTATION PROVING THE PERSON'S IDENTITY AND FILE IT WITH THE LEGAL AFFAIRS BUREAU...
AH, I SEE.
AND HOW MUCH TIME WOULD THAT TAKE?
LET ME SEE... I THINK I COULD HAVE IT DONE IN TWO WEEKS.
I'm quite busy at the moment...
FOR REAL ?!
WAAAH! I'M SORRY, EVERY-ONE...
BUT WHERE ON EARTH COULD IT HAVE GONE...?
Here.

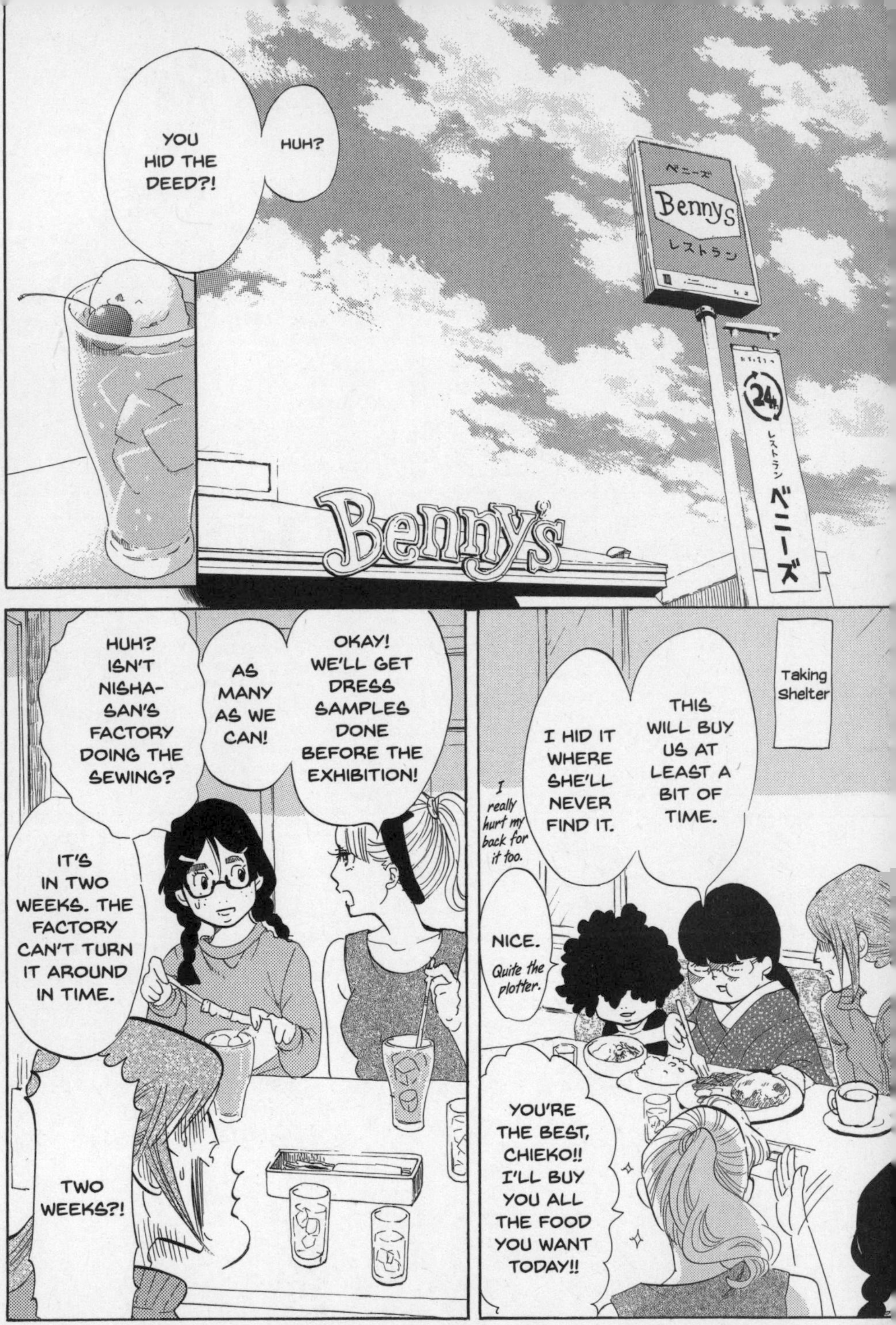
HUH?
YOU HID THE DEED?!
ベニーズ
Bennys
レストラン
24h
レストラン
ベニーズ
Benny's
Taking Shelter
THIS WILL BUY US AT LEAST A BIT OF TIME.
I HID IT WHERE SHE'LL NEVER FIND IT.
I really hurt my back for it too.
NICE.
Quite the plotter.
YOU'RE THE BEST, CHIEKO!! I'LL BUY YOU ALL THE FOOD YOU WANT TODAY!!
OKAY! WE'LL GET DRESS SAMPLES DONE BEFORE THE EXHIBITION!
AS MANY AS WE CAN!
HUH? ISN'T NISHA-SAN'S FACTORY DOING THE SEWING?
IT'S IN TWO WEEKS. THE FACTORY CAN'T TURN IT AROUND IN TIME.
TWO WEEKS?!

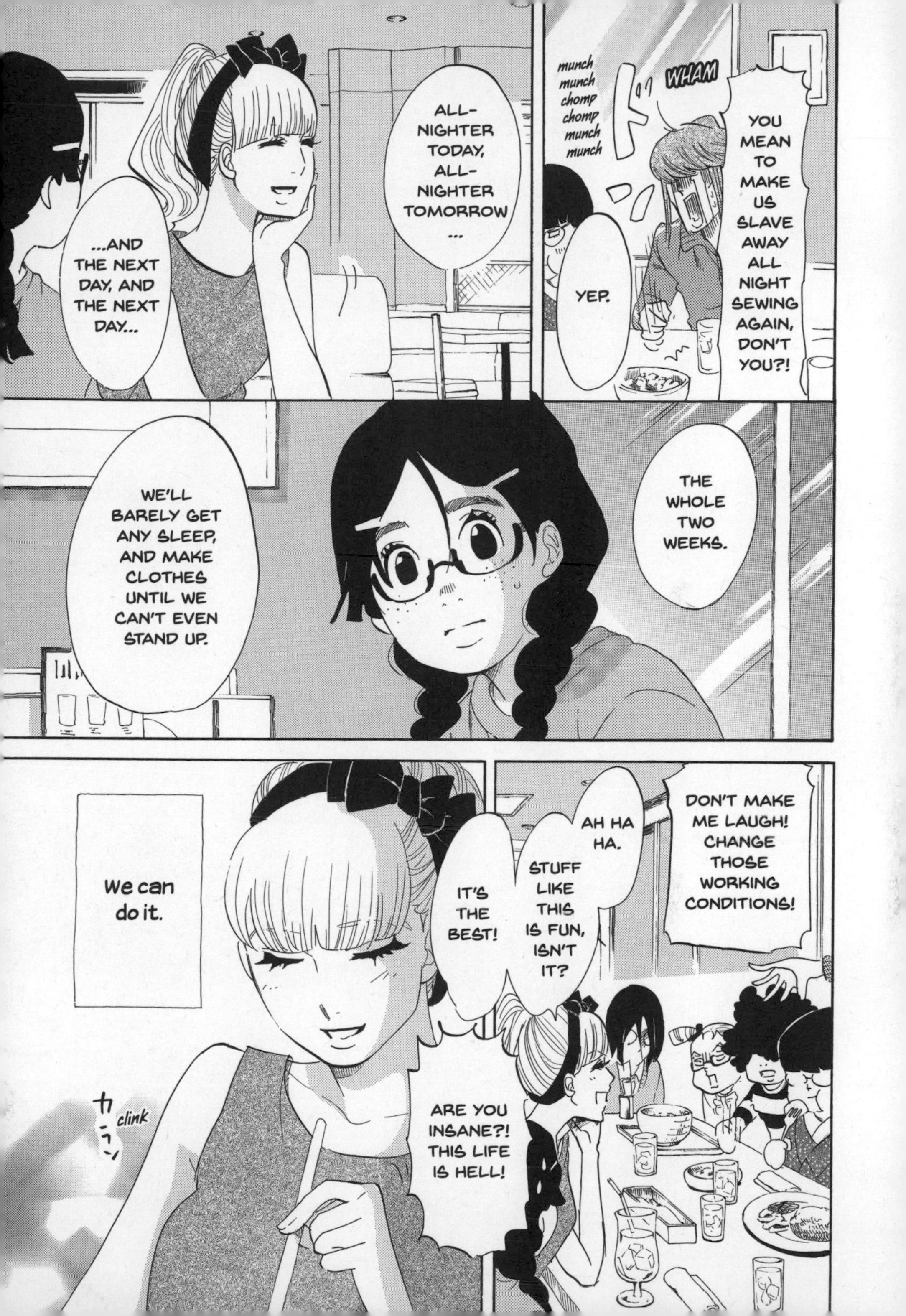
WHAM
YOU MEAN TO MAKE US SLAVE AWAY ALL NIGHT SEWING AGAIN, DON'T YOU?!
munch munch chomp chomp munch munch
YEP.
ALL-NIGHTER TODAY, ALL-NIGHTER TOMORROW...
...AND THE NEXT DAY, AND THE NEXT DAY...
THE WHOLE TWO WEEKS.
WE'LL BARELY GET ANY SLEEP, AND MAKE CLOTHES UNTIL WE CAN'T EVEN STAND UP.
DON'T MAKE ME LAUGH! CHANGE THOSE WORKING CONDITIONS!
AH HA HA.
STUFF LIKE THIS IS FUN, ISN'T IT?
IT'S THE BEST!
We can do it.
clink
ARE YOU INSANE?! THIS LIFE IS HELL!

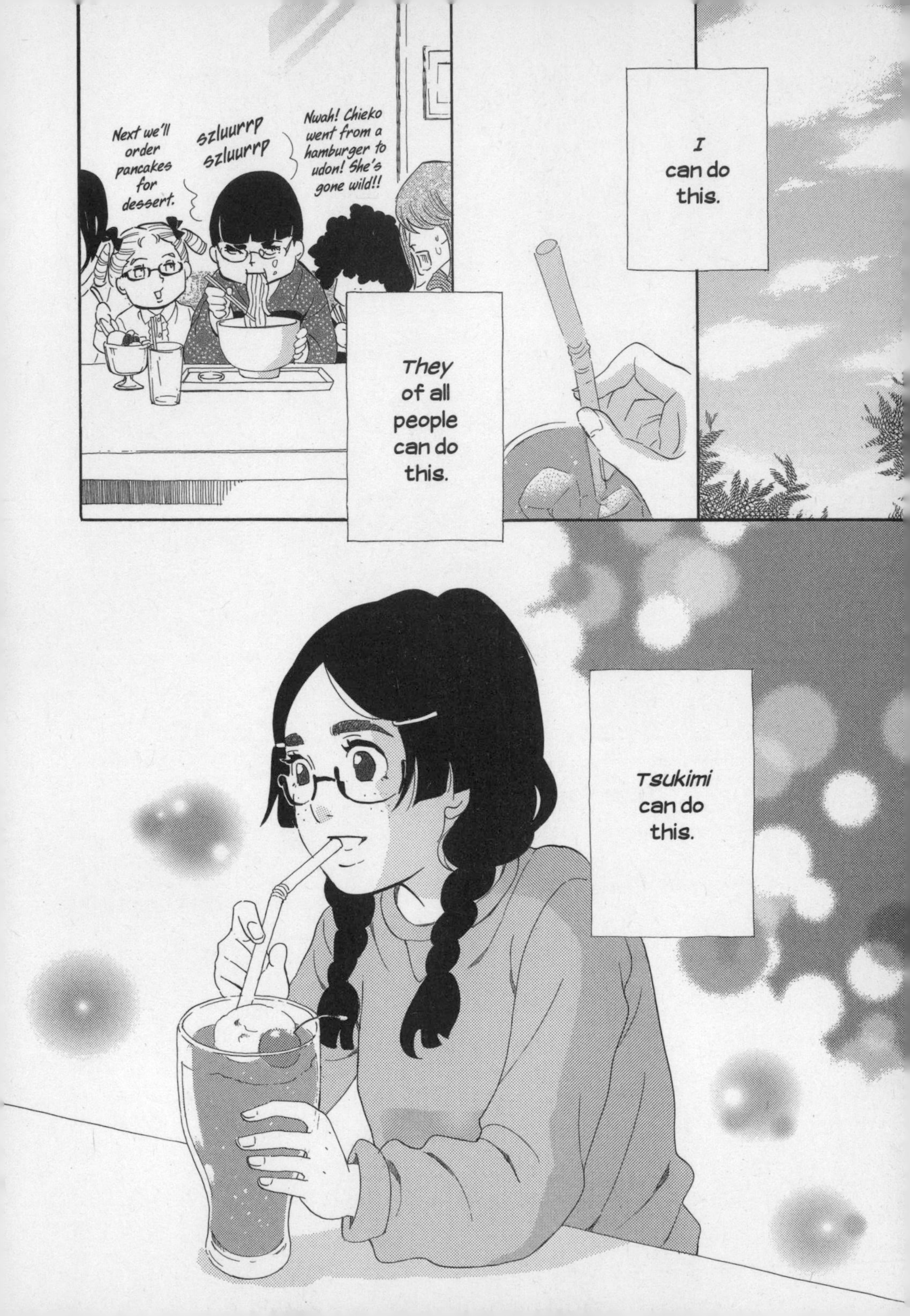
I can do this.
Nwah! Chieko went from a hamburger to udon! She's gone wild!!
szluurrp szluurrp
Next we'll order pancakes for dessert.
They of all people can do this.
Tsukimi can do this.

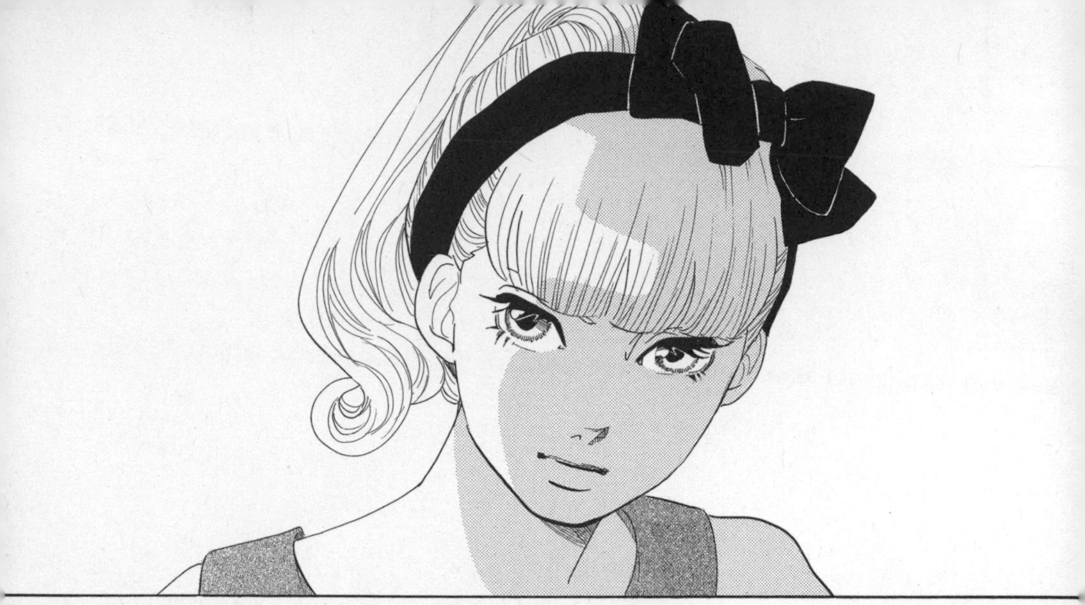

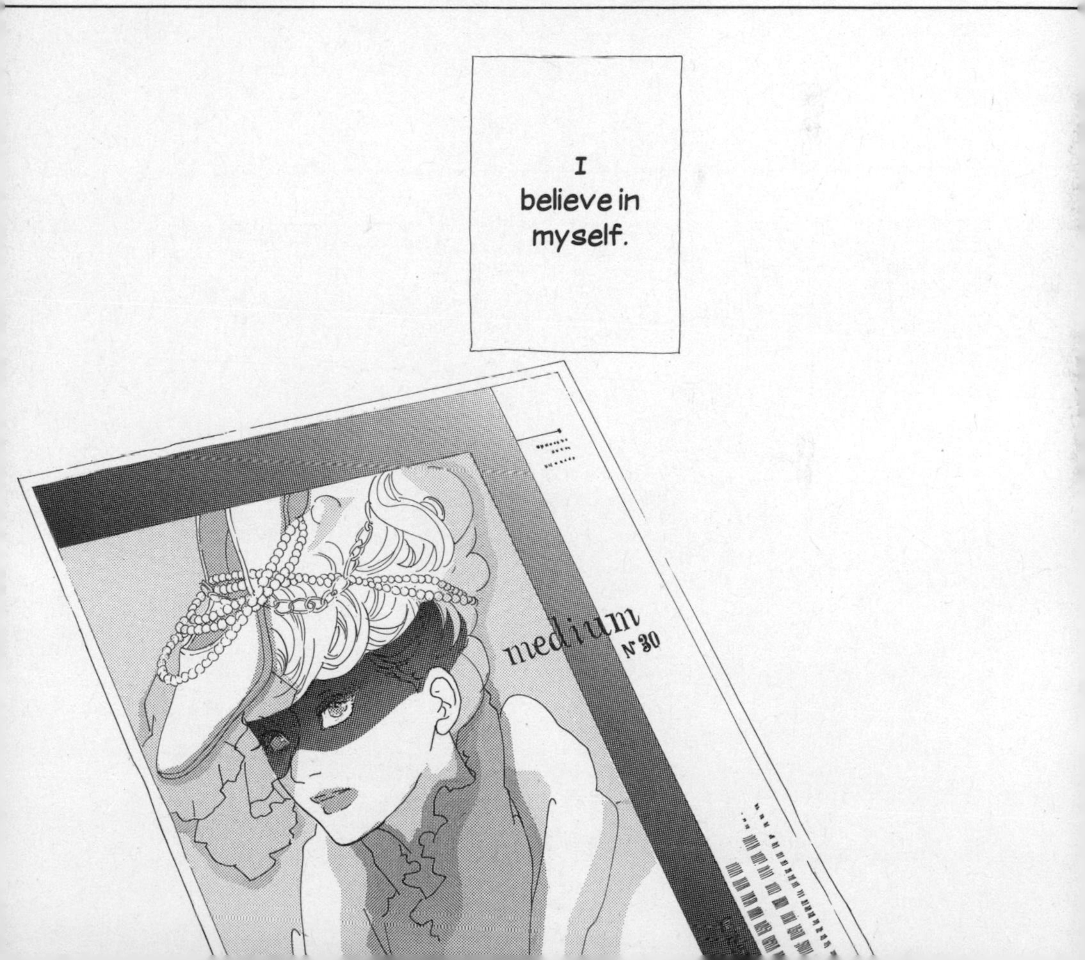
I believe in myself.
medium
N°30

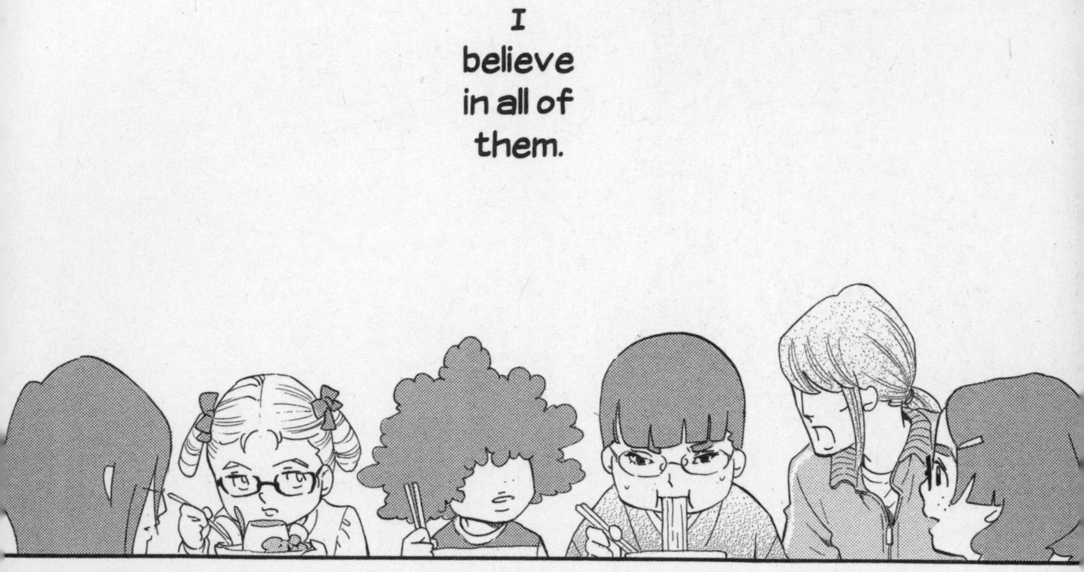
I believe in all of them.

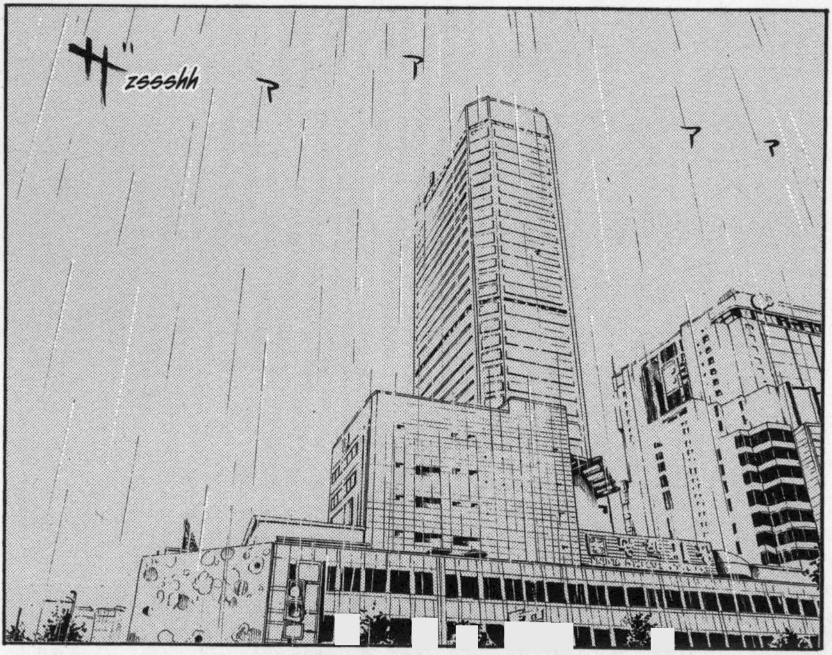
ザ zssshh アアアア

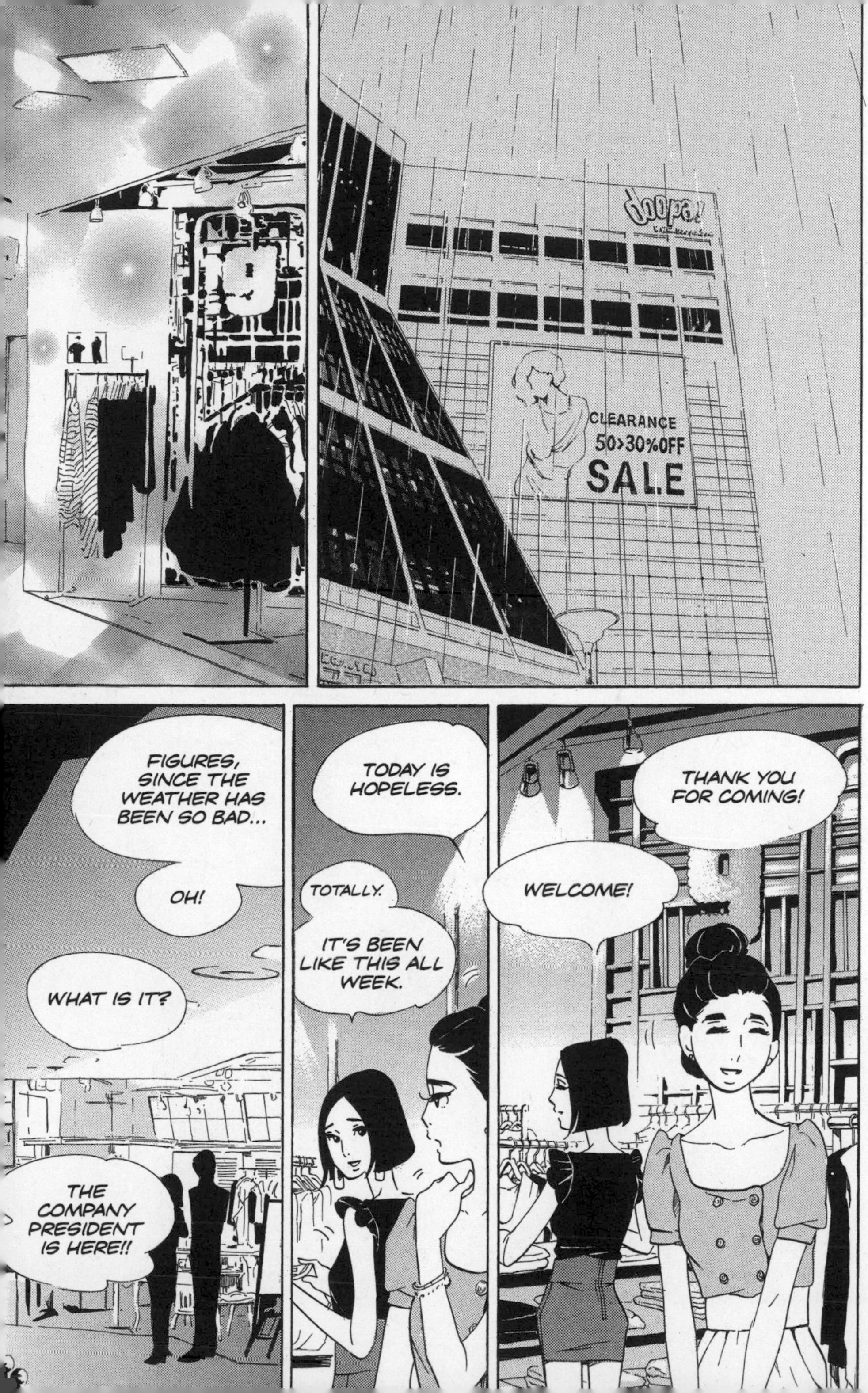

doopa!
CLEARANCE
50>30%OFF
SALE
THANK YOU FOR COMING!
WELCOME!
TODAY IS HOPELESS.
TOTALLY.
IT'S BEEN LIKE THIS ALL WEEK.
FIGURES, SINCE THE WEATHER HAS BEEN SO BAD...
OH!
WHAT IS IT?
THE COMPANY PRESIDENT IS HERE!!

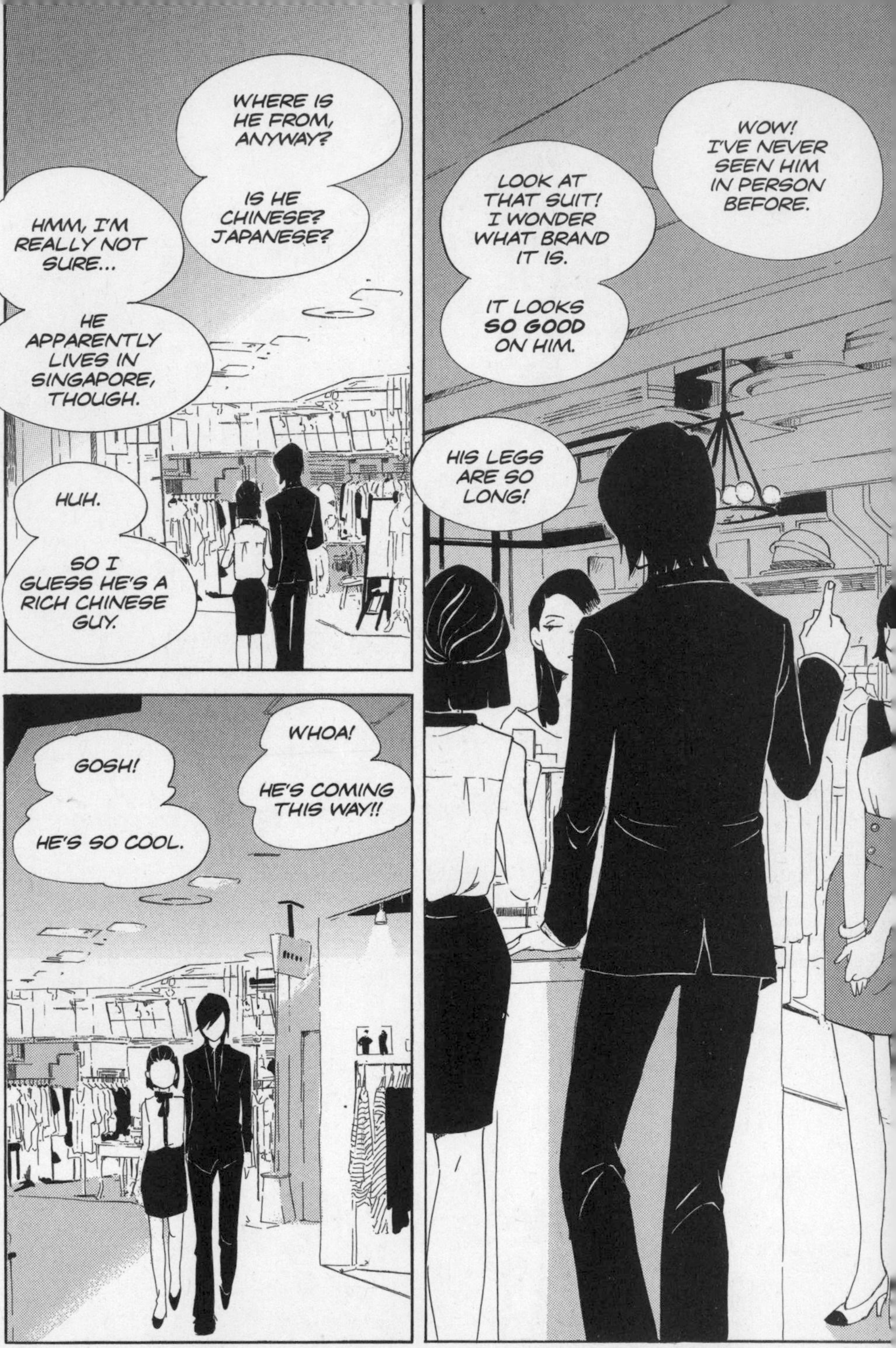
WOW! I'VE NEVER SEEN HIM IN PERSON BEFORE.
LOOK AT THAT SUIT! I WONDER WHAT BRAND IT IS.
IT LOOKS SO GOOD ON HIM.
HIS LEGS ARE SO LONG!
WHERE IS HE FROM, ANYWAY?
IS HE CHINESE? JAPANESE?
HMM, I'M REALLY NOT SURE...
HE APPARENTLY LIVES IN SINGAPORE, THOUGH.
HUH.
SO I GUESS HE'S A RICH CHINESE GUY.
WHOA!
HE'S COMING THIS WAY!!
GOSH!
HE'S SO COOL.

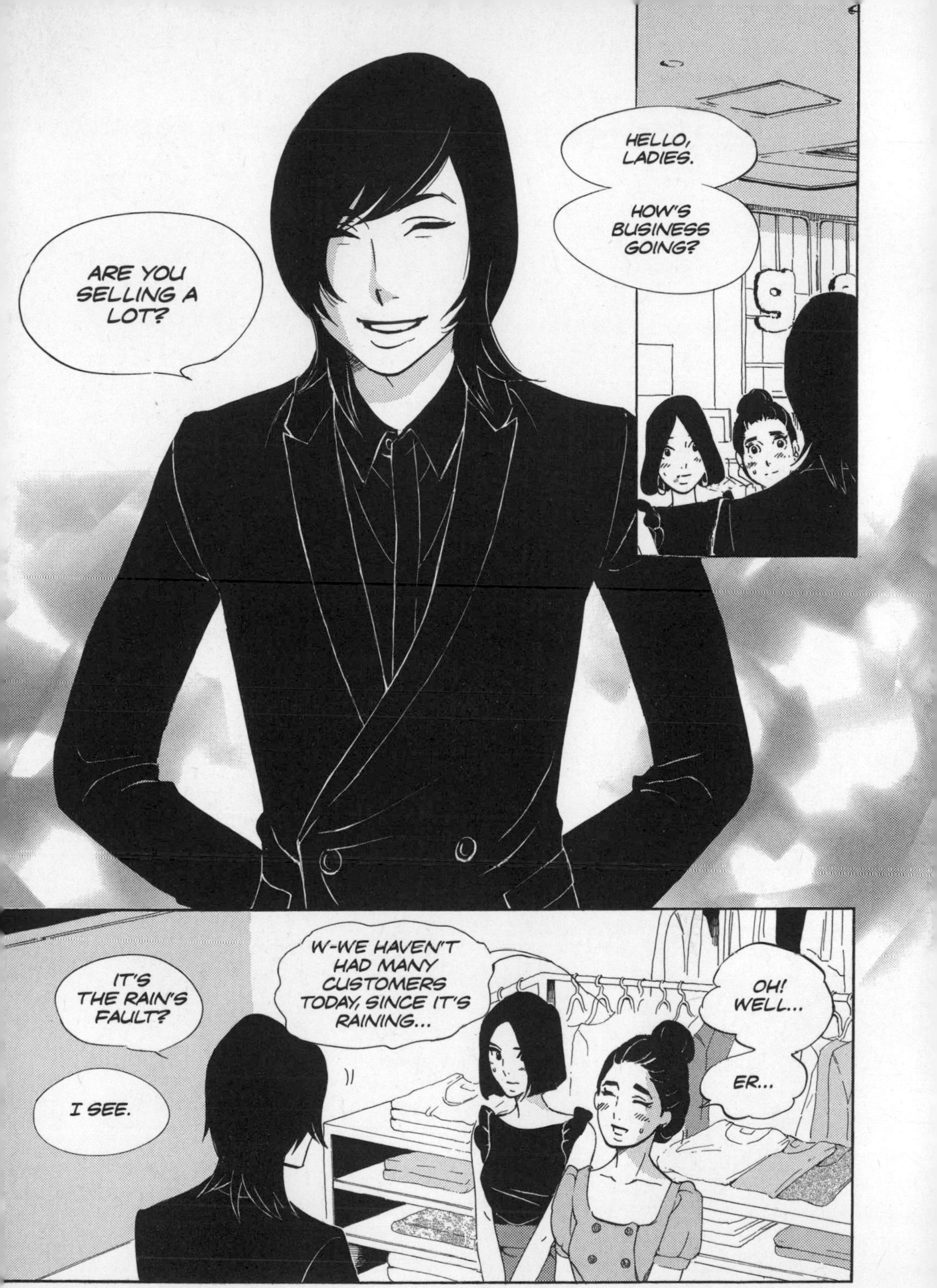
HELLO, LADIES.
HOW'S BUSINESS GOING?
ARE YOU SELLING A LOT?
OH! WELL...
ER...
W-WE HAVEN'T HAD MANY CUSTOMERS TODAY, SINCE IT'S RAINING...
IT'S THE RAIN'S FAULT?
I SEE.

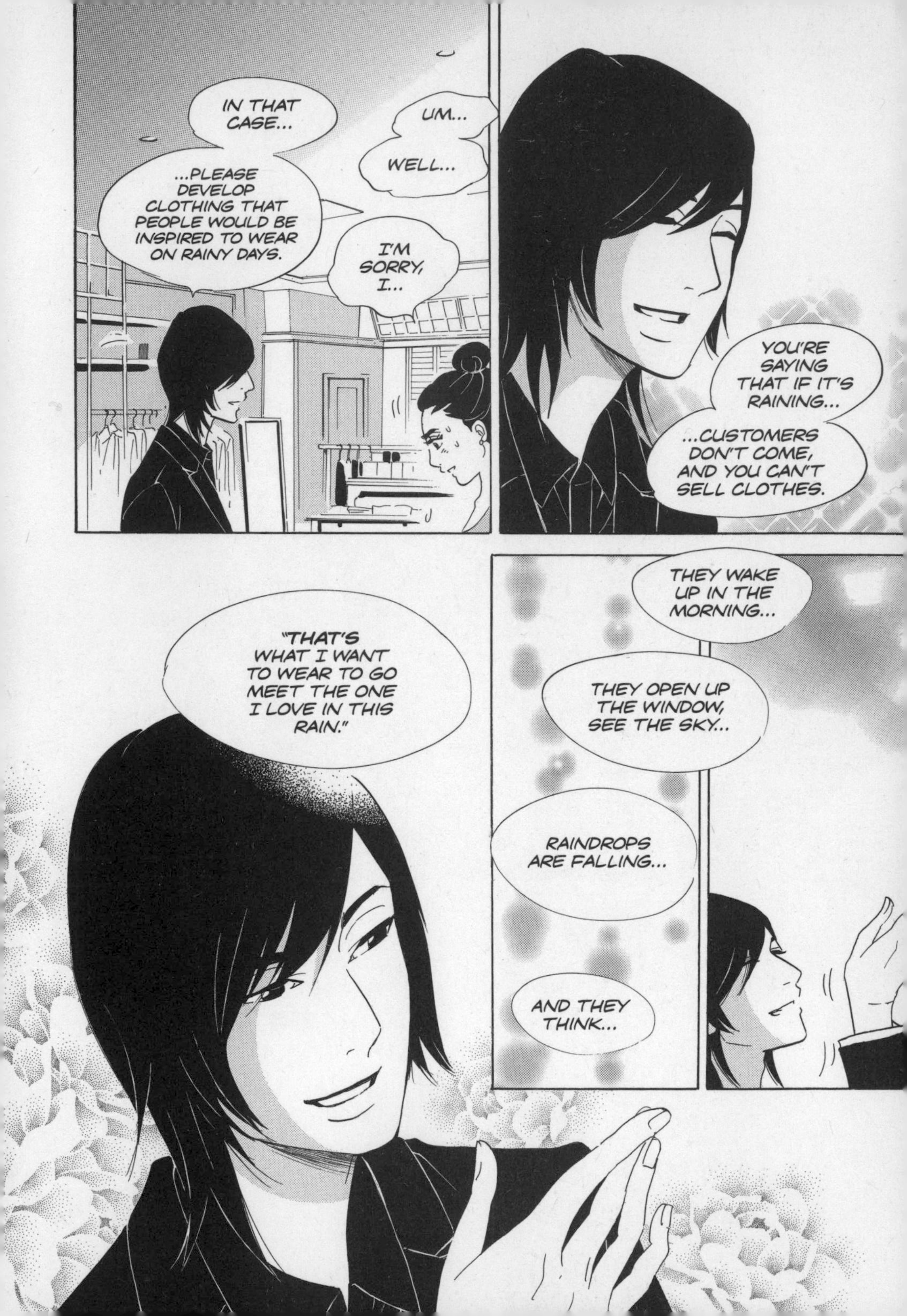
YOU'RE SAYING THAT IF IT'S RAINING...
...CUSTOMERS DON'T COME, AND YOU CAN'T SELL CLOTHES.
UM...
WELL...
IN THAT CASE...
...PLEASE DEVELOP CLOTHING THAT PEOPLE WOULD BE INSPIRED TO WEAR ON RAINY DAYS.
I'M SORRY, I...
THEY WAKE UP IN THE MORNING...
THEY OPEN UP THE WINDOW, SEE THE SKY...
RAINDROPS ARE FALLING...
AND THEY THINK...
"THAT'S WHAT I WANT TO WEAR TO GO MEET THE ONE I LOVE IN THIS RAIN."

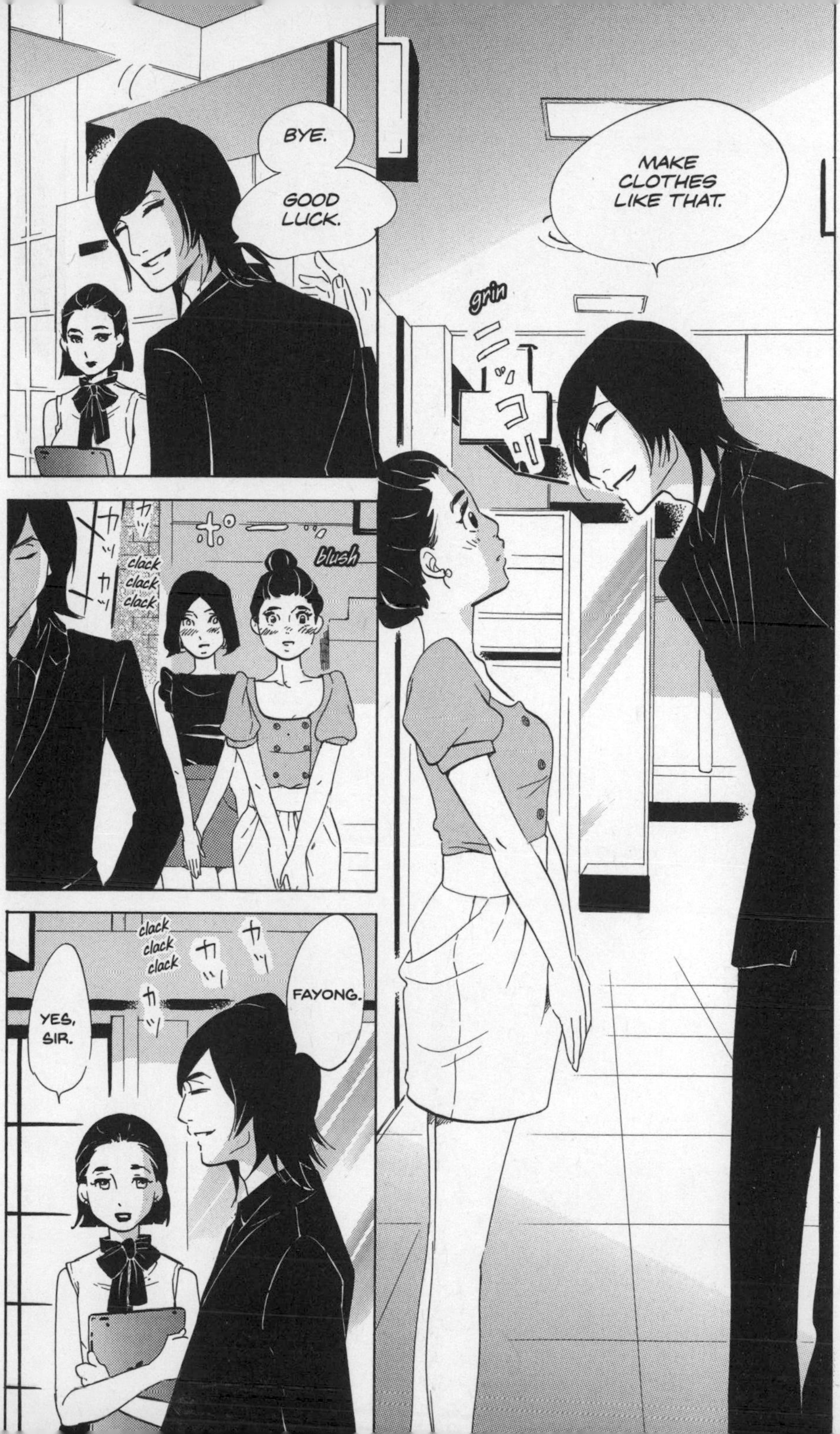
MAKE CLOTHES LIKE THAT.
grin
BYE.
GOOD LUCK.
blush
clack clack clack
FAYONG.
clack clack clack
YES, SIR.

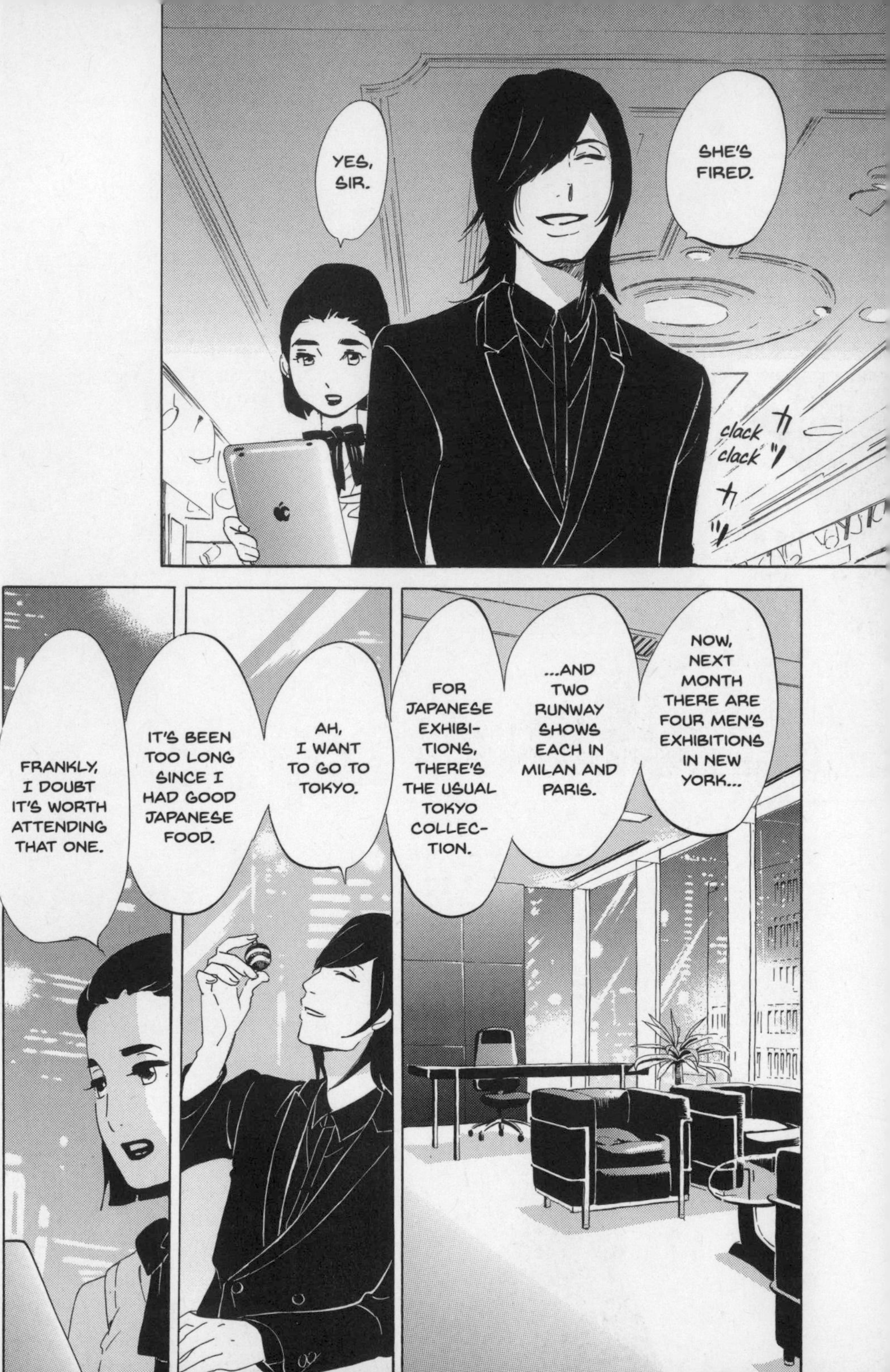
SHE'S FIRED.
YES, SIR.
clack clack
NOW, NEXT MONTH THERE ARE FOUR MEN'S EXHIBITIONS IN NEW YORK...
...AND TWO RUNWAY SHOWS EACH IN MILAN AND PARIS.
FOR JAPANESE EXHIBITIONS, THERE'S THE USUAL TOKYO COLLECTION.
AH, I WANT TO GO TO TOKYO.
IT'S BEEN TOO LONG SINCE I HAD GOOD JAPANESE FOOD.
FRANKLY, I DOUBT IT'S WORTH ATTENDING THAT ONE.

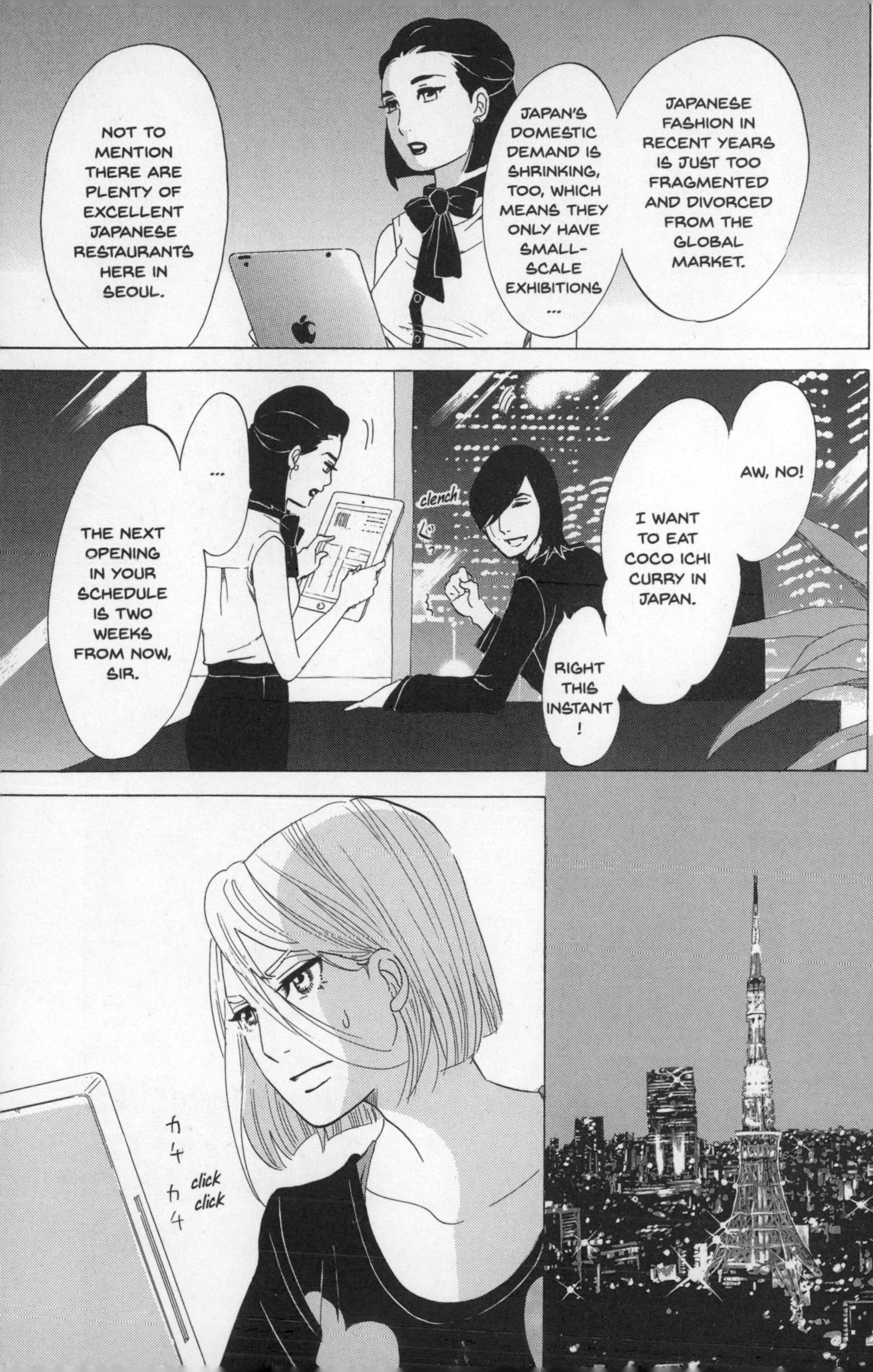
JAPANESE FASHION IN RECENT YEARS IS JUST TOO FRAGMENTED AND DIVORCED FROM THE GLOBAL MARKET.
JAPAN'S DOMESTIC DEMAND IS SHRINKING, TOO, WHICH MEANS THEY ONLY HAVE SMALL-SCALE EXHIBITIONS ...
NOT TO MENTION THERE ARE PLENTY OF EXCELLENT JAPANESE RESTAURANTS HERE IN SEOUL.
AW, NO!
I WANT TO EAT COCO ICHI CURRY IN JAPAN.
RIGHT THIS INSTANT!
clench
...
THE NEXT OPENING IN YOUR SCHEDULE IS TWO WEEKS FROM NOW, SIR.
カチカチ
click click

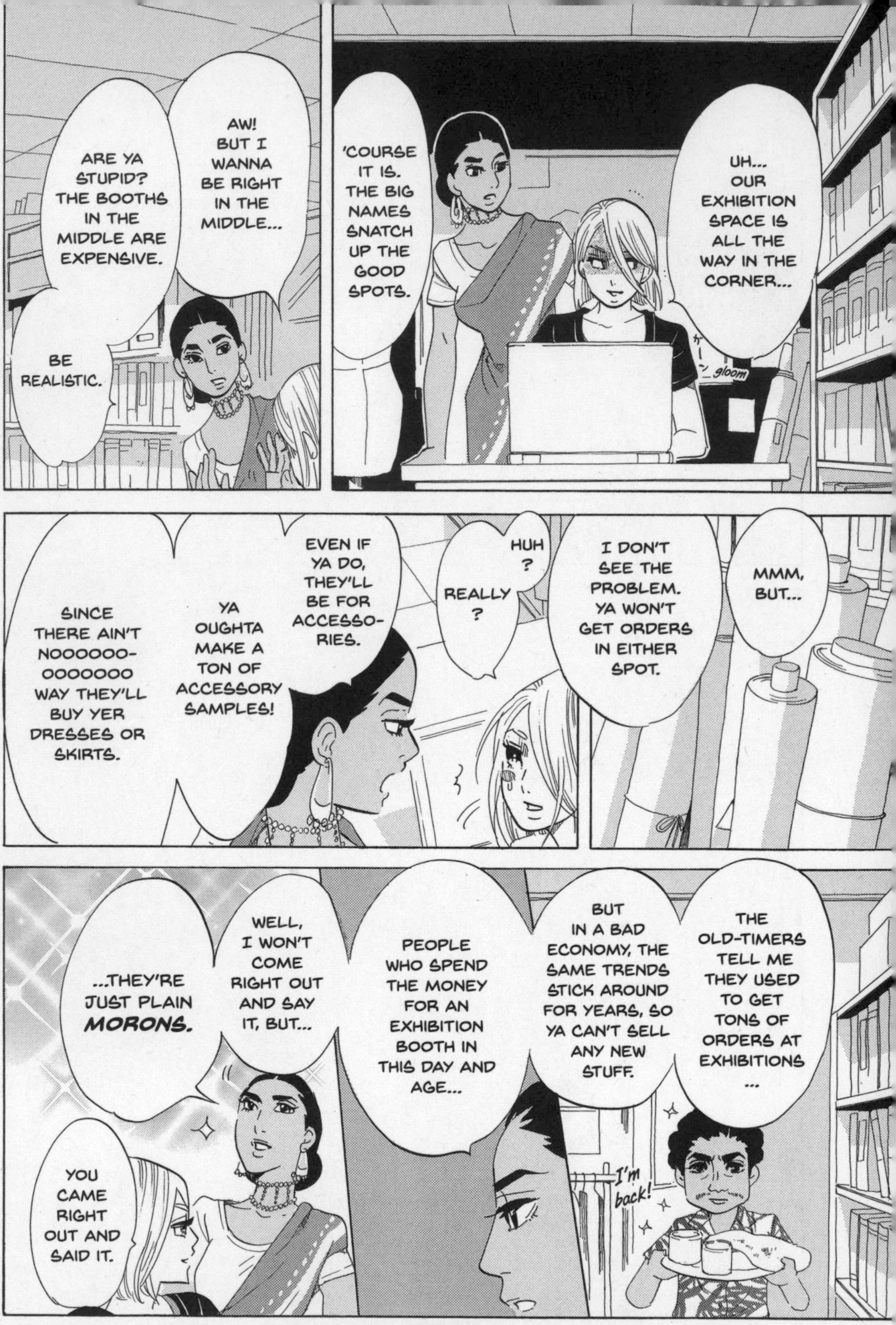
UH... OUR EXHIBITION SPACE IS ALL THE WAY IN THE CORNER...
gloom
'COURSE IT IS. THE BIG NAMES SNATCH UP THE GOOD SPOTS.
AW! BUT I WANNA BE RIGHT IN THE MIDDLE...
ARE YA STUPID? THE BOOTHS IN THE MIDDLE ARE EXPENSIVE.
BE REALISTIC.
MMM, BUT...
I DON'T SEE THE PROBLEM. YA WON'T GET ORDERS IN EITHER SPOT.
HUH? REALLY?
EVEN IF YA DO, THEY'LL BE FOR ACCESSO-RIES.
YA OUGHTA MAKE A TON OF ACCESSORY SAMPLES!
SINCE THERE AIN'T NOOOOOO-OOOOOOO WAY THEY'LL BUY YER DRESSES OR SKIRTS.
THE OLD-TIMERS TELL ME THEY USED TO GET TONS OF ORDERS AT EXHIBITIONS ...
BUT IN A BAD ECONOMY, THE SAME TRENDS STICK AROUND FOR YEARS, SO YA CAN'T SELL ANY NEW STUFF.
PEOPLE WHO SPEND THE MONEY FOR AN EXHIBITION BOOTH IN THIS DAY AND AGE...
I'm back!
WELL, I WON'T COME RIGHT OUT AND SAY IT, BUT...
...THEY'RE JUST PLAIN **MORONS.**
YOU CAME RIGHT OUT AND SAID IT.

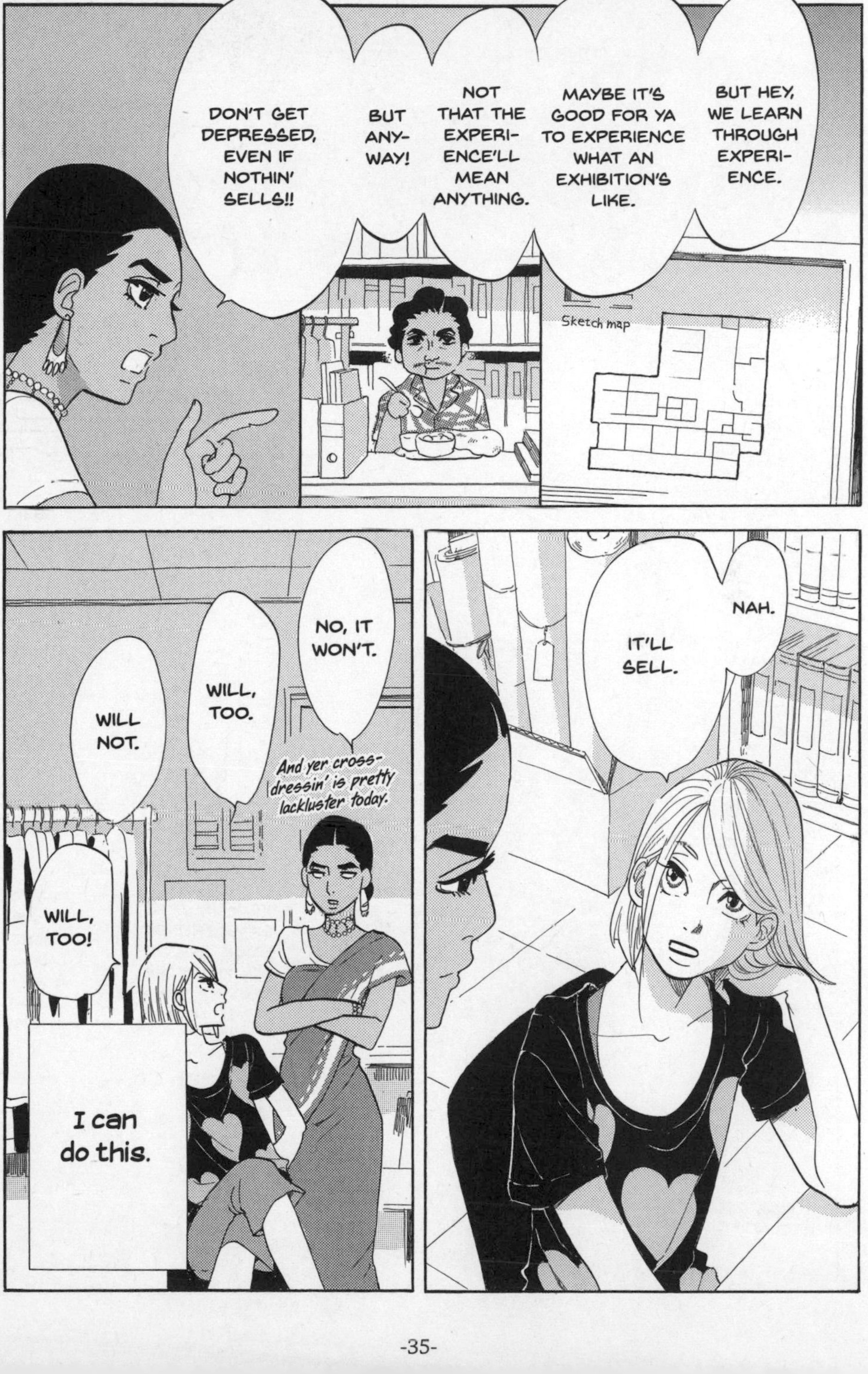
BUT HEY, WE LEARN THROUGH EXPERIENCE.
MAYBE IT'S GOOD FOR YA TO EXPERIENCE WHAT AN EXHIBITION'S LIKE.
NOT THAT THE EXPERIENCE'LL MEAN ANYTHING.
BUT ANYWAY!
DON'T GET DEPRESSED, EVEN IF NOTHIN' SELLS!!
Sketch map
NAH.
IT'LL SELL.
NO, IT WON'T.
WILL, TOO.
WILL NOT.
And yer cross-dressin' is pretty lackluster today.
WILL, TOO!
I can do this.

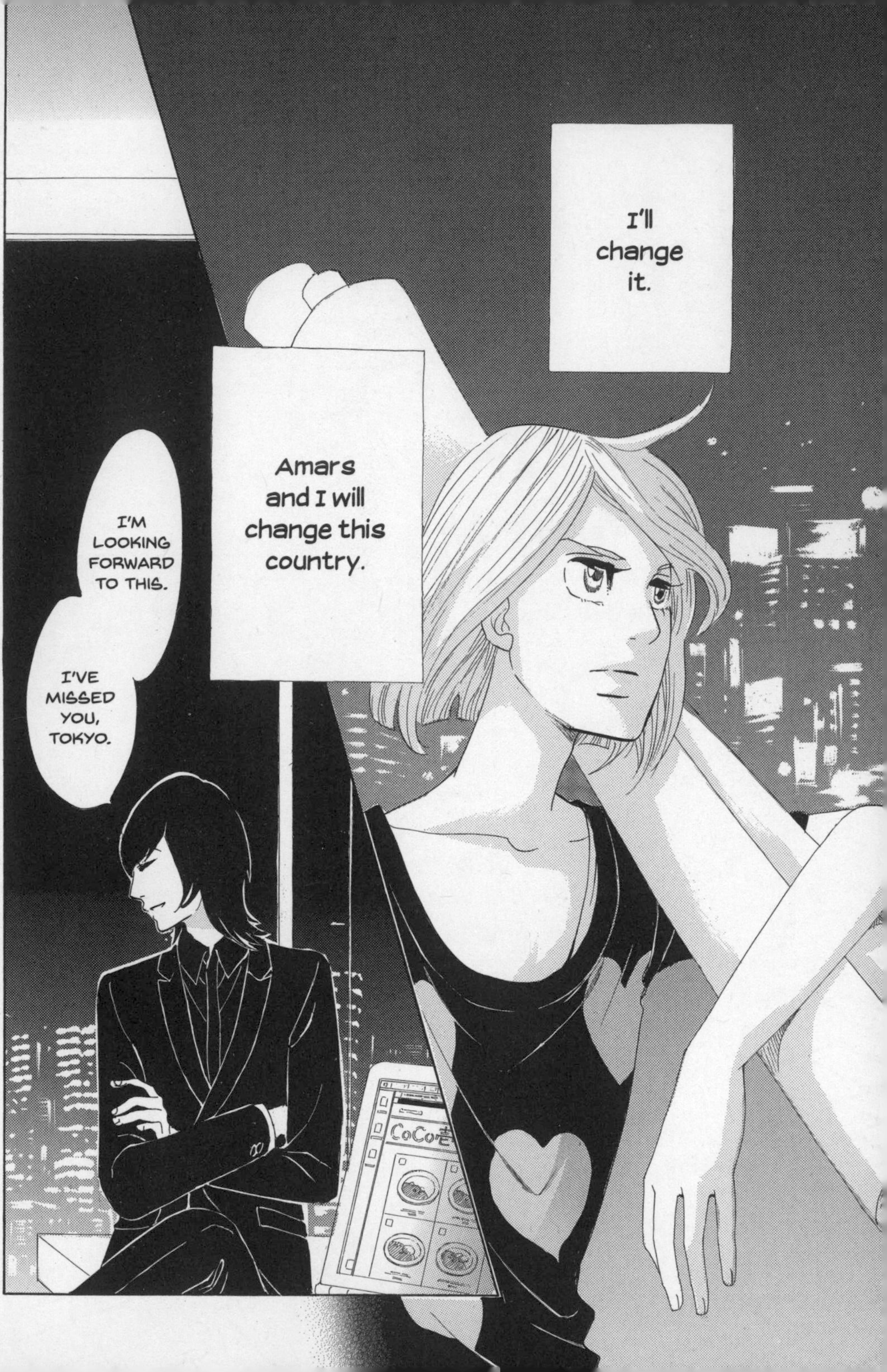
I'll change it.
Amars and I will change this country.
I'M LOOKING FORWARD TO THIS.
I'VE MISSED YOU, TOKYO.

Episode 56

The Toxic Princess

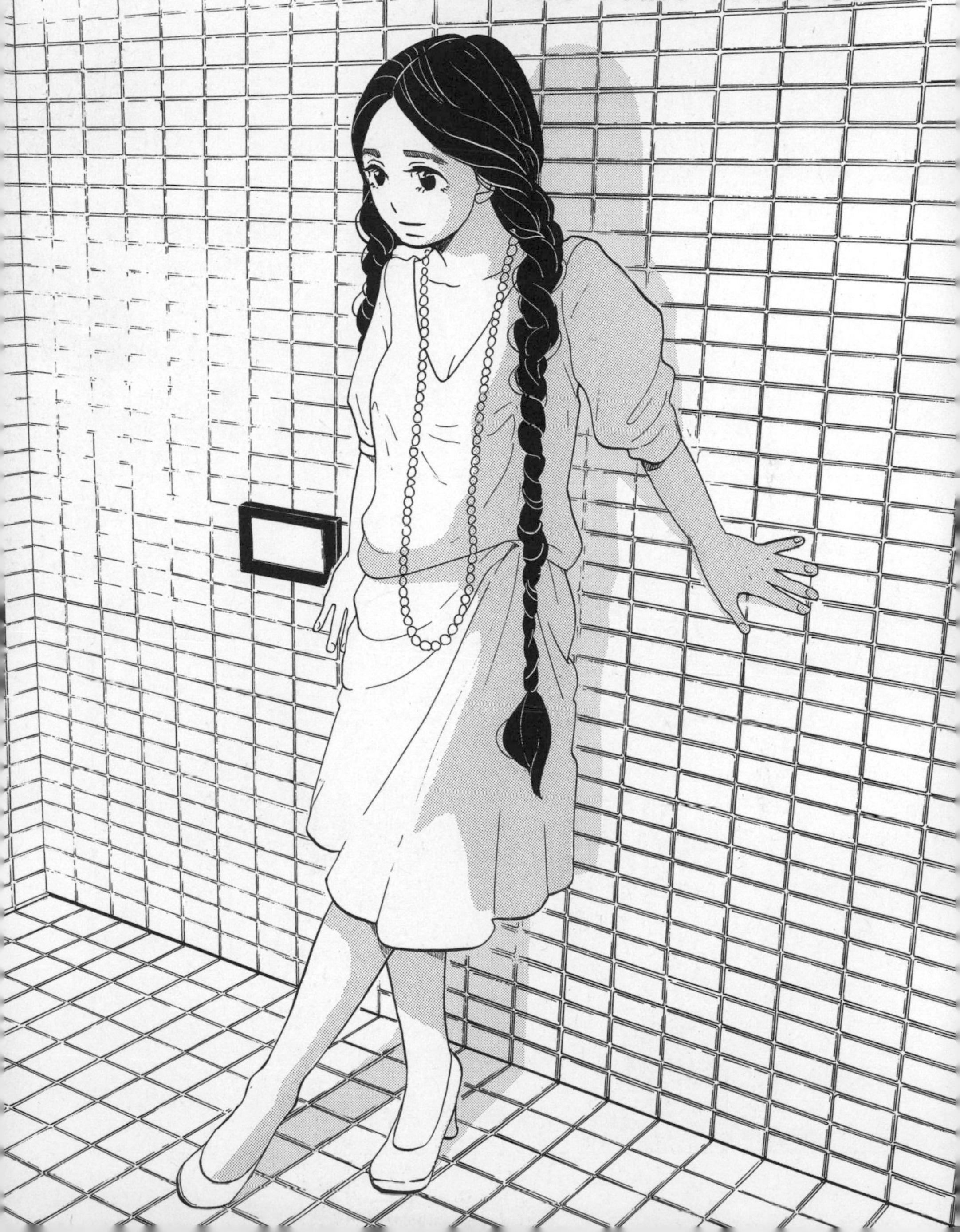

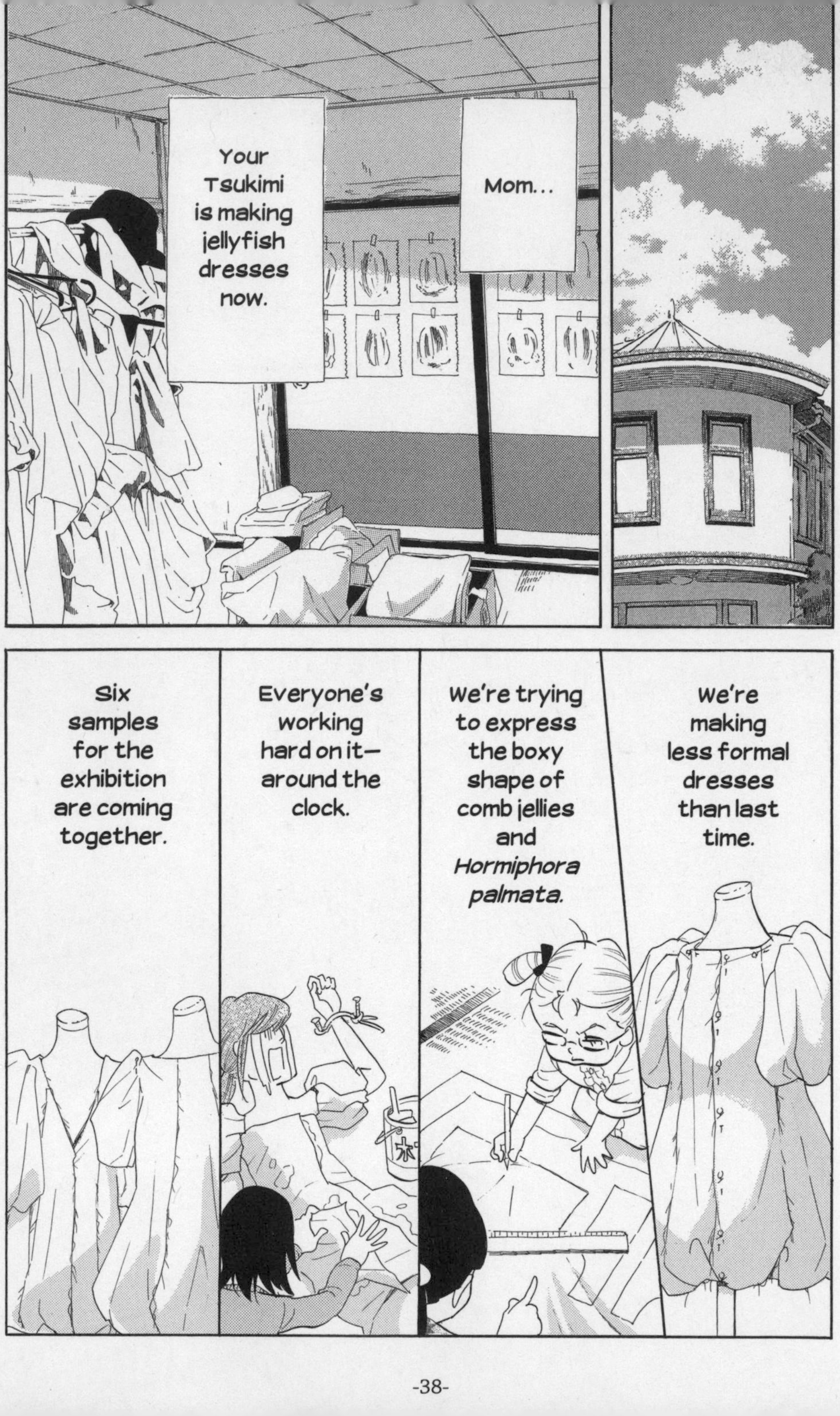
Mom...
Your Tsukimi is making jellyfish dresses now.
We're making less formal dresses than last time.
We're trying to express the boxy shape of comb jellies and *Hormiphora palmata.*
Everyone's working hard on it—around the clock.
Six samples for the exhibition are coming together.

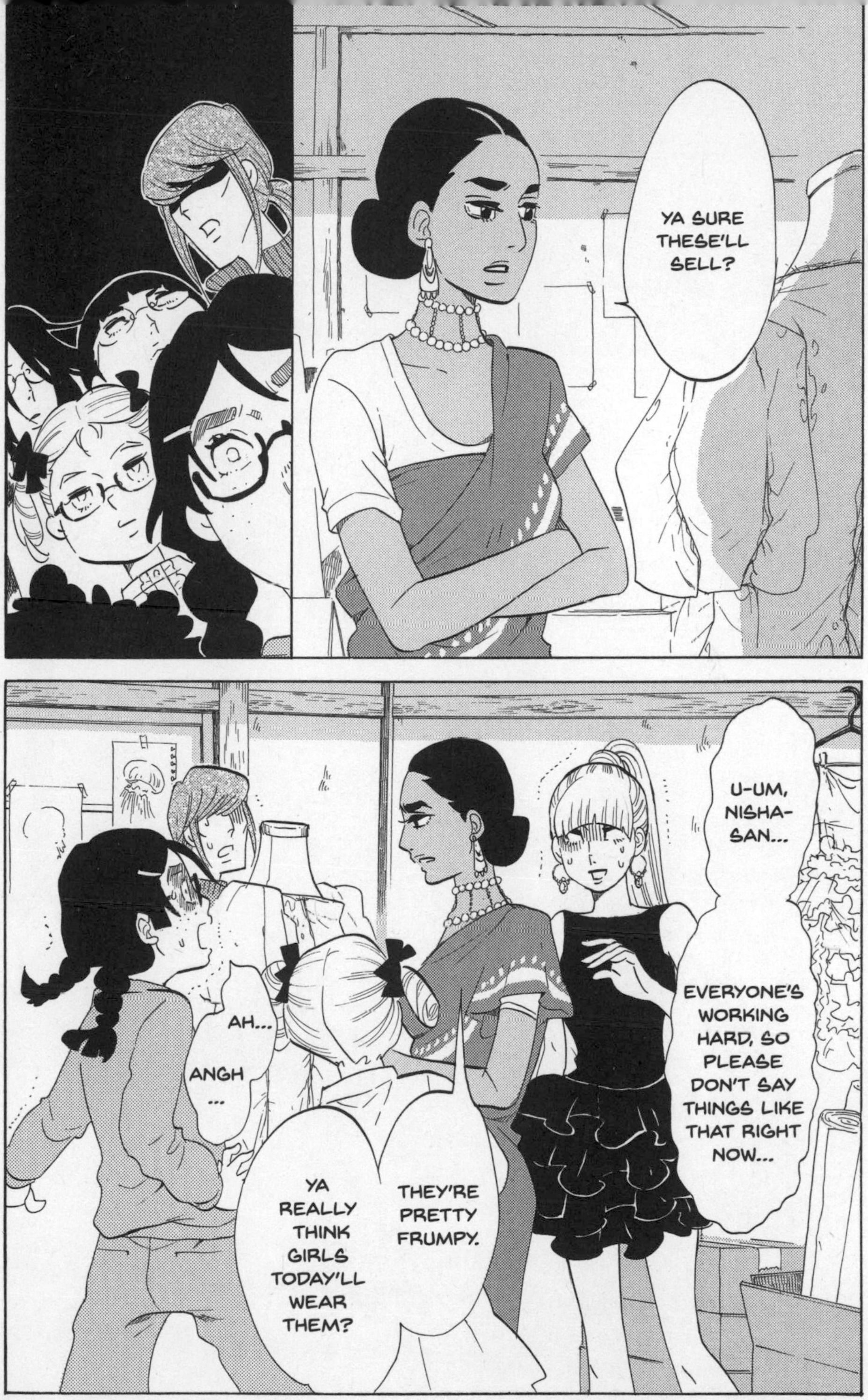
YA SURE THESE'LL SELL?
U-UM, NISHA-SAN...
EVERYONE'S WORKING HARD, SO PLEASE DON'T SAY THINGS LIKE THAT RIGHT NOW...
THEY'RE PRETTY FRUMPY.
YA REALLY THINK GIRLS TODAY'LL WEAR THEM?
AH...
ANGH ...

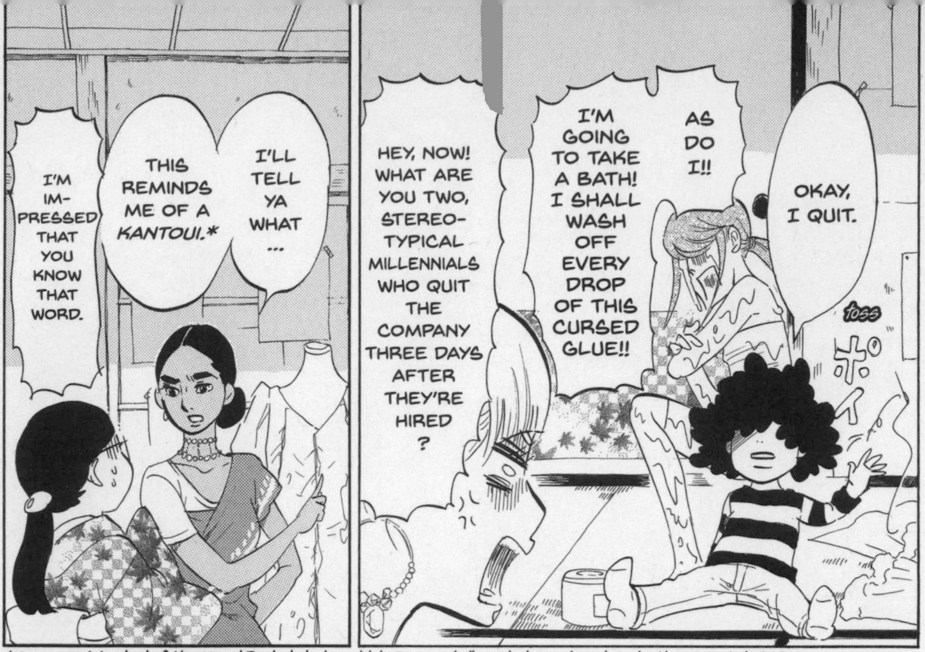
OKAY, I QUIT.
toss
AS DO I!!
I'M GOING TO TAKE A BATH! I SHALL WASH OFF EVERY DROP OF THIS CURSED GLUE!!
HEY, NOW! WHAT ARE YOU TWO, STEREO-TYPICAL MILLENNIALS WHO QUIT THE COMPANY THREE DAYS AFTER THEY'RE HIRED ?
I'LL TELL YA WHAT ...
THIS REMINDS ME OF A KANTOUI.*
I'M IM-PRESSED THAT YOU KNOW THAT WORD.

*A garment typical of the Yayoi Period, during which Queen Himiko ruled over her domain, the Yamatai state.

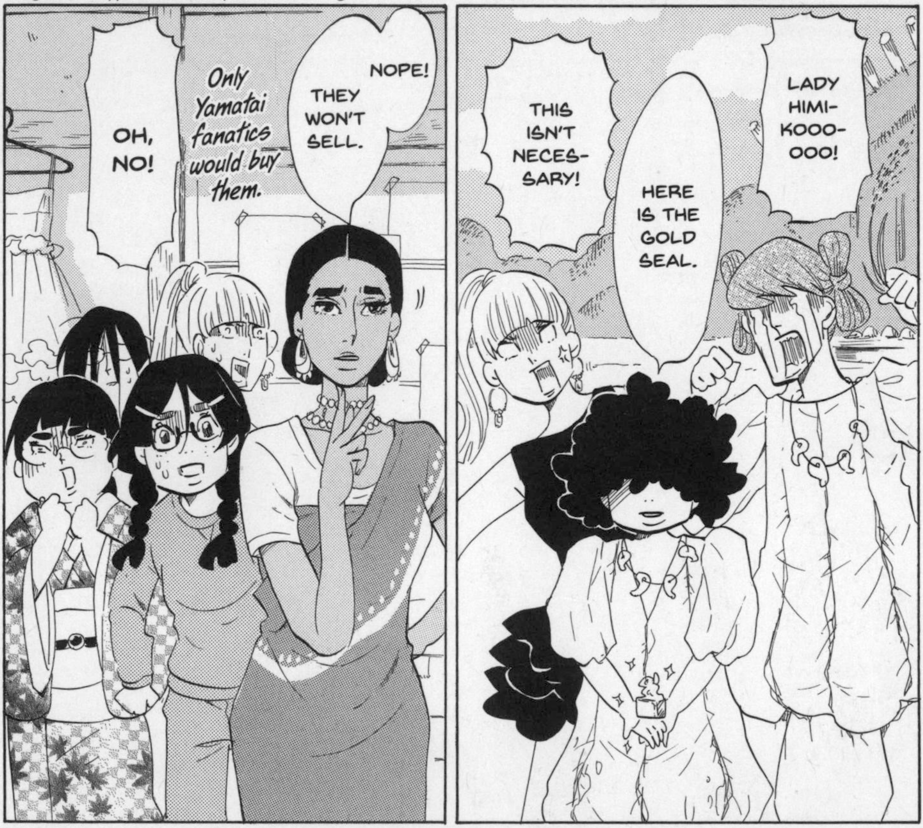
LADY HIMI-KOOO-OOO!
THIS ISN'T NECES-SARY!
HERE IS THE GOLD SEAL.
NOPE! THEY WON'T SELL.
Only Yamatai fanatics would buy them.
OH, NO!

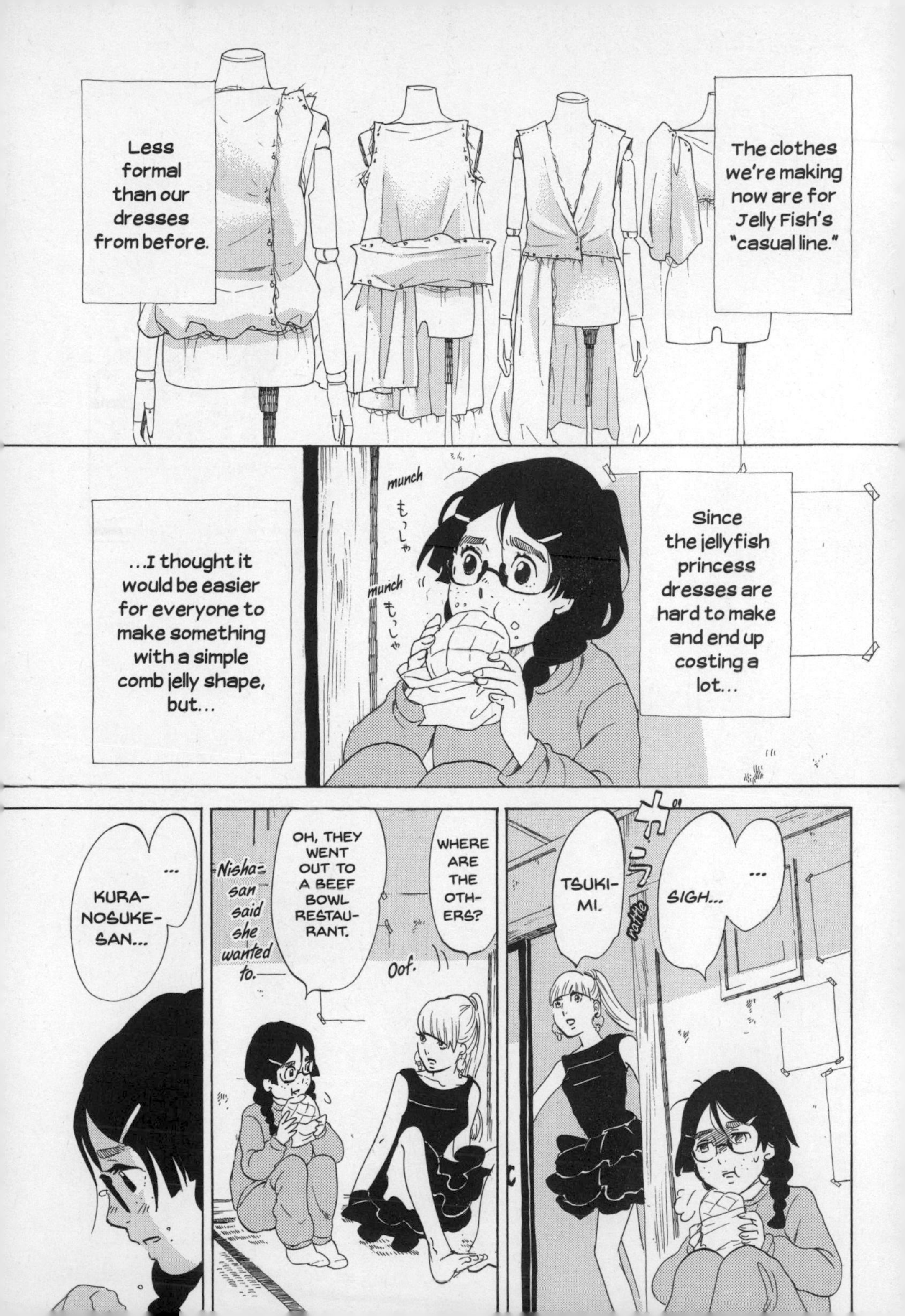

The clothes we're making now are for Jelly Fish's "casual line."
Less formal than our dresses from before.
Since the jellyfish princess dresses are hard to make and end up costing a lot...
munch
もっしゃ
munch
もっしゃ
...I thought it would be easier for everyone to make something with a simple comb jelly shape, but...
... SIGH...
rattle
TSUKI-MI.
WHERE ARE THE OTH-ERS?
OH, THEY WENT OUT TO A BEEF BOWL RESTAU-RANT.
Nisha-san said she wanted to.
Oof.
... KURA-NOSUKE-SAN...

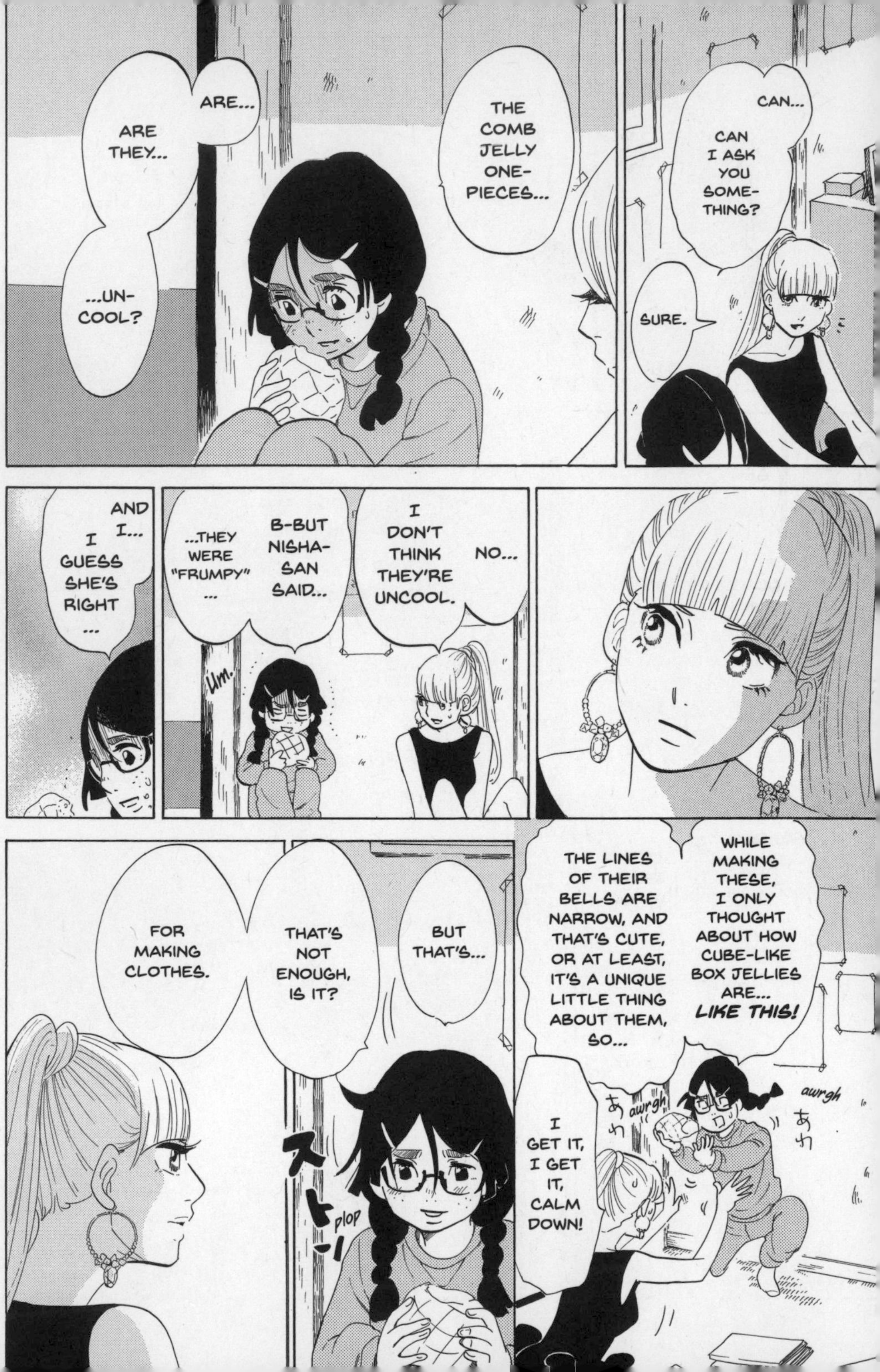
CAN...
CAN I ASK YOU SOME-THING?
SURE.
THE COMB JELLY ONE-PIECES...
ARE...
ARE THEY...
...UN-COOL?
NO...
I DON'T THINK THEY'RE UNCOOL.
B-BUT NISHA-SAN SAID...
...THEY WERE "FRUMPY"...
Um.
AND I...
I GUESS SHE'S RIGHT...
WHILE MAKING THESE, I ONLY THOUGHT ABOUT HOW CUBE-LIKE BOX JELLIES ARE... ***LIKE THIS!***
THE LINES OF THEIR BELLS ARE NARROW, AND THAT'S CUTE, OR AT LEAST, IT'S A UNIQUE LITTLE THING ABOUT THEM, SO...
awrgh
awrgh
I GET IT, I GET IT, CALM DOWN!
BUT THAT'S...
THAT'S NOT ENOUGH, IS IT?
FOR MAKING CLOTHES.
plop

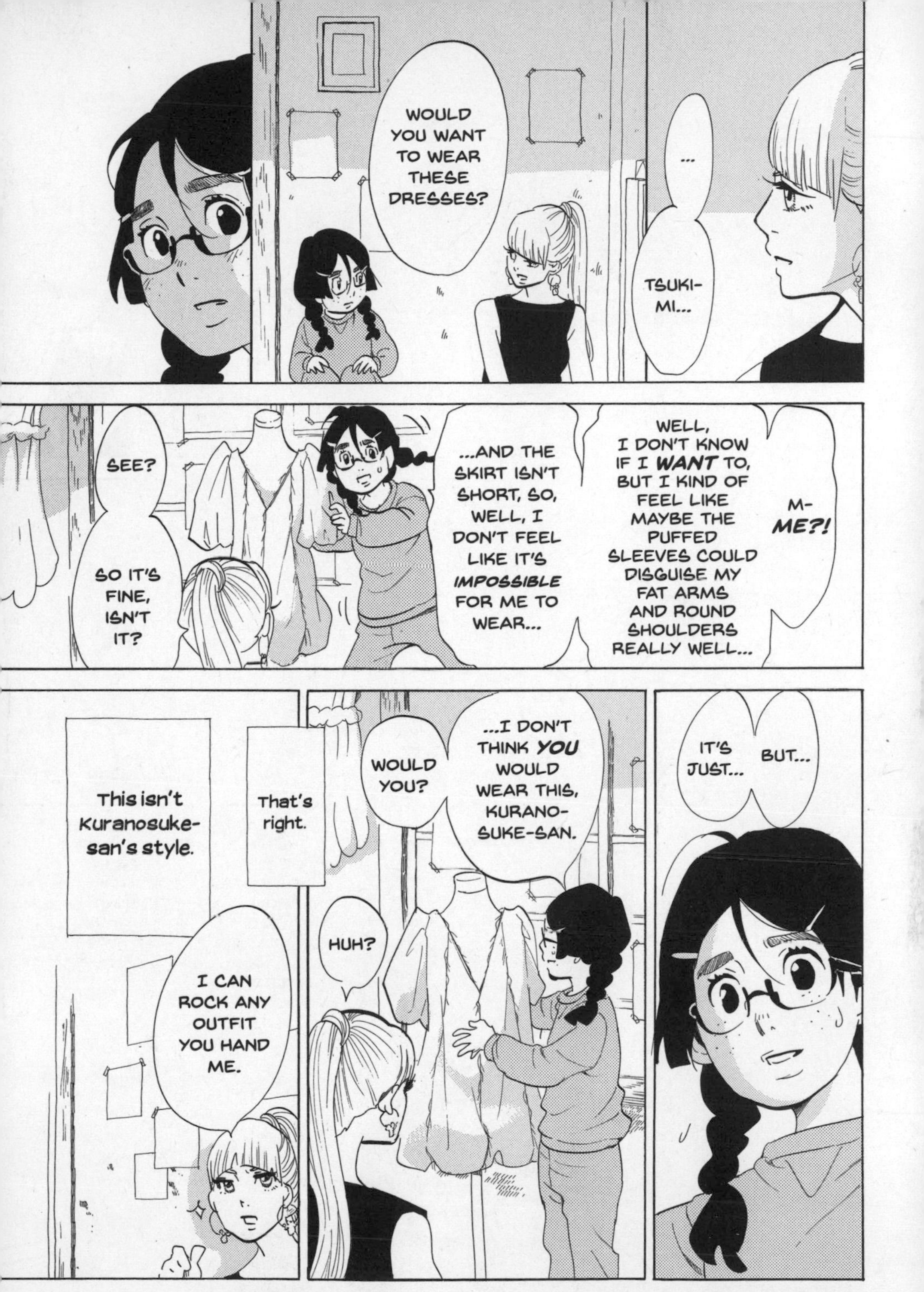
...
TSUKIMI...
WOULD YOU WANT TO WEAR THESE DRESSES?
M-ME?!
WELL, I DON'T KNOW IF I **WANT** TO, BUT I KIND OF FEEL LIKE MAYBE THE PUFFED SLEEVES COULD DISGUISE MY FAT ARMS AND ROUND SHOULDERS REALLY WELL...
...AND THE SKIRT ISN'T SHORT, SO, WELL, I DON'T FEEL LIKE IT'S *IMPOSSIBLE* FOR ME TO WEAR...
SEE?
SO IT'S FINE, ISN'T IT?
BUT...
IT'S JUST...
...I DON'T THINK **YOU** WOULD WEAR THIS, KURANOSUKE-SAN.
WOULD YOU?
HUH?
That's right.
This isn't Kuranosuke-san's style.
I CAN ROCK ANY OUTFIT YOU HAND ME.

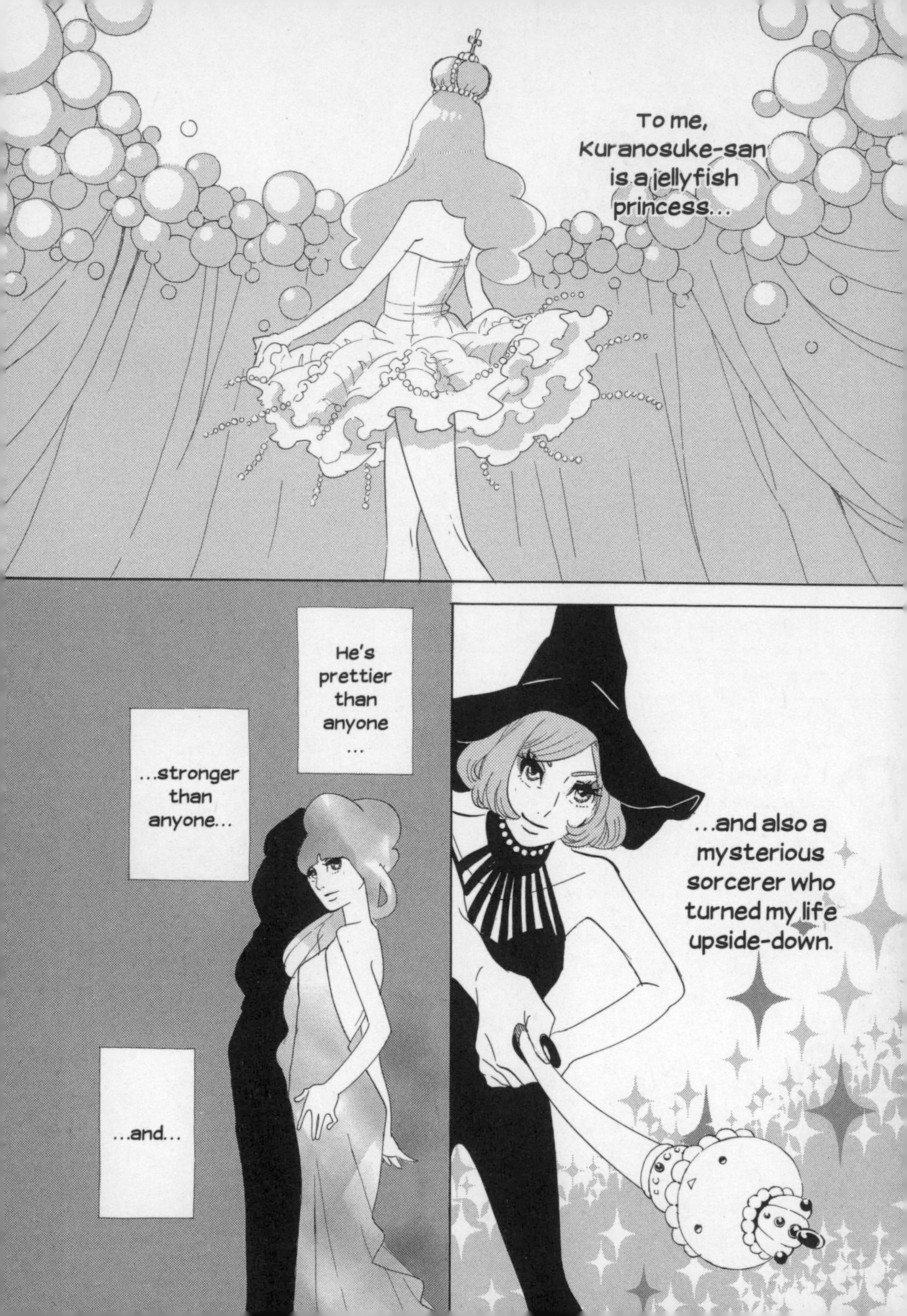
To me, Kuranosuke-san is a jellyfish princess...
He's prettier than anyone ...
...stronger than anyone...
...and...
...and also a mysterious sorcerer who turned my life upside-down.

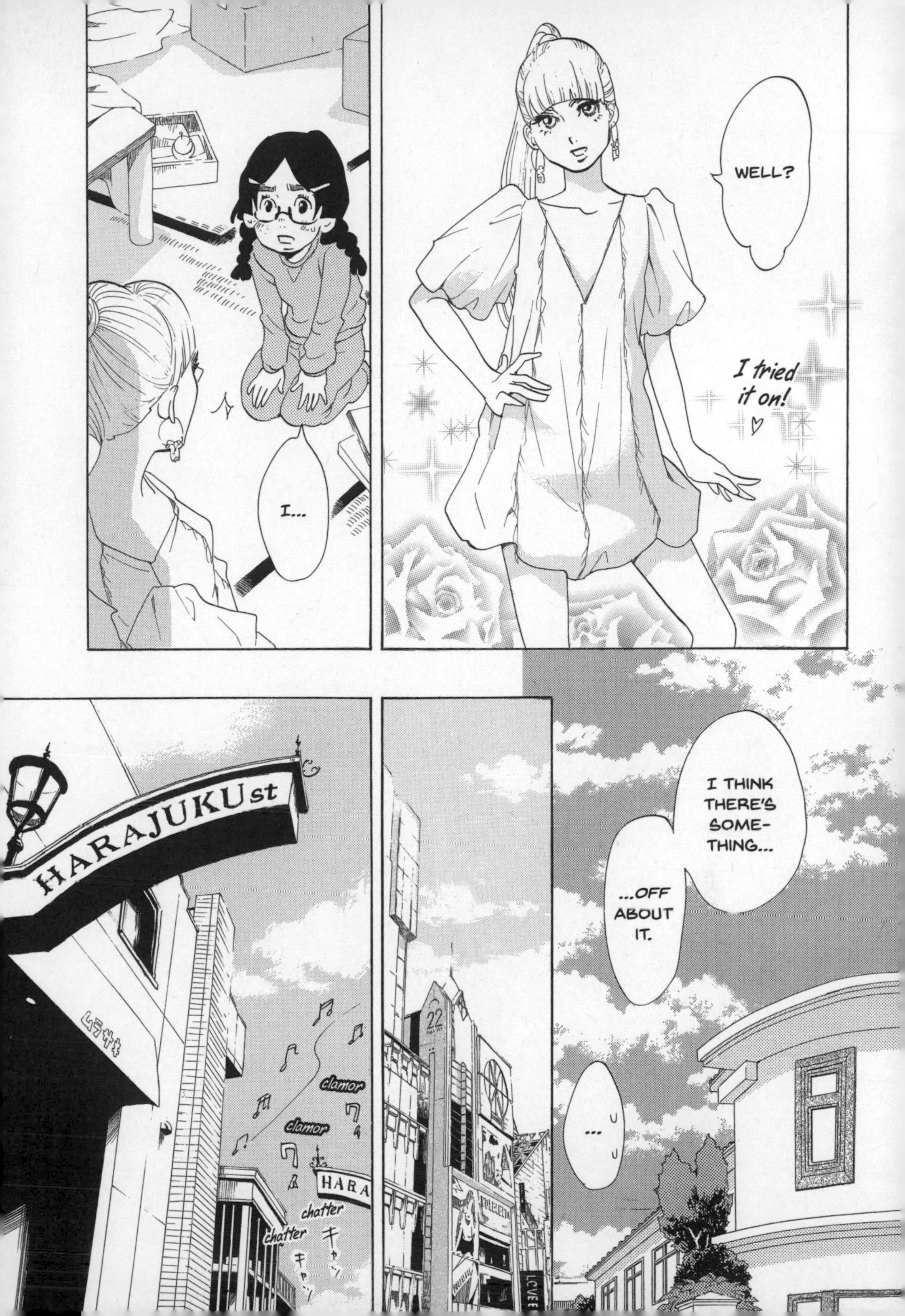
WELL?
I tried it on!
I...
I THINK THERE'S SOME-THING...
...OFF ABOUT IT.
...
22
HARAJUKU st
ムラサキ
clamor
ワ
clamor
ワ
HARA
chatter
キャッ
chatter
キャッ

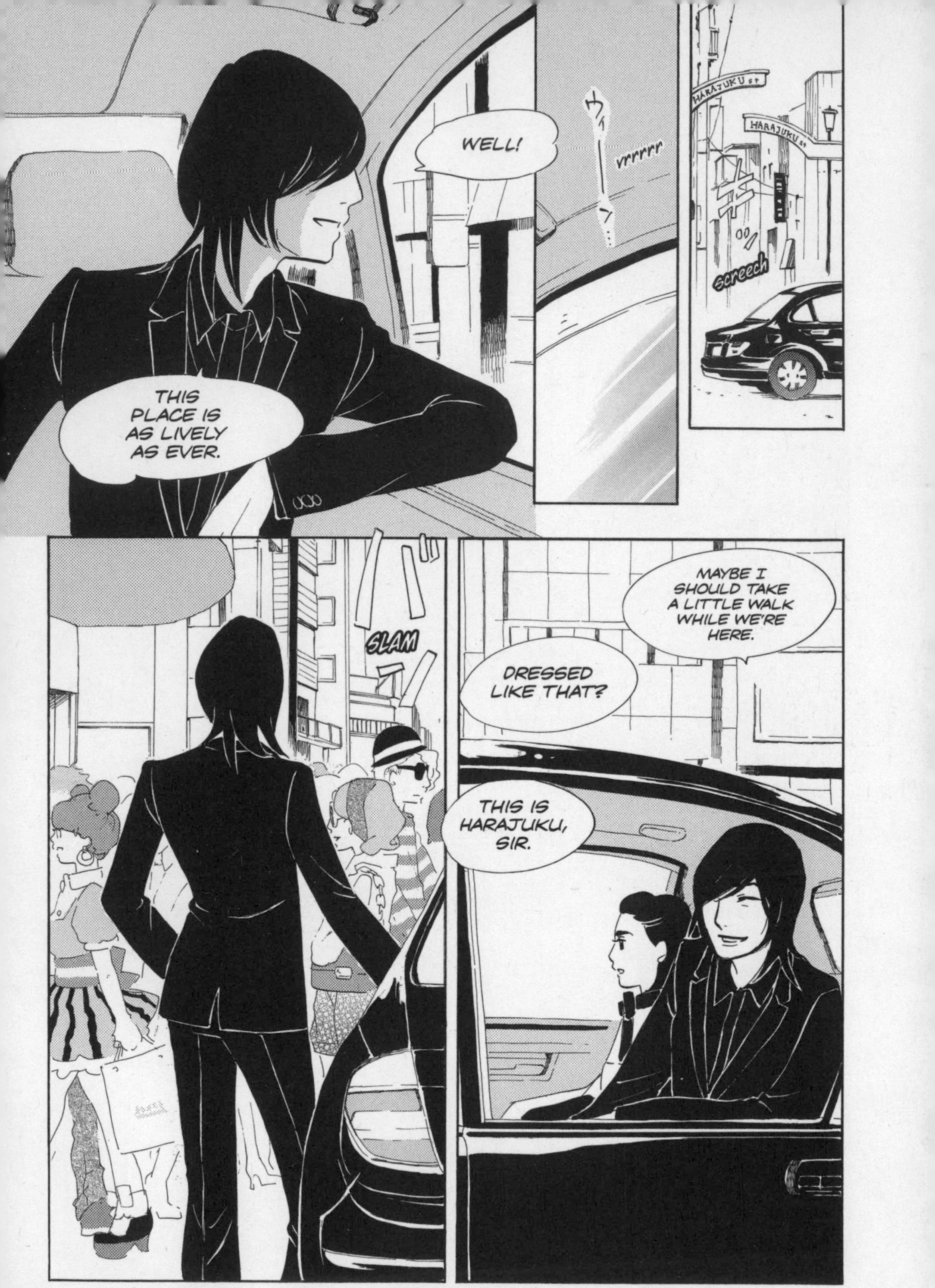
HARAJUKU st
HARAJUKU st
screech
WELL!
vrrrrr
THIS PLACE IS AS LIVELY AS EVER.
MAYBE I SHOULD TAKE A LITTLE WALK WHILE WE'RE HERE.
DRESSED LIKE THAT?
THIS IS HARAJUKU, SIR.
SLAM

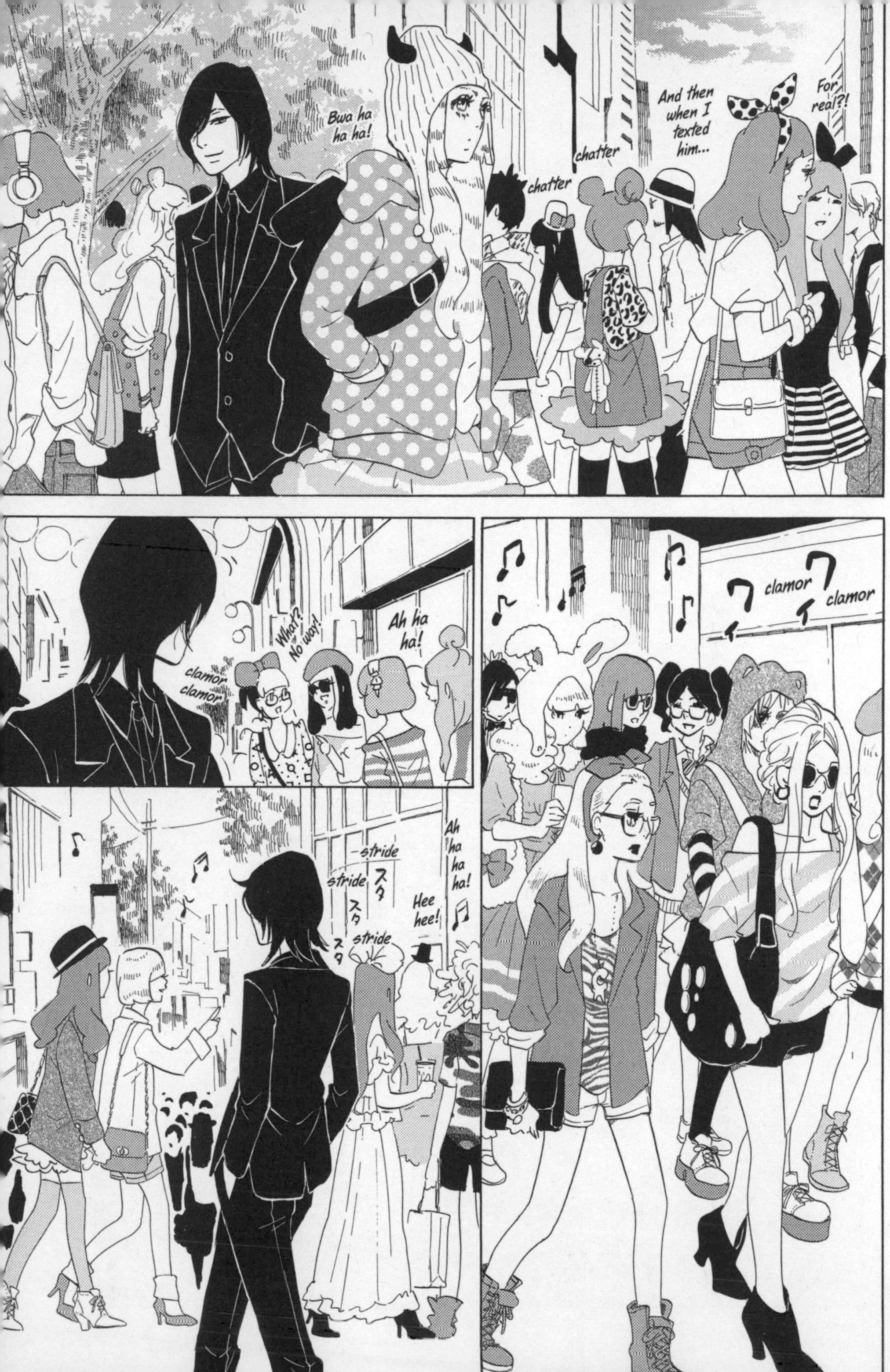
For real?!
And then when I texted him...
chatter
chatter
Bwa ha ha ha!
ワイ clamor
ワイ clamor
Ah ha ha!
What?! No way!
clamor clamor
Ah ha ha ha!
Hee hee!
stride スタ
stride スタ
stride スタ

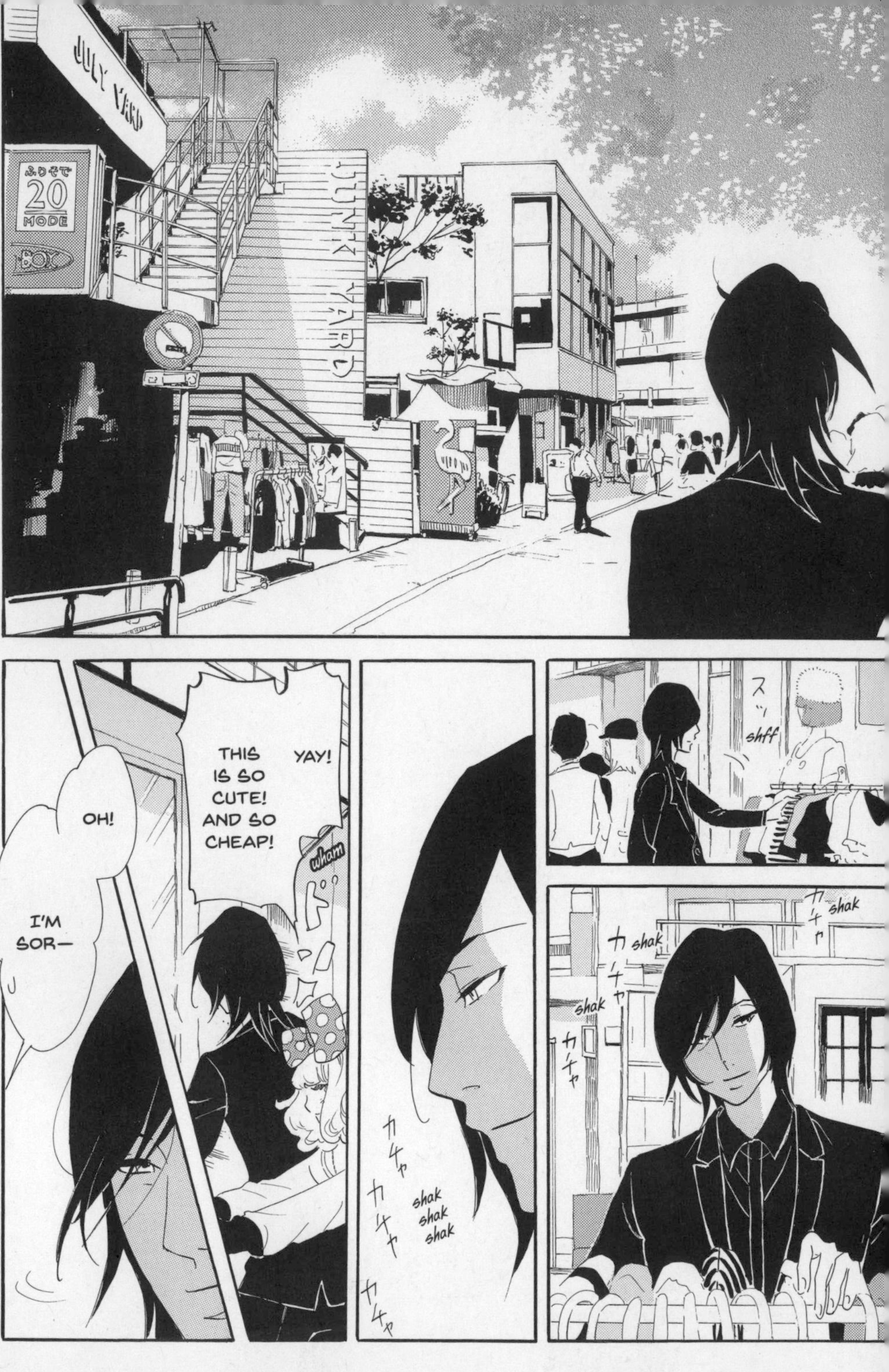
JULY YARD
ふりそで
20
MODE
BOX
JUNK YARD
スッ
shff
カチャ
shak
カチャ
shak
shak
カチャ
カチャ
カチャ
カチャ
shak
shak
shak
wham
ド
YAY!
THIS IS SO CUTE! AND SO CHEAP!
OH!
I'M SOR—

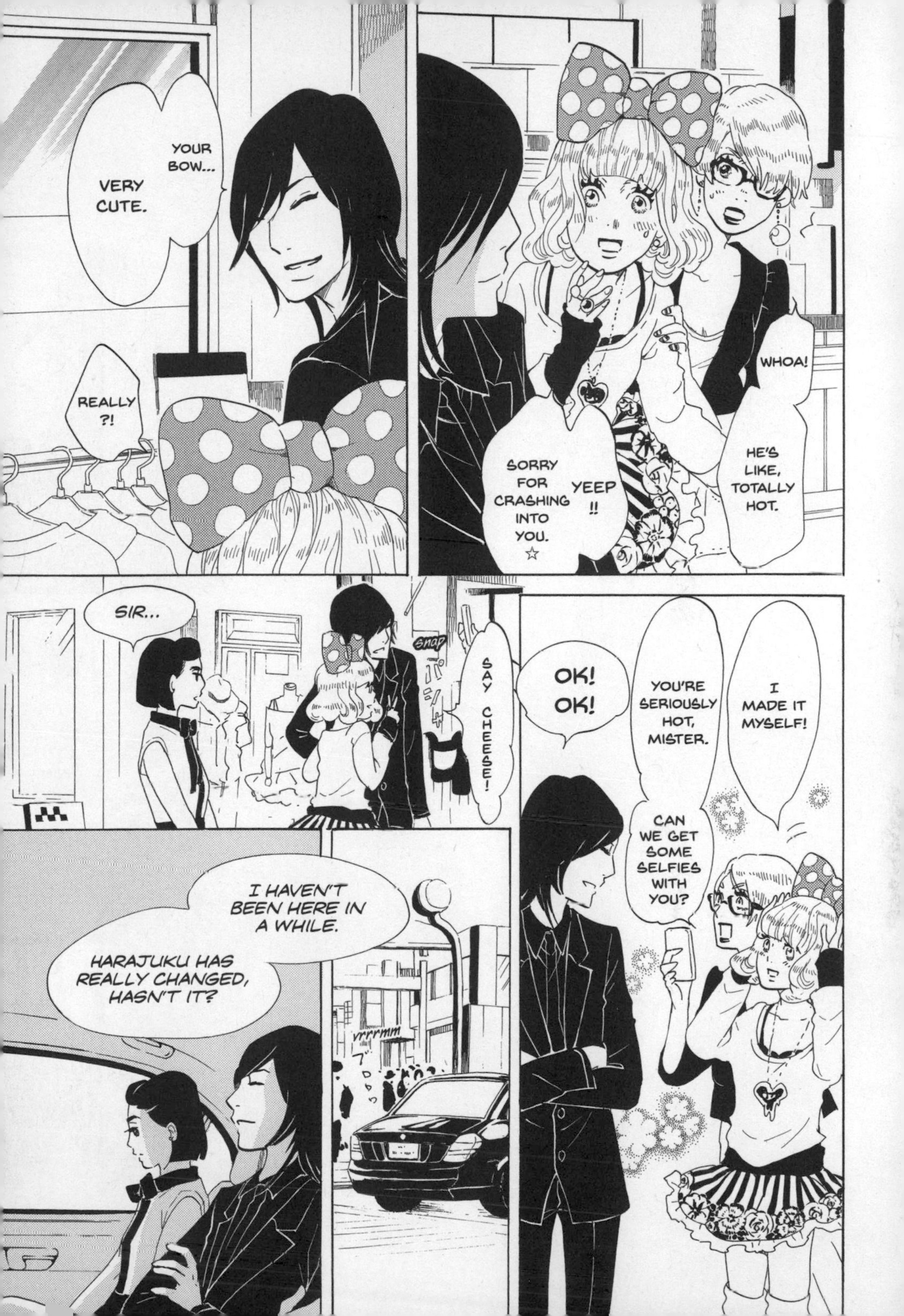
WHOA!
HE'S LIKE, TOTALLY HOT.
YEEP!!
SORRY FOR CRASHING INTO YOU. ☆
YOUR BOW...
VERY CUTE.
REALLY?!
I MADE IT MYSELF!
YOU'RE SERIOUSLY HOT, MISTER.
OK! OK!
CAN WE GET SOME SELFIES WITH YOU?
SAY CHEESE!
snap
SIR...
vrrrmm
I HAVEN'T BEEN HERE IN A WHILE.
HARAJUKU HAS REALLY CHANGED, HASN'T IT?

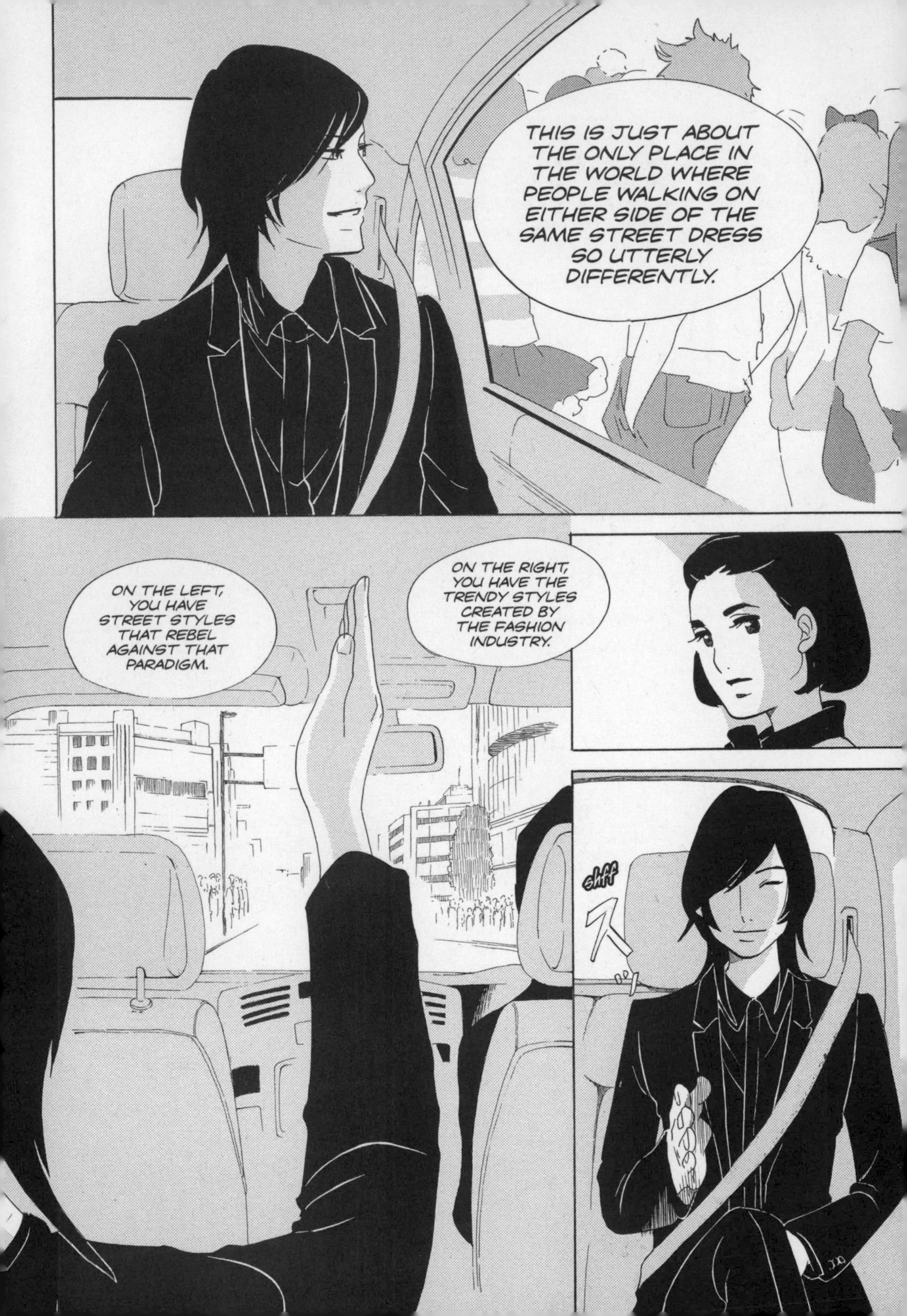
THIS IS JUST ABOUT THE ONLY PLACE IN THE WORLD WHERE PEOPLE WALKING ON EITHER SIDE OF THE SAME STREET DRESS SO UTTERLY DIFFERENTLY.
ON THE RIGHT, YOU HAVE THE TRENDY STYLES CREATED BY THE FASHION INDUSTRY.
ON THE LEFT, YOU HAVE STREET STYLES THAT REBEL AGAINST THAT PARADIGM.
shff

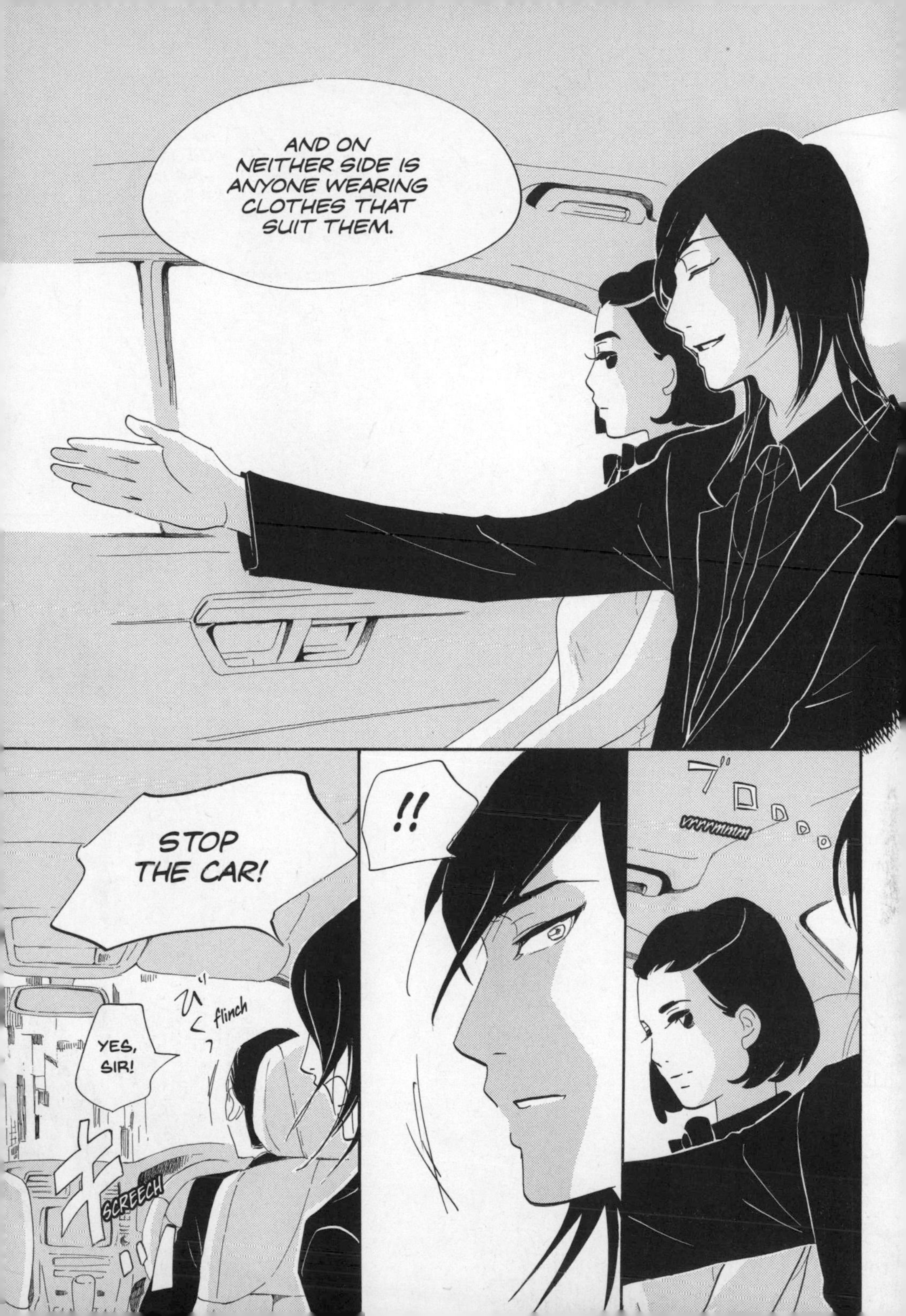
AND ON NEITHER SIDE IS ANYONE WEARING CLOTHES THAT SUIT THEM.
vrrrrmmm
!!
STOP THE CAR!
flinch
YES, SIR!
SCREECH

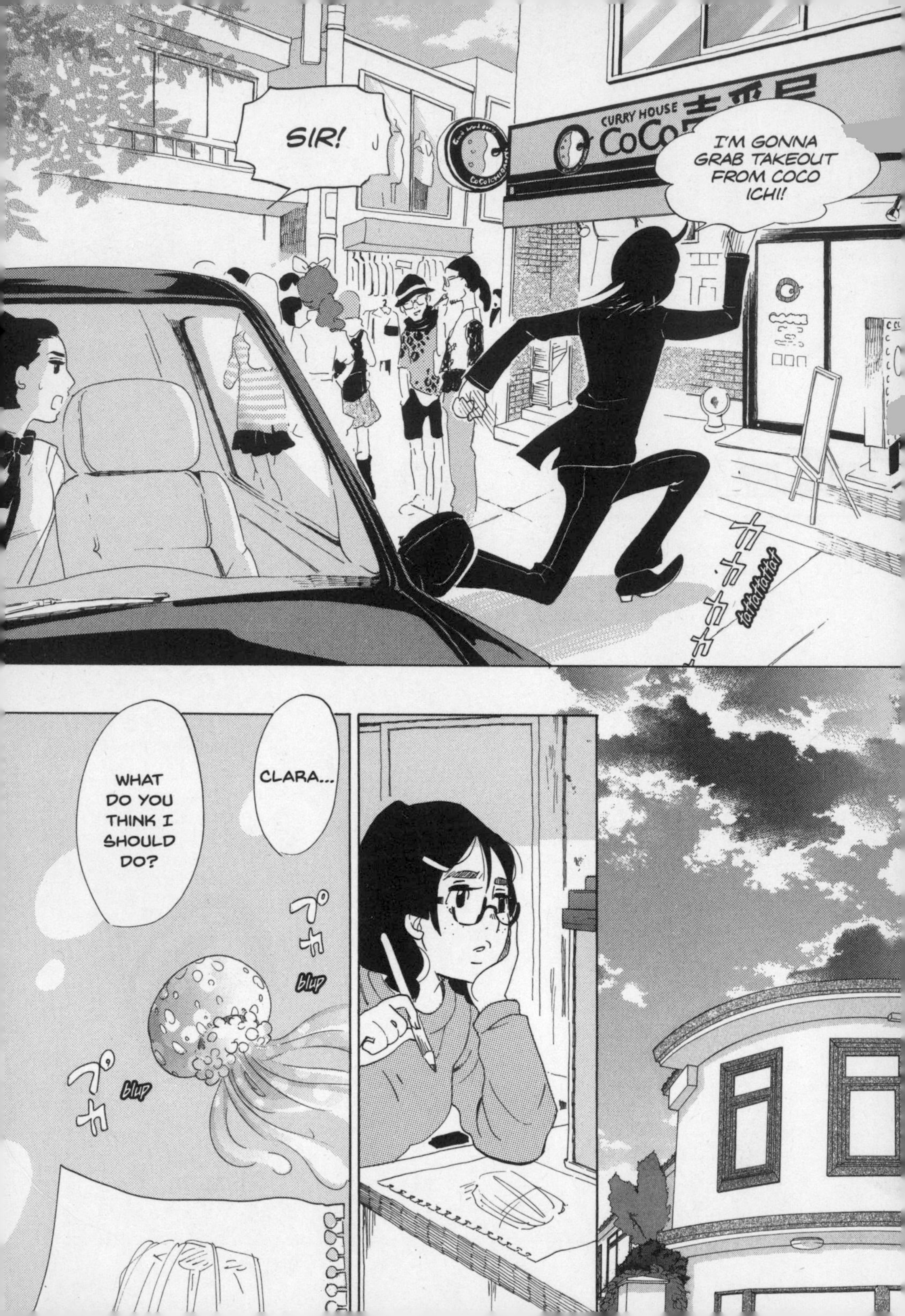
CURRY HOUSE
CoCo
I'M GONNA GRAB TAKEOUT FROM COCO ICHI!
SIR!
タタタタタ
tattattattat
CLARA...
WHAT DO YOU THINK I SHOULD DO?
プチ
blup
プチ
blup

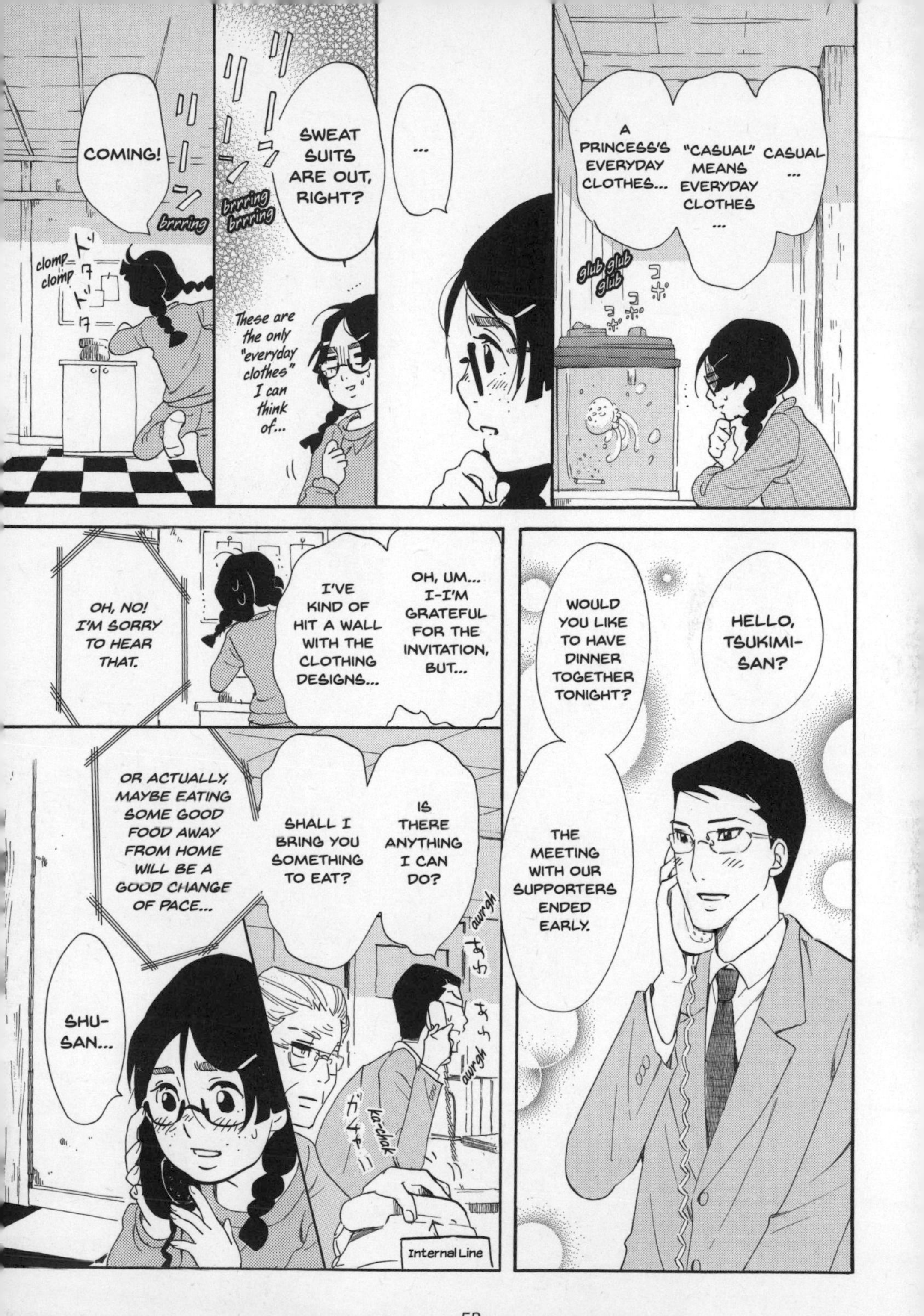
CASUAL ...
"CASUAL" MEANS EVERYDAY CLOTHES ...
A PRINCESS'S EVERYDAY CLOTHES...
glub glub glub
...
SWEAT SUITS ARE OUT, RIGHT?
brrrring brrrring
These are the only "everyday clothes" I can think of...
brrring
COMING!
clomp clomp
HELLO, TSUKIMI-SAN?
WOULD YOU LIKE TO HAVE DINNER TOGETHER TONIGHT?
THE MEETING WITH OUR SUPPORTERS ENDED EARLY.
OH, UM... I-I'M GRATEFUL FOR THE INVITATION, BUT...
I'VE KIND OF HIT A WALL WITH THE CLOTHING DESIGNS...
OH, NO! I'M SORRY TO HEAR THAT.
IS THERE ANYTHING I CAN DO?
SHALL I BRING YOU SOMETHING TO EAT?
OR ACTUALLY, MAYBE EATING SOME GOOD FOOD AWAY FROM HOME WILL BE A GOOD CHANGE OF PACE...
awrgh
awrgh
SHU-SAN...
ka-chak
Internal Line

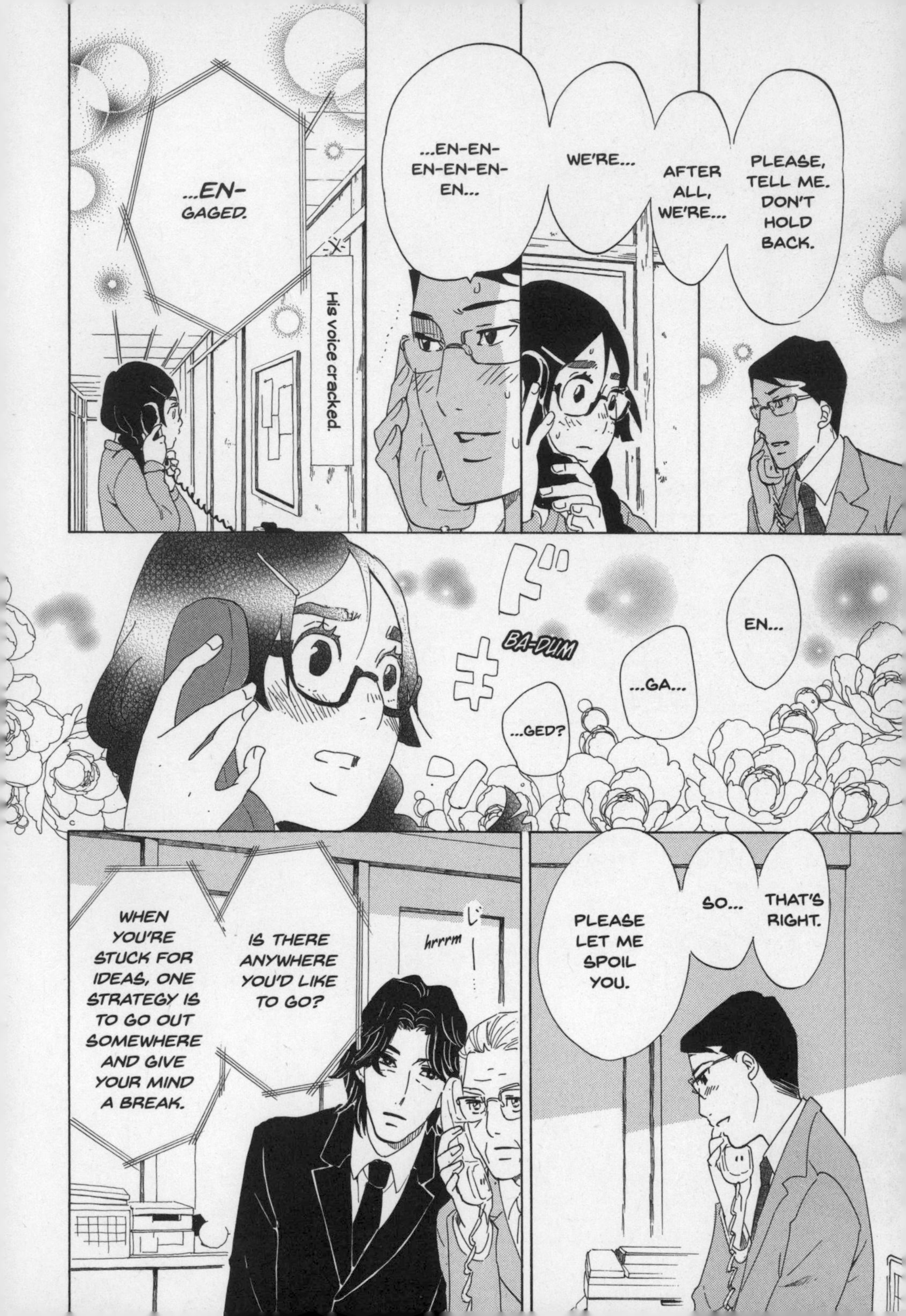
PLEASE, TELL ME. DON'T HOLD BACK.
AFTER ALL, WE'RE...
WE'RE...
...EN-EN-EN-EN-EN-EN...
...EN-GAGED.
His voice cracked.
BA-DUM
EN...
...GA...
...GED?
THAT'S RIGHT.
SO...
PLEASE LET ME SPOIL YOU.
hrrrm
IS THERE ANYWHERE YOU'D LIKE TO GO?
WHEN YOU'RE STUCK FOR IDEAS, ONE STRATEGY IS TO GO OUT SOMEWHERE AND GIVE YOUR MIND A BREAK.

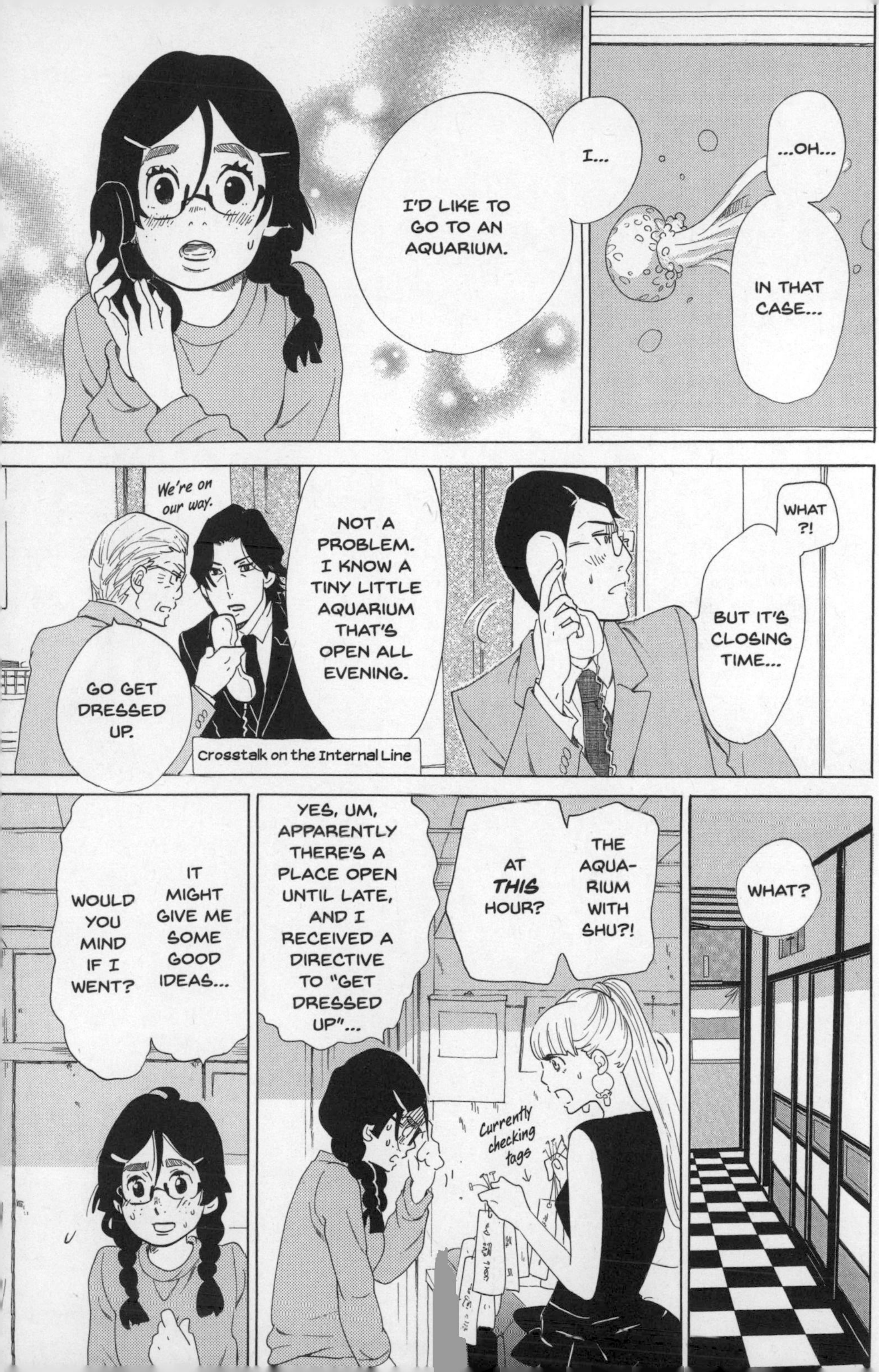
...OH...
IN THAT CASE...
I...
I'D LIKE TO GO TO AN AQUARIUM.
WHAT?!
BUT IT'S CLOSING TIME...
NOT A PROBLEM. I KNOW A TINY LITTLE AQUARIUM THAT'S OPEN ALL EVENING.
We're on our way.
GO GET DRESSED UP.
Crosstalk on the Internal Line
WHAT?
THE AQUA-RIUM WITH SHU?!
AT THIS HOUR?
YES, UM, APPARENTLY THERE'S A PLACE OPEN UNTIL LATE, AND I RECEIVED A DIRECTIVE TO "GET DRESSED UP"...
Currently checking tags
IT MIGHT GIVE ME SOME GOOD IDEAS...
WOULD YOU MIND IF I WENT?

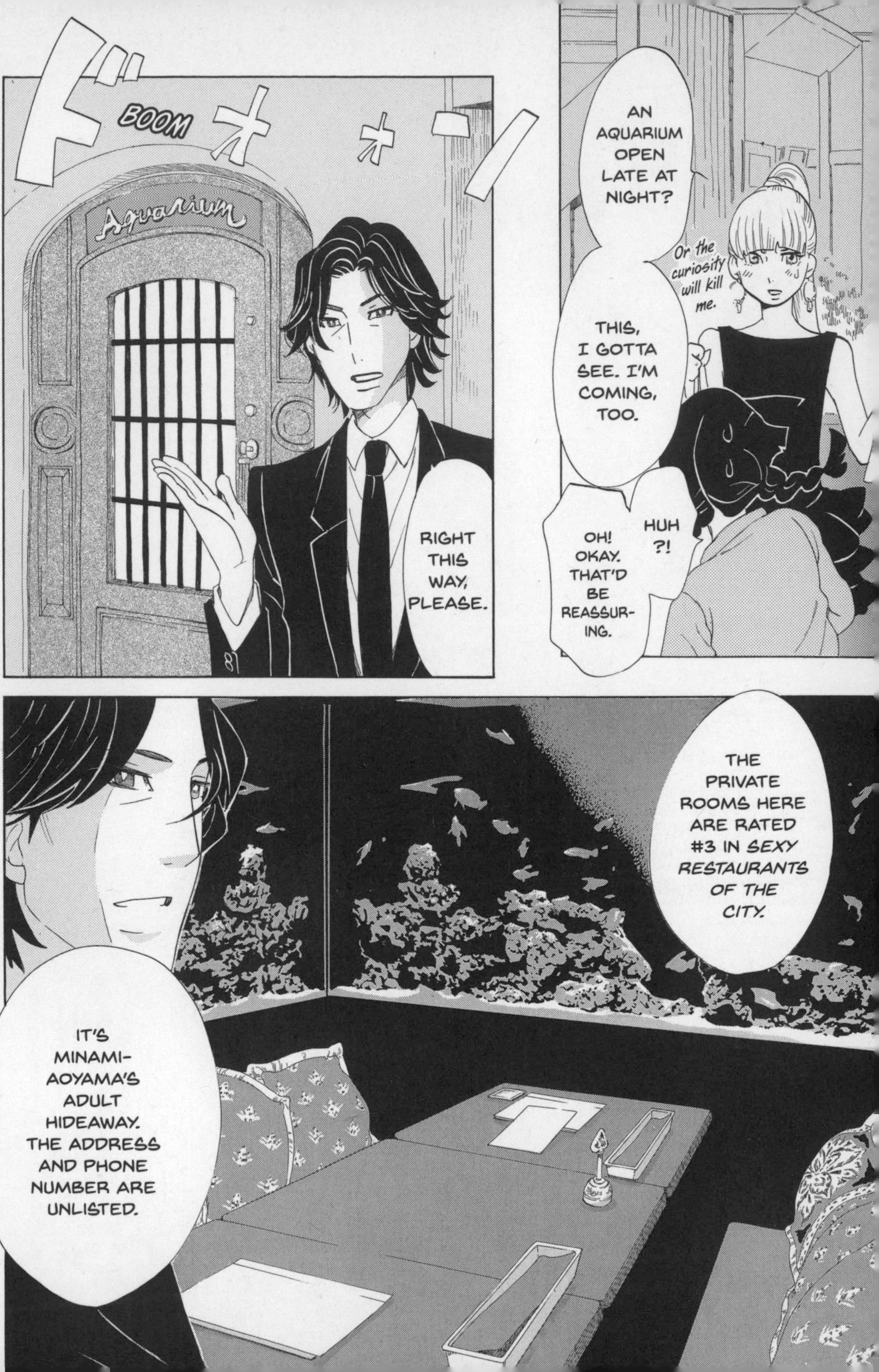
AN AQUARIUM OPEN LATE AT NIGHT?
Or the curiosity will kill me.
THIS, I GOTTA SEE. I'M COMING, TOO.
HUH?!
OH! OKAY. THAT'D BE REASSURING.
ドオォーン
BOOM
Aquarium
RIGHT THIS WAY, PLEASE.
THE PRIVATE ROOMS HERE ARE RATED #3 IN *SEXY RESTAURANTS OF THE CITY.*
IT'S MINAMI-AOYAMA'S ADULT HIDEAWAY. THE ADDRESS AND PHONE NUMBER ARE UNLISTED.

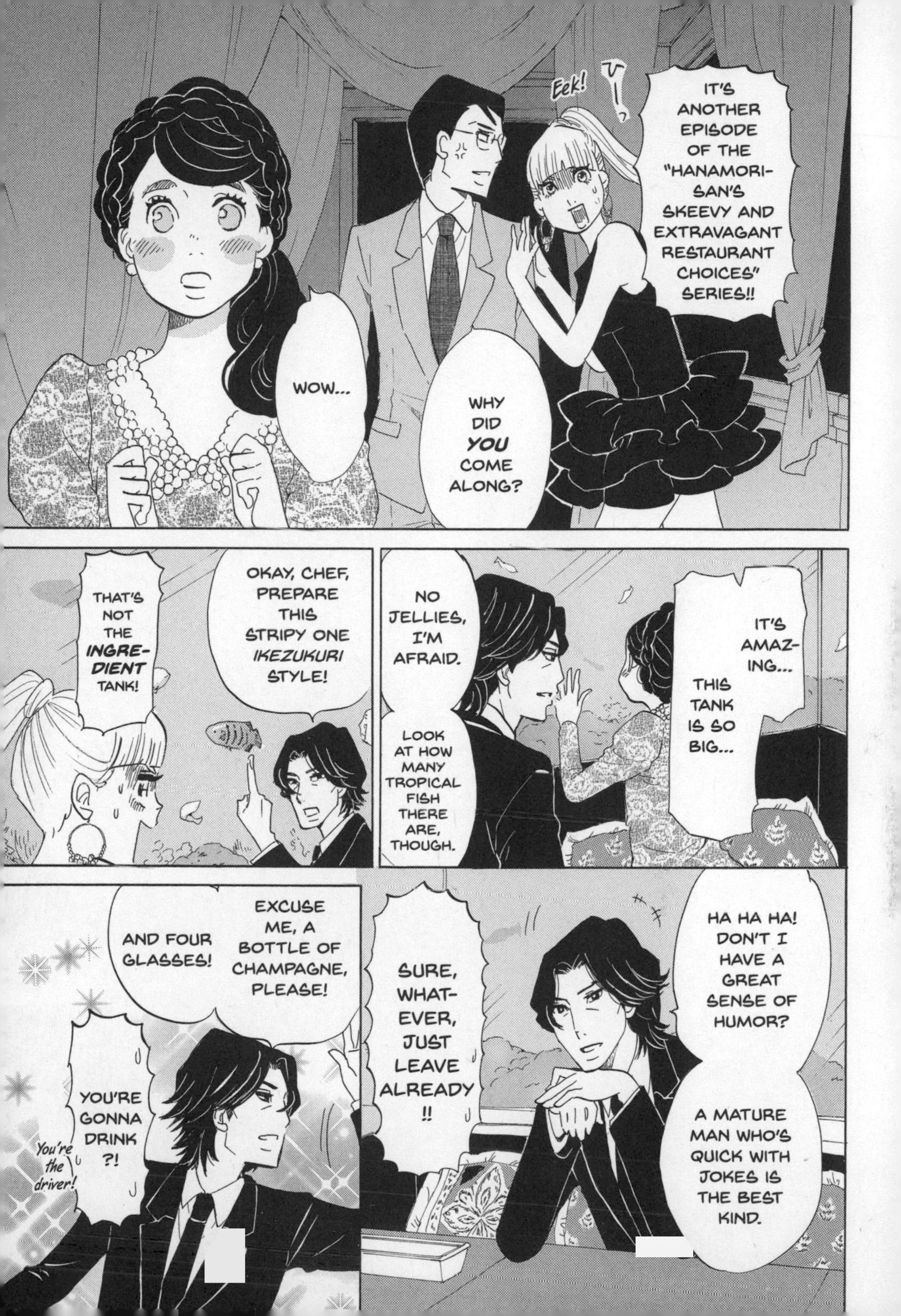
IT'S ANOTHER EPISODE OF THE "HANAMORI-SAN'S SKEEVY AND EXTRAVAGANT RESTAURANT CHOICES" SERIES!!
Eek!
WHY DID *YOU* COME ALONG?
WOW...
IT'S AMAZ-ING...
THIS TANK IS SO BIG...
NO JELLIES, I'M AFRAID.
LOOK AT HOW MANY TROPICAL FISH THERE ARE, THOUGH.
OKAY, CHEF, PREPARE THIS STRIPY ONE *IKEZUKURI* STYLE!
THAT'S NOT THE *INGREDIENT* TANK!
HA HA HA! DON'T I HAVE A GREAT SENSE OF HUMOR?
A MATURE MAN WHO'S QUICK WITH JOKES IS THE BEST KIND.
SURE, WHATEVER, JUST LEAVE ALREADY!!
EXCUSE ME, A BOTTLE OF CHAMPAGNE, PLEASE!
AND FOUR GLASSES!
YOU'RE GONNA DRINK?!
You're the driver!

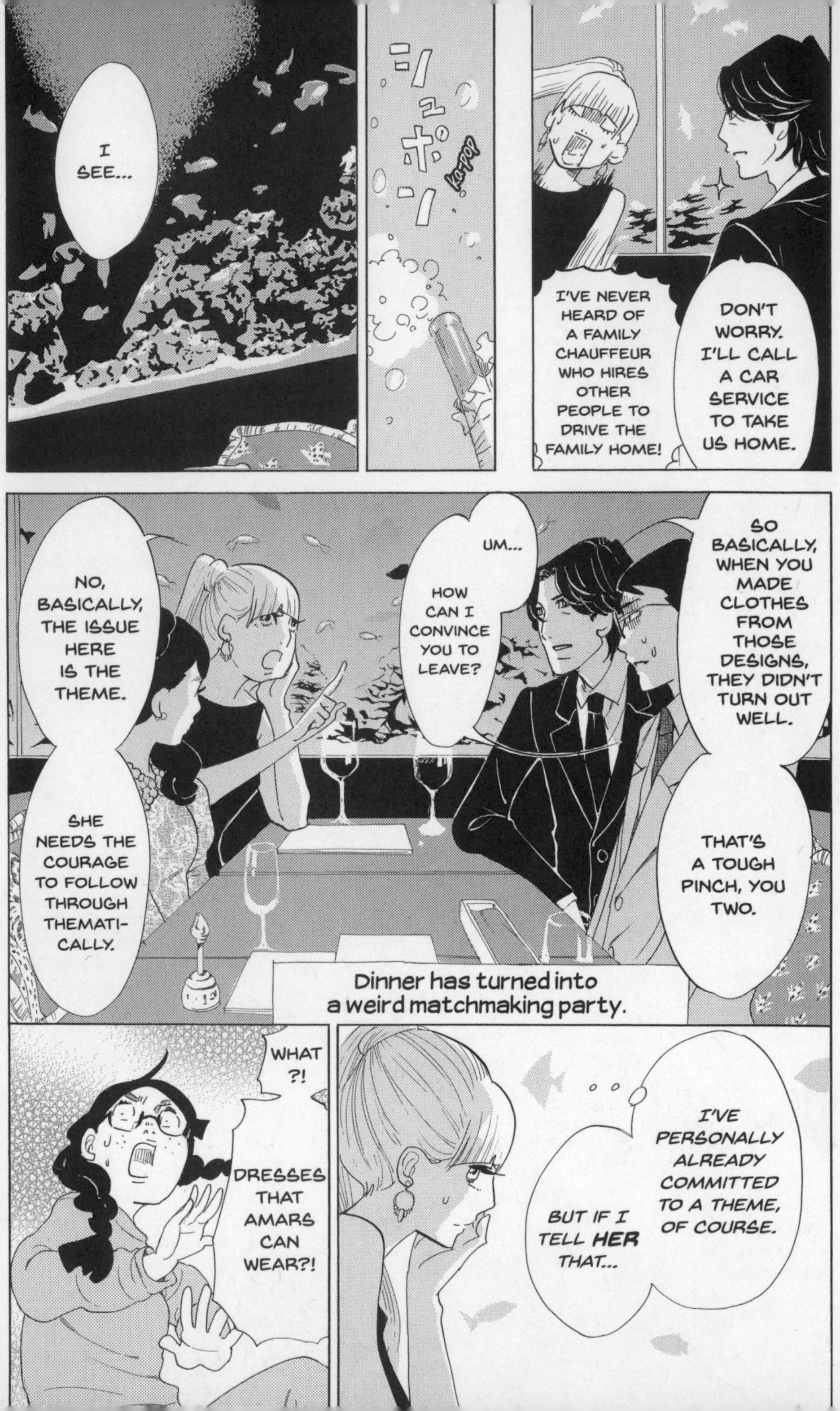
DON'T WORRY. I'LL CALL A CAR SERVICE TO TAKE US HOME.
I'VE NEVER HEARD OF A FAMILY CHAUFFEUR WHO HIRES OTHER PEOPLE TO DRIVE THE FAMILY HOME!
KA-POP
I SEE...
SO BASICALLY, WHEN YOU MADE CLOTHES FROM THOSE DESIGNS, THEY DIDN'T TURN OUT WELL.
THAT'S A TOUGH PINCH, YOU TWO.
UM...
HOW CAN I CONVINCE YOU TO LEAVE?
NO, BASICALLY, THE ISSUE HERE IS THE THEME.
SHE NEEDS THE COURAGE TO FOLLOW THROUGH THEMATI-CALLY.
Dinner has turned into a weird matchmaking party.
I'VE PERSONALLY ALREADY COMMITTED TO A THEME, OF COURSE.
BUT IF I TELL HER THAT...
WHAT?!
DRESSES THAT AMARS CAN WEAR?!

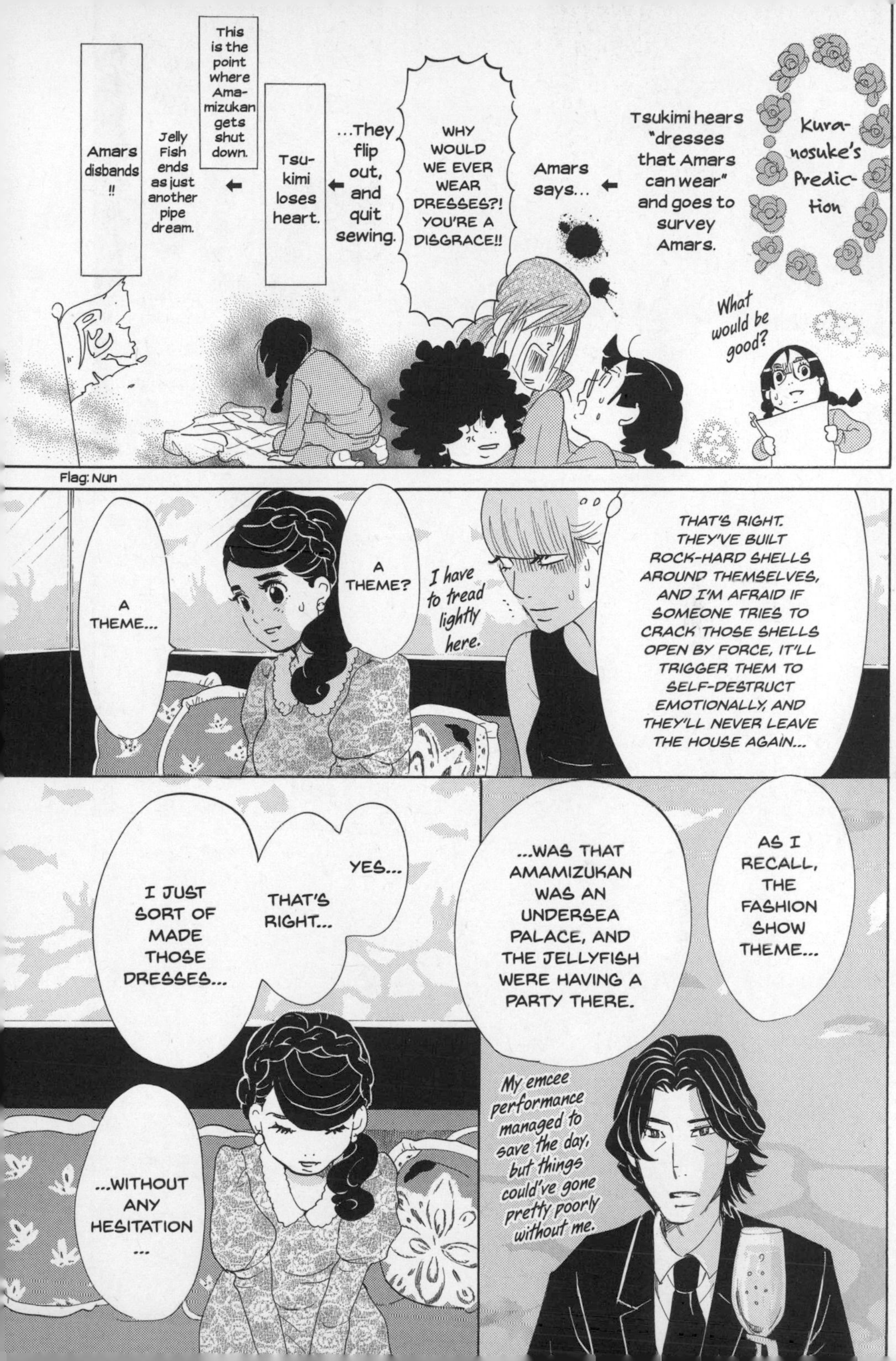
Kuranosuke's Prediction
What would be good?
Tsukimi hears "dresses that Amars can wear" and goes to survey Amars.
Amars says...
WHY WOULD WE EVER WEAR DRESSES?! YOU'RE A DISGRACE!!
...They flip out, and quit sewing.
Tsukimi loses heart.
This is the point where Amamizukan gets shut down.
Jelly Fish ends as just another pipe dream.
Amars disbands!!
尼
Flag: Nun
THAT'S RIGHT. THEY'VE BUILT ROCK-HARD SHELLS AROUND THEMSELVES, AND I'M AFRAID IF SOMEONE TRIES TO CRACK THOSE SHELLS OPEN BY FORCE, IT'LL TRIGGER THEM TO SELF-DESTRUCT EMOTIONALLY, AND THEY'LL NEVER LEAVE THE HOUSE AGAIN...
I have to tread lightly here.
A THEME?
A THEME...
AS I RECALL, THE FASHION SHOW THEME...
...WAS THAT AMAMIZUKAN WAS AN UNDERSEA PALACE, AND THE JELLYFISH WERE HAVING A PARTY THERE.
My emcee performance managed to save the day, but things could've gone pretty poorly without me.
YES... THAT'S RIGHT...
I JUST SORT OF MADE THOSE DRESSES...
...WITHOUT ANY HESITATION ...

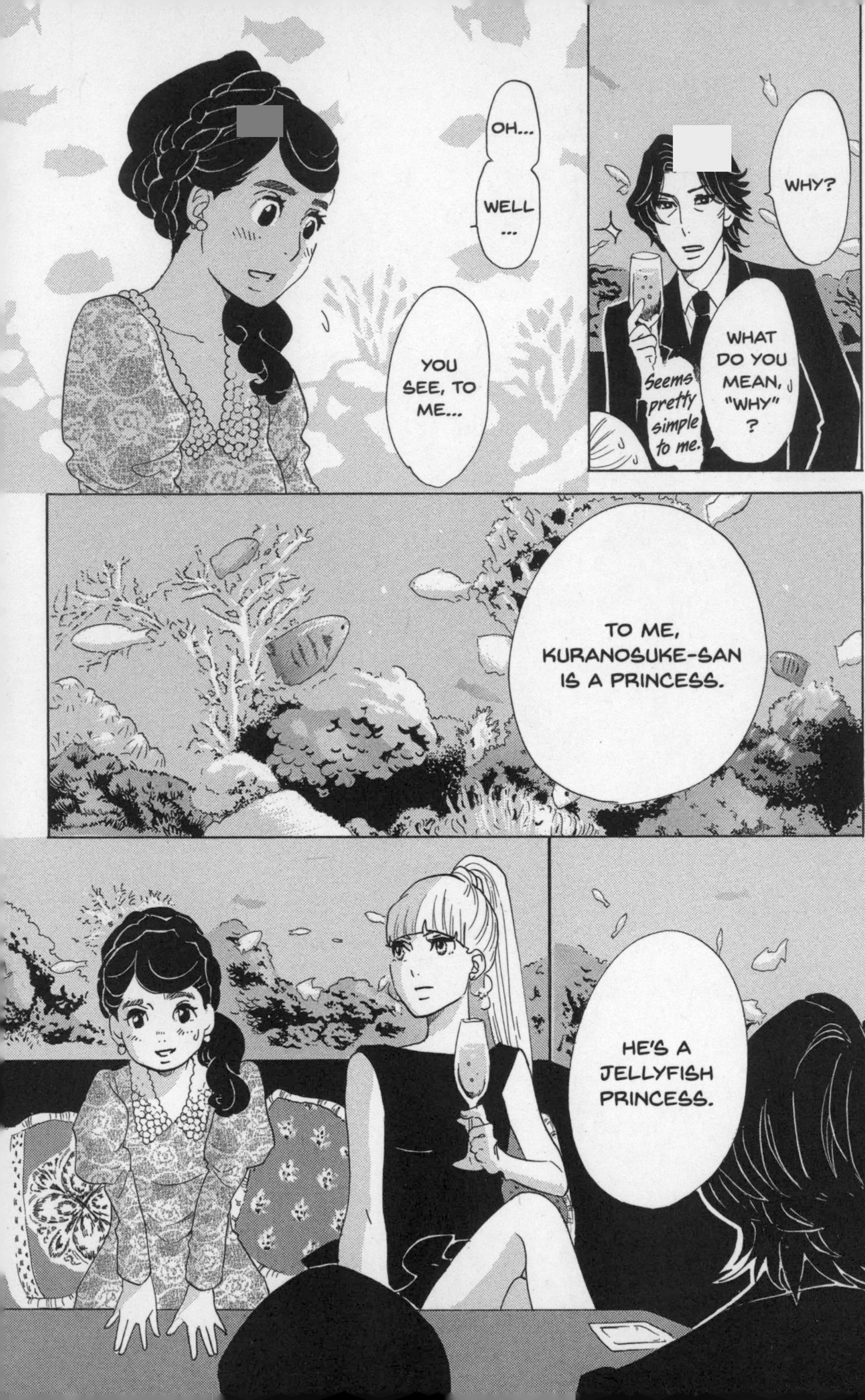
WHY?
WHAT DO YOU MEAN, "WHY"?
Seems pretty simple to me.
OH... WELL...
YOU SEE, TO ME...
TO ME, KURANOSUKE-SAN IS A PRINCESS.
HE'S A JELLYFISH PRINCESS.

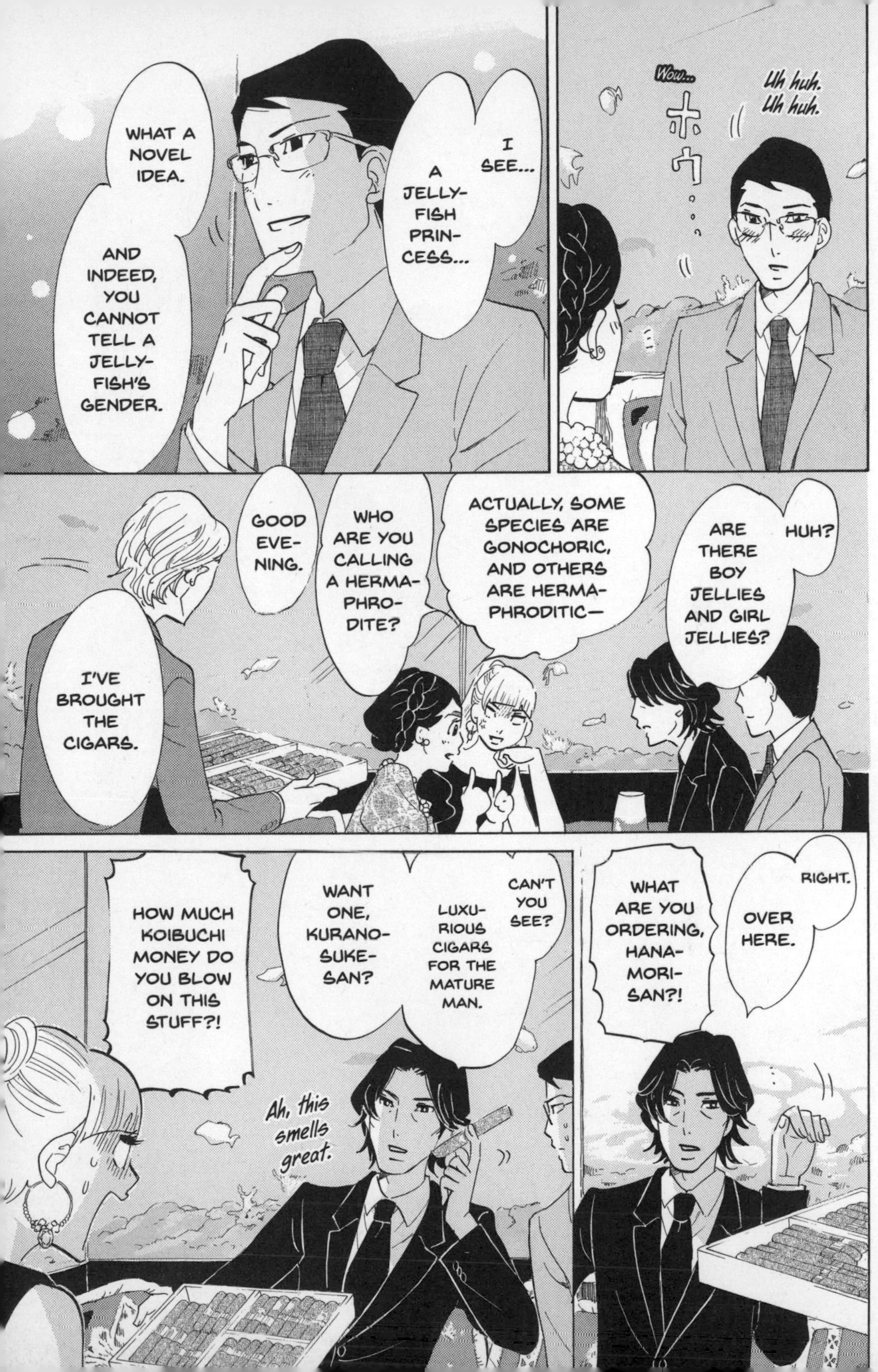
Wow...
ホウ
Uh huh. Uh huh.
I SEE...
A JELLYFISH PRINCESS...
WHAT A NOVEL IDEA.
AND INDEED, YOU CANNOT TELL A JELLYFISH'S GENDER.
HUH?
ARE THERE BOY JELLIES AND GIRL JELLIES?
ACTUALLY, SOME SPECIES ARE GONOCHORIC, AND OTHERS ARE HERMAPHRODITIC—
WHO ARE YOU CALLING A HERMAPHRODITE?
GOOD EVENING.
I'VE BROUGHT THE CIGARS.
RIGHT.
OVER HERE.
WHAT ARE YOU ORDERING, HANAMORI-SAN?!
CAN'T YOU SEE?
LUXURIOUS CIGARS FOR THE MATURE MAN.
WANT ONE, KURANOSUKE-SAN?
HOW MUCH KOIBUCHI MONEY DO YOU BLOW ON THIS STUFF?!
Ah, this smells great.

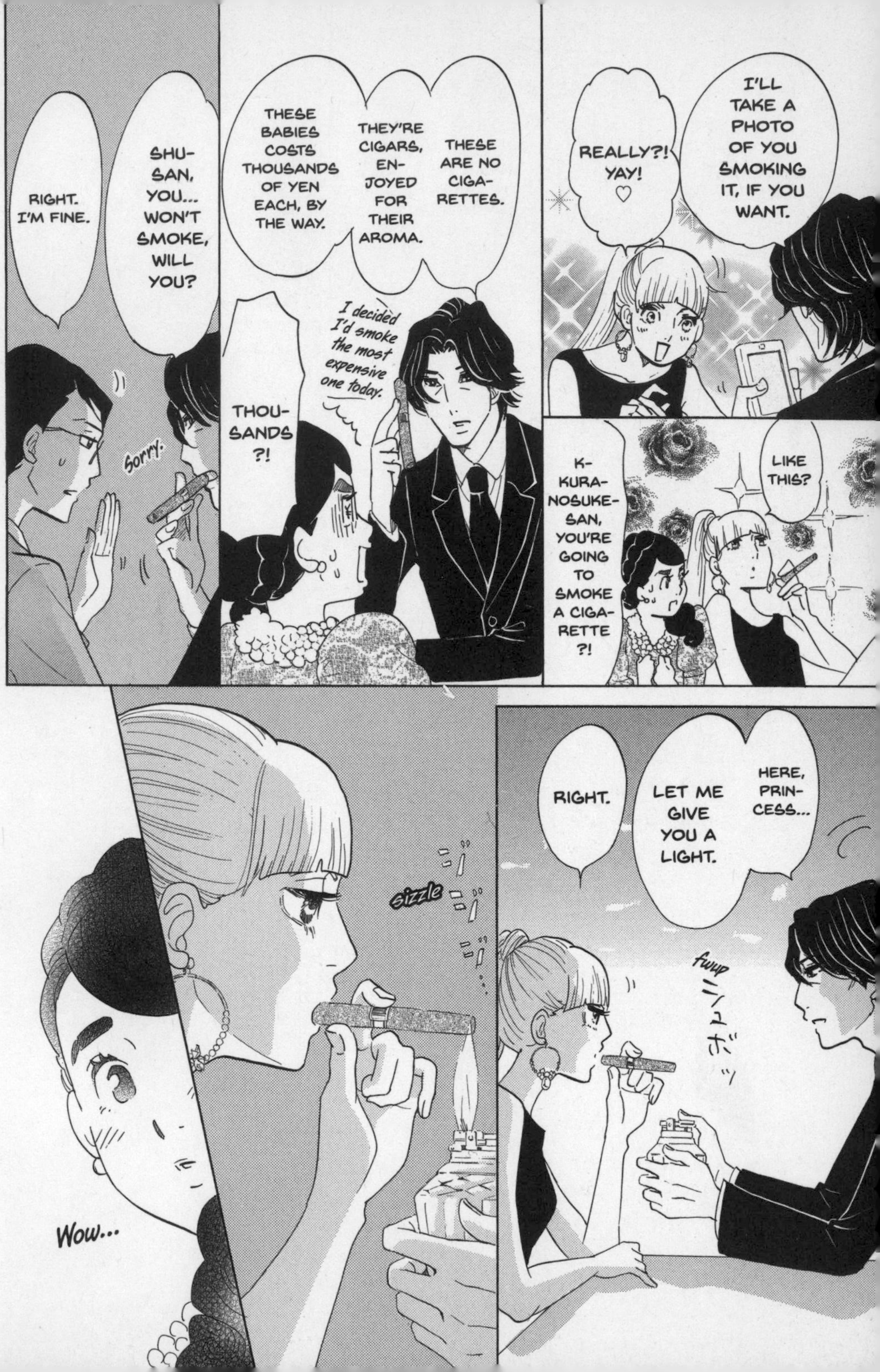
I'LL TAKE A PHOTO OF YOU SMOKING IT, IF YOU WANT.
REALLY?! YAY! ♡
LIKE THIS?
K-KURANOSUKE-SAN, YOU'RE GOING TO SMOKE A CIGARETTE?!
THESE ARE NO CIGARETTES.
THEY'RE CIGARS, ENJOYED FOR THEIR AROMA.
THESE BABIES COSTS THOUSANDS OF YEN EACH, BY THE WAY.
I decided I'd smoke the most expensive one today.
THOUSANDS?!
SHU-SAN, YOU... WON'T SMOKE, WILL YOU?
RIGHT. I'M FINE.
Sorry.
HERE, PRINCESS...
LET ME GIVE YOU A LIGHT.
RIGHT.
fwup
シュボッ
sizzle
Wow...

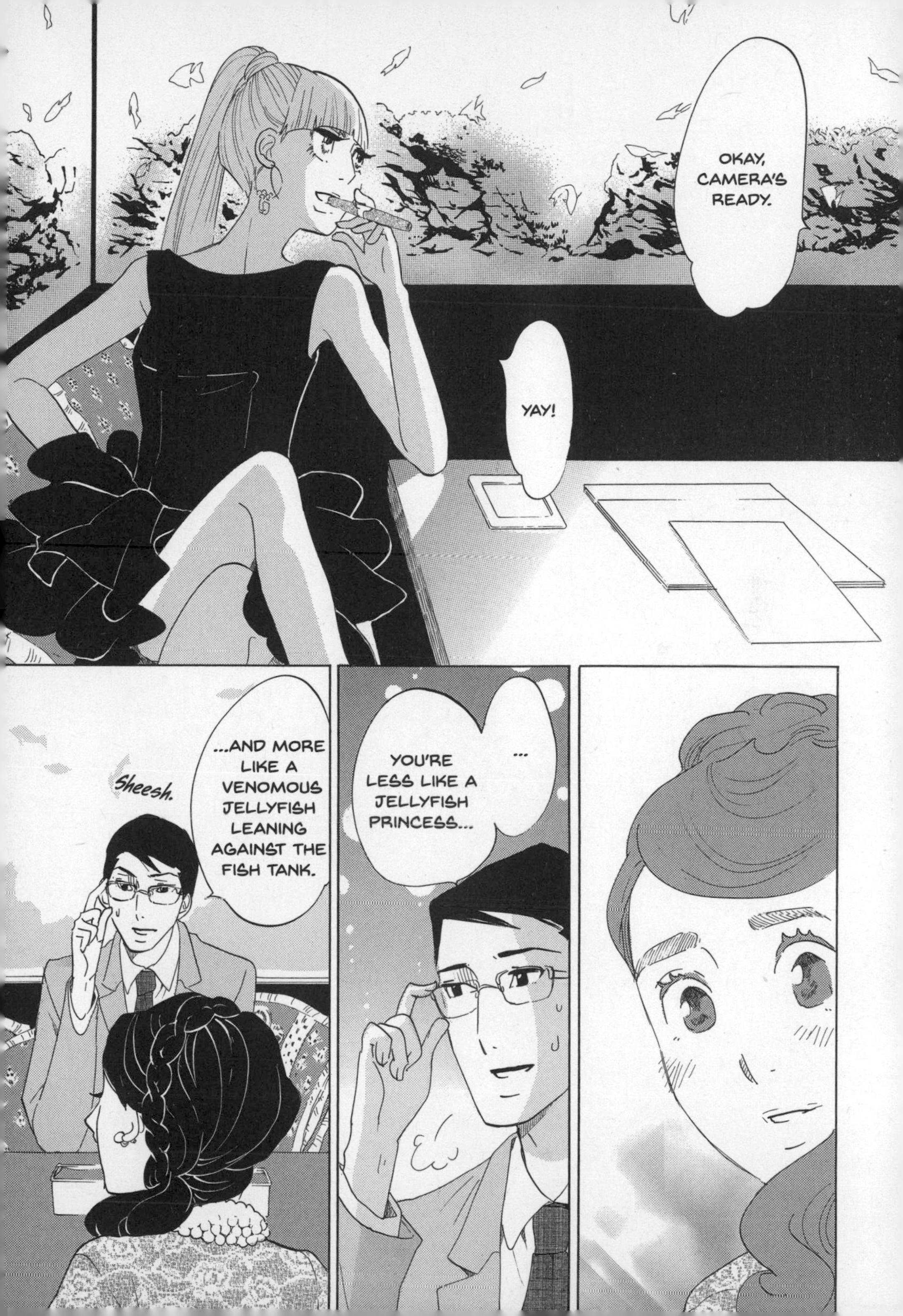
OKAY, CAMERA'S READY.
YAY!
...
YOU'RE LESS LIKE A JELLYFISH PRINCESS...
...AND MORE LIKE A VENOMOUS JELLYFISH LEANING AGAINST THE FISH TANK.
Sheesh.

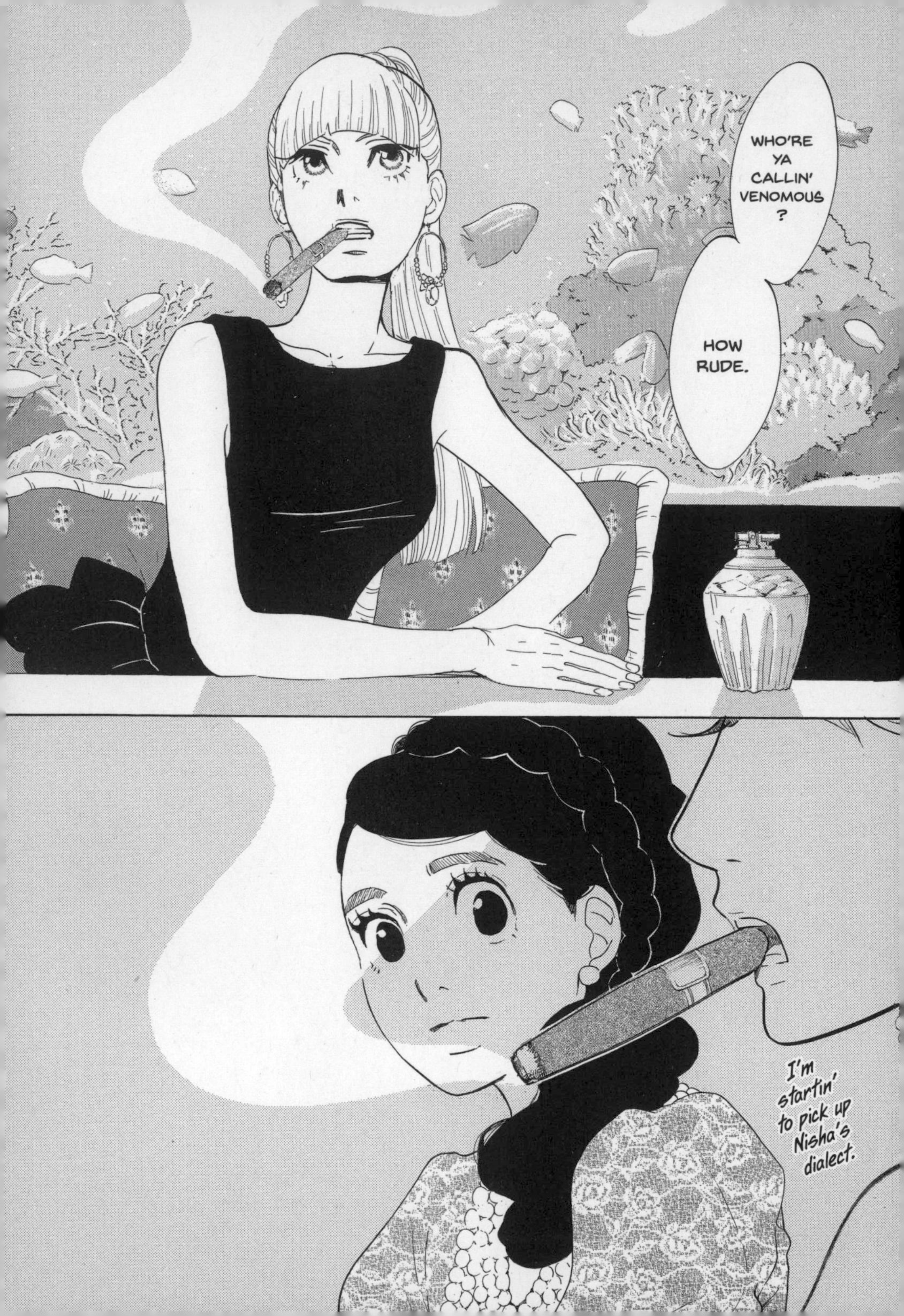
WHO'RE YA CALLIN' VENOMOUS?
HOW RUDE.
I'm startin' to pick up Nisha's dialect.

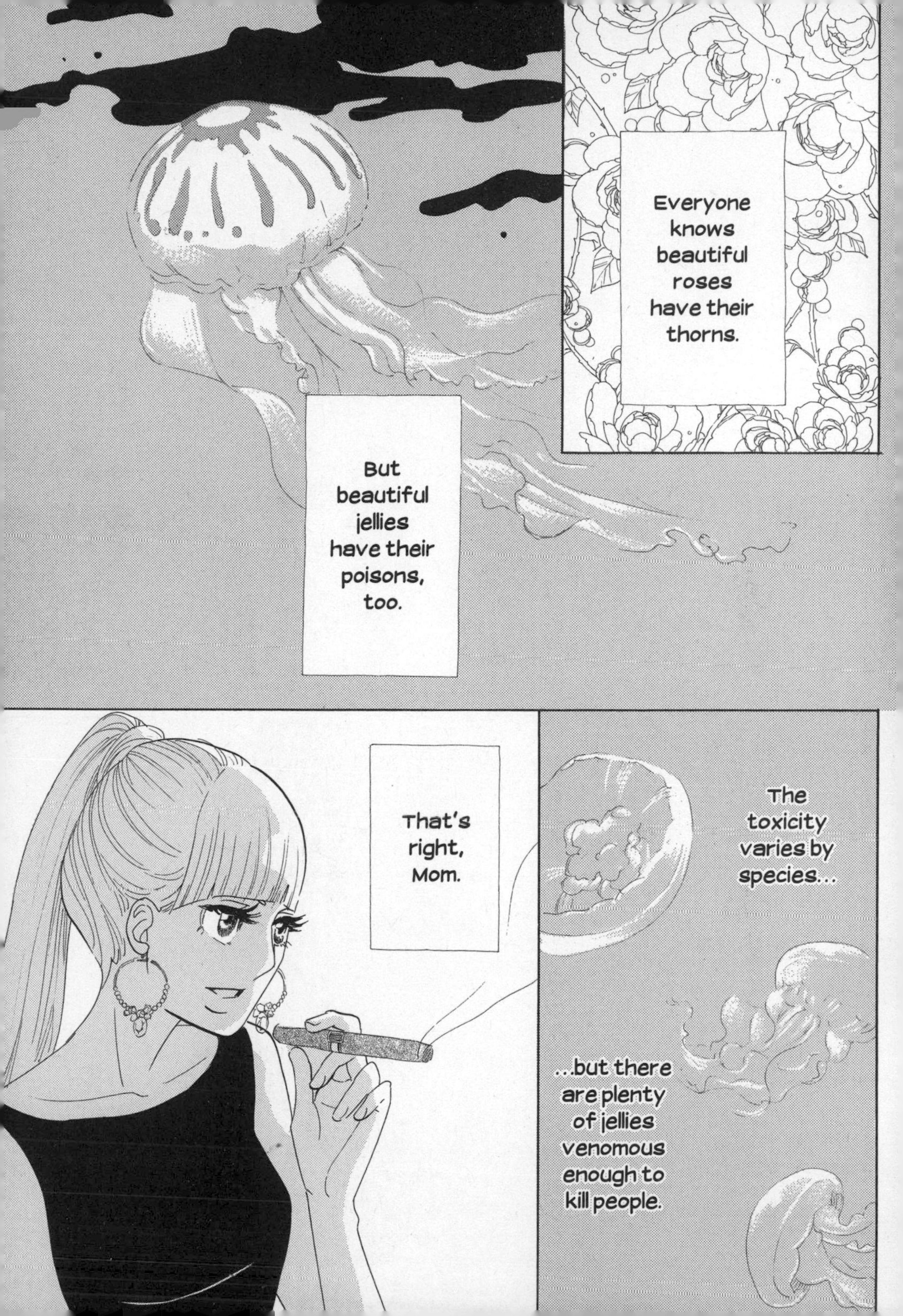
Everyone knows beautiful roses have their thorns.
But beautiful jellies have their poisons, too.
The toxicity varies by species...
...but there are plenty of jellies venomous enough to kill people.
That's right, Mom.

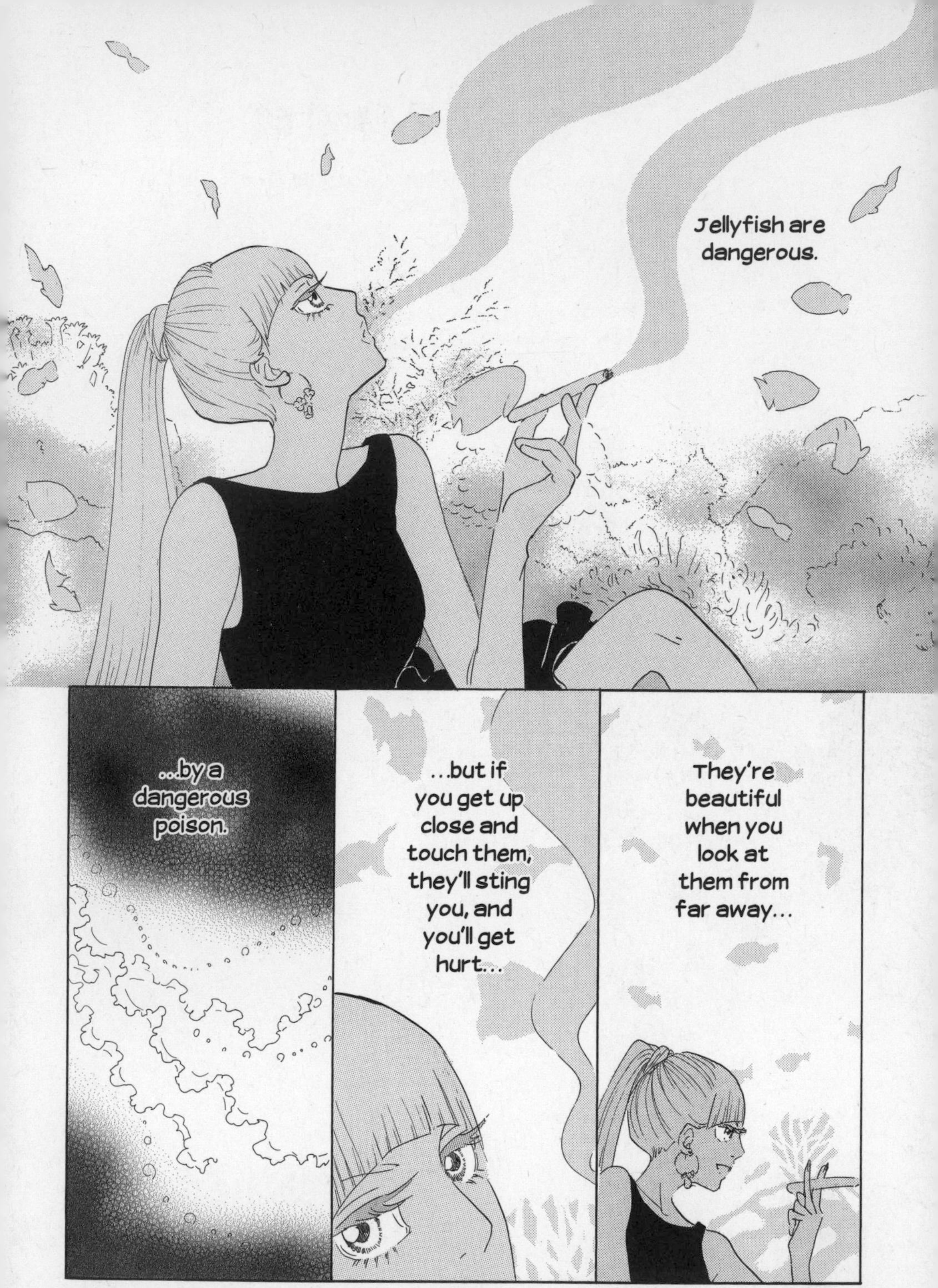
Jellyfish are dangerous.
They're beautiful when you look at them from far away...
...but if you get up close and touch them, they'll sting you, and you'll get hurt...
...by a dangerous poison.

Episode 57
Tsukimi Paints it Black

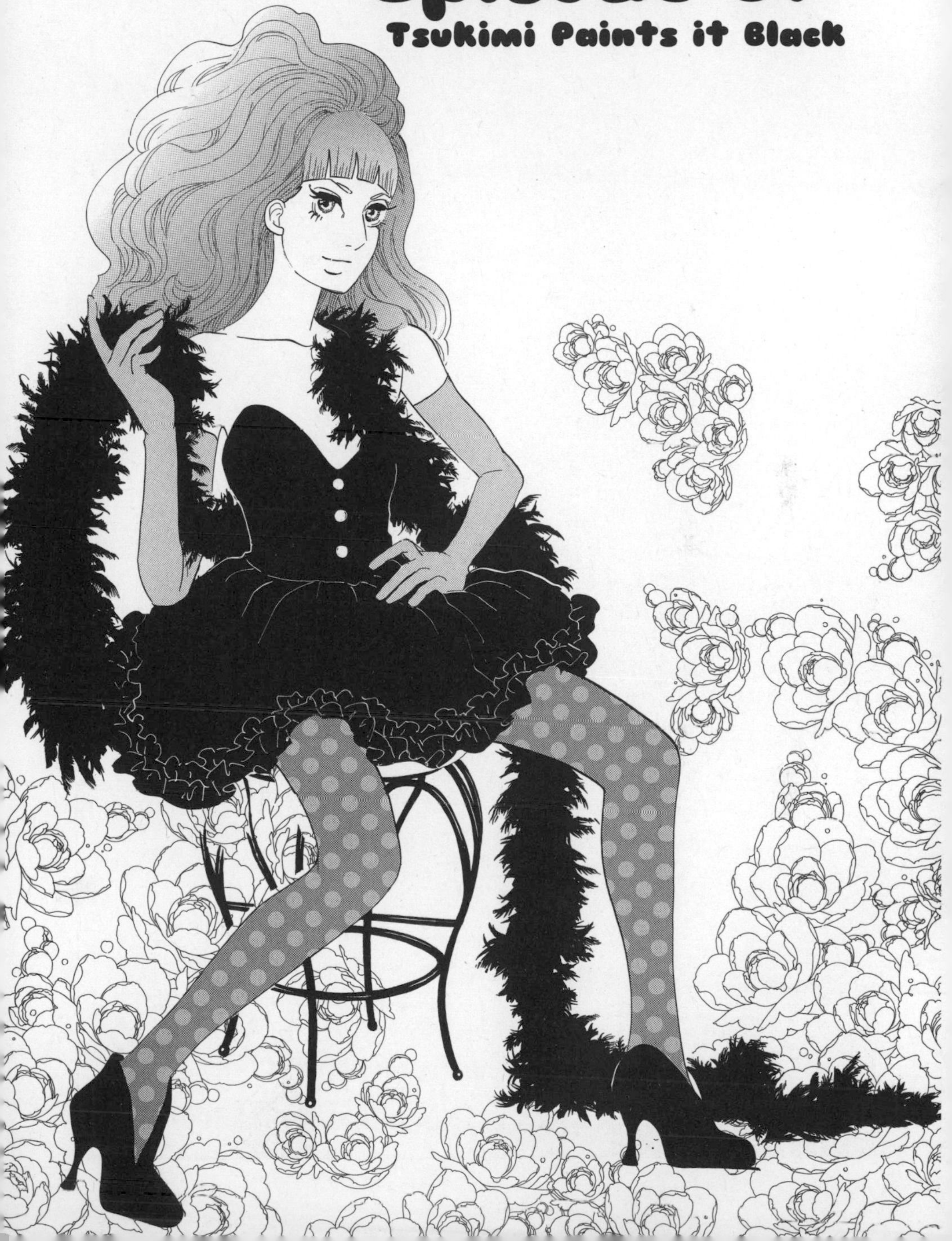

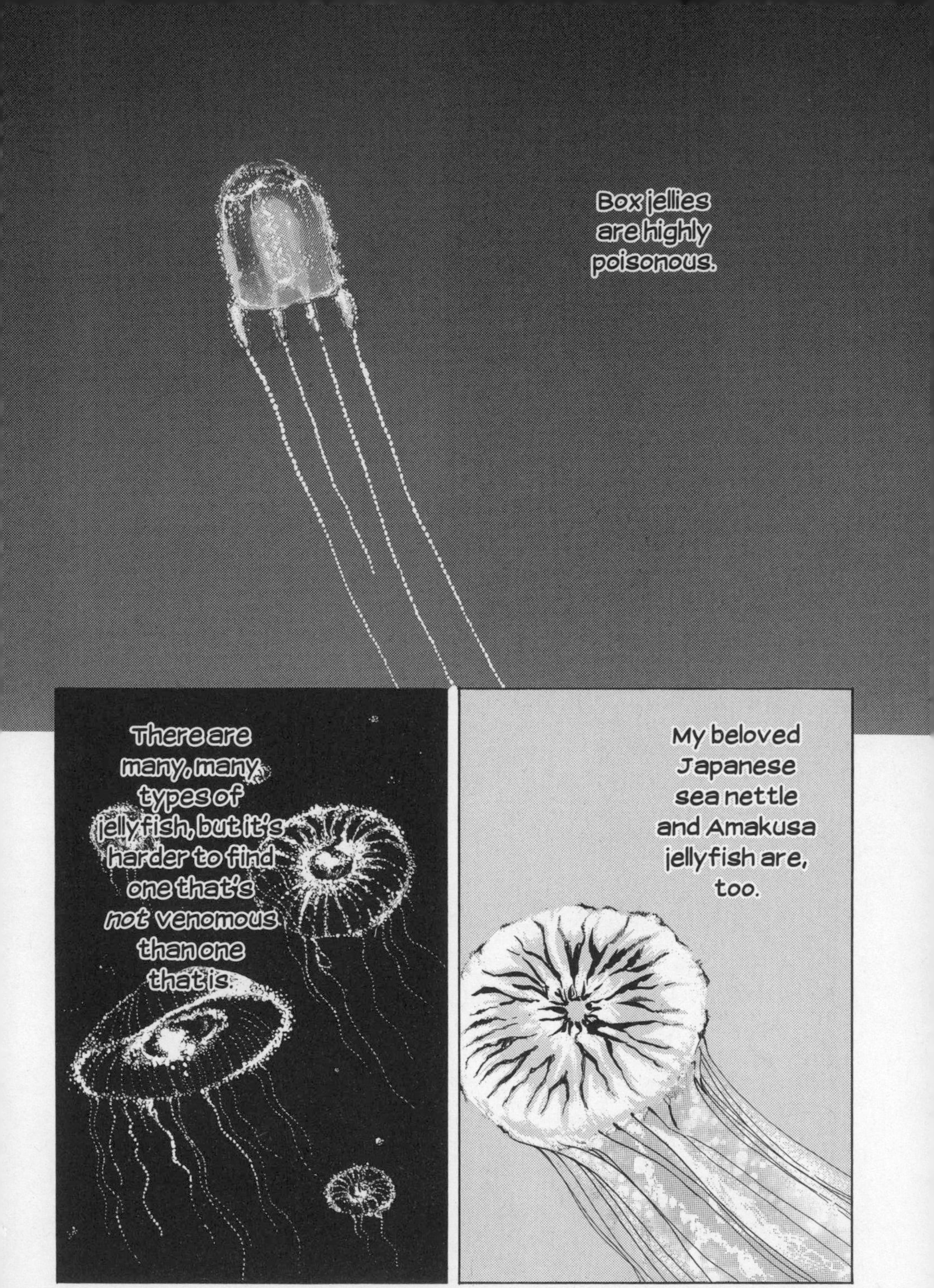
Box jellies are highly poisonous.
My beloved Japanese sea nettle and Amakusa jellyfish are, too.
There are many, many types of jellyfish, but it's harder to find one that's *not* venomous than one that is.

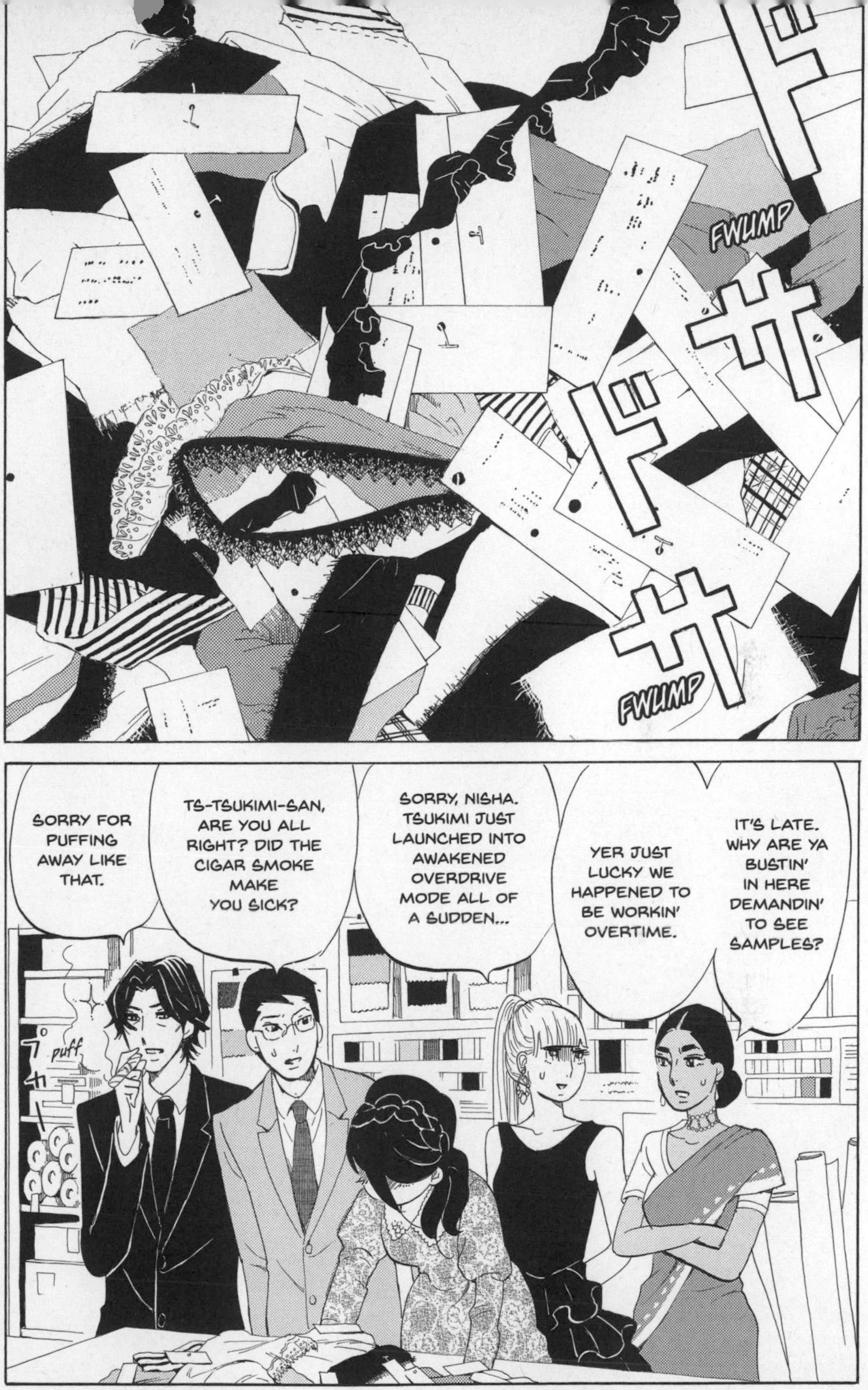
FWUMP
FWUMP
IT'S LATE. WHY ARE YA BUSTIN' IN HERE DEMANDIN' TO SEE SAMPLES?
YER JUST LUCKY WE HAPPENED TO BE WORKIN' OVERTIME.
SORRY, NISHA. TSUKIMI JUST LAUNCHED INTO AWAKENED OVERDRIVE MODE ALL OF A SUDDEN...
TS-TSUKIMI-SAN, ARE YOU ALL RIGHT? DID THE CIGAR SMOKE MAKE YOU SICK?
SORRY FOR PUFFING AWAY LIKE THAT.
puff

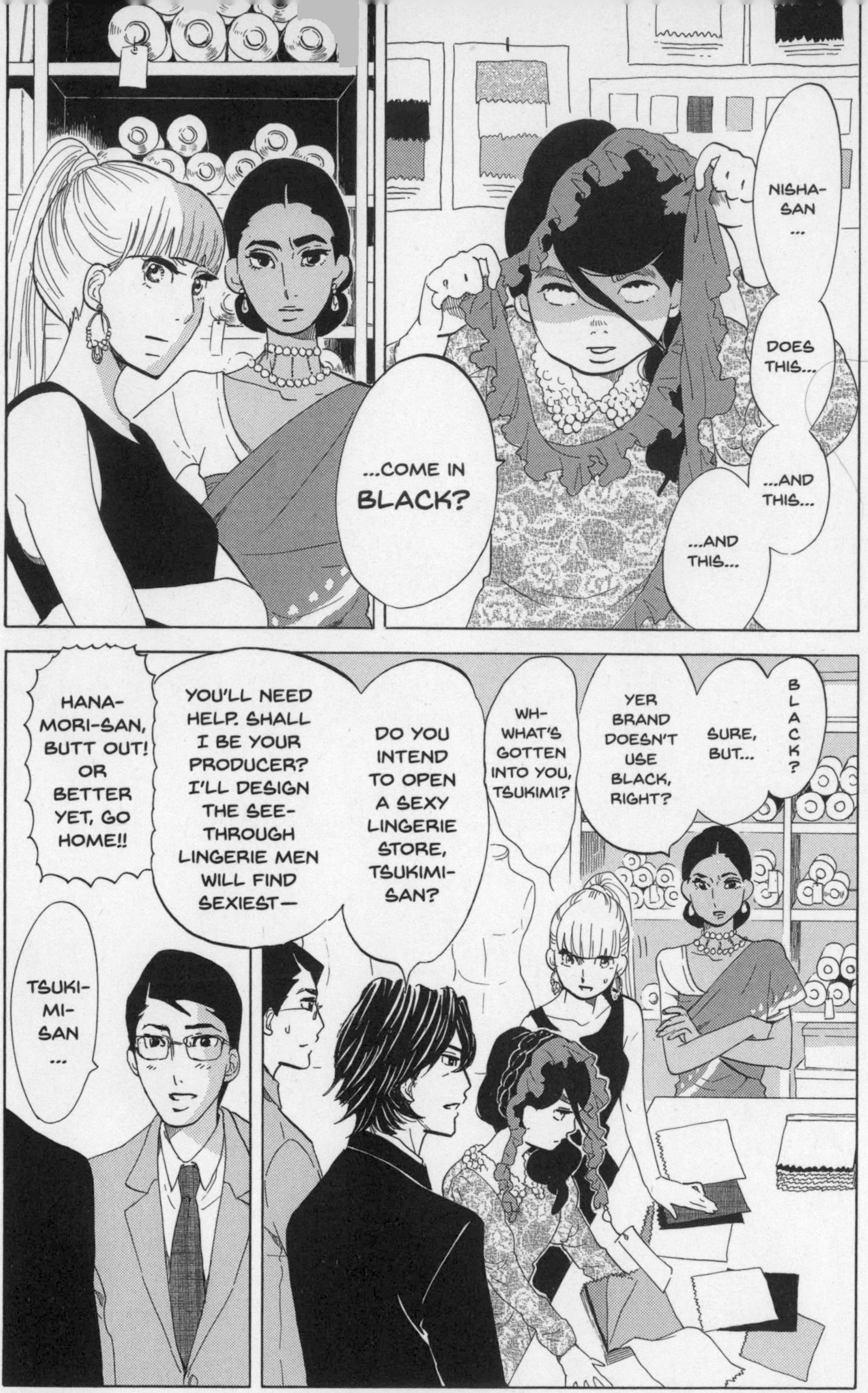
NISHA-SAN...
DOES THIS...
...AND THIS...
...AND THIS...
...COME IN BLACK?
BLACK?
SURE, BUT...
YER BRAND DOESN'T USE BLACK, RIGHT?
WH-WHAT'S GOTTEN INTO YOU, TSUKIMI?
DO YOU INTEND TO OPEN A SEXY LINGERIE STORE, TSUKIMI-SAN?
YOU'LL NEED HELP. SHALL I BE YOUR PRODUCER? I'LL DESIGN THE SEE-THROUGH LINGERIE MEN WILL FIND SEXIEST—
HANA-MORI-SAN, BUTT OUT! OR BETTER YET, GO HOME!!
TSUKI-MI-SAN...

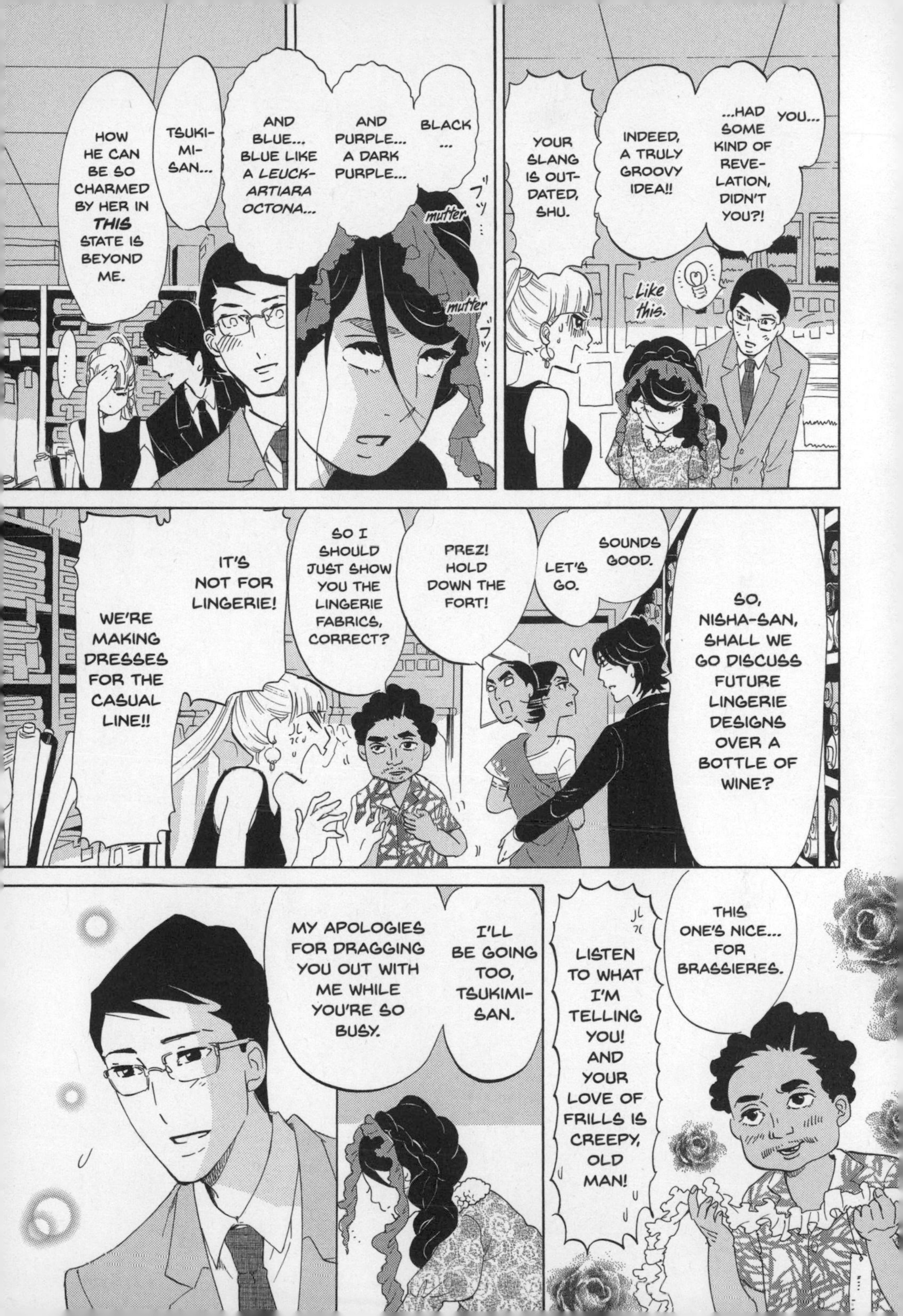
YOU...
...HAD SOME KIND OF REVELATION, DIDN'T YOU?!
INDEED, A TRULY GROOVY IDEA!!
YOUR SLANG IS OUT-DATED, SHU.
Like this.
BLACK...
AND PURPLE... A DARK PURPLE...
AND BLUE... BLUE LIKE A *LEUCKARTIARA OCTONA*...
mutter
mutter
TSUKIMI-SAN...
HOW HE CAN BE SO CHARMED BY HER IN ***THIS*** STATE IS BEYOND ME.
...
SO, NISHA-SAN, SHALL WE GO DISCUSS FUTURE LINGERIE DESIGNS OVER A BOTTLE OF WINE?
SOUNDS GOOD.
LET'S GO.
PREZ! HOLD DOWN THE FORT!
SO I SHOULD JUST SHOW YOU THE LINGERIE FABRICS, CORRECT?
IT'S NOT FOR LINGERIE!
WE'RE MAKING DRESSES FOR THE CASUAL LINE!!
THIS ONE'S NICE... FOR BRASSIERES.
LISTEN TO WHAT I'M TELLING YOU! AND YOUR LOVE OF FRILLS IS CREEPY, OLD MAN!
I'LL BE GOING TOO, TSUKIMI-SAN.
MY APOLOGIES FOR DRAGGING YOU OUT WITH ME WHILE YOU'RE SO BUSY.

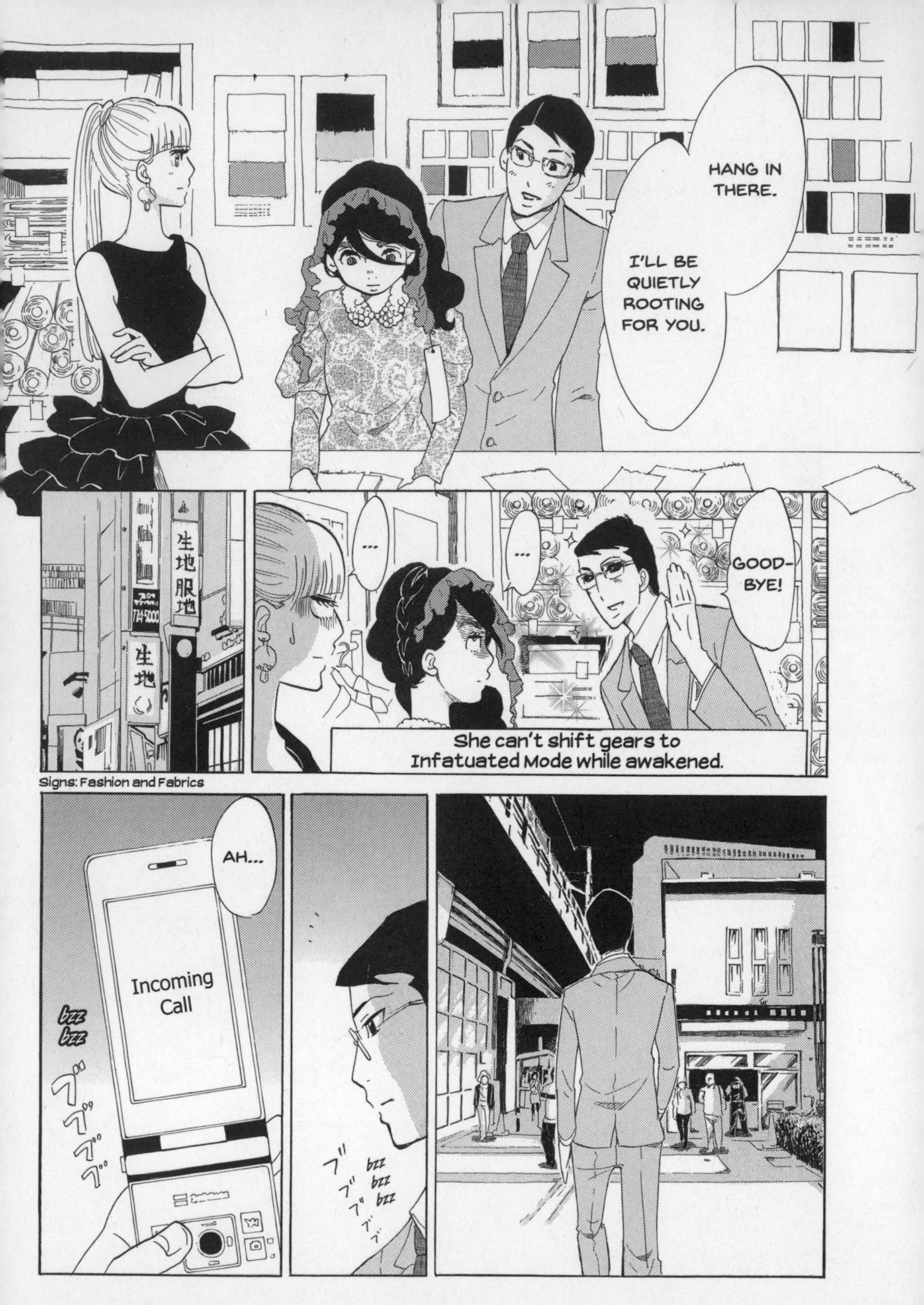
HANG IN THERE.
I'LL BE QUIETLY ROOTING FOR YOU.
GOOD-BYE!
...
...
She can't shift gears to Infatuated Mode while awakened.
Signs: Fashion and Fabrics
bzz bzz bzz
AH...
Incoming Call
bzz bzz

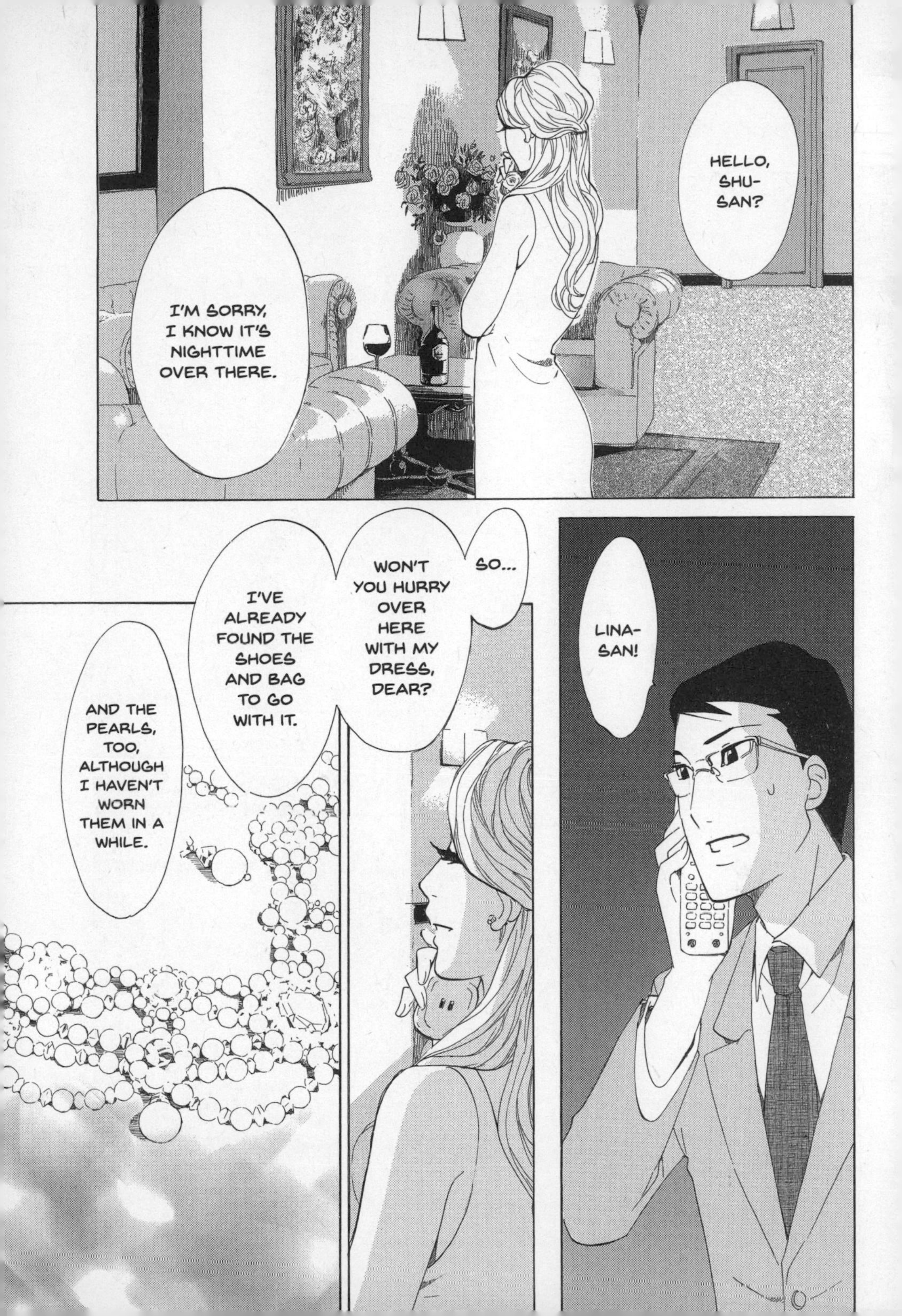
HELLO, SHU-SAN?
I'M SORRY, I KNOW IT'S NIGHTTIME OVER THERE.
LINA-SAN!
SO...
WON'T YOU HURRY OVER HERE WITH MY DRESS, DEAR?
I'VE ALREADY FOUND THE SHOES AND BAG TO GO WITH IT.
AND THE PEARLS, TOO, ALTHOUGH I HAVEN'T WORN THEM IN A WHILE.

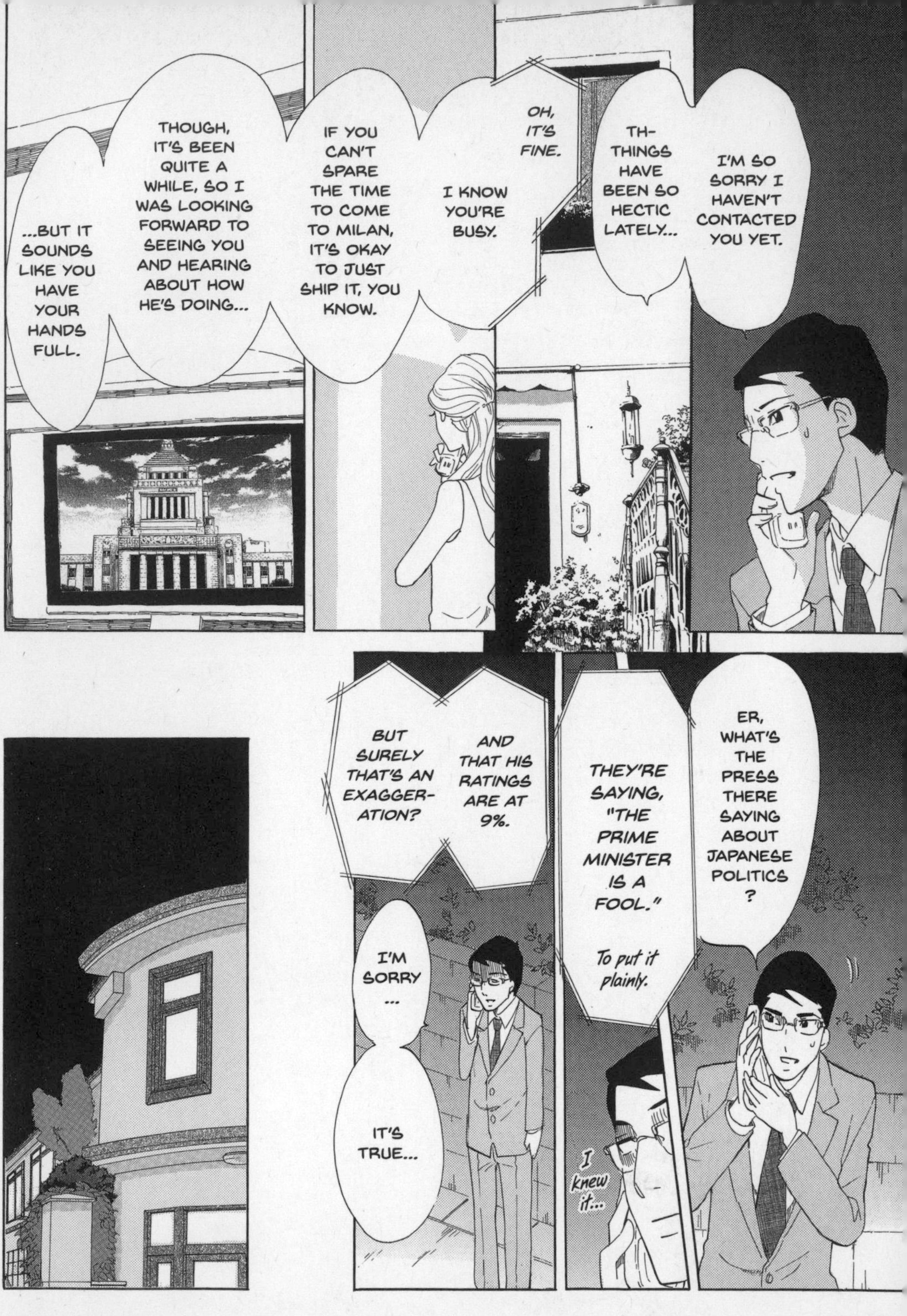
I'M SO SORRY I HAVEN'T CONTACTED YOU YET.
TH-THINGS HAVE BEEN SO HECTIC LATELY...
OH, IT'S FINE.
I KNOW YOU'RE BUSY.
IF YOU CAN'T SPARE THE TIME TO COME TO MILAN, IT'S OKAY TO JUST SHIP IT, YOU KNOW.
THOUGH, IT'S BEEN QUITE A WHILE, SO I WAS LOOKING FORWARD TO SEEING YOU AND HEARING ABOUT HOW HE'S DOING...
...BUT IT SOUNDS LIKE YOU HAVE YOUR HANDS FULL.
ER, WHAT'S THE PRESS THERE SAYING ABOUT JAPANESE POLITICS?
THEY'RE SAYING, "THE PRIME MINISTER IS A FOOL."
To put it plainly.
I knew it...
AND THAT HIS RATINGS ARE AT 9%.
BUT SURELY THAT'S AN EXAGGER-ATION?
I'M SORRY...
IT'S TRUE...

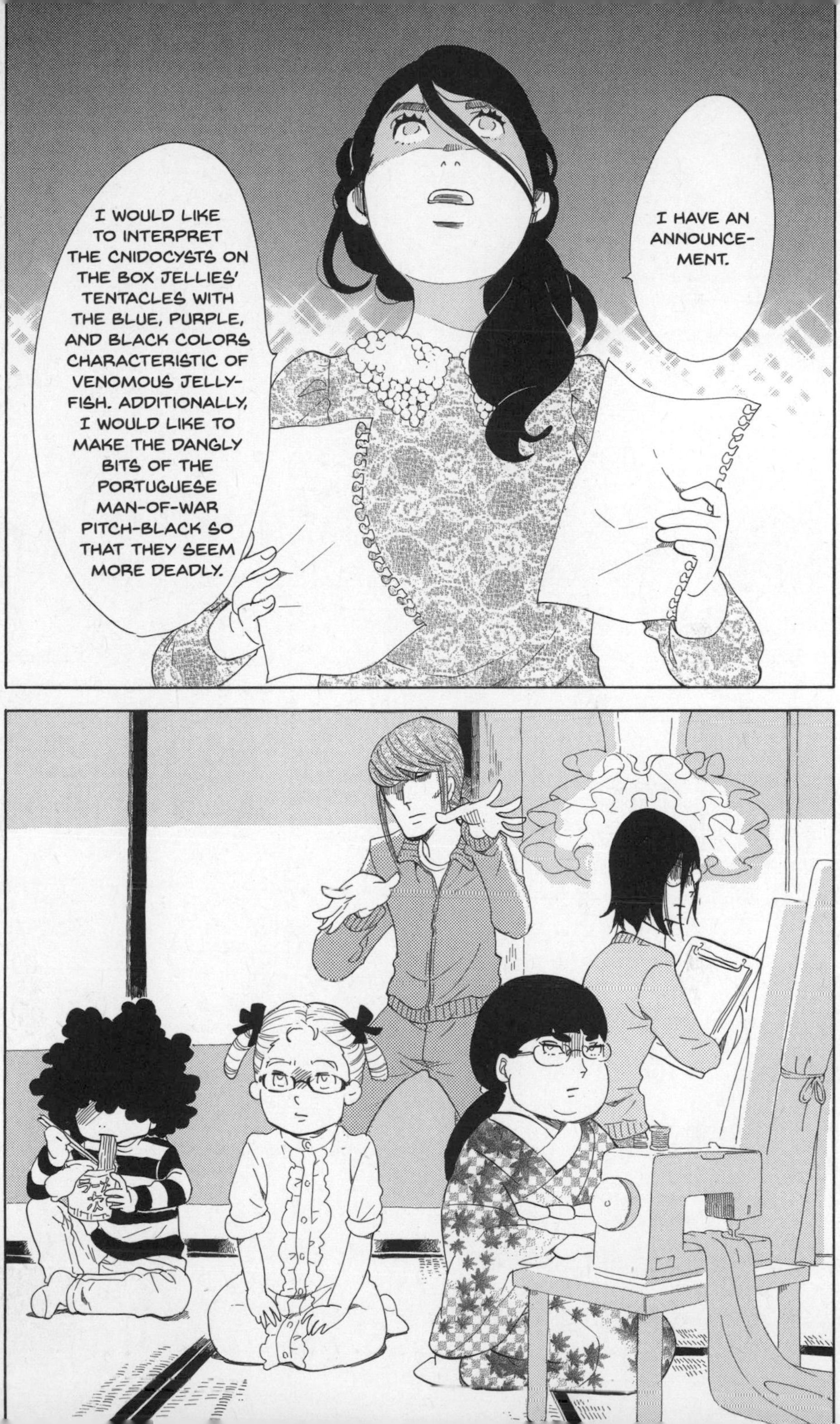
I HAVE AN ANNOUNCE-MENT.
I WOULD LIKE TO INTERPRET THE CNIDOCYSTS ON THE BOX JELLIES' TENTACLES WITH THE BLUE, PURPLE, AND BLACK COLORS CHARACTERISTIC OF VENOMOUS JELLY-FISH. ADDITIONALLY, I WOULD LIKE TO MAKE THE DANGLY BITS OF THE PORTUGUESE MAN-OF-WAR PITCH-BLACK SO THAT THEY SEEM MORE DEADLY.

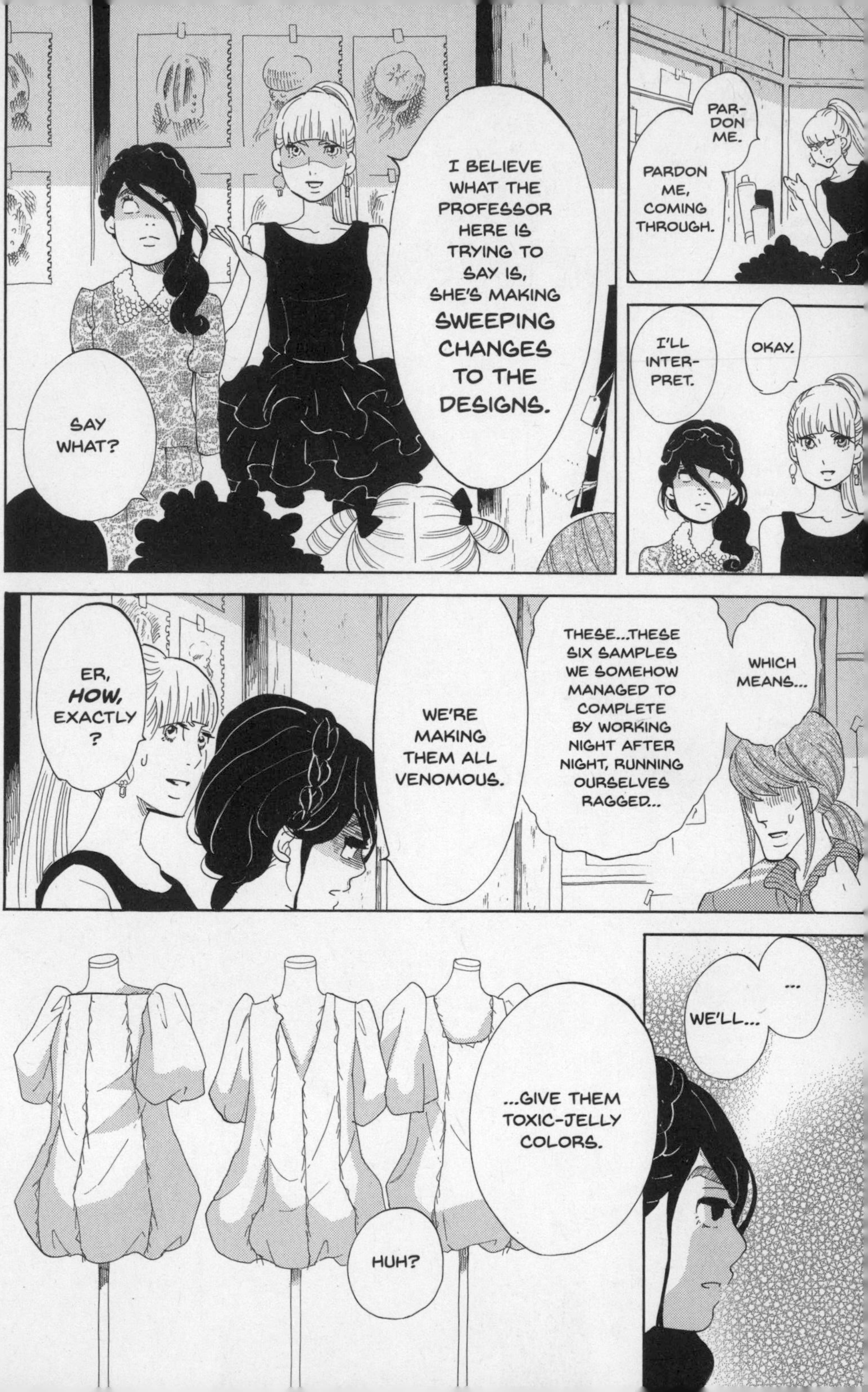
PAR-DON ME.
PARDON ME, COMING THROUGH.
OKAY.
I'LL INTER-PRET.
I BELIEVE WHAT THE PROFESSOR HERE IS TRYING TO SAY IS, SHE'S MAKING SWEEPING CHANGES TO THE DESIGNS.
SAY WHAT?
WHICH MEANS...
THESE...THESE SIX SAMPLES WE SOMEHOW MANAGED TO COMPLETE BY WORKING NIGHT AFTER NIGHT, RUNNING OURSELVES RAGGED...
WE'RE MAKING THEM ALL VENOMOUS.
ER, HOW, EXACTLY?
...
WE'LL...
...GIVE THEM TOXIC-JELLY COLORS.
HUH?

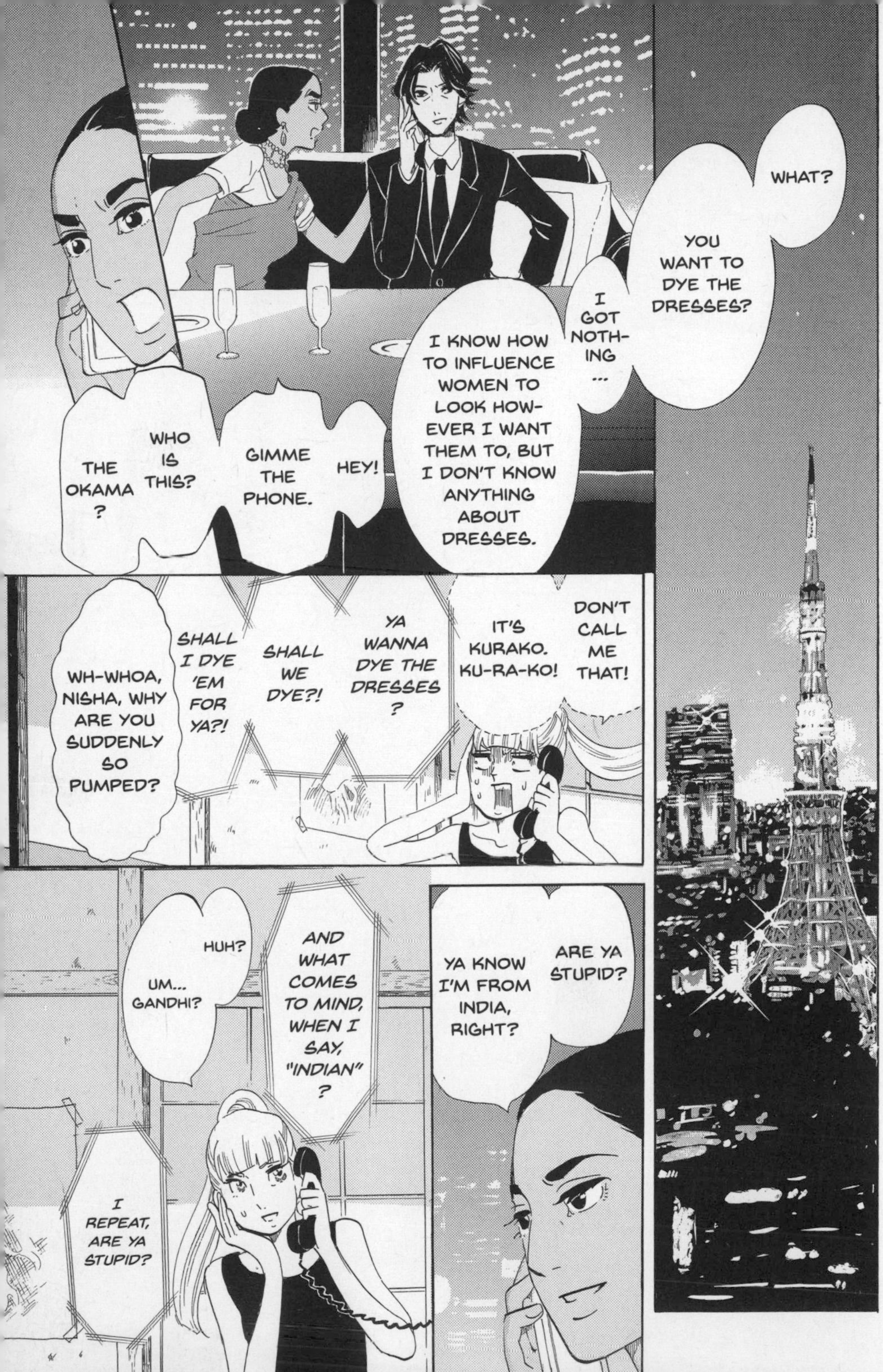
WHAT?
YOU WANT TO DYE THE DRESSES?
I GOT NOTHING...
I KNOW HOW TO INFLUENCE WOMEN TO LOOK HOWEVER I WANT THEM TO, BUT I DON'T KNOW ANYTHING ABOUT DRESSES.
HEY!
GIMME THE PHONE.
WHO IS THIS?
THE OKAMA?
DON'T CALL ME THAT!
IT'S KURAKO. KU-RA-KO!
YA WANNA DYE THE DRESSES?
SHALL WE DYE?!
SHALL I DYE 'EM FOR YA?!
WH-WHOA, NISHA, WHY ARE YOU SUDDENLY SO PUMPED?
ARE YA STUPID?
YA KNOW I'M FROM INDIA, RIGHT?
AND WHAT COMES TO MIND, WHEN I SAY, "INDIAN"?
HUH?
UM... GANDHI?
I REPEAT, ARE YA STUPID?

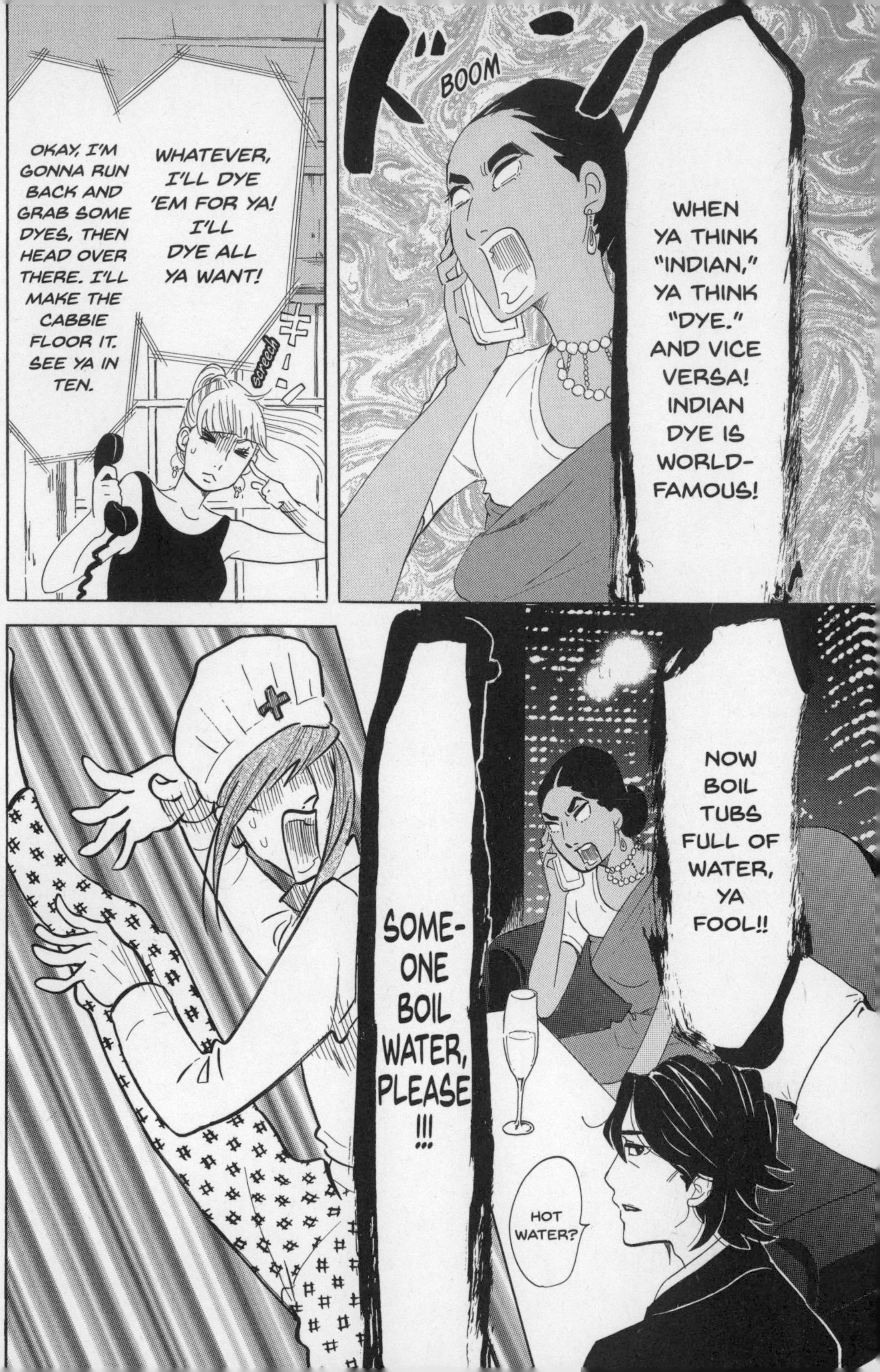
BOOM
WHEN YA THINK "INDIAN," YA THINK "DYE." AND VICE VERSA! INDIAN DYE IS WORLD-FAMOUS!
WHATEVER, I'LL DYE 'EM FOR YA! I'LL DYE ALL YA WANT!
OKAY, I'M GONNA RUN BACK AND GRAB SOME DYES, THEN HEAD OVER THERE. I'LL MAKE THE CABBIE FLOOR IT. SEE YA IN TEN.
screech
NOW BOIL TUBS FULL OF WATER, YA FOOL!!
HOT WATER?
SOME-ONE BOIL WATER, PLEASE!!!

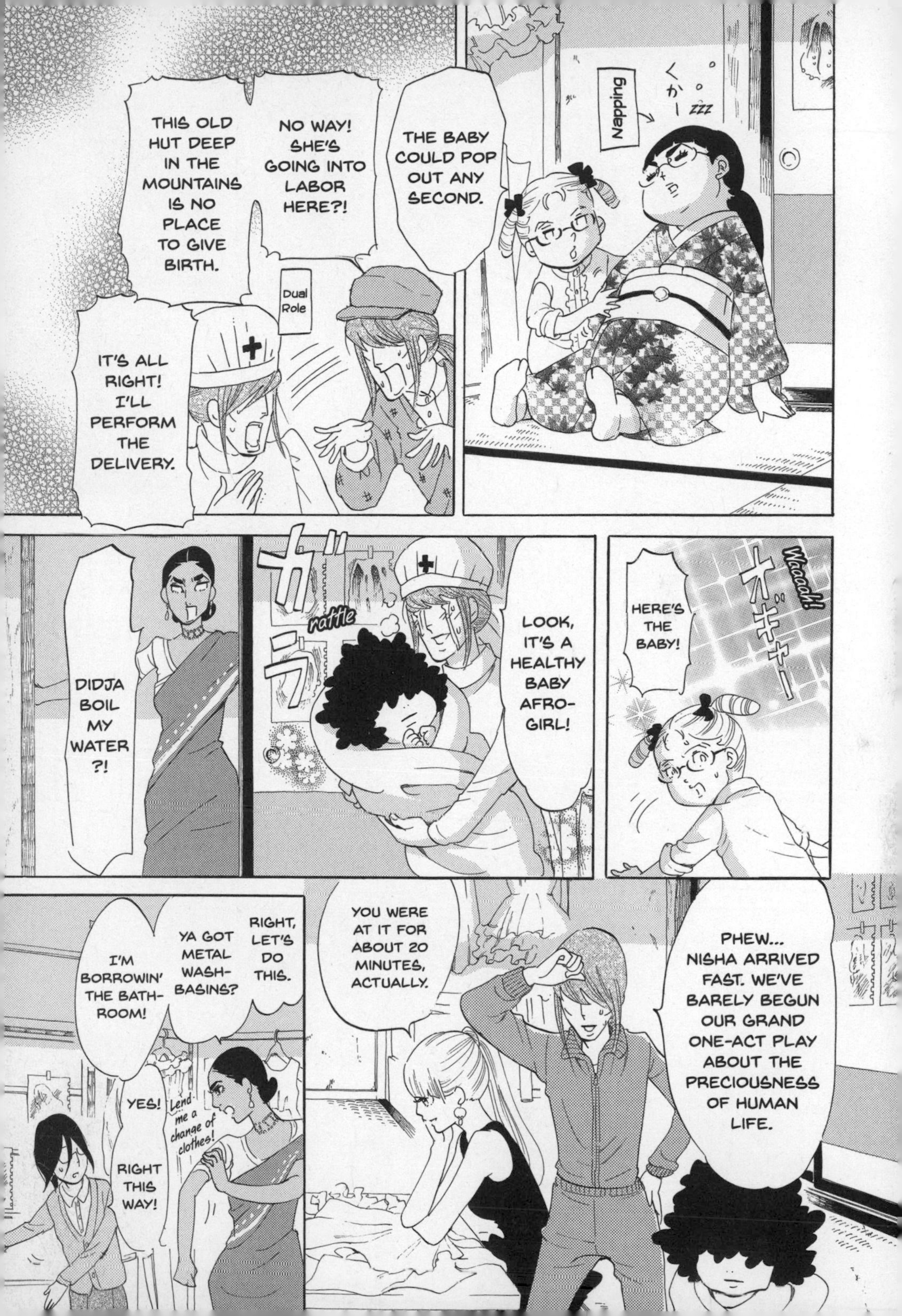

Napping
くかー
zzz
THE BABY COULD POP OUT ANY SECOND.
NO WAY! SHE'S GOING INTO LABOR HERE?!
THIS OLD HUT DEEP IN THE MOUNTAINS IS NO PLACE TO GIVE BIRTH.
Dual Role
IT'S ALL RIGHT! I'LL PERFORM THE DELIVERY.
Waaaah!
オギャー
HERE'S THE BABY!
LOOK, IT'S A HEALTHY BABY AFRO-GIRL!
ガラ
rattle
DIDJA BOIL MY WATER?!
PHEW... NISHA ARRIVED FAST. WE'VE BARELY BEGUN OUR GRAND ONE-ACT PLAY ABOUT THE PRECIOUSNESS OF HUMAN LIFE.
YOU WERE AT IT FOR ABOUT 20 MINUTES, ACTUALLY.
RIGHT, LET'S DO THIS.
YA GOT METAL WASH-BASINS?
I'M BORROWIN' THE BATH-ROOM!
YES!
Lend me a change of clothes!
RIGHT THIS WAY!

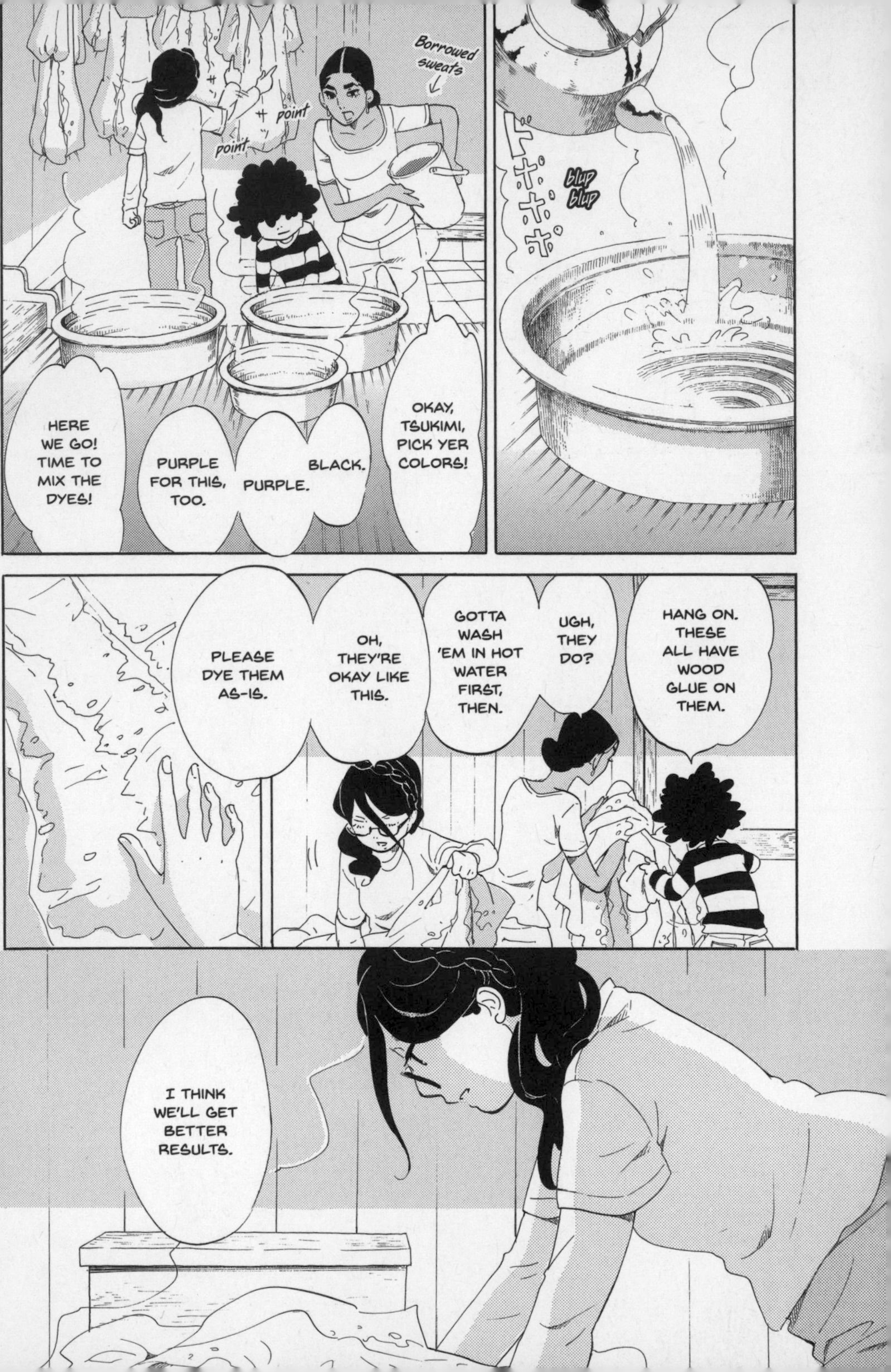
blup blup
Borrowed sweats
point
point
OKAY, TSUKIMI, PICK YER COLORS!
BLACK.
PURPLE.
PURPLE FOR THIS, TOO.
HERE WE GO! TIME TO MIX THE DYES!
HANG ON. THESE ALL HAVE WOOD GLUE ON THEM.
UGH, THEY DO?
GOTTA WASH 'EM IN HOT WATER FIRST, THEN.
OH, THEY'RE OKAY LIKE THIS.
PLEASE DYE THEM AS-IS.
I THINK WE'LL GET BETTER RESULTS.

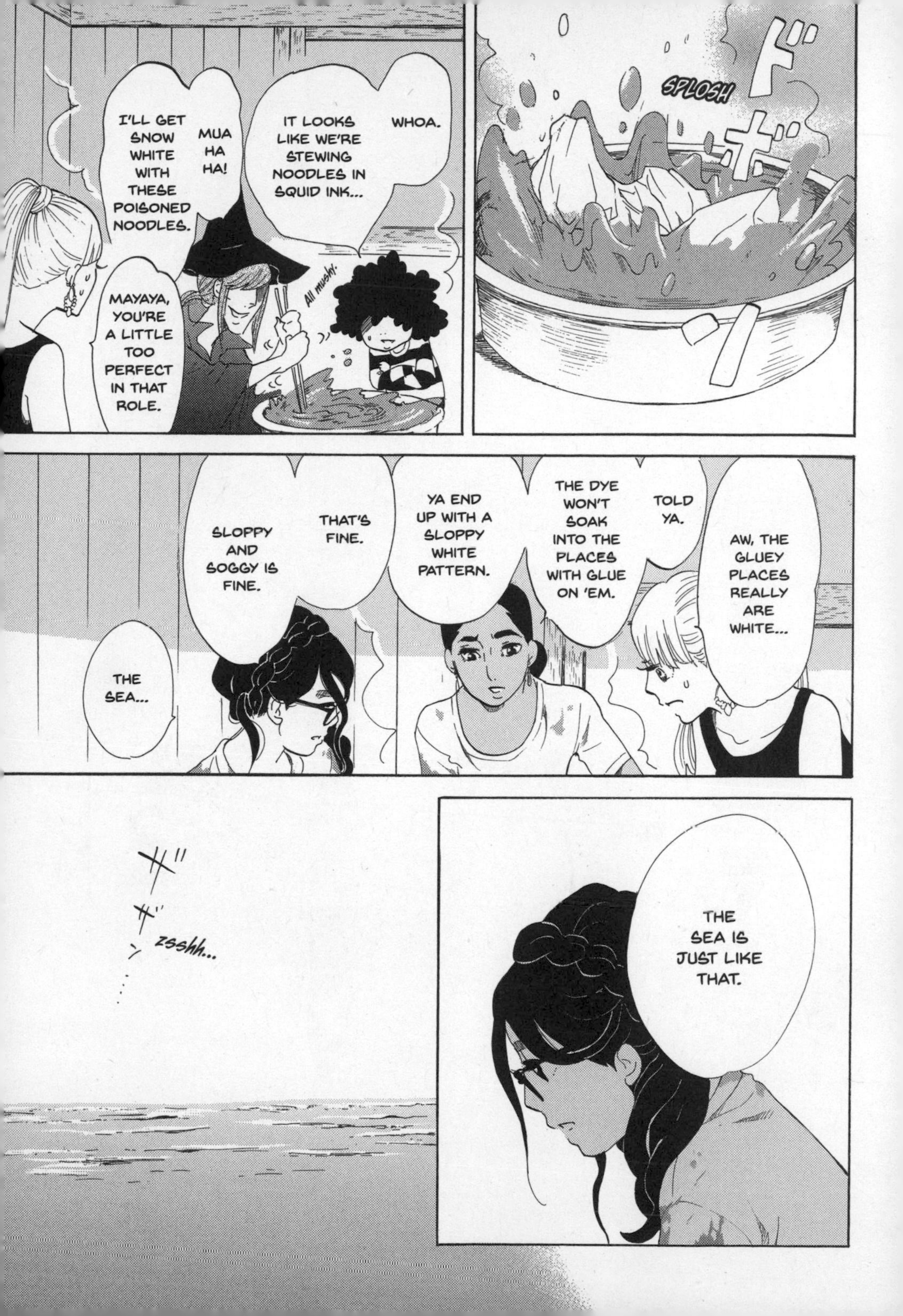
ド
ボ
SPLOSH
WHOA.
IT LOOKS LIKE WE'RE STEWING NOODLES IN SQUID INK...
MUA HA HA!
I'LL GET SNOW WHITE WITH THESE POISONED NOODLES.
All mushy.
MAYAYA, YOU'RE A LITTLE TOO PERFECT IN THAT ROLE.
AW, THE GLUEY PLACES REALLY ARE WHITE...
TOLD YA.
THE DYE WON'T SOAK INTO THE PLACES WITH GLUE ON 'EM.
YA END UP WITH A SLOPPY WHITE PATTERN.
THAT'S FINE.
SLOPPY AND SOGGY IS FINE.
THE SEA...
THE SEA IS JUST LIKE THAT.
ザ
ザ
ン
zsshh...

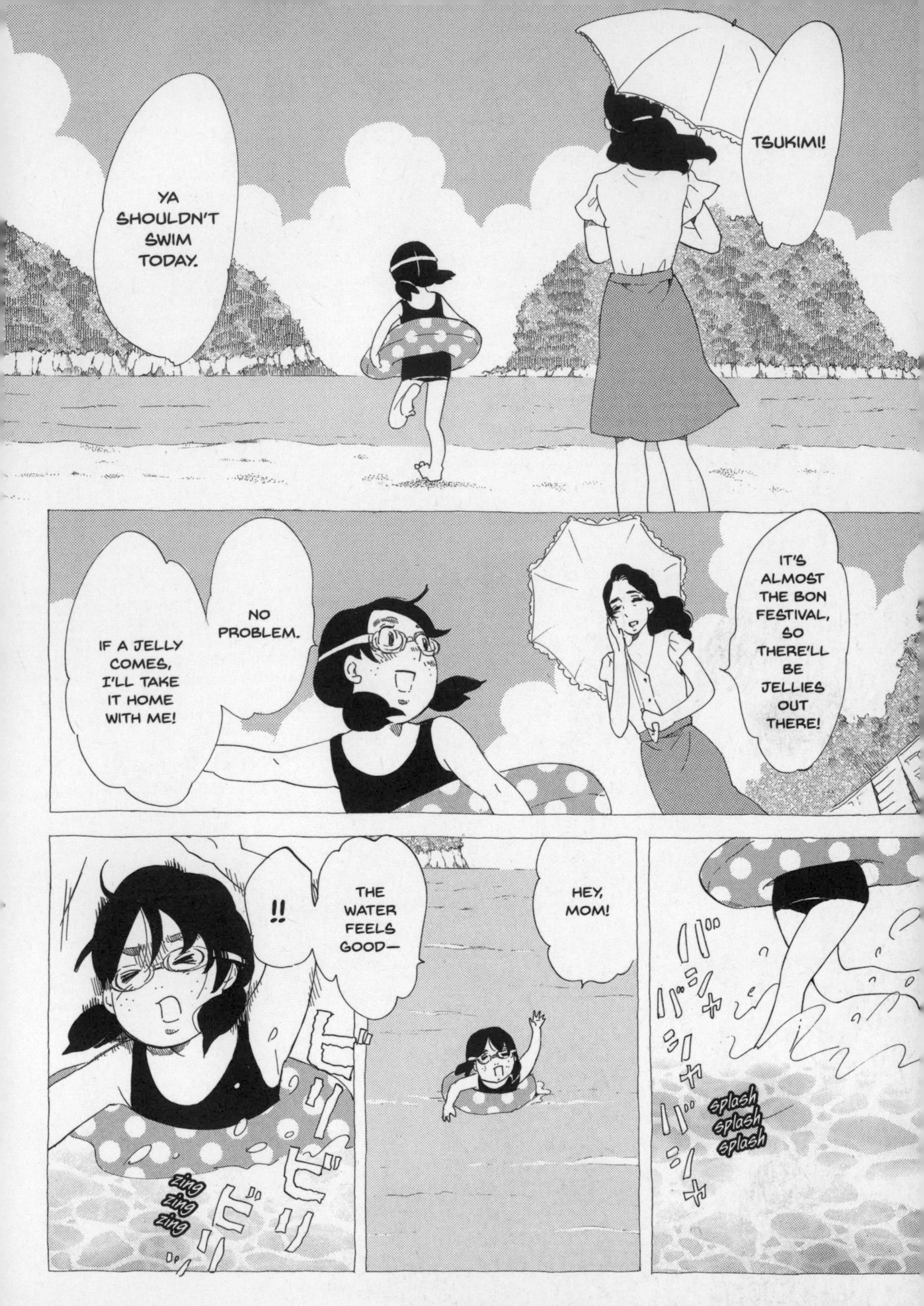
TSUKIMI!
YA SHOULDN'T SWIM TODAY.
IT'S ALMOST THE BON FESTIVAL, SO THERE'LL BE JELLIES OUT THERE!
NO PROBLEM.
IF A JELLY COMES, I'LL TAKE IT HOME WITH ME!
splash splash splash
HEY, MOM!
THE WATER FEELS GOOD—
!!
zing zing zing

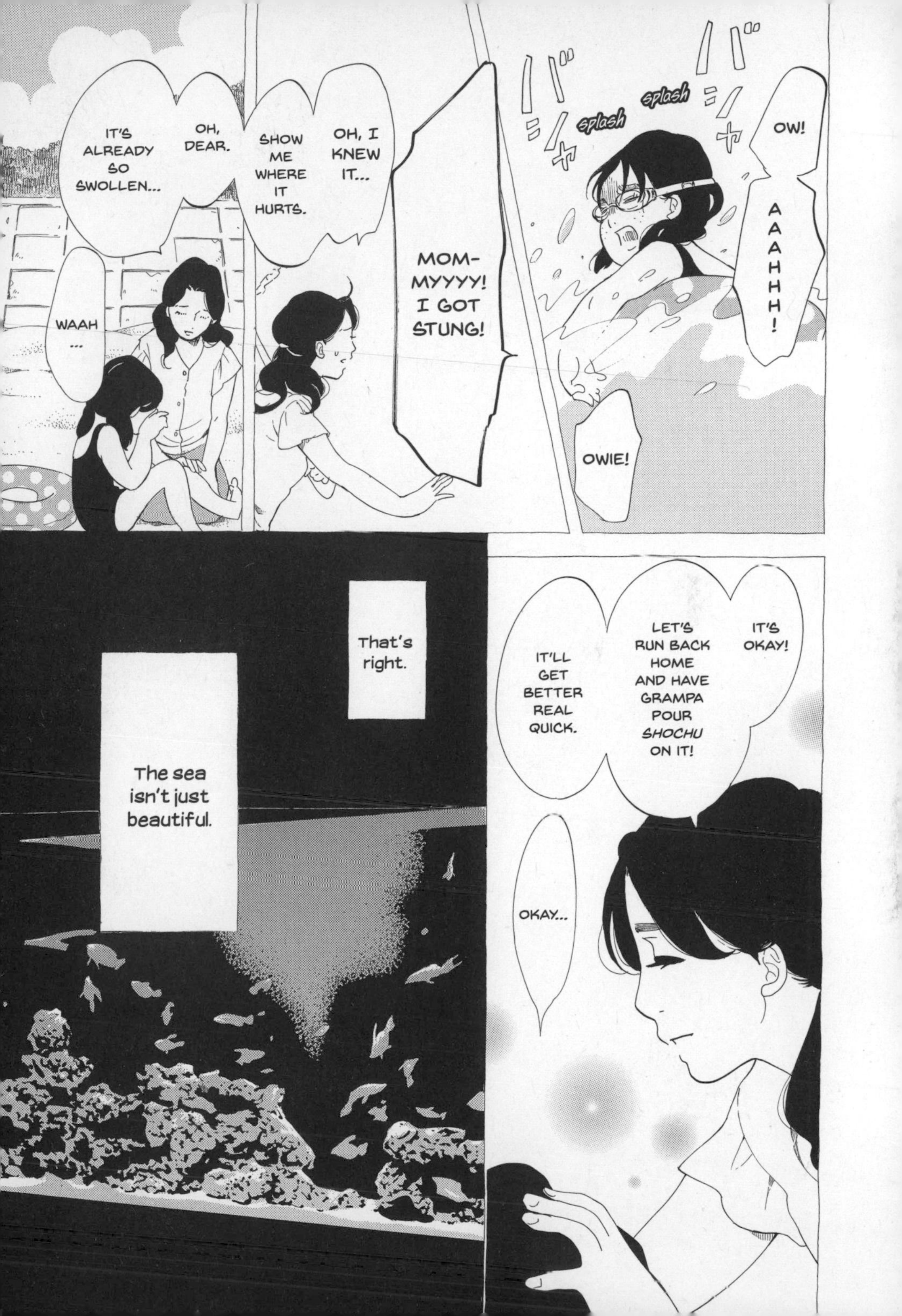
splash
splash
OW!
AAAAHHH!
OWIE!
MOM-MYYYY! I GOT STUNG!
OH, I KNEW IT...
SHOW ME WHERE IT HURTS.
OH, DEAR.
IT'S ALREADY SO SWOLLEN...
WAAH ...
IT'S OKAY!
LET'S RUN BACK HOME AND HAVE GRAMPA POUR *SHOCHU* ON IT!
IT'LL GET BETTER REAL QUICK.
OKAY...
That's right.
The sea isn't just beautiful.

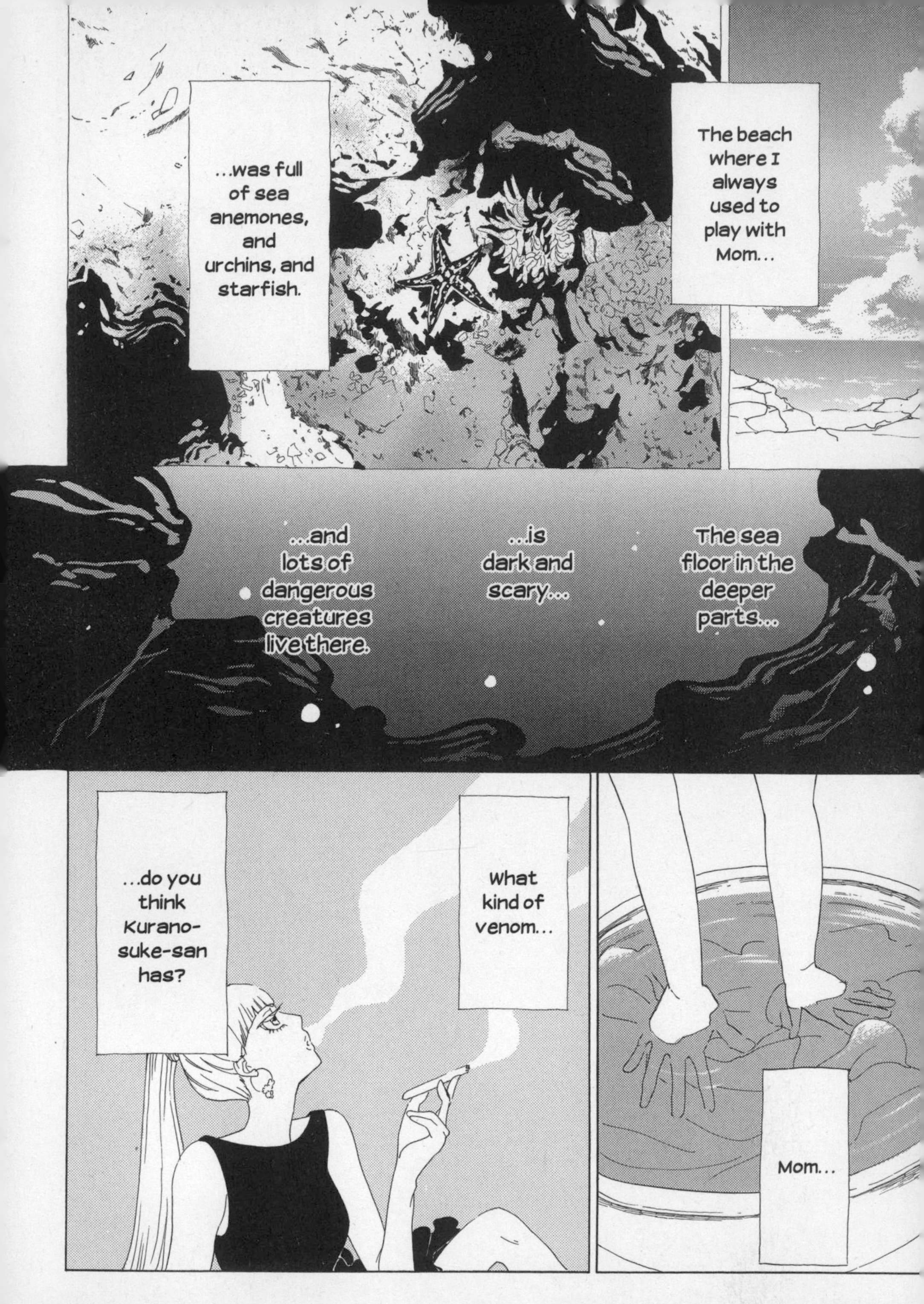
The beach where I always used to play with Mom...
...was full of sea anemones, and urchins, and starfish.
The sea floor in the deeper parts...
...is dark and scary...
...and lots of dangerous creatures live there.
Mom...
What kind of venom...
...do you think Kurano-suke-san has?

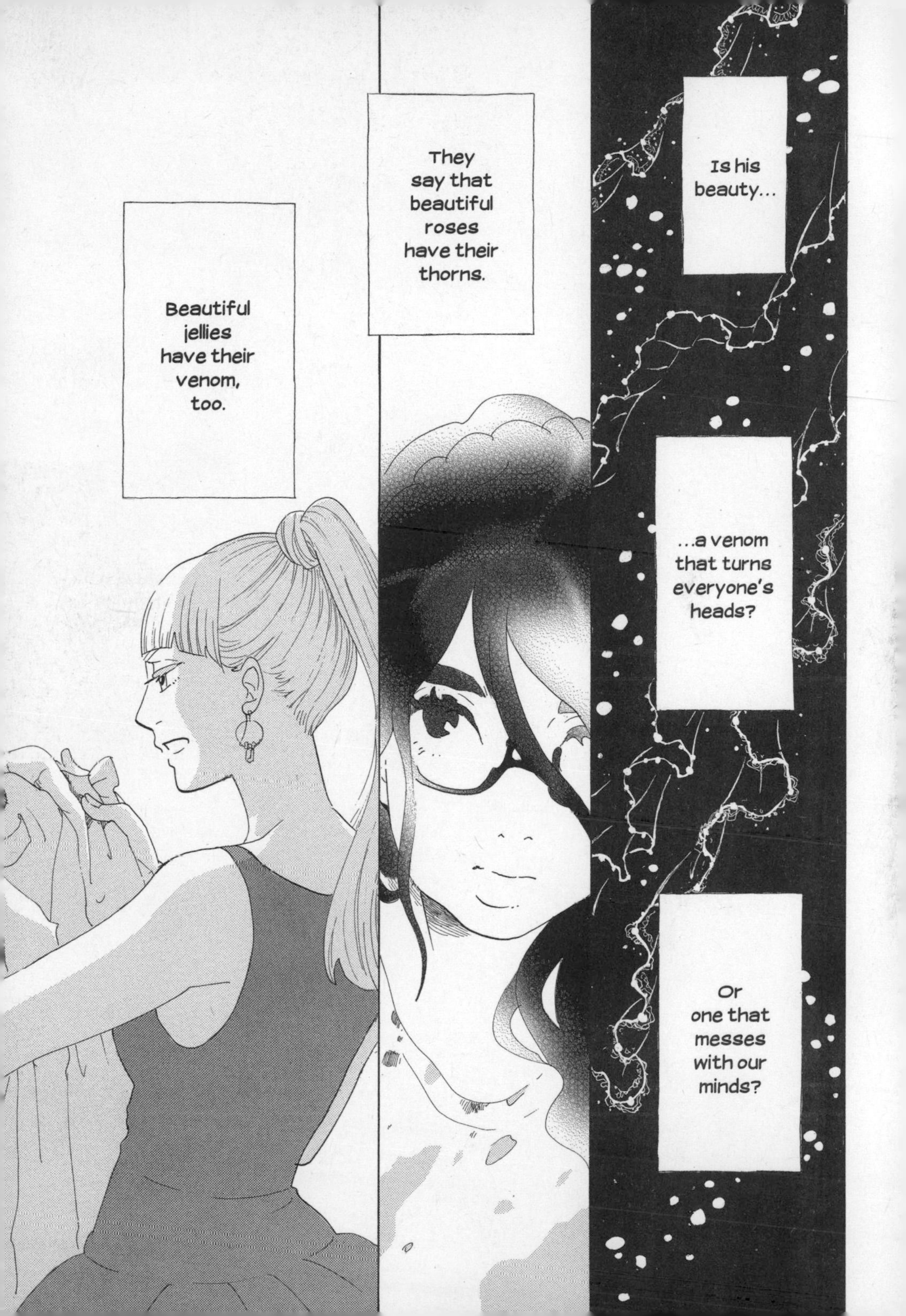
Is his beauty...
...a venom that turns everyone's heads?
Or one that messes with our minds?
They say that beautiful roses have their thorns.
Beautiful jellies have their venom, too.

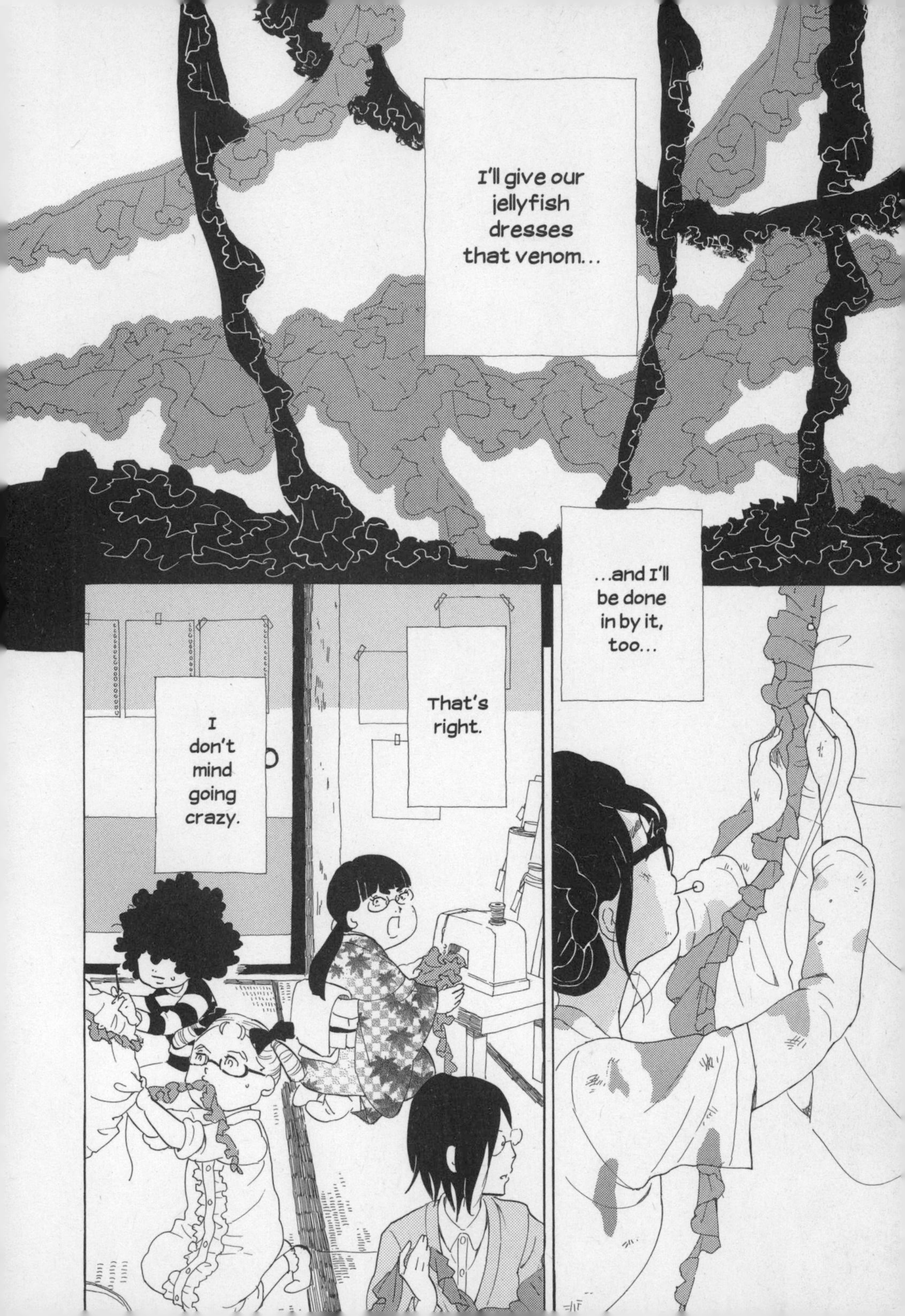
I'll give our jellyfish dresses that venom...
...and I'll be done in by it, too...
That's right.
I don't mind going crazy.

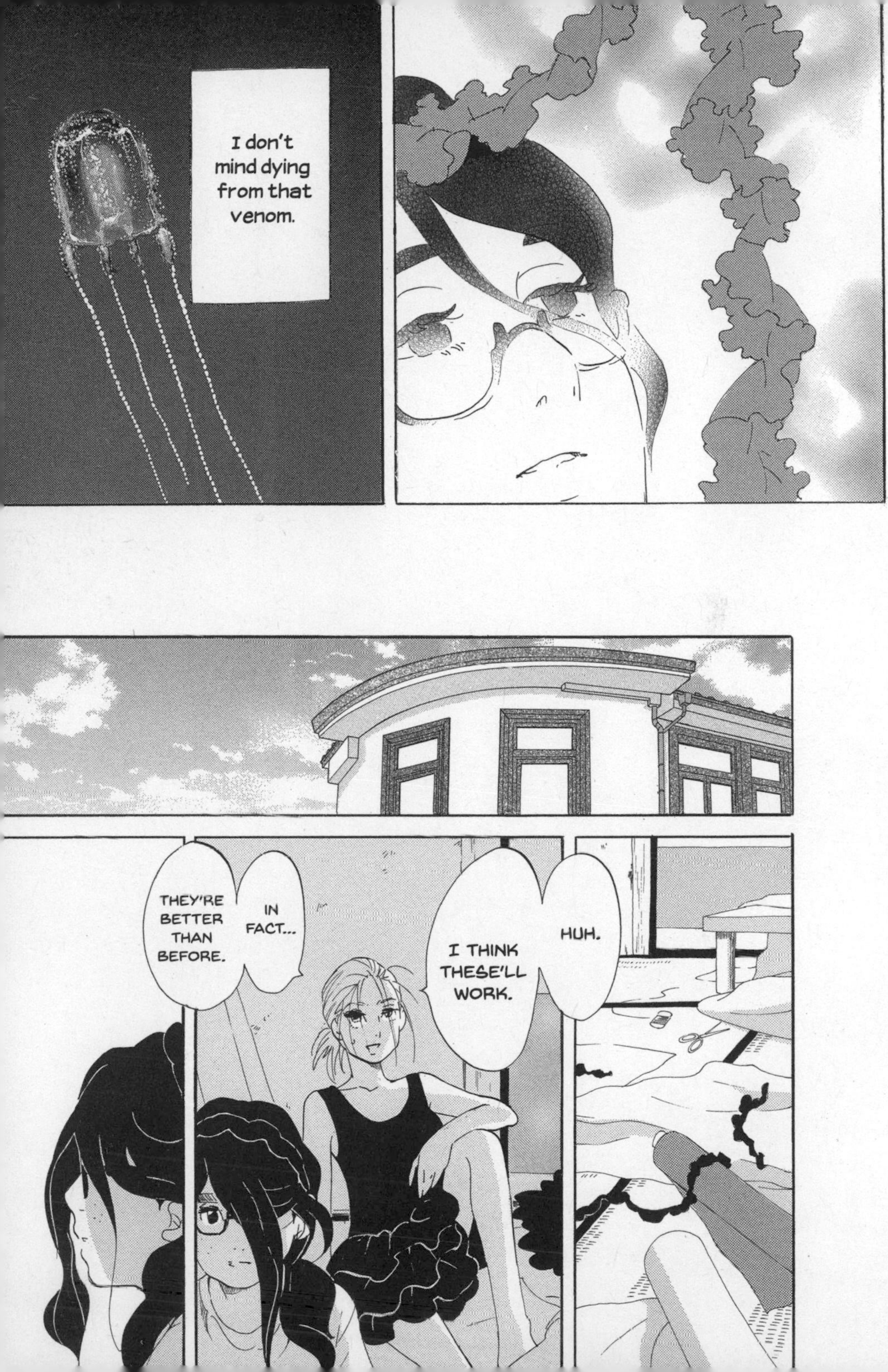
I don't mind dying from that venom.
HUH.
I THINK THESE'LL WORK.
IN FACT...
THEY'RE BETTER THAN BEFORE.

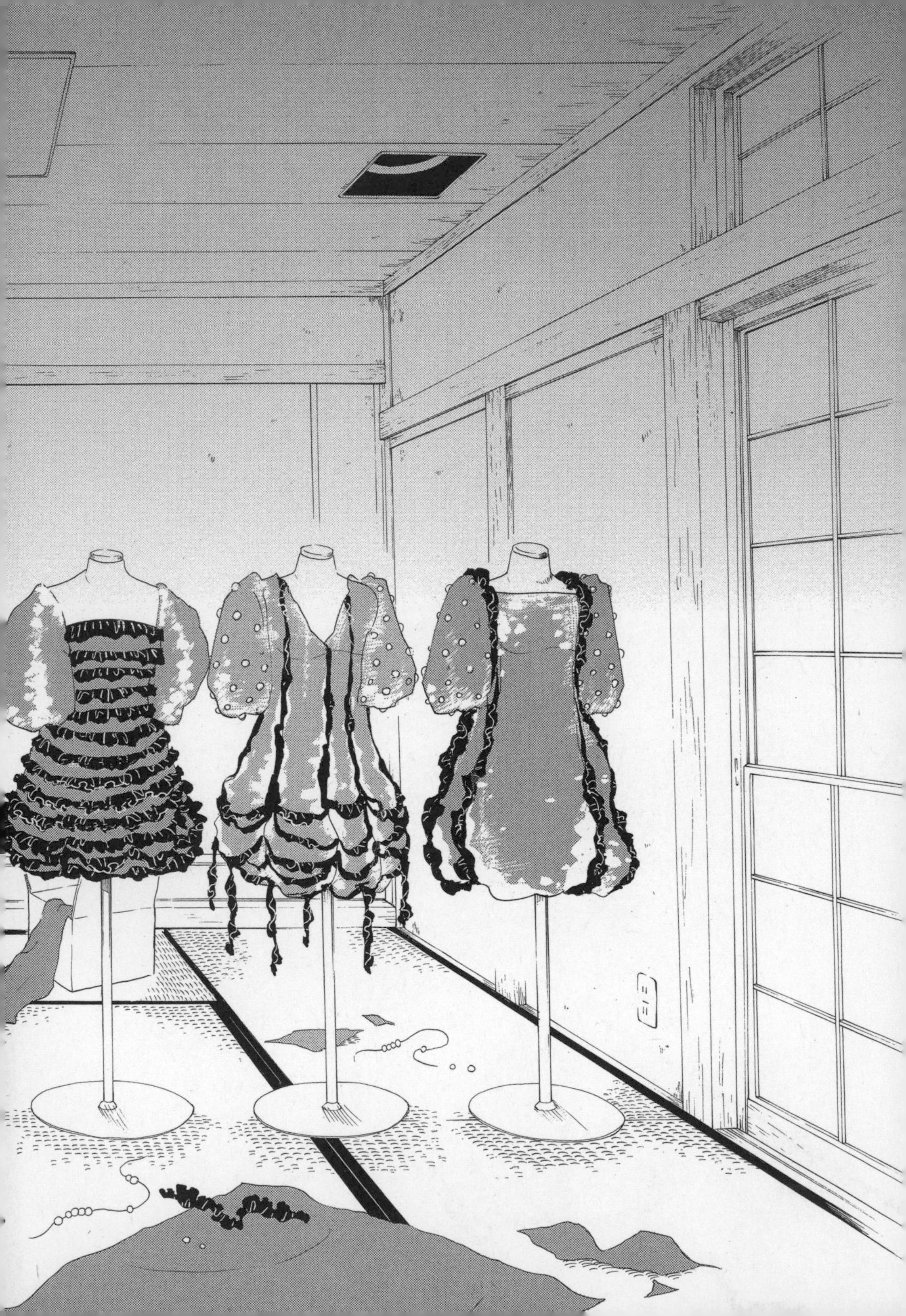

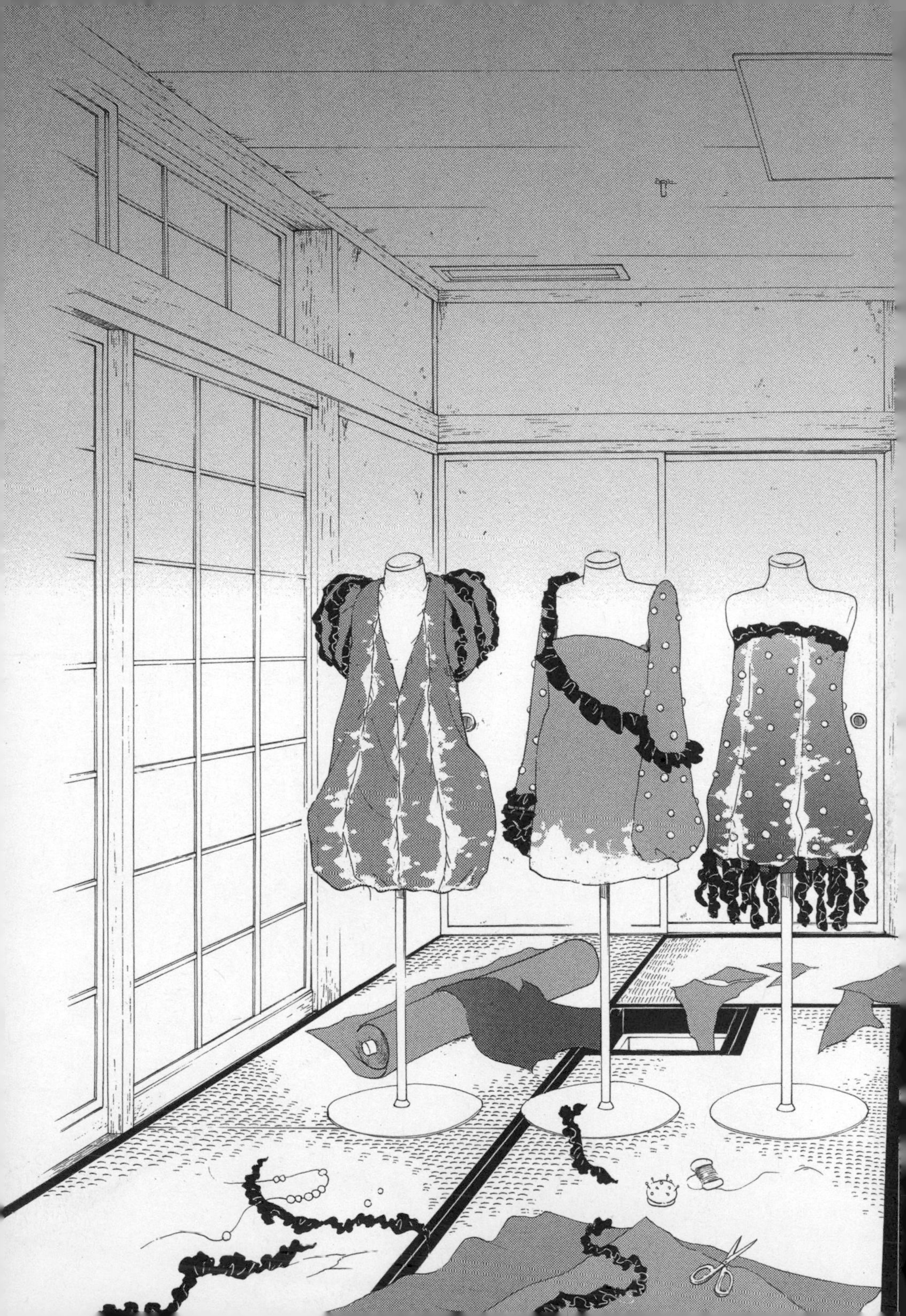

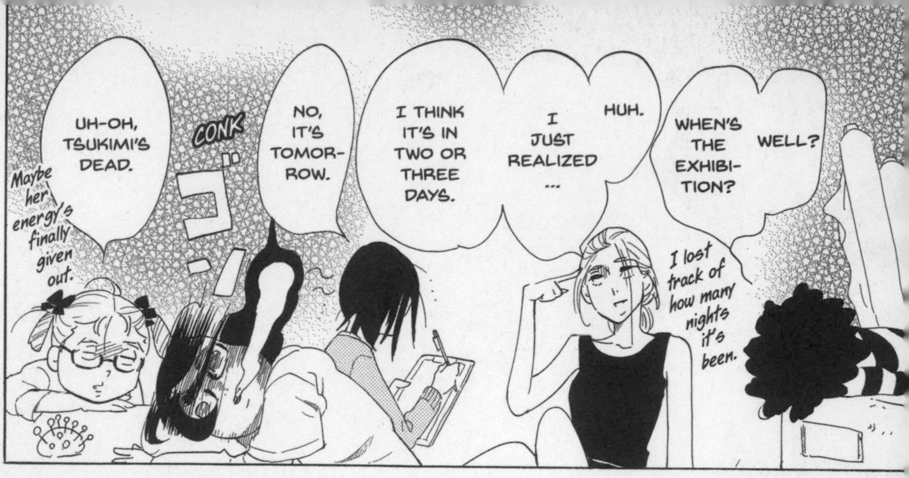
WELL?
WHEN'S THE EXHIBITION?
I lost track of how many nights it's been.
HUH.
I JUST REALIZED ...
I THINK IT'S IN TWO OR THREE DAYS.
NO, IT'S TOMORROW.
CONK
ゴン
UH-OH, TSUKIMI'S DEAD.
Maybe her energy's finally given out.

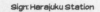

Sign: Harajuku Station

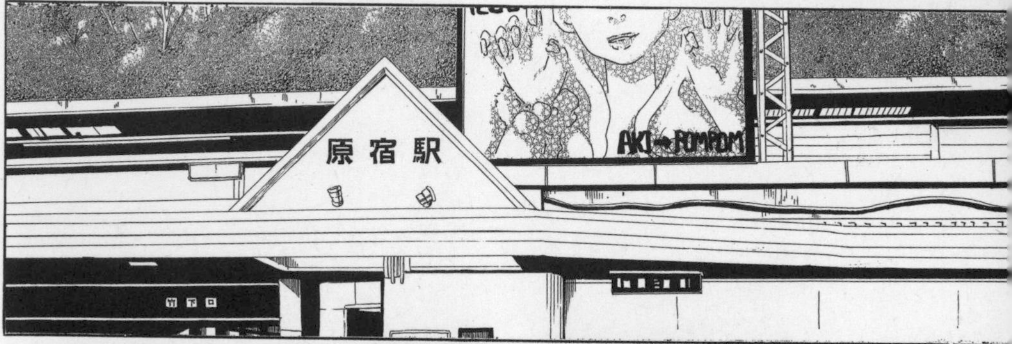
原宿駅
AKI POMPOM

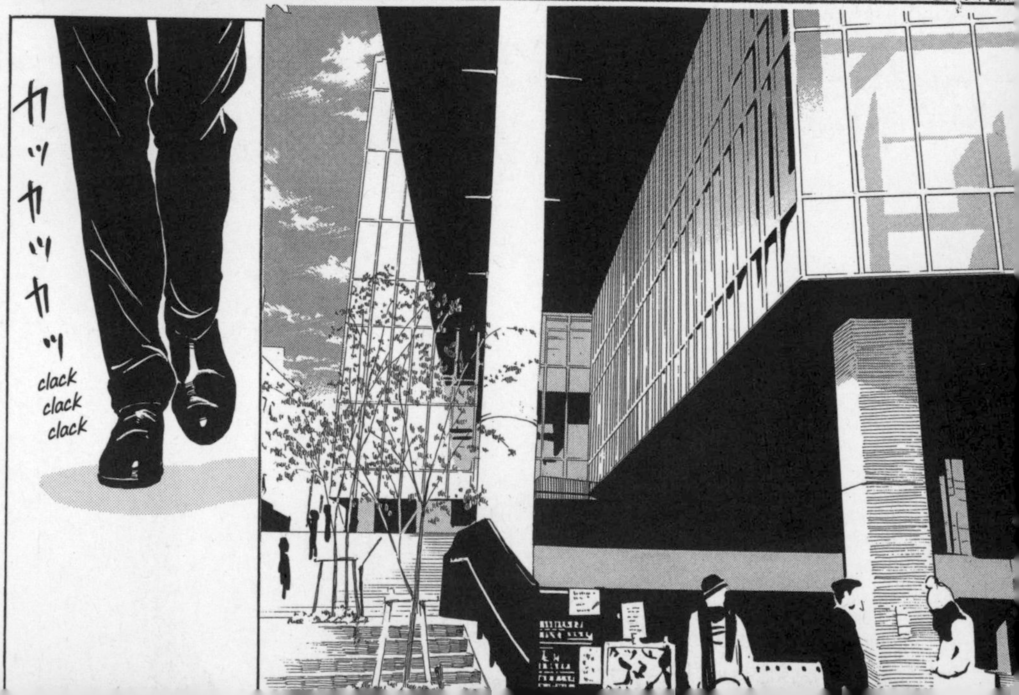
カッカッカッ
clack clack clack

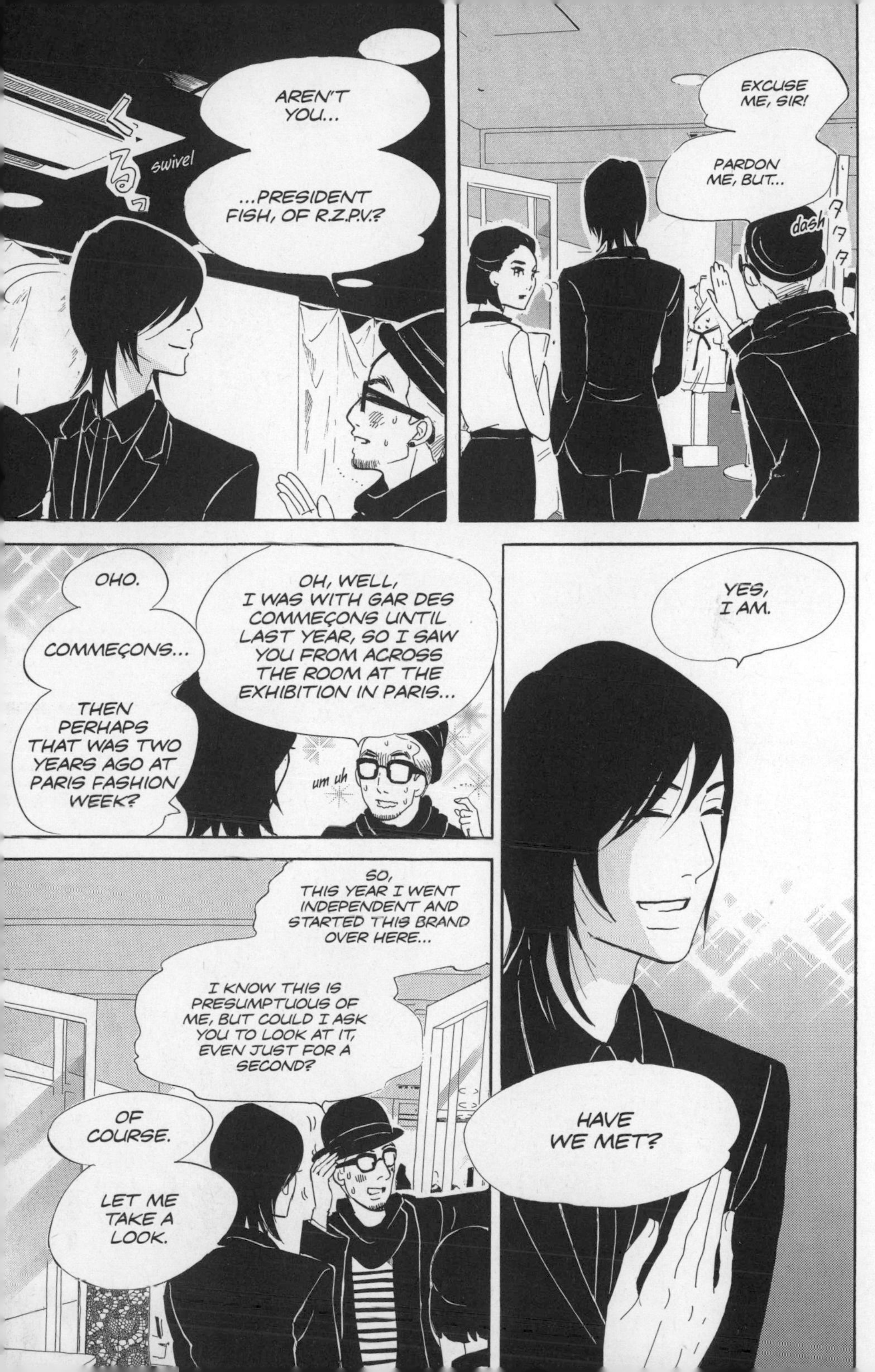
EXCUSE ME, SIR!
PARDON ME, BUT...
dash
AREN'T YOU...
...PRESIDENT FISH, OF R.Z.P.V.?
swivel
YES, I AM.
HAVE WE MET?
OH, WELL, I WAS WITH GAR DES COMMEÇONS UNTIL LAST YEAR, SO I SAW YOU FROM ACROSS THE ROOM AT THE EXHIBITION IN PARIS...
OHO.
COMMEÇONS...
THEN PERHAPS THAT WAS TWO YEARS AGO AT PARIS FASHION WEEK?
um uh
SO, THIS YEAR I WENT INDEPENDENT AND STARTED THIS BRAND OVER HERE...
I KNOW THIS IS PRESUMPTUOUS OF ME, BUT COULD I ASK YOU TO LOOK AT IT, EVEN JUST FOR A SECOND?
OF COURSE.
LET ME TAKE A LOOK.

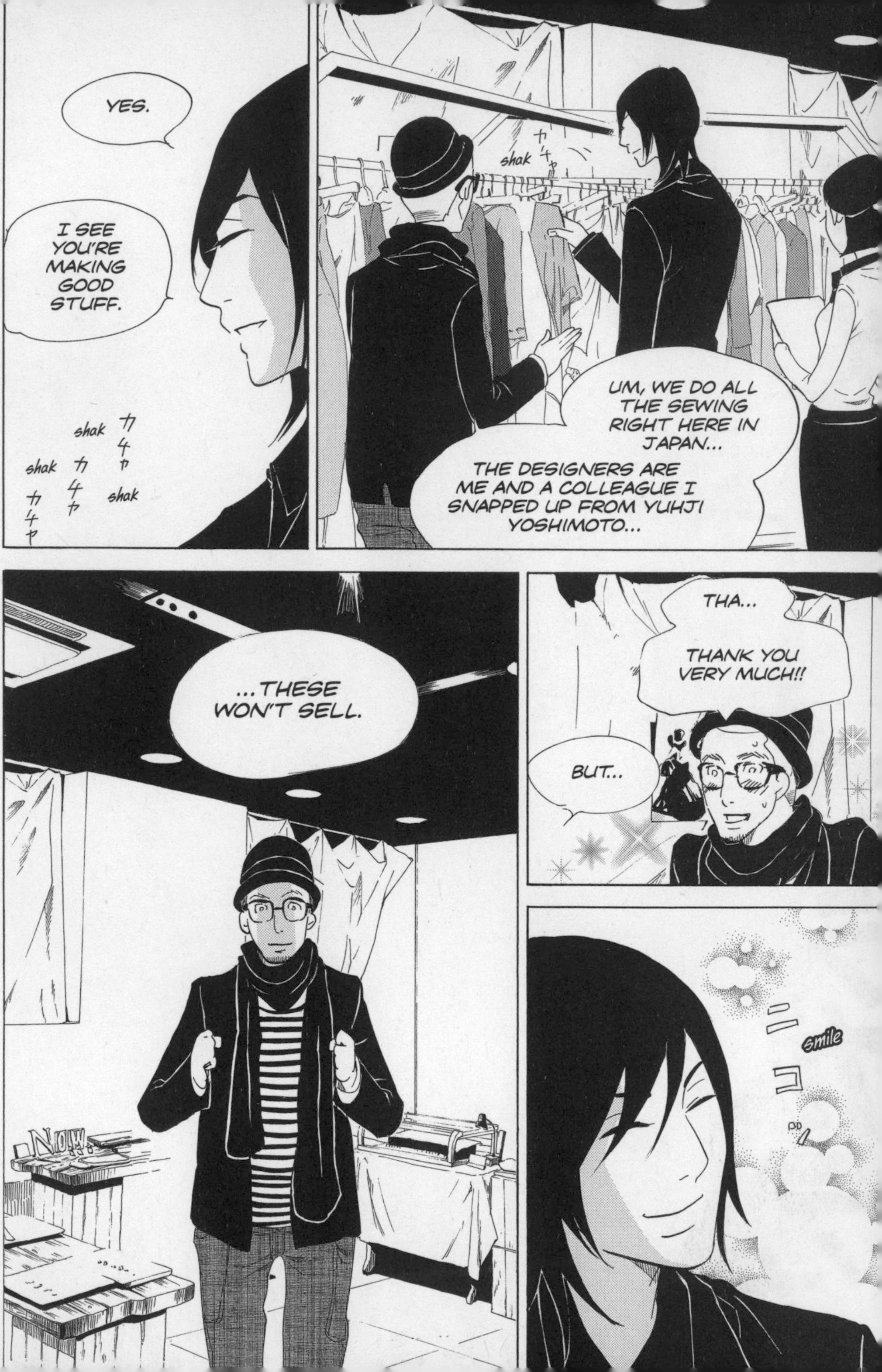
shak カチャ
UM, WE DO ALL THE SEWING RIGHT HERE IN JAPAN...
THE DESIGNERS ARE ME AND A COLLEAGUE I SNAPPED UP FROM YUHJI YOSHIMOTO...
YES.
I SEE YOU'RE MAKING GOOD STUFF.
shak カチャ
shak カチャ
shak カチャ
THA...
THANK YOU VERY MUCH!!
BUT...
ニコ
smile
...THESE WON'T SELL.

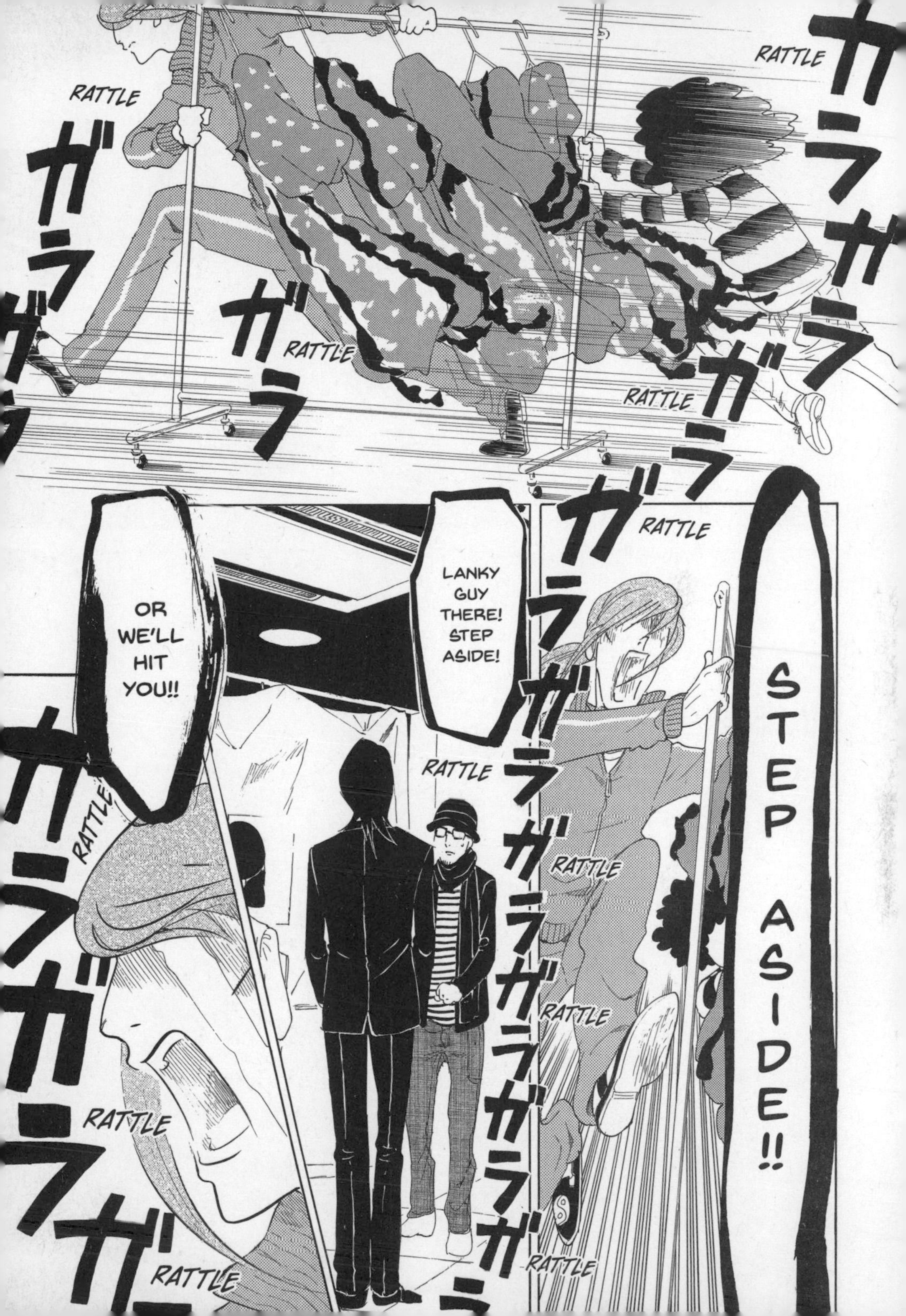

カラガラ
RATTLE
RATTLE
ガラガラ
ガラ
RATTLE
RATTLE
ガラガラ
RATTLE
STEP ASIDE!!
RATTLE
RATTLE
RATTLE
LANKY GUY THERE! STEP ASIDE!
RATTLE
OR WE'LL HIT YOU!!
RATTLE
RATTLE
RATTLE

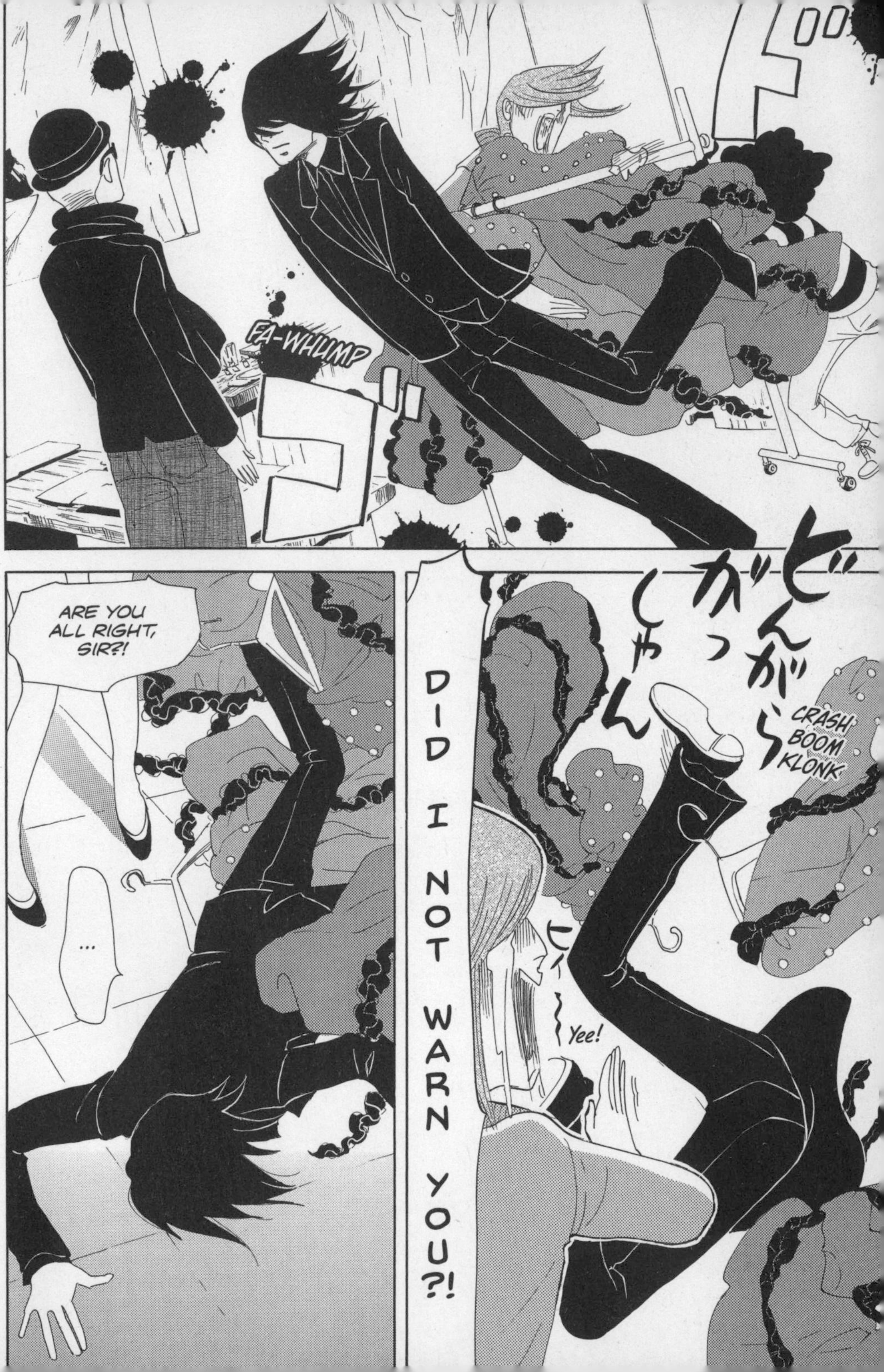
FA-WHUMP
どんがらがっしゃん
CRASH BOOM KLONK
Yee!
DID I NOT WARN YOU?!
ARE YOU ALL RIGHT, SIR?!
...

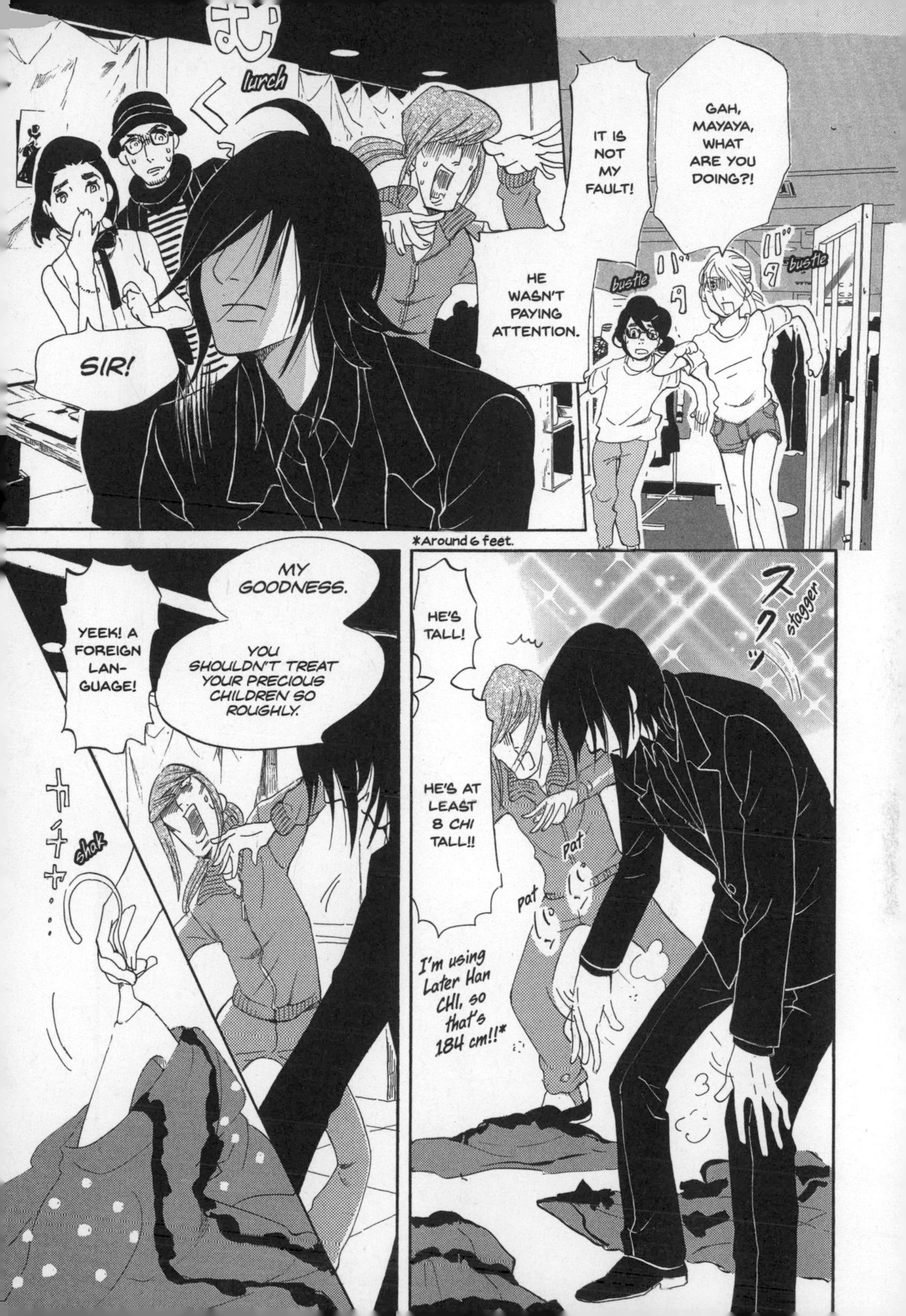
GAH, MAYAYA, WHAT ARE YOU DOING?!
IT IS NOT MY FAULT!
bustle
bustle
HE WASN'T PAYING ATTENTION.
lurch
SIR!
*Around 6 feet.
stagger
HE'S TALL!
HE'S AT LEAST 8 CHI TALL!!
pat
pat
I'm using Later Han CHI, so that's 184 cm!!*
MY GOODNESS.
YOU SHOULDN'T TREAT YOUR PRECIOUS CHILDREN SO ROUGHLY.
YEEK! A FOREIGN LAN-GUAGE!
shak

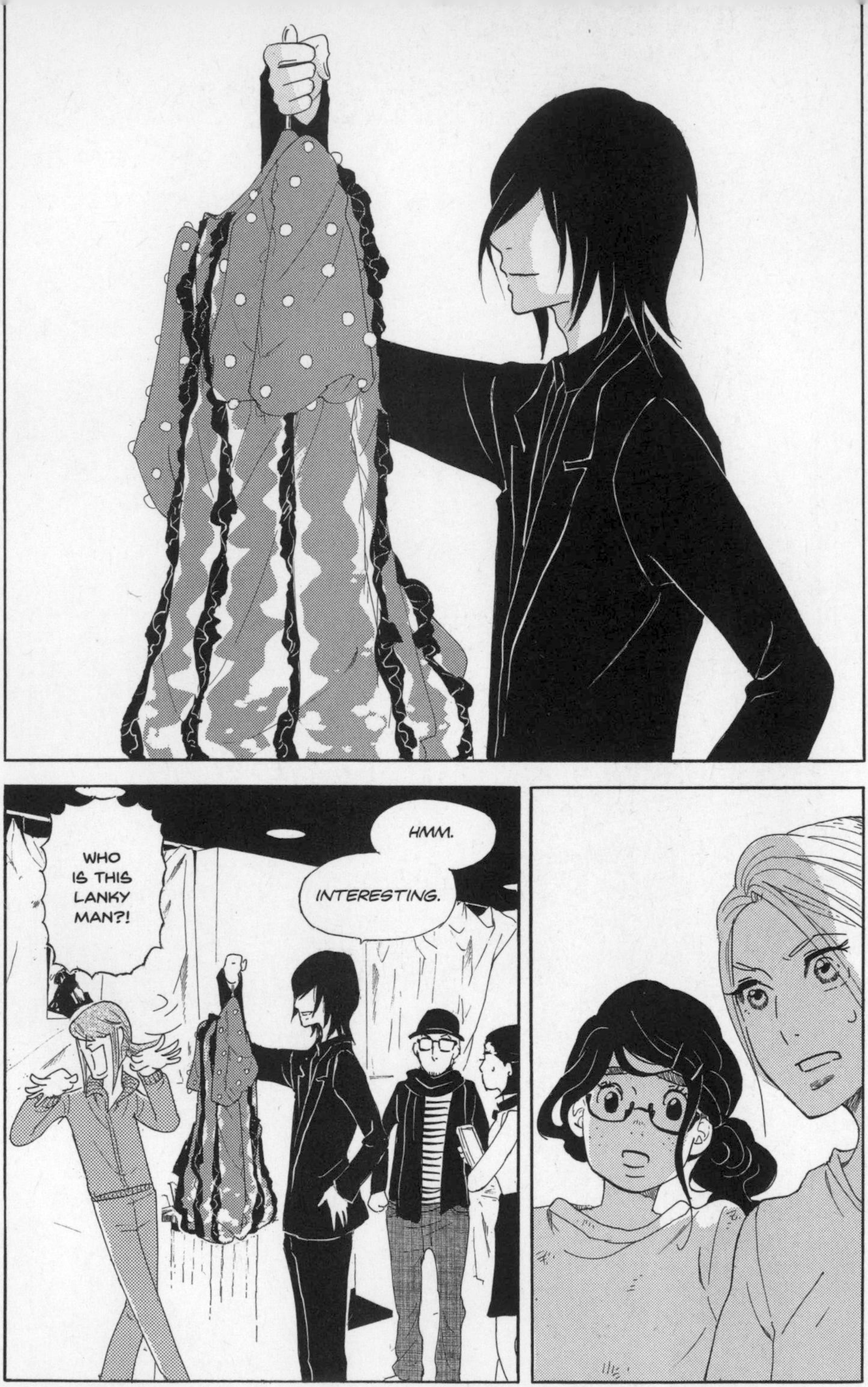
HMM.
INTERESTING.
WHO IS THIS LANKY MAN?!

Episode 58

Fashion Wars: The Don of Asia

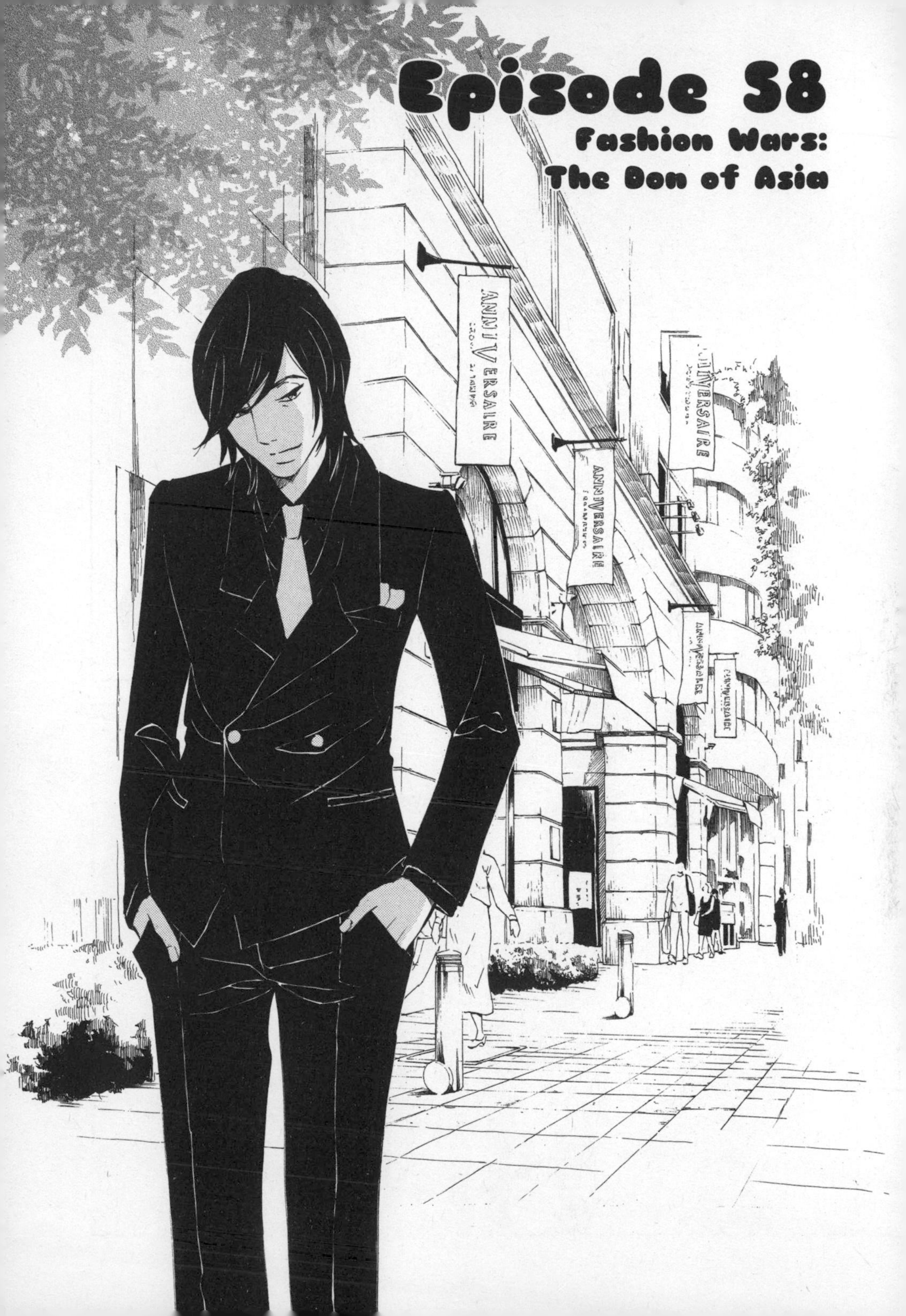
ANNIVERSAIRE
ANNIVERSAIRE
ANNIVERSAIRE
ANNIVERSAIRE

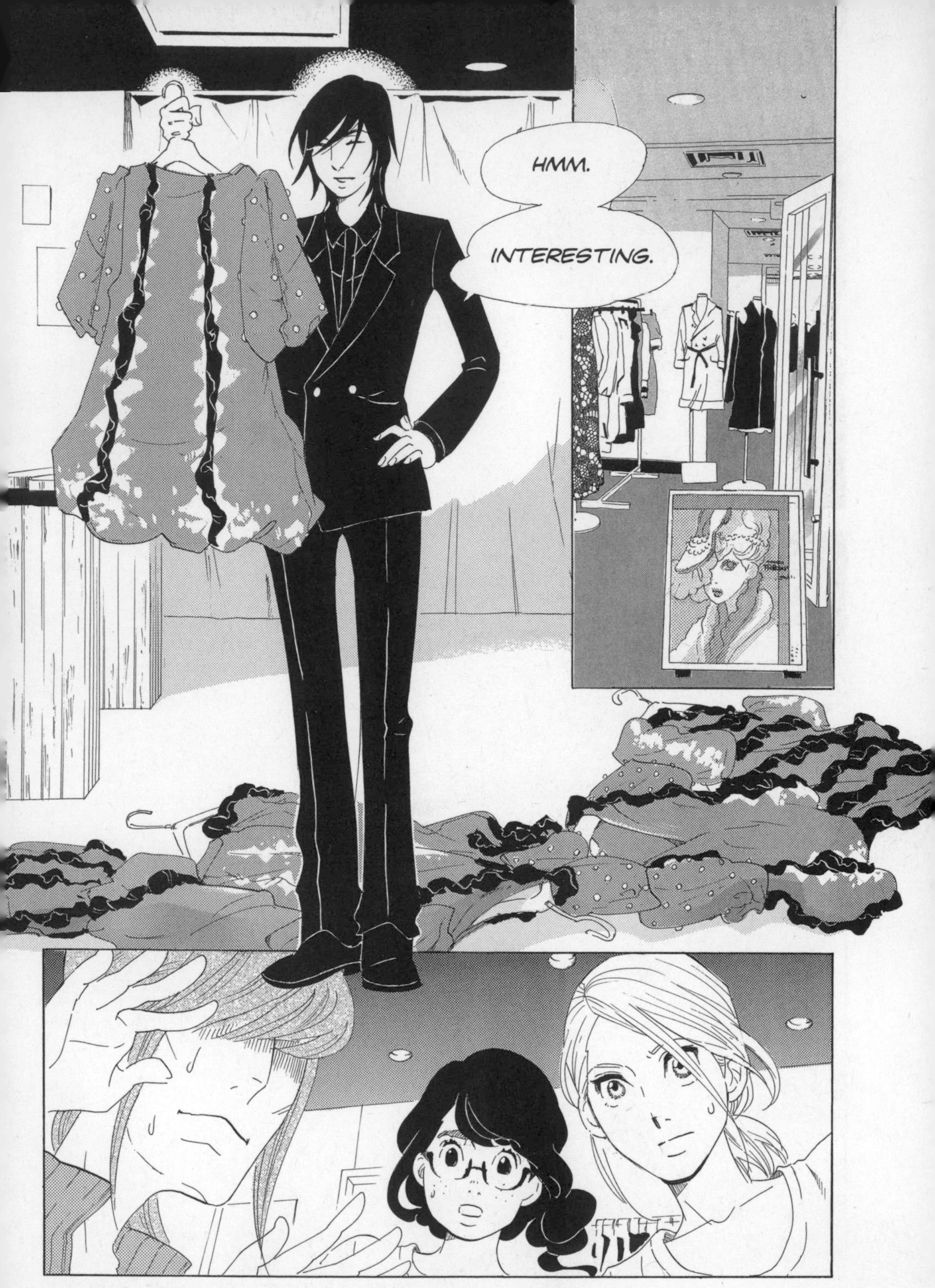
HMM.
INTERESTING.

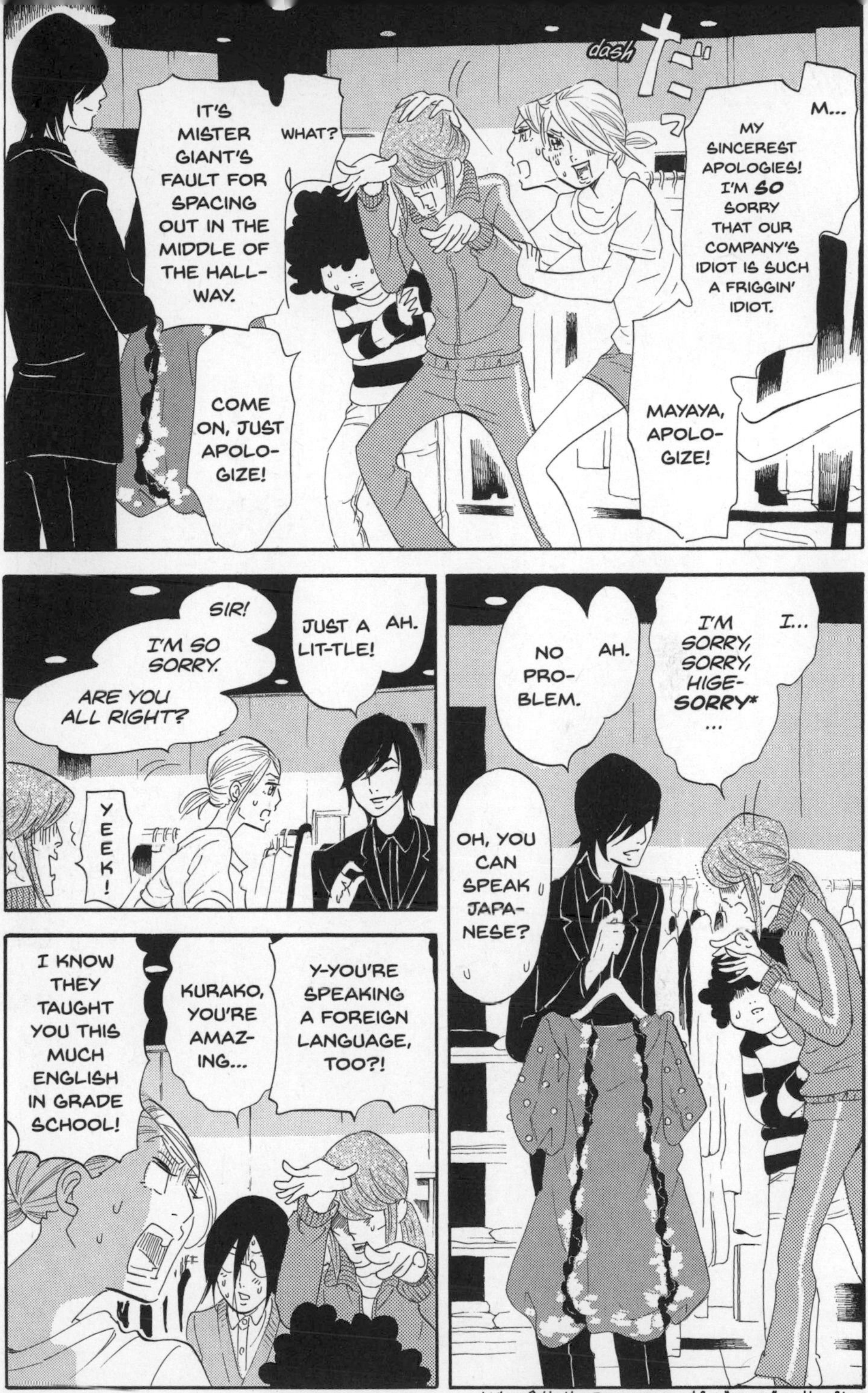
M...
MY SINCEREST APOLOGIES! I'M SO SORRY THAT OUR COMPANY'S IDIOT IS SUCH A FRIGGIN' IDIOT.
dash
WHAT?
IT'S MISTER GIANT'S FAULT FOR SPACING OUT IN THE MIDDLE OF THE HALL-WAY.
MAYAYA, APOLO-GIZE!
COME ON, JUST APOLO-GIZE!
I...
I'M SORRY, SORRY, HIGE-SORRY* ...
AH.
NO PRO-BLEM.
OH, YOU CAN SPEAK JAPA-NESE?
AH.
JUST A LIT-TLE!
SIR! I'M SO SORRY. ARE YOU ALL RIGHT?
YEEK!
Y-YOU'RE SPEAKING A FOREIGN LANGUAGE, TOO?!
KURAKO, YOU'RE AMAZ-ING...
I KNOW THEY TAUGHT YOU THIS MUCH ENGLISH IN GRADE SCHOOL!

**Higesôri* is the Japanese word for "razor," and is often used in Japan as a punny rhyme while apologizing.

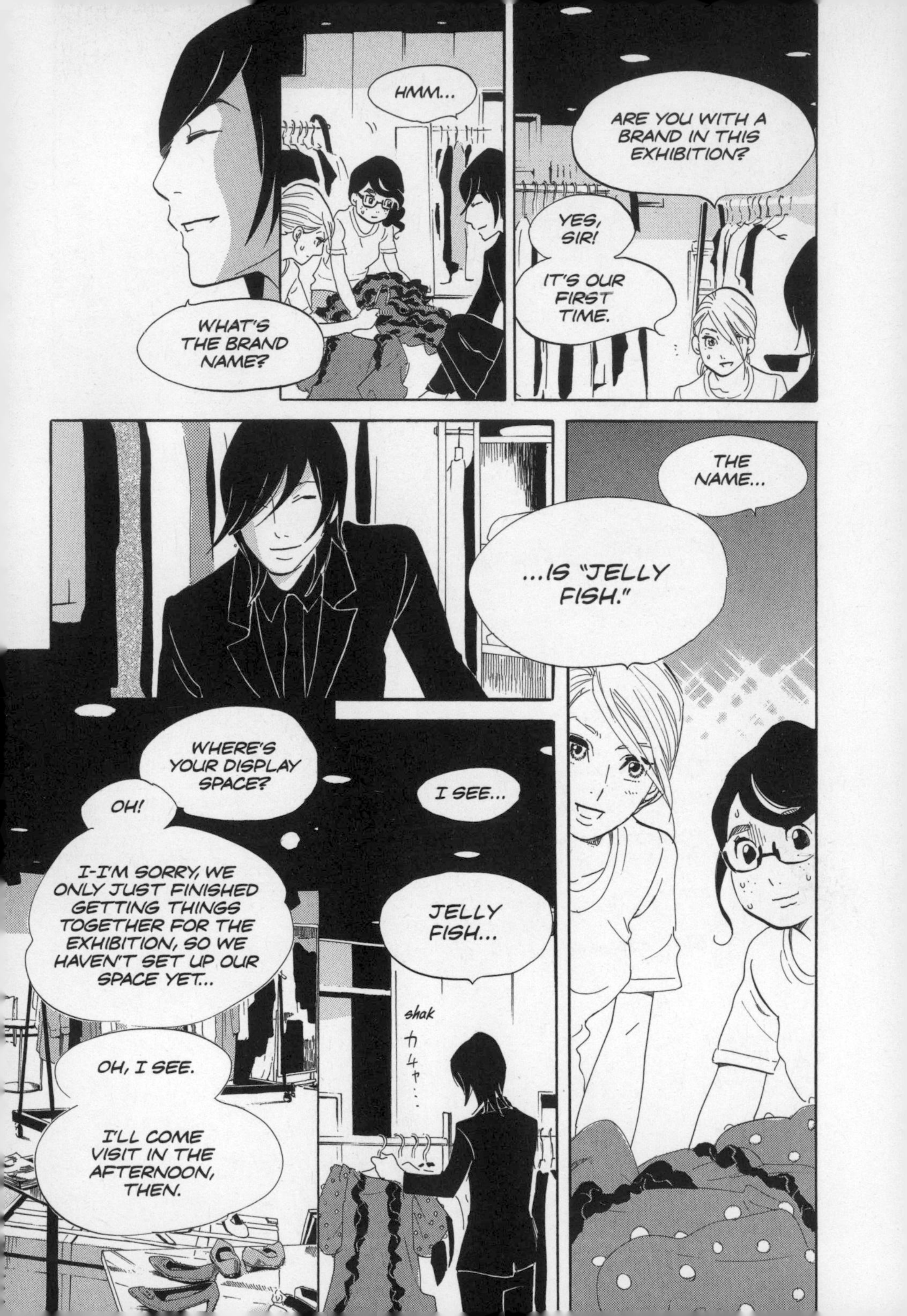
ARE YOU WITH A BRAND IN THIS EXHIBITION?
YES, SIR!
IT'S OUR FIRST TIME.
HMM...
WHAT'S THE BRAND NAME?
THE NAME...
...IS "JELLY FISH."
I SEE...
JELLY FISH...
WHERE'S YOUR DISPLAY SPACE?
OH!
I-I'M SORRY, WE ONLY JUST FINISHED GETTING THINGS TOGETHER FOR THE EXHIBITION, SO WE HAVEN'T SET UP OUR SPACE YET...
shak
カチャ・・
OH, I SEE.
I'LL COME VISIT IN THE AFTERNOON, THEN.

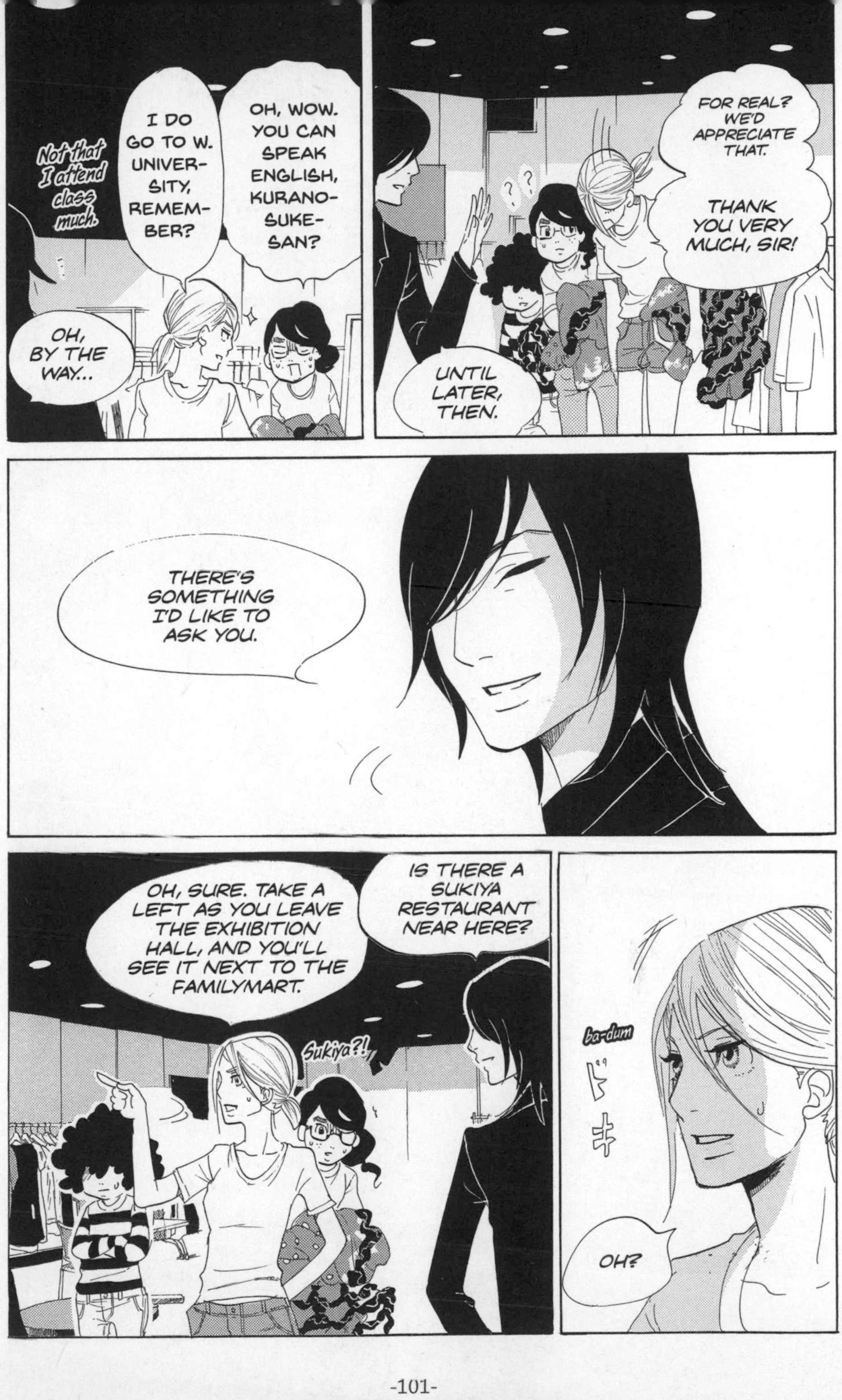
FOR REAL? WE'D APPRECIATE THAT.
THANK YOU VERY MUCH, SIR!
UNTIL LATER, THEN.
OH, WOW. YOU CAN SPEAK ENGLISH, KURANOSUKE-SAN?
I DO GO TO W. UNIVERSITY, REMEMBER?
Not that I attend class much.
OH, BY THE WAY...
THERE'S SOMETHING I'D LIKE TO ASK YOU.
ba-dum
ドキ
OH?
IS THERE A SUKIYA RESTAURANT NEAR HERE?
OH, SURE. TAKE A LEFT AS YOU LEAVE THE EXHIBITION HALL, AND YOU'LL SEE IT NEXT TO THE FAMILYMART.
Sukiya?!

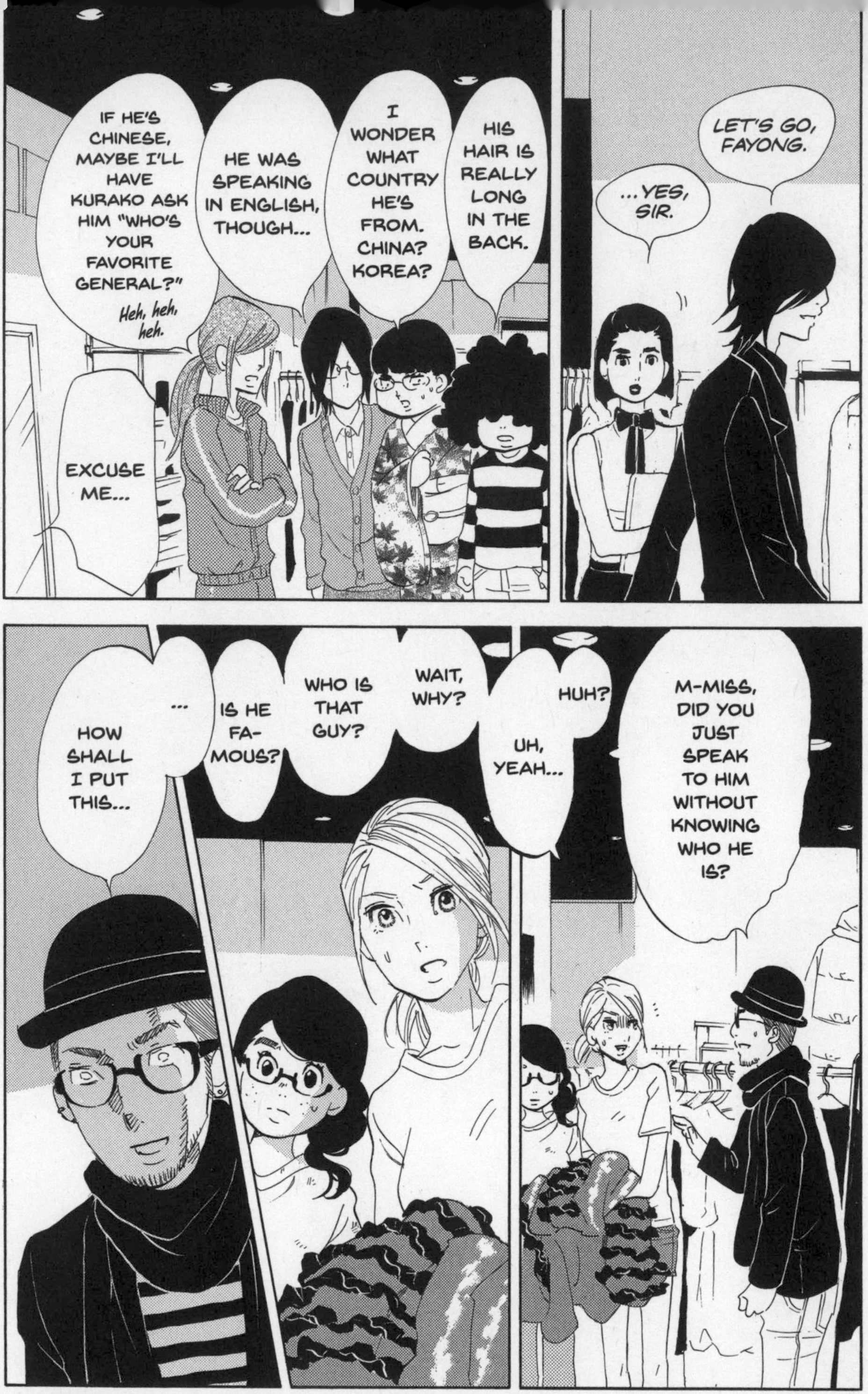
LET'S GO, FAYONG.
...YES, SIR.
HIS HAIR IS REALLY LONG IN THE BACK.
I WONDER WHAT COUNTRY HE'S FROM. CHINA? KOREA?
HE WAS SPEAKING IN ENGLISH, THOUGH...
IF HE'S CHINESE, MAYBE I'LL HAVE KURAKO ASK HIM "WHO'S YOUR FAVORITE GENERAL?"
Heh, heh, heh.
EXCUSE ME...
M-MISS, DID YOU JUST SPEAK TO HIM WITHOUT KNOWING WHO HE IS?
HUH?
UH, YEAH...
WAIT, WHY?
WHO IS THAT GUY?
IS HE FA-MOUS?
...
HOW SHALL I PUT THIS...

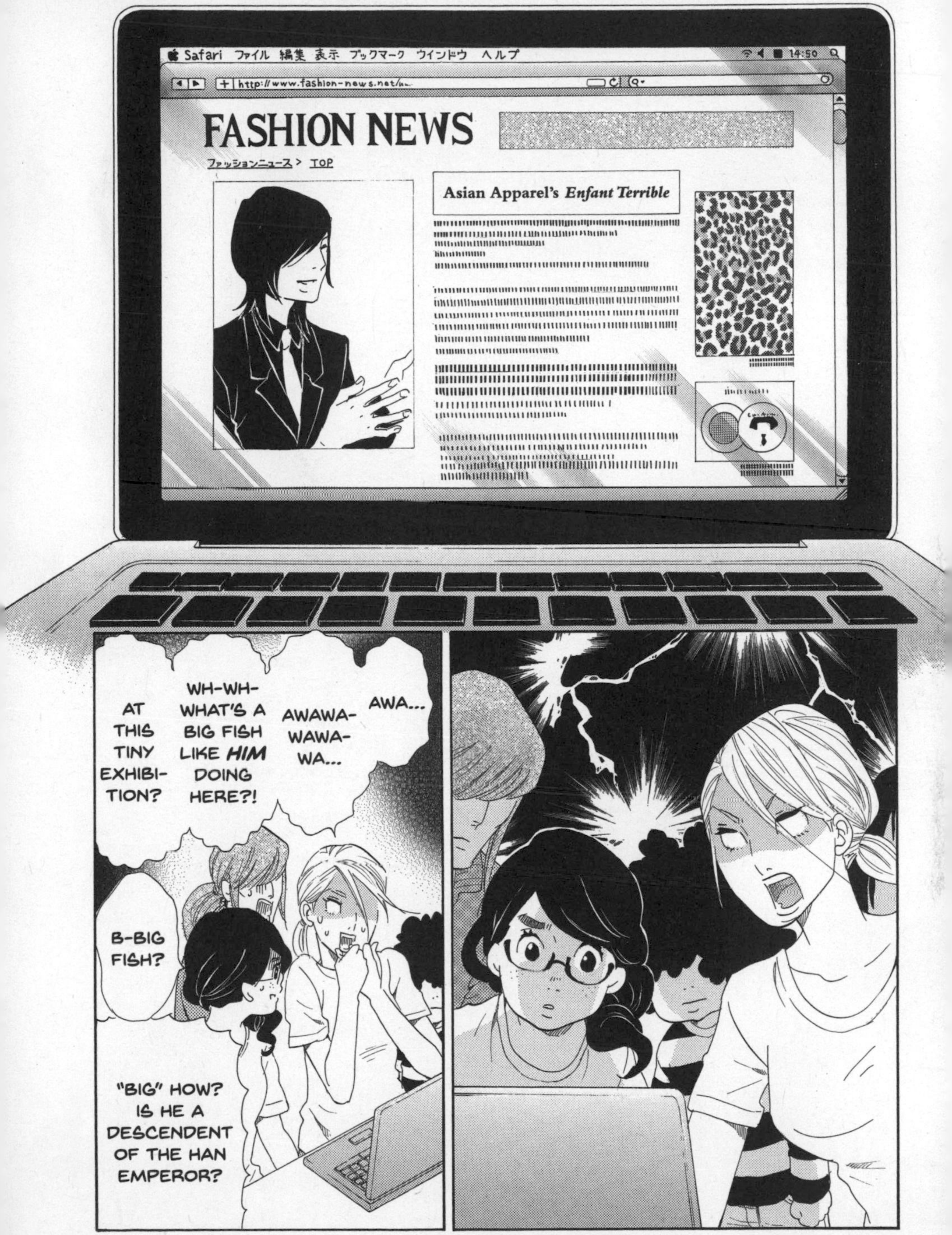
Safari ファイル 編集 表示 ブックマーク ウインドウ ヘルプ
14:50
http://www.fashion-news.net/
FASHION NEWS
ファッションニュース > TOP
Asian Apparel's *Enfant Terrible*
AWA...
AWAWA-WAWA-WA...
WH-WH-WHAT'S A BIG FISH LIKE *HIM* DOING HERE?!
AT THIS TINY EXHIBITION?
B-BIG FISH?
"BIG" HOW? IS HE A DESCENDENT OF THE HAN EMPEROR?

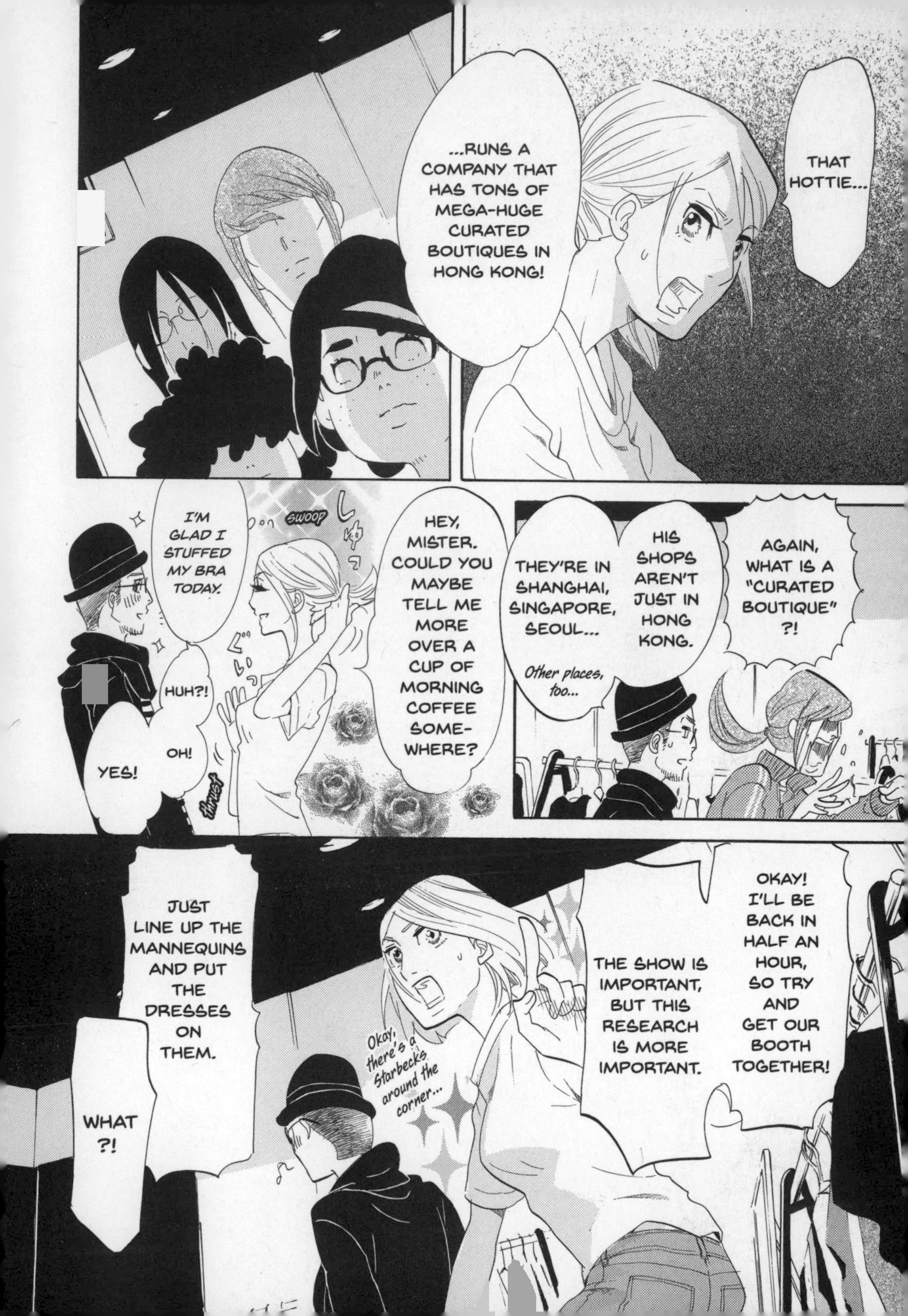
THAT HOTTIE...
...RUNS A COMPANY THAT HAS TONS OF MEGA-HUGE CURATED BOUTIQUES IN HONG KONG!
AGAIN, WHAT IS A "CURATED BOUTIQUE"?!
HIS SHOPS AREN'T JUST IN HONG KONG.
THEY'RE IN SHANGHAI, SINGAPORE, SEOUL...
Other places, too...
HEY, MISTER. COULD YOU MAYBE TELL ME MORE OVER A CUP OF MORNING COFFEE SOMEWHERE?
swoop
I'M GLAD I STUFFED MY BRA TODAY.
HUH?!
OH!
YES!
thrust
OKAY! I'LL BE BACK IN HALF AN HOUR, SO TRY AND GET OUR BOOTH TOGETHER!
THE SHOW IS IMPORTANT, BUT THIS RESEARCH IS MORE IMPORTANT.
Okay, there's a Starbecks around the corner...
JUST LINE UP THE MANNEQUINS AND PUT THE DRESSES ON THEM.
WHAT?!

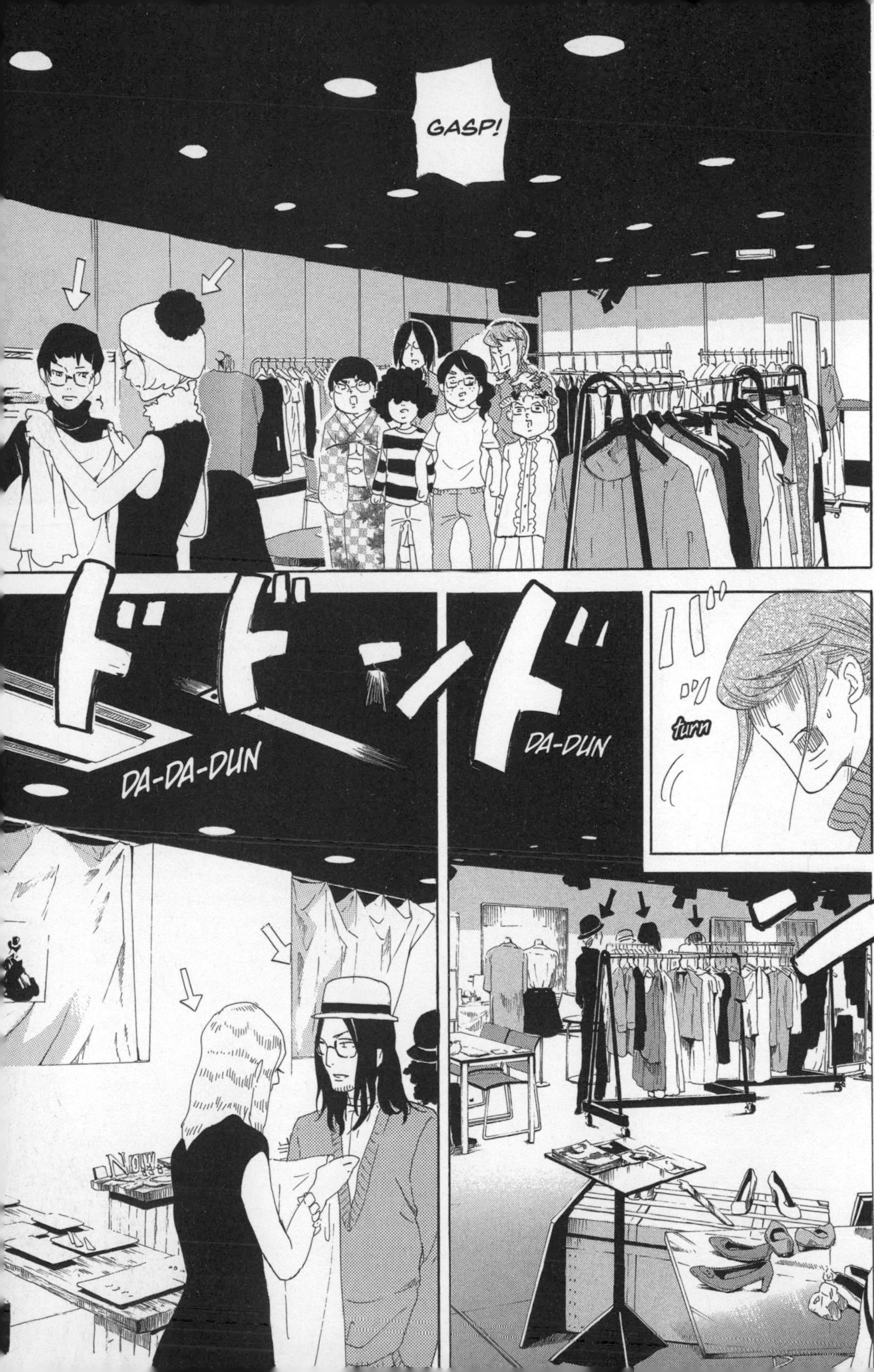
GASP!
turn
DA-DUN
DA-DA-DUN

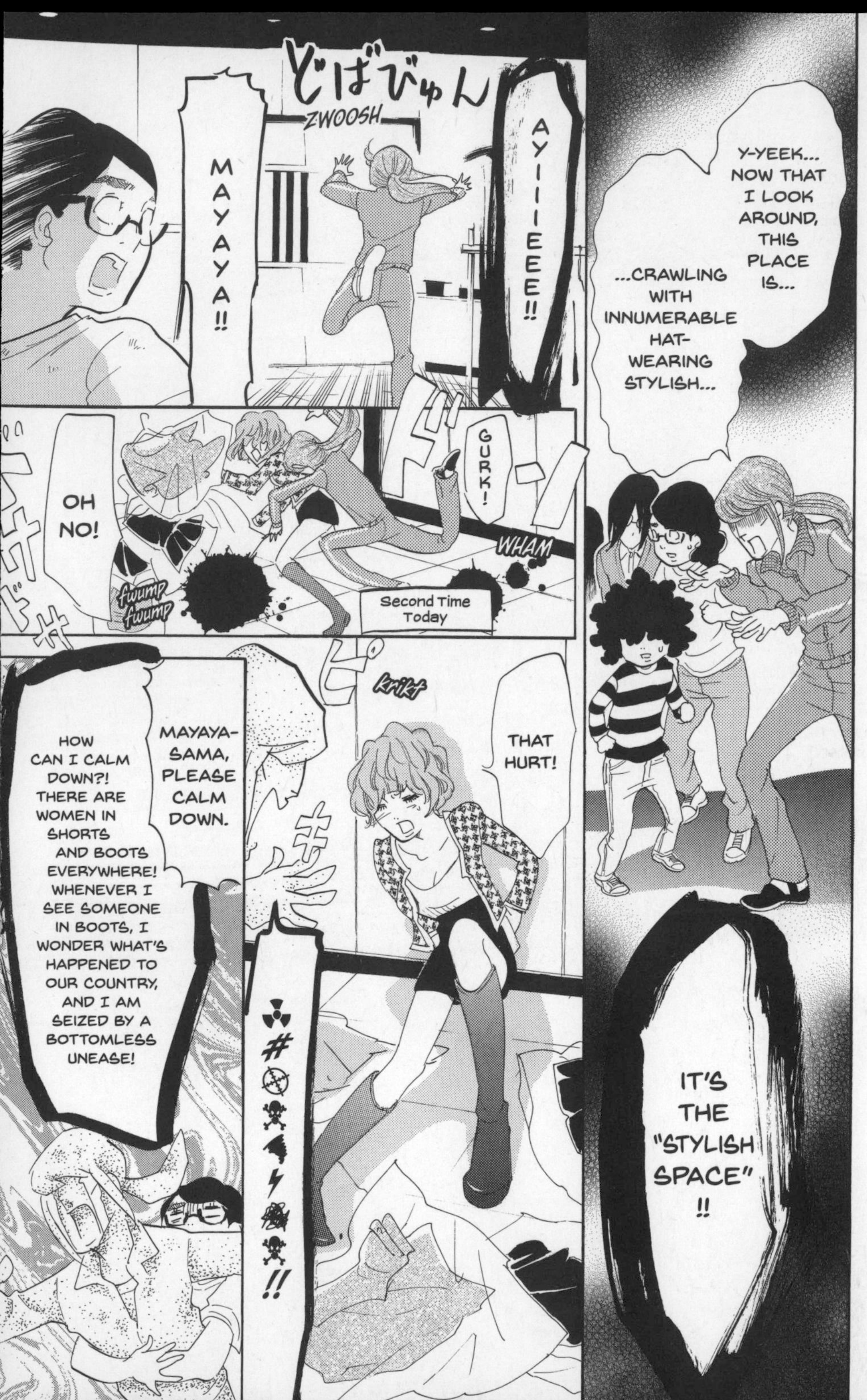
Y-YEEK... NOW THAT I LOOK AROUND, THIS PLACE IS...
...CRAWLING WITH INNUMERABLE HAT-WEARING STYLISH...
IT'S THE "STYLISH SPACE" !!
どばびゅん
ZWOOSH
AYIIIEEE!!
MAYAYA!!
GURK!
WHAM
Second Time Today
OH NO!
fwuump fwuump
krikt
THAT HURT!
MAYAYA-SAMA, PLEASE CALM DOWN.
HOW CAN I CALM DOWN?! THERE ARE WOMEN IN SHORTS AND BOOTS EVERYWHERE! WHENEVER I SEE SOMEONE IN BOOTS, I WONDER WHAT'S HAPPENED TO OUR COUNTRY, AND I AM SEIZED BY A BOTTOMLESS UNEASE!
!!

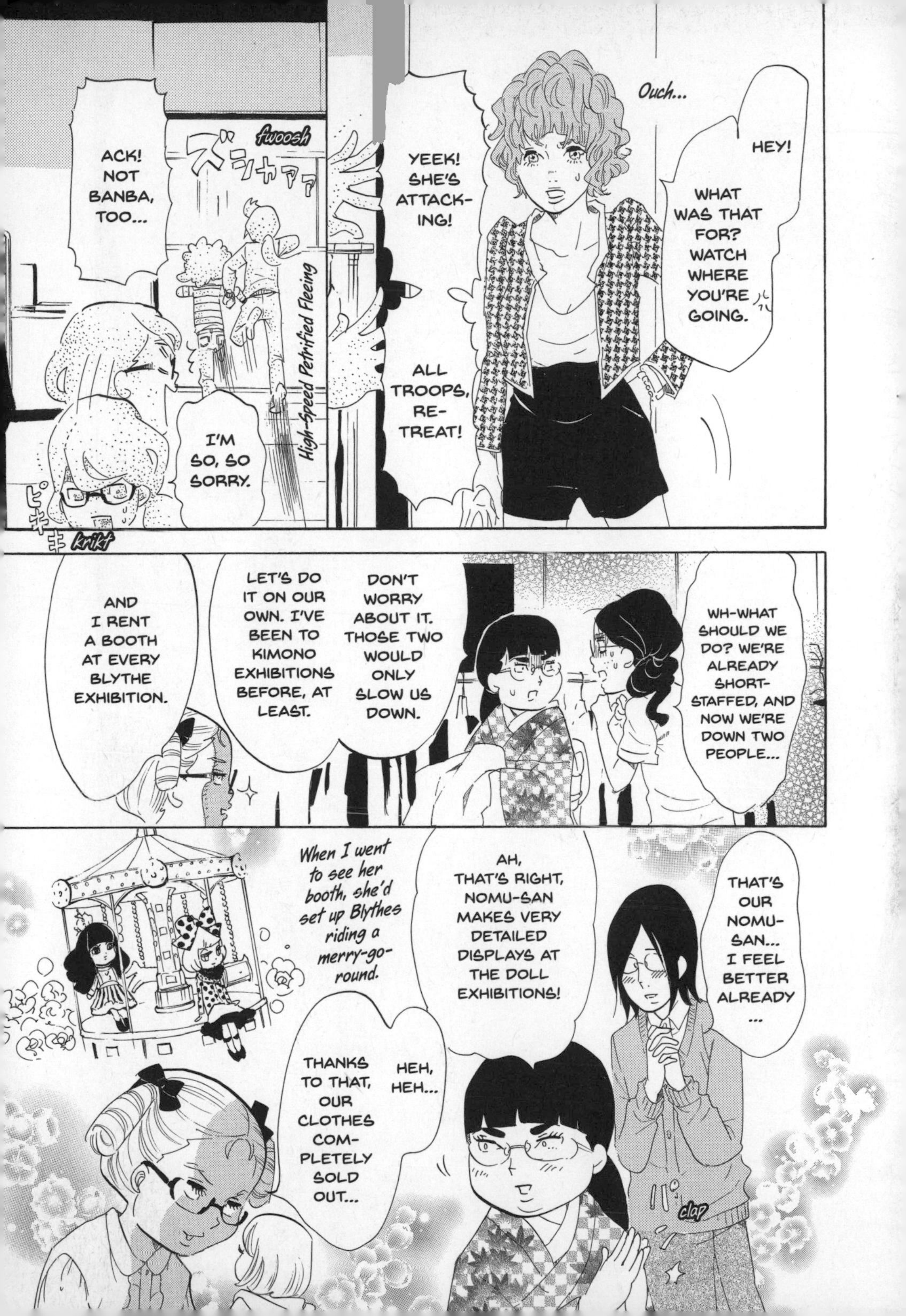
Ouch...
HEY!
WHAT WAS THAT FOR? WATCH WHERE YOU'RE GOING.
YEEK! SHE'S ATTACKING!
ALL TROOPS, RE-TREAT!
fwoosh
High-Speed Petrified Fleeing
ACK! NOT BANBA, TOO...
I'M SO, SO SORRY.
krikt
WH-WHAT SHOULD WE DO? WE'RE ALREADY SHORT-STAFFED, AND NOW WE'RE DOWN TWO PEOPLE...
DON'T WORRY ABOUT IT. THOSE TWO WOULD ONLY SLOW US DOWN.
LET'S DO IT ON OUR OWN. I'VE BEEN TO KIMONO EXHIBITIONS BEFORE, AT LEAST.
AND I RENT A BOOTH AT EVERY BLYTHE EXHIBITION.
THAT'S OUR NOMU-SAN... I FEEL BETTER ALREADY...
AH, THAT'S RIGHT, NOMU-SAN MAKES VERY DETAILED DISPLAYS AT THE DOLL EXHIBITIONS!
When I went to see her booth, she'd set up Blythes riding a merry-go-round.
clap
HEH, HEH...
THANKS TO THAT, OUR CLOTHES COMPLETELY SOLD OUT...

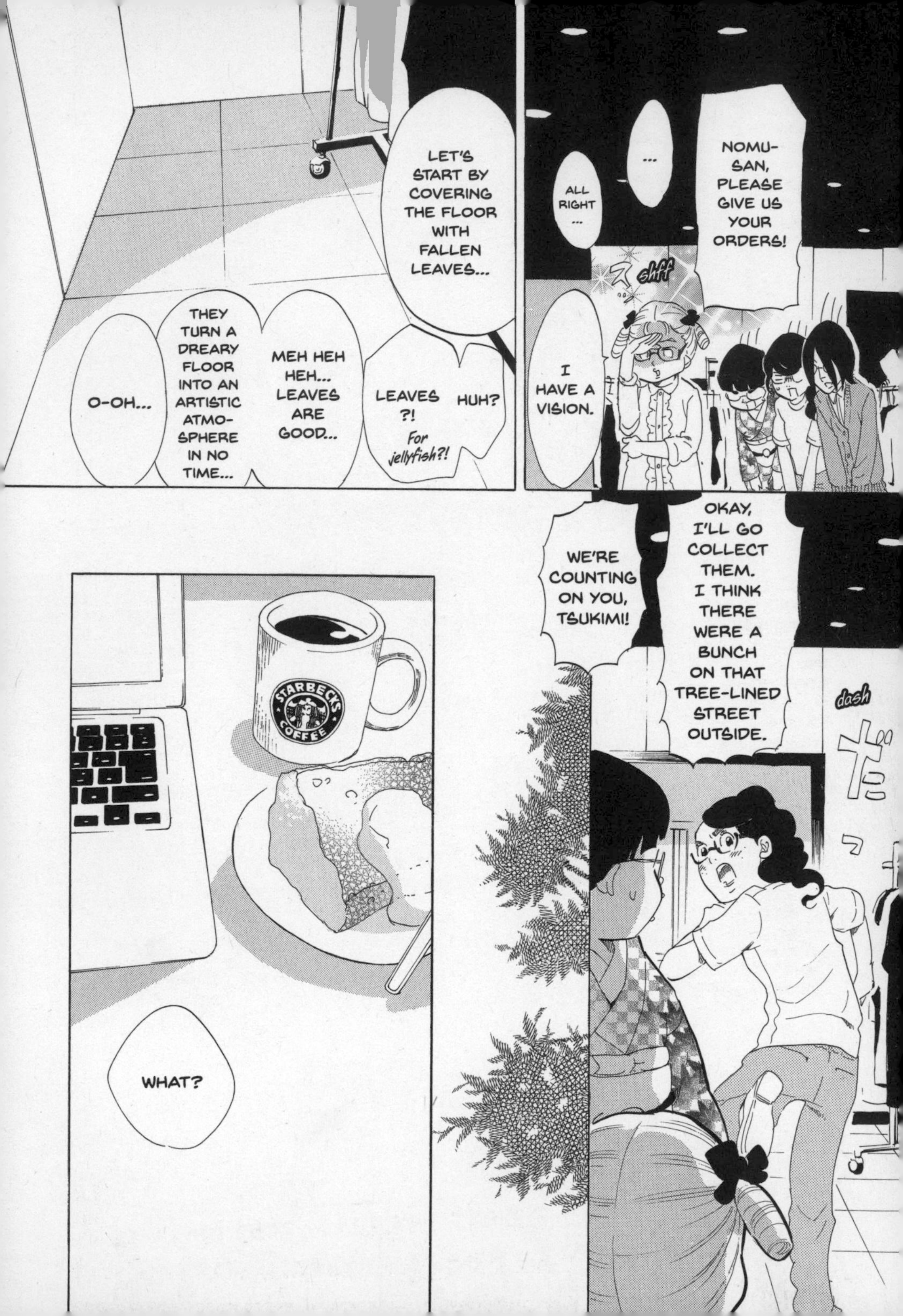
NOMU-SAN, PLEASE GIVE US YOUR ORDERS!
...
ALL RIGHT ...
shff
I HAVE A VISION.
LET'S START BY COVERING THE FLOOR WITH FALLEN LEAVES...
HUH?
LEAVES?!
For jellyfish?!
MEH HEH HEH... LEAVES ARE GOOD...
THEY TURN A DREARY FLOOR INTO AN ARTISTIC ATMOSPHERE IN NO TIME...
O-OH...
OKAY, I'LL GO COLLECT THEM. I THINK THERE WERE A BUNCH ON THAT TREE-LINED STREET OUTSIDE.
WE'RE COUNTING ON YOU, TSUKIMI!
dash
STARBECKS COFFEE
WHAT?

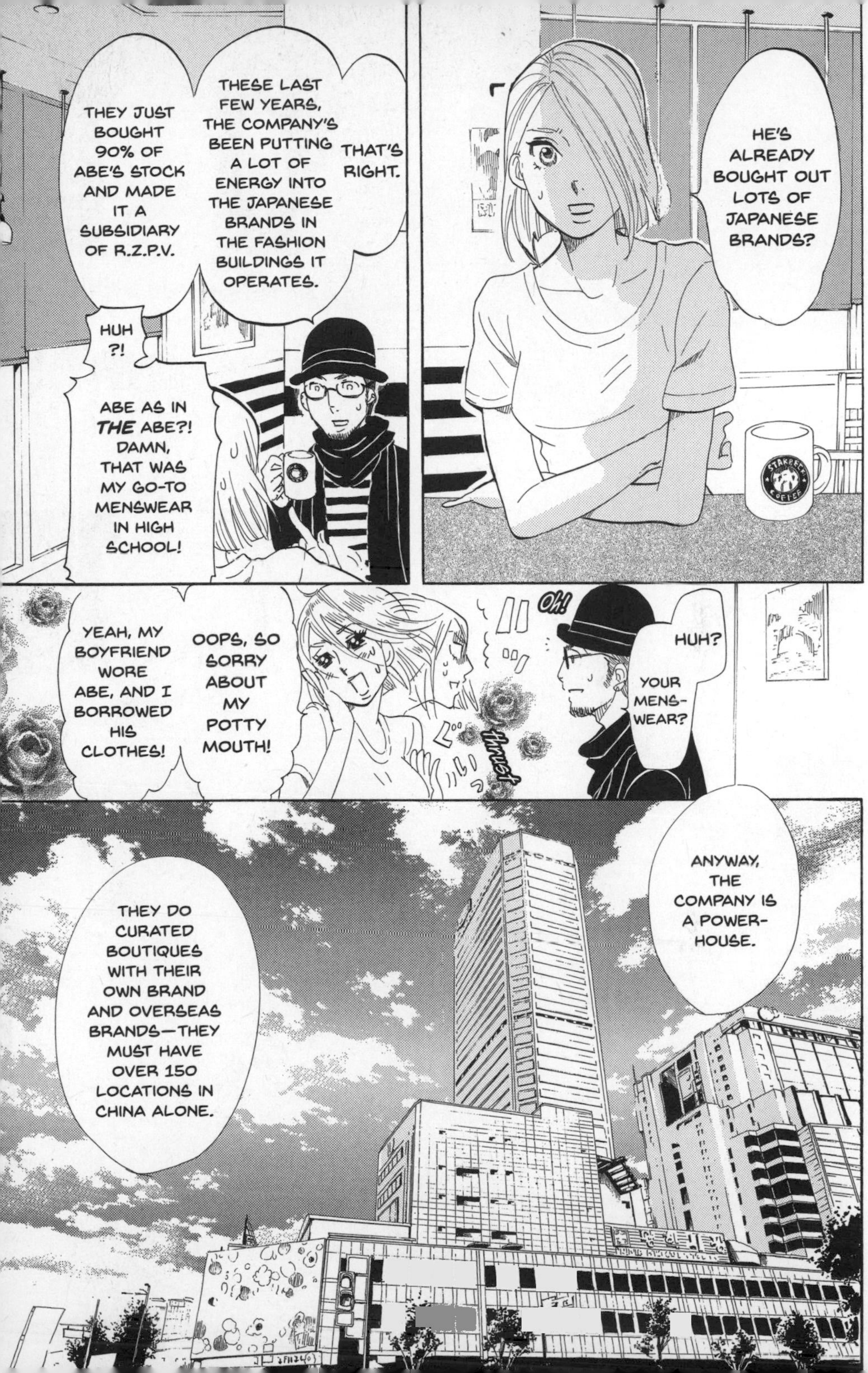
HE'S ALREADY BOUGHT OUT LOTS OF JAPANESE BRANDS?
THAT'S RIGHT.
THESE LAST FEW YEARS, THE COMPANY'S BEEN PUTTING A LOT OF ENERGY INTO THE JAPANESE BRANDS IN THE FASHION BUILDINGS IT OPERATES.
THEY JUST BOUGHT 90% OF ABE'S STOCK AND MADE IT A SUBSIDIARY OF R.Z.P.V.
HUH ?!
ABE AS IN ***THE*** ABE?! DAMN, THAT WAS MY GO-TO MENSWEAR IN HIGH SCHOOL!
OH!
HUH?
YOUR MENS-WEAR?
thrust
OOPS, SO SORRY ABOUT MY POTTY MOUTH!
YEAH, MY BOYFRIEND WORE ABE, AND I BORROWED HIS CLOTHES!
ANYWAY, THE COMPANY IS A POWER-HOUSE.
THEY DO CURATED BOUTIQUES WITH THEIR OWN BRAND AND OVERSEAS BRANDS—THEY MUST HAVE OVER 150 LOCATIONS IN CHINA ALONE.

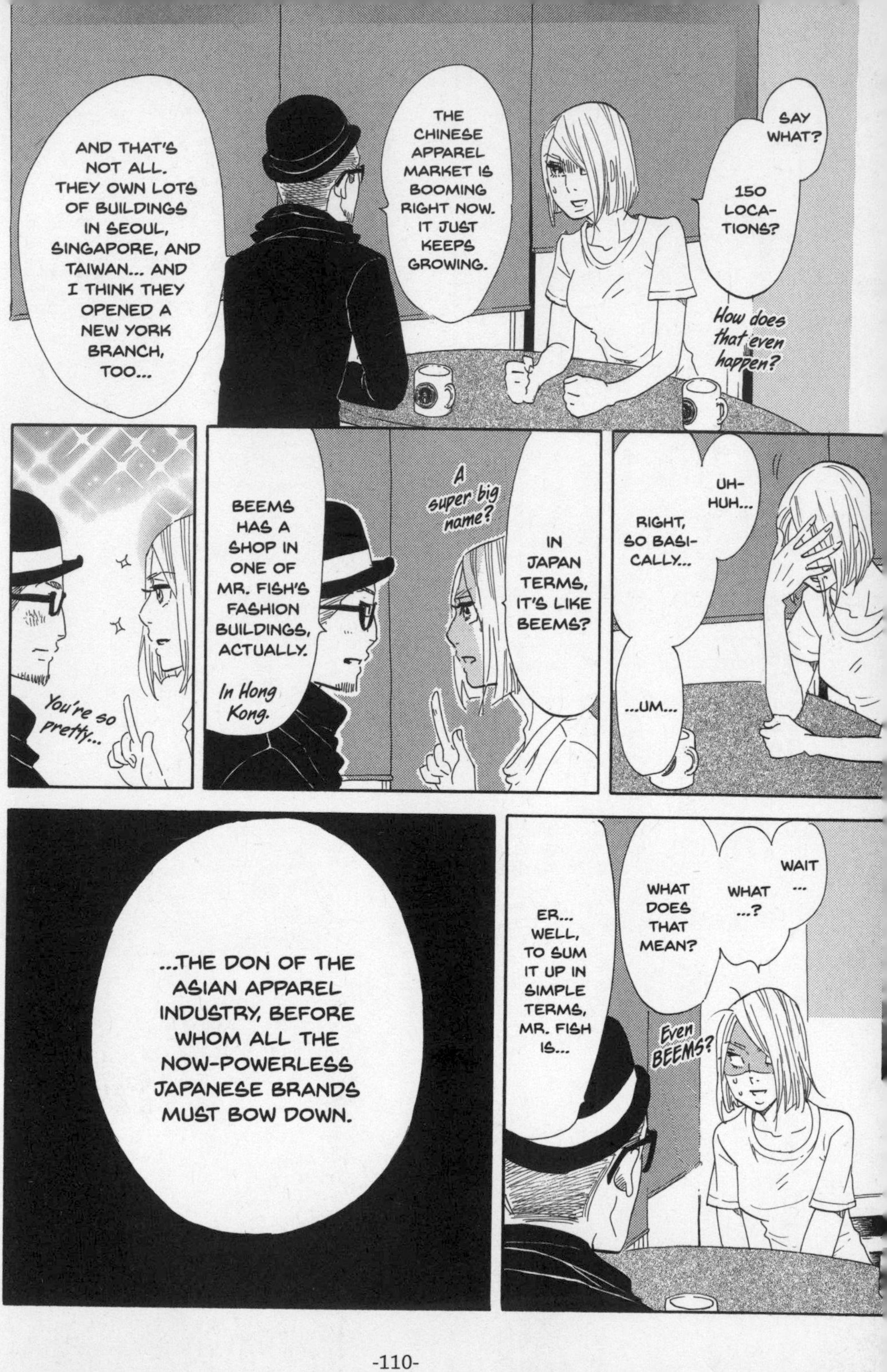
SAY WHAT?
150 LOCATIONS?
How does that even happen?
THE CHINESE APPAREL MARKET IS BOOMING RIGHT NOW. IT JUST KEEPS GROWING.
AND THAT'S NOT ALL. THEY OWN LOTS OF BUILDINGS IN SEOUL, SINGAPORE, AND TAIWAN... AND I THINK THEY OPENED A NEW YORK BRANCH, TOO...
UH-HUH...
RIGHT, SO BASICALLY...
...UM...
IN JAPAN TERMS, IT'S LIKE BEEMS?
A super big name?
BEEMS HAS A SHOP IN ONE OF MR. FISH'S FASHION BUILDINGS, ACTUALLY.
In Hong Kong.
You're so pretty...
WAIT...
WHAT...?
WHAT DOES THAT MEAN?
Even BEEMS?
ER... WELL, TO SUM IT UP IN SIMPLE TERMS, MR. FISH IS...
...THE DON OF THE ASIAN APPAREL INDUSTRY, BEFORE WHOM ALL THE NOW-POWERLESS JAPANESE BRANDS MUST BOW DOWN.

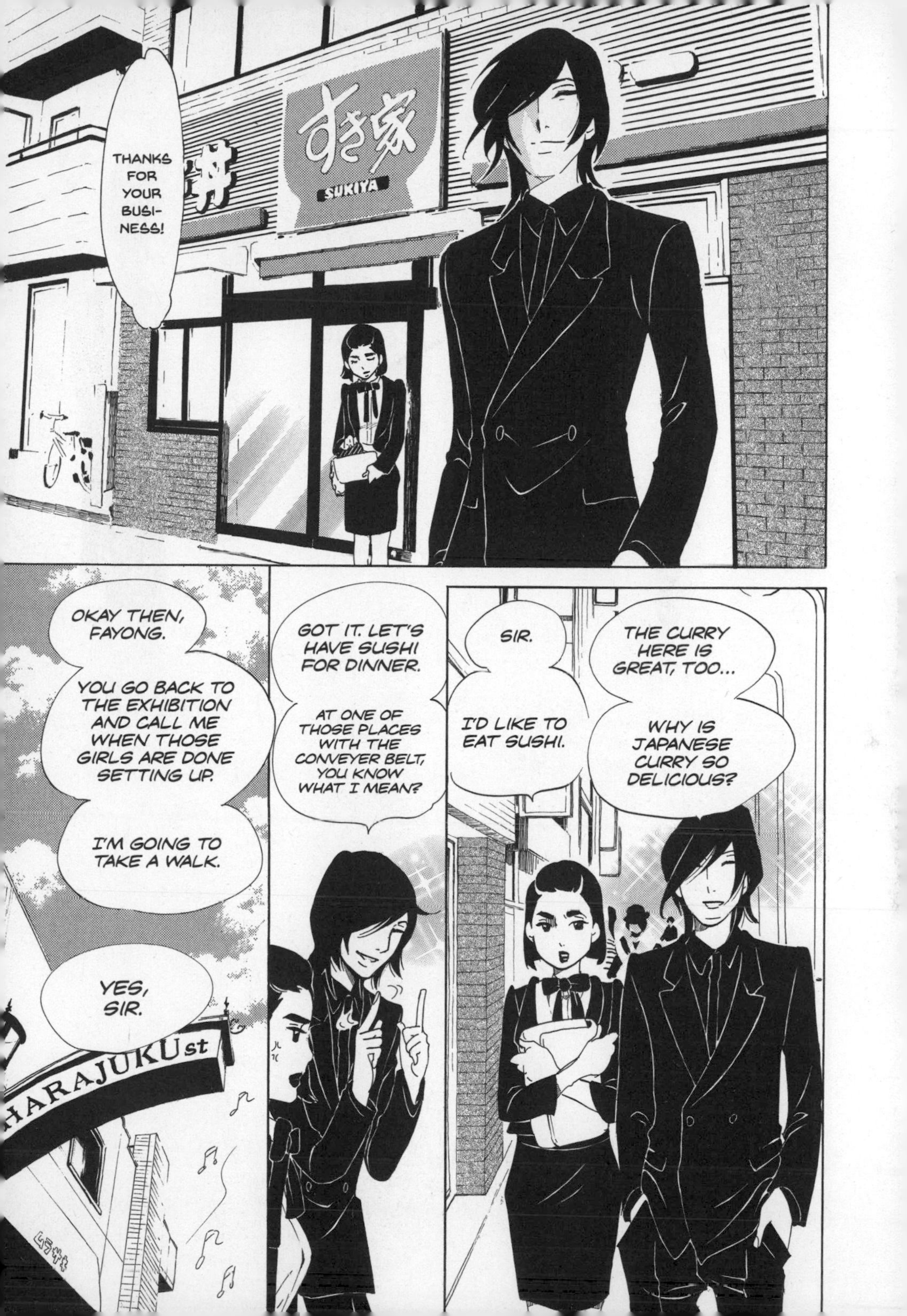
すき家
SUKIYA
THANKS FOR YOUR BUSINESS!
THE CURRY HERE IS GREAT, TOO...
WHY IS JAPANESE CURRY SO DELICIOUS?
SIR.
I'D LIKE TO EAT SUSHI.
GOT IT. LET'S HAVE SUSHI FOR DINNER.
AT ONE OF THOSE PLACES WITH THE CONVEYER BELT, YOU KNOW WHAT I MEAN?
OKAY THEN, FAYONG.
YOU GO BACK TO THE EXHIBITION AND CALL ME WHEN THOSE GIRLS ARE DONE SETTING UP.
I'M GOING TO TAKE A WALK.
YES, SIR.
HARAJUKU st

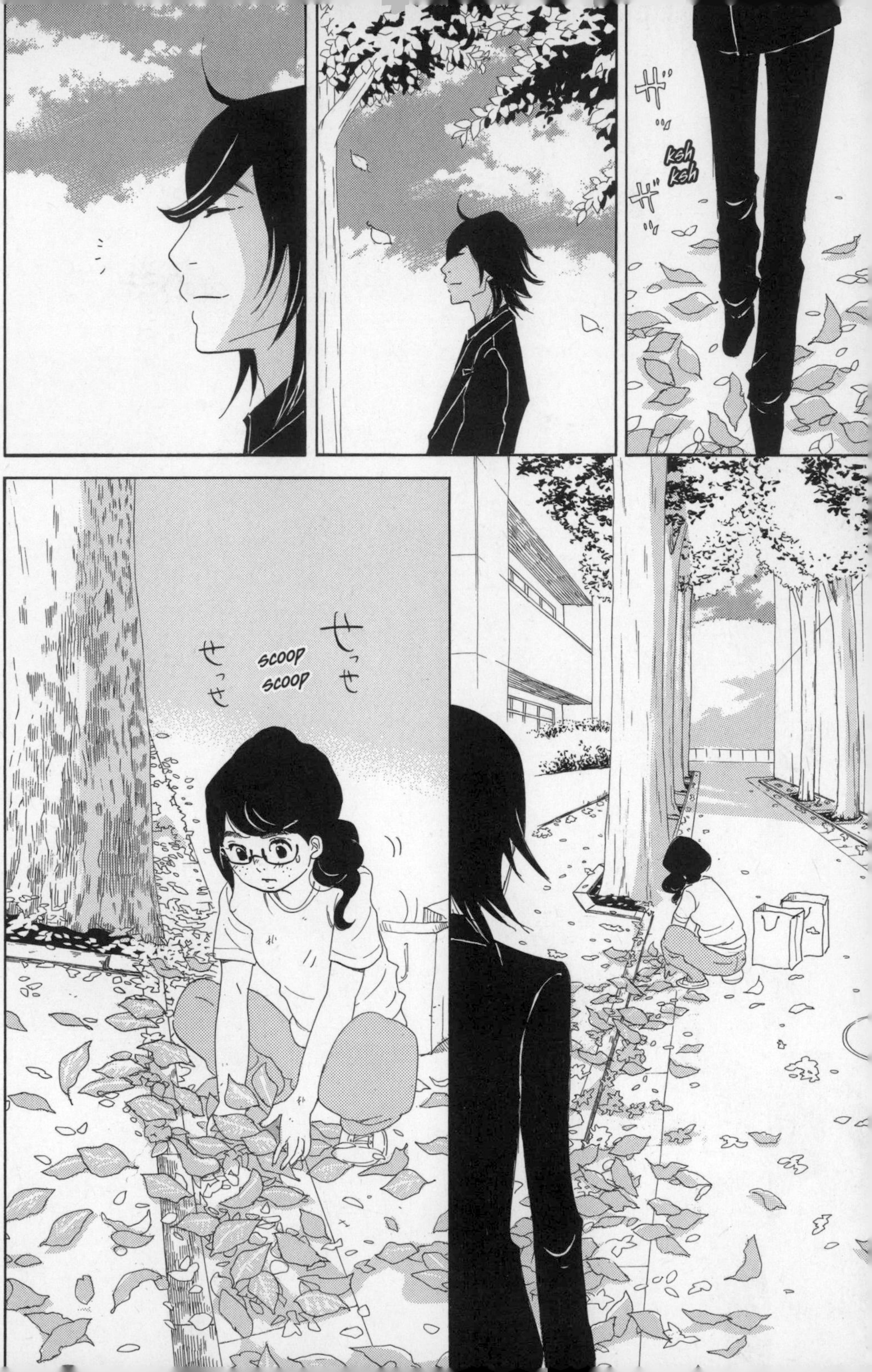
ザッ
ksh ksh
ザッ
せっせ
せっせ
scoop scoop

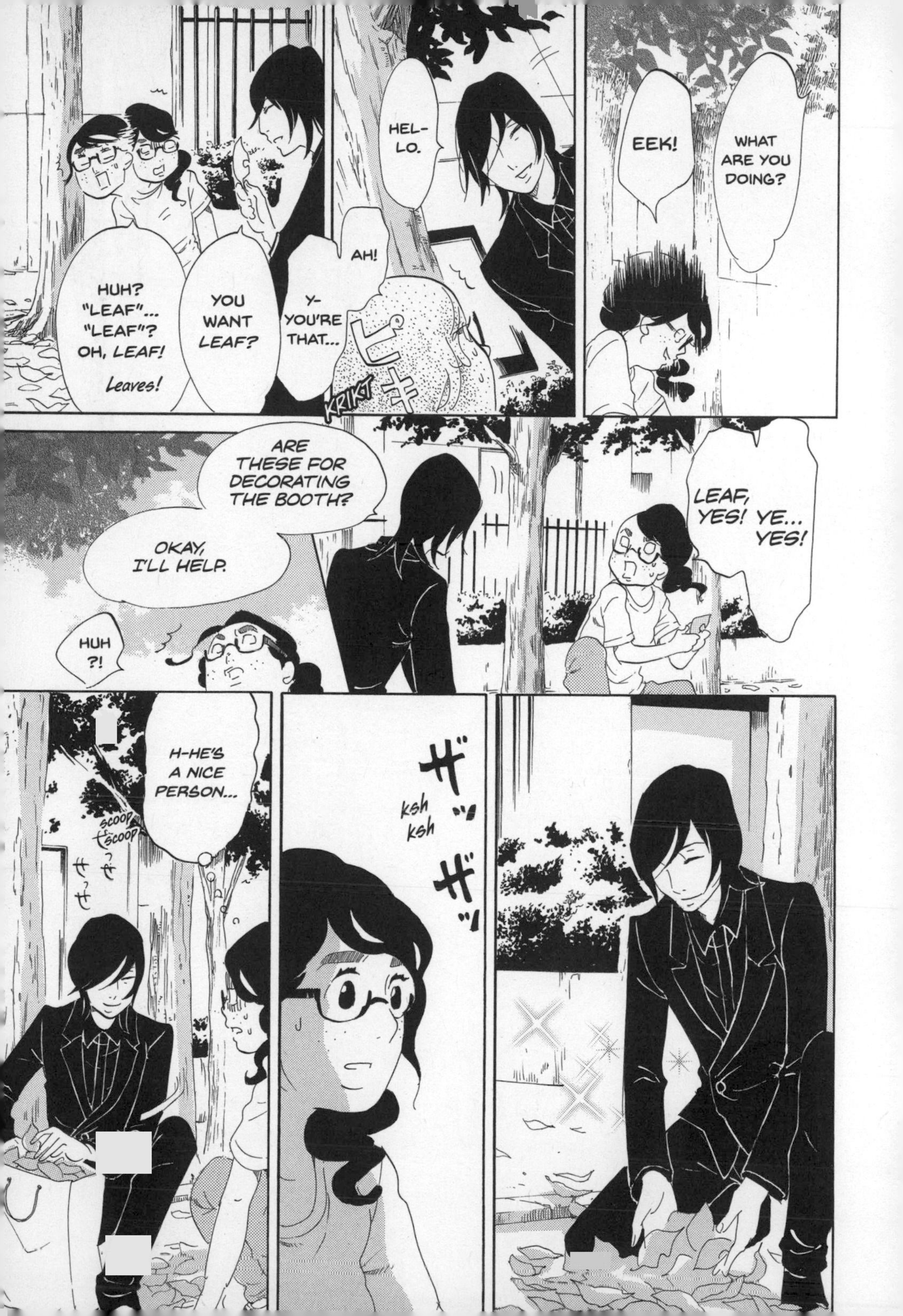
WHAT ARE YOU DOING?
EEK!
HEL-LO.
AH!
Y-YOU'RE THAT...
ピキ
KRIKT
YOU WANT LEAF?
HUH? "LEAF"... "LEAF"? OH, LEAF!
Leaves!
LEAF, YES! YE... YES!
ARE THESE FOR DECORATING THE BOOTH?
OKAY, I'LL HELP.
HUH ?!
ザッ ザッ
ksh ksh
H-HE'S A NICE PERSON...
せっせ
scoop scoop

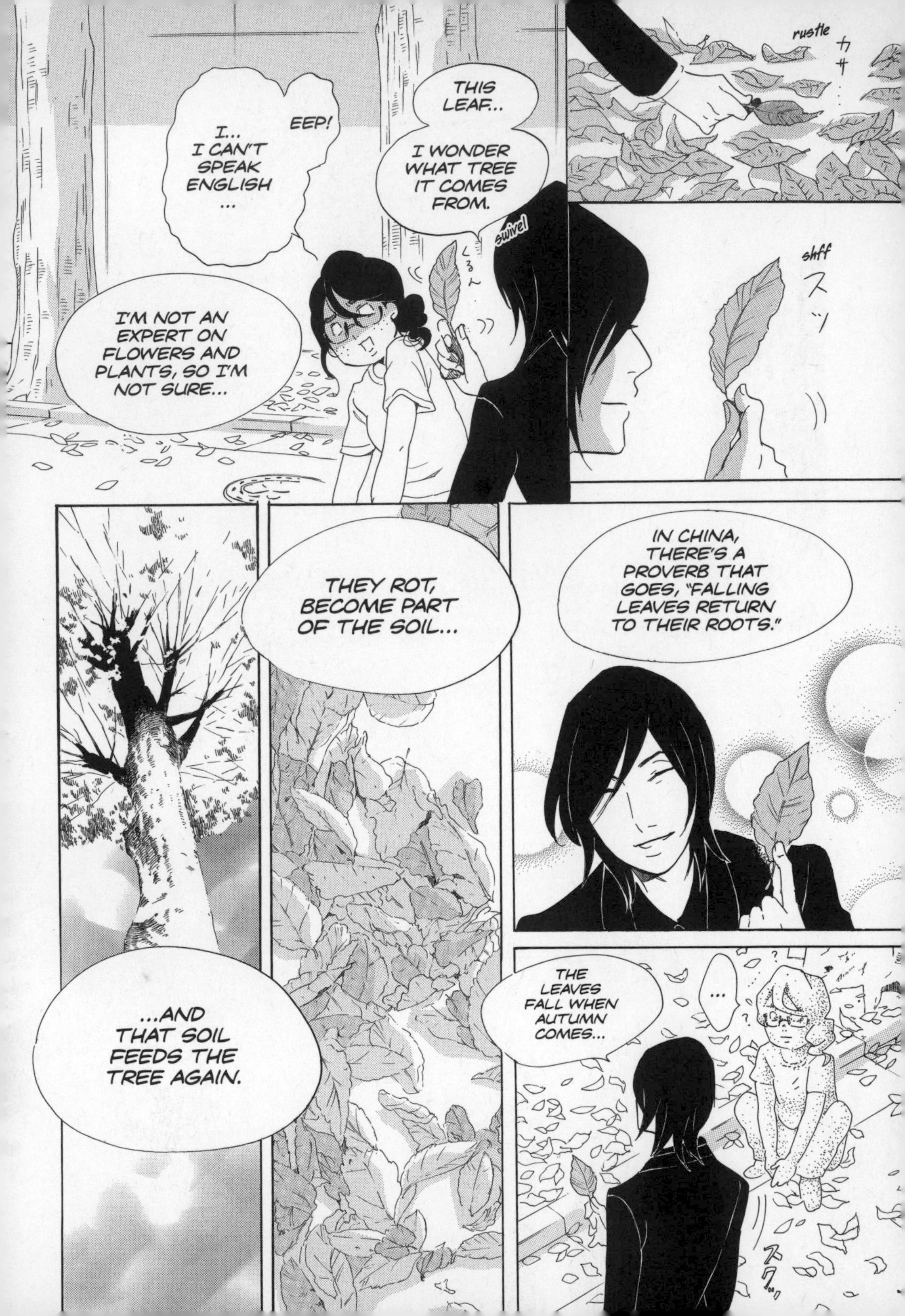
rustle
カサ
shff
スッ
THIS LEAF...
I WONDER WHAT TREE IT COMES FROM.
swivel
くるん
EEP!
I... I CAN'T SPEAK ENGLISH...
I'M NOT AN EXPERT ON FLOWERS AND PLANTS, SO I'M NOT SURE...
IN CHINA, THERE'S A PROVERB THAT GOES, "FALLING LEAVES RETURN TO THEIR ROOTS."
THE LEAVES FALL WHEN AUTUMN COMES...
...
THEY ROT, BECOME PART OF THE SOIL...
...AND THAT SOIL FEEDS THE TREE AGAIN.

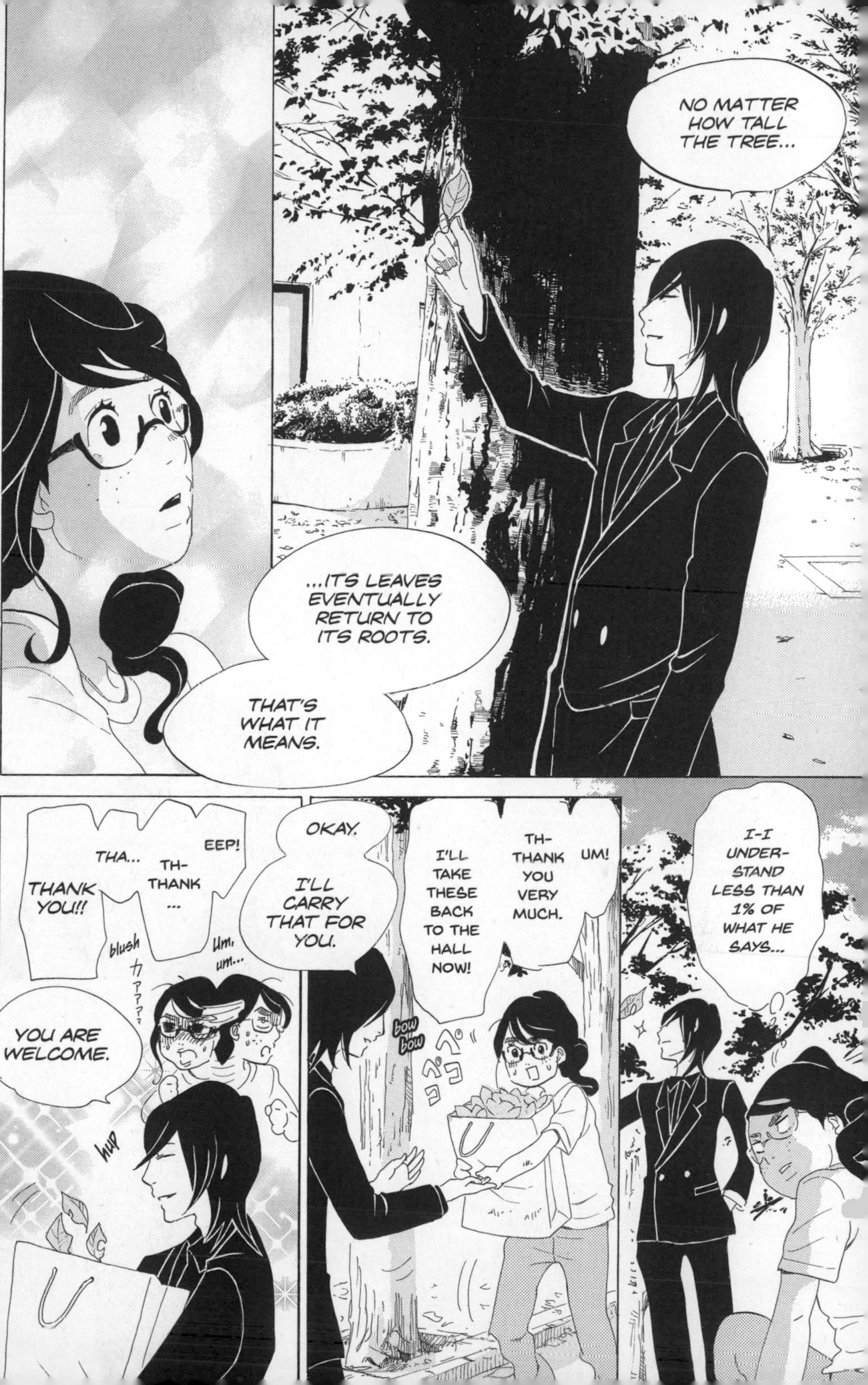

NO MATTER HOW TALL THE TREE...
...ITS LEAVES EVENTUALLY RETURN TO ITS ROOTS.
THAT'S WHAT IT MEANS.
I-I UNDERSTAND LESS THAN 1% OF WHAT HE SAYS...
UM!
TH-THANK YOU VERY MUCH.
I'LL TAKE THESE BACK TO THE HALL NOW!
bow bow
OKAY.
I'LL CARRY THAT FOR YOU.
EEP!
TH-THANK ...
THA...
THANK YOU!!
Um, um...
blush
YOU ARE WELCOME.
hup

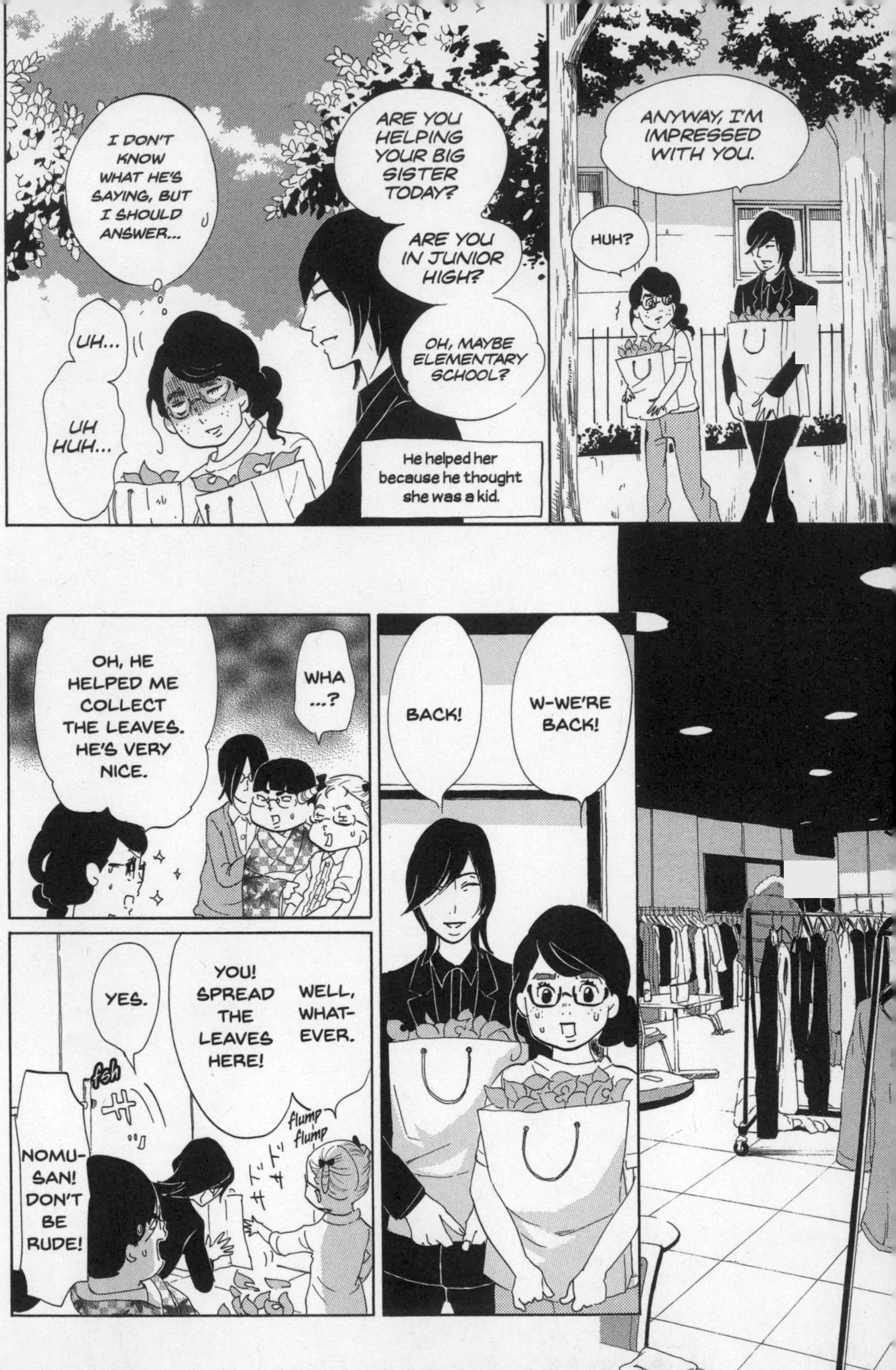
ANYWAY, I'M IMPRESSED WITH YOU.
HUH?
ARE YOU HELPING YOUR BIG SISTER TODAY?
ARE YOU IN JUNIOR HIGH?
I DON'T KNOW WHAT HE'S SAYING, BUT I SHOULD ANSWER...
OH, MAYBE ELEMENTARY SCHOOL?
UH...
UH HUH...
He helped her because he thought she was a kid.
W-WE'RE BACK!
BACK!
WHA ...?
OH, HE HELPED ME COLLECT THE LEAVES. HE'S VERY NICE.
WELL, WHATEVER.
YOU! SPREAD THE LEAVES HERE!
YES.
fsh
flump flump
NOMU-SAN! DON'T BE RUDE!

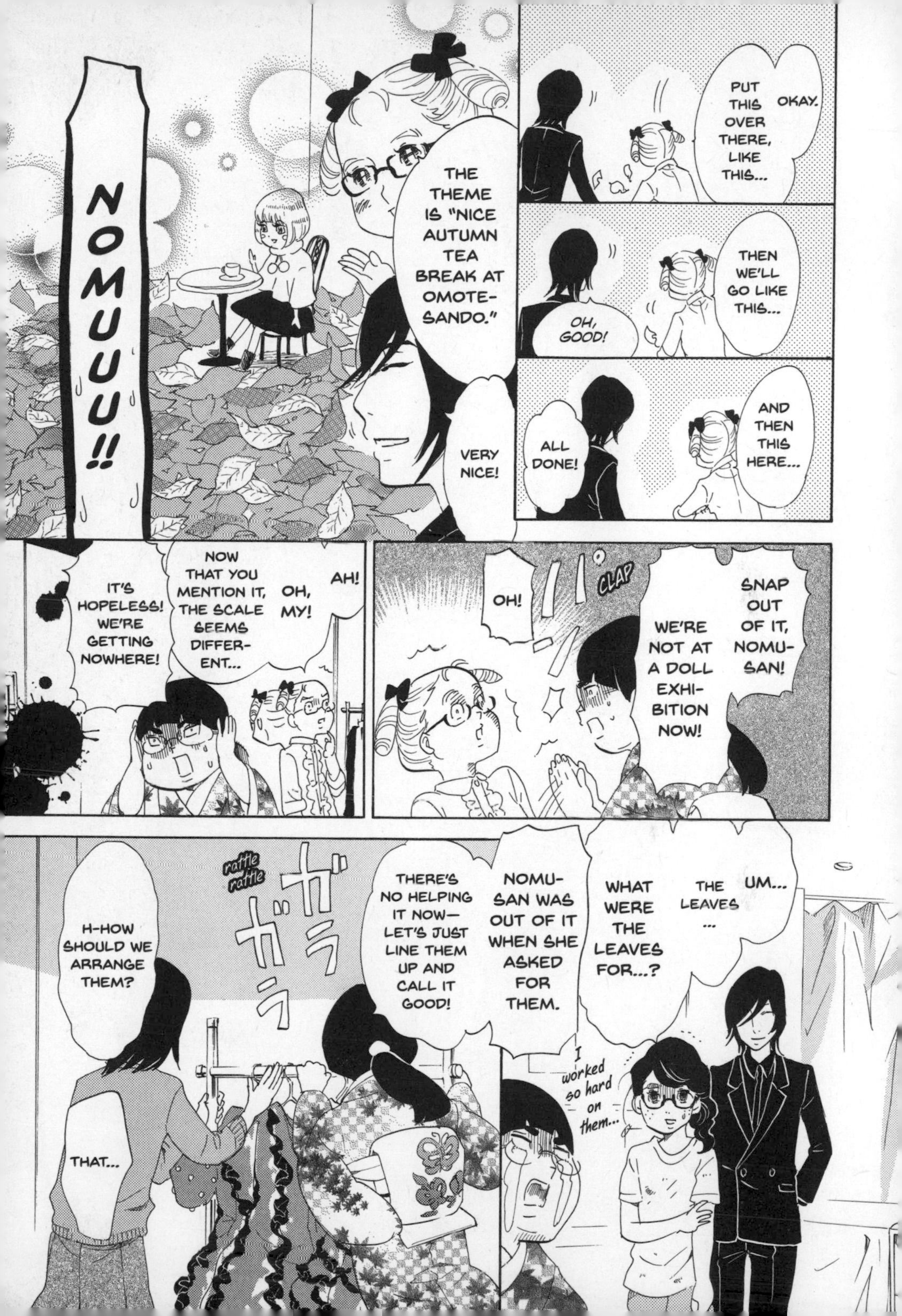

PUT THIS OVER THERE, LIKE THIS...
OKAY.
THEN WE'LL GO LIKE THIS...
OH, GOOD!
AND THEN THIS HERE...
ALL DONE!
THE THEME IS "NICE AUTUMN TEA BREAK AT OMOTE-SANDO."
VERY NICE!
NOMUUUU!!
SNAP OUT OF IT, NOMU-SAN!
WE'RE NOT AT A DOLL EXHIBITION NOW!
CLAP
OH!
AH!
OH, MY!
NOW THAT YOU MENTION IT, THE SCALE SEEMS DIFFERENT...
IT'S HOPELESS! WE'RE GETTING NOWHERE!
UM...
THE LEAVES...
WHAT WERE THE LEAVES FOR...?
NOMU-SAN WAS OUT OF IT WHEN SHE ASKED FOR THEM.
I worked so hard on them...
THERE'S NO HELPING IT NOW—LET'S JUST LINE THEM UP AND CALL IT GOOD!
ガラガラ
rattle rattle
H-HOW SHOULD WE ARRANGE THEM?
THAT...

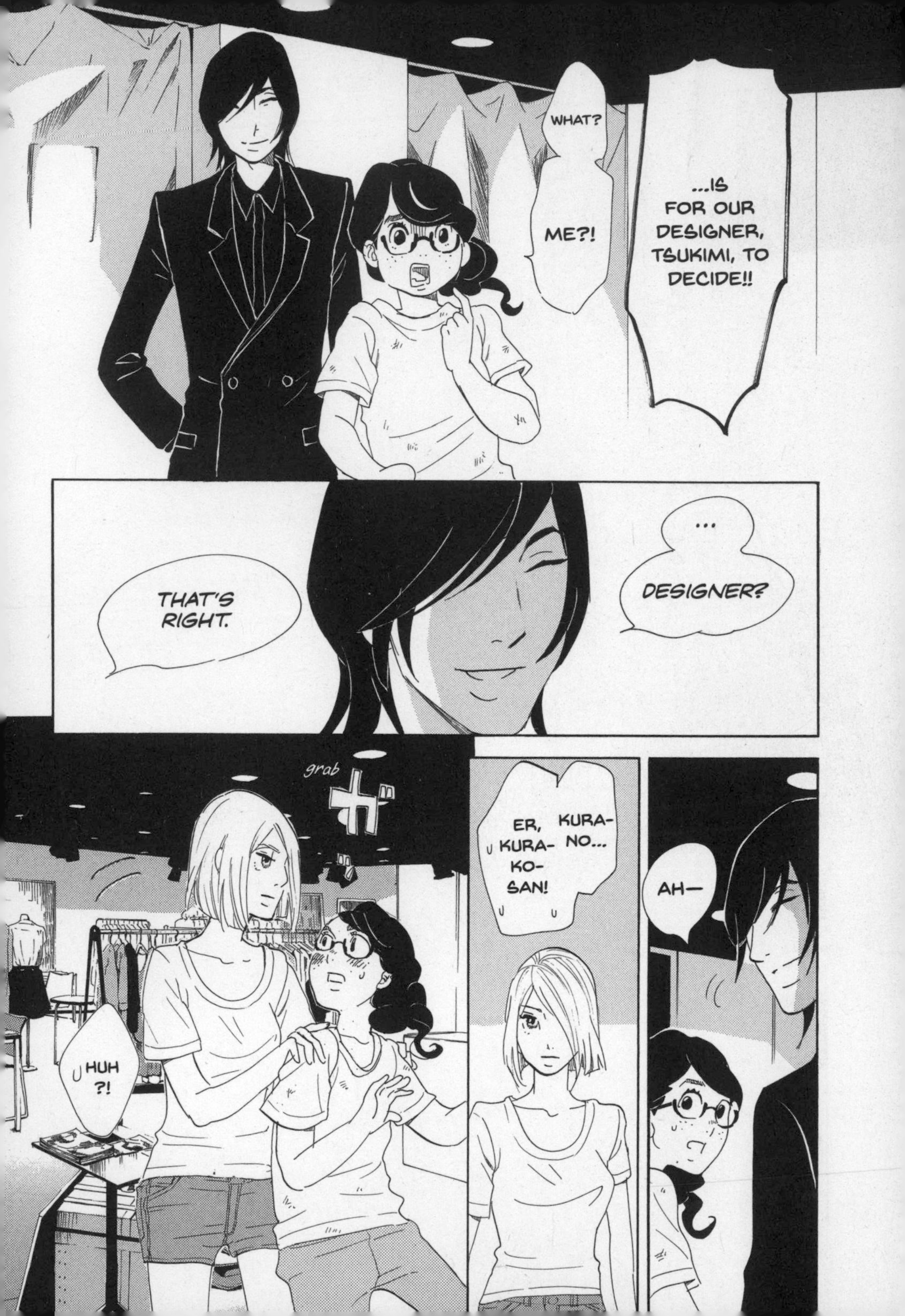
...IS FOR OUR DESIGNER, TSUKIMI, TO DECIDE!!
WHAT? ME?!
... DESIGNER?
THAT'S RIGHT.
AH—
ER, KURA-NO... KURA-KO-SAN!
grab
HUH ?!

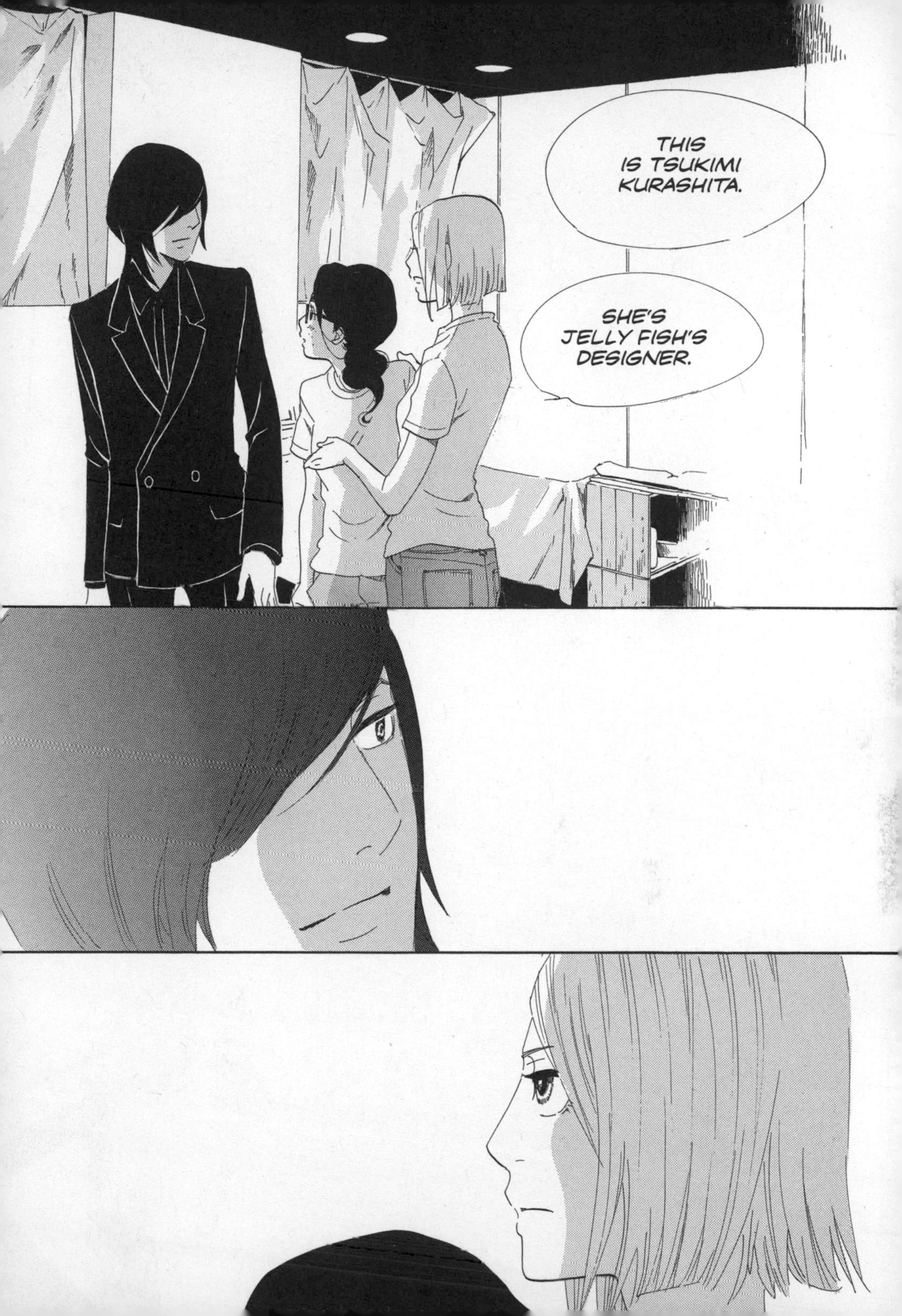
THIS IS TSUKIMI KURASHITA.
SHE'S JELLY FISH'S DESIGNER.

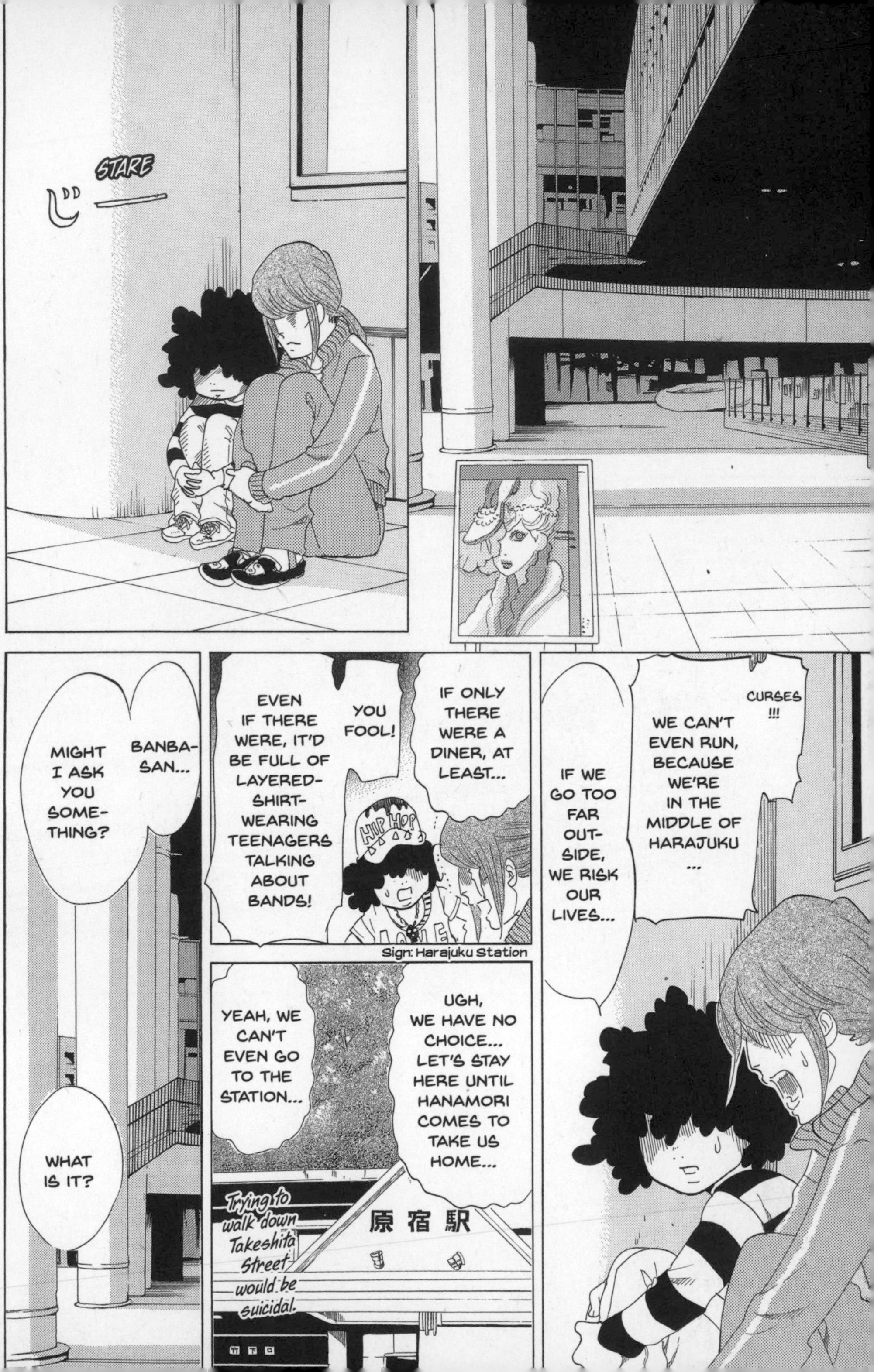
STARE
じーー
CURSES!!!
WE CAN'T EVEN RUN, BECAUSE WE'RE IN THE MIDDLE OF HARAJUKU...
IF WE GO TOO FAR OUTSIDE, WE RISK OUR LIVES...
IF ONLY THERE WERE A DINER, AT LEAST...
YOU FOOL!
EVEN IF THERE WERE, IT'D BE FULL OF LAYERED-SHIRT-WEARING TEENAGERS TALKING ABOUT BANDS!
HIP HOP
Sign: Harajuku Station
UGH, WE HAVE NO CHOICE... LET'S STAY HERE UNTIL HANAMORI COMES TO TAKE US HOME...
YEAH, WE CAN'T EVEN GO TO THE STATION...
原宿駅
Trying to walk down Takeshita Street would be suicidal.
BANBA-SAN...
MIGHT I ASK YOU SOMETHING?
WHAT IS IT?

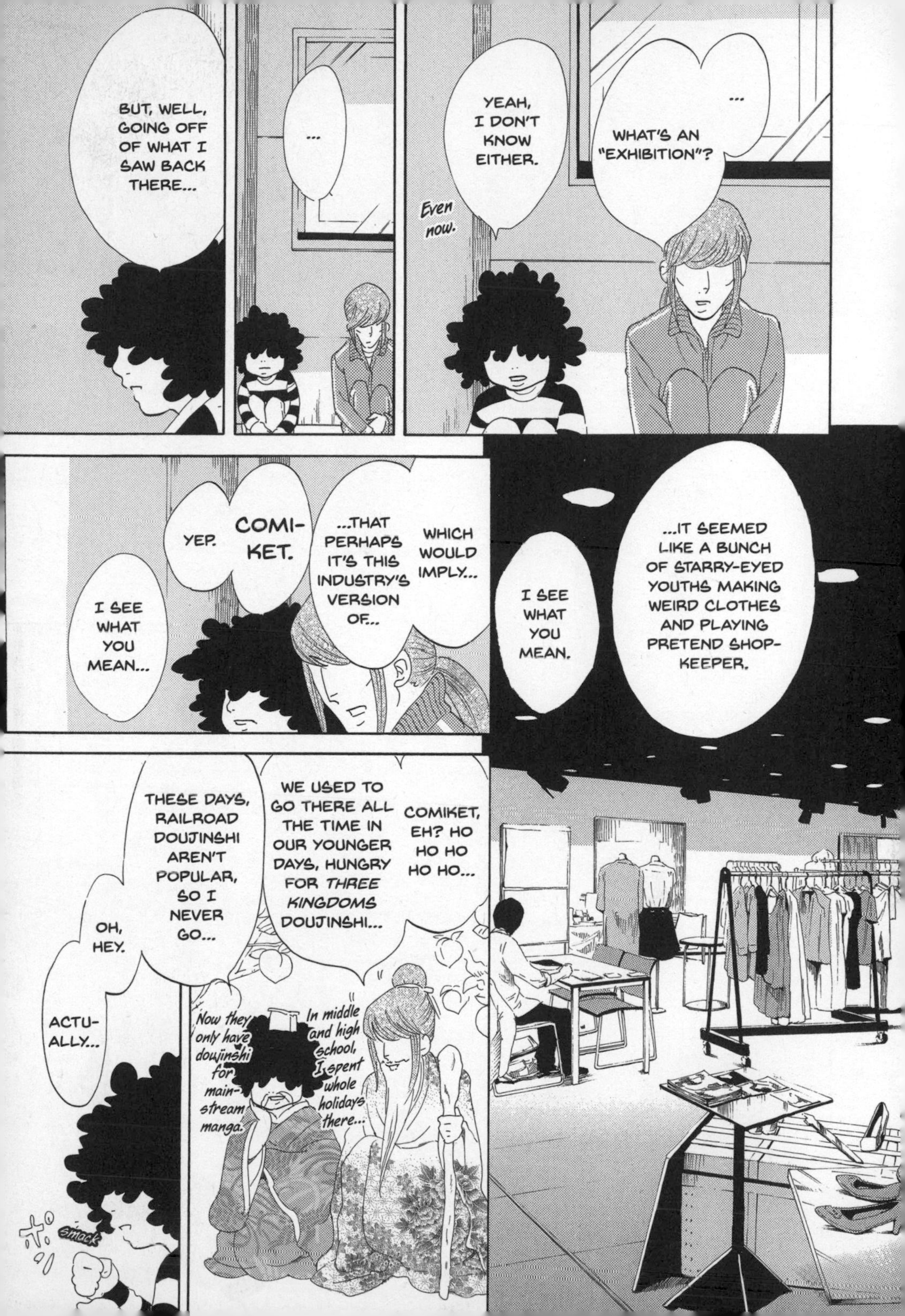
...
WHAT'S AN "EXHIBITION"?
YEAH, I DON'T KNOW EITHER.
Even now.
...
BUT, WELL, GOING OFF OF WHAT I SAW BACK THERE...
...IT SEEMED LIKE A BUNCH OF STARRY-EYED YOUTHS MAKING WEIRD CLOTHES AND PLAYING PRETEND SHOP-KEEPER.
I SEE WHAT YOU MEAN.
WHICH WOULD IMPLY...
...THAT PERHAPS IT'S THIS INDUSTRY'S VERSION OF...
COMI-KET.
YEP.
I SEE WHAT YOU MEAN...
COMIKET, EH? HO HO HO HO...
WE USED TO GO THERE ALL THE TIME IN OUR YOUNGER DAYS, HUNGRY FOR *THREE KINGDOMS* DOUJINSHI...
THESE DAYS, RAILROAD DOUJINSHI AREN'T POPULAR, SO I NEVER GO...
In middle and high school, I spent whole holidays there...
Now they only have doujinshi for main-stream manga.
OH, HEY.
ACTU-ALLY...
smack

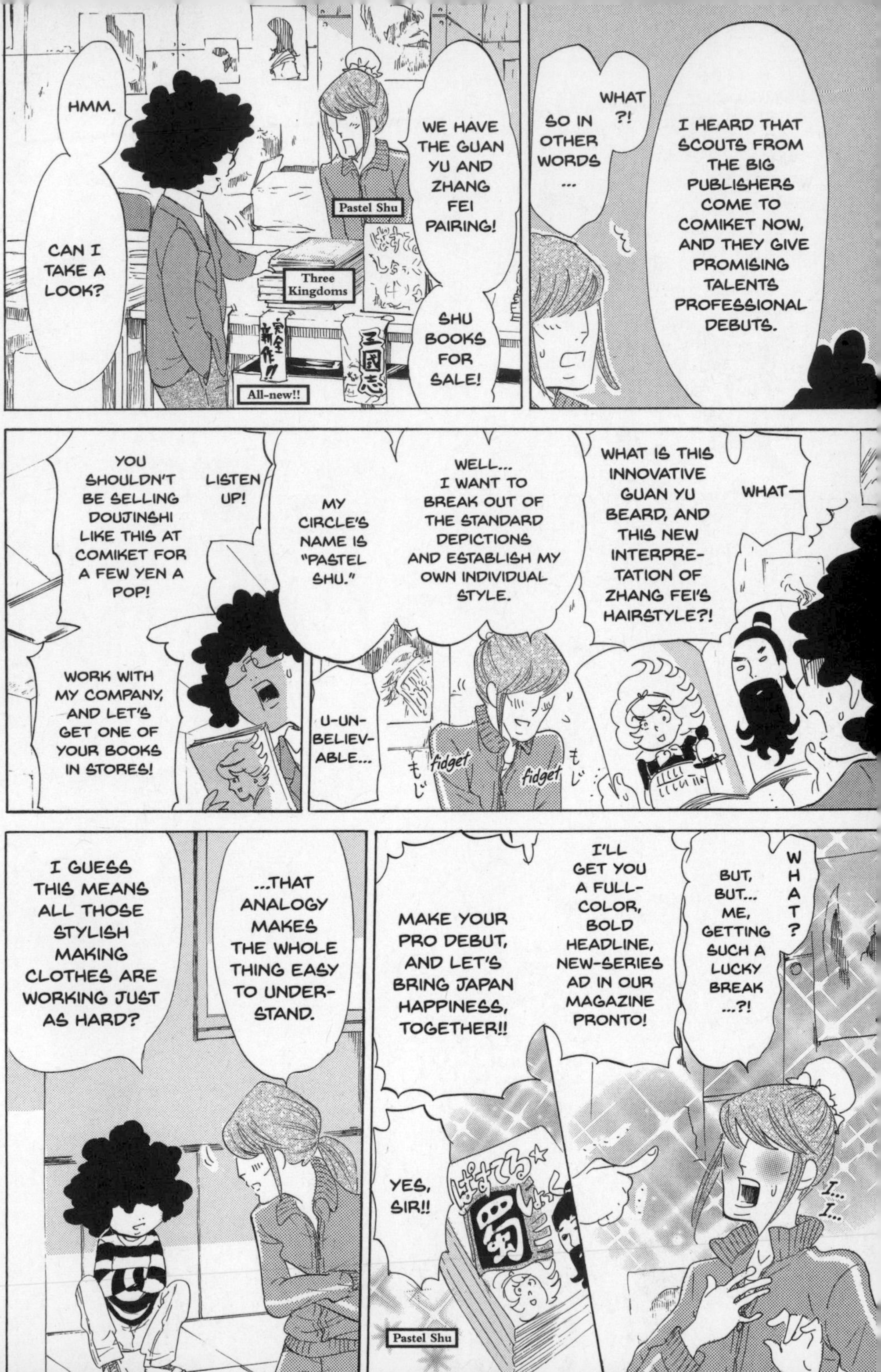
I HEARD THAT SCOUTS FROM THE BIG PUBLISHERS COME TO COMIKET NOW, AND THEY GIVE PROMISING TALENTS PROFESSIONAL DEBUTS.
WHAT ?!
SO IN OTHER WORDS ...
WE HAVE THE GUAN YU AND ZHANG FEI PAIRING!
SHU BOOKS FOR SALE!
Pastel Shu
Three Kingdoms
三國志
完全新作!!
All-new!!
HMM.
CAN I TAKE A LOOK?
WHAT—
WHAT IS THIS INNOVATIVE GUAN YU BEARD, AND THIS NEW INTERPRETATION OF ZHANG FEI'S HAIRSTYLE?!
WELL... I WANT TO BREAK OUT OF THE STANDARD DEPICTIONS AND ESTABLISH MY OWN INDIVIDUAL STYLE.
MY CIRCLE'S NAME IS "PASTEL SHU."
fidget もじ
fidget もじ
LISTEN UP!
YOU SHOULDN'T BE SELLING DOUJINSHI LIKE THIS AT COMIKET FOR A FEW YEN A POP!
U-UN-BELIEV-ABLE...
WORK WITH MY COMPANY, AND LET'S GET ONE OF YOUR BOOKS IN STORES!
WHAT?
BUT, BUT... ME, GETTING SUCH A LUCKY BREAK ...?!
I... I...
I'LL GET YOU A FULL-COLOR, BOLD HEADLINE, NEW-SERIES AD IN OUR MAGAZINE PRONTO!
MAKE YOUR PRO DEBUT, AND LET'S BRING JAPAN HAPPINESS, TOGETHER!!
YES, SIR!!
蜀
Pastel Shu
...THAT ANALOGY MAKES THE WHOLE THING EASY TO UNDER-STAND.
I GUESS THIS MEANS ALL THOSE STYLISH MAKING CLOTHES ARE WORKING JUST AS HARD?

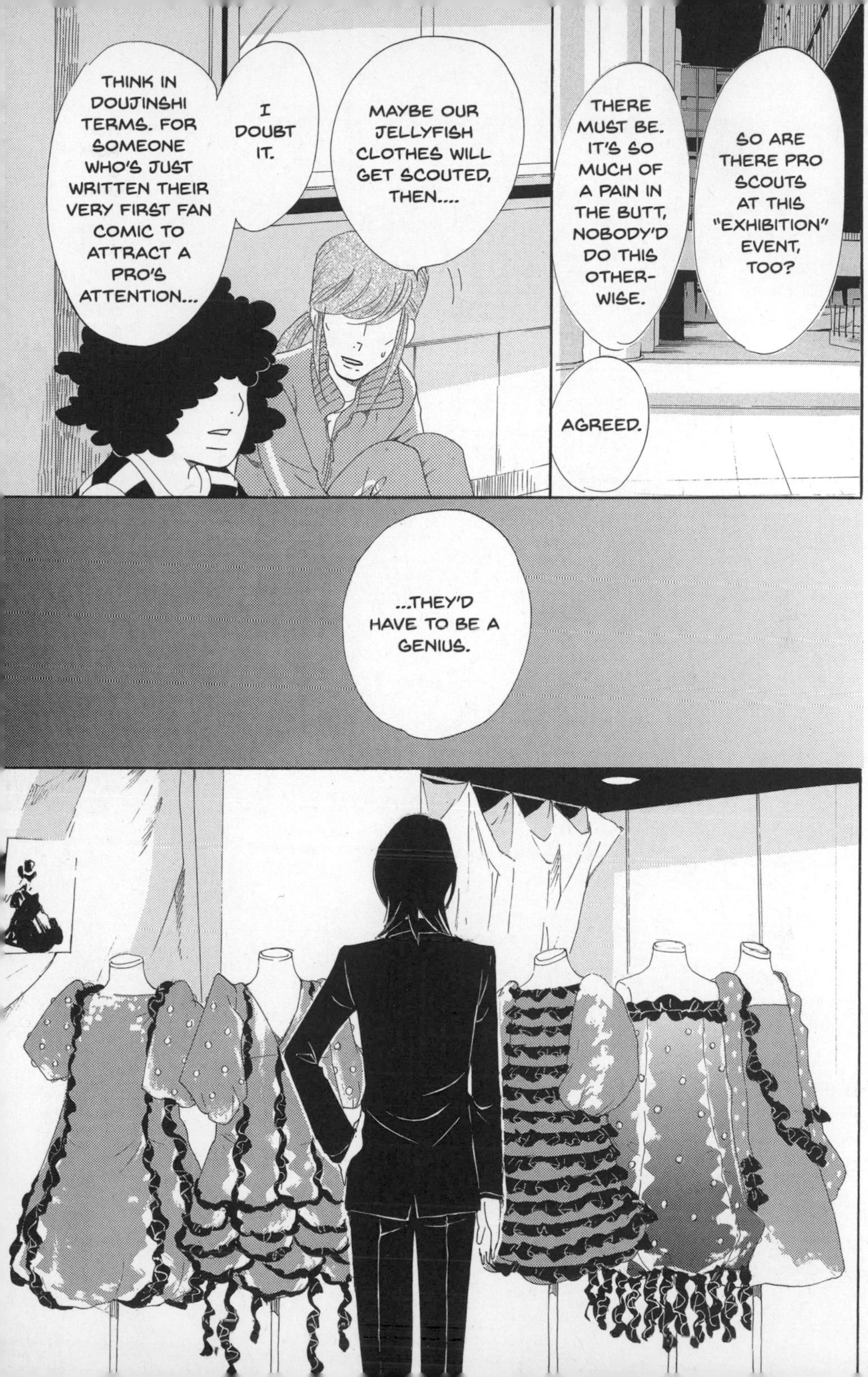
SO ARE THERE PRO SCOUTS AT THIS "EXHIBITION" EVENT, TOO?
THERE MUST BE. IT'S SO MUCH OF A PAIN IN THE BUTT, NOBODY'D DO THIS OTHER-WISE.
AGREED.
MAYBE OUR JELLYFISH CLOTHES WILL GET SCOUTED, THEN....
I DOUBT IT.
THINK IN DOUJINSHI TERMS. FOR SOMEONE WHO'S JUST WRITTEN THEIR VERY FIRST FAN COMIC TO ATTRACT A PRO'S ATTENTION...
...THEY'D HAVE TO BE A GENIUS.

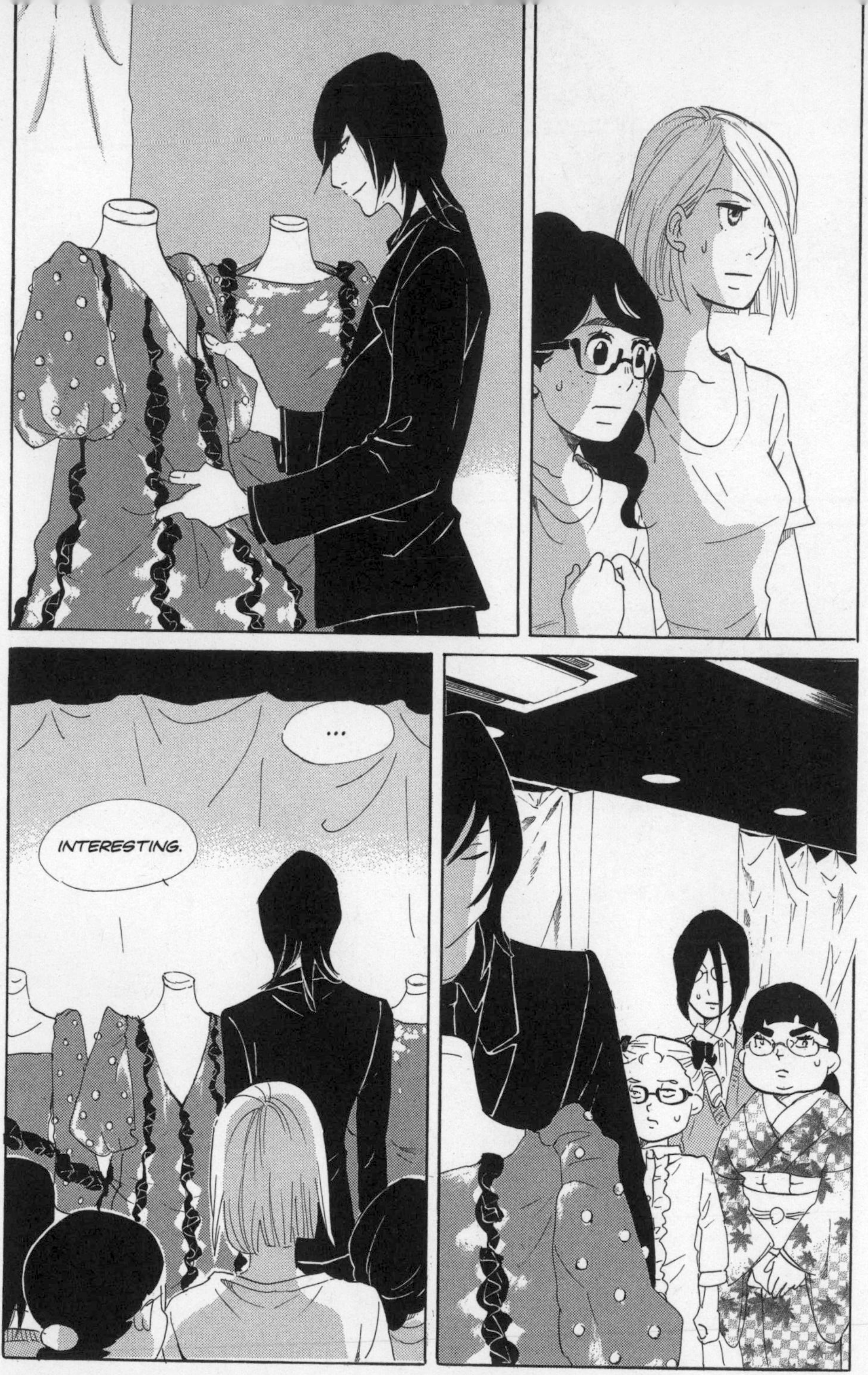
...
INTERESTING.

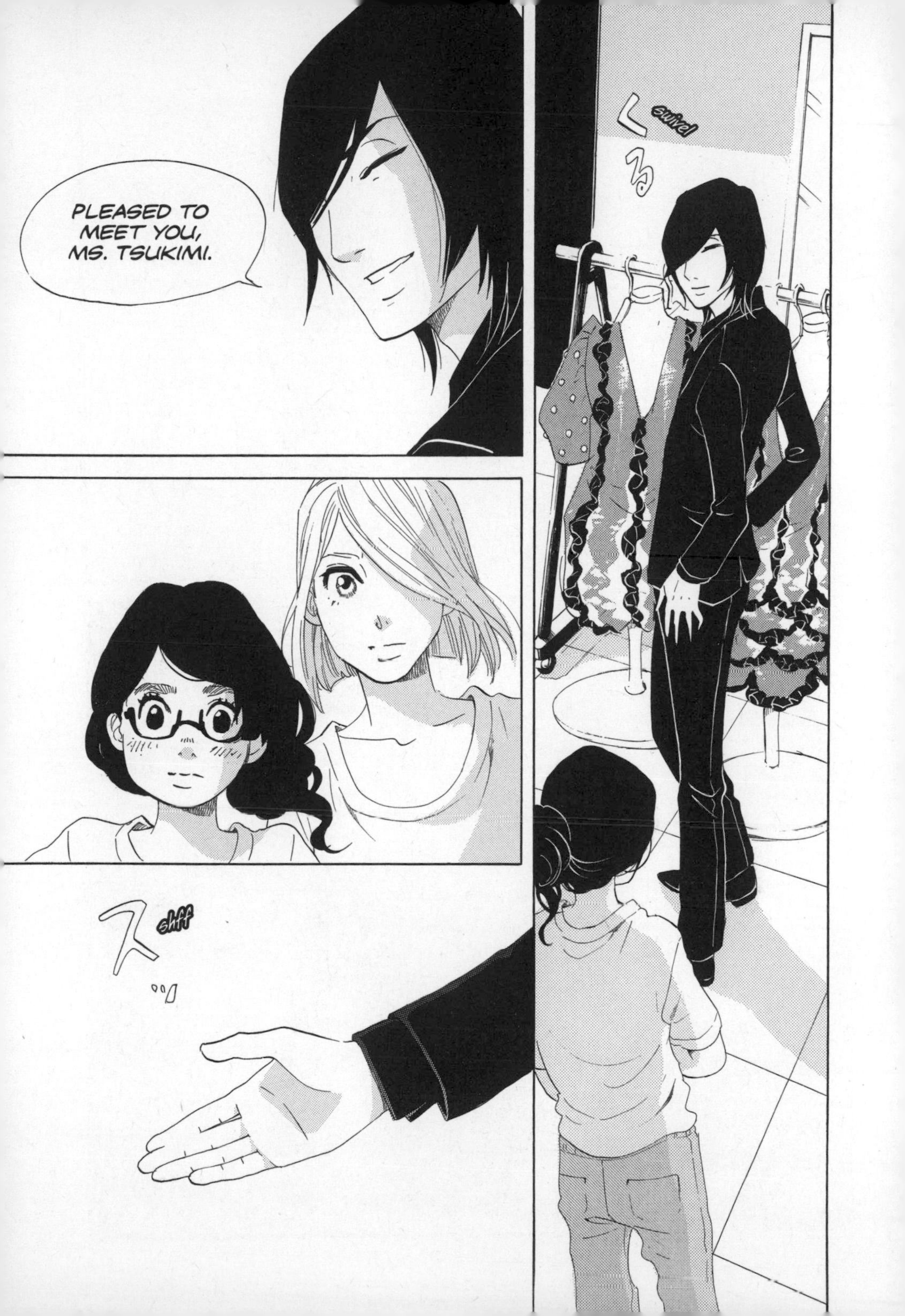
くる swivel
PLEASED TO MEET YOU, MS. TSUKIMI.
スッ shff

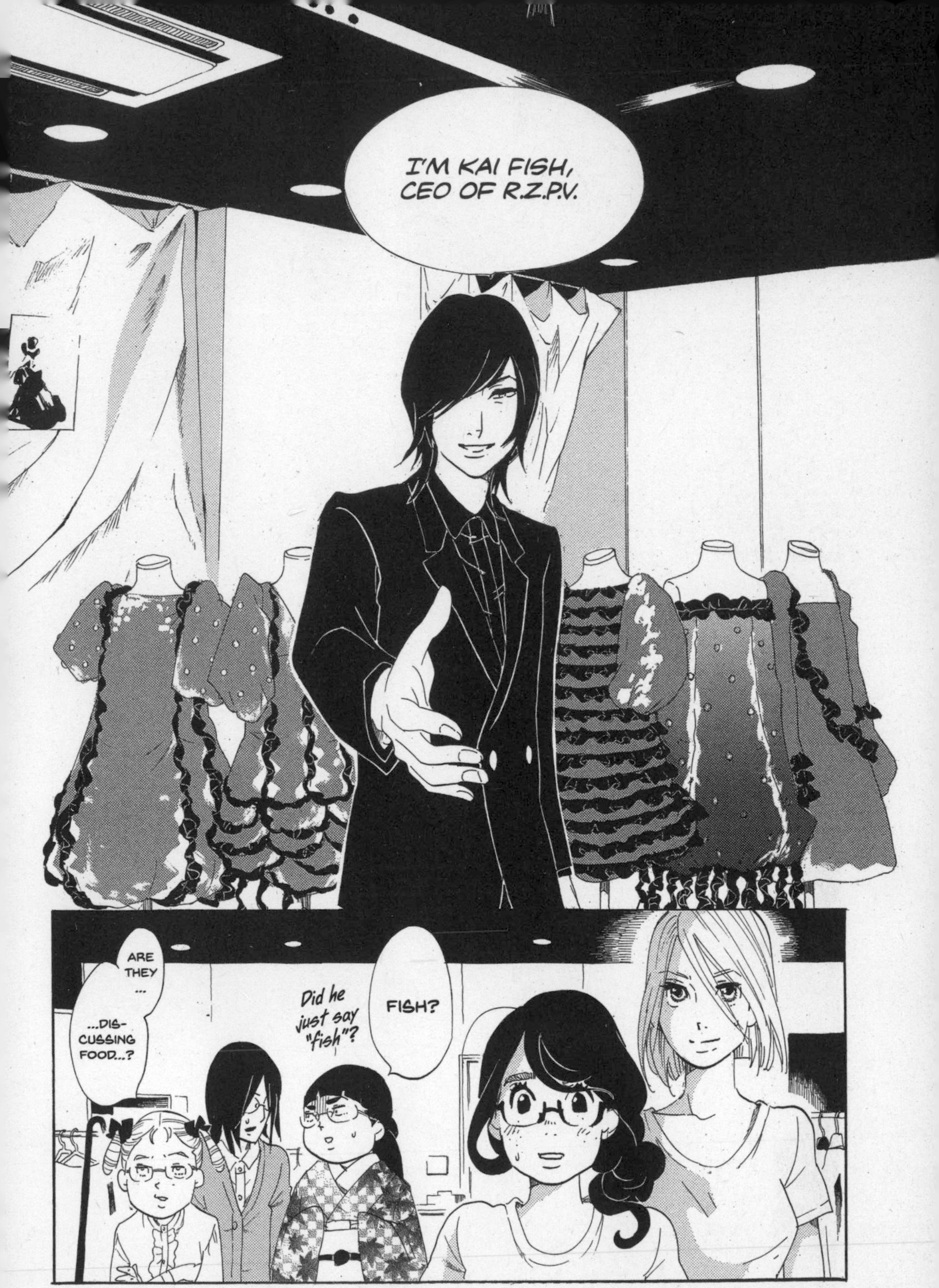
I'M KAI FISH, CEO OF R.Z.P.V.
FISH?
Did he just say "fish"?
ARE THEY ...
...DISCUSSING FOOD...?

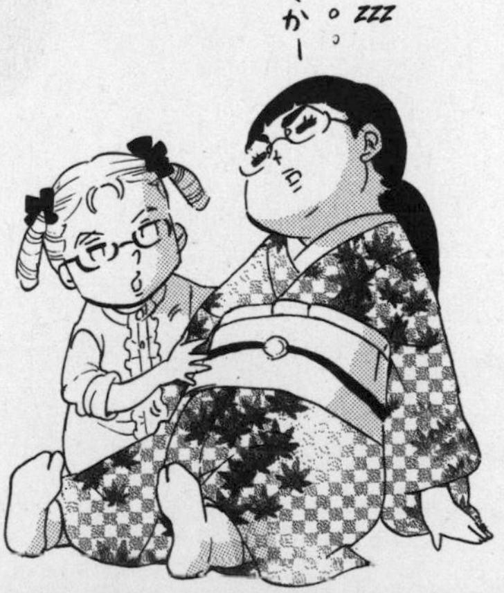
くかー
zzz

Episode 59

Fish Loves You (Yeah, Yeah, Yeah)

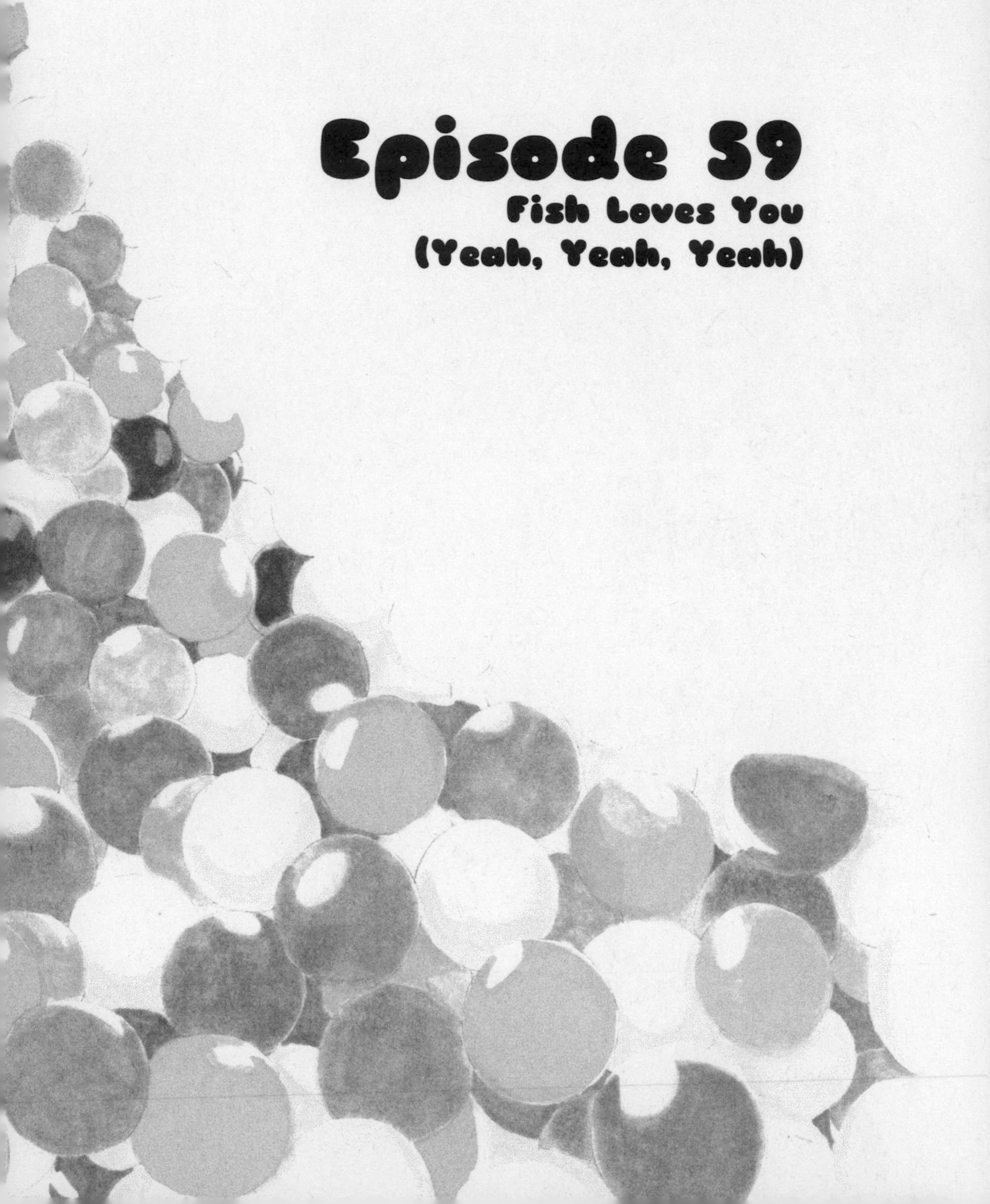

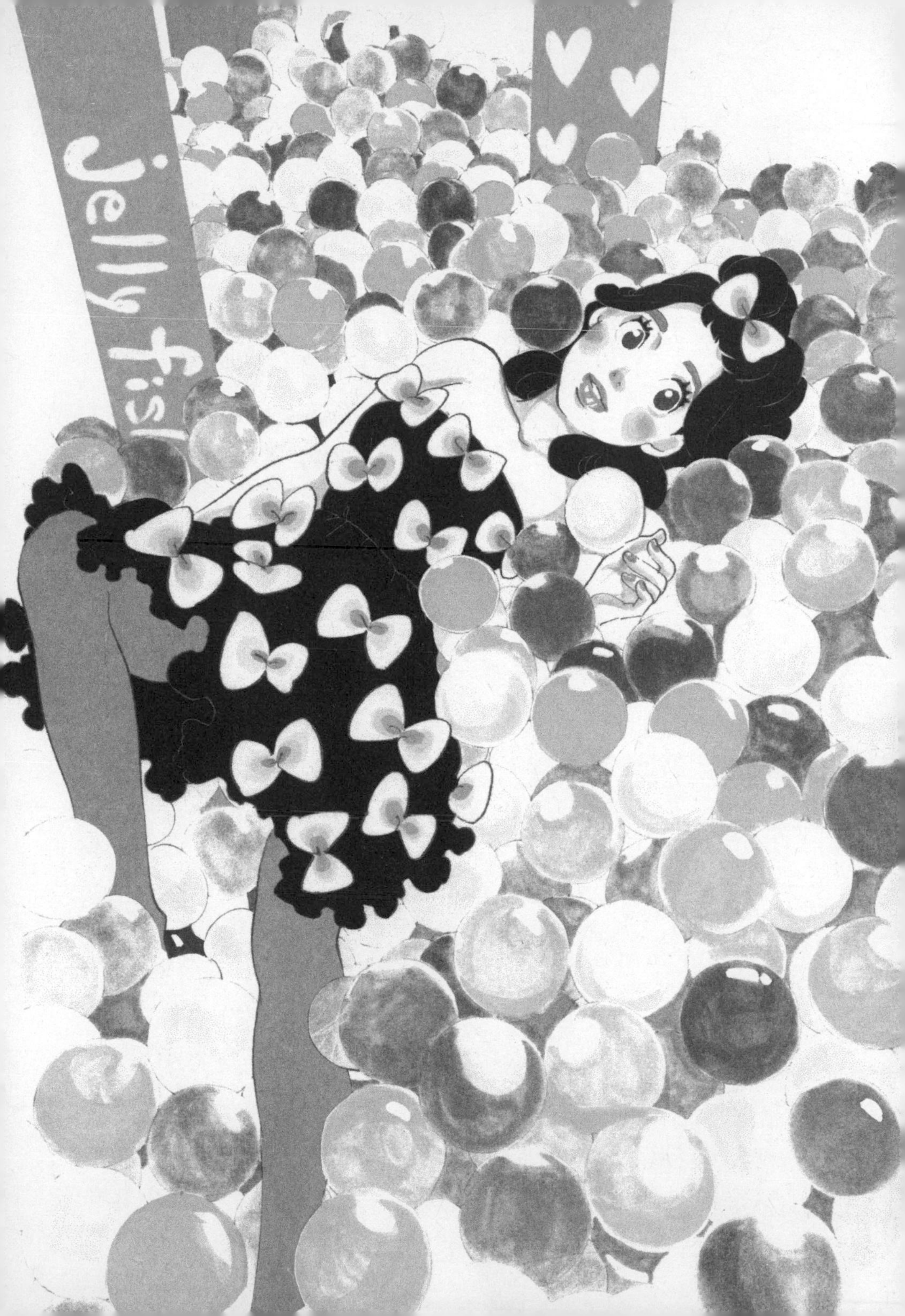
Jelly fis

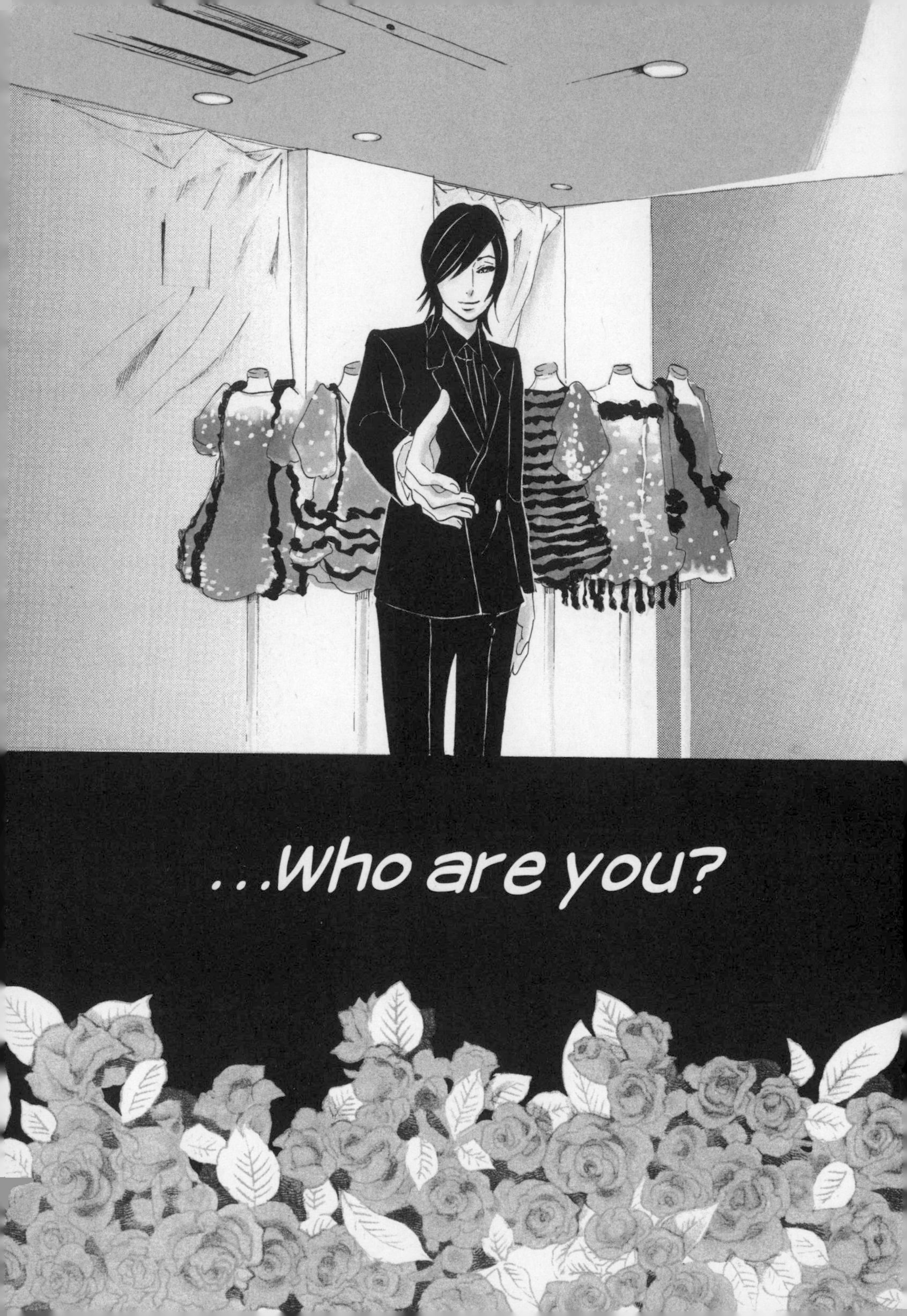
...who are you?

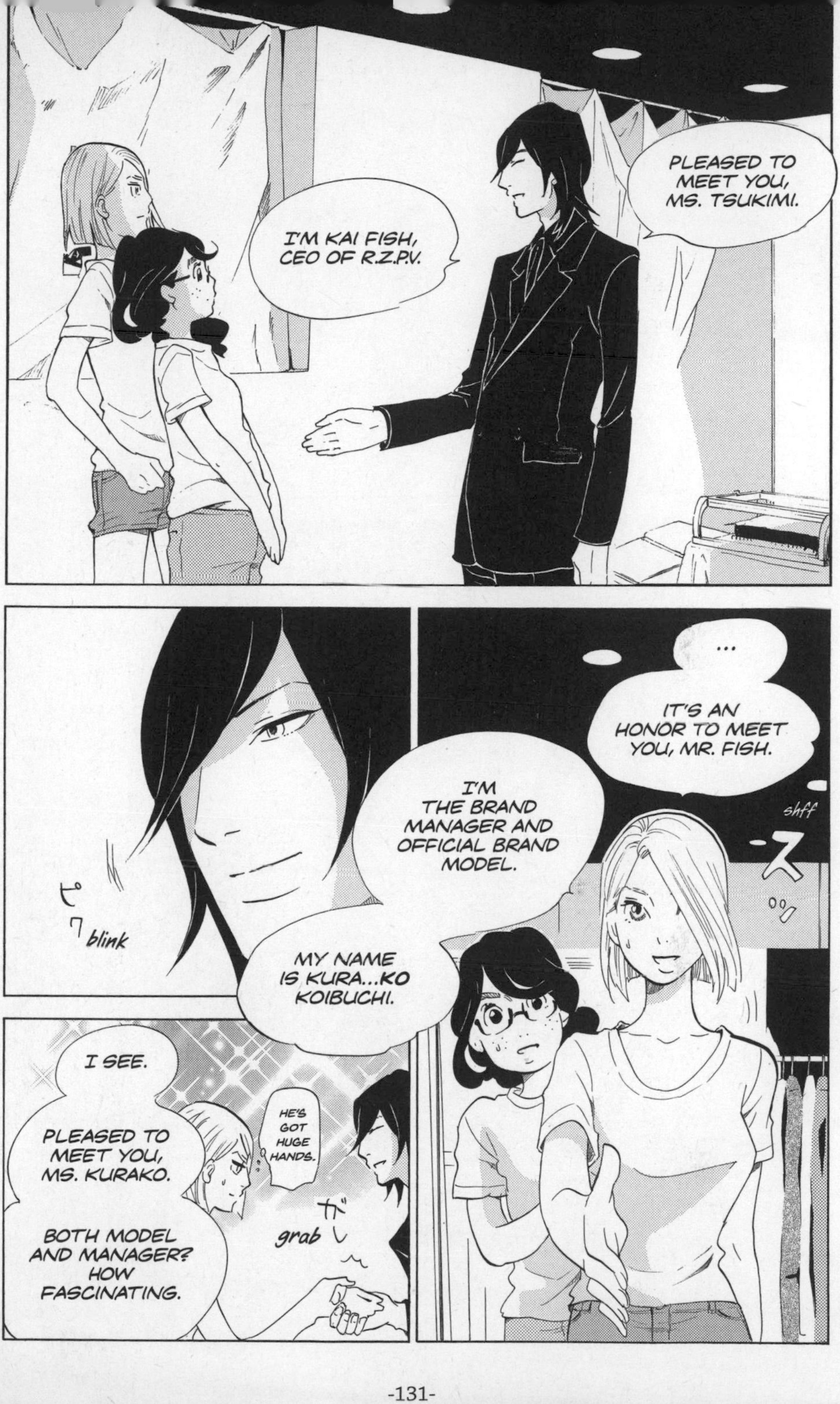
PLEASED TO MEET YOU, MS. TSUKIMI.
I'M KAI FISH, CEO OF R.Z.P.V.
...
IT'S AN HONOR TO MEET YOU, MR. FISH.
shff
ス
I'M THE BRAND MANAGER AND OFFICIAL BRAND MODEL.
MY NAME IS KURA...KO KOIBUCHI.
ピク
blink
HE'S GOT HUGE HANDS.
I SEE.
PLEASED TO MEET YOU, MS. KURAKO.
BOTH MODEL AND MANAGER? HOW FASCINATING.
ガシ
grab

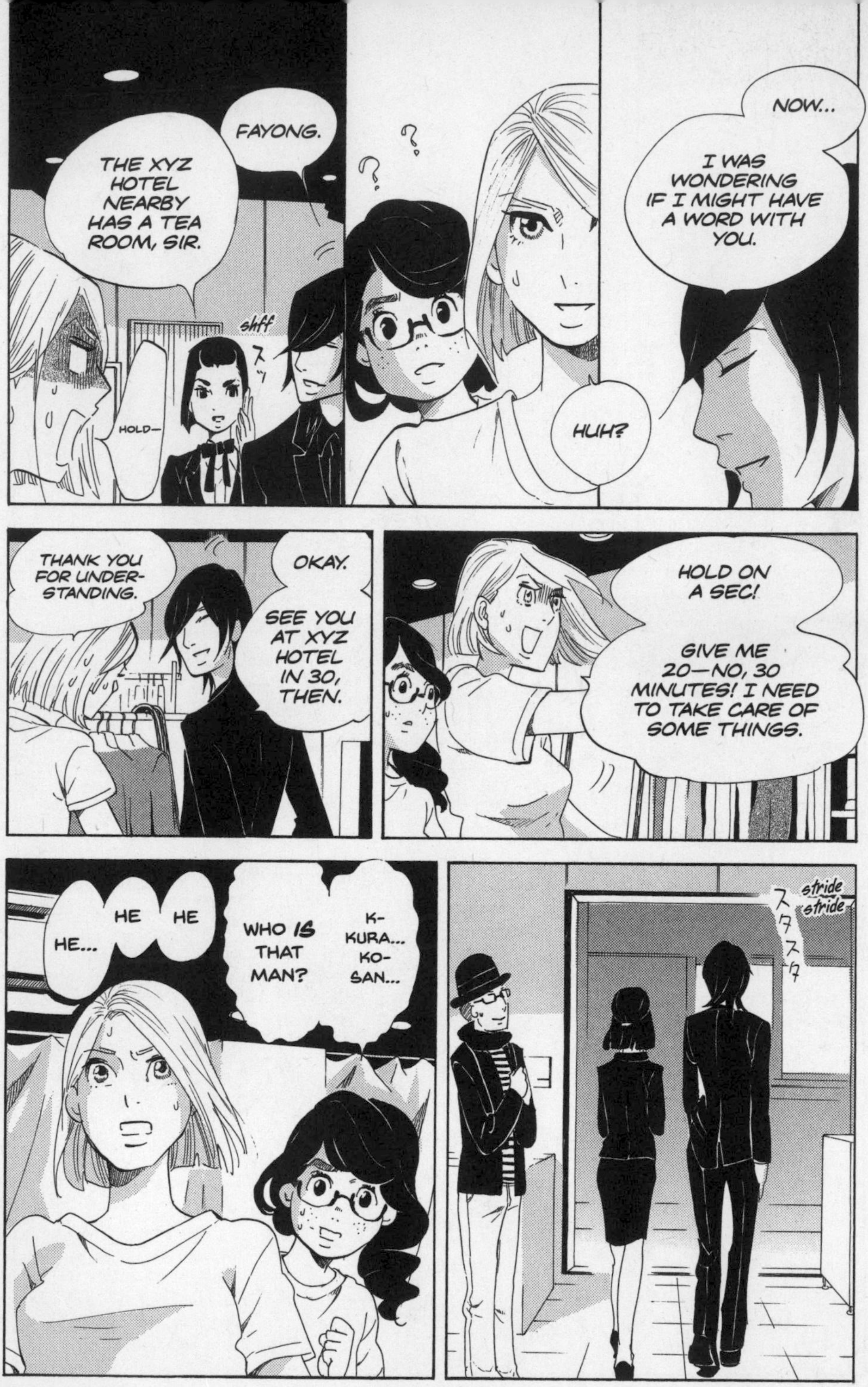
NOW...
I WAS WONDERING IF I MIGHT HAVE A WORD WITH YOU.
HUH?
?
?
FAYONG.
THE XYZ HOTEL NEARBY HAS A TEA ROOM, SIR.
shff
スッ
HOLD—
HOLD ON A SEC!
GIVE ME 20—NO, 30 MINUTES! I NEED TO TAKE CARE OF SOME THINGS.
OKAY.
SEE YOU AT XYZ HOTEL IN 30, THEN.
THANK YOU FOR UNDERSTANDING.
stride stride
スタスタ
K-KURA... KO-SAN...
WHO *IS* THAT MAN?
HE... HE HE

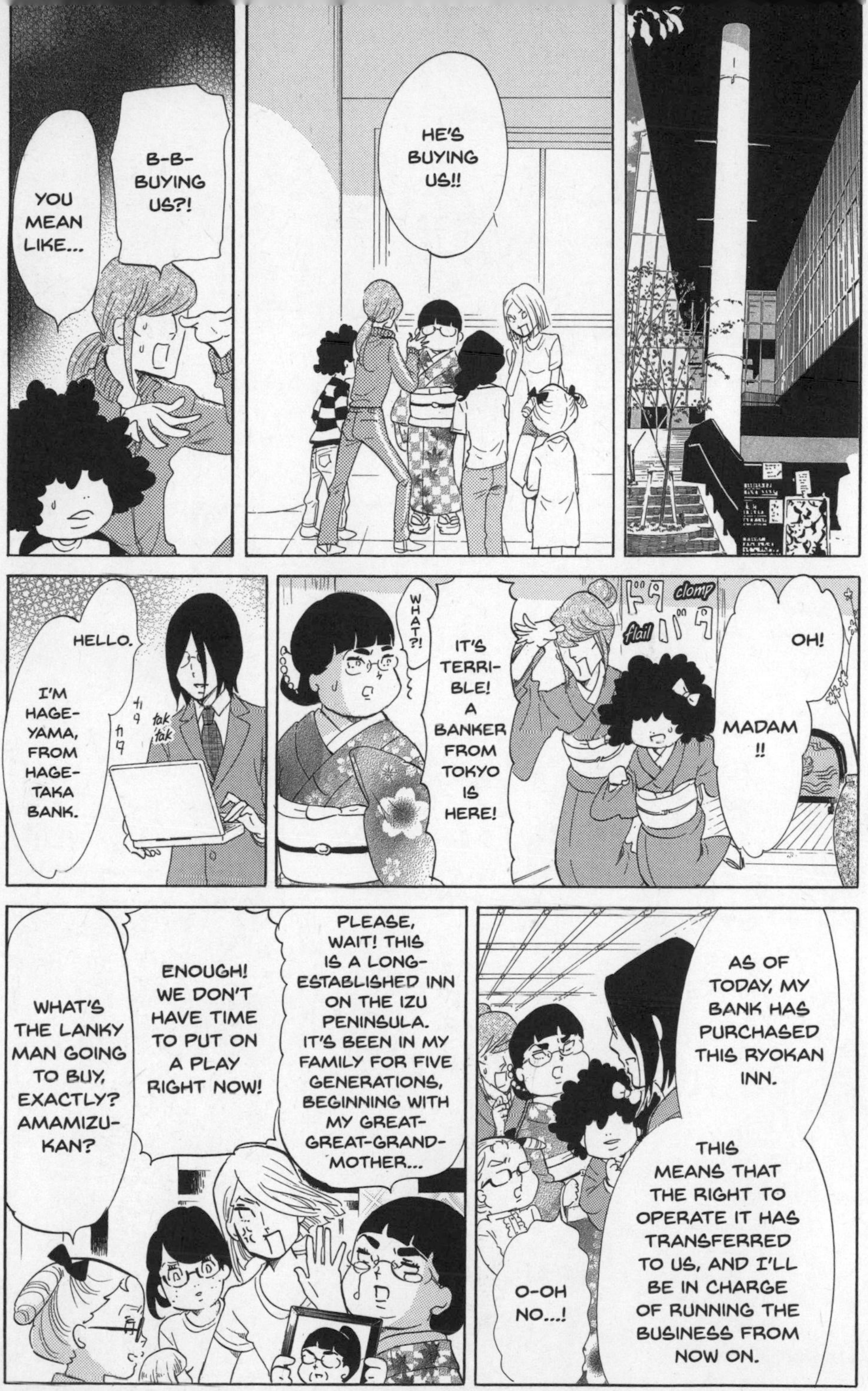
HE'S BUYING US!!
B-B-BUYING US?!
YOU MEAN LIKE...
OH! MADAM!!
ドタ clomp
バタ flail
IT'S TERRIBLE! A BANKER FROM TOKYO IS HERE!
WHAT?!
HELLO.
I'M HAGE-YAMA, FROM HAGE-TAKA BANK.
カタ カタ tak tak
AS OF TODAY, MY BANK HAS PURCHASED THIS RYOKAN INN.
THIS MEANS THAT THE RIGHT TO OPERATE IT HAS TRANSFERRED TO US, AND I'LL BE IN CHARGE OF RUNNING THE BUSINESS FROM NOW ON.
O-OH NO...!
PLEASE, WAIT! THIS IS A LONG-ESTABLISHED INN ON THE IZU PENINSULA. IT'S BEEN IN MY FAMILY FOR FIVE GENERATIONS, BEGINNING WITH MY GREAT-GREAT-GRAND-MOTHER...
ENOUGH! WE DON'T HAVE TIME TO PUT ON A PLAY RIGHT NOW!
WHAT'S THE LANKY MAN GOING TO BUY, EXACTLY? AMAMIZU-KAN?

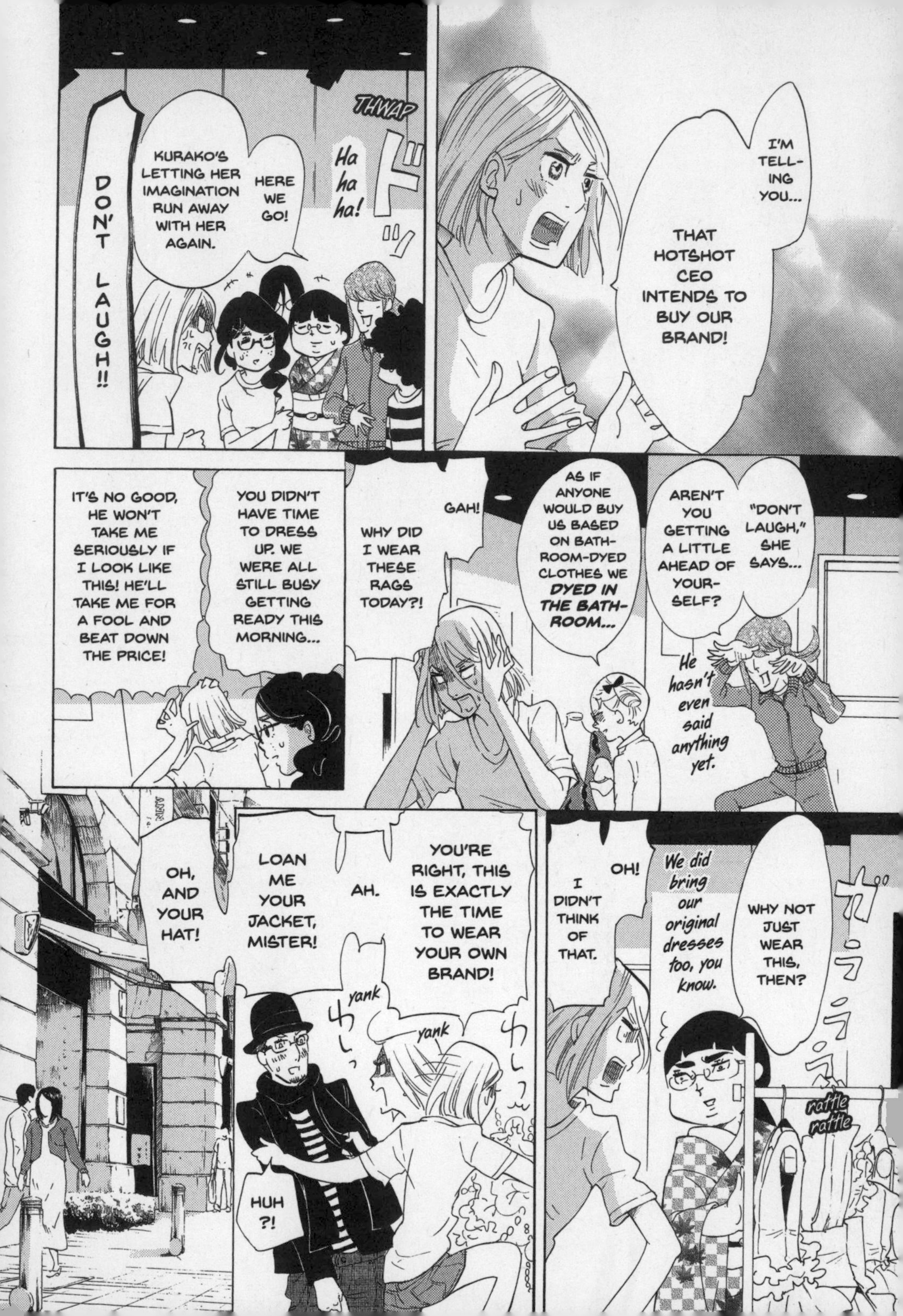
I'M TELLING YOU...
THAT HOTSHOT CEO INTENDS TO BUY OUR BRAND!
THWAP
DON'T LAUGH!!
KURAKO'S LETTING HER IMAGINATION RUN AWAY WITH HER AGAIN.
HERE WE GO!
Ha ha ha!
"DON'T LAUGH," SHE SAYS...
AREN'T YOU GETTING A LITTLE AHEAD OF YOURSELF?
He hasn't even said anything yet.
AS IF ANYONE WOULD BUY US BASED ON BATH-ROOM-DYED CLOTHES WE DYED IN THE BATHROOM...
GAH!
WHY DID I WEAR THESE RAGS TODAY?!
YOU DIDN'T HAVE TIME TO DRESS UP. WE WERE ALL STILL BUSY GETTING READY THIS MORNING...
IT'S NO GOOD, HE WON'T TAKE ME SERIOUSLY IF I LOOK LIKE THIS! HE'LL TAKE ME FOR A FOOL AND BEAT DOWN THE PRICE!
WHY NOT JUST WEAR THIS, THEN?
rattle rattle
We did bring our original dresses too, you know.
OH!
I DIDN'T THINK OF THAT.
YOU'RE RIGHT, THIS IS EXACTLY THE TIME TO WEAR YOUR OWN BRAND!
AH.
LOAN ME YOUR JACKET, MISTER!
OH, AND YOUR HAT!
yank
yank
HUH ?!

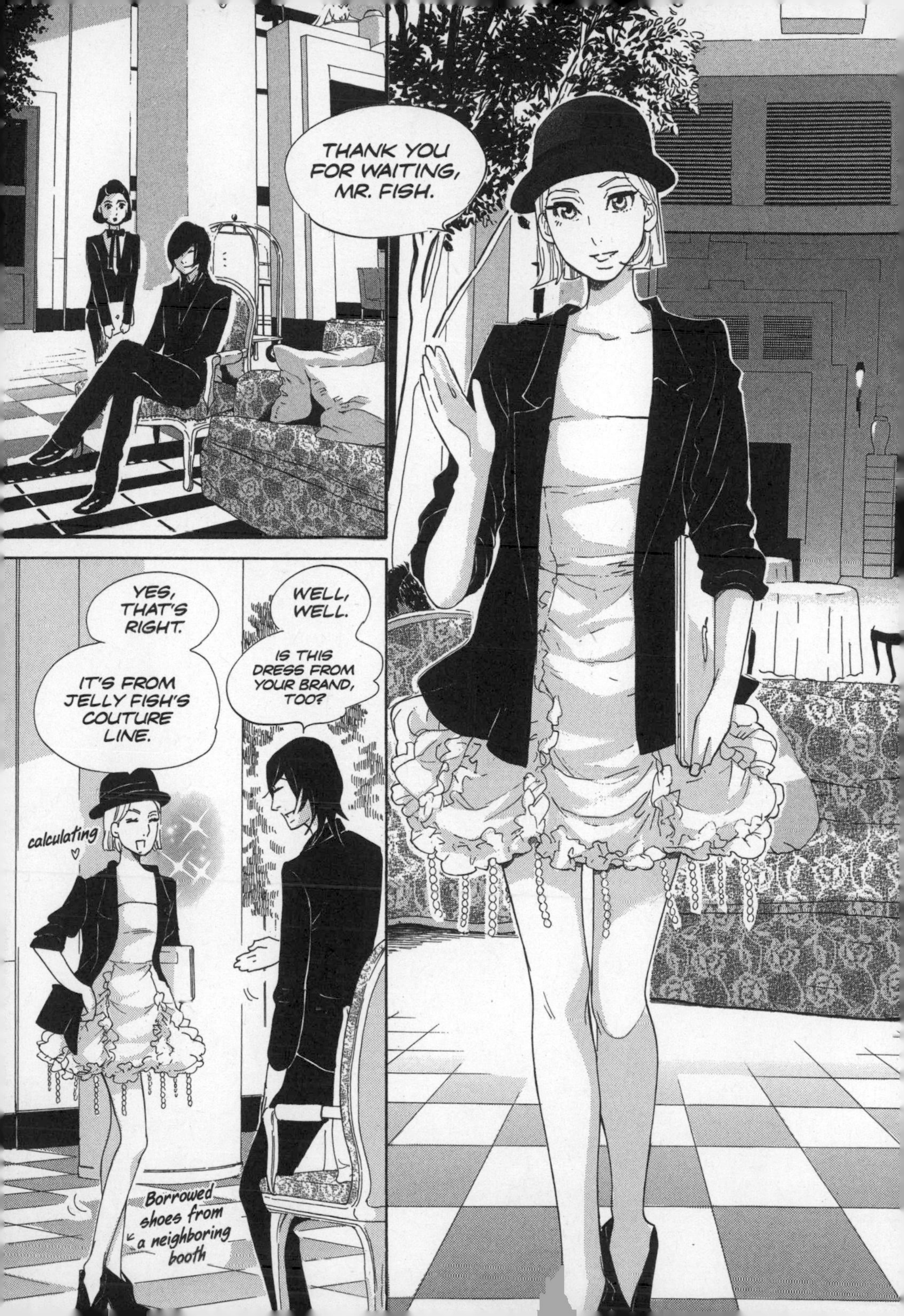
THANK YOU FOR WAITING, MR. FISH.
WELL, WELL.
IS THIS DRESS FROM YOUR BRAND, TOO?
YES, THAT'S RIGHT.
IT'S FROM JELLY FISH'S COUTURE LINE.
calculating
Borrowed shoes from a neighboring booth

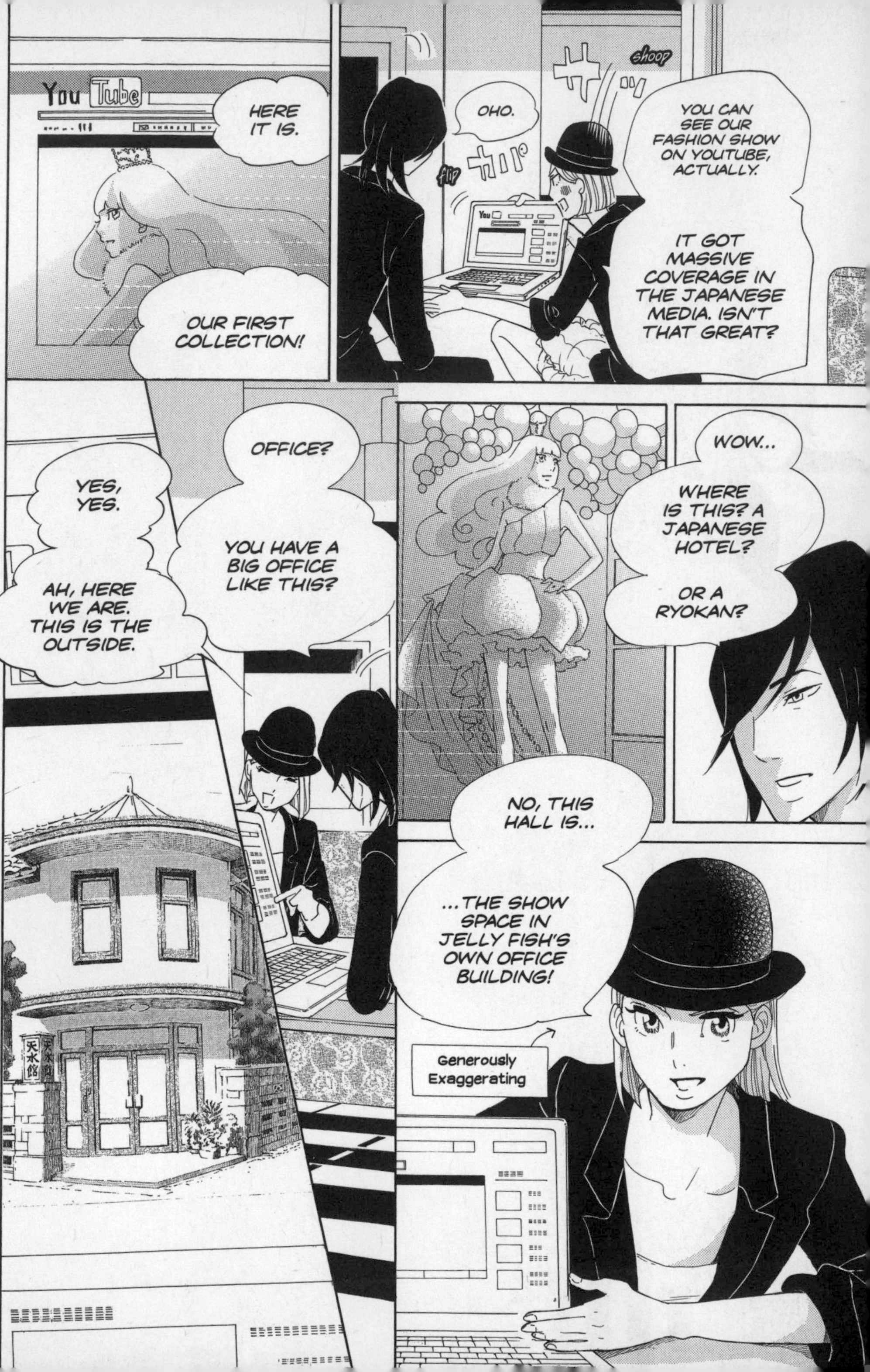
shoop
YOU CAN SEE OUR FASHION SHOW ON YOUTUBE, ACTUALLY.
flip
OHO.
IT GOT MASSIVE COVERAGE IN THE JAPANESE MEDIA. ISN'T THAT GREAT?
YouTube
HERE IT IS.
OUR FIRST COLLECTION!
WOW...
WHERE IS THIS? A JAPANESE HOTEL?
OR A RYOKAN?
NO, THIS HALL IS...
...THE SHOW SPACE IN JELLY FISH'S OWN OFFICE BUILDING!
Generously Exaggerating
OFFICE?
YOU HAVE A BIG OFFICE LIKE THIS?
YES, YES.
AH, HERE WE ARE. THIS IS THE OUTSIDE.
天水館

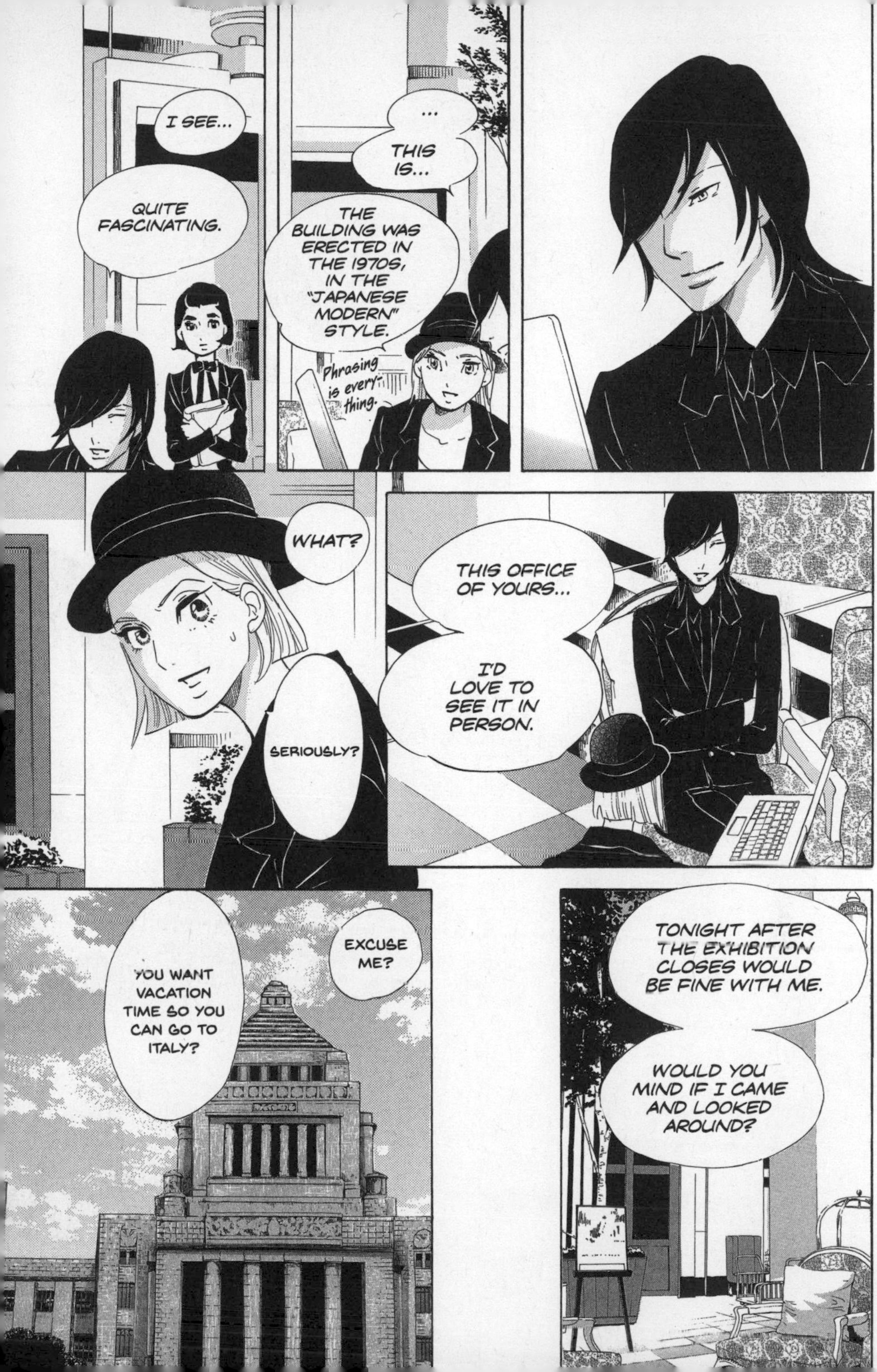
... THIS IS...
THE BUILDING WAS ERECTED IN THE 1970S, IN THE "JAPANESE MODERN" STYLE.
Phrasing is every-thing.
I SEE...
QUITE FASCINATING.
THIS OFFICE OF YOURS...
I'D LOVE TO SEE IT IN PERSON.
WHAT?
SERIOUSLY?
TONIGHT AFTER THE EXHIBITION CLOSES WOULD BE FINE WITH ME.
WOULD YOU MIND IF I CAME AND LOOKED AROUND?
EXCUSE ME?
YOU WANT VACATION TIME SO YOU CAN GO TO ITALY?

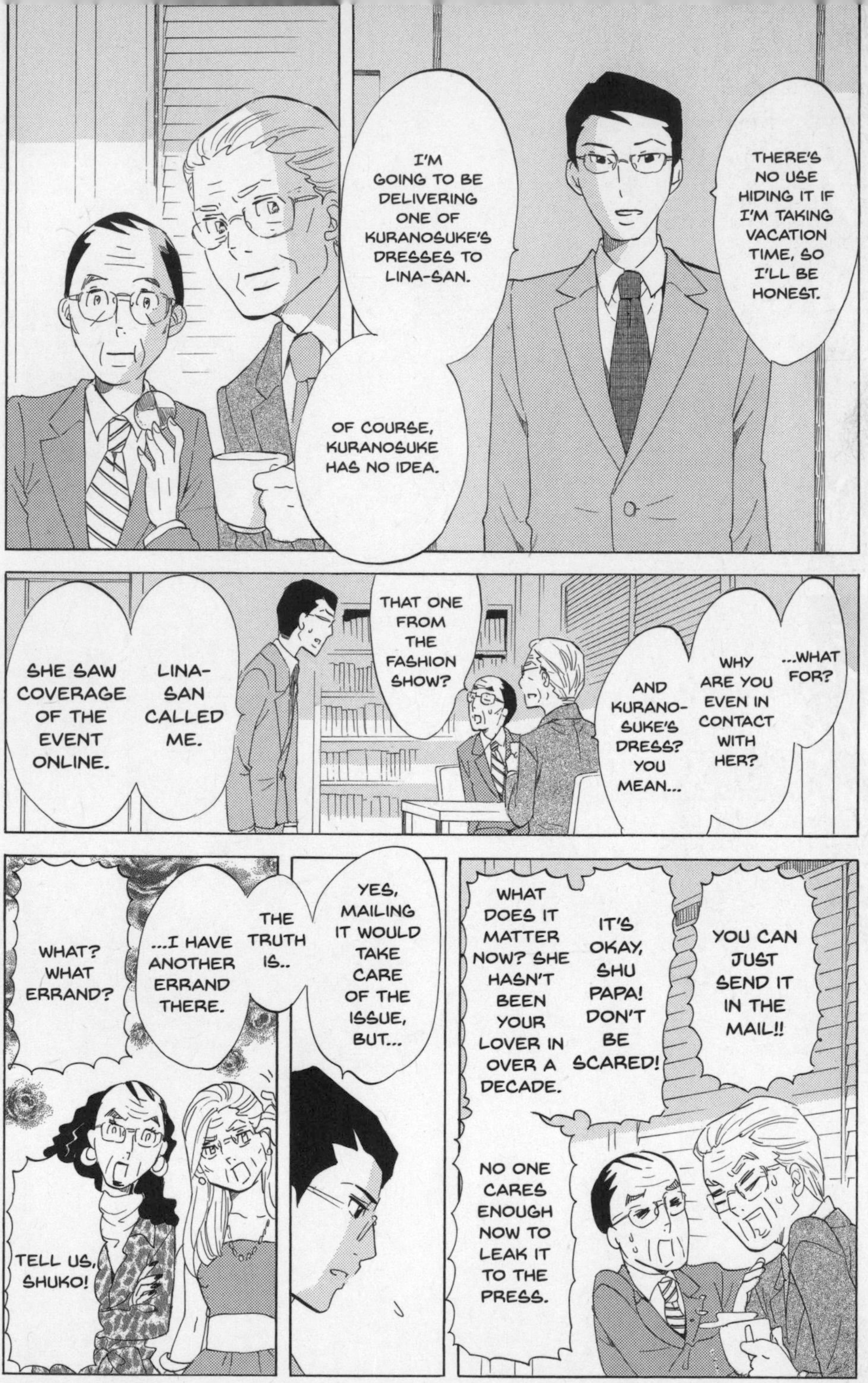
THERE'S NO USE HIDING IT IF I'M TAKING VACATION TIME, SO I'LL BE HONEST.
I'M GOING TO BE DELIVERING ONE OF KURANOSUKE'S DRESSES TO LINA-SAN.
OF COURSE, KURANOSUKE HAS NO IDEA.
...WHAT FOR?
WHY ARE YOU EVEN IN CONTACT WITH HER?
AND KURANOSUKE'S DRESS? YOU MEAN...
THAT ONE FROM THE FASHION SHOW?
LINA-SAN CALLED ME.
SHE SAW COVERAGE OF THE EVENT ONLINE.
YOU CAN JUST SEND IT IN THE MAIL!!
IT'S OKAY, SHU PAPA! DON'T BE SCARED!
WHAT DOES IT MATTER NOW? SHE HASN'T BEEN YOUR LOVER IN OVER A DECADE.
NO ONE CARES ENOUGH NOW TO LEAK IT TO THE PRESS.
YES, MAILING IT WOULD TAKE CARE OF THE ISSUE, BUT...
THE TRUTH IS..
...I HAVE ANOTHER ERRAND THERE.
WHAT? WHAT ERRAND?
TELL US, SHUKO!

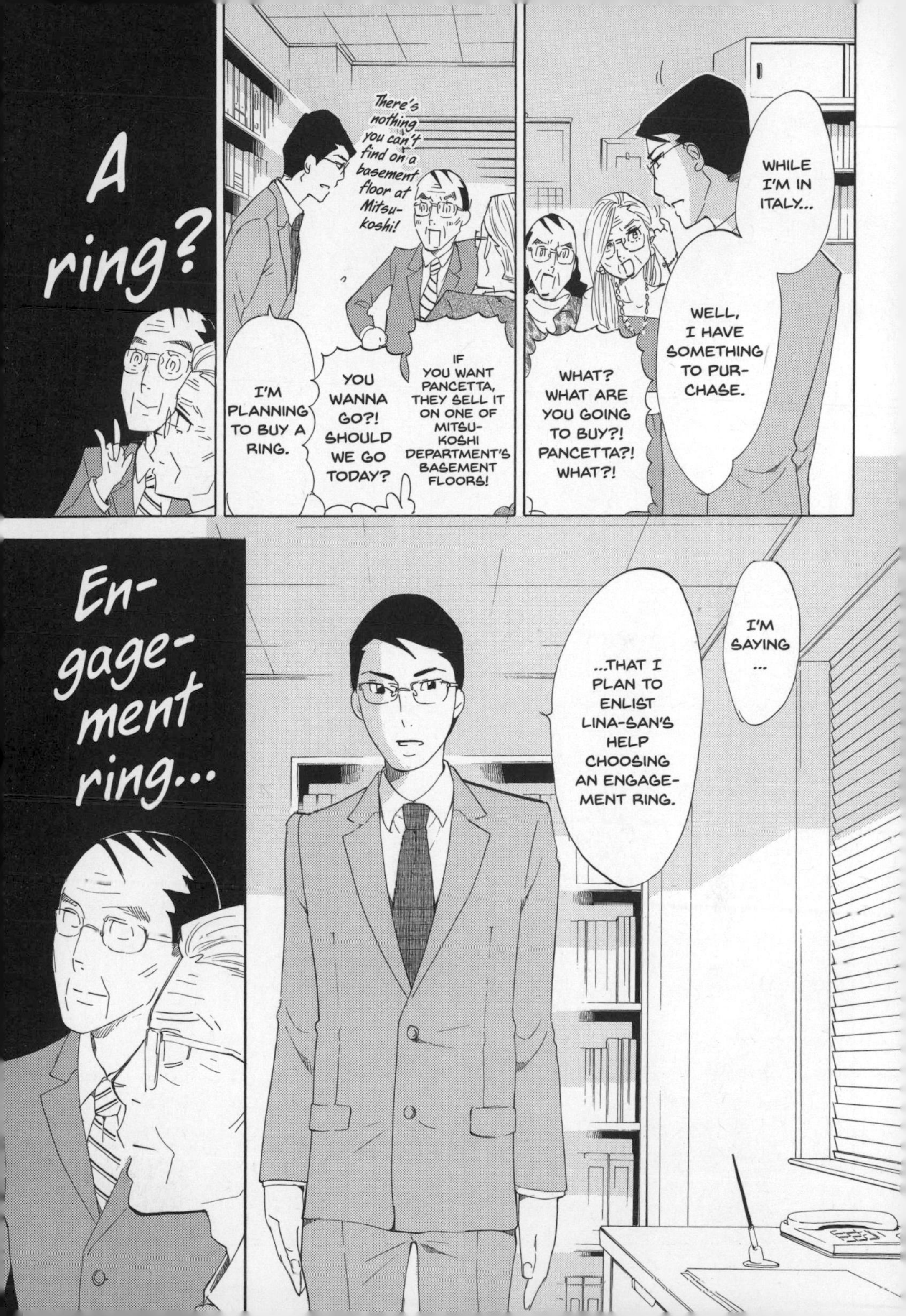
WHILE I'M IN ITALY...
WELL, I HAVE SOMETHING TO PURCHASE.
WHAT? WHAT ARE YOU GOING TO BUY?! PANCETTA?! WHAT?!
There's nothing you can't find on a basement floor at Mitsukoshi!
IF YOU WANT PANCETTA, THEY SELL IT ON ONE OF MITSUKOSHI DEPARTMENT'S BASEMENT FLOORS!
YOU WANNA GO?! SHOULD WE GO TODAY?
I'M PLANNING TO BUY A RING.
A ring?
I'M SAYING ...
...THAT I PLAN TO ENLIST LINA-SAN'S HELP CHOOSING AN ENGAGEMENT RING.
Engagement ring...

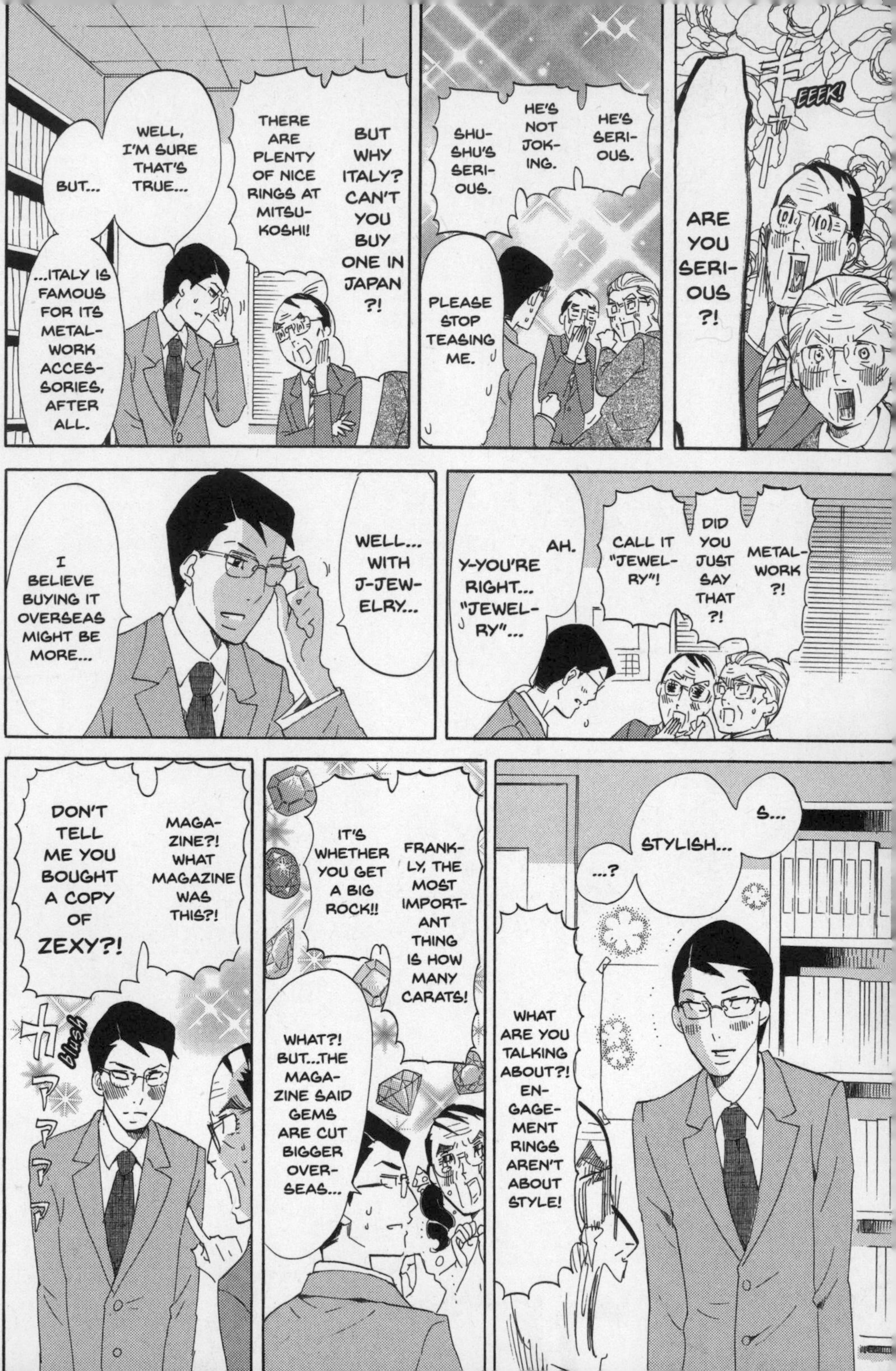

EEEK!
ARE YOU SERIOUS?!
HE'S SERIOUS.
HE'S NOT JOKING.
SHU-SHU'S SERIOUS.
PLEASE STOP TEASING ME.
BUT WHY ITALY? CAN'T YOU BUY ONE IN JAPAN?!
THERE ARE PLENTY OF NICE RINGS AT MITSUKOSHI!
WELL, I'M SURE THAT'S TRUE...
BUT...
...ITALY IS FAMOUS FOR ITS METALWORK ACCESSORIES, AFTER ALL.
METALWORK?!
DID YOU JUST SAY THAT?!
CALL IT "JEWELRY"!
AH.
Y-YOU'RE RIGHT... "JEWELRY"...
WELL... WITH J-JEWELRY...
I BELIEVE BUYING IT OVERSEAS MIGHT BE MORE...
S...
STYLISH...
...?
WHAT ARE YOU TALKING ABOUT?! ENGAGEMENT RINGS AREN'T ABOUT STYLE!
FRANKLY, THE MOST IMPORTANT THING IS HOW MANY CARATS!
IT'S WHETHER YOU GET A BIG ROCK!!
WHAT?! BUT...THE MAGAZINE SAID GEMS ARE CUT BIGGER OVERSEAS...
MAGAZINE?! WHAT MAGAZINE WAS THIS?!
DON'T TELL ME YOU BOUGHT A COPY OF ZEXY?!
blush

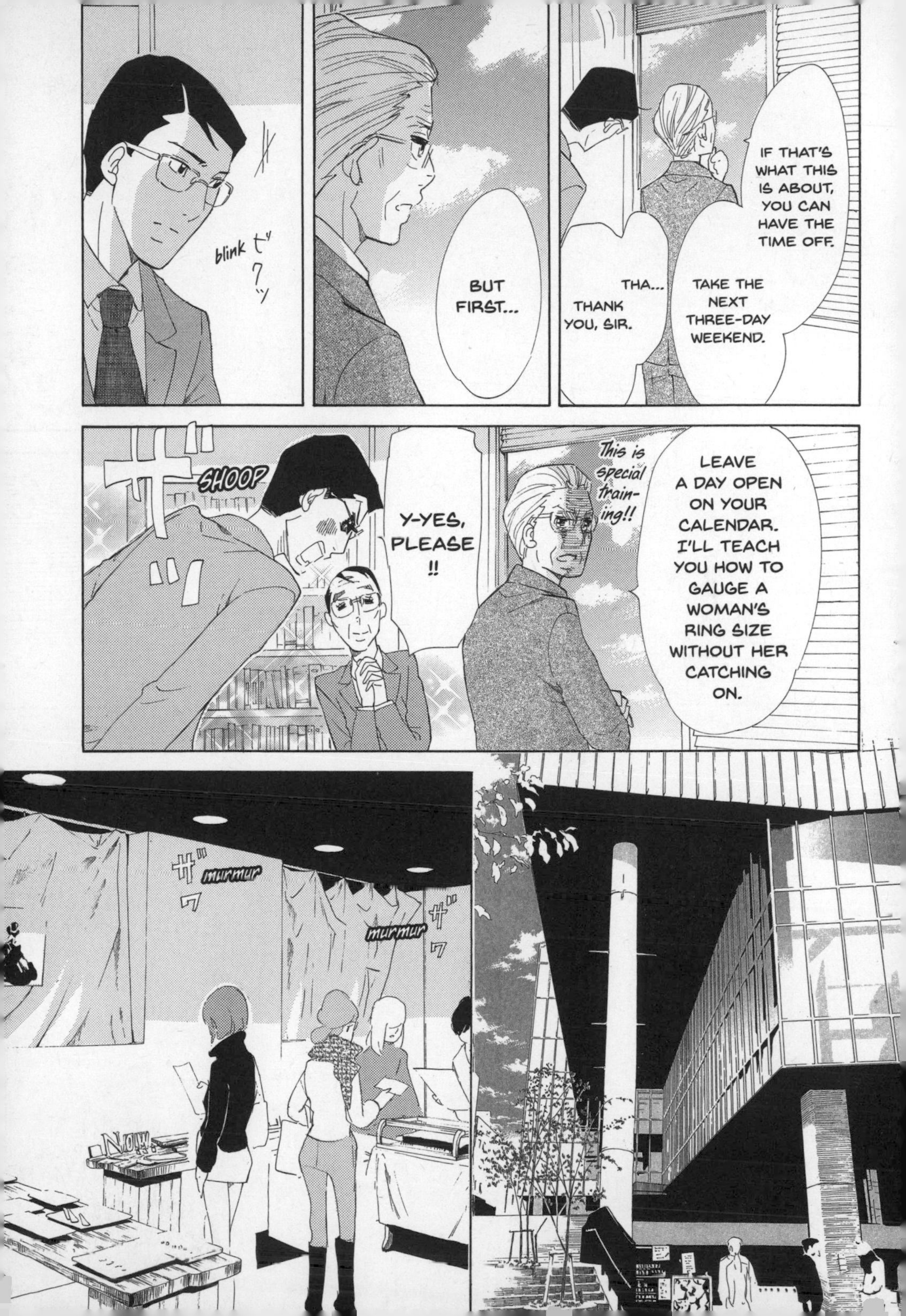
IF THAT'S WHAT THIS IS ABOUT, YOU CAN HAVE THE TIME OFF.
TAKE THE NEXT THREE-DAY WEEKEND.
THA...
THANK YOU, SIR.
BUT FIRST...
blink
LEAVE A DAY OPEN ON YOUR CALENDAR. I'LL TEACH YOU HOW TO GAUGE A WOMAN'S RING SIZE WITHOUT HER CATCHING ON.
This is special training!!
Y-YES, PLEASE!!
SHOOP
murmur
murmur

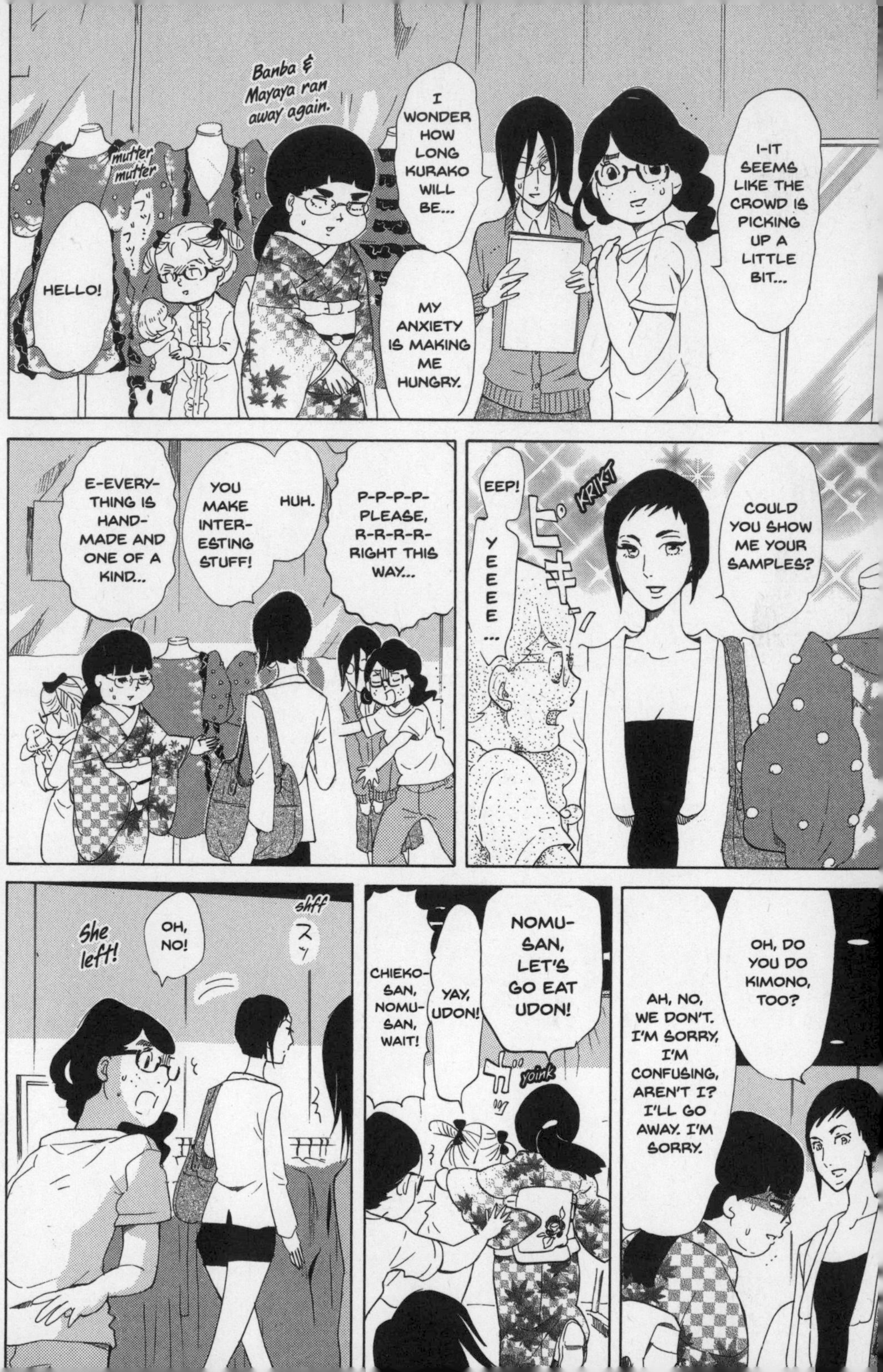
I-IT SEEMS LIKE THE CROWD IS PICKING UP A LITTLE BIT...
I WONDER HOW LONG KURAKO WILL BE...
MY ANXIETY IS MAKING ME HUNGRY.
Banba & Mayaya ran away again.
mutter mutter
HELLO!
COULD YOU SHOW ME YOUR SAMPLES?
KRIKT
EEP!
YEEEE...
P-P-P-P-PLEASE, R-R-R-R-RIGHT THIS WAY...
HUH.
YOU MAKE INTERESTING STUFF!
E-EVERYTHING IS HANDMADE AND ONE OF A KIND...
OH, DO YOU DO KIMONO, TOO?
AH, NO, WE DON'T. I'M SORRY, I'M CONFUSING, AREN'T I? I'LL GO AWAY. I'M SORRY.
NOMU-SAN, LET'S GO EAT UDON!
YAY, UDON!
CHIEKO-SAN, NOMU-SAN, WAIT!
yoink
shff
OH, NO!
She left!

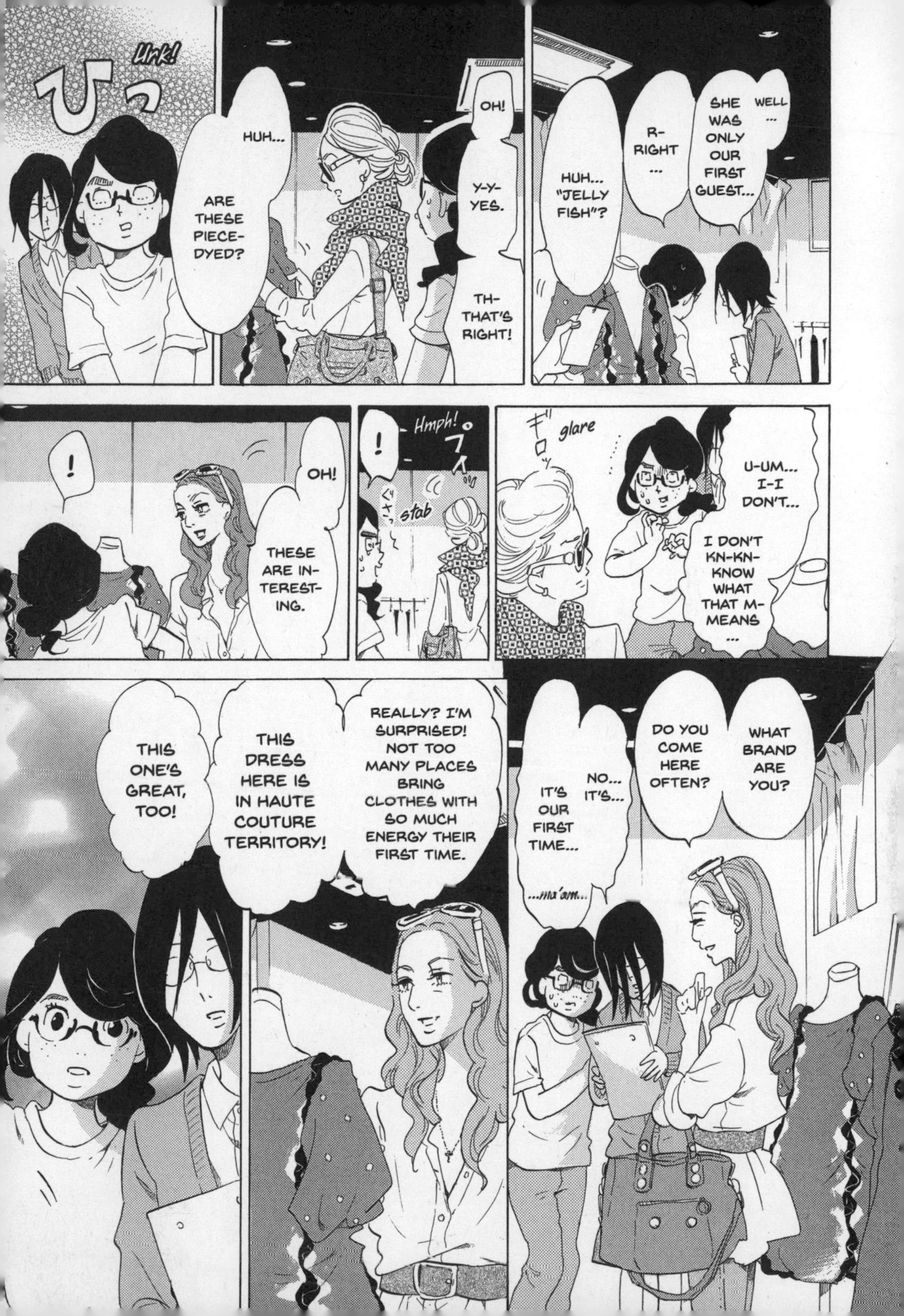
WELL...
SHE WAS ONLY OUR FIRST GUEST...
R-RIGHT...
HUH... "JELLY FISH"?
OH!
Y-Y-YES.
TH-THAT'S RIGHT!
HUH... ARE THESE PIECE-DYED?
ひっ
Unk!
ギロッ
glare
U-UM... I-I DON'T...
I DON'T KN-KN-KNOW WHAT THAT M-MEANS...
プイ
Hmph!
!
stab
OH! THESE ARE IN-TEREST-ING.
!
WHAT BRAND ARE YOU?
DO YOU COME HERE OFTEN?
NO... IT'S...
IT'S OUR FIRST TIME...
...ma'am...
REALLY? I'M SURPRISED! NOT TOO MANY PLACES BRING CLOTHES WITH SO MUCH ENERGY THEIR FIRST TIME.
THIS DRESS HERE IS IN HAUTE COUTURE TERRITORY!
THIS ONE'S GREAT, TOO!

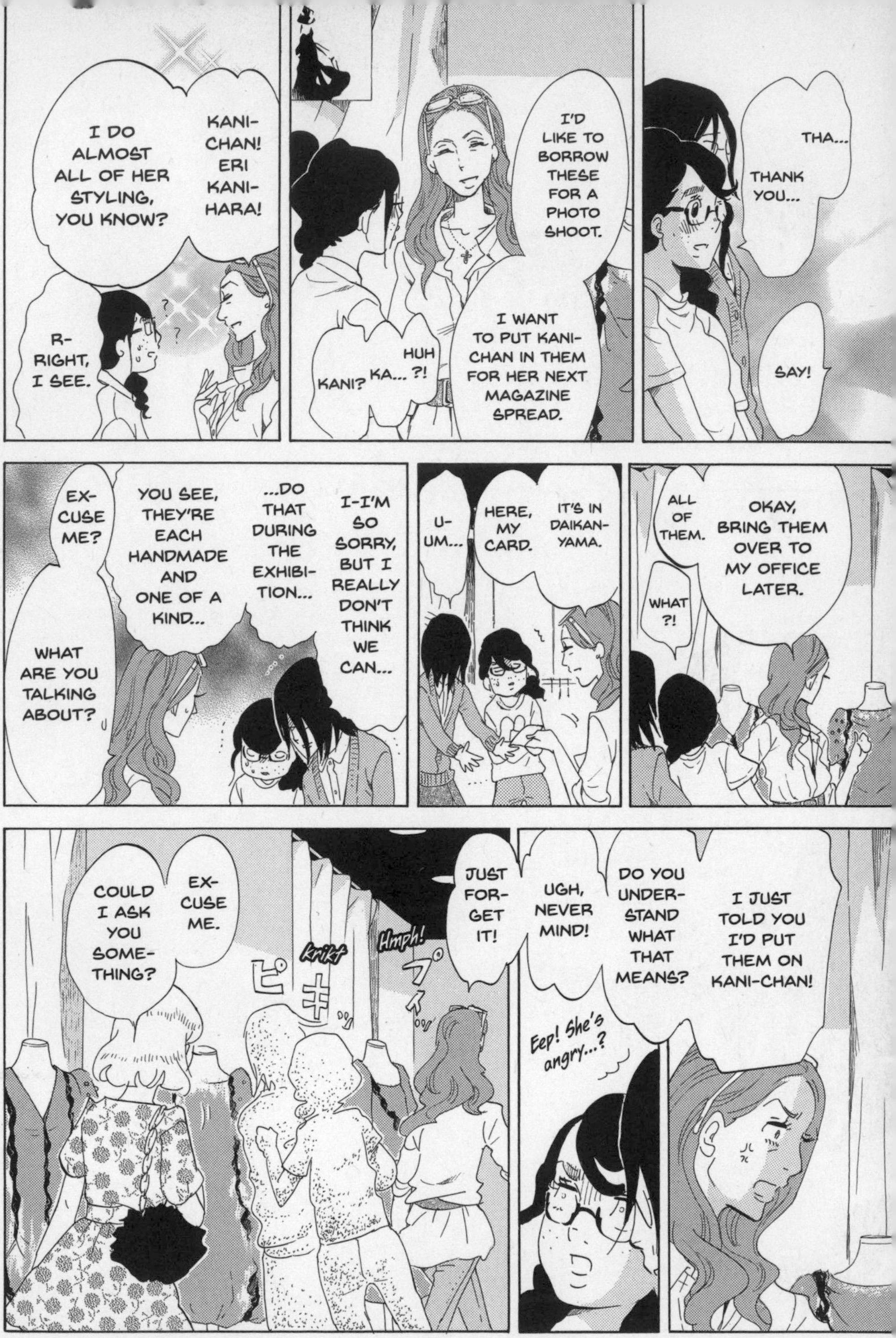
THA...
THANK YOU...
SAY!
I'D LIKE TO BORROW THESE FOR A PHOTO SHOOT.
I WANT TO PUT KANI-CHAN IN THEM FOR HER NEXT MAGAZINE SPREAD.
HUH KA...?!
KANI?
KANI-CHAN! ERI KANI-HARA!
I DO ALMOST ALL OF HER STYLING, YOU KNOW?
R-RIGHT, I SEE.
OKAY, BRING THEM OVER TO MY OFFICE LATER.
ALL OF THEM.
WHAT?!
IT'S IN DAIKAN-YAMA.
HERE, MY CARD.
U-UM...
I-I'M SO SORRY, BUT I REALLY DON'T THINK WE CAN...
...DO THAT DURING THE EXHIBITION...
YOU SEE, THEY'RE EACH HANDMADE AND ONE OF A KIND...
EX-CUSE ME?
WHAT ARE YOU TALKING ABOUT?
I JUST TOLD YOU I'D PUT THEM ON KANI-CHAN!
DO YOU UNDER-STAND WHAT THAT MEANS?
UGH, NEVER MIND!
JUST FOR-GET IT!
Eep! She's angry...?
Hmph!
krikt
EX-CUSE ME.
COULD I ASK YOU SOME-THING?

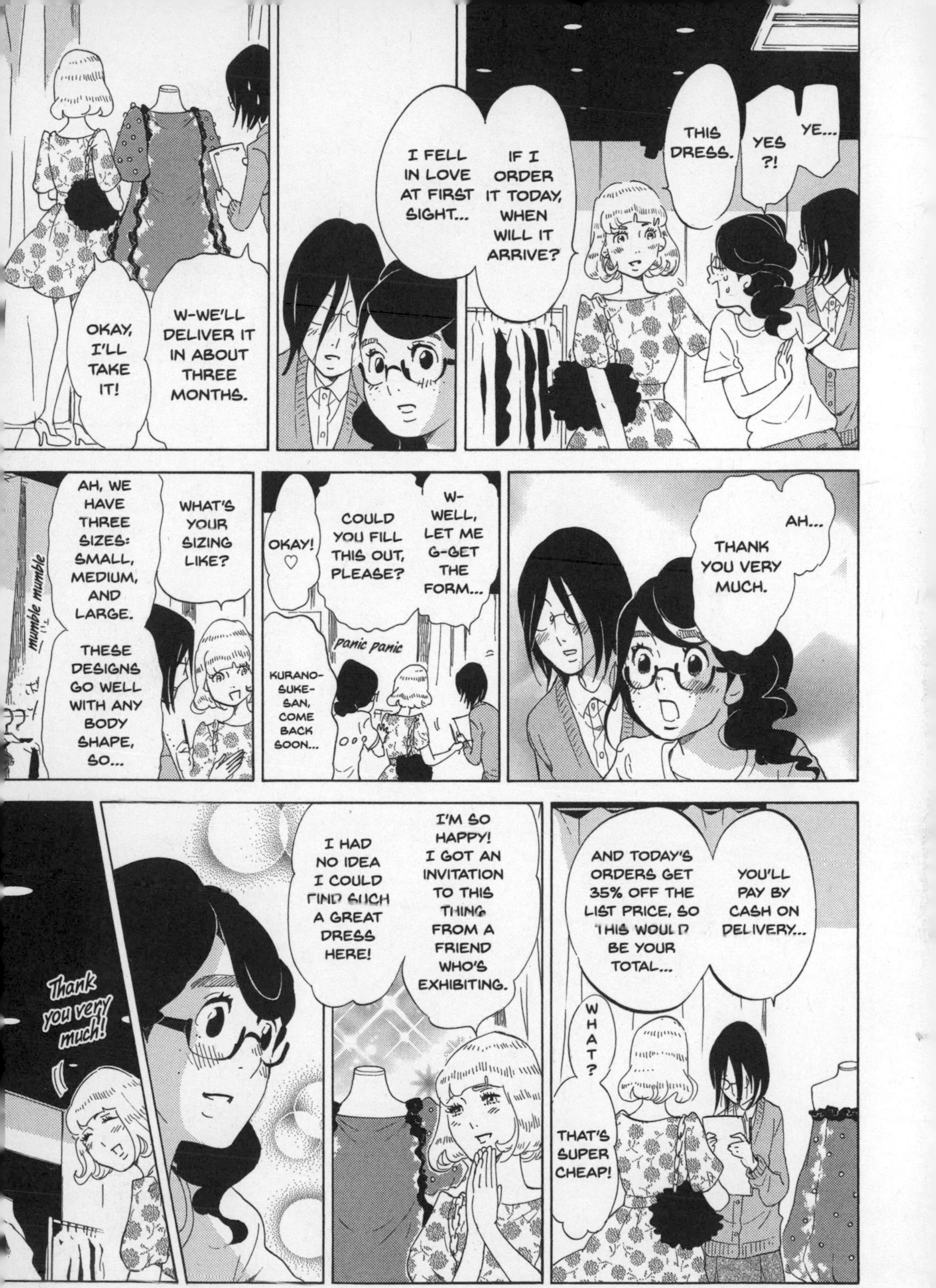
YE...
YES ?!
THIS DRESS.
IF I ORDER IT TODAY, WHEN WILL IT ARRIVE?
I FELL IN LOVE AT FIRST SIGHT...
W-WE'LL DELIVER IT IN ABOUT THREE MONTHS.
OKAY, I'LL TAKE IT!
AH...
THANK YOU VERY MUCH.
W-WELL, LET ME G-GET THE FORM...
COULD YOU FILL THIS OUT, PLEASE?
OKAY! ♡
panic panic
KURANOSUKE-SAN, COME BACK SOON...
WHAT'S YOUR SIZING LIKE?
AH, WE HAVE THREE SIZES: SMALL, MEDIUM, AND LARGE.
mumble mumble
THESE DESIGNS GO WELL WITH ANY BODY SHAPE, SO...
YOU'LL PAY BY CASH ON DELIVERY...
AND TODAY'S ORDERS GET 35% OFF THE LIST PRICE, SO THIS WOULD BE YOUR TOTAL...
WHAT?
THAT'S SUPER CHEAP!
I'M SO HAPPY! I GOT AN INVITATION TO THIS THING FROM A FRIEND WHO'S EXHIBITING.
I HAD NO IDEA I COULD FIND SUCH A GREAT DRESS HERE!
Thank you very much!

tattat
たたっ

HEY!

I'M SORRY!

pause
ピ
ク
〃

WAH!

THIS ONE'S EVEN CUTER!

What?!

Tee-hee!
☆

CANCEL THAT LAST ONE-PIECE ORDER, PLEASE!

stare
じ～

No, no, I'm an architect, but I designed the flagship store for one of the ex-hibitors, so they always invite me to this event, and per—

That's not easy in this climate, you know. What? You're independent? So are you in boutiques, then? When was your debut collection?

Oh, so you want to sell online?

No Reaction	Talks Incessantly, Then Doesn't Buy	A Pain to Deal With, and Doesn't Even Buy

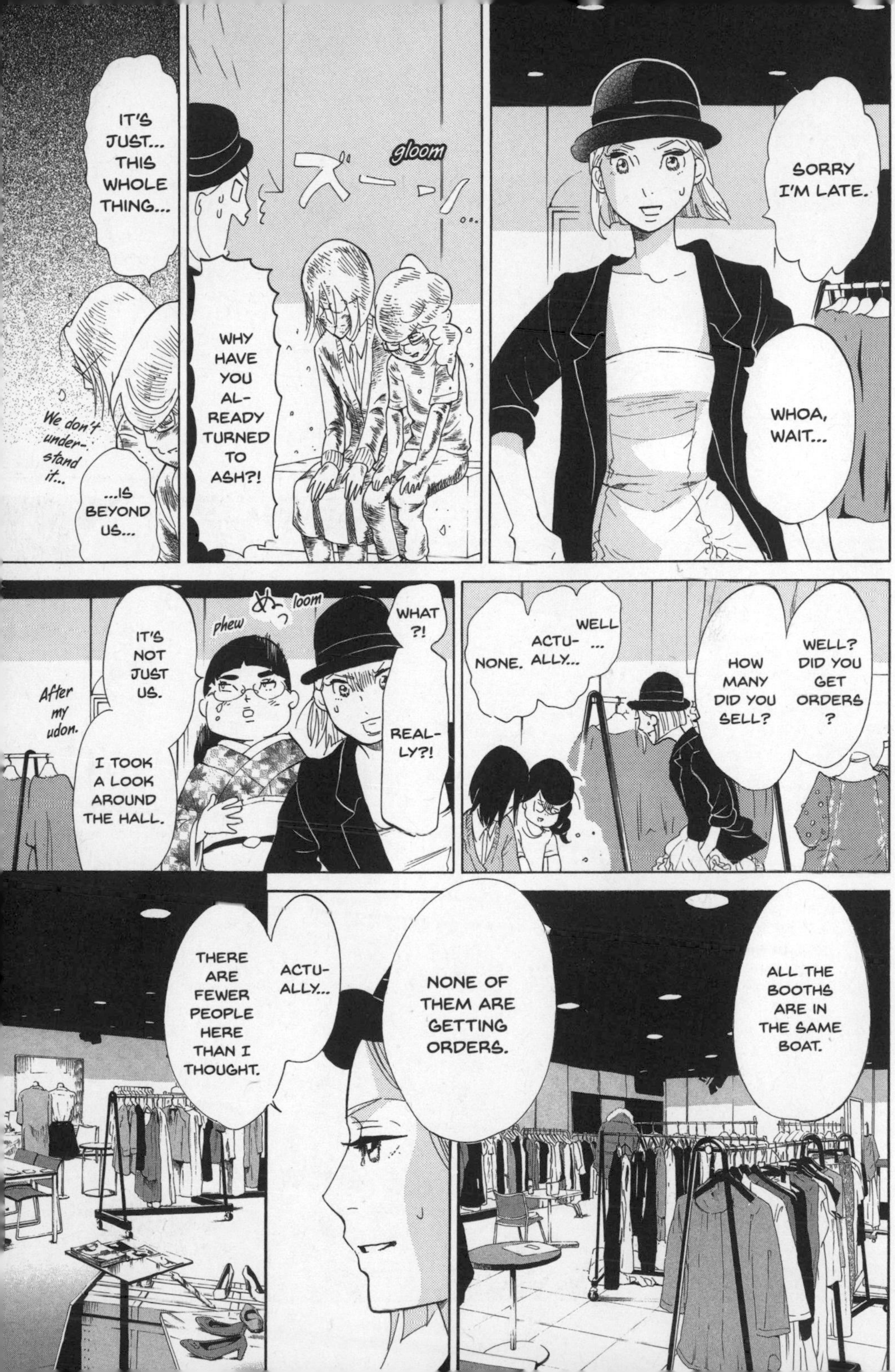
SORRY I'M LATE.
WHOA, WAIT...
gloom
WHY HAVE YOU AL-READY TURNED TO ASH?!
IT'S JUST... THIS WHOLE THING...
We don't under-stand it...
...IS BEYOND US...
WELL? DID YOU GET ORDERS?
HOW MANY DID YOU SELL?
WELL...
ACTU-ALLY...
NONE.
WHAT?!
REAL-LY?!
loom
phew
IT'S NOT JUST US.
After my udon.
I TOOK A LOOK AROUND THE HALL.
ALL THE BOOTHS ARE IN THE SAME BOAT.
NONE OF THEM ARE GETTING ORDERS.
ACTU-ALLY...
THERE ARE FEWER PEOPLE HERE THAN I THOUGHT.

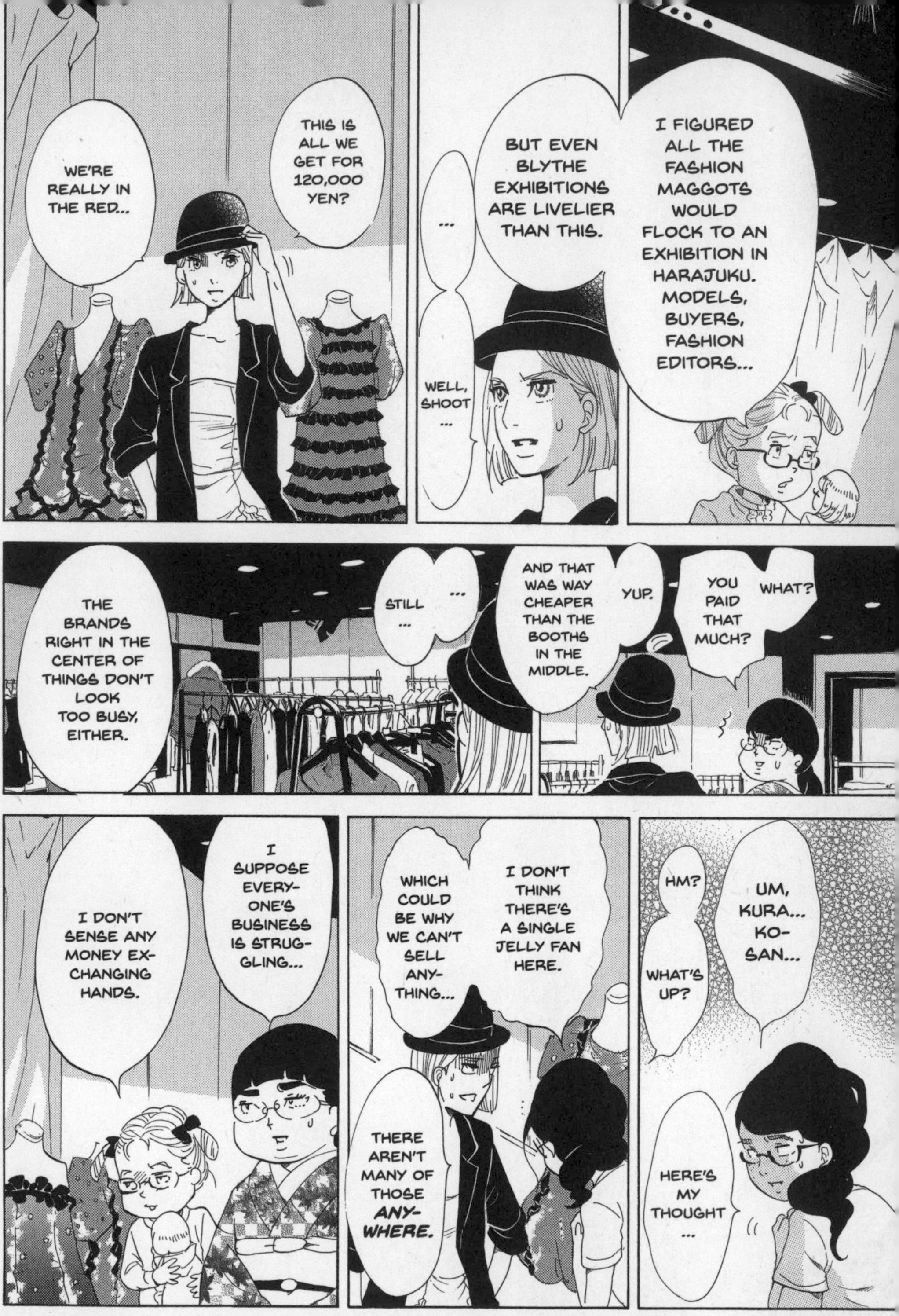
I FIGURED ALL THE FASHION MAGGOTS WOULD FLOCK TO AN EXHIBITION IN HARAJUKU. MODELS, BUYERS, FASHION EDITORS...
BUT EVEN BLYTHE EXHIBITIONS ARE LIVELIER THAN THIS.
...
WELL, SHOOT ...
THIS IS ALL WE GET FOR 120,000 YEN?
WE'RE REALLY IN THE RED...
WHAT?
YOU PAID THAT MUCH?
YUP.
AND THAT WAS WAY CHEAPER THAN THE BOOTHS IN THE MIDDLE.
...
STILL ...
THE BRANDS RIGHT IN THE CENTER OF THINGS DON'T LOOK TOO BUSY, EITHER.
UM, KURA... KO-SAN...
HM?
WHAT'S UP?
HERE'S MY THOUGHT ...
I DON'T THINK THERE'S A SINGLE JELLY FAN HERE.
WHICH COULD BE WHY WE CAN'T SELL ANYTHING...
THERE AREN'T MANY OF THOSE ANYWHERE.
I SUPPOSE EVERYONE'S BUSINESS IS STRUGGLING...
I DON'T SENSE ANY MONEY EXCHANGING HANDS.

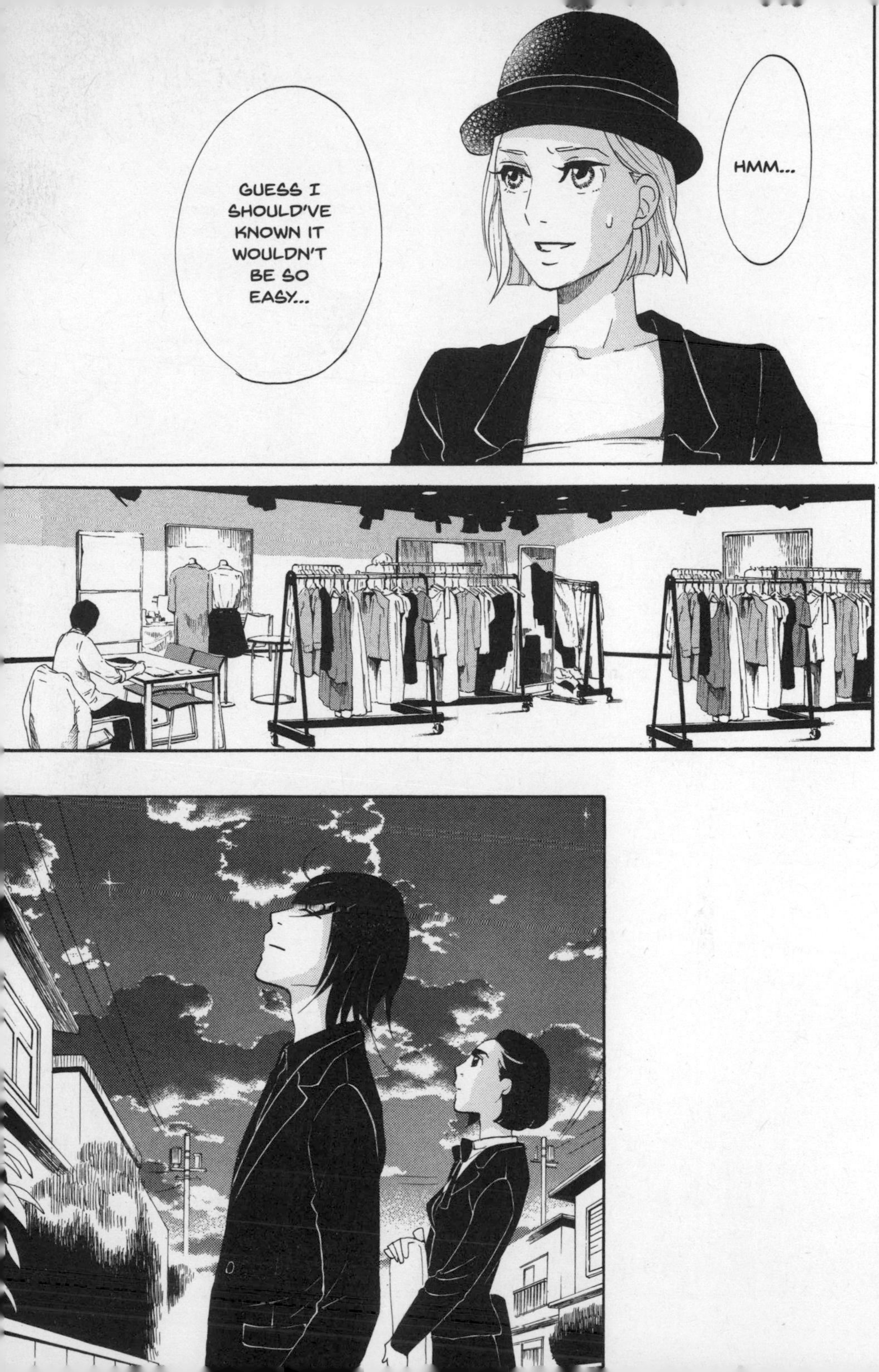
HMM...
GUESS I SHOULD'VE KNOWN IT WOULDN'T BE SO EASY...

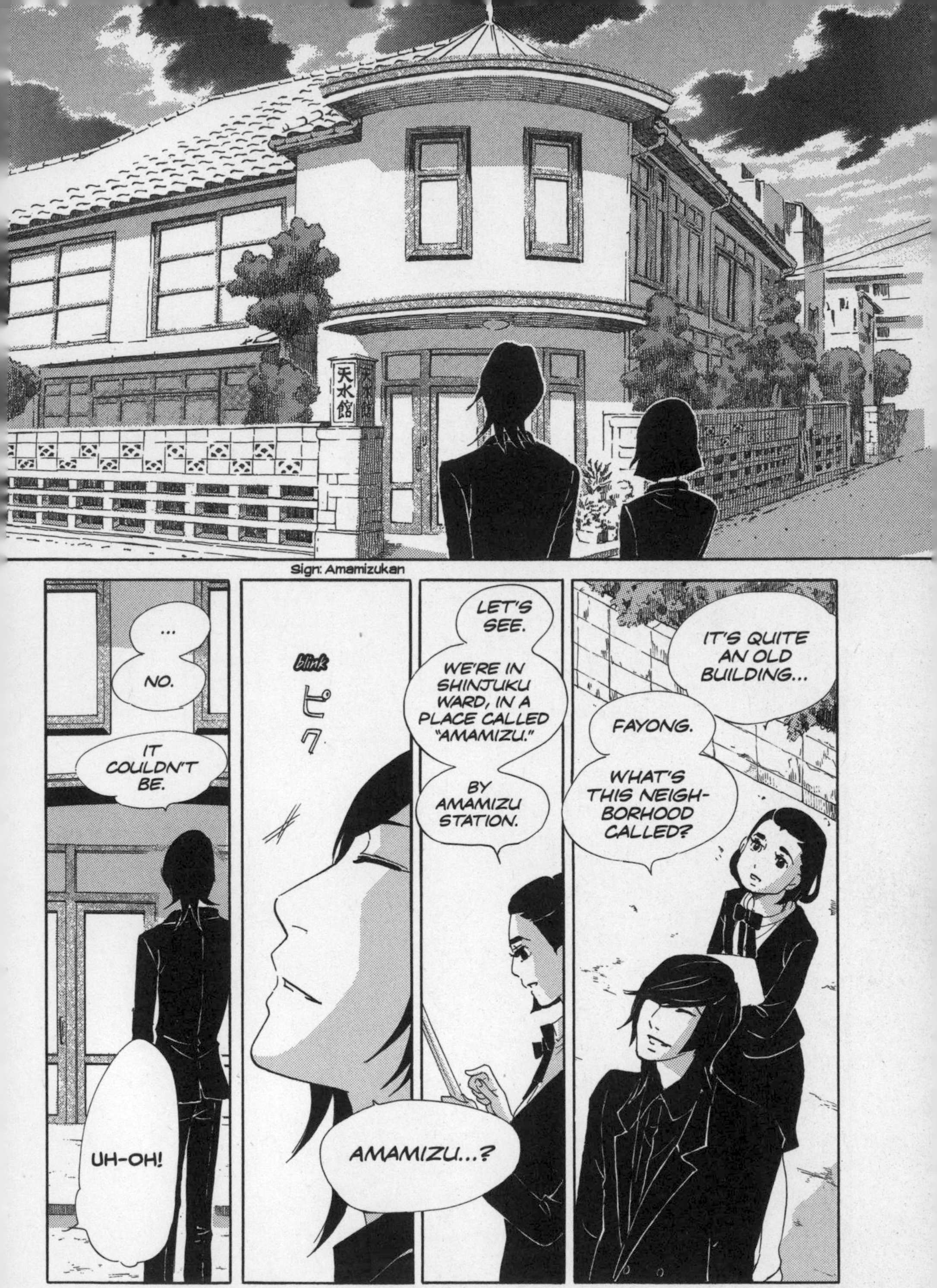
天水館
Sign: Amamizukan
IT'S QUITE AN OLD BUILDING...
FAYONG.
WHAT'S THIS NEIGHBORHOOD CALLED?
LET'S SEE.
WE'RE IN SHINJUKU WARD, IN A PLACE CALLED "AMAMIZU."
BY AMAMIZU STATION.
blink
ピク
AMAMIZU...?
...
NO.
IT COULDN'T BE.
UH-OH!

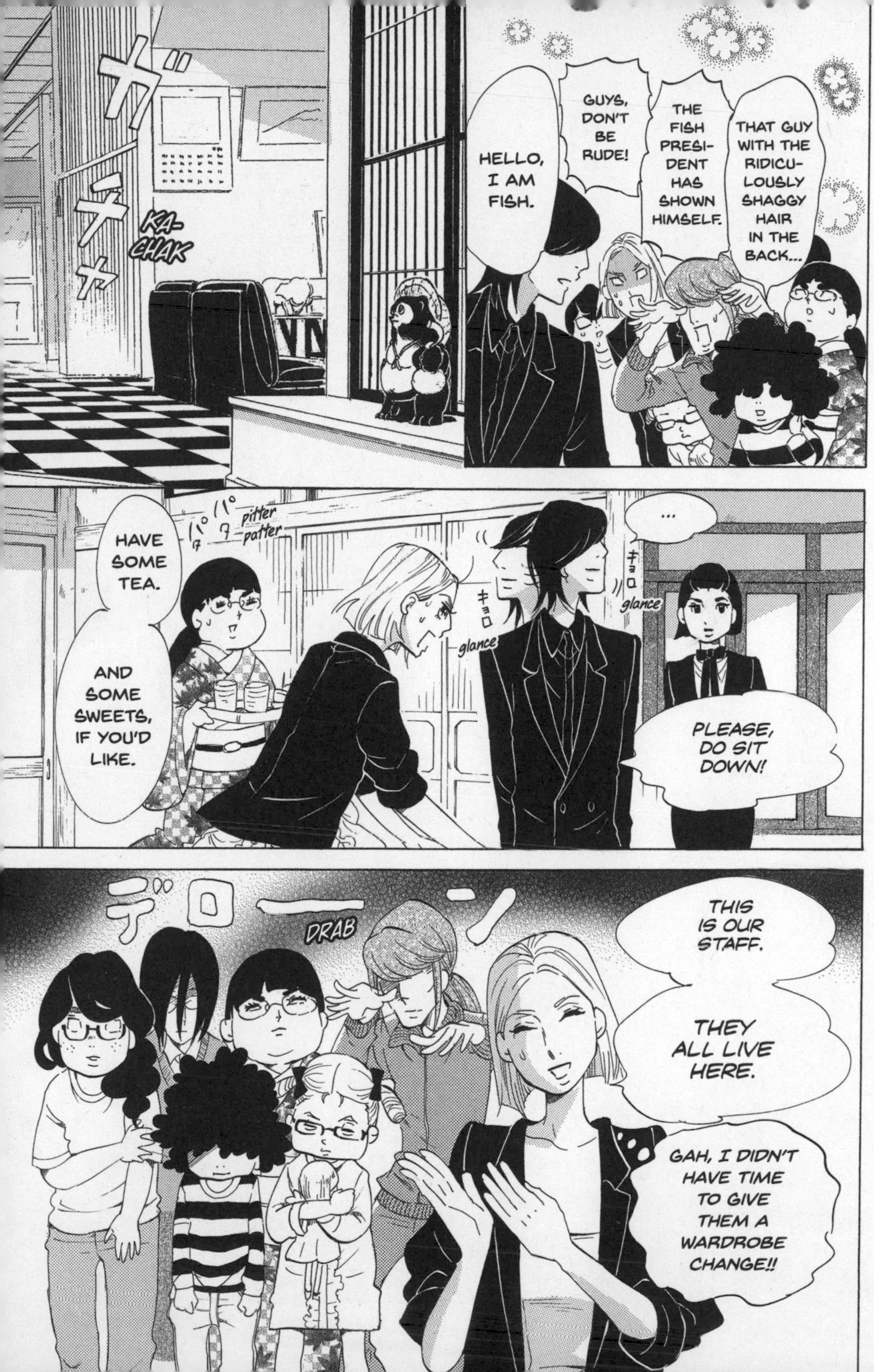
THAT GUY WITH THE RIDICULOUSLY SHAGGY HAIR IN THE BACK...
THE FISH PRESIDENT HAS SHOWN HIMSELF.
GUYS, DON'T BE RUDE!
HELLO, I AM FISH.
ガチャ
KA-CHAK
...
キョロ
glance
PLEASE, DO SIT DOWN!
キョロ
glance
パタパタ
pitter patter
HAVE SOME TEA.
AND SOME SWEETS, IF YOU'D LIKE.
THIS IS OUR STAFF.
THEY ALL LIVE HERE.
GAH, I DIDN'T HAVE TIME TO GIVE THEM A WARDROBE CHANGE!!
デローン
DRAB

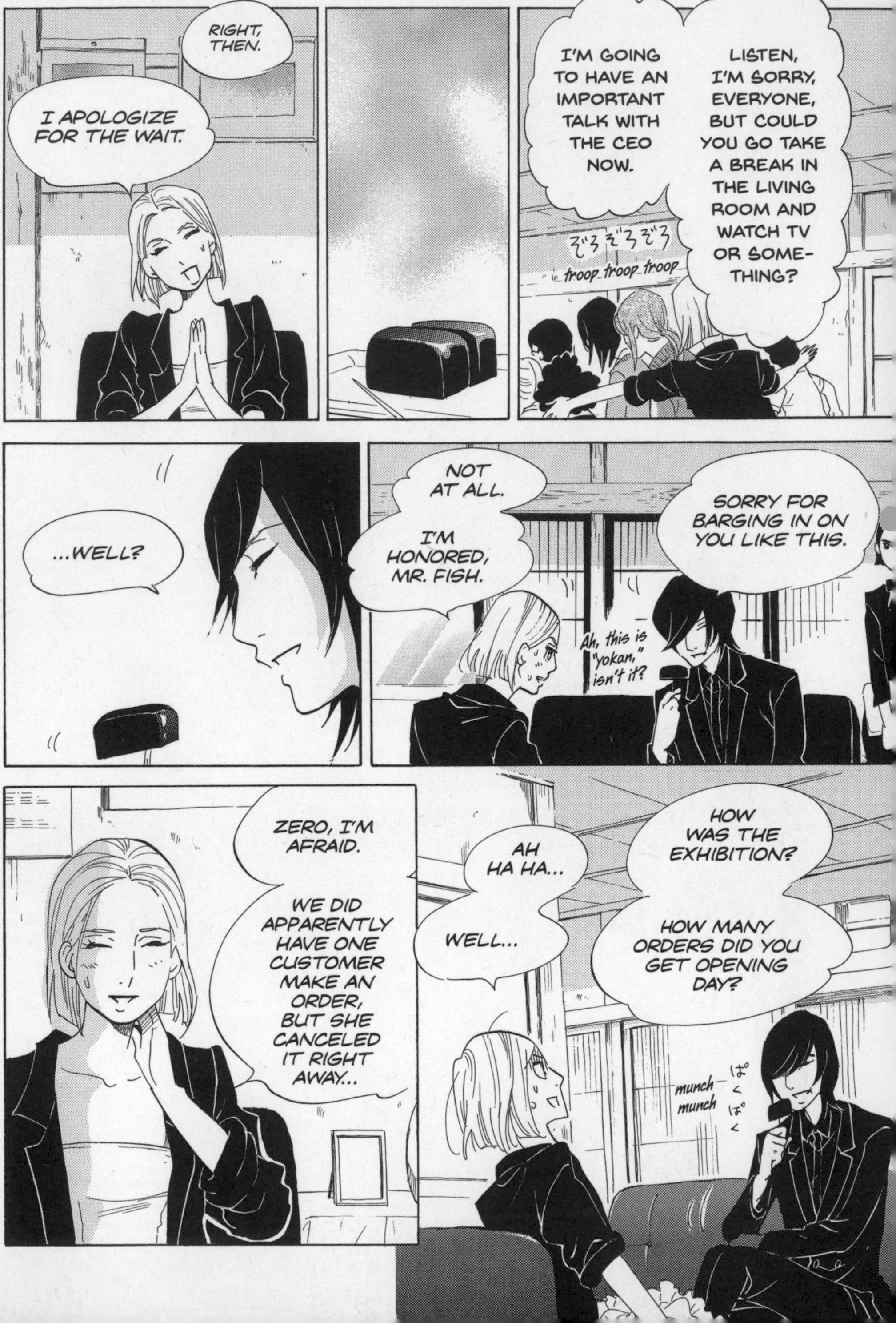
LISTEN, I'M SORRY, EVERYONE, BUT COULD YOU GO TAKE A BREAK IN THE LIVING ROOM AND WATCH TV OR SOME-THING?
I'M GOING TO HAVE AN IMPORTANT TALK WITH THE CEO NOW.
ぞろぞろぞろ
troop troop troop
RIGHT, THEN.
I APOLOGIZE FOR THE WAIT.
SORRY FOR BARGING IN ON YOU LIKE THIS.
NOT AT ALL.
I'M HONORED, MR. FISH.
Ah, this is "yokan," isn't it?
...WELL?
HOW WAS THE EXHIBITION?
HOW MANY ORDERS DID YOU GET OPENING DAY?
AH HA HA...
WELL...
ぱくぱく
munch munch
ZERO, I'M AFRAID.
WE DID APPARENTLY HAVE ONE CUSTOMER MAKE AN ORDER, BUT SHE CANCELED IT RIGHT AWAY...

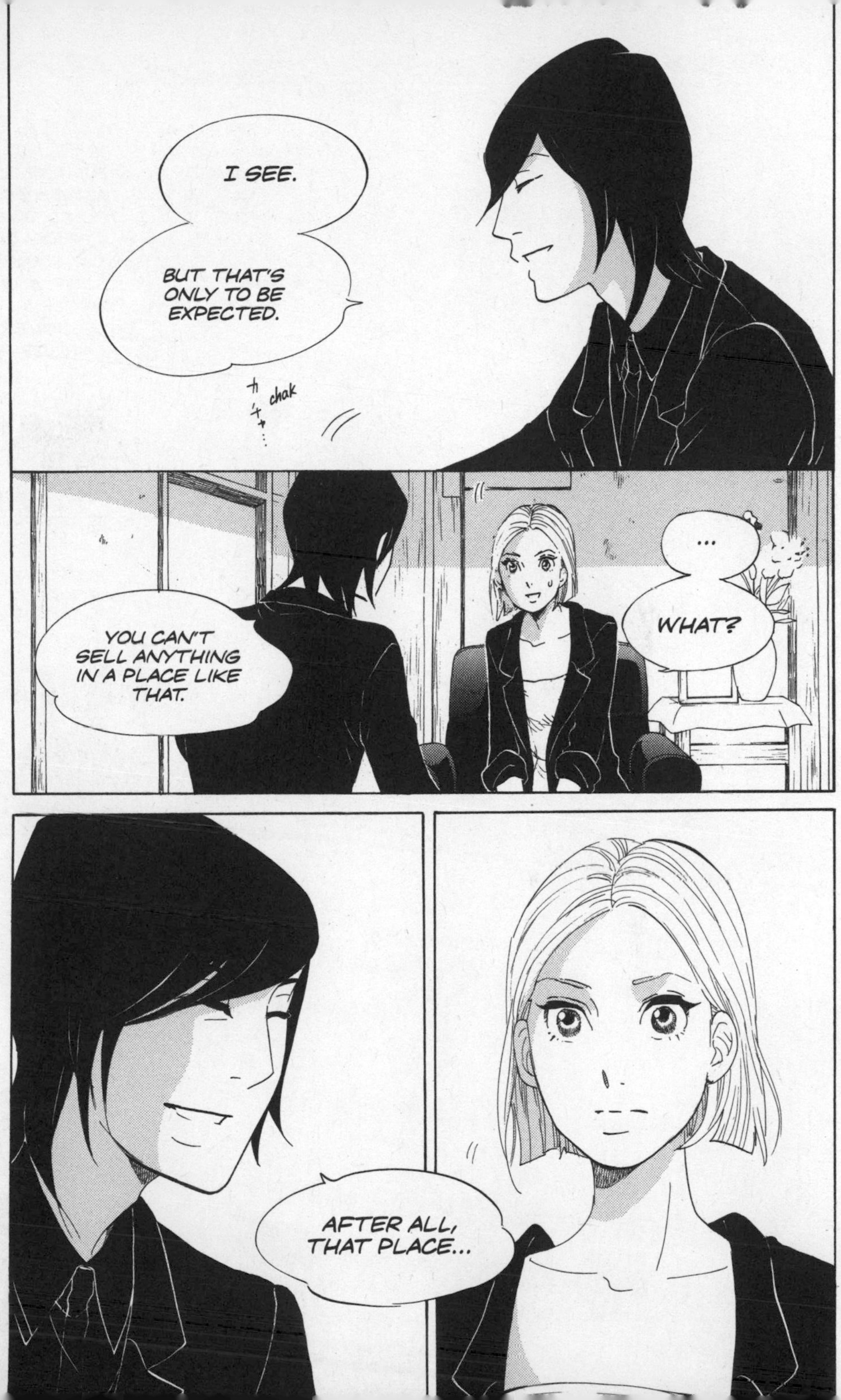
I SEE.
BUT THAT'S ONLY TO BE EXPECTED.
カチャ…
chak
...
WHAT?
YOU CAN'T SELL ANYTHING IN A PLACE LIKE THAT.
AFTER ALL, THAT PLACE...

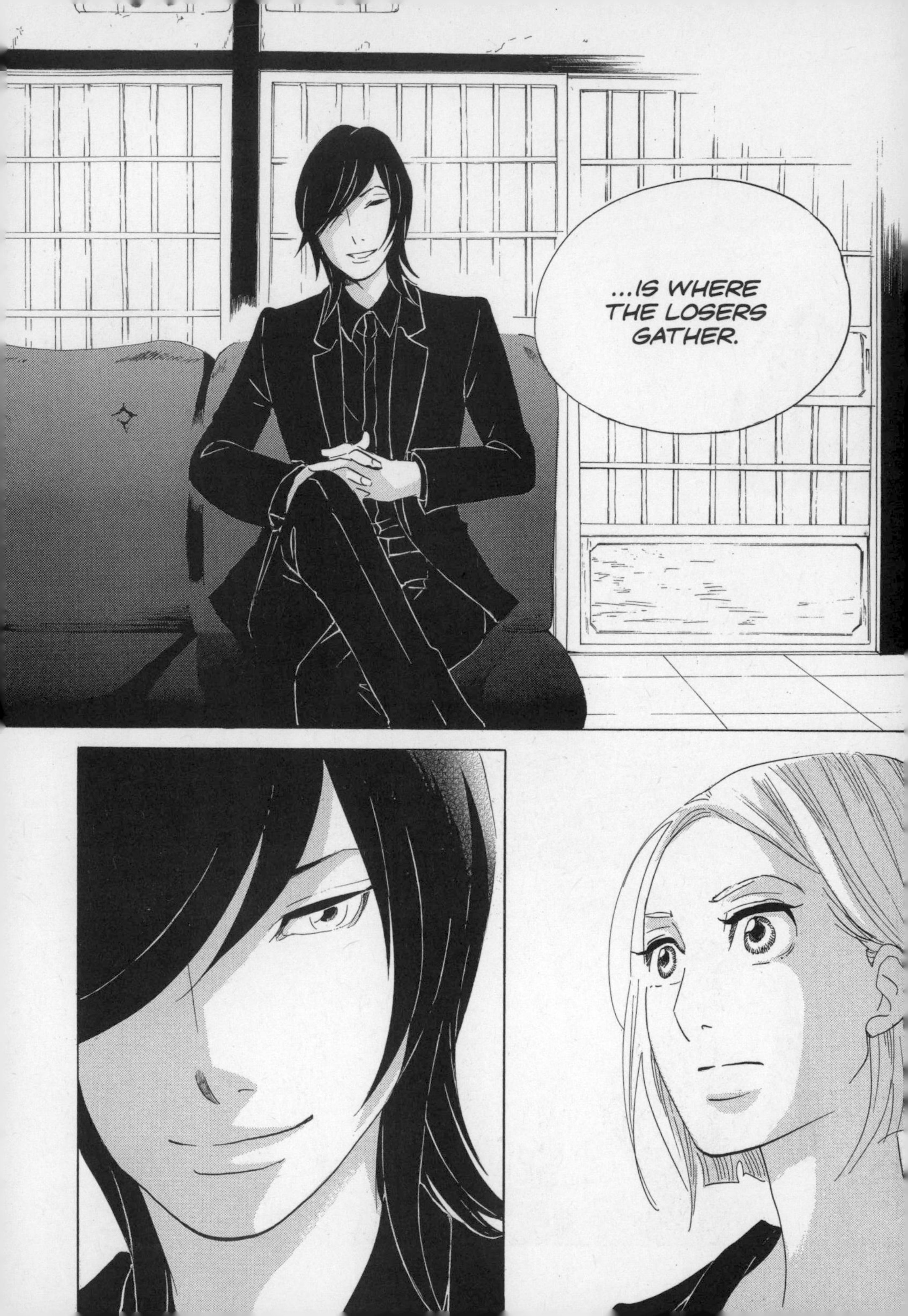
...IS WHERE THE LOSERS GATHER.

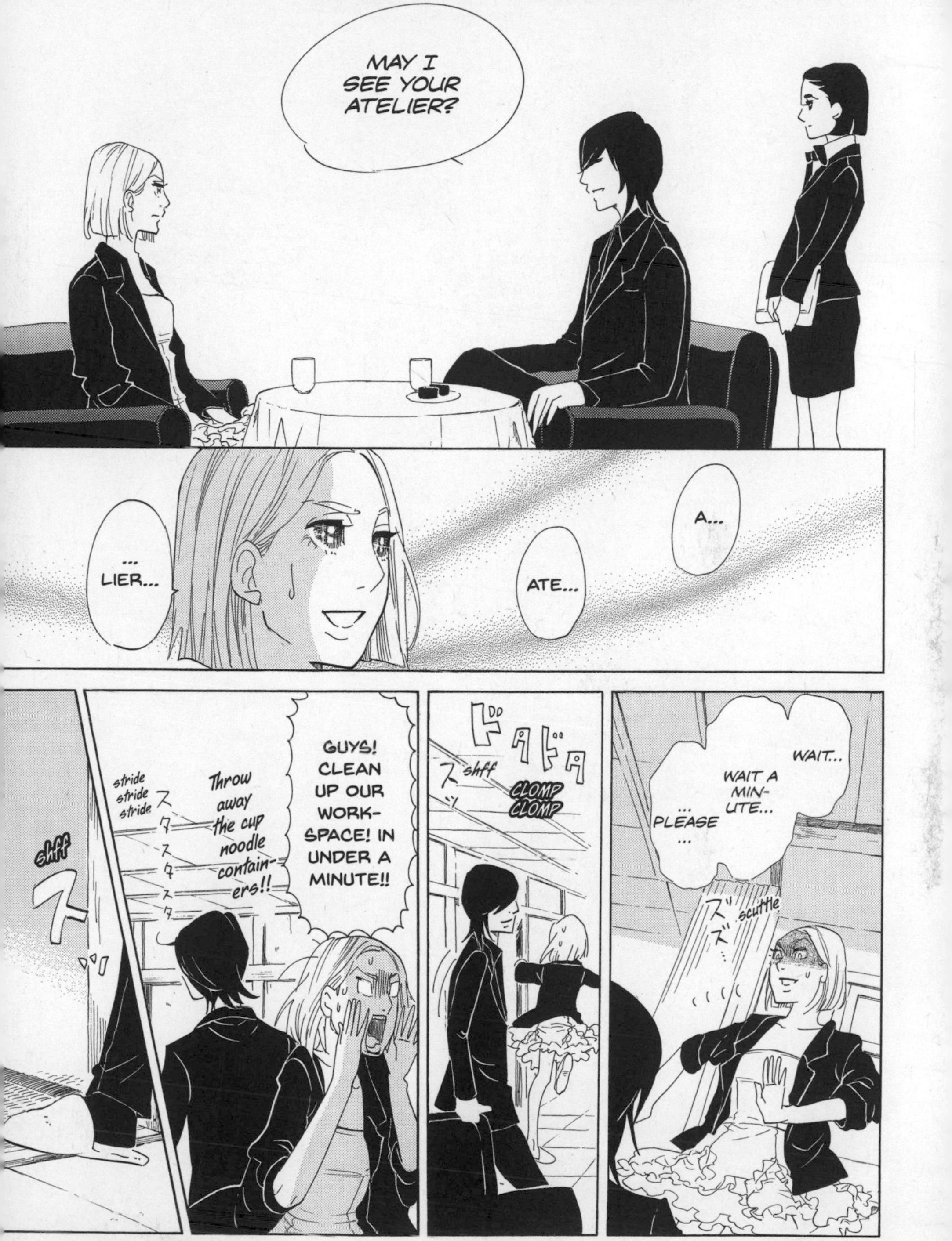
MAY I SEE YOUR ATELIER?
A...
ATE...
...LIER...
WAIT...
WAIT A MIN-UTE...
...PLEASE...
scuttle
shff
CLOMP CLOMP
GUYS! CLEAN UP OUR WORK-SPACE! IN UNDER A MINUTE!!
Throw away the cup noodle contain-ers!!
stride stride stride
shff

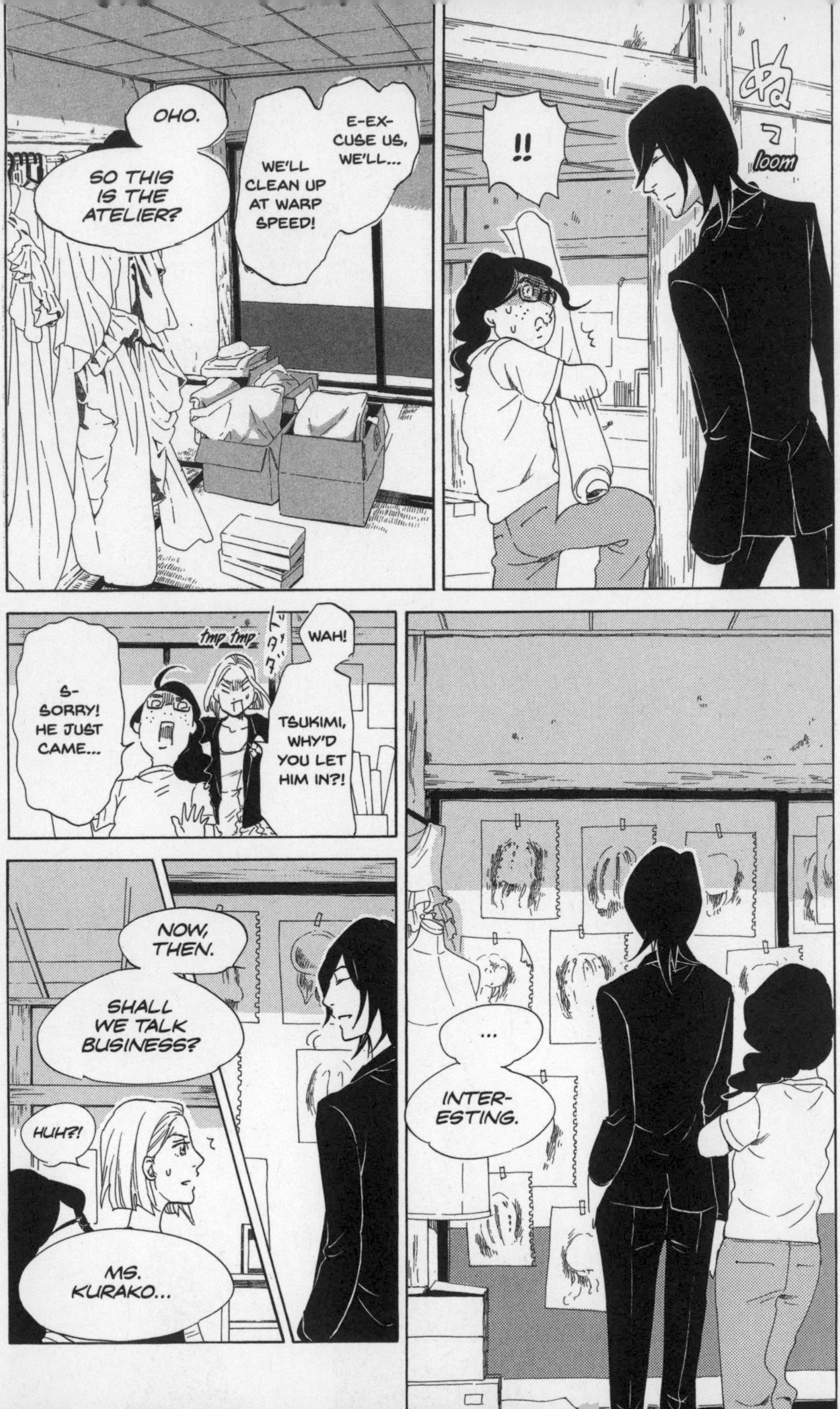

!!
loom
E-EXCUSE US, WE'LL...
WE'LL CLEAN UP AT WARP SPEED!
OHO.
SO THIS IS THE ATELIER?
...
INTERESTING.
WAH!
TSUKIMI, WHY'D YOU LET HIM IN?!
tmp tmp
S-SORRY! HE JUST CAME...
NOW, THEN.
SHALL WE TALK BUSINESS?
HUH?!
MS. KURAKO...

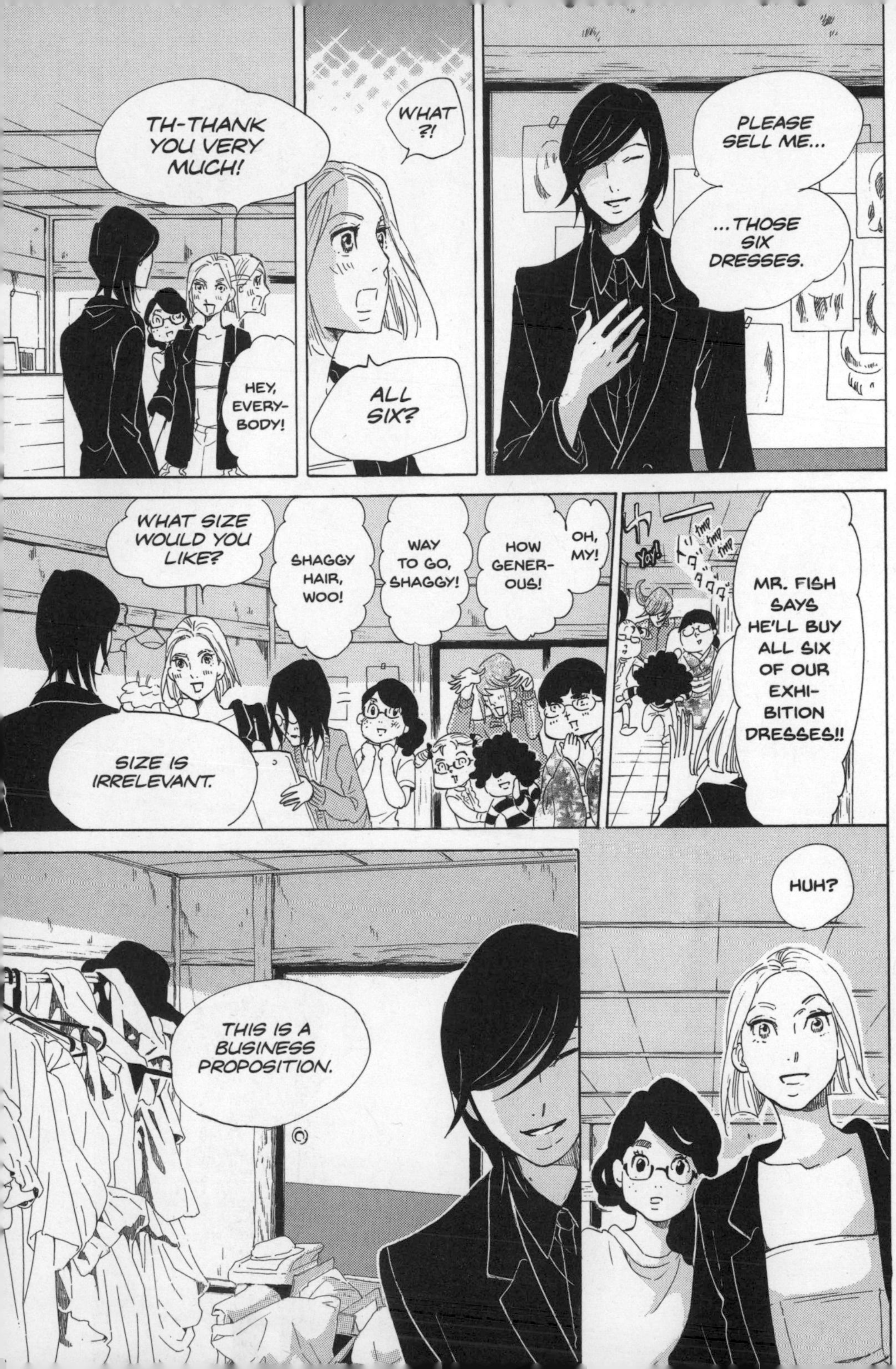
PLEASE SELL ME...
...THOSE SIX DRESSES.
WHAT ?!
ALL SIX?
TH-THANK YOU VERY MUCH!
HEY, EVERY-BODY!
Yay!
tmp tmp tmp
MR. FISH SAYS HE'LL BUY ALL SIX OF OUR EXHI-BITION DRESSES!!
OH, MY!
HOW GENER-OUS!
WAY TO GO, SHAGGY!
SHAGGY HAIR, WOO!
WHAT SIZE WOULD YOU LIKE?
SIZE IS IRRELEVANT.
HUH?
THIS IS A BUSINESS PROPOSITION.

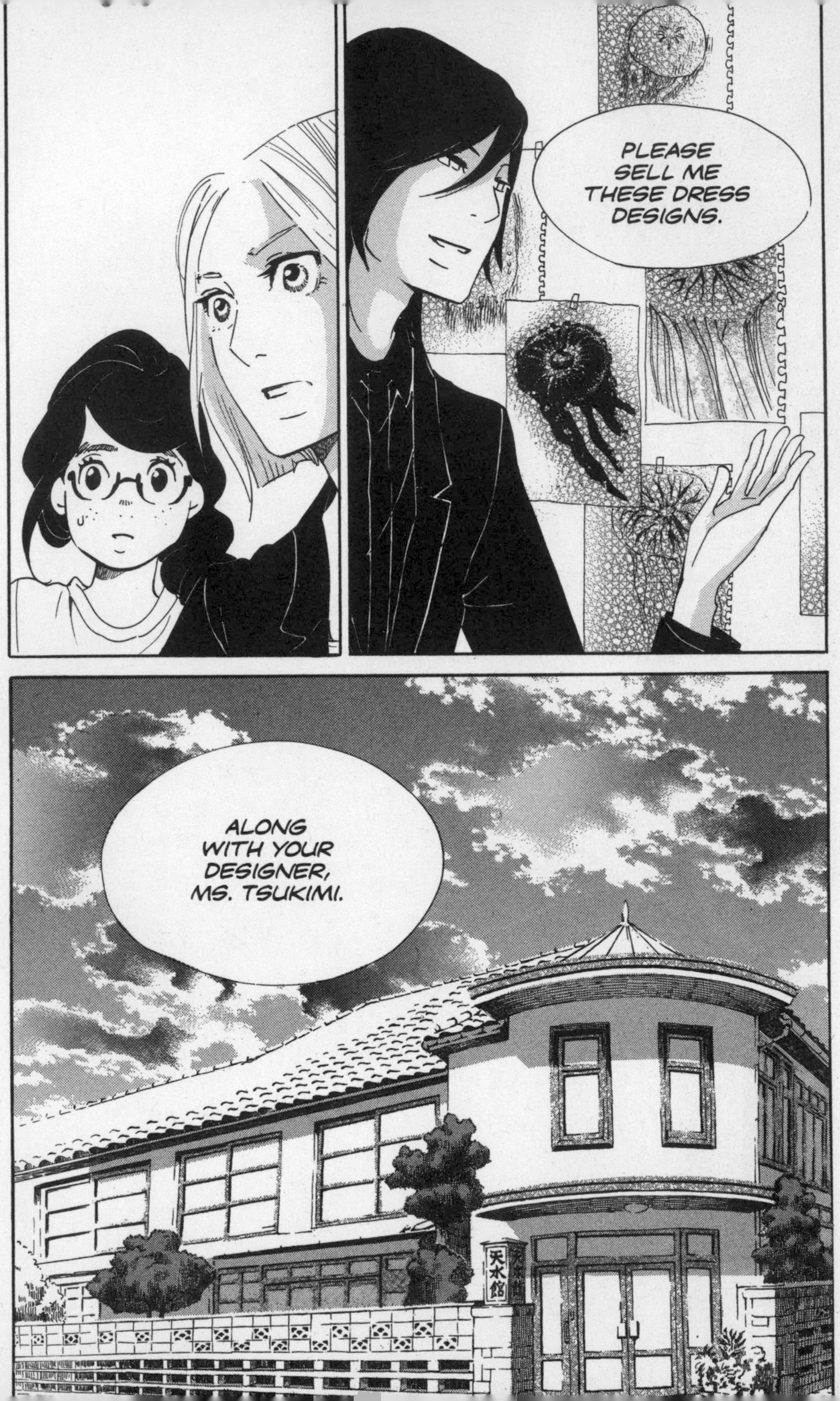
PLEASE SELL ME THESE DRESS DESIGNS.
ALONG WITH YOUR DESIGNER, MS. TSUKIMI.
天水館

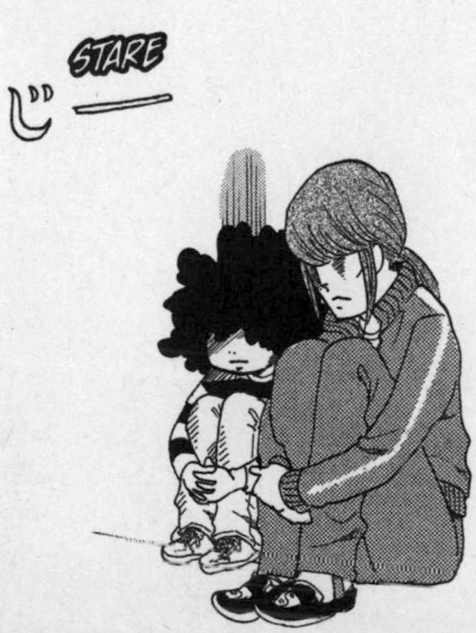
STARE
じー

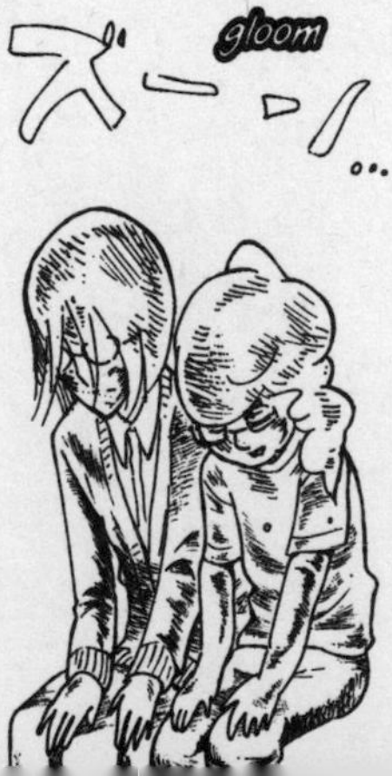
ズーン…
gloom

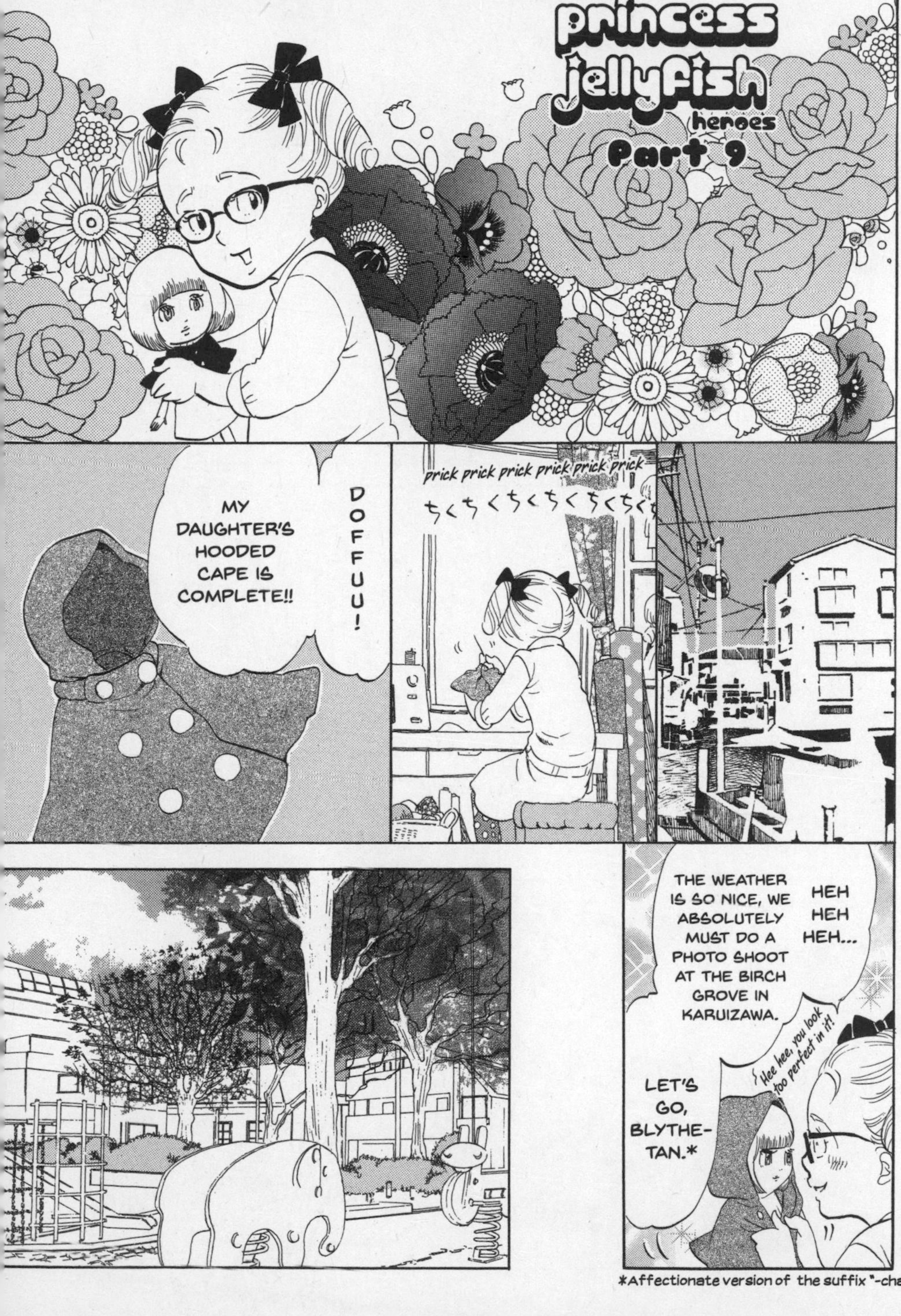
princess jellyfish heroes
Part 9
prick prick prick prick prick prick
ちくちくちくちくちくちく
DOFFUU!
MY DAUGHTER'S HOODED CAPE IS COMPLETE!!
HEH HEH HEH...
THE WEATHER IS SO NICE, WE ABSOLUTELY MUST DO A PHOTO SHOOT AT THE BIRCH GROVE IN KARUIZAWA.
Hee hee, you look too perfect in it!
LET'S GO, BLYTHE-TAN.*

*Affectionate version of the suffix "-chan."

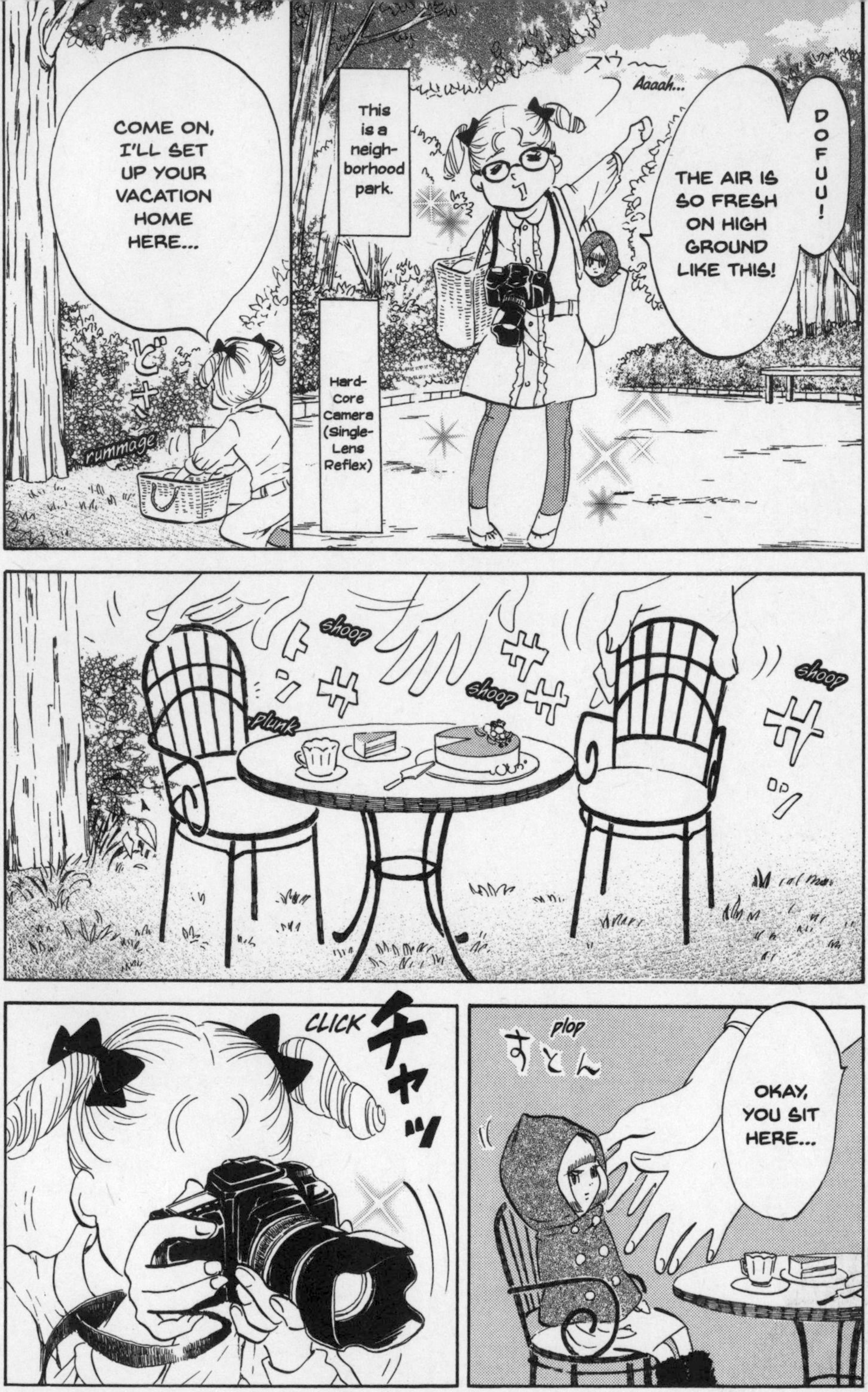
DOFUU!
スウ〜
Aaaah...
THE AIR IS SO FRESH ON HIGH GROUND LIKE THIS!
This is a neighborhood park.
Hard-Core Camera (Single-Lens Reflex)
COME ON, I'LL SET UP YOUR VACATION HOME HERE...
rummage
shoop
サ
shoop
サ
サ
shoop
トン
サ
plunk
plop
すとん
OKAY, YOU SIT HERE...
CLICK
チャッ

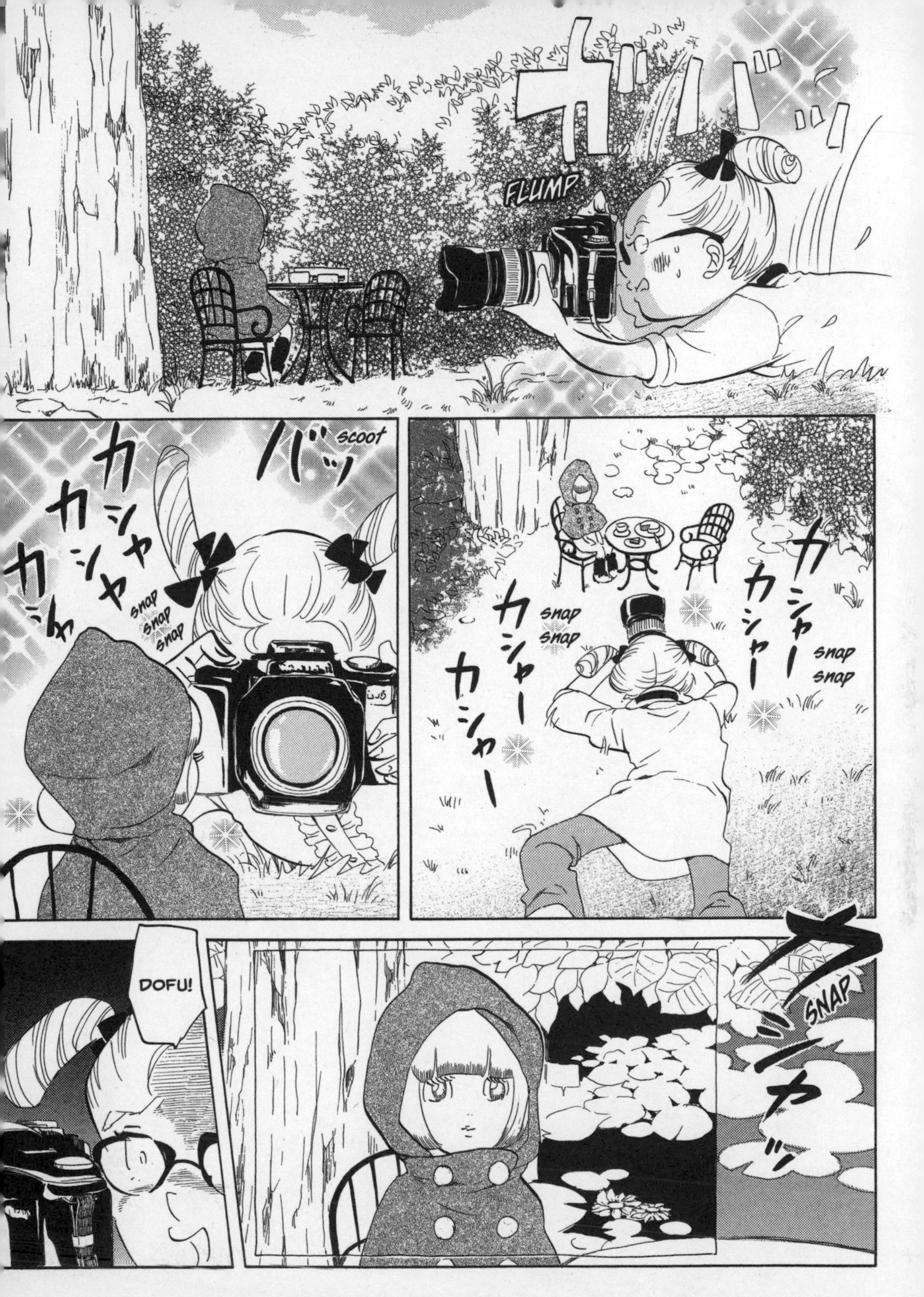

FLUMP
カシャー
カシャー
snap snap
カシャー
カシャー
snap snap
バッ
scoot
カシャ
カシャ
カシャ
snap
snap
snap
SNAP
DOFU!

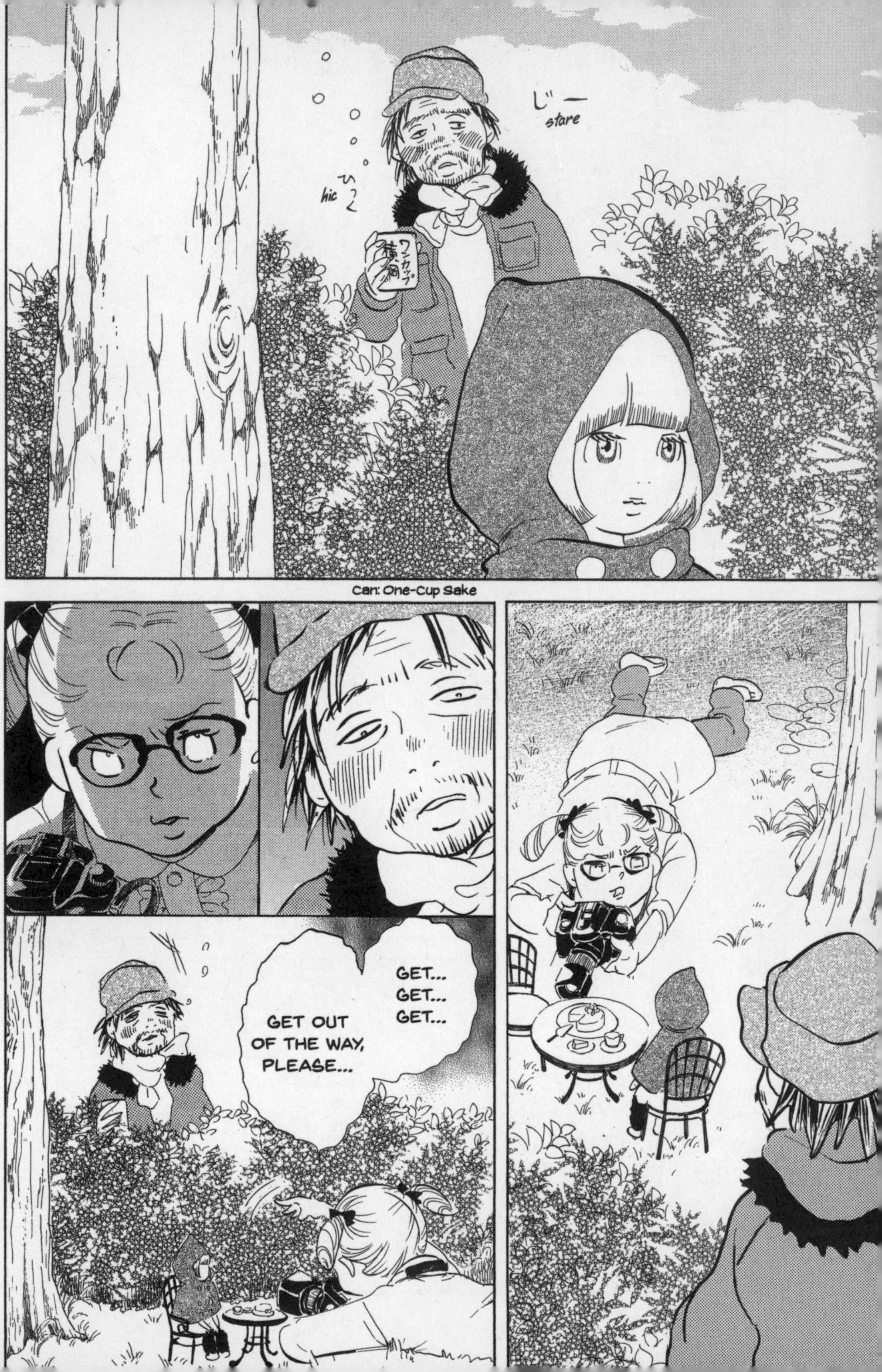

じー
stare
ひっく
hic
ワンカップ
Can: One-Cup Sake
GET... GET... GET...
GET OUT OF THE WAY, PLEASE...

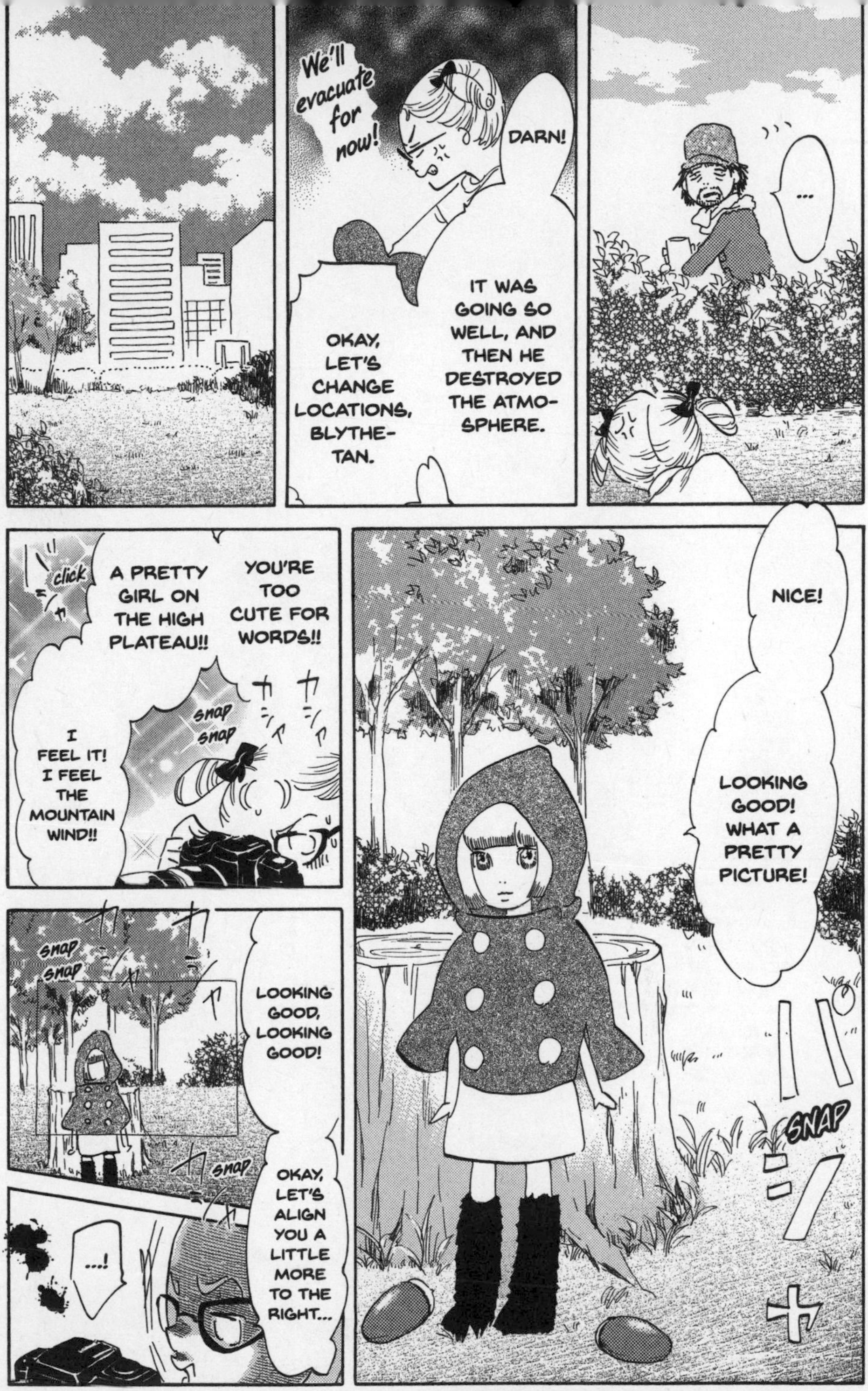
...
DARN!
We'll evacuate for now!
IT WAS GOING SO WELL, AND THEN HE DESTROYED THE ATMO-SPHERE.
OKAY, LET'S CHANGE LOCATIONS, BLYTHE-TAN.
NICE!
LOOKING GOOD! WHAT A PRETTY PICTURE!
SNAP
click
YOU'RE TOO CUTE FOR WORDS!!
A PRETTY GIRL ON THE HIGH PLATEAU!!
snap snap
I FEEL IT! I FEEL THE MOUNTAIN WIND!!
LOOKING GOOD, LOOKING GOOD!
snap snap
snap
OKAY, LET'S ALIGN YOU A LITTLE MORE TO THE RIGHT...
...!

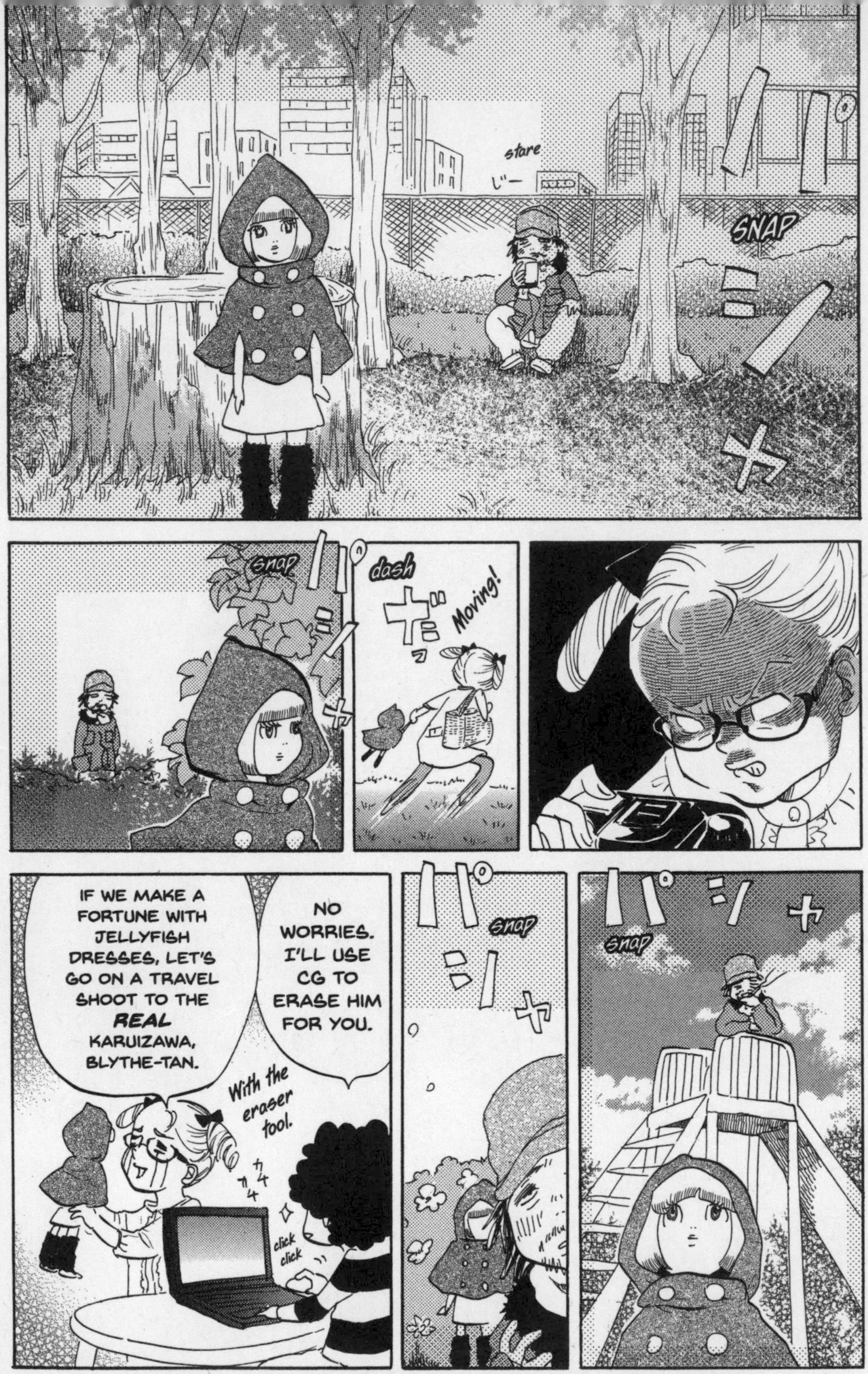
stare
じー
SNAP
dash
Moving!
snap
snap
snap
NO WORRIES. I'LL USE CG TO ERASE HIM FOR YOU.
IF WE MAKE A FORTUNE WITH JELLYFISH DRESSES, LET'S GO ON A TRAVEL SHOOT TO THE **REAL** KARUIZAWA, BLYTHE-TAN.
With the eraser tool.
click click

Princess Jellyfish Heroes Part 9/End

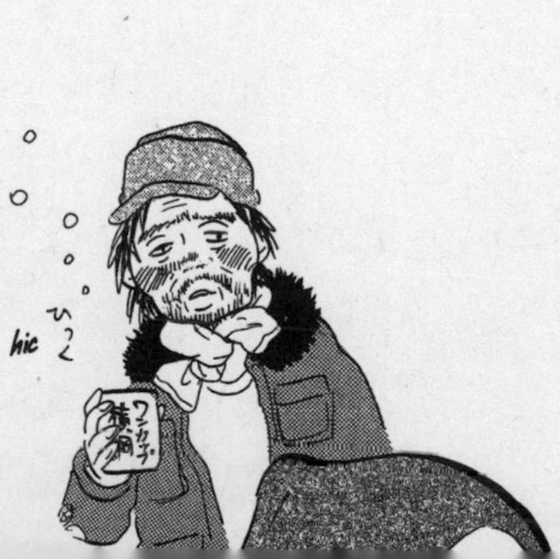
ワンカップ
ひっく
hic

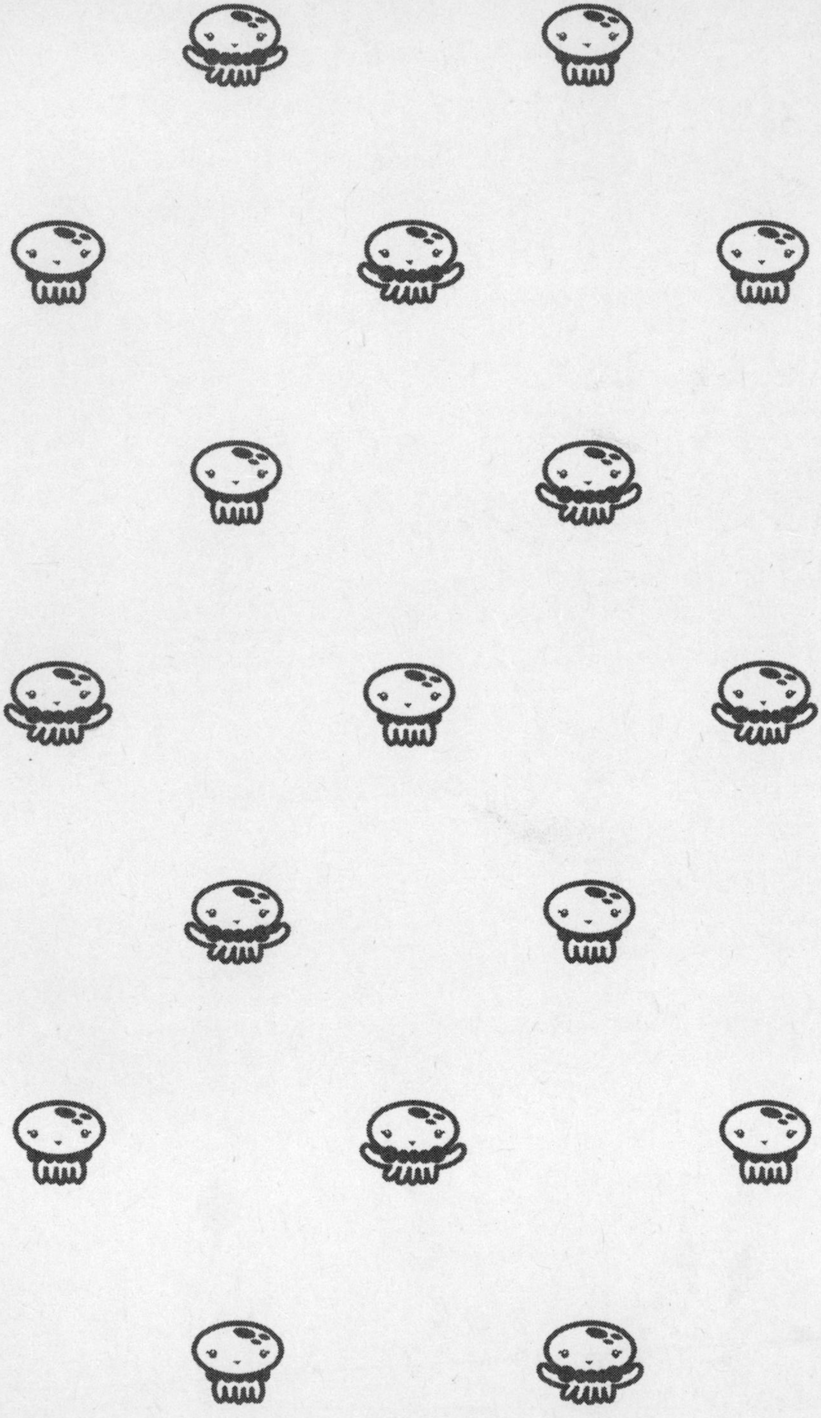

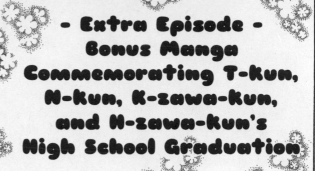

- Extra Episode - Bonus Manga Commemorating T-Kun, N-Kun, K-zawa-Kun, and H-zawa-Kun's High School Graduation

Akiko Higashimura

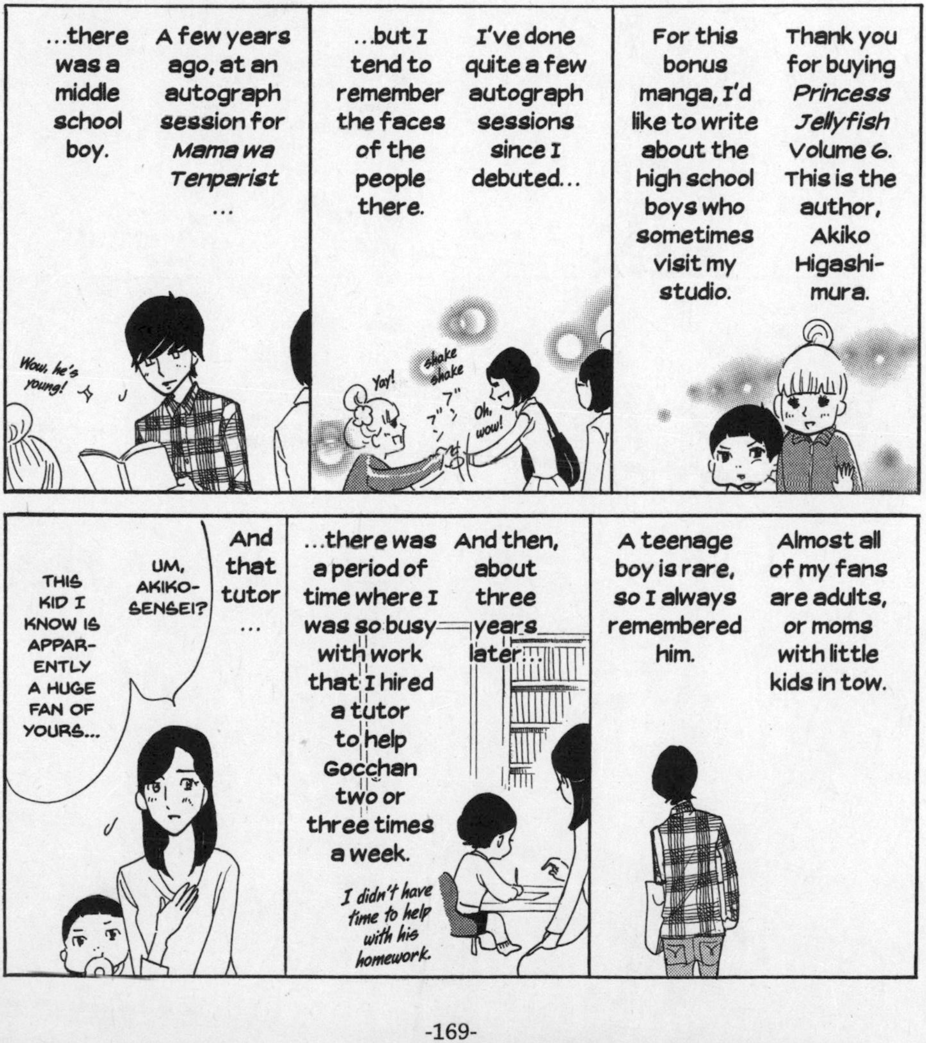
Thank you for buying *Princess Jellyfish* Volume 6. This is the author, Akiko Higashimura.
For this bonus manga, I'd like to write about the high school boys who sometimes visit my studio.
I've done quite a few autograph sessions since I debuted...
...but I tend to remember the faces of the people there.
shake shake
Yay!
Oh, wow!
A few years ago, at an autograph session for *Mama wa Tenparist*...
...there was a middle school boy.
Wow, he's young!
Almost all of my fans are adults, or moms with little kids in tow.
A teenage boy is rare, so I always remembered him.
And then, about three years later...
...there was a period of time where I was so busy with work that I hired a tutor to help Gocchan two or three times a week.
I didn't have time to help with his homework.
And that tutor...
UM, AKIKO-SENSEI?
THIS KID I KNOW IS APPARENTLY A HUGE FAN OF YOURS...

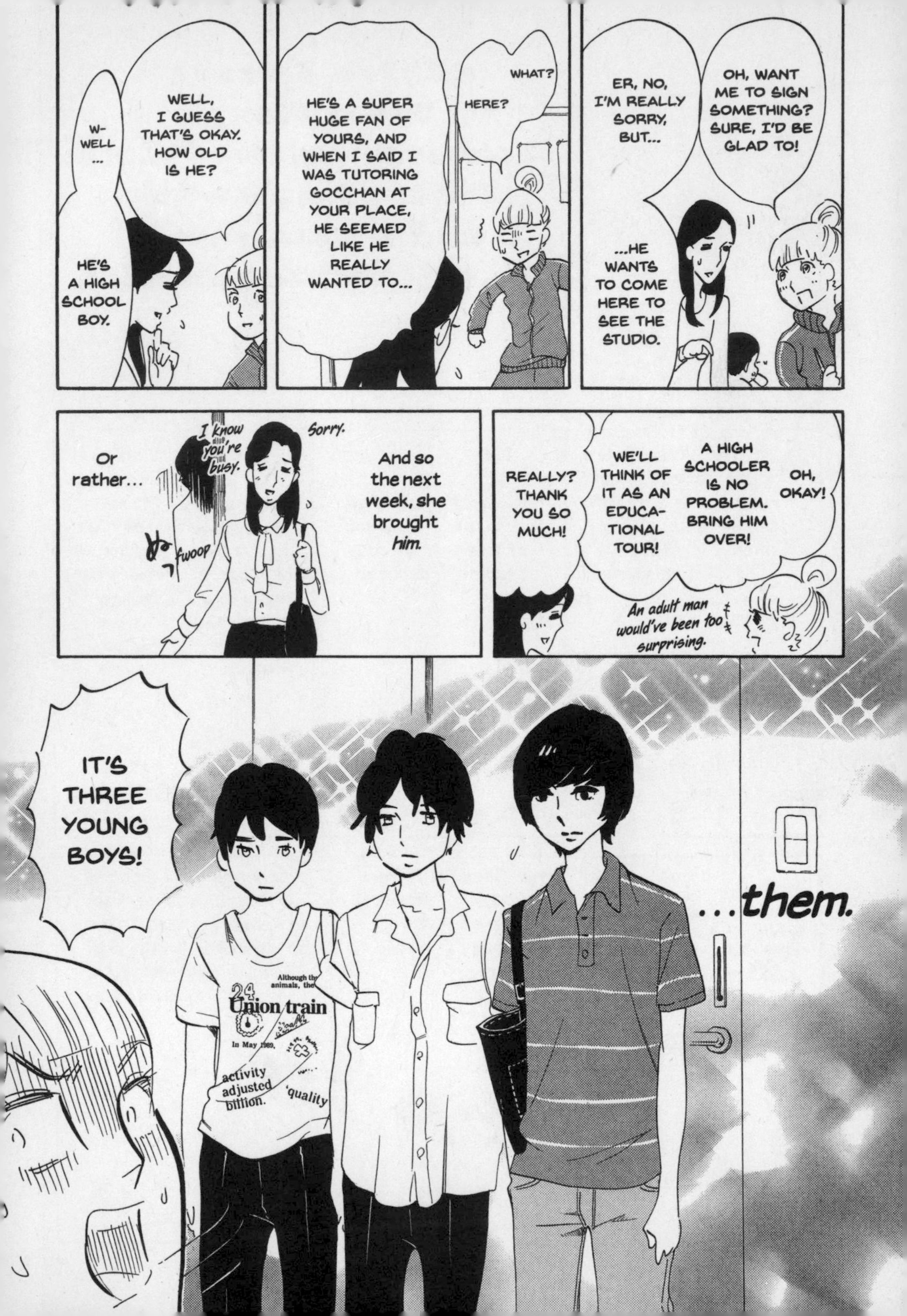
OH, WANT ME TO SIGN SOMETHING? SURE, I'D BE GLAD TO!
ER, NO, I'M REALLY SORRY, BUT...
...HE WANTS TO COME HERE TO SEE THE STUDIO.
WHAT?
HERE?
HE'S A SUPER HUGE FAN OF YOURS, AND WHEN I SAID I WAS TUTORING GOCCHAN AT YOUR PLACE, HE SEEMED LIKE HE REALLY WANTED TO...
WELL, I GUESS THAT'S OKAY. HOW OLD IS HE?
W-WELL...
HE'S A HIGH SCHOOL BOY.
OH, OKAY!
A HIGH SCHOOLER IS NO PROBLEM. BRING HIM OVER!
WE'LL THINK OF IT AS AN EDUCATIONAL TOUR!
REALLY? THANK YOU SO MUCH!
An adult man would've been too surprising.
Sorry.
I know you're busy.
And so the next week, she brought him.
Or rather...
fwoop
...them.
IT'S THREE YOUNG BOYS!
24
Although th
animals, the
Union train
In May 1989,
activity adjusted billion.
'quality

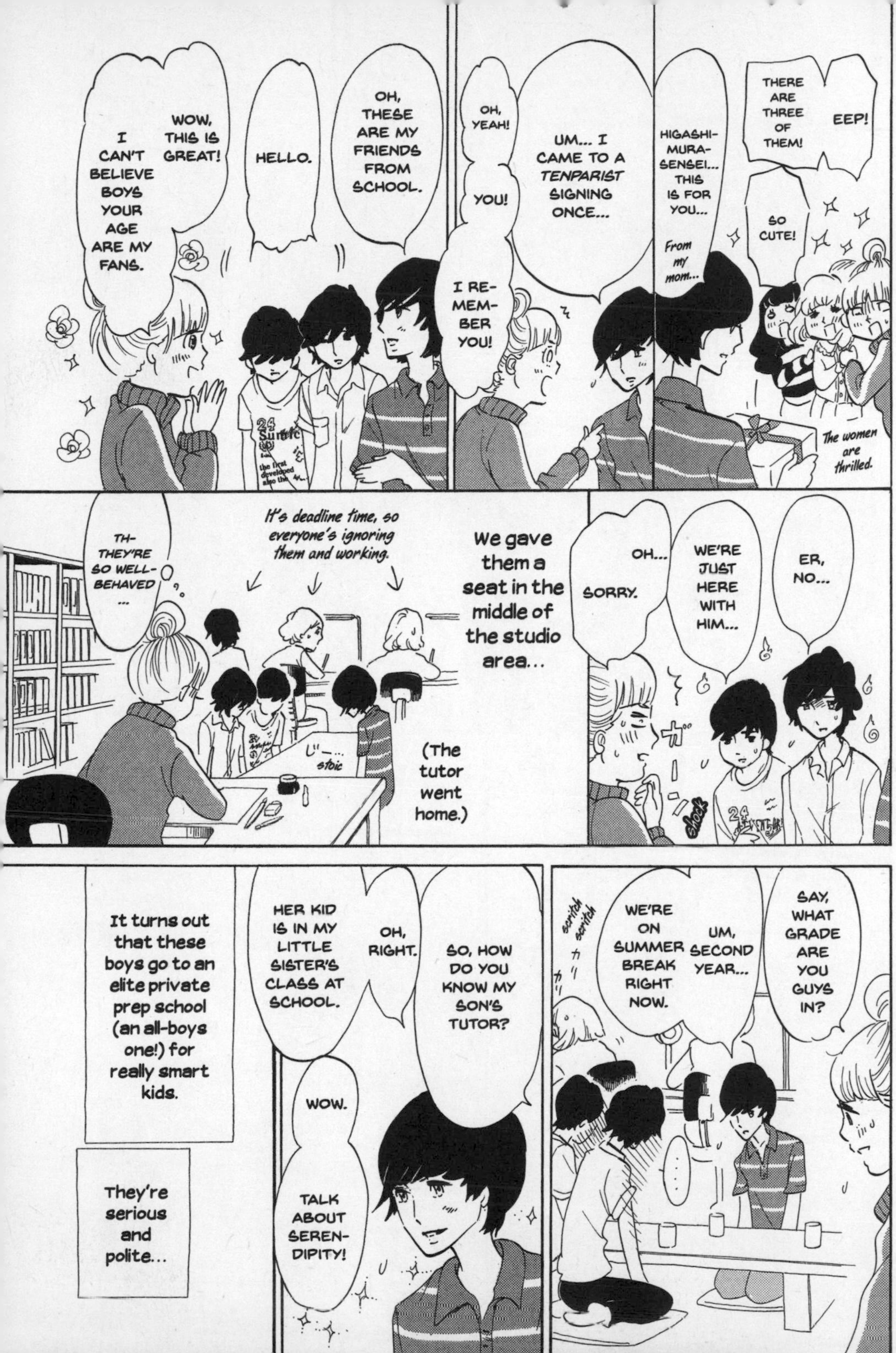
EEP!
THERE ARE THREE OF THEM!
HIGASHIMURA-SENSEI... THIS IS FOR YOU...
From my mom...
SO CUTE!
The women are thrilled.
UM... I CAME TO A *TENPARIST* SIGNING ONCE...
OH, YEAH! YOU!
I REMEMBER YOU!
OH, THESE ARE MY FRIENDS FROM SCHOOL.
HELLO.
WOW, THIS IS GREAT!
I CAN'T BELIEVE BOYS YOUR AGE ARE MY FANS.
ER, NO...
WE'RE JUST HERE WITH HIM...
OH...
SORRY.
shock
We gave them a seat in the middle of the studio area...
It's deadline time, so everyone's ignoring them and working.
TH-THEY'RE SO WELL-BEHAVED...
stoic
(The tutor went home.)
SAY, WHAT GRADE ARE YOU GUYS IN?
UM, SECOND YEAR...
WE'RE ON SUMMER BREAK RIGHT NOW.
scritch scritch
SO, HOW DO YOU KNOW MY SON'S TUTOR?
OH, RIGHT.
HER KID IS IN MY LITTLE SISTER'S CLASS AT SCHOOL.
WOW.
TALK ABOUT SERENDIPITY!
It turns out that these boys go to an elite private prep school (an all-boys one!) for really smart kids.
They're serious and polite...

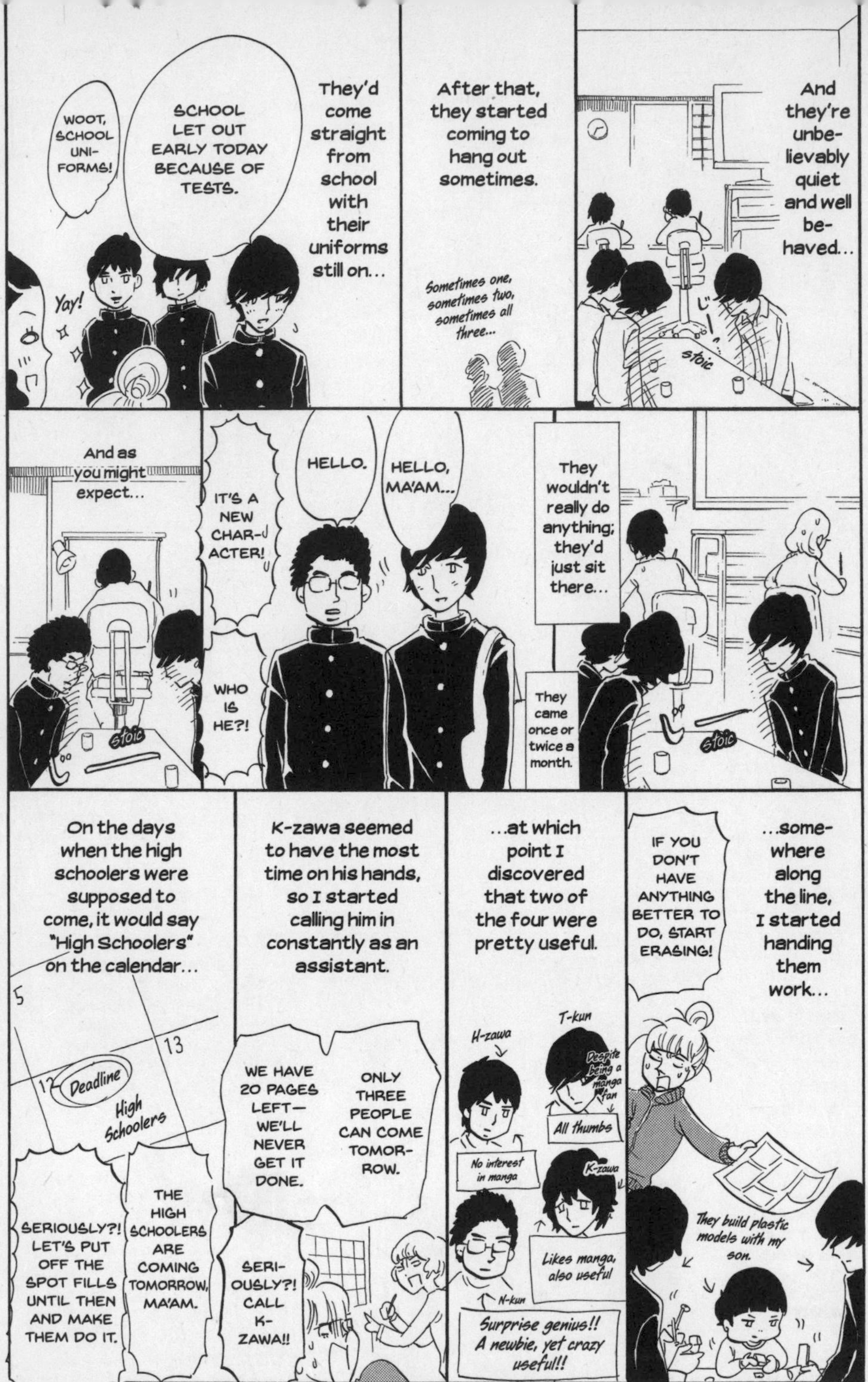
And they're unbe-lievably quiet and well be-haved...
stoic
After that, they started coming to hang out sometimes.
Sometimes one, sometimes two, sometimes all three...
They'd come straight from school with their uniforms still on...
SCHOOL LET OUT EARLY TODAY BECAUSE OF TESTS.
WOOT, SCHOOL UNI-FORMS!
Yay!
They wouldn't really do anything; they'd just sit there...
They came once or twice a month.
stoic
HELLO, MA'AM...
HELLO.
IT'S A NEW CHAR-ACTER!
WHO IS HE?!
And as you might expect...
stoic
...some-where along the line, I started handing them work...
IF YOU DON'T HAVE ANYTHING BETTER TO DO, START ERASING!
They build plastic models with my son.
...at which point I discovered that two of the four were pretty useful.
T-kun
Despite being a manga fan
All thumbs
H-zawa
No interest in manga
K-zawa
Likes manga, also useful
N-kun
Surprise genius!! A newbie, yet crazy useful!!
K-zawa seemed to have the most time on his hands, so I started calling him in constantly as an assistant.
ONLY THREE PEOPLE CAN COME TOMOR-ROW.
WE HAVE 20 PAGES LEFT—WE'LL NEVER GET IT DONE.
SERI-OUSLY?! CALL K-ZAWA!!
On the days when the high schoolers were supposed to come, it would say "High Schoolers" on the calendar...
5
13
12
Deadline
High Schoolers
THE HIGH SCHOOLERS ARE COMING TOMORROW, MA'AM.
SERIOUSLY?! LET'S PUT OFF THE SPOT FILLS UNTIL THEN AND MAKE THEM DO IT.

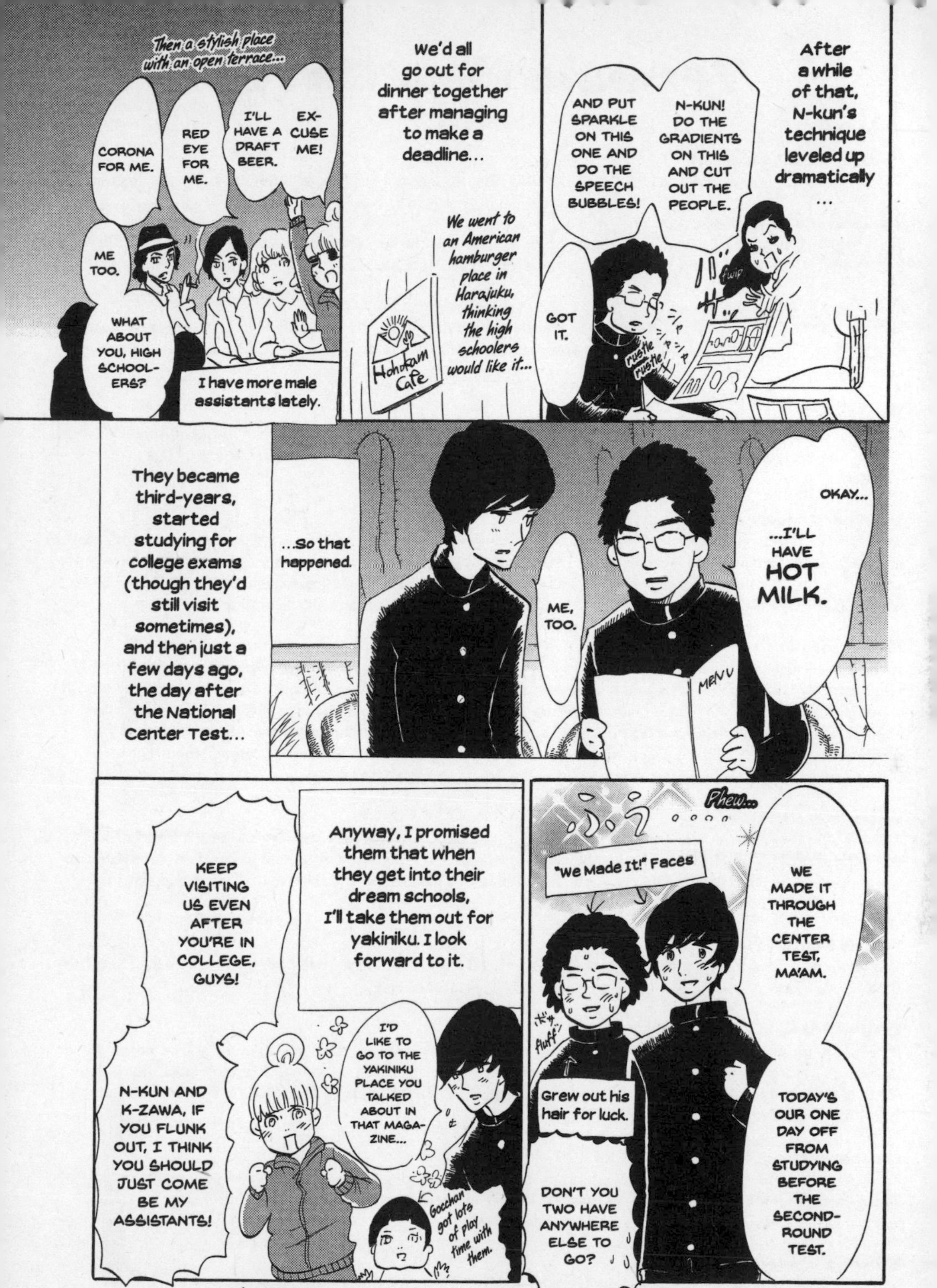
After a while of that, N-kun's technique leveled up dramatically…
N-KUN! DO THE GRADIENTS ON THIS AND CUT OUT THE PEOPLE.
AND PUT SPARKLE ON THIS ONE AND DO THE SPEECH BUBBLES!
fwip
GOT IT.
rustle rustle
We'd all go out for dinner together after managing to make a deadline…
We went to an American hamburger place in Harajuku, thinking the high schoolers would like it…
Hohokam Cafe
Then a stylish place with an open terrace…
EX-CUSE ME!
I'LL HAVE A DRAFT BEER.
RED EYE FOR ME.
CORONA FOR ME.
ME TOO.
WHAT ABOUT YOU, HIGH SCHOOL-ERS?
I have more male assistants lately.
OKAY…
…I'LL HAVE HOT MILK.
ME, TOO.
MENU
…So that happened.
They became third-years, started studying for college exams (though they'd still visit sometimes), and then just a few days ago, the day after the National Center Test…
Phew…
WE MADE IT THROUGH THE CENTER TEST, MA'AM.
"We Made It!" Faces
fluff
Grew out his hair for luck.
TODAY'S OUR ONE DAY OFF FROM STUDYING BEFORE THE SECOND-ROUND TEST.
DON'T YOU TWO HAVE ANYWHERE ELSE TO GO?
Anyway, I promised them that when they get into their dream schools, I'll take them out for yakiniku. I look forward to it.
KEEP VISITING US EVEN AFTER YOU'RE IN COLLEGE, GUYS!
I'D LIKE TO GO TO THE YAKINIKU PLACE YOU TALKED ABOUT IN THAT MAGA-ZINE…
N-KUN AND K-ZAWA, IF YOU FLUNK OUT, I THINK YOU SHOULD JUST COME BE MY ASSISTANTS!
Gocchan got lots of play time with them.

The End

Translation Notes

The Exhibition Game, page 4
This chapter's title is a reference to Francis Veber's 1998 film *Le Dîner de Cons*, known in English as *The Dinner Game*.

Machaaki and Joe Shishido, page 11
Joe Shishido is an actor who is well-known for his yakuza roles in the late 1950s and 60s, like in *Branded to Kill* (1967) directed by Seijun Suzuki. For more on the all-around entertainer Machaaki, see Volume 5 translation notes.

Not a Copy Robot, page 14
The "Copy Robot" is a robot in Fujiko F. Fujio's manga (the creators of *Doraemon* and *Perman*). The robot can turn into an identical copy of someone, but when you push the button where its nose is, it will go back to its default faceless state.

The Toxic Princess, page 37
The Japanese title is *Tsukimi no Dokudoku Princess*, which fits the title pattern of a couple of different American horror-comedy films: *Dance of the Dead* (*Akuma no Dokudoku Party*), and *The Toxic Avenger* (*Akuma no Dokudoku Monster*).

This reminds me of a kantoui., page 40
A *kantoui* is a type of garment which is a solid panel of cloth folded in two, with a hole for the head at the top, similar to a poncho. *Kantoui* aren't worn in Japan today, and this word wouldn't usually come up in everyday conversation. Most people think of *kantoui* as the standard dress in the Yayoi Period (approx. 300 BCE-300 CE), which is what makes Mayaya and Banba think of the legendary-and-historical shaman Queen Himiko.

Himiko, page 40
Himiko is a female ruler mentioned in Chinese historical annals, including *Records of the Three Kingdoms*, where Wei's emperor Cao Rui gives her a gold seal in return for tributes she sent him. Almost nothing is known for certain about Himiko, including which part of modern-day Japan her kingdom of "Yamatai" corresponds to. There's just enough information available to tickle a writer's imagination, making her a popular figure in print fiction, TV, and film. In addition to the jelly-style *kantoui*, Banba's Himiko cosplay features a necklace of comma-shaped beads—these are examples of the *magatama* mentioned in the Volume 5 translation notes.

Ikezukuri Style, page 57
Some restaurants in Japan allow you to pick a fish from the tank and have the chef fillet and slice it into sashimi while the animal is still alive. This is called *ikezukuri* or *ikizukuri*. Usually, the sashimi pieces are then placed back on the body of the fish and served. Of course, the fish tank here is decorative, and the fish in it aren't supposed to be eaten.

Tsukimi Paints It Black, page 67
The Japanese title of this chapter is a reference to another Seijun Suzuki film titled *Kaikyo, Chi ni Somete* (*Blood-Red Water in the Channel*) from 1961. "*Chi ni somete*" means "dye it blood-red."

Fractured Fashion, page 91
If you read this page and thought, "Wait, 'Gar des Commeçons' doesn't sound like real French," you're quite right. In fact, it's a rearrangement of the name "Comme des Garçons," which is a real Japanese fashion label. This volume is full of fractured fashion, including R.Z.P.V., a riff on the R.S.V.P. label; Yuhji Yoshimoto, a riff on Yohji Yamamoto; and BEEMS, a riff on BEAMS.

Comiket and Doujinshi, page 121
Doujinshi are fan-made media (often comics) that are based on existing media, or other fandoms such as trains. Twice a year, there is a massive grassroots market called Comiket (Comic Market), where authors can sell their self-published and alternative work to the fan community.

Mama wa Tenparist, page 169
Mama wa Tenparist is a previous manga by Higashimura-sensei about her experiences raising Gocchan.

DEAREST READERS!

HOW HAVE YOU BEEN?!
I'VE BEEN DOING
THE SAME THING, AS ALWAYS.
I'M HOLED UP IN MY HOUSE
AND DRAWING MANGA,
WHILE WATCHING YOUTUBE!!
I GOTTA SAY, I LOOK AT
MY LIFE RIGHT NOW, AND...
THERE'S NOTHING I'D CHANGE!
IT'S PERFECT!!
I DON'T NEED ANYTHING
OTHER THAN YOUTUBE
TO LIVE!!

-AKIKO HIGASHIMURA

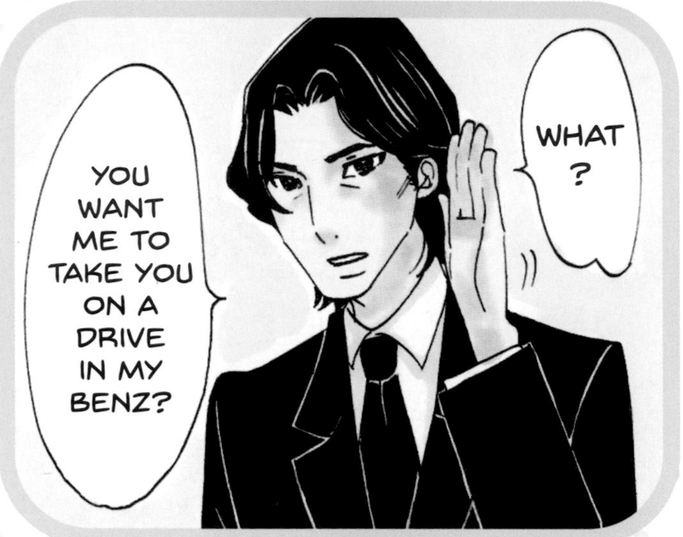
WHAT?
YOU WANT ME TO TAKE YOU ON A DRIVE IN MY BENZ?

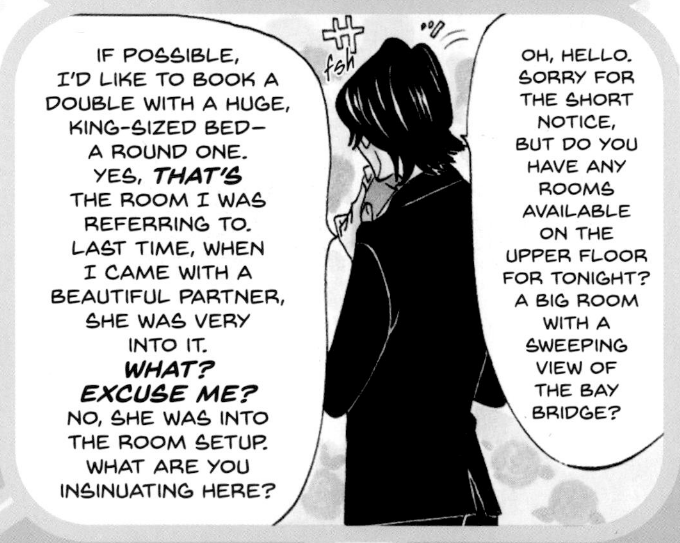
OH, HELLO. SORRY FOR THE SHORT NOTICE, BUT DO YOU HAVE ANY ROOMS AVAILABLE ON THE UPPER FLOOR FOR TONIGHT? A BIG ROOM WITH A SWEEPING VIEW OF THE BAY BRIDGE?
fsh
IF POSSIBLE, I'D LIKE TO BOOK A DOUBLE WITH A HUGE, KING-SIZED BED— A ROUND ONE. YES, THAT'S THE ROOM I WAS REFERRING TO. LAST TIME, WHEN I CAME WITH A BEAUTIFUL PARTNER, SHE WAS VERY INTO IT. WHAT? EXCUSE ME? NO, SHE WAS INTO THE ROOM SETUP. WHAT ARE YOU INSINUATING HERE?

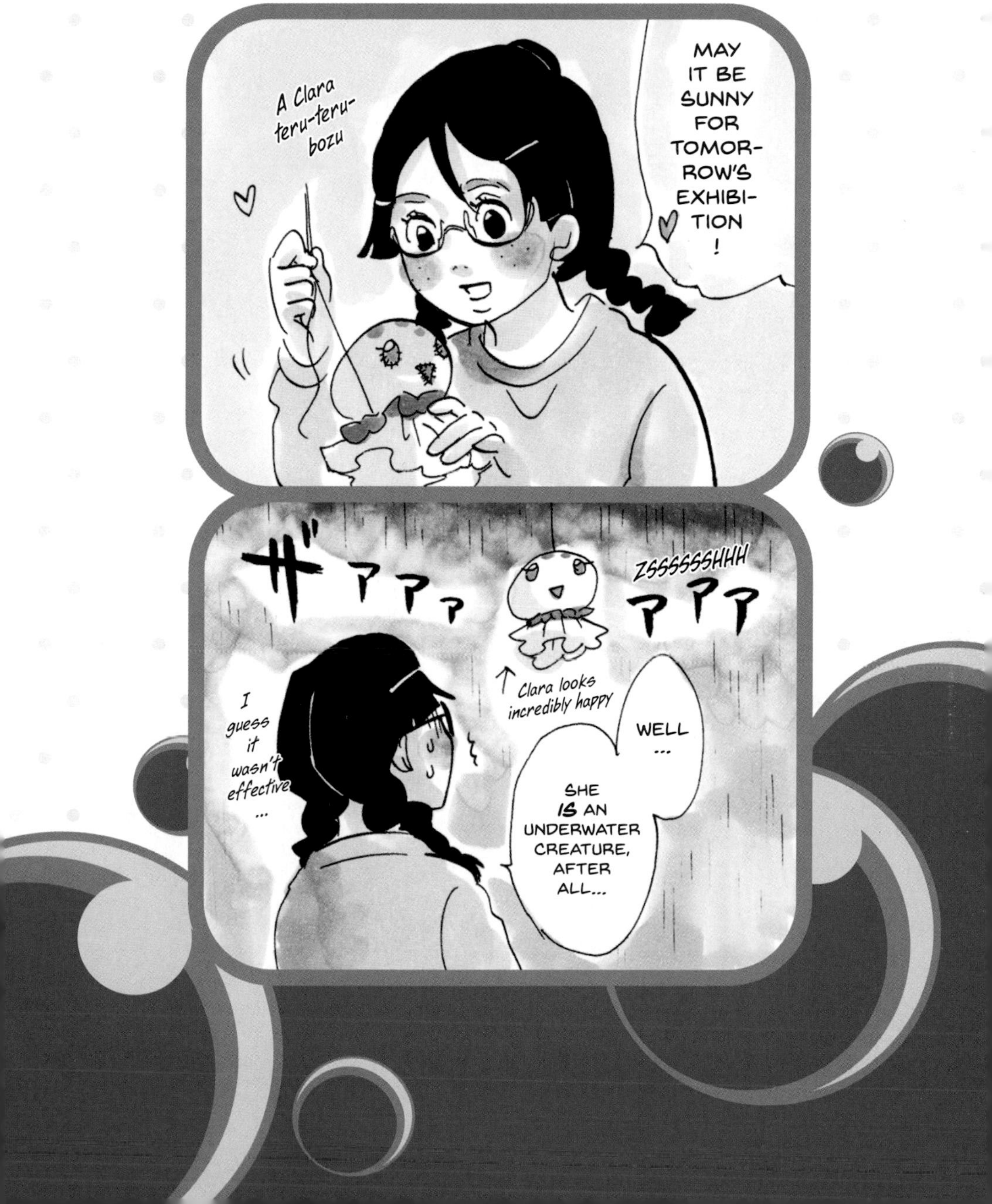
MAY IT BE SUNNY FOR TOMORROW'S EXHIBITION!
A Clara teru-teru-bozu
ZSSSSSSHHH
ザアアァ アアア
↑ Clara looks incredibly happy
WELL...
SHE **IS** AN UNDERWATER CREATURE, AFTER ALL...
I guess it wasn't effective...

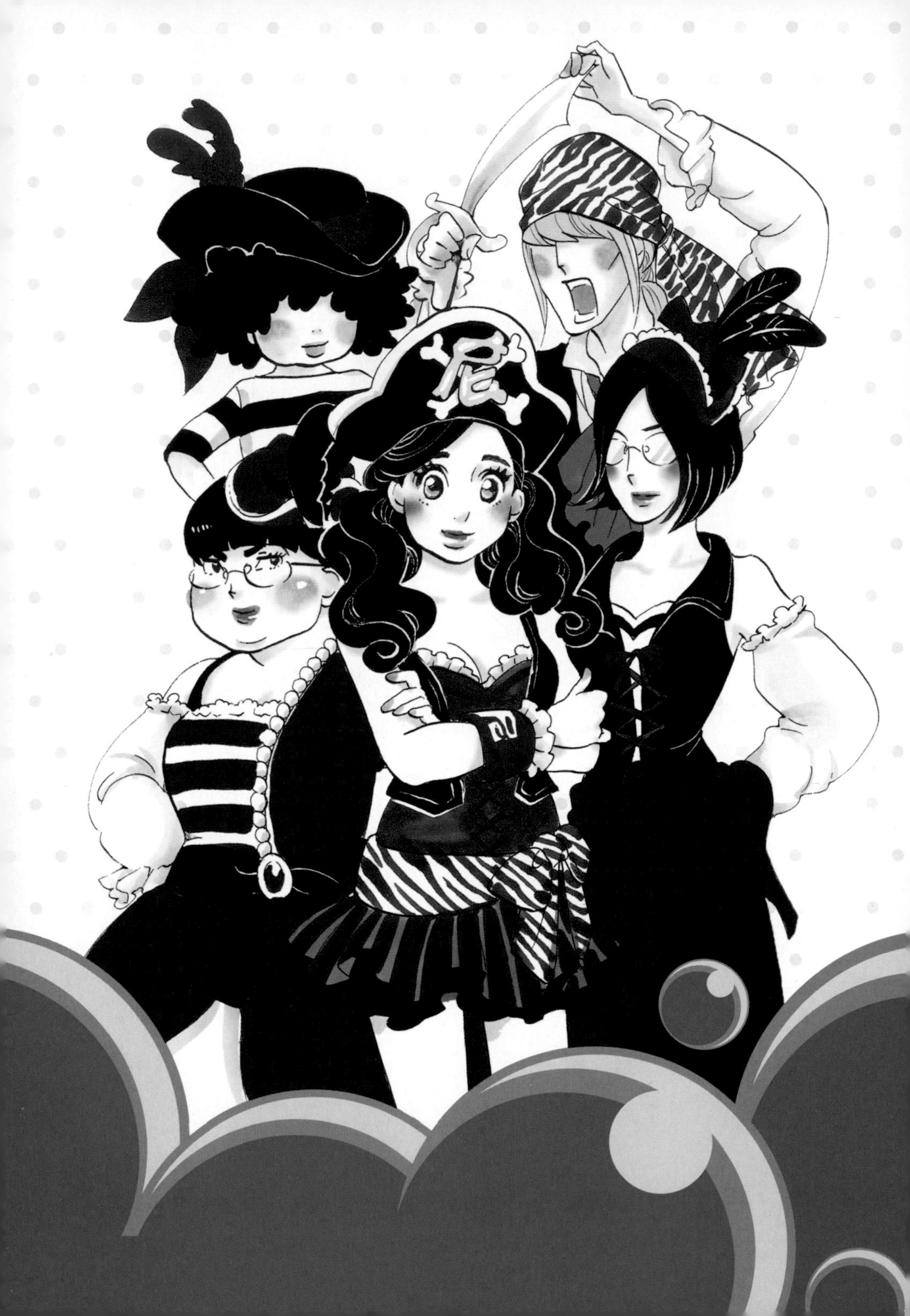
危

DEAREST READERS!

THANKS FOR ALL
YOUR HARD WORK!!
SO, HOW ARE THINGS
GOING LATELY?
I BET YOU'RE HIDING AWAY
IN YOUR HOUSE AND WATCHING
A BUNCH OF CONCERT DVDS,
AM I RIGHT?!
WHAT? *...ME?!*
WELL, IF YOU REALLY
WANNA KNOW...
*OF COURSE I'M
ROCKING ALONG!!*
I'M WAVING AROUND THIS
HAND FAN I GOT AT A CONCERT—
EVEN WHILE I'M WORKING!!
SOMEONE PLEASE COME
AND STOP ME!!

-AKIKO HIGASHIMURA

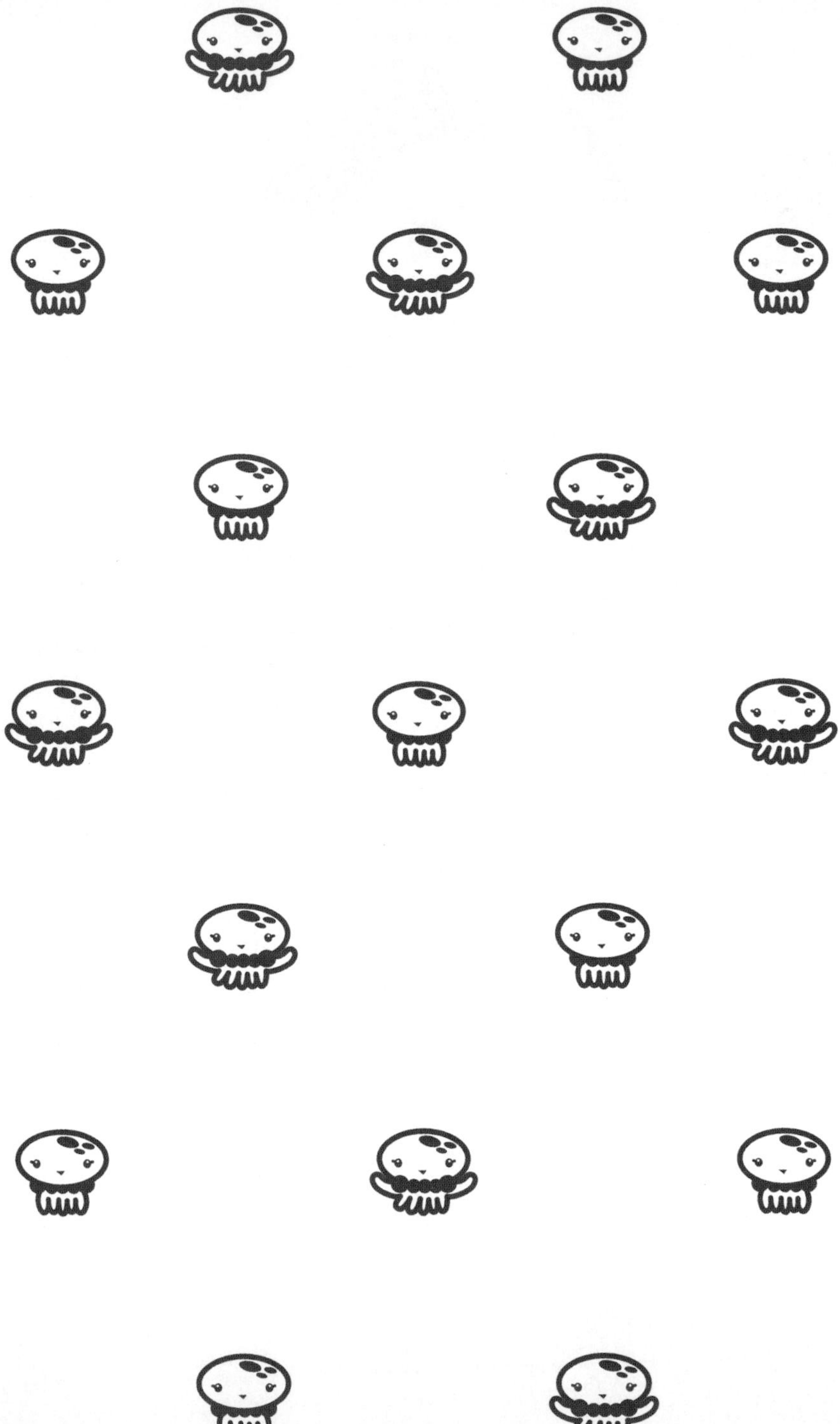

Episode 60

Singapore Thrilling

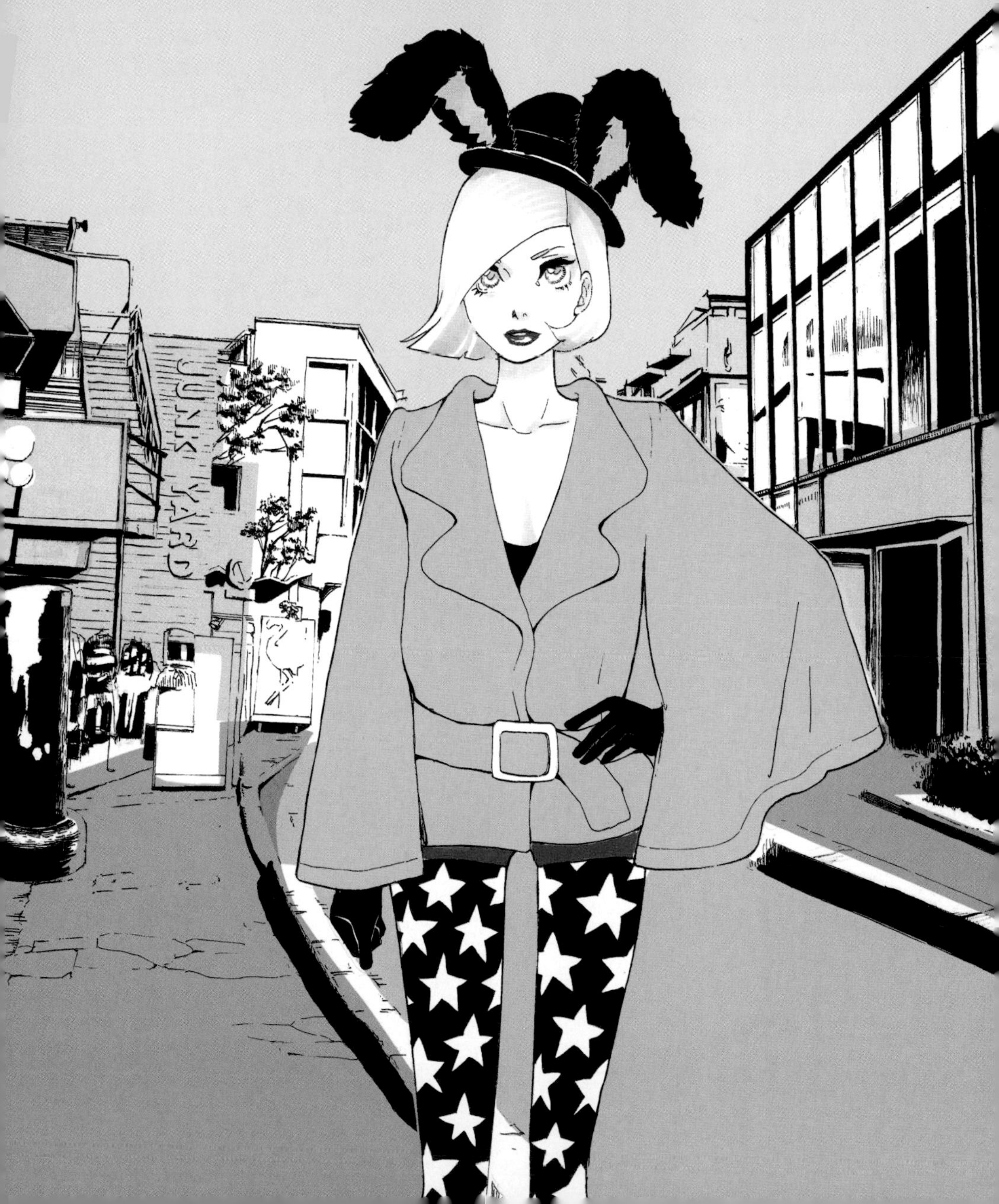
JUNK YARD

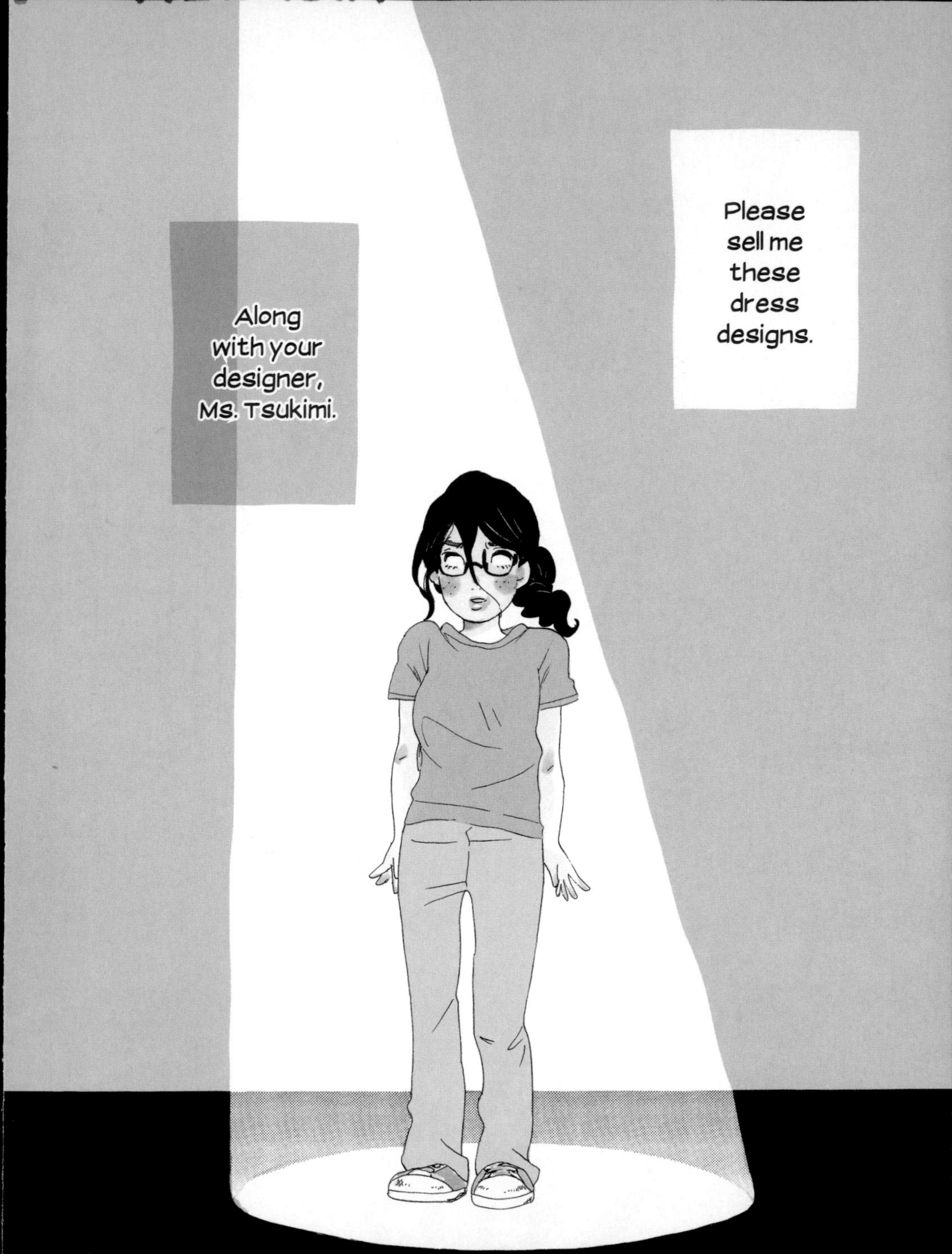
Please sell me these dress designs.
Along with your designer, Ms. Tsukimi.

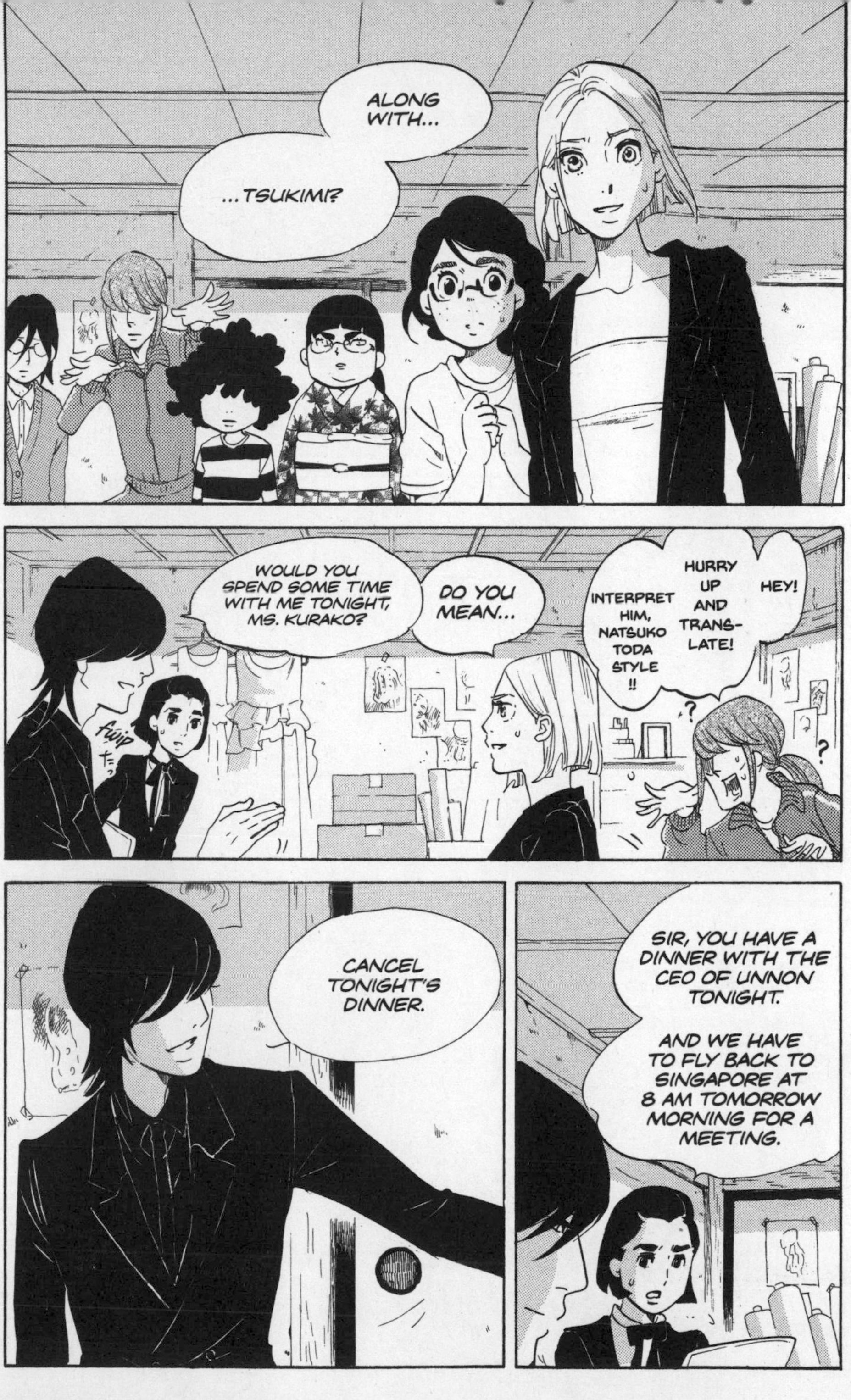
ALONG WITH...
...TSUKIMI?
HEY!
HURRY UP AND TRANSLATE!
INTERPRET HIM, NATSUKO TODA STYLE !!
DO YOU MEAN...
WOULD YOU SPEND SOME TIME WITH ME TONIGHT, MS. KURAKO?
fwip
SIR, YOU HAVE A DINNER WITH THE CEO OF UNNON TONIGHT.
AND WE HAVE TO FLY BACK TO SINGAPORE AT 8 AM TOMORROW MORNING FOR A MEETING.
CANCEL TONIGHT'S DINNER.

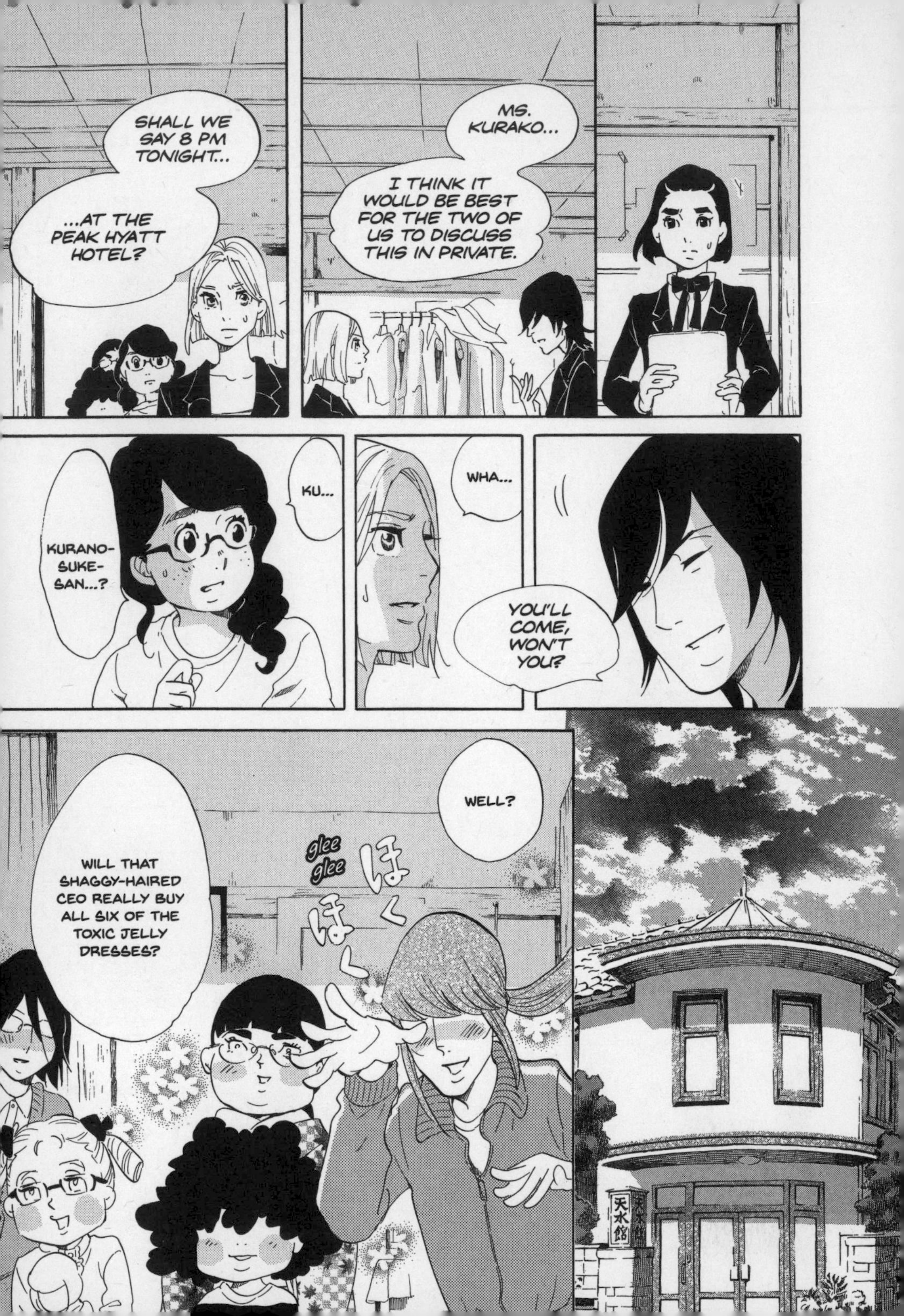
MS. KURAKO...
I THINK IT WOULD BE BEST FOR THE TWO OF US TO DISCUSS THIS IN PRIVATE.
SHALL WE SAY 8 PM TONIGHT...
...AT THE PEAK HYATT HOTEL?
YOU'LL COME, WON'T YOU?
WHA...
KU...
KURANO-SUKE-SAN...?
天水館
WELL?
ほくほく
glee glee
WILL THAT SHAGGY-HAIRED CEO REALLY BUY ALL SIX OF THE TOXIC JELLY DRESSES?

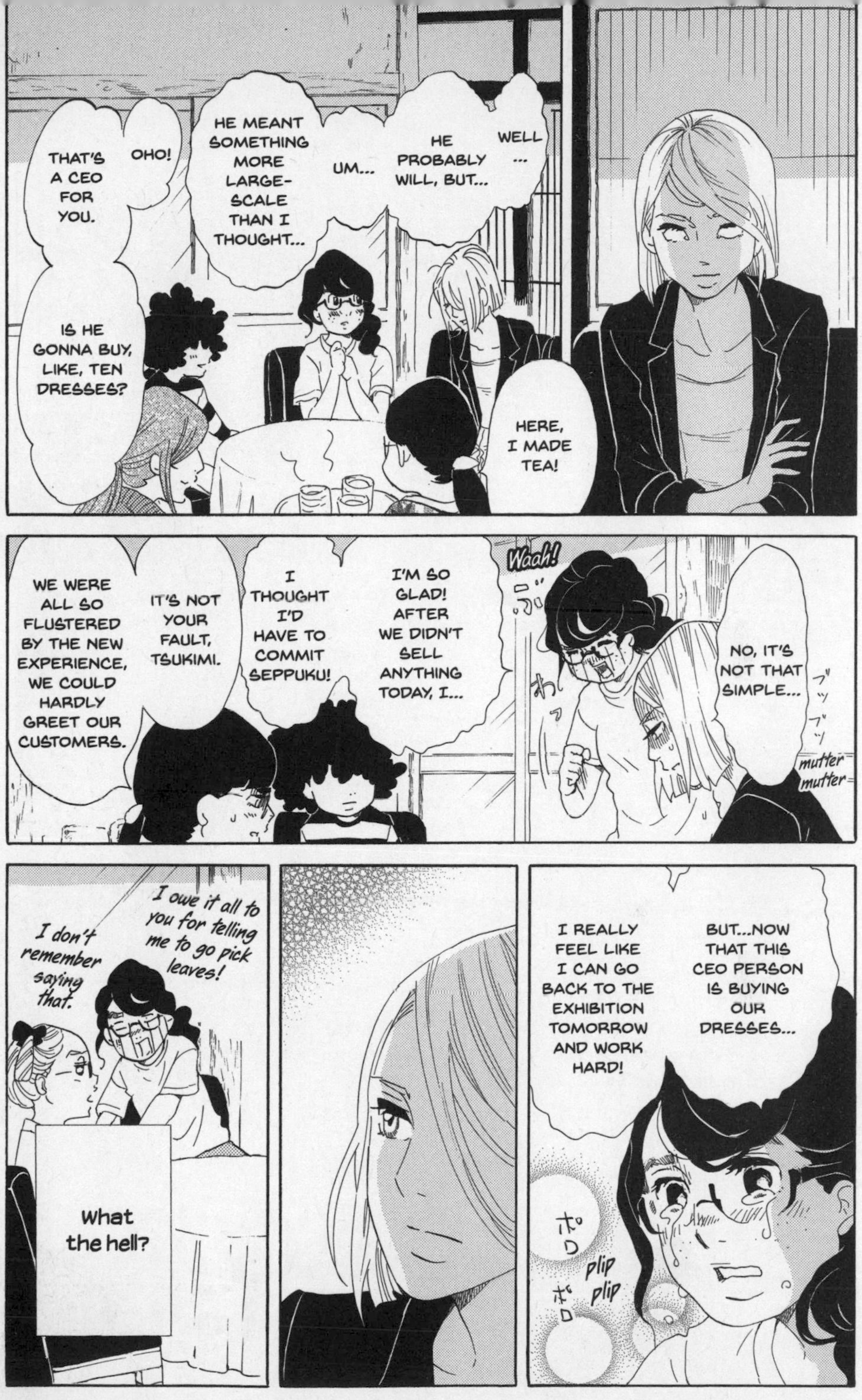
WELL ...
HE PROBABLY WILL, BUT...
UM...
HE MEANT SOMETHING MORE LARGE-SCALE THAN I THOUGHT...
OHO!
THAT'S A CEO FOR YOU.
IS HE GONNA BUY, LIKE, TEN DRESSES?
HERE, I MADE TEA!
Waah!
NO, IT'S NOT THAT SIMPLE...
mutter mutter
I'M SO GLAD! AFTER WE DIDN'T SELL ANYTHING TODAY, I...
I THOUGHT I'D HAVE TO COMMIT SEPPUKU!
IT'S NOT YOUR FAULT, TSUKIMI.
WE WERE ALL SO FLUSTERED BY THE NEW EXPERIENCE, WE COULD HARDLY GREET OUR CUSTOMERS.
BUT...NOW THAT THIS CEO PERSON IS BUYING OUR DRESSES...
I REALLY FEEL LIKE I CAN GO BACK TO THE EXHIBITION TOMORROW AND WORK HARD!
plip plip
I owe it all to you for telling me to go pick leaves!
I don't remember saying that.
What the hell?

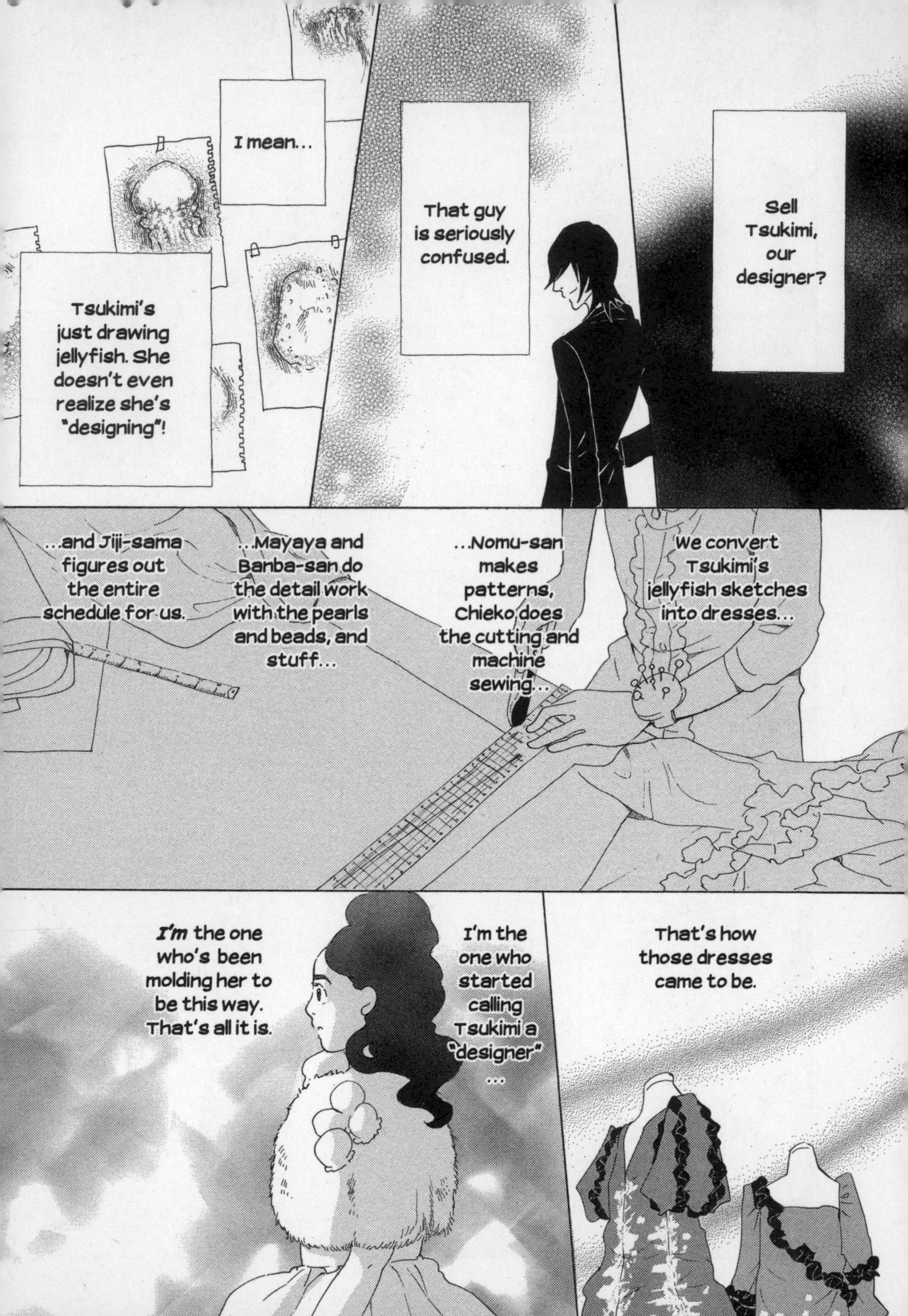
Sell Tsukimi, our designer?
That guy is seriously confused.
I mean...
Tsukimi's just drawing jellyfish. She doesn't even realize she's "designing"!
We convert Tsukimi's jellyfish sketches into dresses...
...Nomu-san makes patterns, Chieko does the cutting and machine sewing...
...Mayaya and Banba-san do the detail work with the pearls and beads, and stuff...
...and Jiji-sama figures out the entire schedule for us.
That's how those dresses came to be.
I'm the one who started calling Tsukimi a "designer"...
I'm the one who's been molding her to be this way. That's all it is.

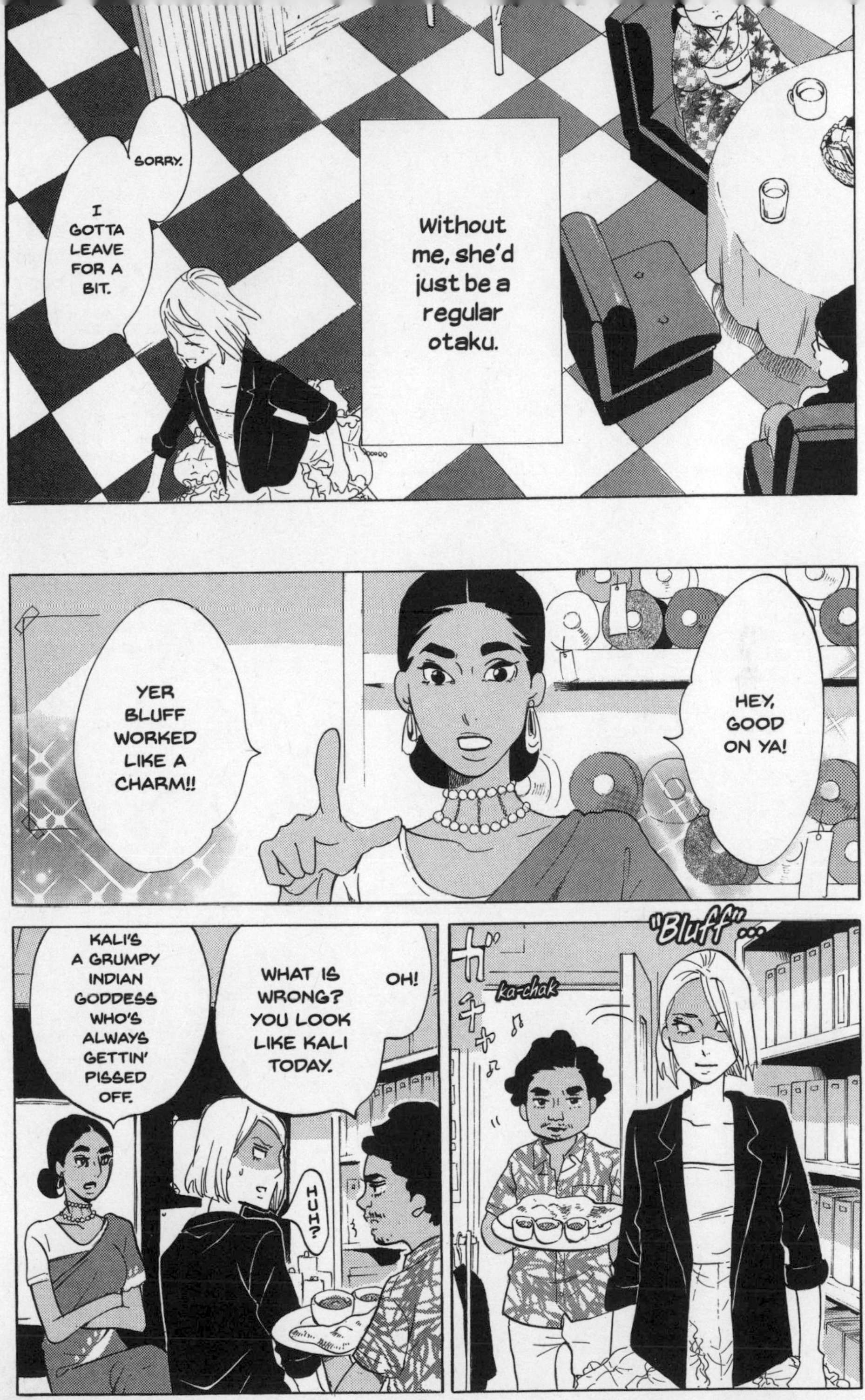
Without me, she'd just be a regular otaku.
SORRY.
I GOTTA LEAVE FOR A BIT.
HEY, GOOD ON YA!
YER BLUFF WORKED LIKE A CHARM!!
"Bluff"...
ガチャ
ka-chak
OH!
WHAT IS WRONG? YOU LOOK LIKE KALI TODAY.
KALI'S A GRUMPY INDIAN GODDESS WHO'S ALWAYS GETTIN' PISSED OFF.
HUH?

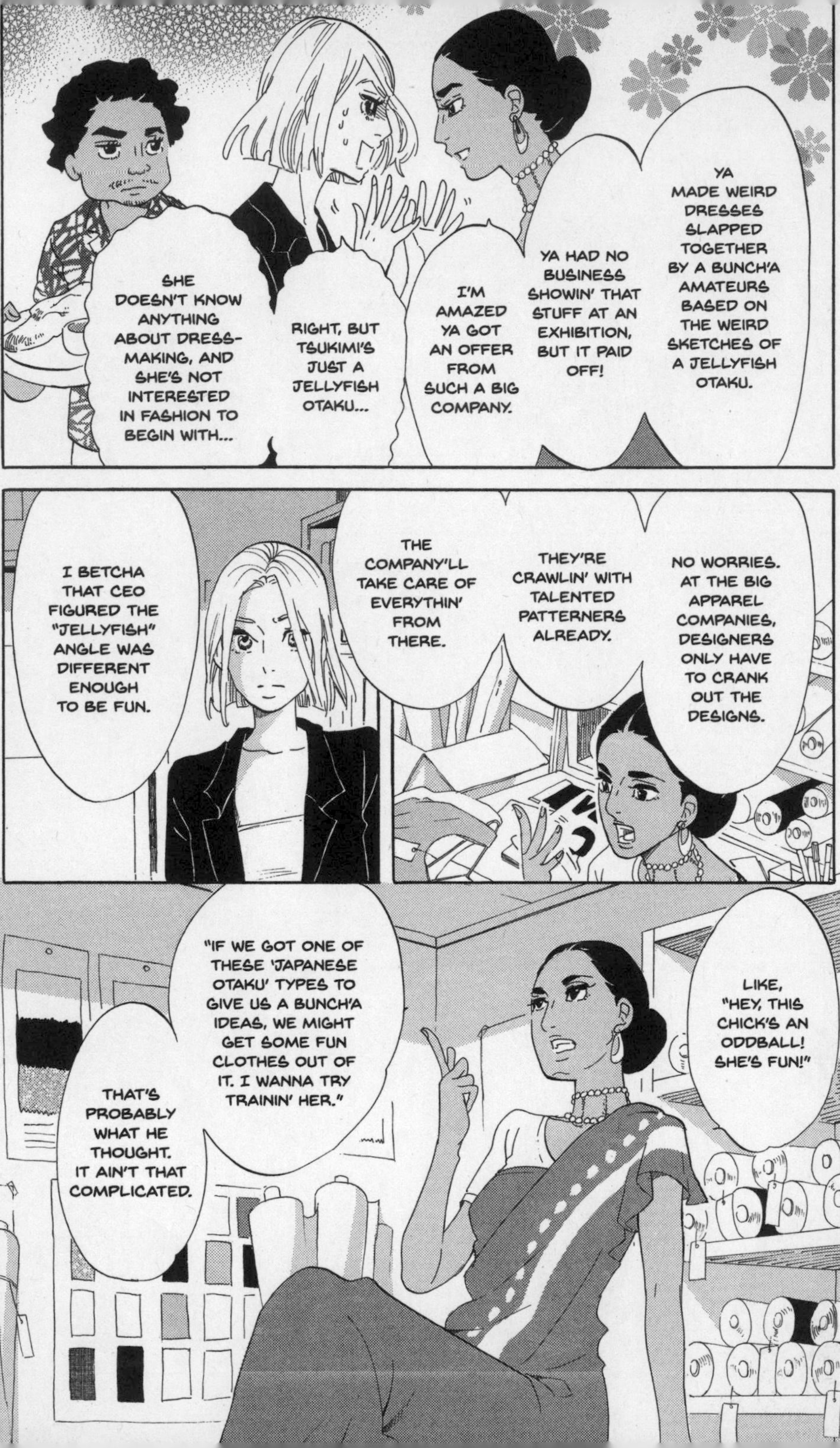
YA MADE WEIRD DRESSES SLAPPED TOGETHER BY A BUNCH'A AMATEURS BASED ON THE WEIRD SKETCHES OF A JELLYFISH OTAKU.
YA HAD NO BUSINESS SHOWIN' THAT STUFF AT AN EXHIBITION, BUT IT PAID OFF!
I'M AMAZED YA GOT AN OFFER FROM SUCH A BIG COMPANY.
RIGHT, BUT TSUKIMI'S JUST A JELLYFISH OTAKU...
SHE DOESN'T KNOW ANYTHING ABOUT DRESS-MAKING, AND SHE'S NOT INTERESTED IN FASHION TO BEGIN WITH...
NO WORRIES. AT THE BIG APPAREL COMPANIES, DESIGNERS ONLY HAVE TO CRANK OUT THE DESIGNS.
THEY'RE CRAWLIN' WITH TALENTED PATTERNERS ALREADY.
THE COMPANY'LL TAKE CARE OF EVERYTHIN' FROM THERE.
I BETCHA THAT CEO FIGURED THE "JELLYFISH" ANGLE WAS DIFFERENT ENOUGH TO BE FUN.
LIKE, "HEY, THIS CHICK'S AN ODDBALL! SHE'S FUN!"
"IF WE GOT ONE OF THESE 'JAPANESE OTAKU' TYPES TO GIVE US A BUNCH'A IDEAS, WE MIGHT GET SOME FUN CLOTHES OUT OF IT. I WANNA TRY TRAININ' HER."
THAT'S PROBABLY WHAT HE THOUGHT. IT AIN'T THAT COMPLICATED.

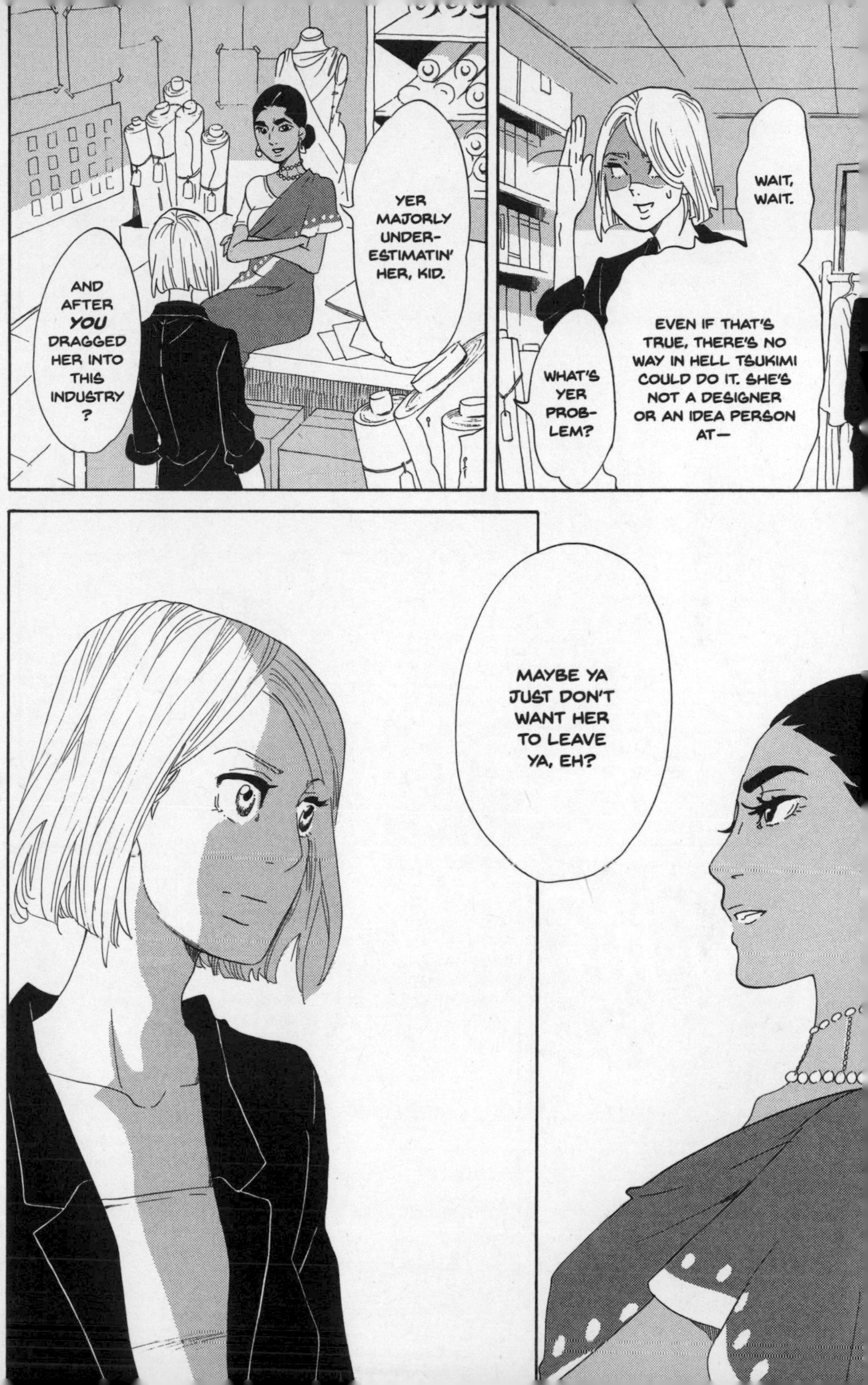
WAIT, WAIT.
EVEN IF THAT'S TRUE, THERE'S NO WAY IN HELL TSUKIMI COULD DO IT. SHE'S NOT A DESIGNER OR AN IDEA PERSON AT—
WHAT'S YER PROB-LEM?
YER MAJORLY UNDER-ESTIMATIN' HER, KID.
AND AFTER ***YOU*** DRAGGED HER INTO THIS INDUSTRY ?
MAYBE YA JUST DON'T WANT HER TO LEAVE YA, EH?

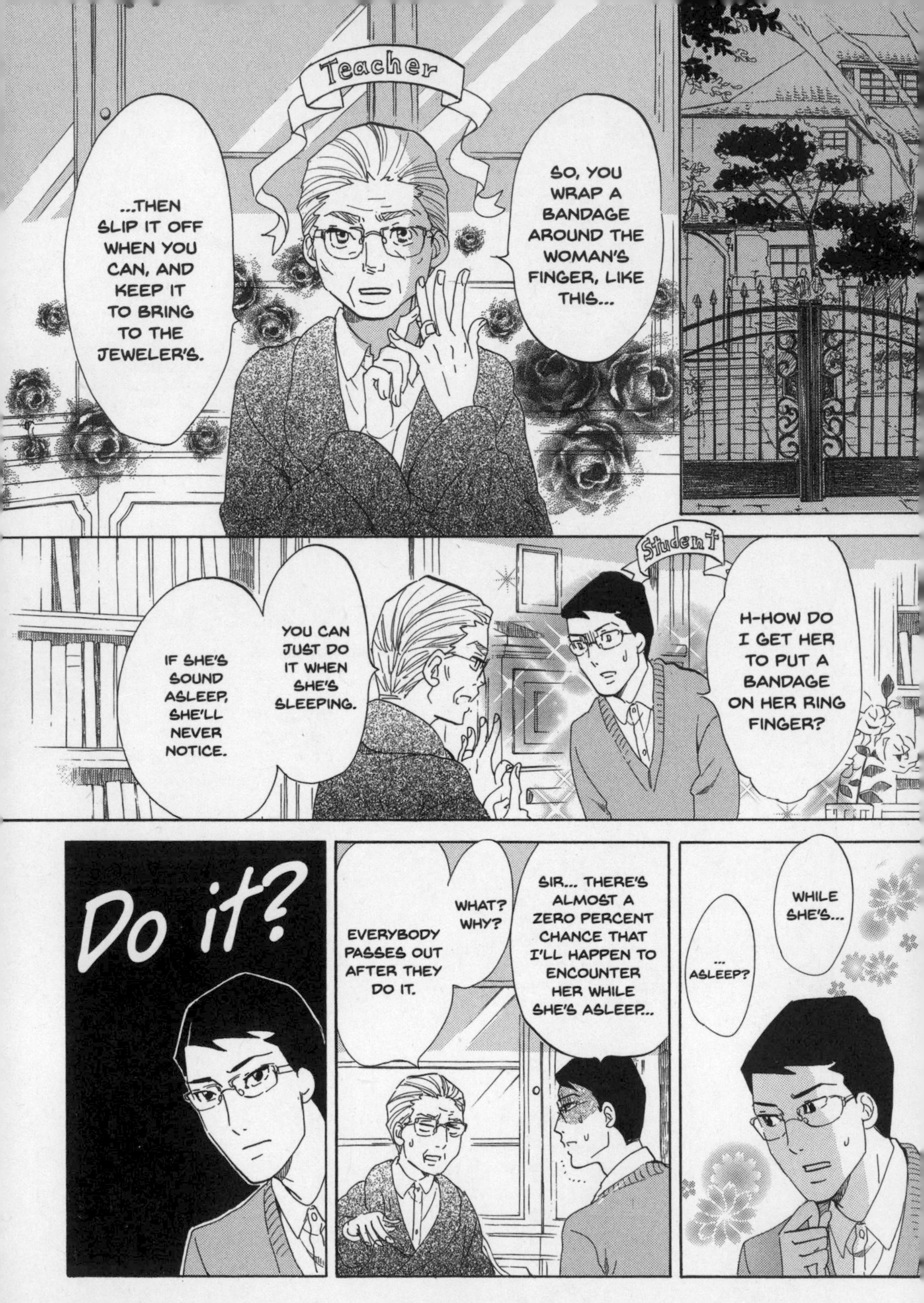
Teacher
SO, YOU WRAP A BANDAGE AROUND THE WOMAN'S FINGER, LIKE THIS...
...THEN SLIP IT OFF WHEN YOU CAN, AND KEEP IT TO BRING TO THE JEWELER'S.
Student
H-HOW DO I GET HER TO PUT A BANDAGE ON HER RING FINGER?
YOU CAN JUST DO IT WHEN SHE'S SLEEPING.
IF SHE'S SOUND ASLEEP, SHE'LL NEVER NOTICE.
WHILE SHE'S...
... ASLEEP?
SIR... THERE'S ALMOST A ZERO PERCENT CHANCE THAT I'LL HAPPEN TO ENCOUNTER HER WHILE SHE'S ASLEEP...
WHAT? WHY?
EVERYBODY PASSES OUT AFTER THEY DO IT.
Do it?

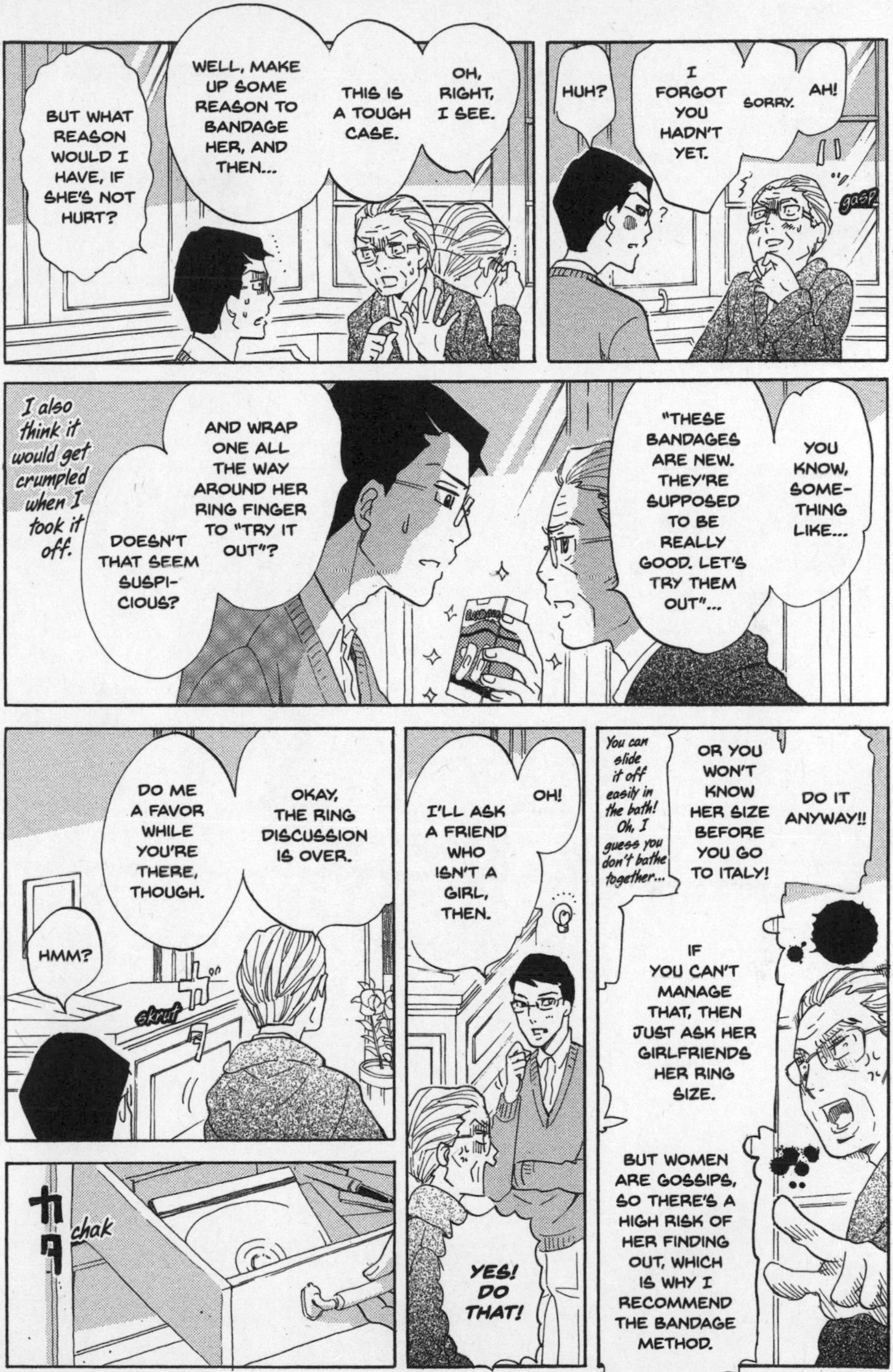

AH!
SORRY.
I FORGOT YOU HADN'T YET.
HUH?
gasp
OH, RIGHT, I SEE.
THIS IS A TOUGH CASE.
WELL, MAKE UP SOME REASON TO BANDAGE HER, AND THEN...
BUT WHAT REASON WOULD I HAVE, IF SHE'S NOT HURT?
YOU KNOW, SOME-THING LIKE...
"THESE BANDAGES ARE NEW. THEY'RE SUPPOSED TO BE REALLY GOOD. LET'S TRY THEM OUT"...
AND WRAP ONE ALL THE WAY AROUND HER RING FINGER TO "TRY IT OUT"?
DOESN'T THAT SEEM SUSPI-CIOUS?
I also think it would get crumpled when I took it off.
DO IT ANYWAY!!
OR YOU WON'T KNOW HER SIZE BEFORE YOU GO TO ITALY!
You can slide it off easily in the bath! Oh, I guess you don't bathe together...
IF YOU CAN'T MANAGE THAT, THEN JUST ASK HER GIRLFRIENDS HER RING SIZE.
BUT WOMEN ARE GOSSIPS, SO THERE'S A HIGH RISK OF HER FINDING OUT, WHICH IS WHY I RECOMMEND THE BANDAGE METHOD.
OH!
I'LL ASK A FRIEND WHO ISN'T A GIRL, THEN.
YES! DO THAT!
OKAY, THE RING DISCUSSION IS OVER.
DO ME A FAVOR WHILE YOU'RE THERE, THOUGH.
HMM?
sknut
カタ
chak

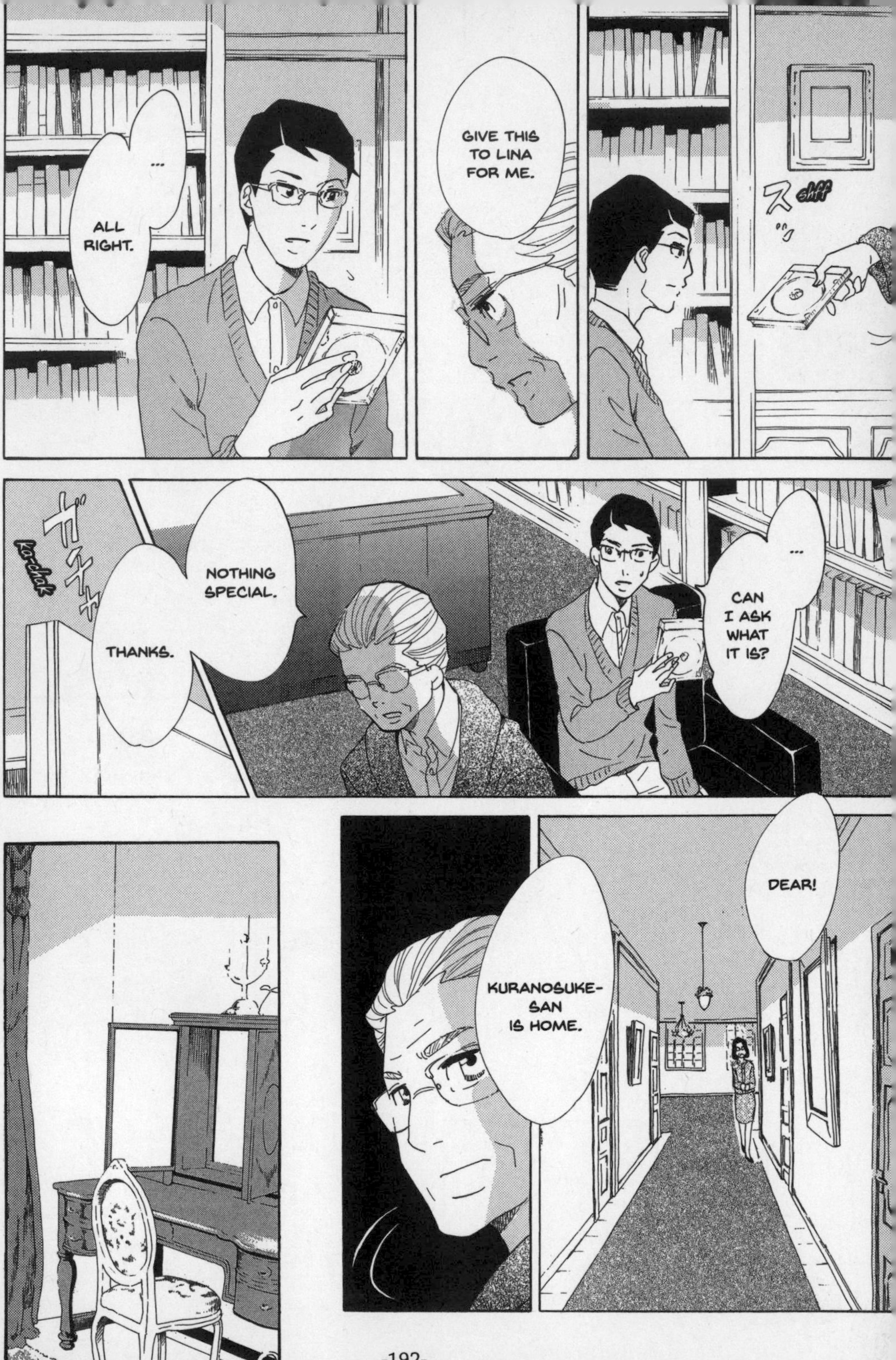
shff
GIVE THIS TO LINA FOR ME.
...
ALL RIGHT.
...
CAN I ASK WHAT IT IS?
NOTHING SPECIAL.
THANKS.
ka-chak
DEAR!
KURANOSUKE-SAN IS HOME.

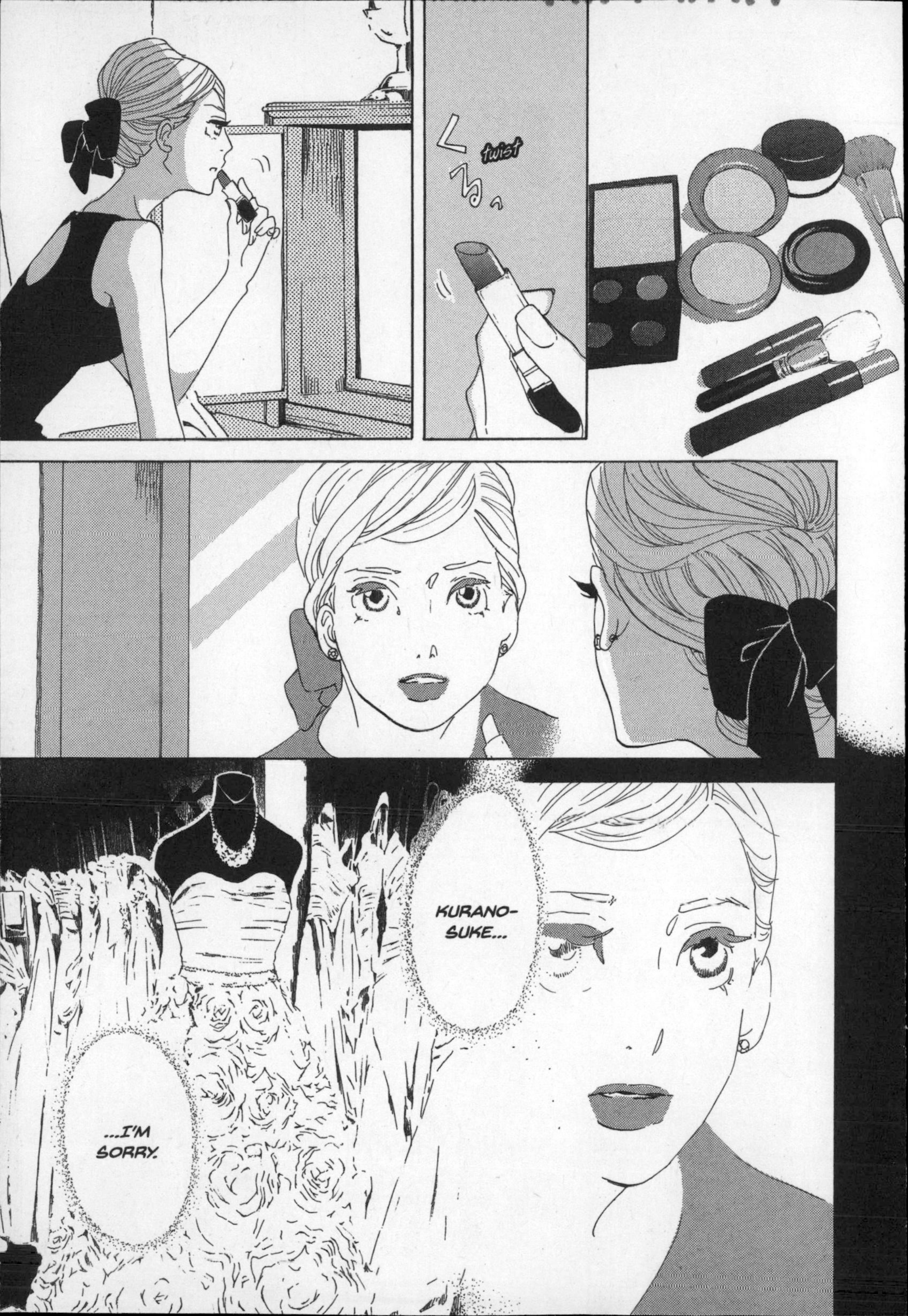
twist
KURANO-SUKE...
...I'M SORRY.

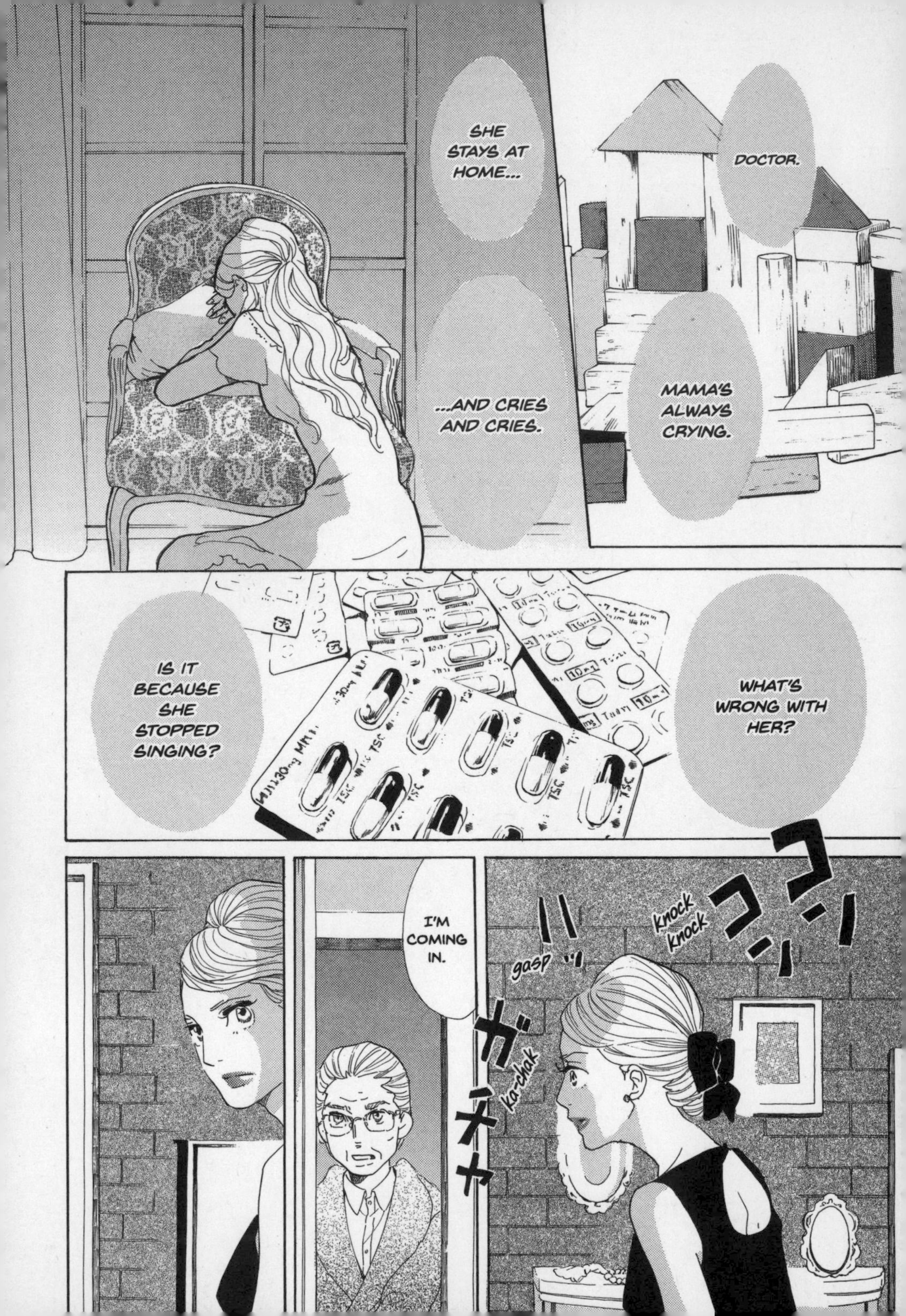
DOCTOR.
MAMA'S ALWAYS CRYING.
SHE STAYS AT HOME...
...AND CRIES AND CRIES.
WHAT'S WRONG WITH HER?
IS IT BECAUSE SHE STOPPED SINGING?
コンコン
knock knock
ハッ
gasp
ガチャ
ka-chak
I'M COMING IN.

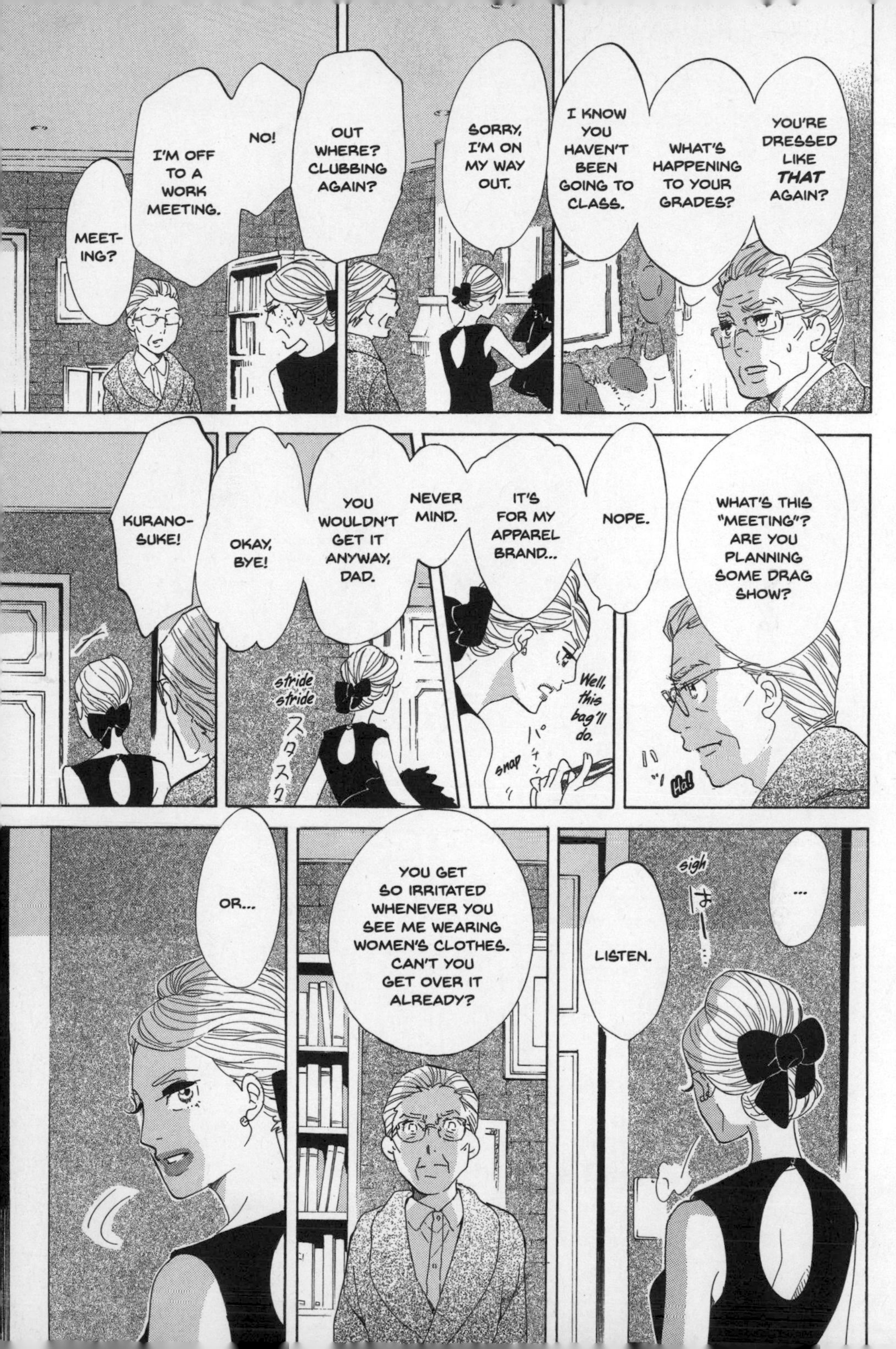

YOU'RE DRESSED LIKE *THAT* AGAIN?
WHAT'S HAPPENING TO YOUR GRADES?
I KNOW YOU HAVEN'T BEEN GOING TO CLASS.
SORRY, I'M ON MY WAY OUT.
OUT WHERE? CLUBBING AGAIN?
NO!
I'M OFF TO A WORK MEETING.
MEET-ING?
WHAT'S THIS "MEETING"? ARE YOU PLANNING SOME DRAG SHOW?
Ha!
NOPE.
IT'S FOR MY APPAREL BRAND...
NEVER MIND.
YOU WOULDN'T GET IT ANYWAY, DAD.
Well, this bag'll do.
snap
OKAY, BYE!
stride stride
スタスタ
KURANO-SUKE!
...
sigh
LISTEN.
YOU GET SO IRRITATED WHENEVER YOU SEE ME WEARING WOMEN'S CLOTHES. CAN'T YOU GET OVER IT ALREADY?
OR...

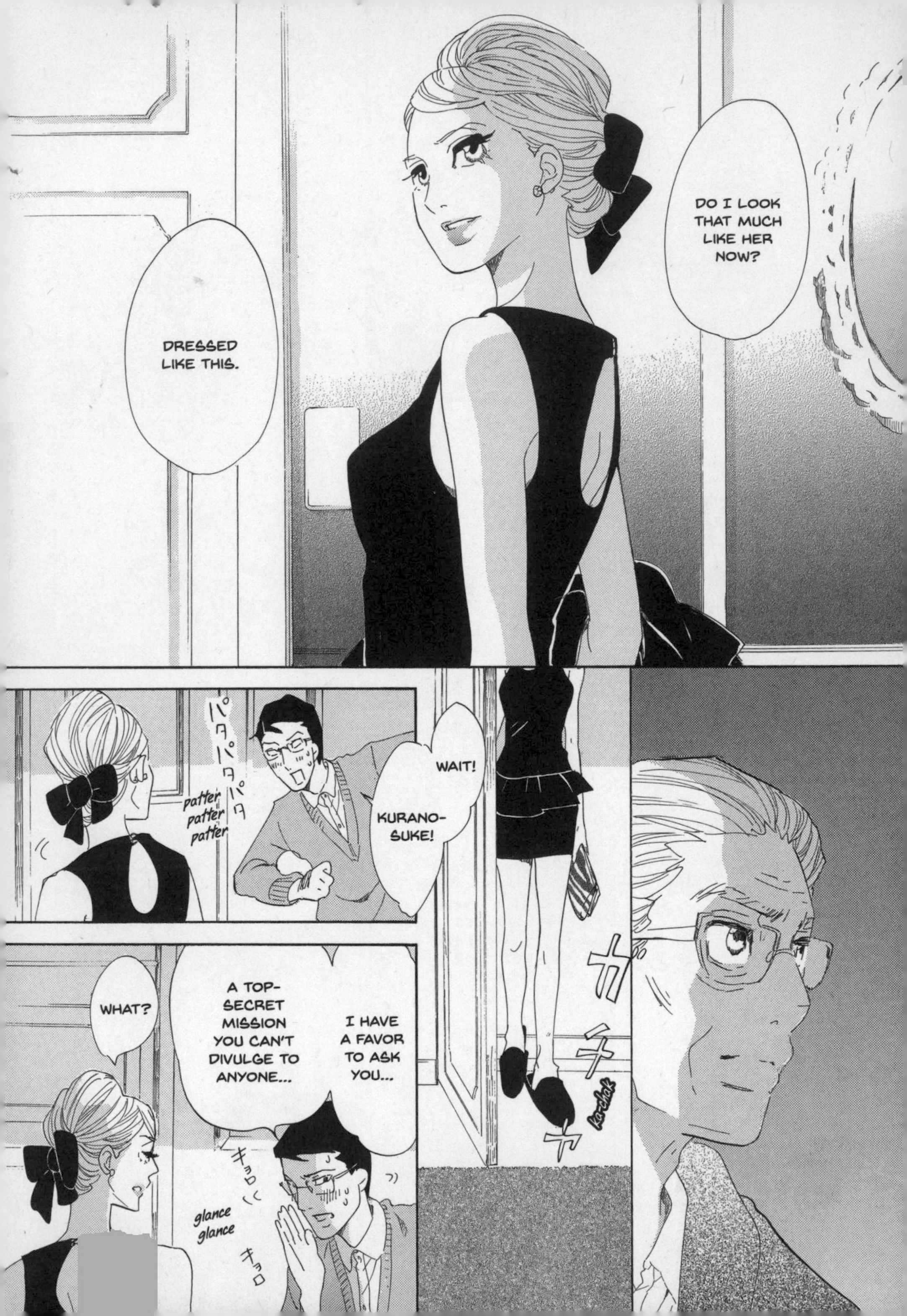
DO I LOOK THAT MUCH LIKE HER NOW?
DRESSED LIKE THIS.
ガチャ
ka-chak
WAIT!
KURANO-SUKE!
パタパタパタ
patter patter patter
I HAVE A FAVOR TO ASK YOU...
A TOP-SECRET MISSION YOU CAN'T DIVULGE TO ANYONE...
WHAT?
キョロキョロ
glance glance

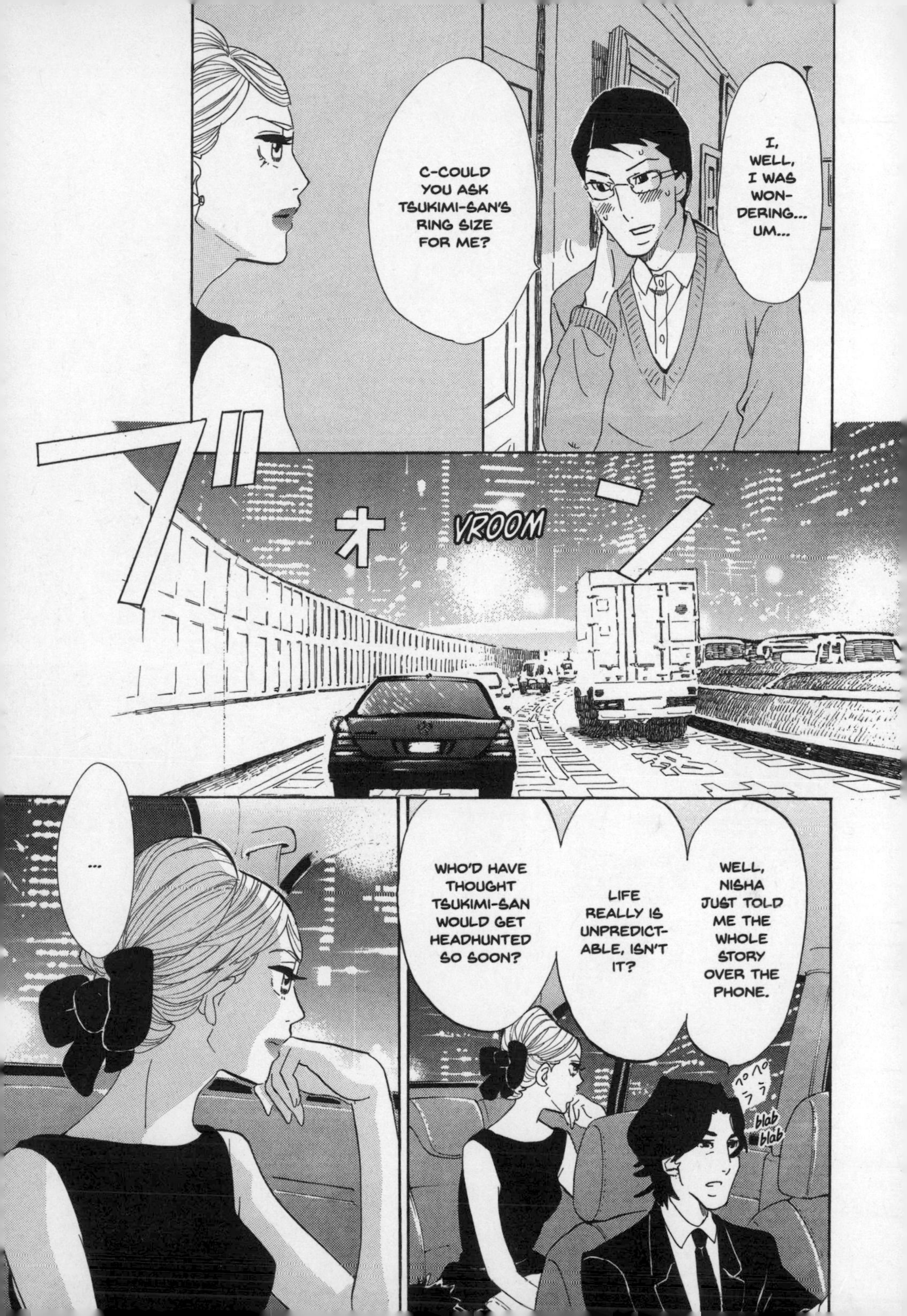
I, WELL, I WAS WON-DERING... UM...
C-COULD YOU ASK TSUKIMI-SAN'S RING SIZE FOR ME?
ブオーン
VROOM
WELL, NISHA JUST TOLD ME THE WHOLE STORY OVER THE PHONE.
LIFE REALLY IS UNPREDICT-ABLE, ISN'T IT?
WHO'D HAVE THOUGHT TSUKIMI-SAN WOULD GET HEADHUNTED SO SOON?
ヘラヘラ
blab blab
...

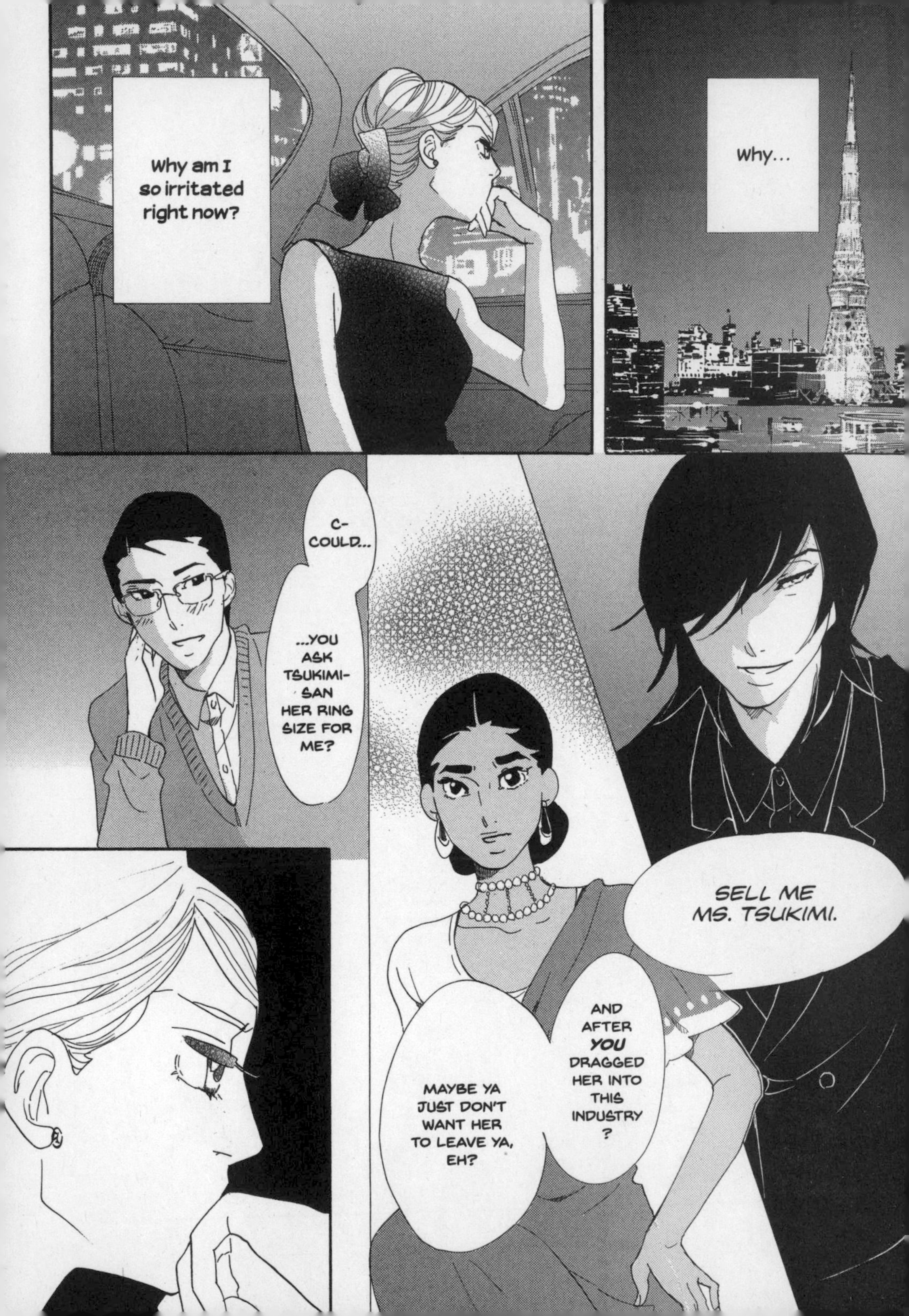
Why...
Why am I so irritated right now?
SELL ME MS. TSUKIMI.
AND AFTER *YOU* DRAGGED HER INTO THIS INDUSTRY?
MAYBE YA JUST DON'T WANT HER TO LEAVE YA, EH?
C-COULD...
...YOU ASK TSUKIMI-SAN HER RING SIZE FOR ME?

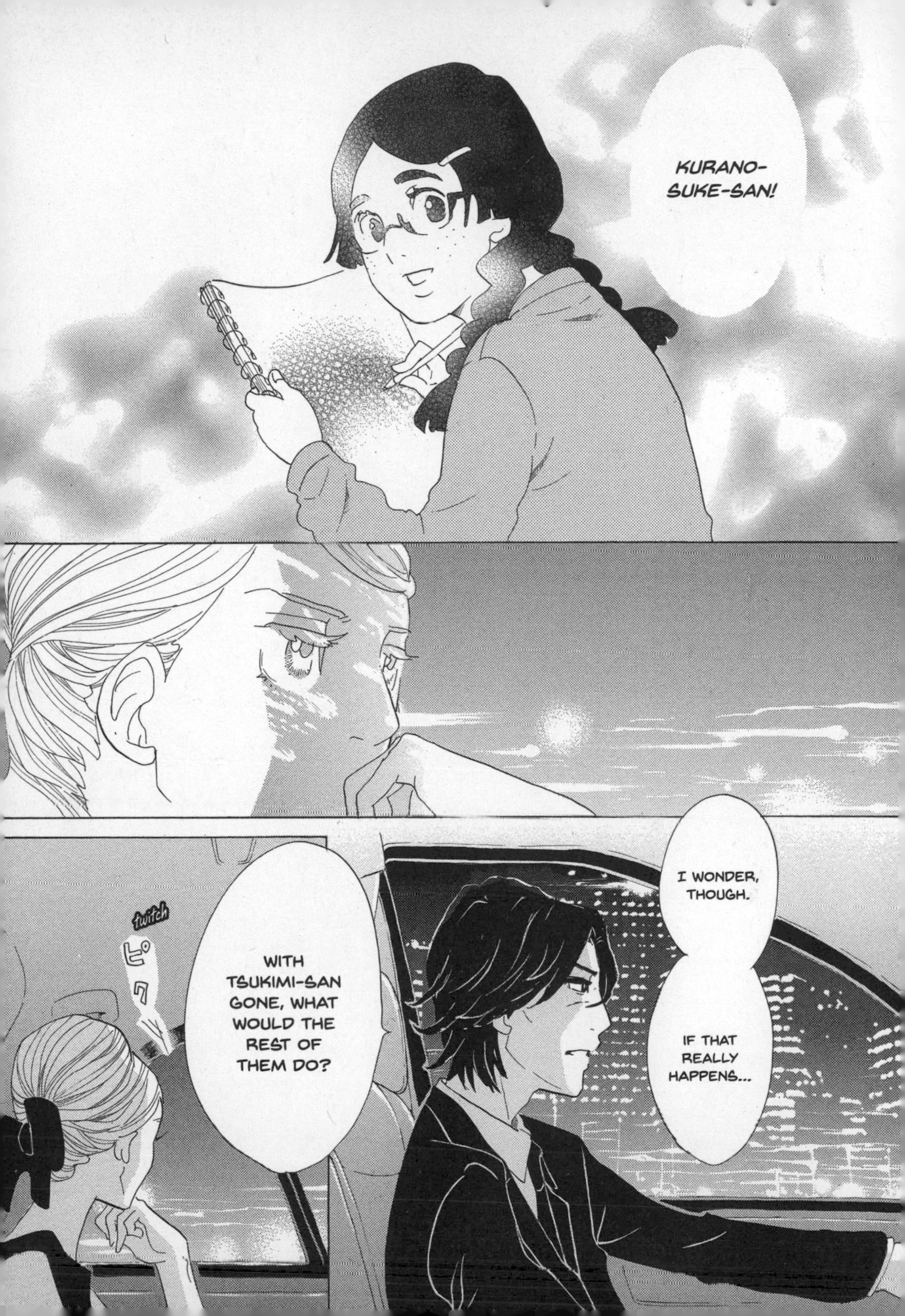
KURANO-SUKE-SAN!
I WONDER, THOUGH.
IF THAT REALLY HAPPENS...
WITH TSUKIMI-SAN GONE, WHAT WOULD THE REST OF THEM DO?
twitch
ピク

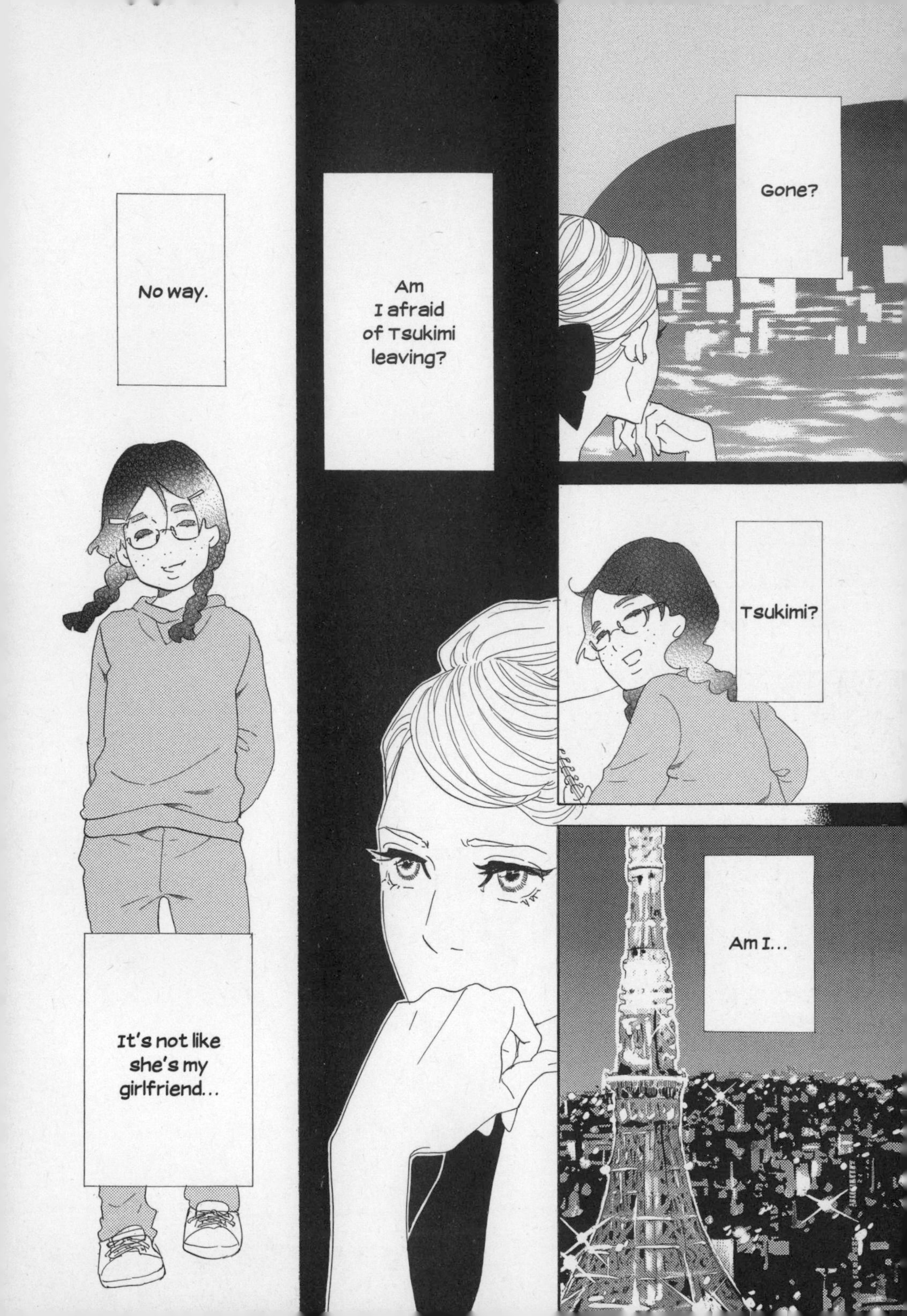
Gone?
Tsukimi?
Am I...
Am I afraid of Tsukimi leaving?
No way.
It's not like she's my girlfriend...

She's not my mother...

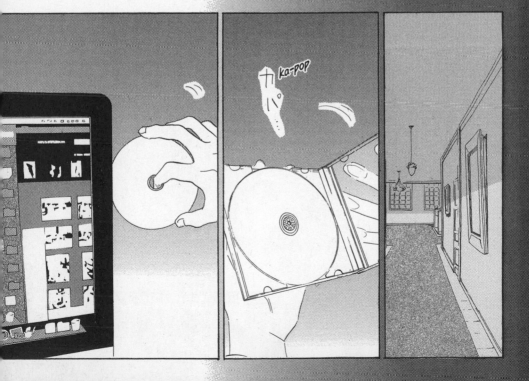

ka-pop

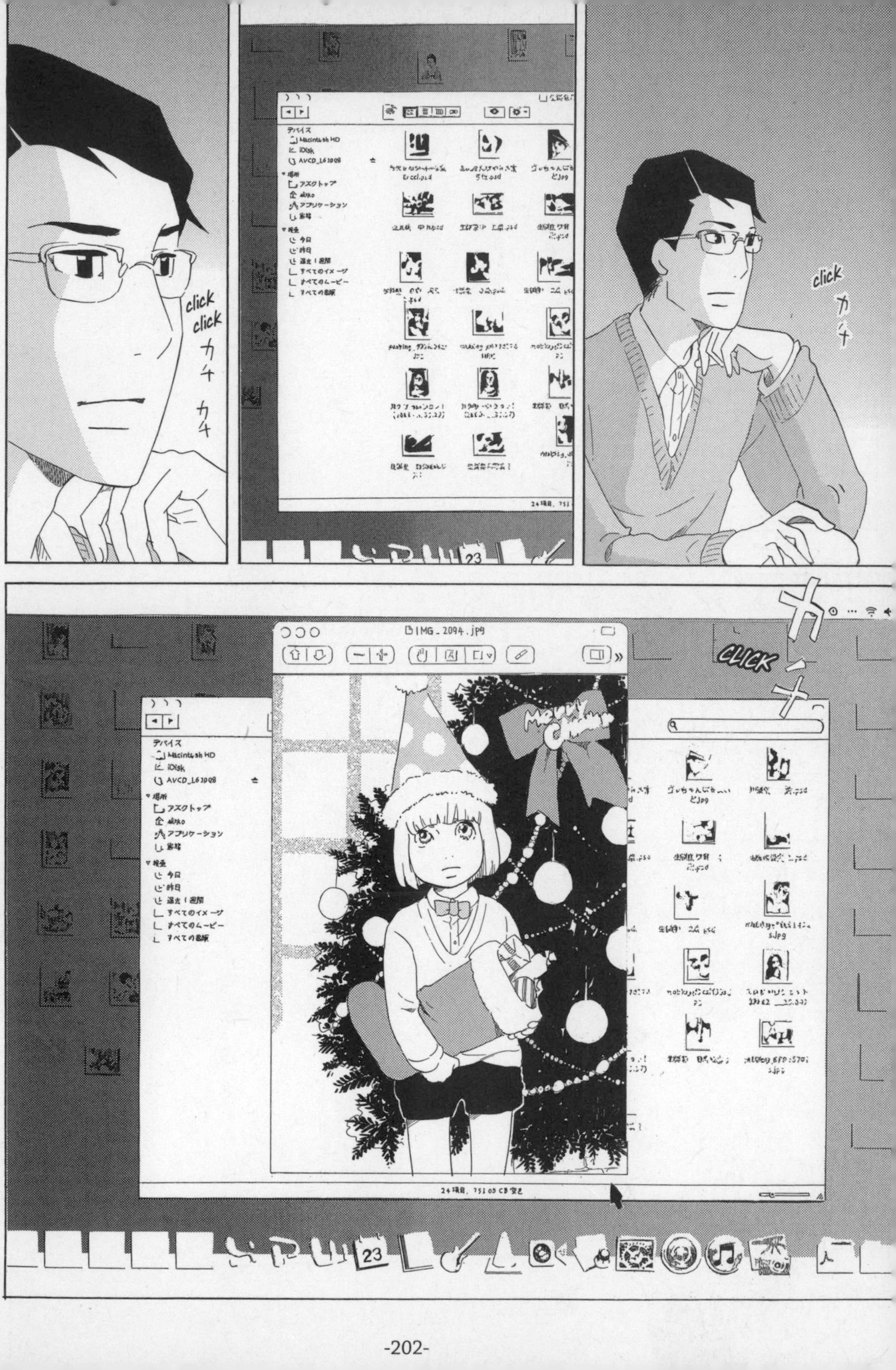
click
カチ
IMG_2094.jpg
click click
カチ
カチ
CLICK
カチ

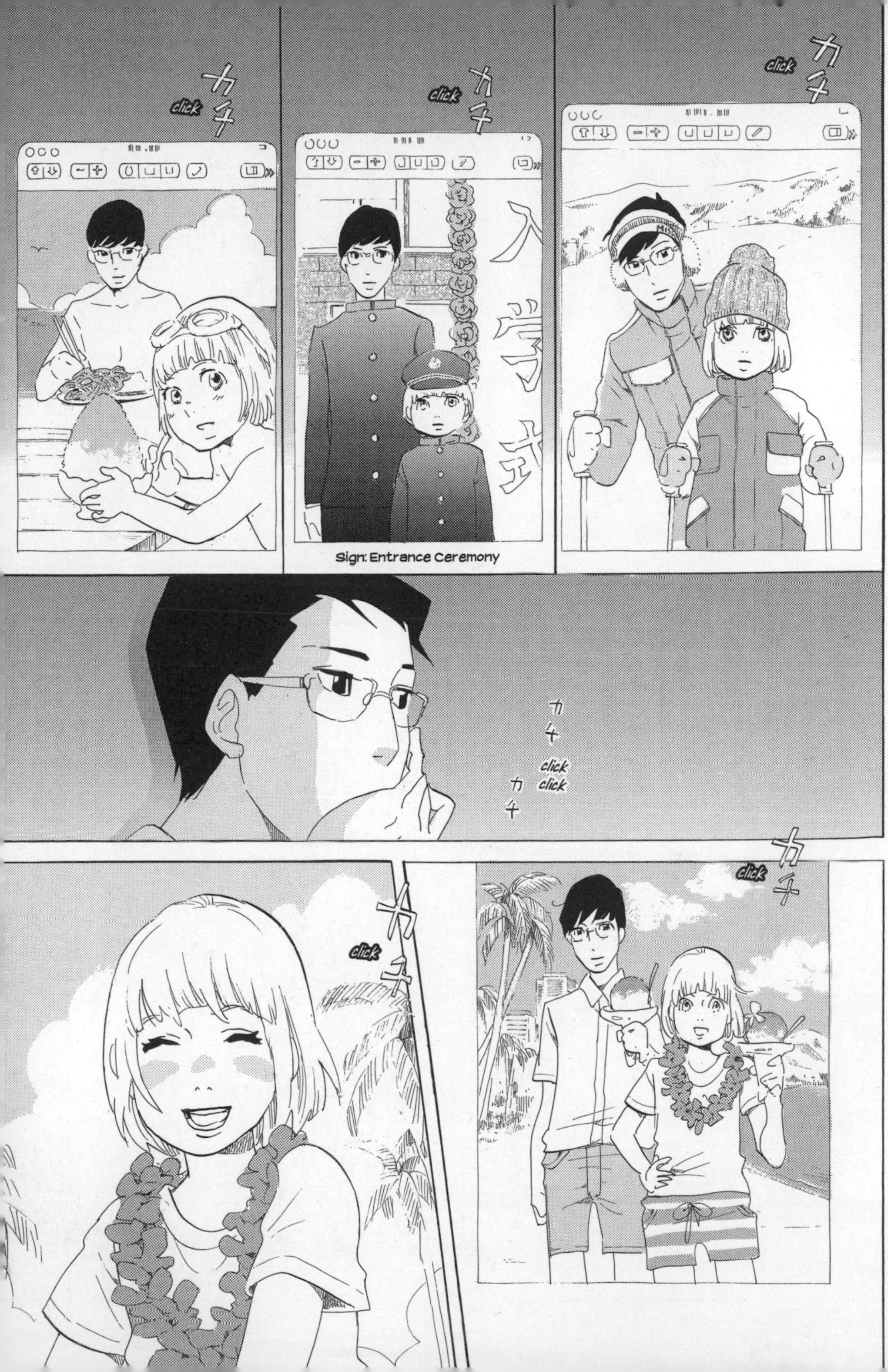
カチ
click
カチ
click
入学式
Sign: Entrance Ceremony
カチ
click
カチ
click
カチ
click
カチ
click
カチ
click
カチ
click

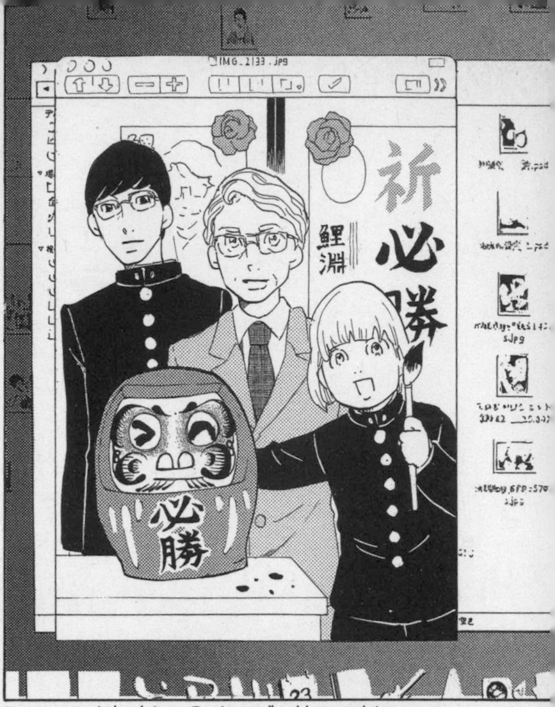
祈
必勝
鯉淵
必勝
Daruma: Certain Victory. Poster: Koibuchi, New Victory.

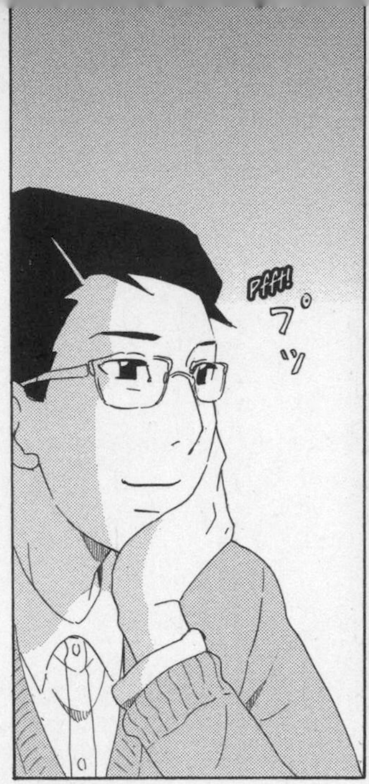
Pfff!
プッ

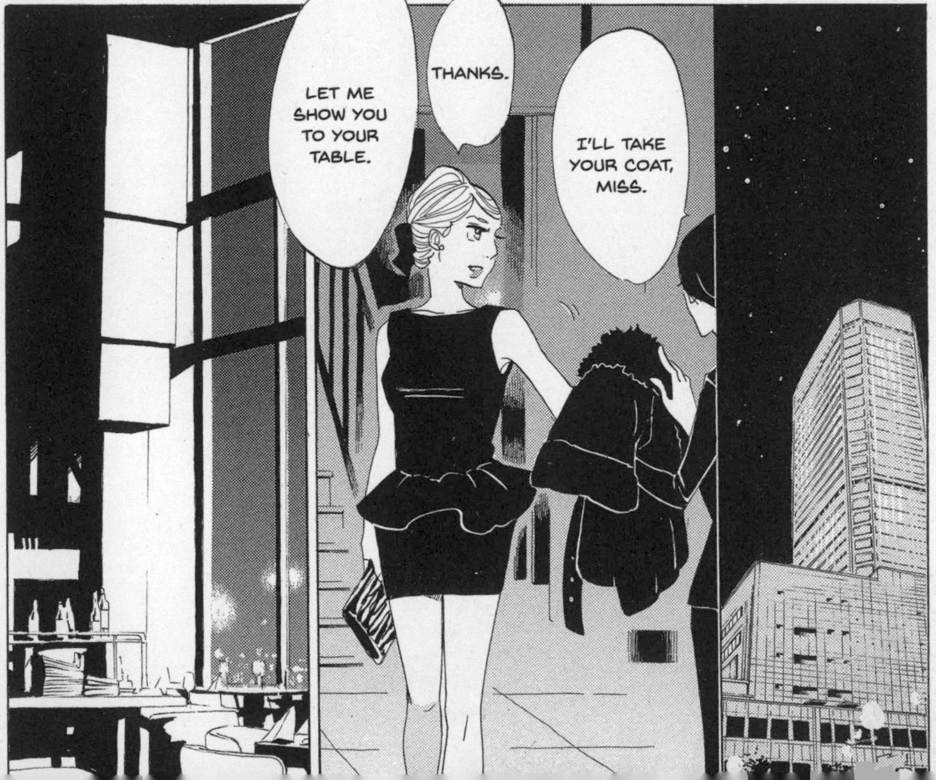
I'LL TAKE YOUR COAT, MISS.
THANKS.
LET ME SHOW YOU TO YOUR TABLE.

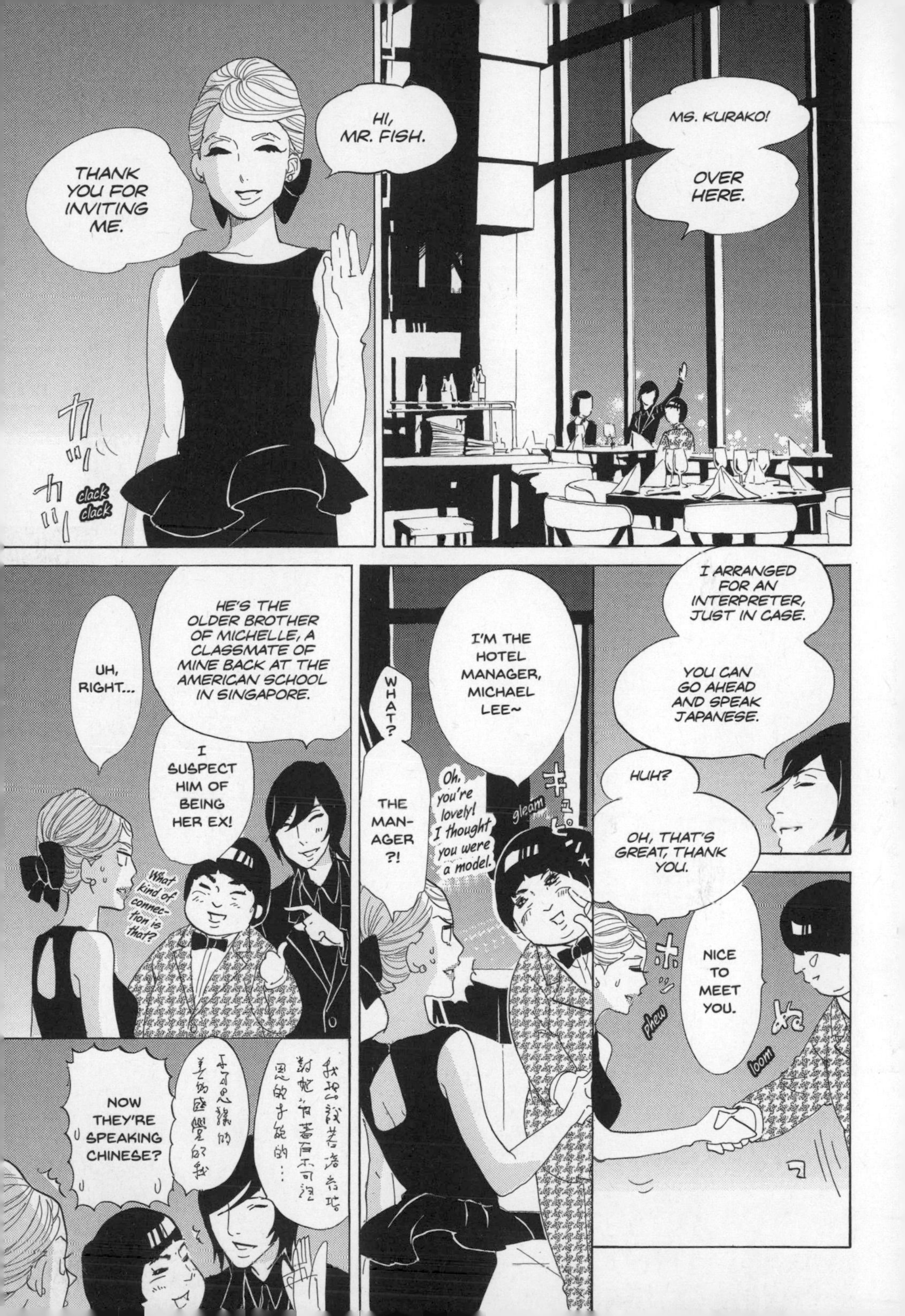
MS. KURAKO!
OVER HERE.
HI, MR. FISH.
THANK YOU FOR INVITING ME.
clack clack
I ARRANGED FOR AN INTERPRETER, JUST IN CASE.
YOU CAN GO AHEAD AND SPEAK JAPANESE.
HUH?
OH, THAT'S GREAT, THANK YOU.
NICE TO MEET YOU.
phew
loom
I'M THE HOTEL MANAGER, MICHAEL LEE~
WHAT?
THE MANAGER?!
gleam
Oh, you're lovely! I thought you were a model.
HE'S THE OLDER BROTHER OF MICHELLE, A CLASSMATE OF MINE BACK AT THE AMERICAN SCHOOL IN SINGAPORE.
UH, RIGHT...
I SUSPECT HIM OF BEING HER EX!
What kind of connection is that?
NOW THEY'RE SPEAKING CHINESE?

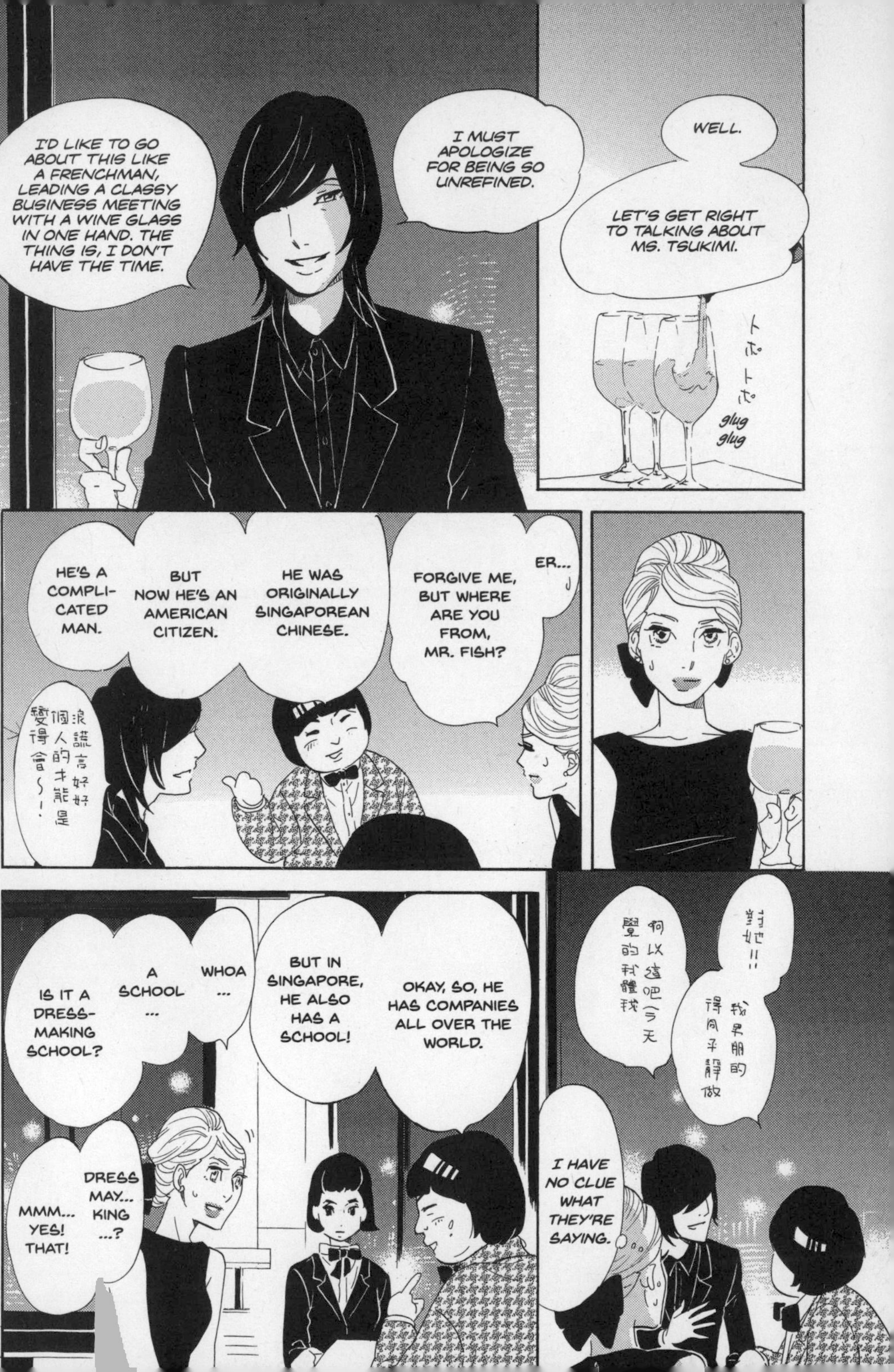
WELL.
LET'S GET RIGHT TO TALKING ABOUT MS. TSUKIMI.
トポトポ
glug glug
I MUST APOLOGIZE FOR BEING SO UNREFINED.
I'D LIKE TO GO ABOUT THIS LIKE A FRENCHMAN, LEADING A CLASSY BUSINESS MEETING WITH A WINE GLASS IN ONE HAND. THE THING IS, I DON'T HAVE THE TIME.
ER...
FORGIVE ME, BUT WHERE ARE YOU FROM, MR. FISH?
HE WAS ORIGINALLY SINGAPOREAN CHINESE.
BUT NOW HE'S AN AMERICAN CITIZEN.
HE'S A COMPLICATED MAN.
浪識言好好個人的才能是變得會～！
對妣!!
我男朋的得向子靜做
啊以這吧今天覺的我體我
I HAVE NO CLUE WHAT THEY'RE SAYING.
OKAY, SO, HE HAS COMPANIES ALL OVER THE WORLD.
BUT IN SINGAPORE, HE ALSO HAS A SCHOOL!
WHOA...
A SCHOOL...
IS IT A DRESS-MAKING SCHOOL?
DRESS MAY... KING...?
MMM... YES! THAT!

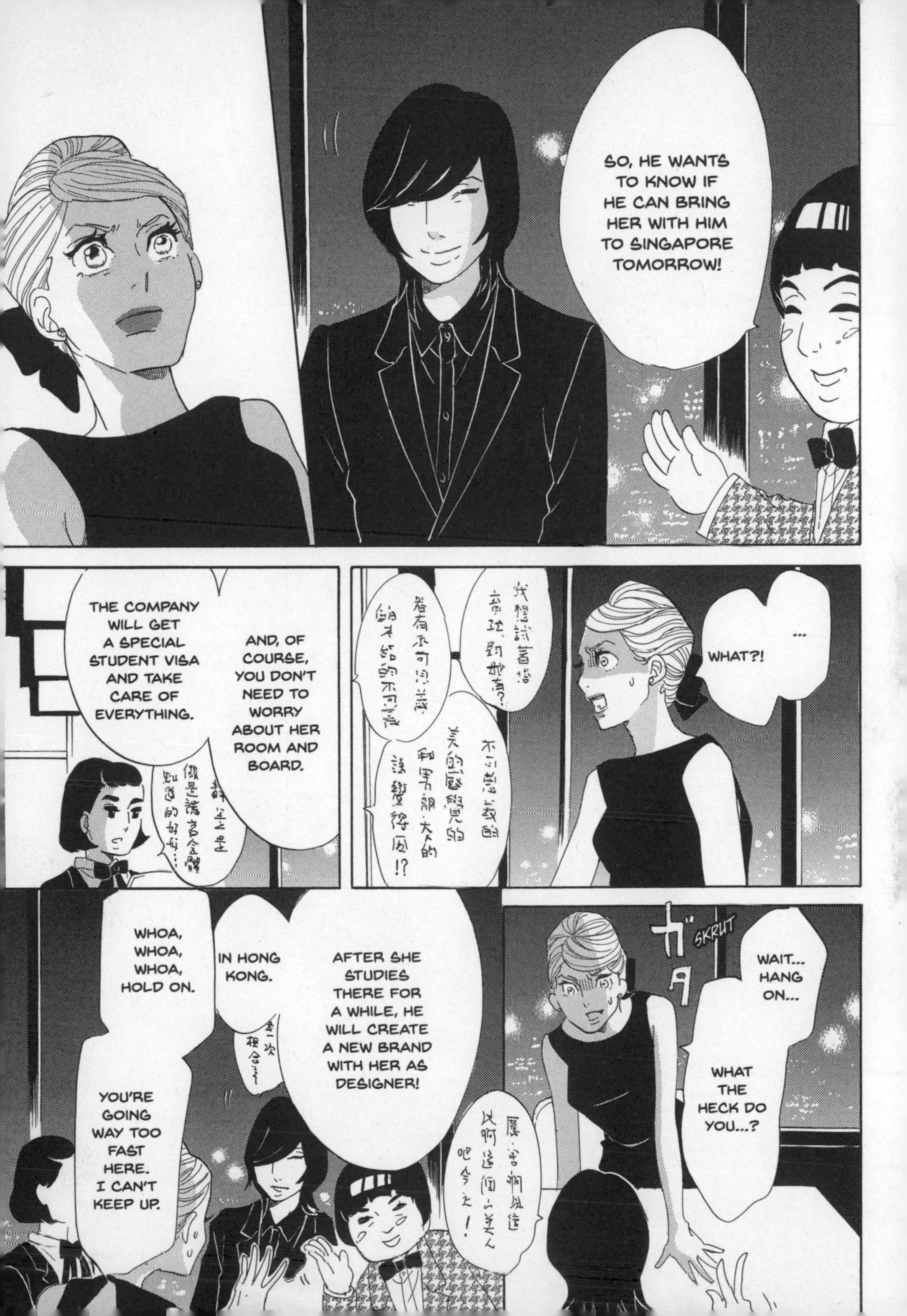
SO, HE WANTS TO KNOW IF HE CAN BRING HER WITH HIM TO SINGAPORE TOMORROW!
...
WHAT?!
THE COMPANY WILL GET A SPECIAL STUDENT VISA AND TAKE CARE OF EVERYTHING.
AND, OF COURSE, YOU DON'T NEED TO WORRY ABOUT HER ROOM AND BOARD.
SKRUT
WAIT... HANG ON...
WHAT THE HECK DO YOU...?
IN HONG KONG.
AFTER SHE STUDIES THERE FOR A WHILE, HE WILL CREATE A NEW BRAND WITH HER AS DESIGNER!
WHOA, WHOA, WHOA, HOLD ON.
YOU'RE GOING WAY TOO FAST HERE. I CAN'T KEEP UP.

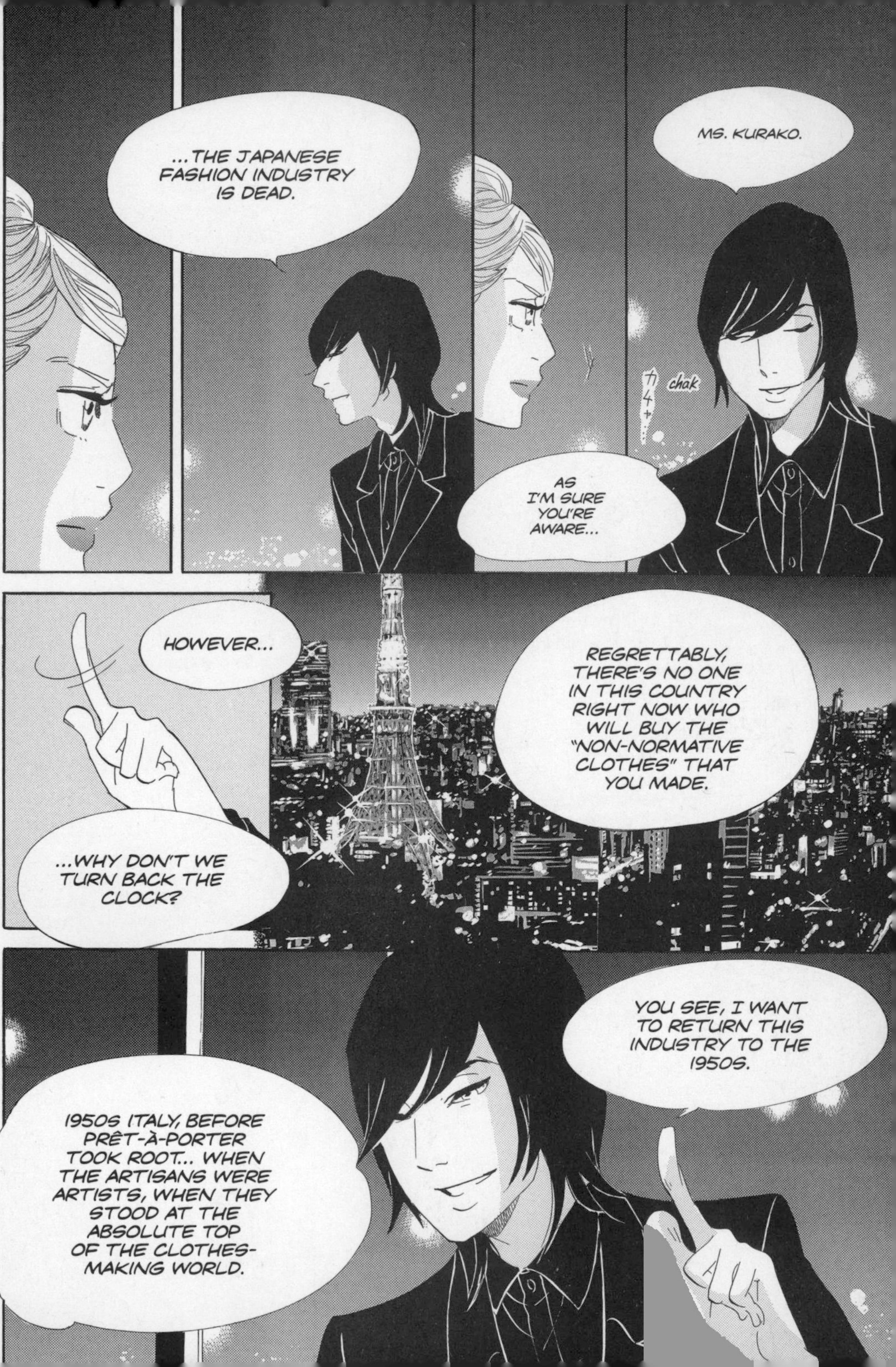
MS. KURAKO.
カチャ
chak
AS I'M SURE YOU'RE AWARE...
...THE JAPANESE FASHION INDUSTRY IS DEAD.
REGRETTABLY, THERE'S NO ONE IN THIS COUNTRY RIGHT NOW WHO WILL BUY THE "NON-NORMATIVE CLOTHES" THAT YOU MADE.
HOWEVER...
...WHY DON'T WE TURN BACK THE CLOCK?
YOU SEE, I WANT TO RETURN THIS INDUSTRY TO THE 1950S.
1950S ITALY, BEFORE PRÊT-À-PORTER TOOK ROOT... WHEN THE ARTISANS WERE ARTISTS, WHEN THEY STOOD AT THE ABSOLUTE TOP OF THE CLOTHES-MAKING WORLD.

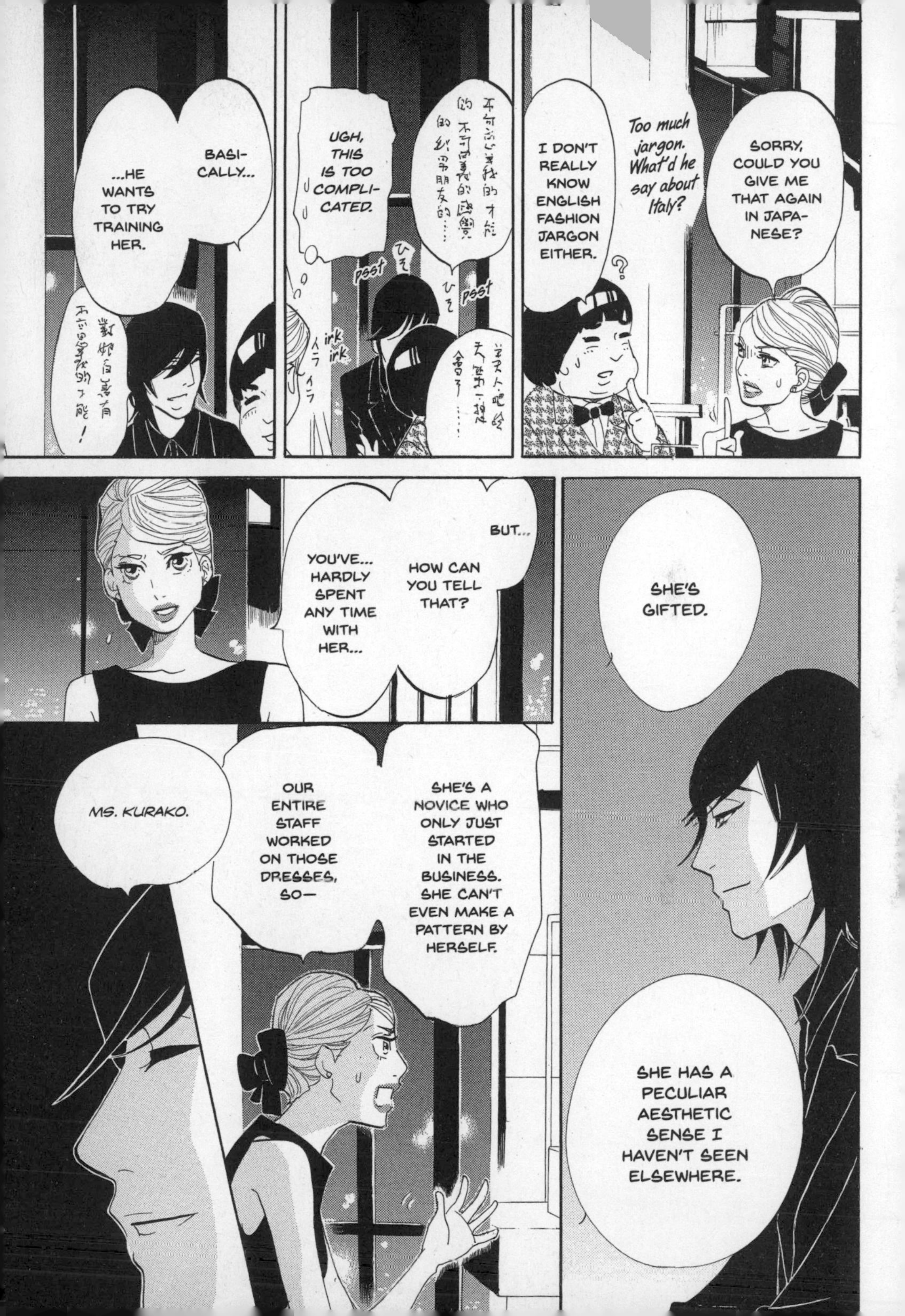
SORRY, COULD YOU GIVE ME THAT AGAIN IN JAPANESE?
Too much jargon. What'd he say about Italy?
I DON'T REALLY KNOW ENGLISH FASHION JARGON EITHER.
psst
psst
UGH, THIS IS TOO COMPLICATED.
irk irk
BASICALLY...
...HE WANTS TO TRY TRAINING HER.
SHE'S GIFTED.
SHE HAS A PECULIAR AESTHETIC SENSE I HAVEN'T SEEN ELSEWHERE.
BUT...
HOW CAN YOU TELL THAT?
YOU'VE... HARDLY SPENT ANY TIME WITH HER...
SHE'S A NOVICE WHO ONLY JUST STARTED IN THE BUSINESS. SHE CAN'T EVEN MAKE A PATTERN BY HERSELF.
OUR ENTIRE STAFF WORKED ON THOSE DRESSES, SO—
MS. KURAKO.

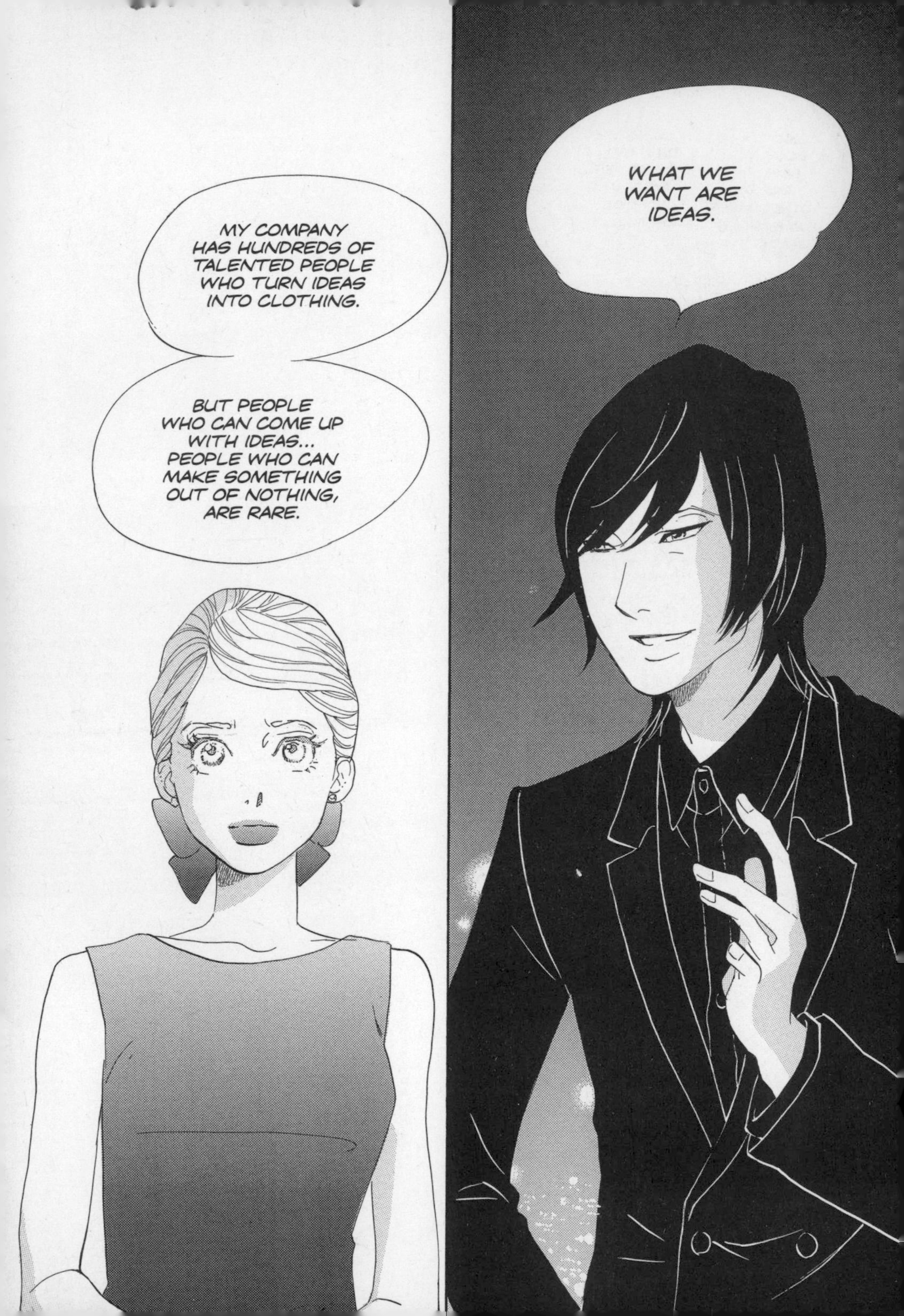
WHAT WE WANT ARE IDEAS.
MY COMPANY HAS HUNDREDS OF TALENTED PEOPLE WHO TURN IDEAS INTO CLOTHING.
BUT PEOPLE WHO CAN COME UP WITH IDEAS... PEOPLE WHO CAN MAKE SOMETHING OUT OF NOTHING, ARE RARE.

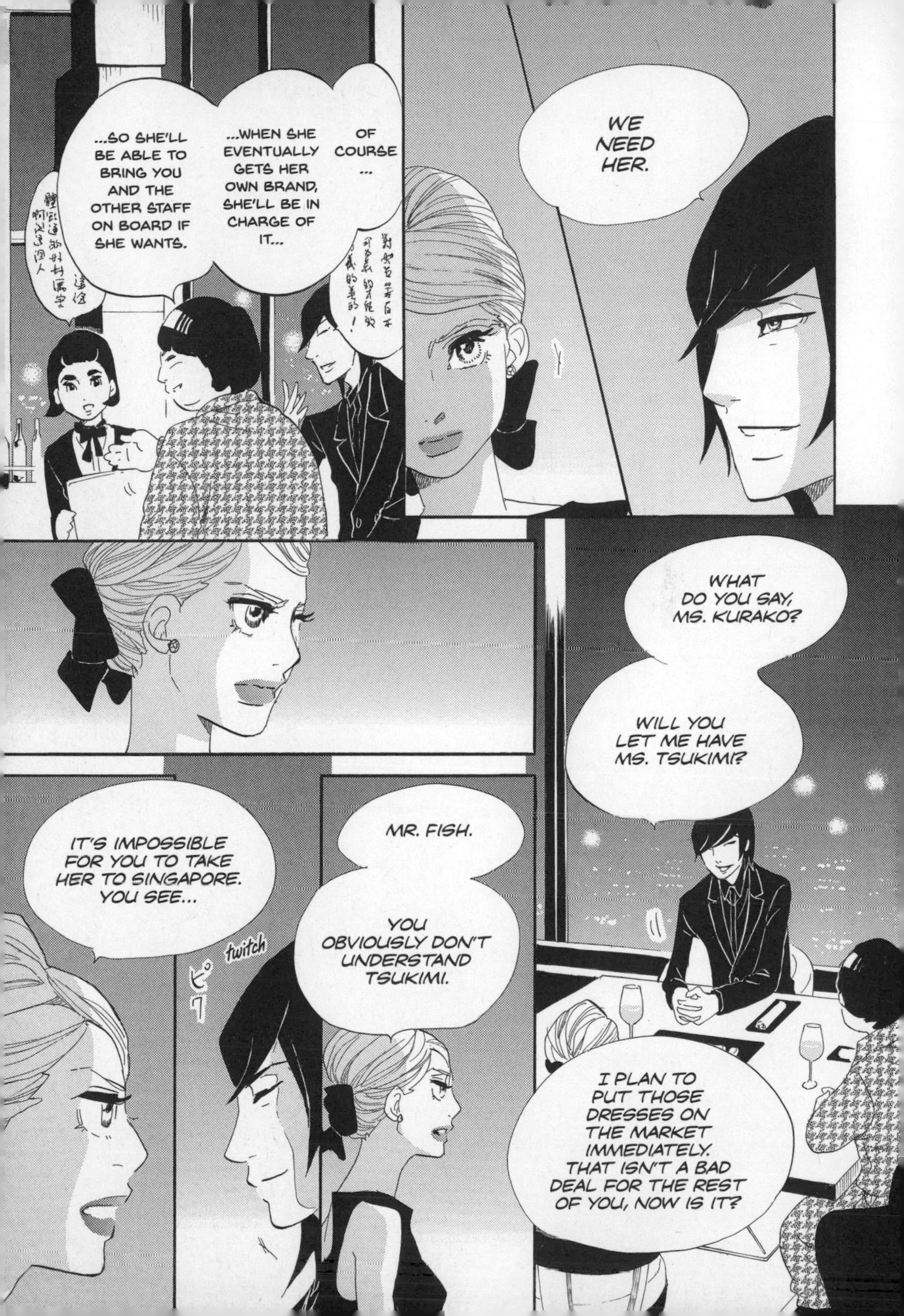
WE NEED HER.
OF COURSE ...
...WHEN SHE EVENTUALLY GETS HER OWN BRAND, SHE'LL BE IN CHARGE OF IT...
...SO SHE'LL BE ABLE TO BRING YOU AND THE OTHER STAFF ON BOARD IF SHE WANTS.
WHAT DO YOU SAY, MS. KURAKO?
WILL YOU LET ME HAVE MS. TSUKIMI?
I PLAN TO PUT THOSE DRESSES ON THE MARKET IMMEDIATELY. THAT ISN'T A BAD DEAL FOR THE REST OF YOU, NOW IS IT?
MR. FISH.
YOU OBVIOUSLY DON'T UNDERSTAND TSUKIMI.
twitch
ピク
IT'S IMPOSSIBLE FOR YOU TO TAKE HER TO SINGAPORE. YOU SEE...

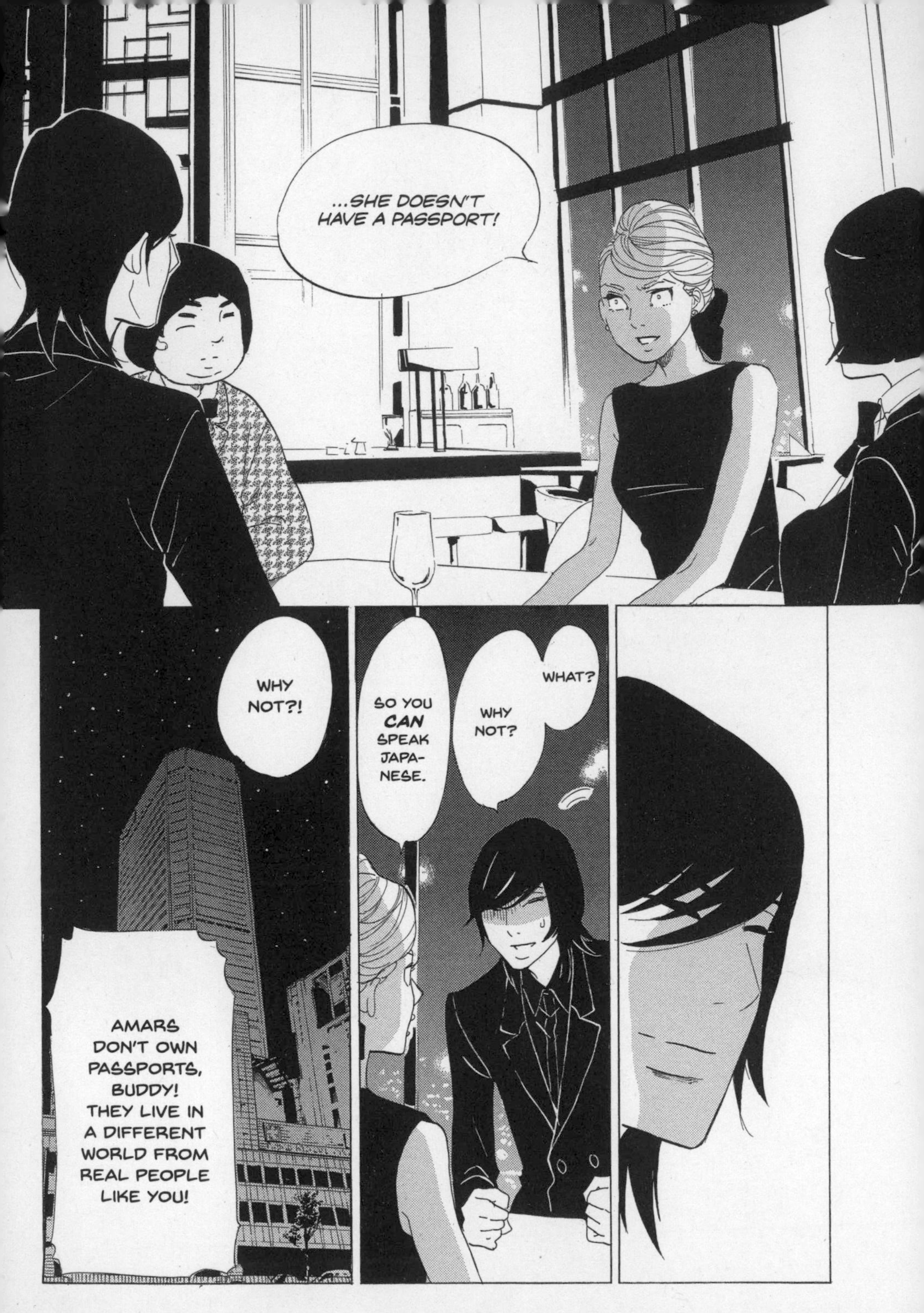
...SHE DOESN'T HAVE A PASSPORT!
WHAT?
WHY NOT?
SO YOU CAN SPEAK JAPANESE.
WHY NOT?!
AMARS DON'T OWN PASSPORTS, BUDDY! THEY LIVE IN A DIFFERENT WORLD FROM REAL PEOPLE LIKE YOU!

Episode 61

The Little Match Girl

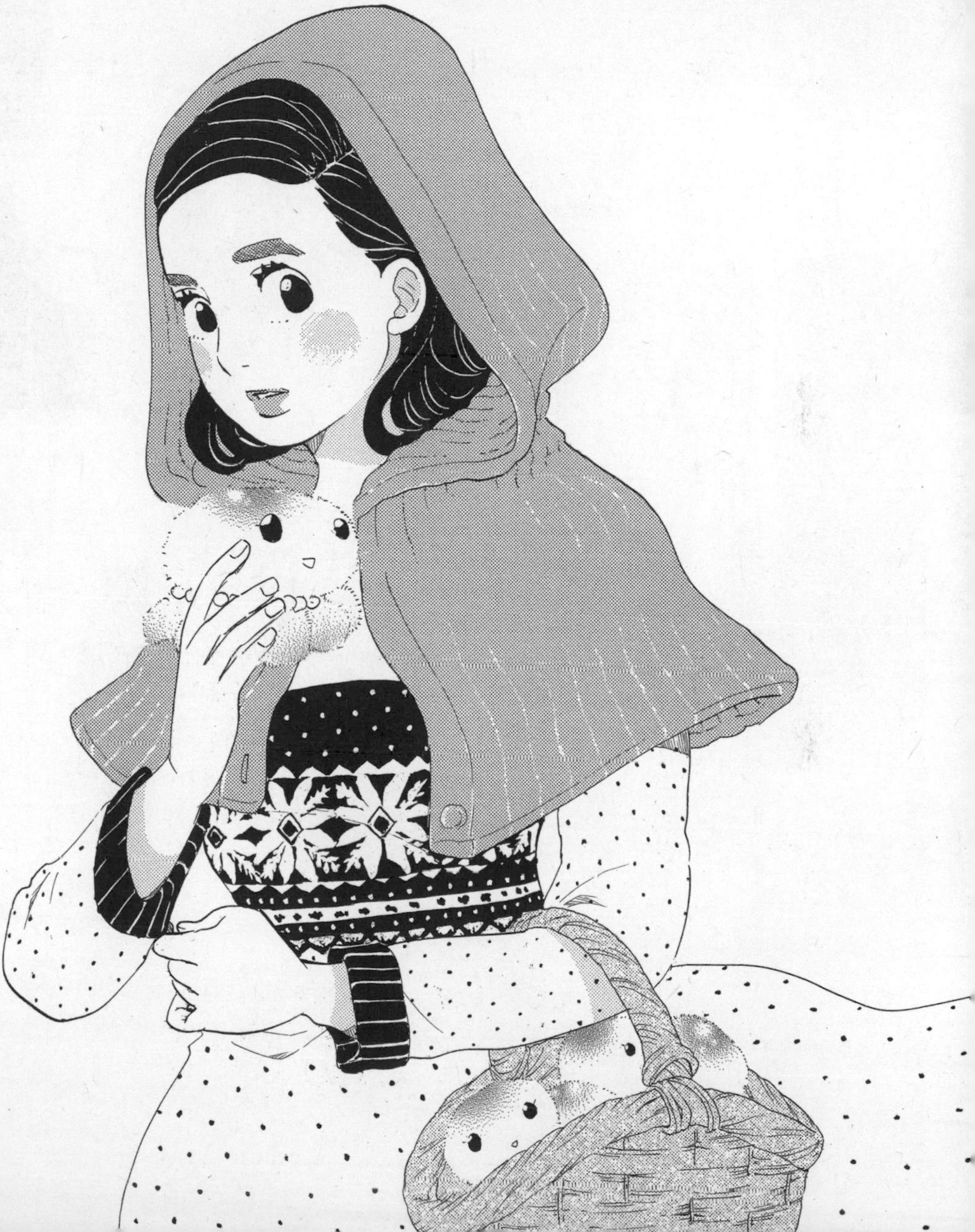

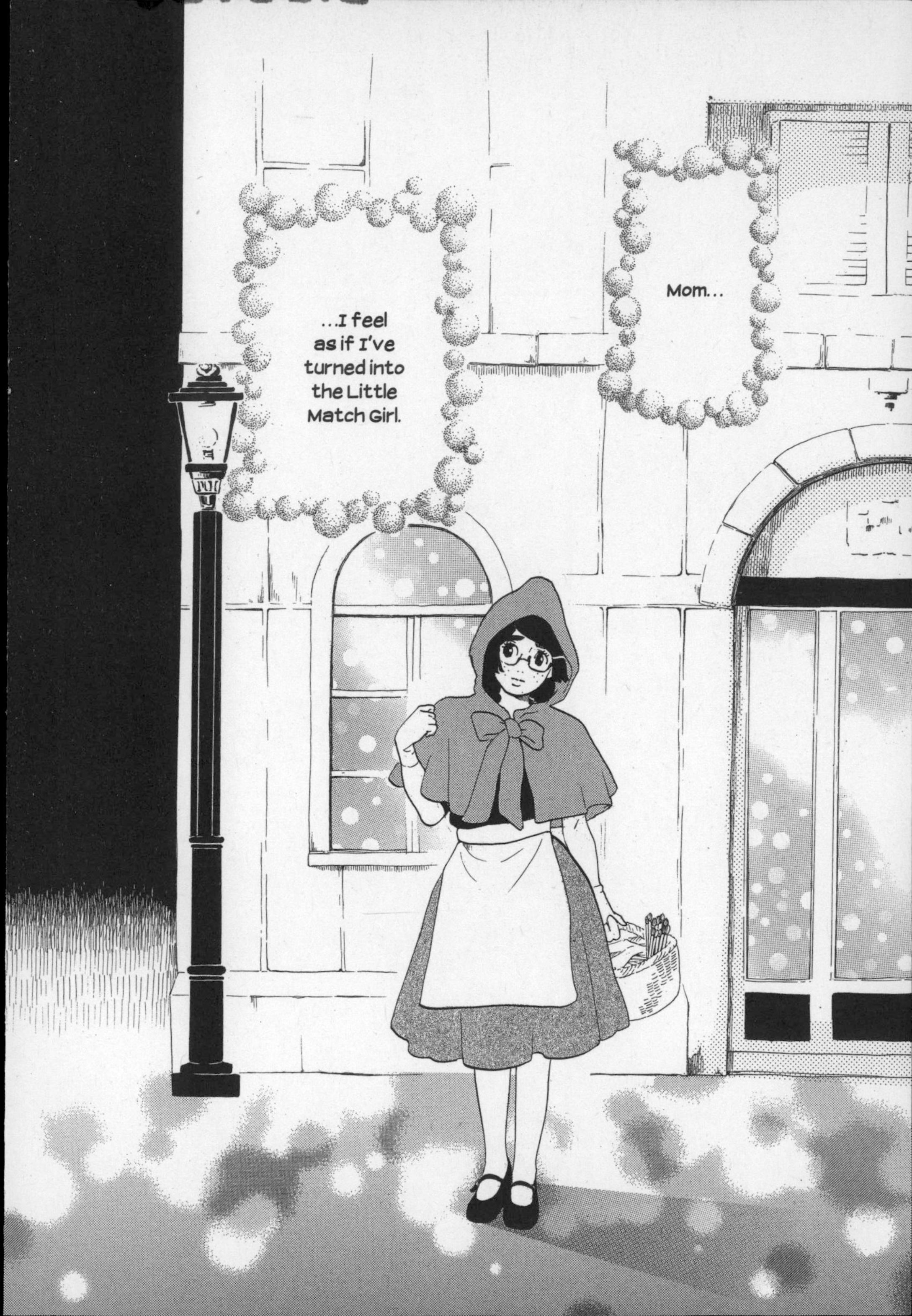
Mom...
...I feel as if I've turned into the Little Match Girl.

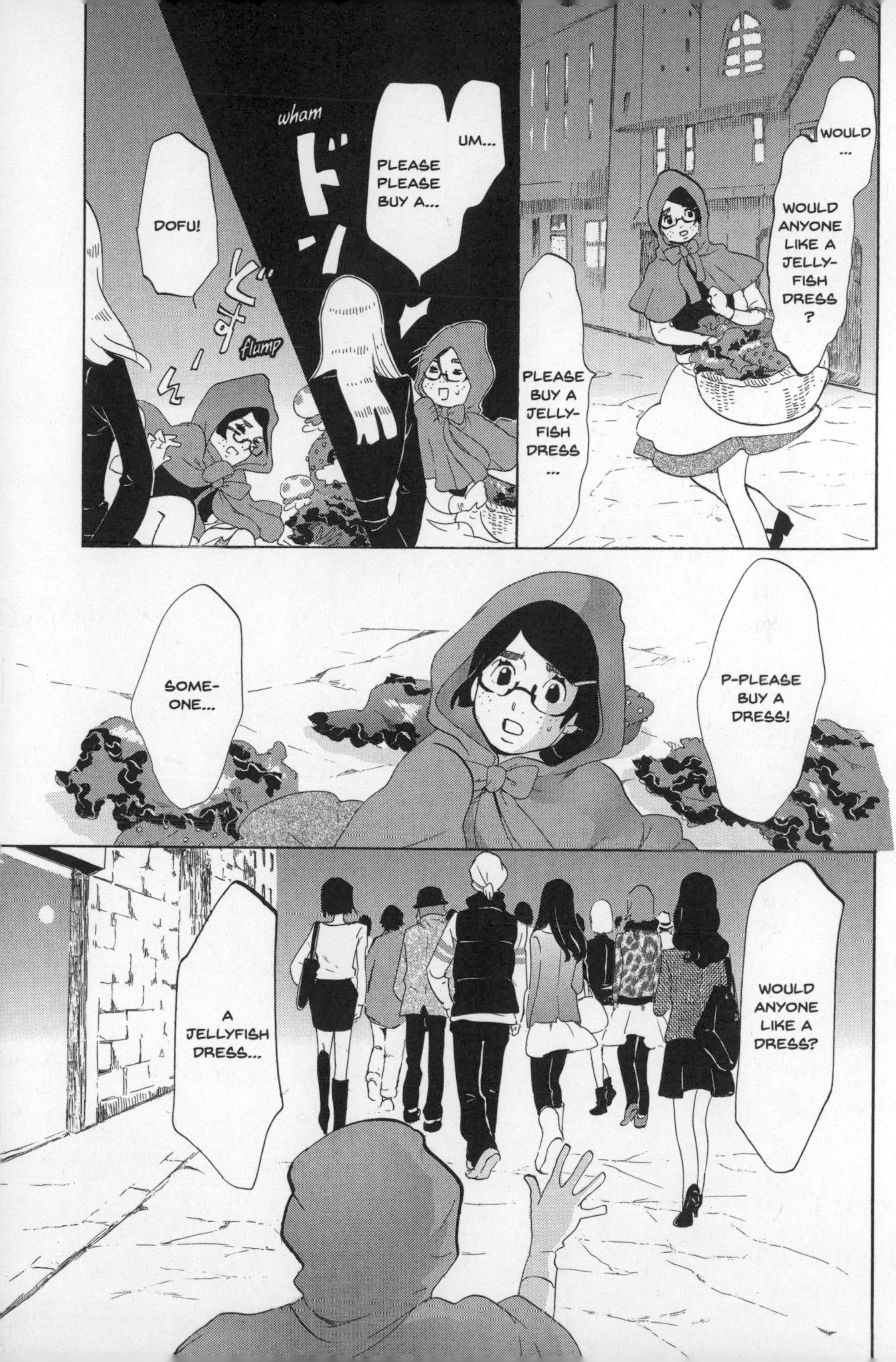
WOULD...
WOULD ANYONE LIKE A JELLY-FISH DRESS?
PLEASE BUY A JELLY-FISH DRESS...
UM...
PLEASE PLEASE BUY A...
wham
DOFU!
flump
P-PLEASE BUY A DRESS!
SOME-ONE...
WOULD ANYONE LIKE A DRESS?
A JELLYFISH DRESS...

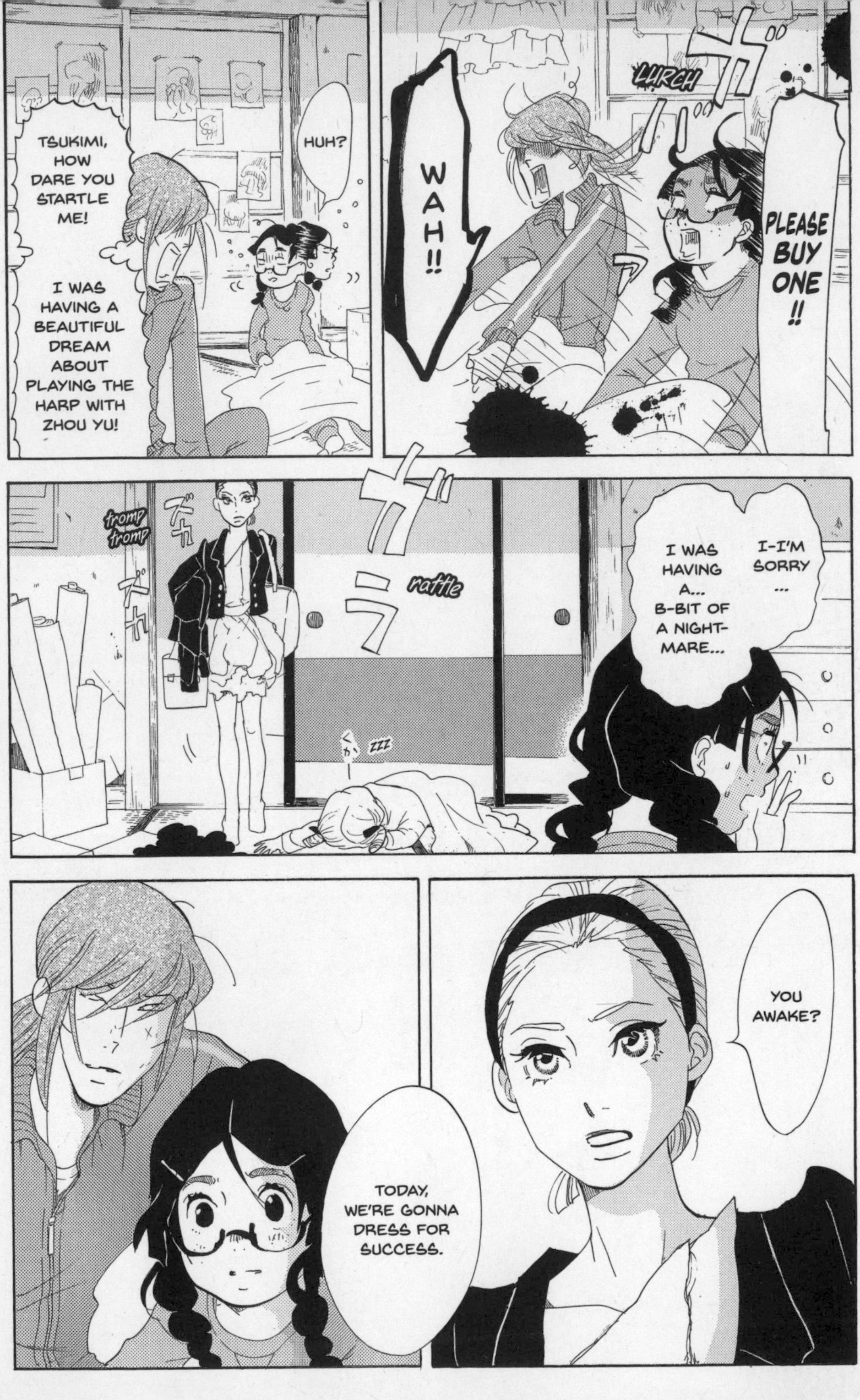
LURCH
PLEASE BUY ONE!!
WAH!!
HUH?
TSUKIMI, HOW DARE YOU STARTLE ME!
I WAS HAVING A BEAUTIFUL DREAM ABOUT PLAYING THE HARP WITH ZHOU YU!
I-I'M SORRY...
I WAS HAVING A... B-BIT OF A NIGHTMARE...
rattle
tromp tromp
zzz
YOU AWAKE?
TODAY, WE'RE GONNA DRESS FOR SUCCESS.

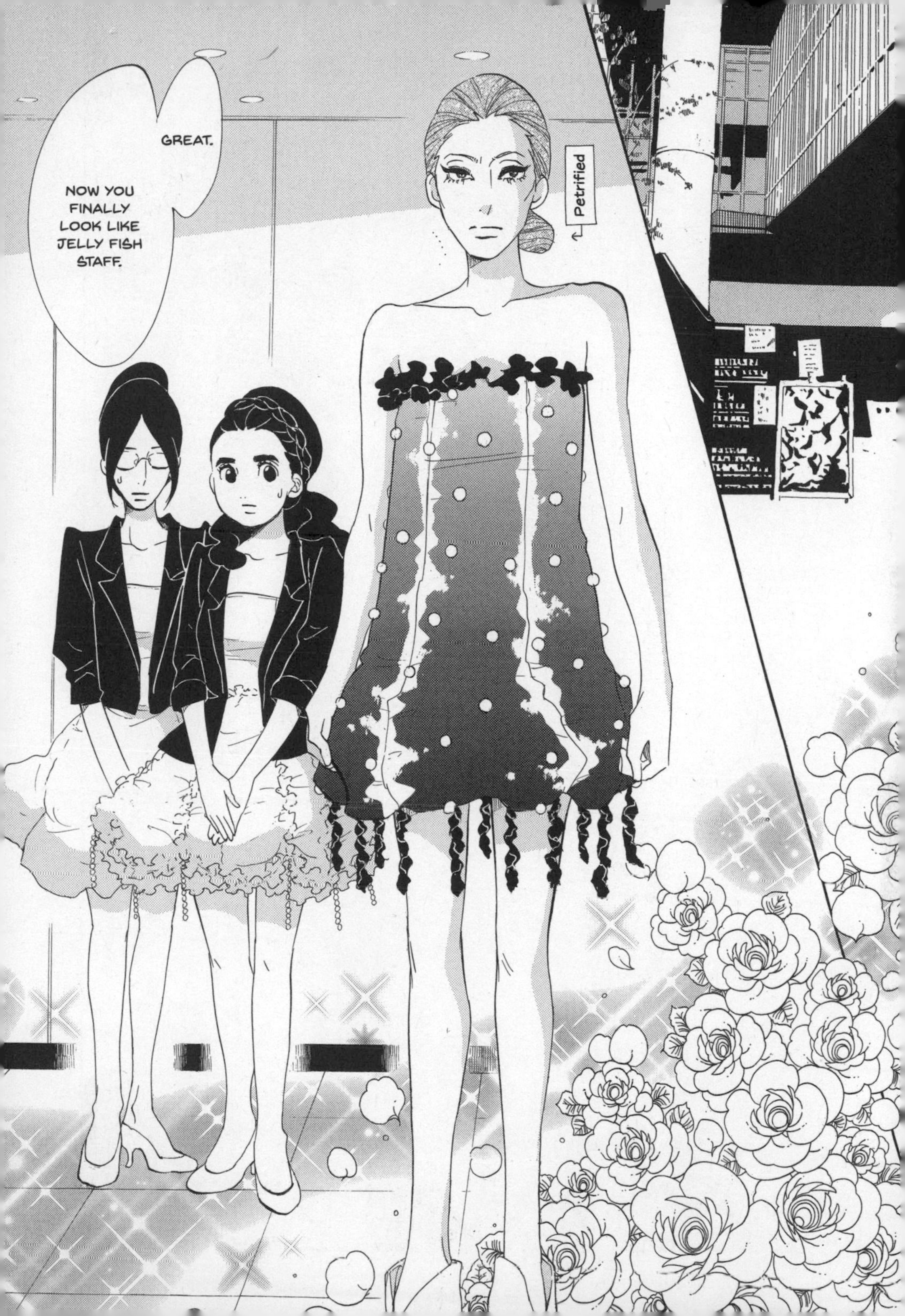
GREAT.
NOW YOU FINALLY LOOK LIKE JELLY FISH STAFF.
Petrified

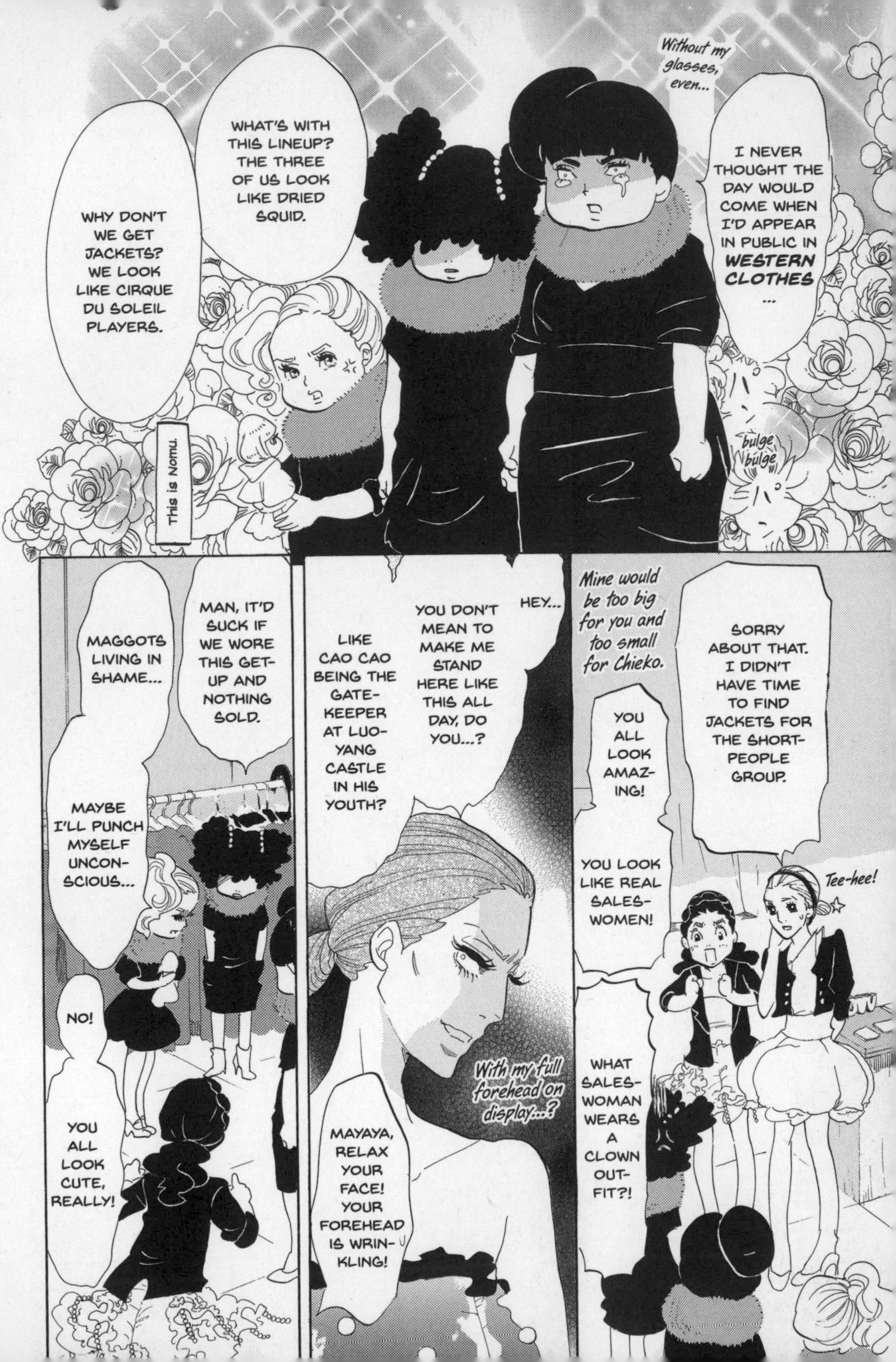
Without my glasses, even...
I NEVER THOUGHT THE DAY WOULD COME WHEN I'D APPEAR IN PUBLIC IN WESTERN CLOTHES...
WHAT'S WITH THIS LINEUP? THE THREE OF US LOOK LIKE DRIED SQUID.
WHY DON'T WE GET JACKETS? WE LOOK LIKE CIRQUE DU SOLEIL PLAYERS.
bulge bulge
This is Nomu.
SORRY ABOUT THAT. I DIDN'T HAVE TIME TO FIND JACKETS FOR THE SHORT-PEOPLE GROUP.
Mine would be too big for you and too small for Chieko.
YOU ALL LOOK AMAZING!
YOU LOOK LIKE REAL SALESWOMEN!
Tee-hee!
WHAT SALESWOMAN WEARS A CLOWN OUTFIT?!
HEY...
YOU DON'T MEAN TO MAKE ME STAND HERE LIKE THIS ALL DAY, DO YOU...?
LIKE CAO CAO BEING THE GATEKEEPER AT LUOYANG CASTLE IN HIS YOUTH?
With my full forehead on display...?
MAYAYA, RELAX YOUR FACE! YOUR FOREHEAD IS WRINKLING!
MAN, IT'D SUCK IF WE WORE THIS GET-UP AND NOTHING SOLD.
MAGGOTS LIVING IN SHAME...
MAYBE I'LL PUNCH MYSELF UNCONSCIOUS...
NO!
YOU ALL LOOK CUTE, REALLY!

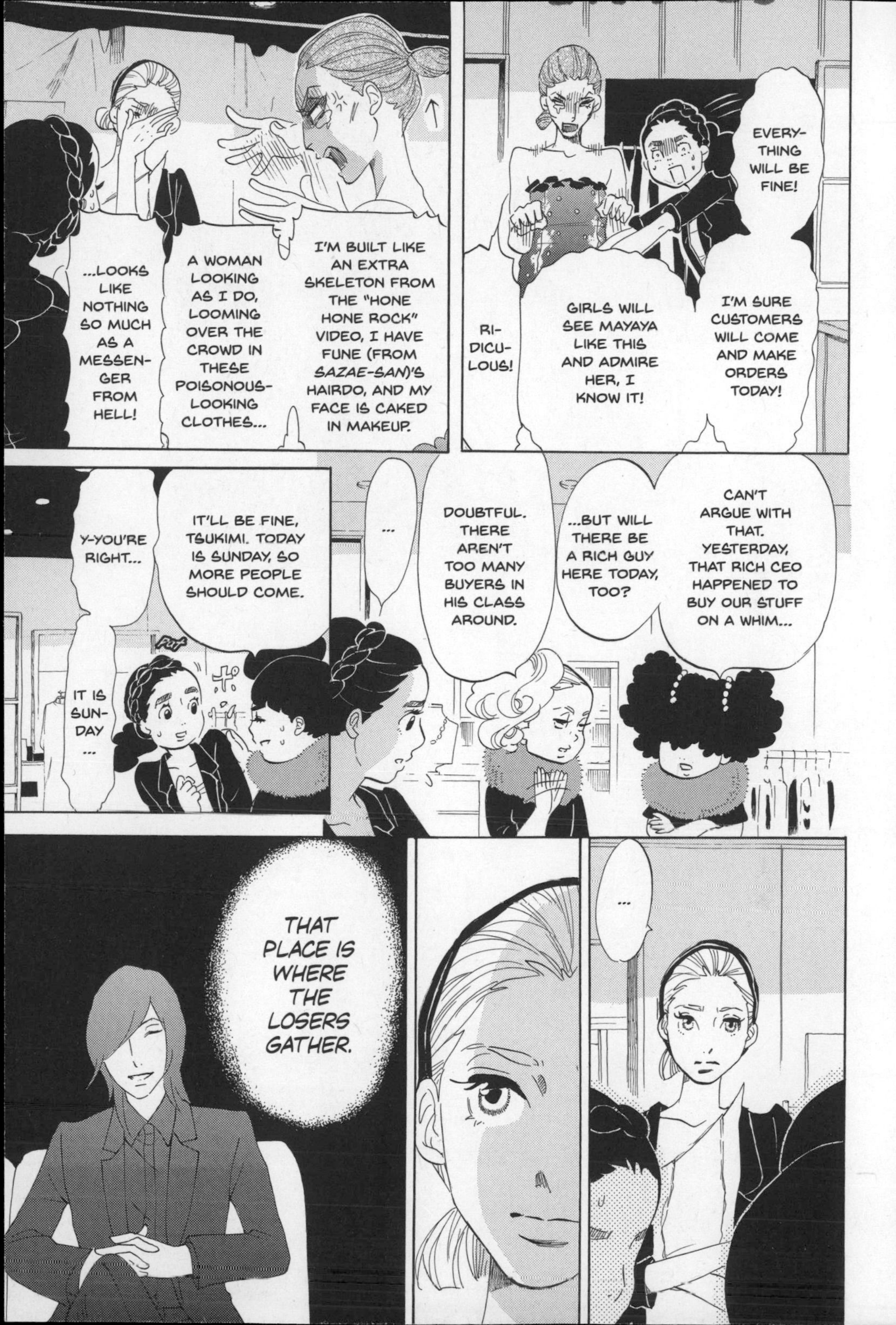
EVERYTHING WILL BE FINE!
I'M SURE CUSTOMERS WILL COME AND MAKE ORDERS TODAY!
GIRLS WILL SEE MAYAYA LIKE THIS AND ADMIRE HER, I KNOW IT!
RIDICULOUS!
I'M BUILT LIKE AN EXTRA SKELETON FROM THE "HONE HONE ROCK" VIDEO, I HAVE FUNE (FROM *SAZAE-SAN*)'S HAIRDO, AND MY FACE IS CAKED IN MAKEUP.
A WOMAN LOOKING AS I DO, LOOMING OVER THE CROWD IN THESE POISONOUS-LOOKING CLOTHES...
...LOOKS LIKE NOTHING SO MUCH AS A MESSENGER FROM HELL!
CAN'T ARGUE WITH THAT. YESTERDAY, THAT RICH CEO HAPPENED TO BUY OUR STUFF ON A WHIM...
...BUT WILL THERE BE A RICH GUY HERE TODAY, TOO?
DOUBTFUL. THERE AREN'T TOO MANY BUYERS IN HIS CLASS AROUND.
...
IT'LL BE FINE, TSUKIMI. TODAY IS SUNDAY, SO MORE PEOPLE SHOULD COME.
Y-YOU'RE RIGHT...
IT IS SUNDAY...
...
THAT PLACE IS WHERE THE LOSERS GATHER.

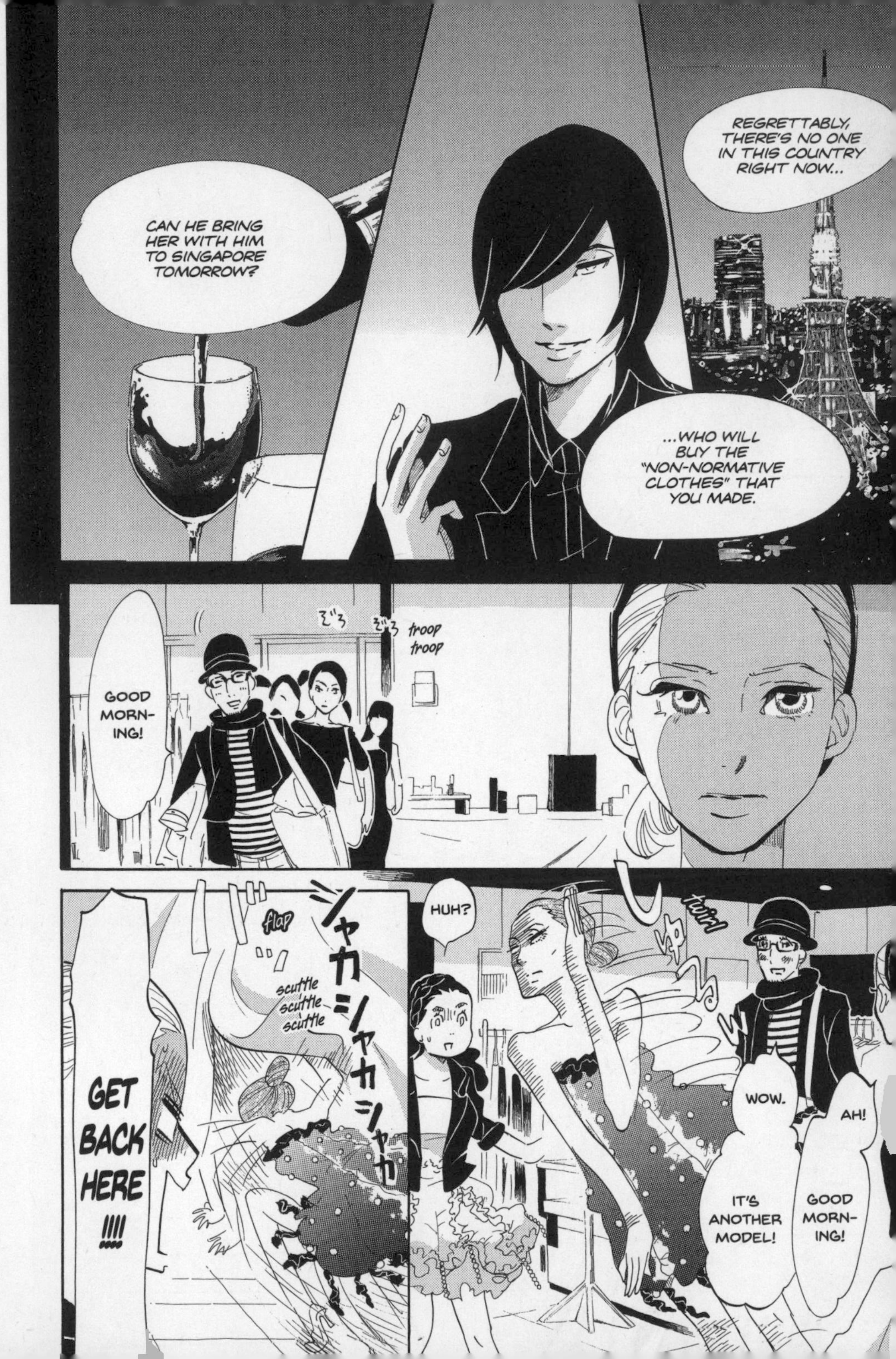
REGRETTABLY, THERE'S NO ONE IN THIS COUNTRY RIGHT NOW...
CAN HE BRING HER WITH HIM TO SINGAPORE TOMORROW?
...WHO WILL BUY THE "NON-NORMATIVE CLOTHES" THAT YOU MADE.
ぞろぞろ
troop troop
GOOD MORNING!
twirl
AH!
GOOD MORNING!
WOW.
IT'S ANOTHER MODEL!
HUH?
シャカシャカシャカ
flap
scuttle scuttle scuttle
GET BACK HERE!!!!

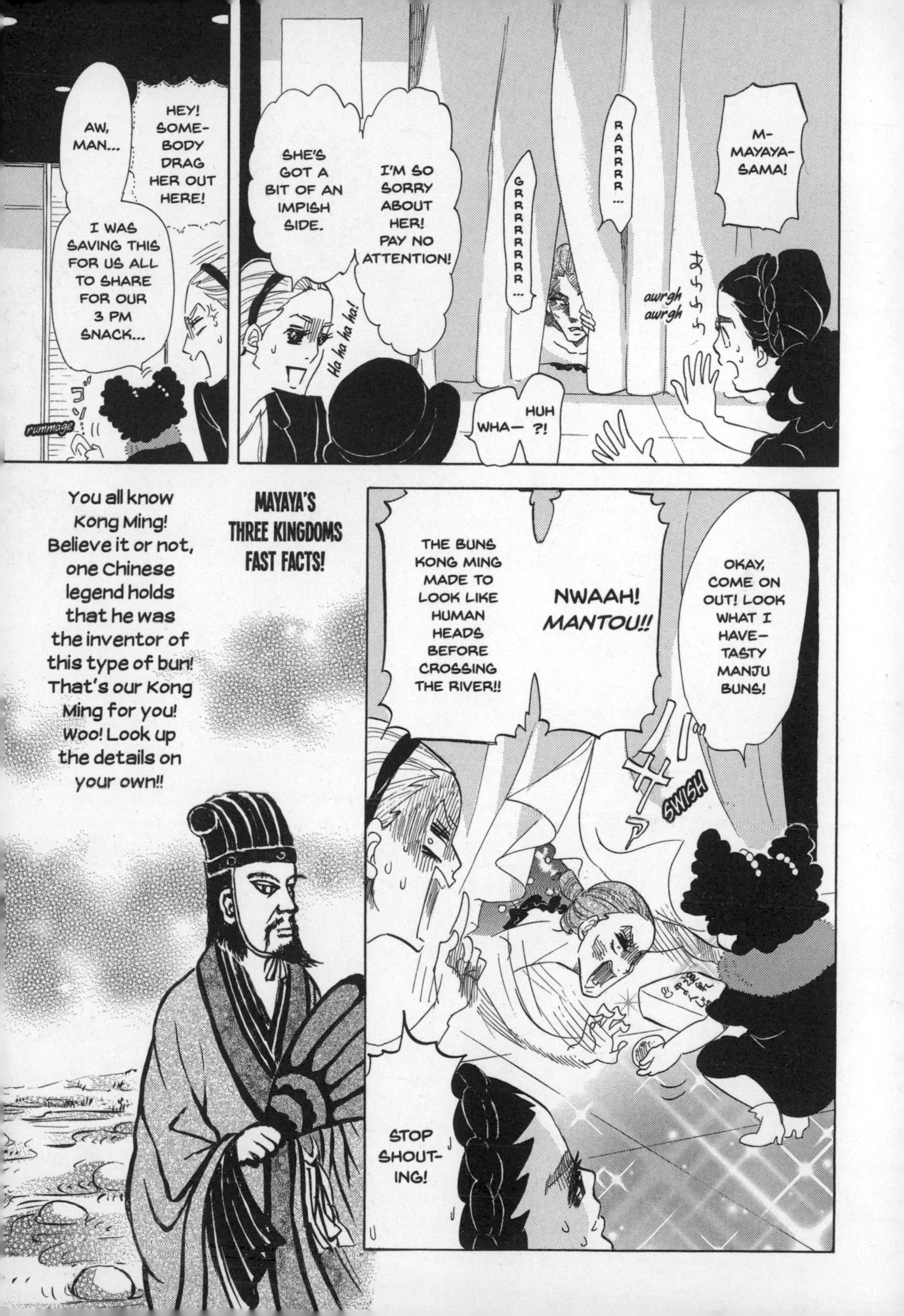
M-MAYAYA-SAMA!
RARRRR...
GRRRRRRRR...
I'M SO SORRY ABOUT HER! PAY NO ATTENTION!
SHE'S GOT A BIT OF AN IMPISH SIDE.
awrgh awrgh
Ha ha ha ha!
HUH WHA— ?!
HEY! SOMEBODY DRAG HER OUT HERE!
AW, MAN...
I WAS SAVING THIS FOR US ALL TO SHARE FOR OUR 3 PM SNACK...
rummage
OKAY, COME ON OUT! LOOK WHAT I HAVE—TASTY MANJU BUNS!
NWAAH! MANTOU!!
THE BUNS KONG MING MADE TO LOOK LIKE HUMAN HEADS BEFORE CROSSING THE RIVER!!
SWISH
STOP SHOUTING!
MAYAYA'S THREE KINGDOMS FAST FACTS!
You all know Kong Ming! Believe it or not, one Chinese legend holds that he was the inventor of this type of bun! That's our Kong Ming for you! Woo! Look up the details on your own!!

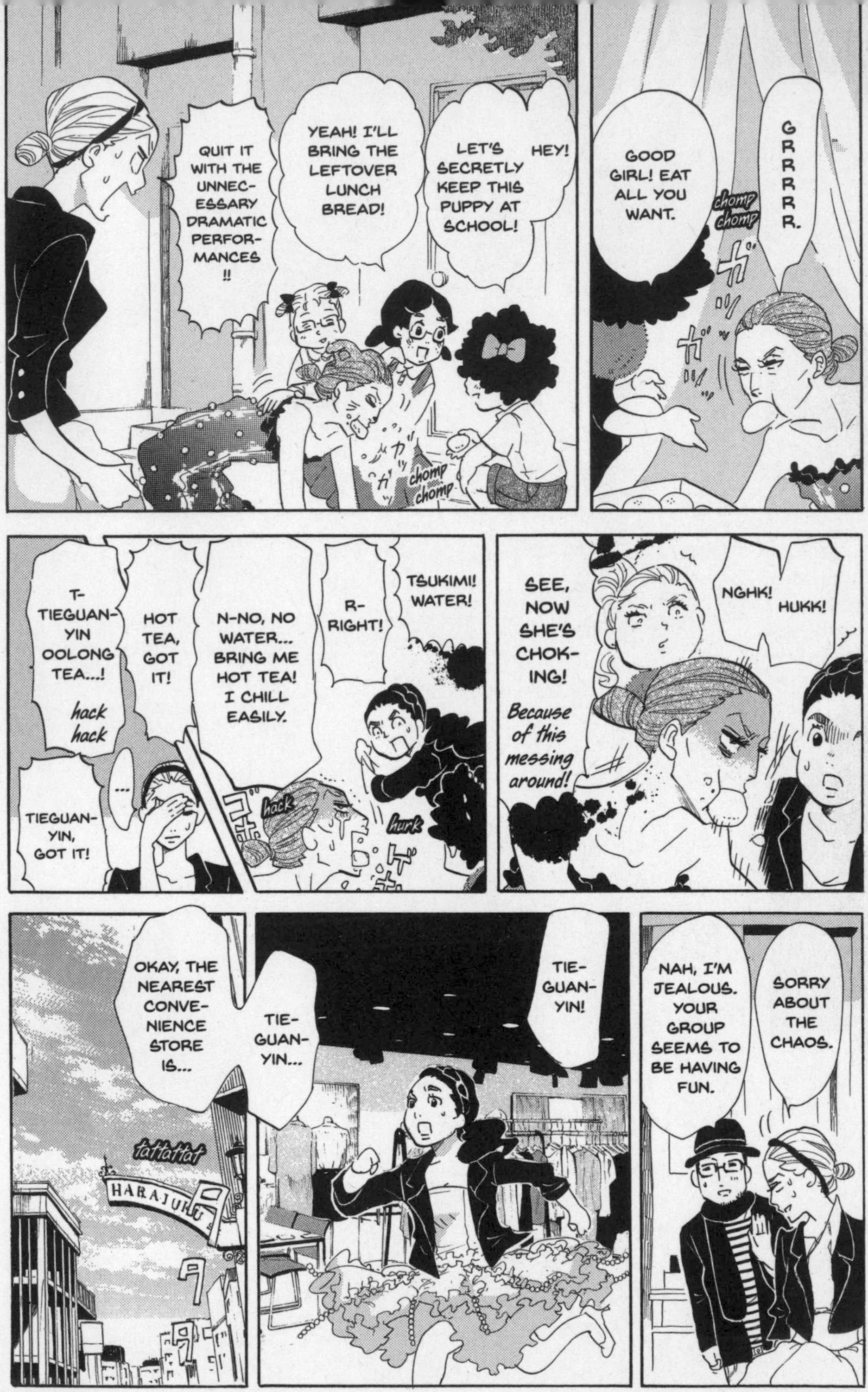
GRRRRR.
GOOD GIRL! EAT ALL YOU WANT.
chomp chomp
HEY!
LET'S SECRETLY KEEP THIS PUPPY AT SCHOOL!
YEAH! I'LL BRING THE LEFTOVER LUNCH BREAD!
QUIT IT WITH THE UNNECESSARY DRAMATIC PERFORMANCES!!
chomp chomp
HUKK!
NGHK!
SEE, NOW SHE'S CHOKING!
Because of this messing around!
TSUKIMI! WATER!
R-RIGHT!
N-NO, NO WATER... BRING ME HOT TEA! I CHILL EASILY.
HOT TEA, GOT IT!
T-TIEGUANYIN OOLONG TEA...!
hack hack
...
TIEGUANYIN, GOT IT!
hack
hurk
SORRY ABOUT THE CHAOS.
NAH, I'M JEALOUS. YOUR GROUP SEEMS TO BE HAVING FUN.
TIEGUANYIN!
TIEGUANYIN...
OKAY, THE NEAREST CONVENIENCE STORE IS...
tattattat
HARAJUKU

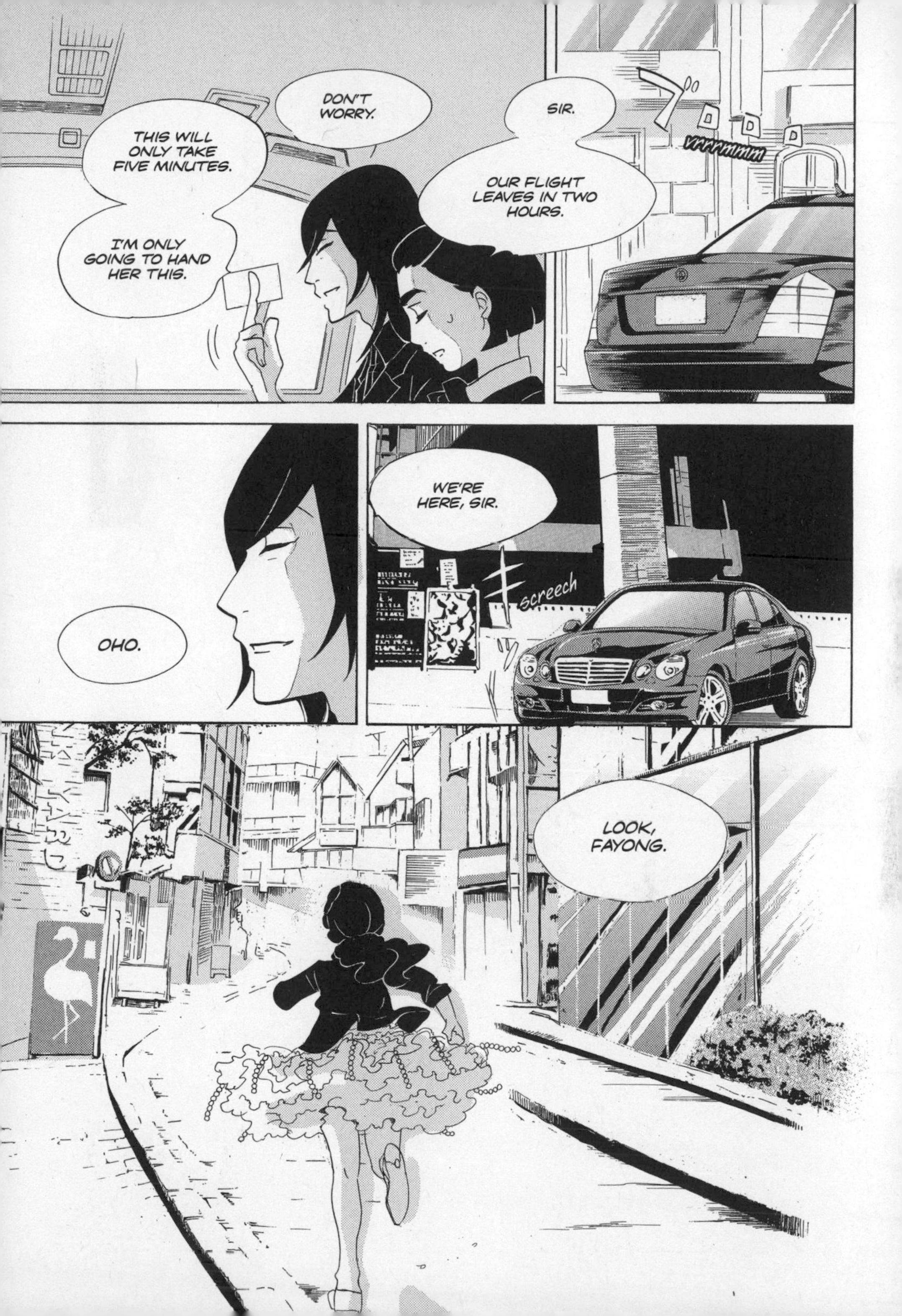
vrrrmmmm
SIR.
OUR FLIGHT LEAVES IN TWO HOURS.
DON'T WORRY.
THIS WILL ONLY TAKE FIVE MINUTES.
I'M ONLY GOING TO HAND HER THIS.
WE'RE HERE, SIR.
screech
OHO.
LOOK, FAYONG.

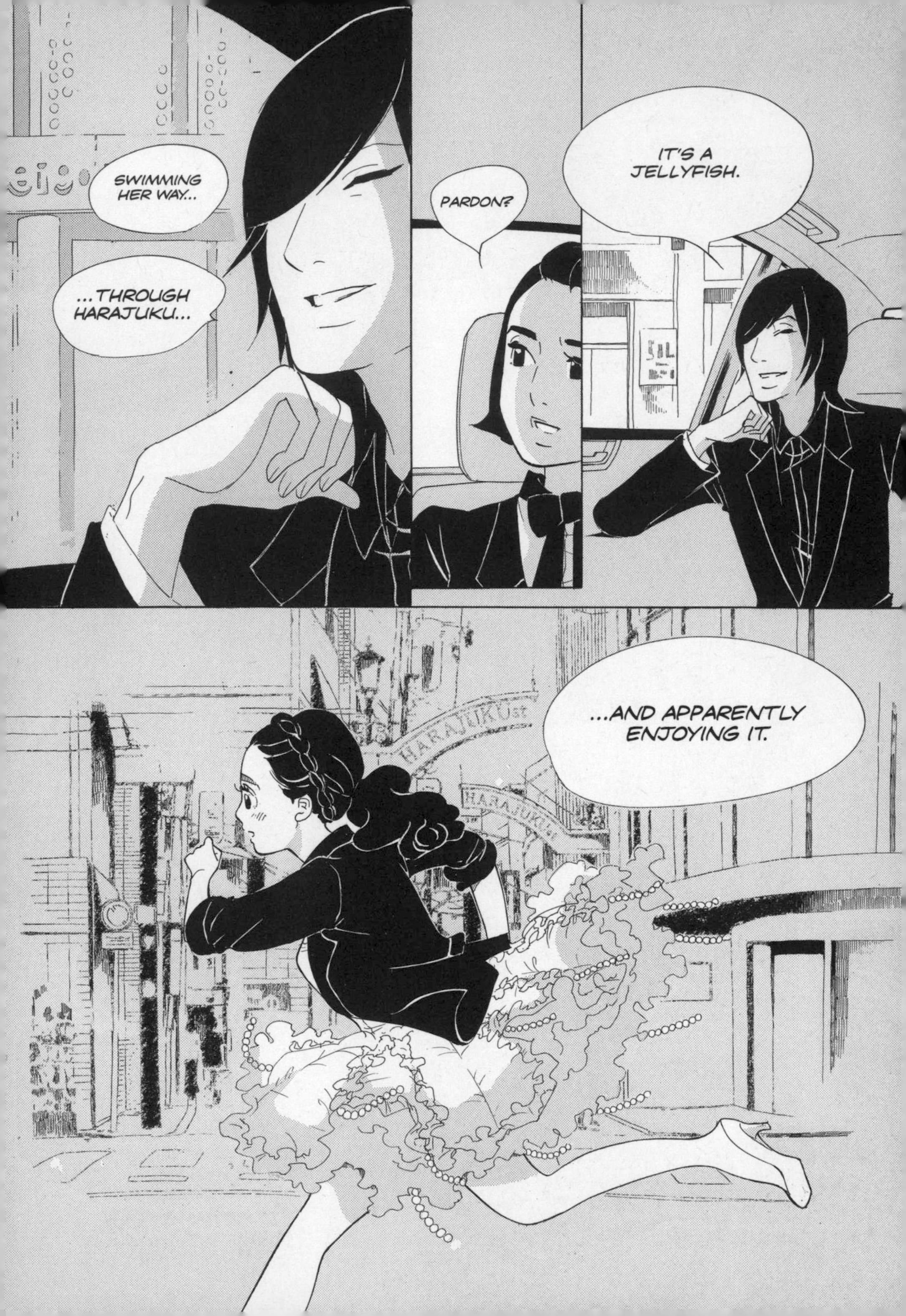
IT'S A JELLYFISH.
PARDON?
SWIMMING HER WAY...
...THROUGH HARAJUKU...
HARAJUKU st
...AND APPARENTLY ENJOYING IT.

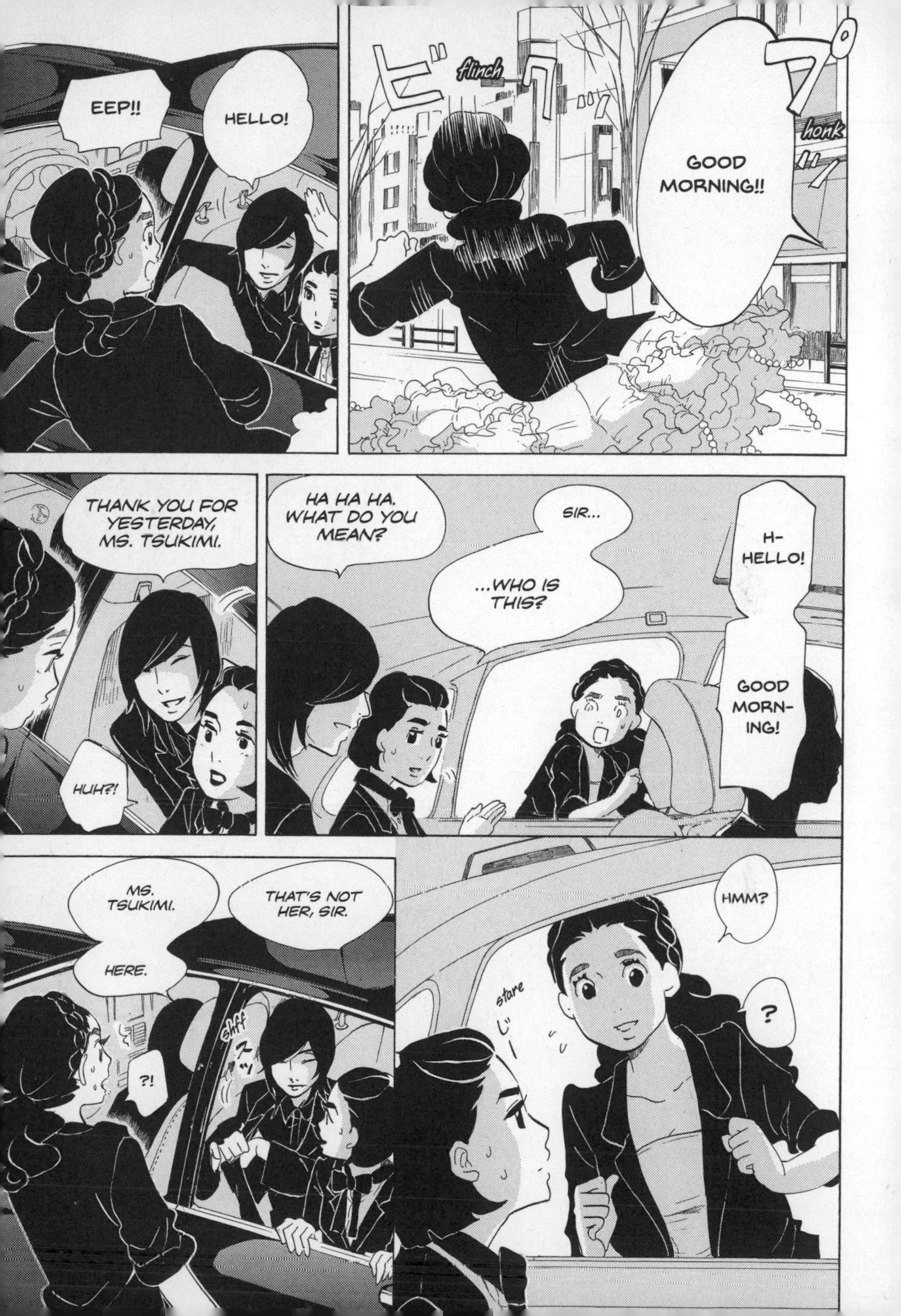
honk
GOOD MORNING!!
flinch
HELLO!
EEP!!
H-HELLO!
GOOD MORN-ING!
SIR...
...WHO IS THIS?
HA HA HA. WHAT DO YOU MEAN?
THANK YOU FOR YESTERDAY, MS. TSUKIMI.
HUH?!
HMM?
stare
?
THAT'S NOT HER, SIR.
MS. TSUKIMI.
HERE.
shff
?!

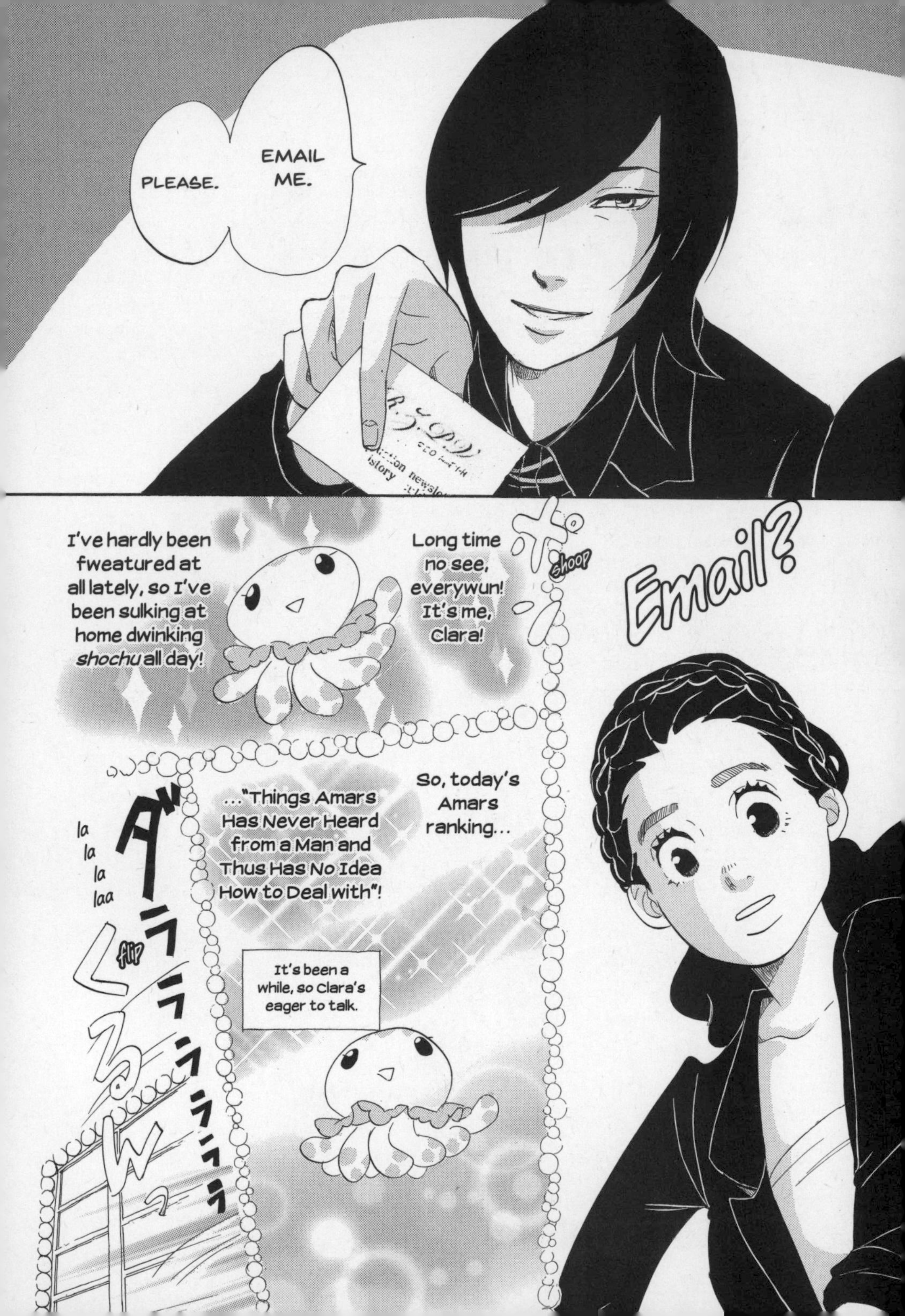
EMAIL ME.
PLEASE.
Email?
shoop
Long time no see, everywun! It's me, Clara!
I've hardly been fweatured at all lately, so I've been sulking at home dwinking *shochu* all day!
So, today's Amars ranking...
..."Things Amars Has Never Heard from a Man and Thus Has No Idea How to Deal with"!
It's been a while, so Clara's eager to talk.
flip
la la la laa

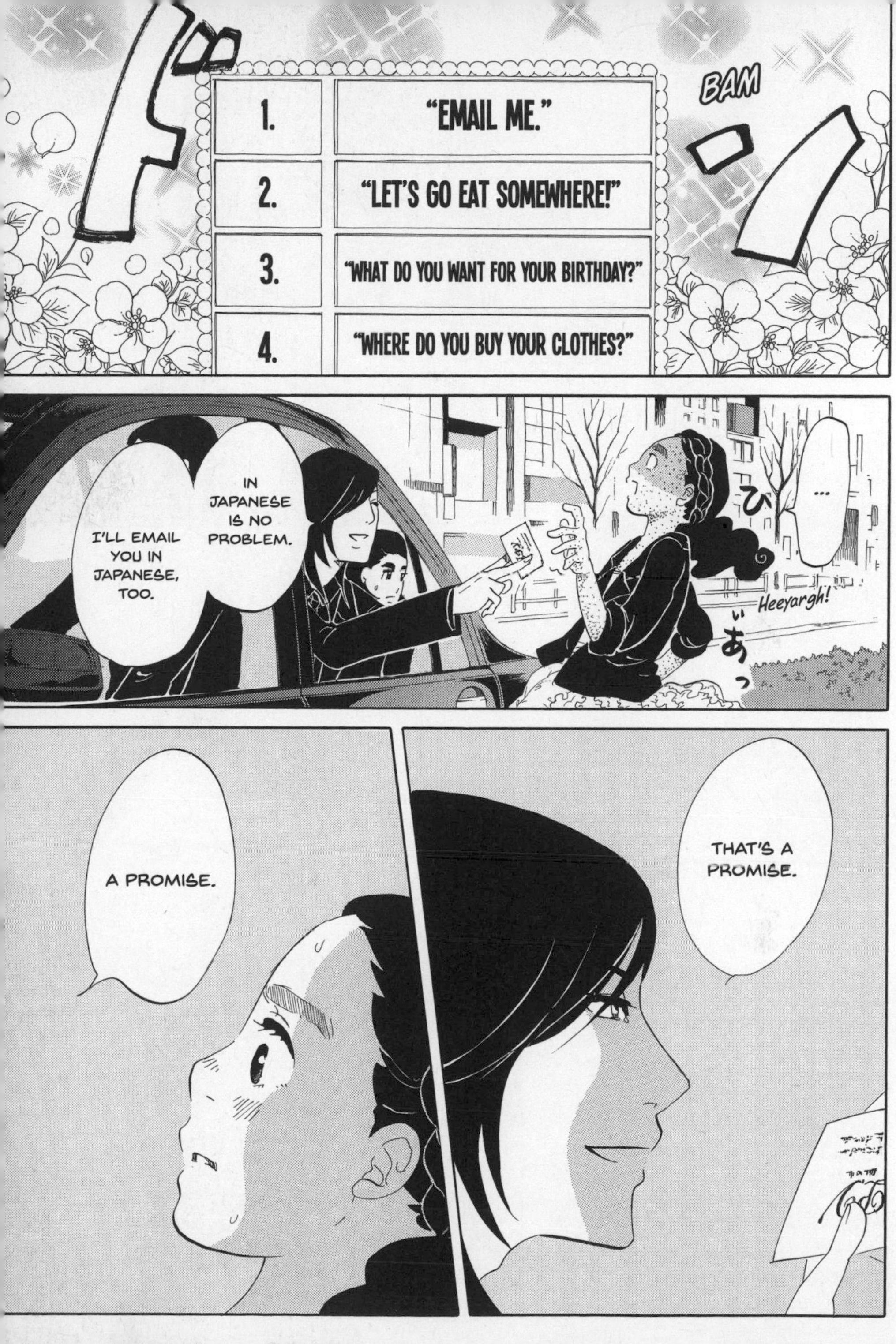
BAM
1. "EMAIL ME."
2. "LET'S GO EAT SOMEWHERE!"
3. "WHAT DO YOU WANT FOR YOUR BIRTHDAY?"
4. "WHERE DO YOU BUY YOUR CLOTHES?"
...
びいあっ
Heeyargh!
IN JAPANESE IS NO PROBLEM.
I'LL EMAIL YOU IN JAPANESE, TOO.
THAT'S A PROMISE.
A PROMISE.

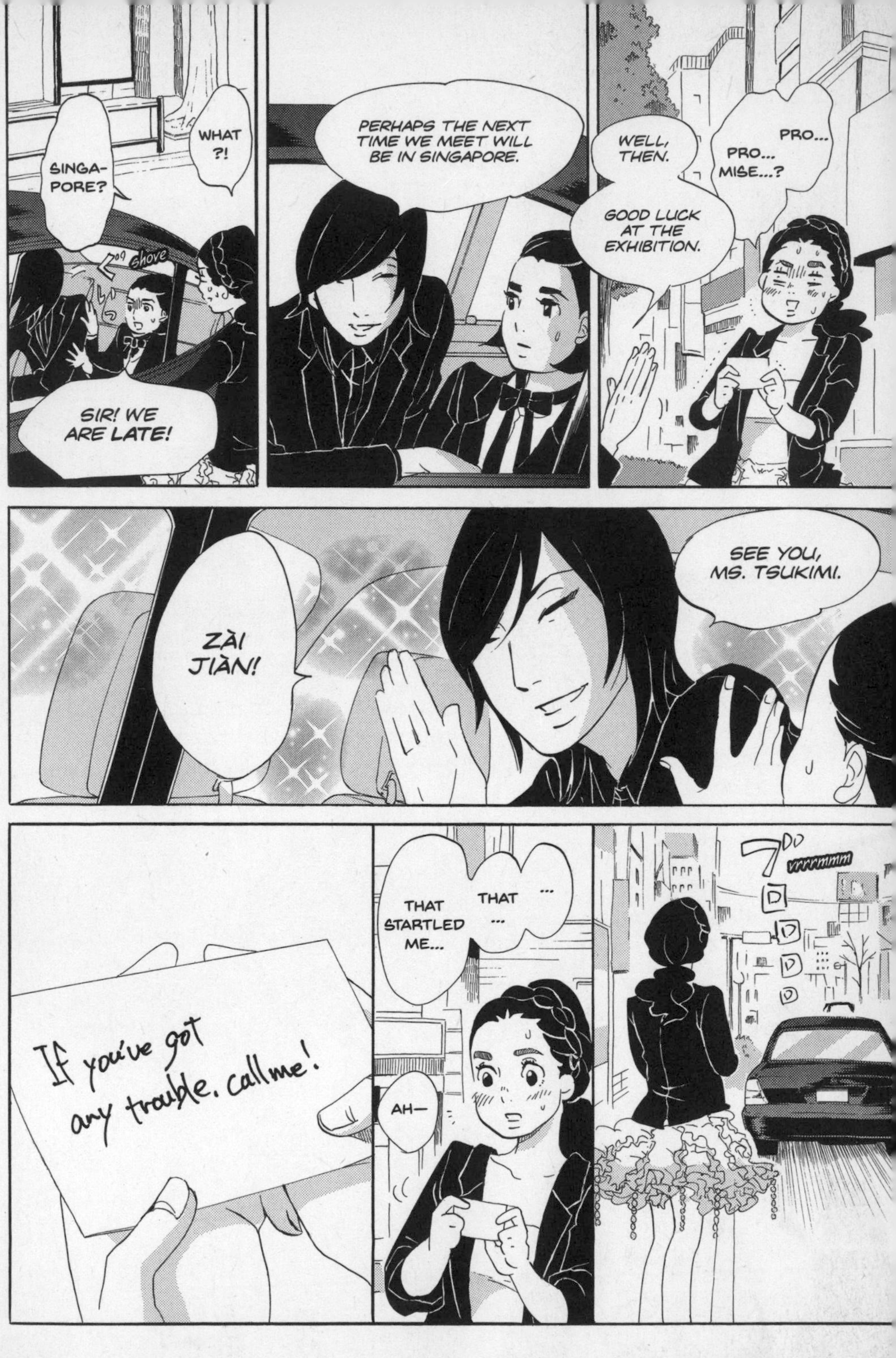
PRO...
PRO... MISE...?
WELL, THEN.
GOOD LUCK AT THE EXHIBITION.
PERHAPS THE NEXT TIME WE MEET WILL BE IN SINGAPORE.
WHAT ?!
SINGA-PORE?
shove
SIR! WE ARE LATE!
SEE YOU, MS. TSUKIMI.
ZÀI JIÀN!
vrrrmmm
THAT ...
THAT STARTLED ME...
AH—
If you've got any trouble. call me!

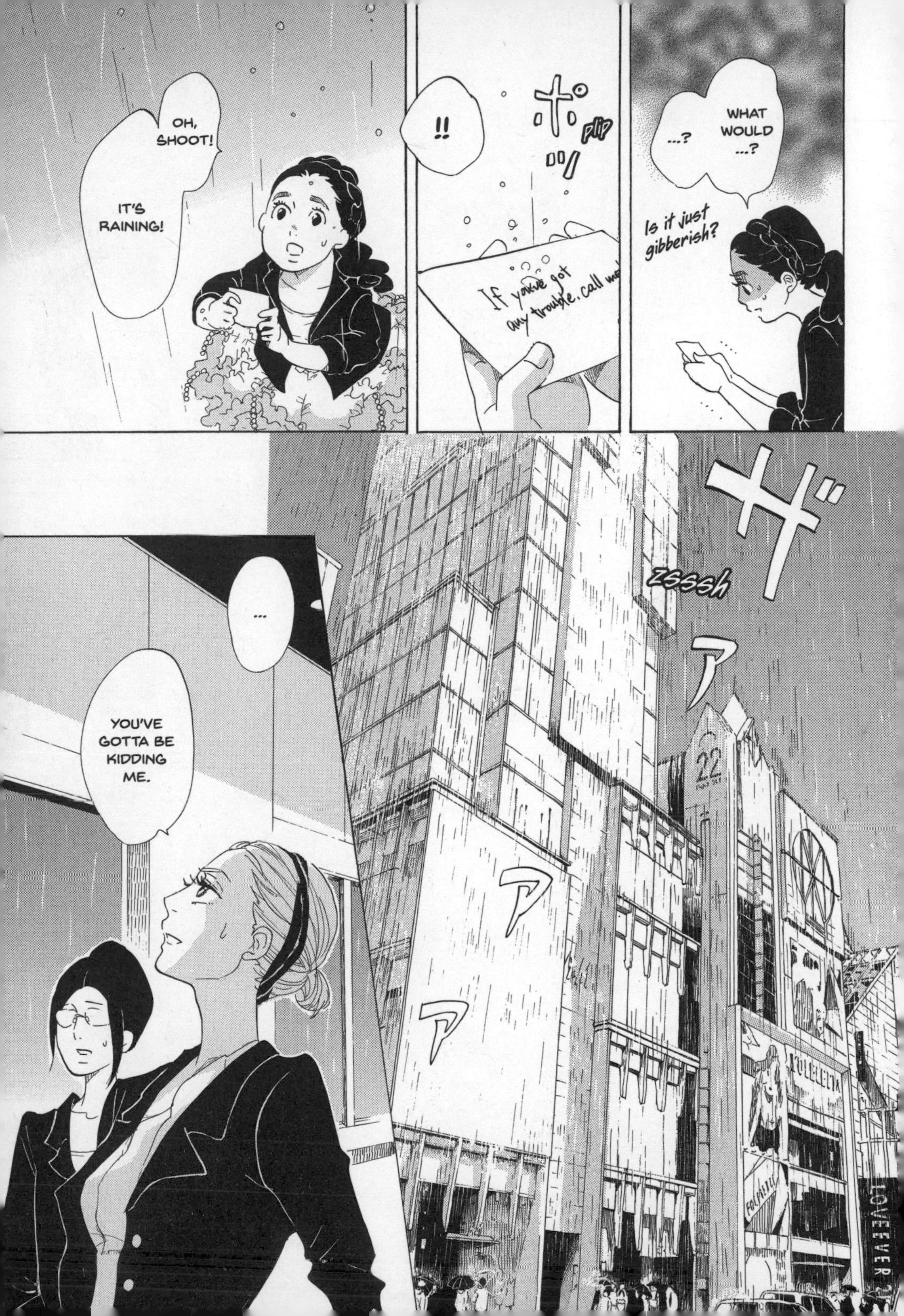
WHAT WOULD ...?
...?
Is it just gibberish?
!!
plip
If you've got any trouble, call me
OH, SHOOT!
IT'S RAINING!
ZSSSH
22
...
YOU'VE GOTTA BE KIDDING ME.

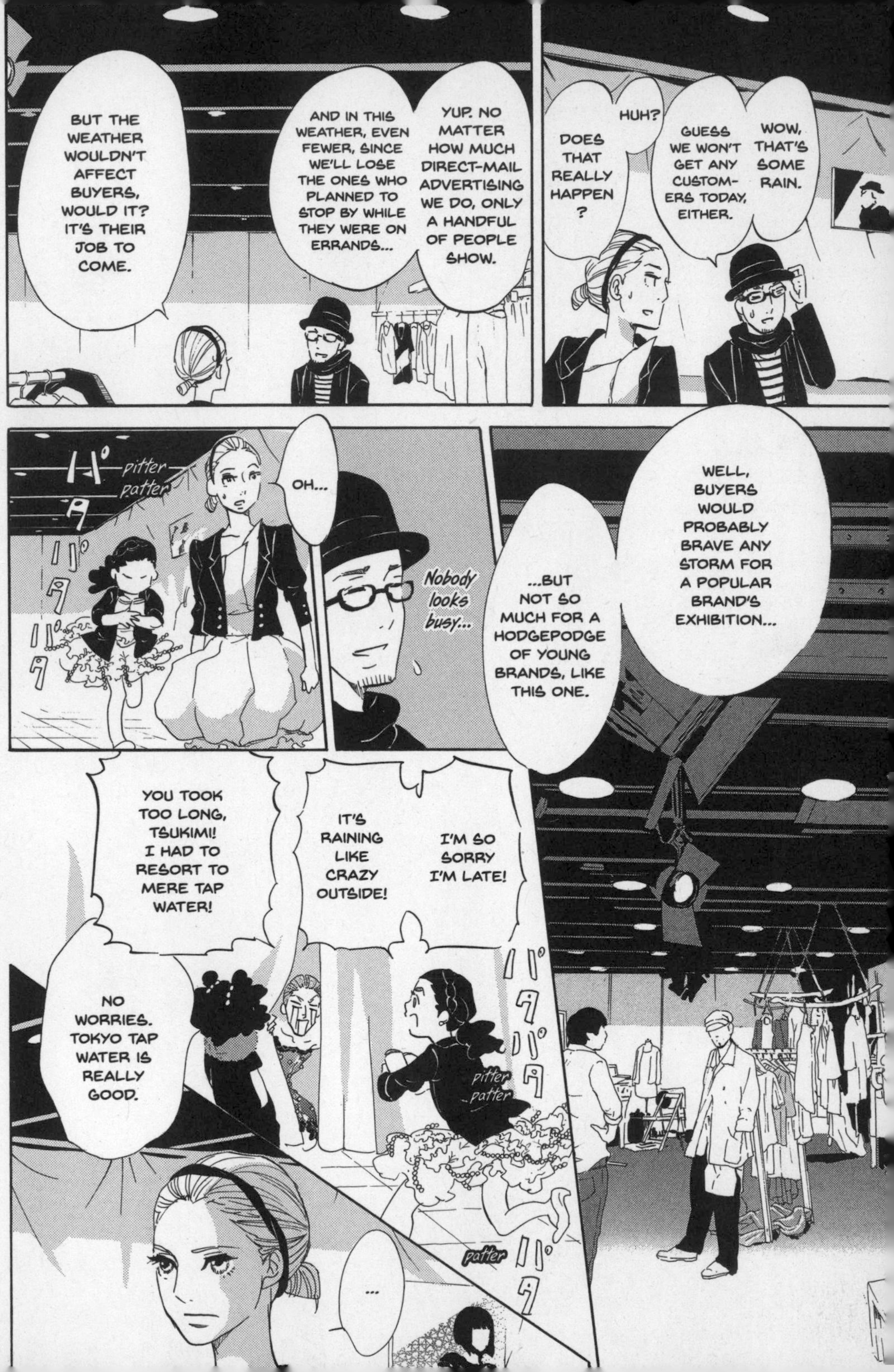
WOW, THAT'S SOME RAIN.
GUESS WE WON'T GET ANY CUSTOM-ERS TODAY, EITHER.
HUH?
DOES THAT REALLY HAPPEN?
YUP. NO MATTER HOW MUCH DIRECT-MAIL ADVERTISING WE DO, ONLY A HANDFUL OF PEOPLE SHOW.
AND IN THIS WEATHER, EVEN FEWER, SINCE WE'LL LOSE THE ONES WHO PLANNED TO STOP BY WHILE THEY WERE ON ERRANDS...
BUT THE WEATHER WOULDN'T AFFECT BUYERS, WOULD IT? IT'S THEIR JOB TO COME.
WELL, BUYERS WOULD PROBABLY BRAVE ANY STORM FOR A POPULAR BRAND'S EXHIBITION...
...BUT NOT SO MUCH FOR A HODGEPODGE OF YOUNG BRANDS, LIKE THIS ONE.
Nobody looks busy...
OH...
pitter patter
I'M SO SORRY I'M LATE!
IT'S RAINING LIKE CRAZY OUTSIDE!
YOU TOOK TOO LONG, TSUKIMI! I HAD TO RESORT TO MERE TAP WATER!
pitter patter
NO WORRIES. TOKYO TAP WATER IS REALLY GOOD.
patter
...

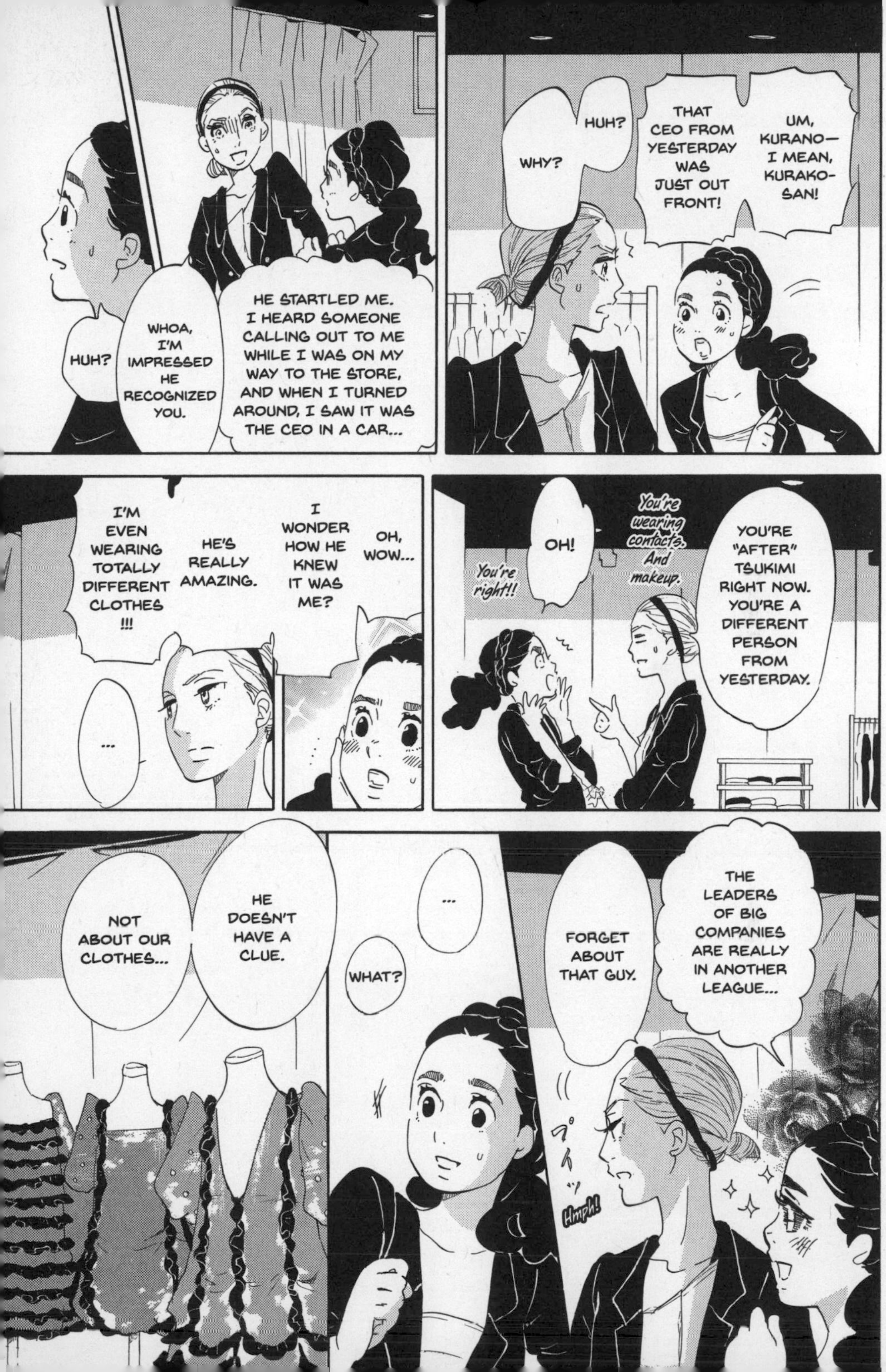
UM, KURANO— I MEAN, KURAKO-SAN!
THAT CEO FROM YESTERDAY WAS JUST OUT FRONT!
HUH?
WHY?
HE STARTLED ME. I HEARD SOMEONE CALLING OUT TO ME WHILE I WAS ON MY WAY TO THE STORE, AND WHEN I TURNED AROUND, I SAW IT WAS THE CEO IN A CAR...
WHOA, I'M IMPRESSED HE RECOGNIZED YOU.
HUH?
YOU'RE "AFTER" TSUKIMI RIGHT NOW. YOU'RE A DIFFERENT PERSON FROM YESTERDAY.
You're wearing contacts. And makeup.
OH!
You're right!!
OH, WOW...
I WONDER HOW HE KNEW IT WAS ME?
HE'S REALLY AMAZING.
I'M EVEN WEARING TOTALLY DIFFERENT CLOTHES!!!
...
THE LEADERS OF BIG COMPANIES ARE REALLY IN ANOTHER LEAGUE...
FORGET ABOUT THAT GUY.
Hmph!
...
WHAT?
HE DOESN'T HAVE A CLUE.
NOT ABOUT OUR CLOTHES...

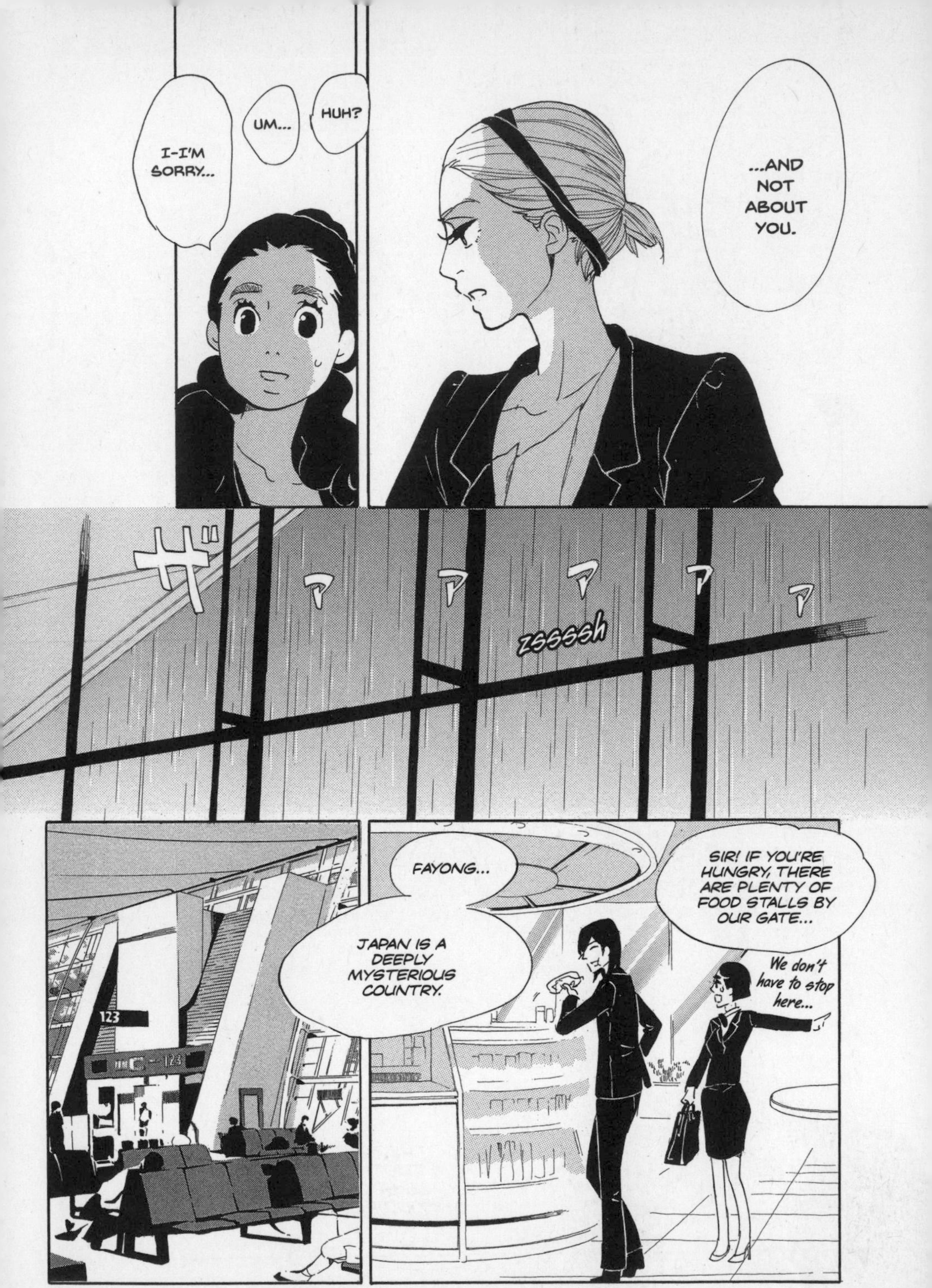
...AND NOT ABOUT YOU.
HUH?
UM...
I-I'M SORRY...
ザァァァァァ
zssssh
SIR! IF YOU'RE HUNGRY, THERE ARE PLENTY OF FOOD STALLS BY OUR GATE...
FAYONG...
JAPAN IS A DEEPLY MYSTERIOUS COUNTRY.
We don't have to stop here...
123

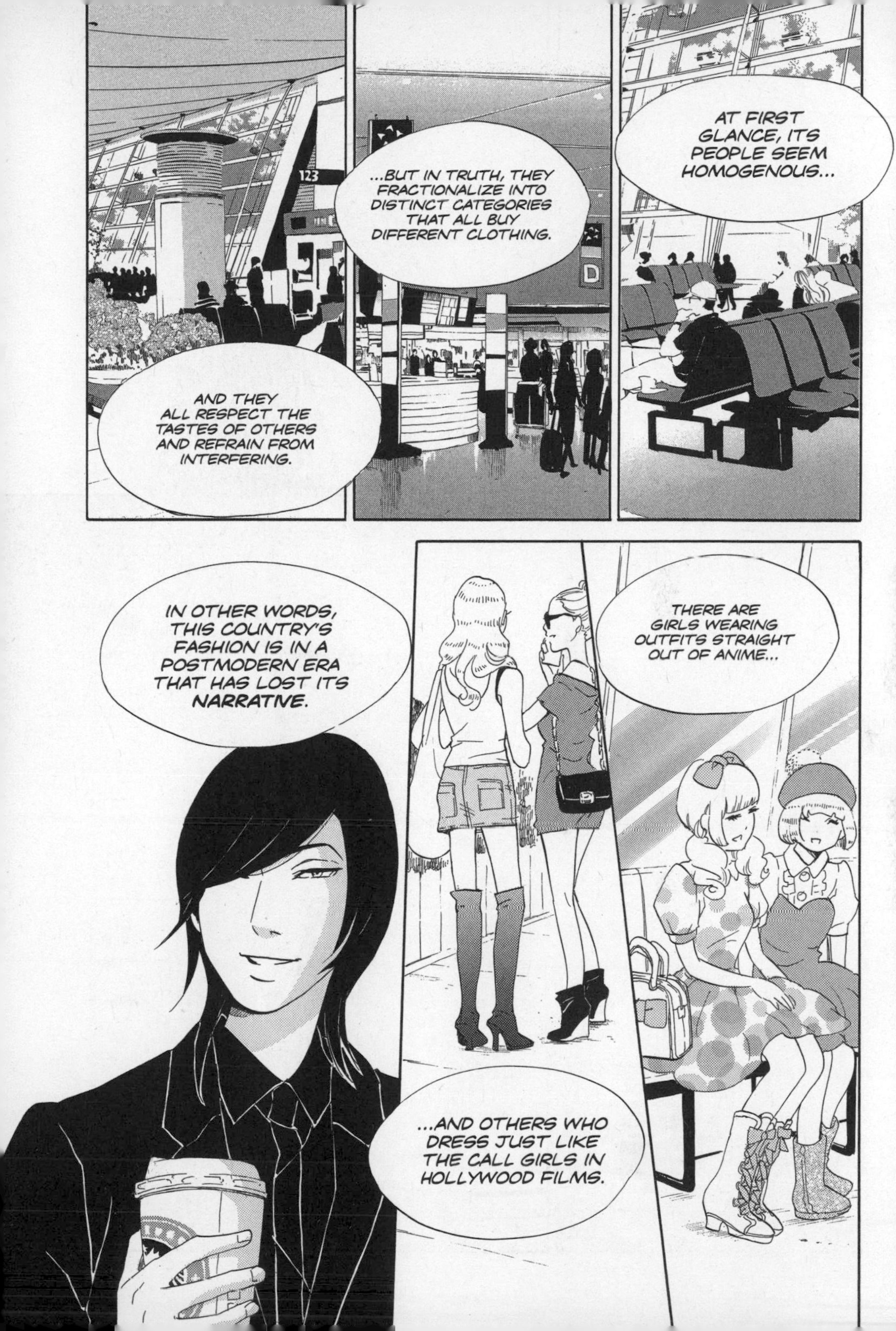

AT FIRST GLANCE, ITS PEOPLE SEEM HOMOGENOUS...
...BUT IN TRUTH, THEY FRACTIONALIZE INTO DISTINCT CATEGORIES THAT ALL BUY DIFFERENT CLOTHING.
AND THEY ALL RESPECT THE TASTES OF OTHERS AND REFRAIN FROM INTERFERING.
THERE ARE GIRLS WEARING OUTFITS STRAIGHT OUT OF ANIME...
...AND OTHERS WHO DRESS JUST LIKE THE CALL GIRLS IN HOLLYWOOD FILMS.
IN OTHER WORDS, THIS COUNTRY'S FASHION IS IN A POSTMODERN ERA THAT HAS LOST ITS NARRATIVE.

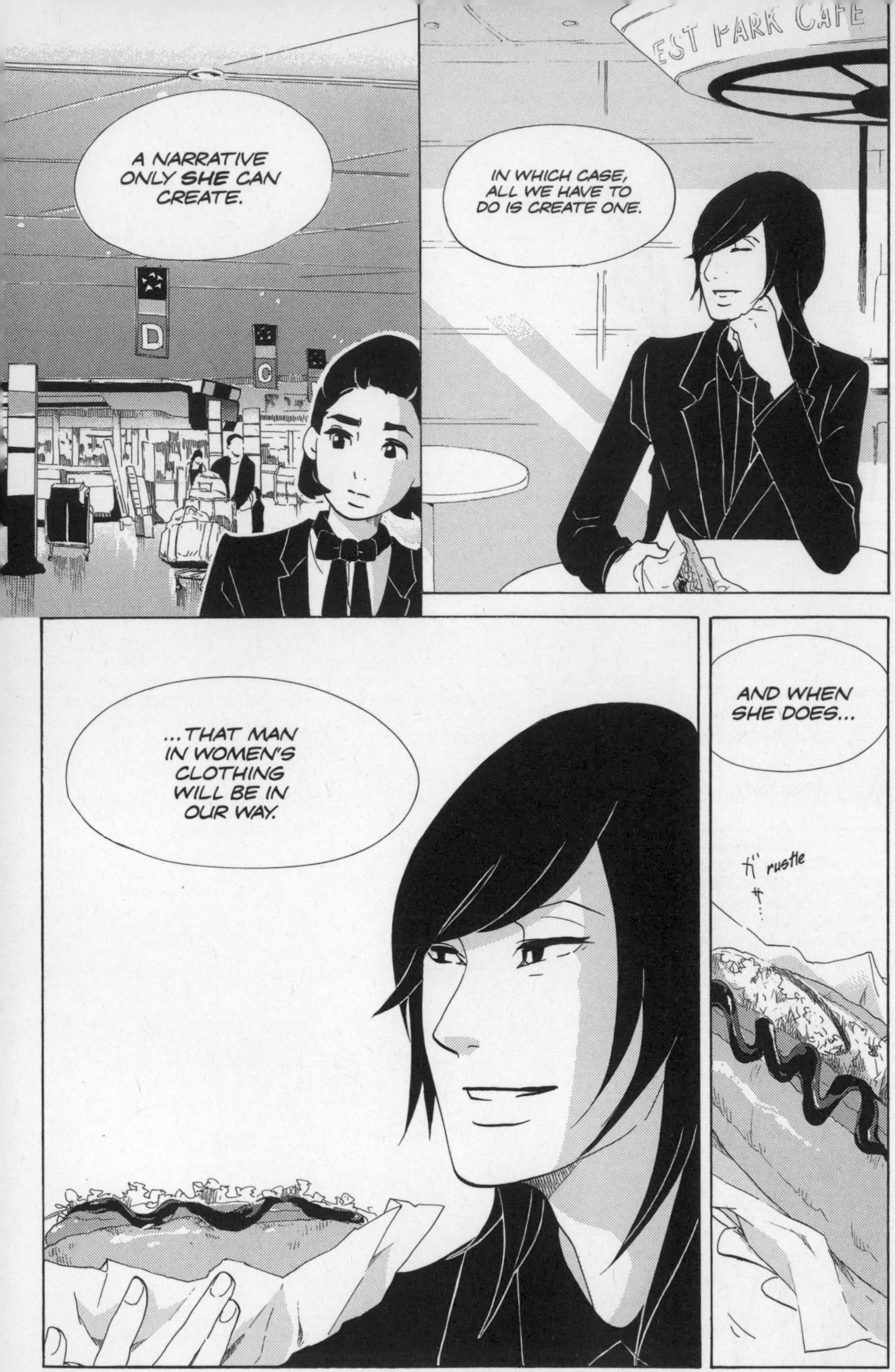
EST PARK CAFE
IN WHICH CASE, ALL WE HAVE TO DO IS CREATE ONE.
A NARRATIVE ONLY SHE CAN CREATE.
AND WHEN SHE DOES...
rustle
...THAT MAN IN WOMEN'S CLOTHING WILL BE IN OUR WAY.

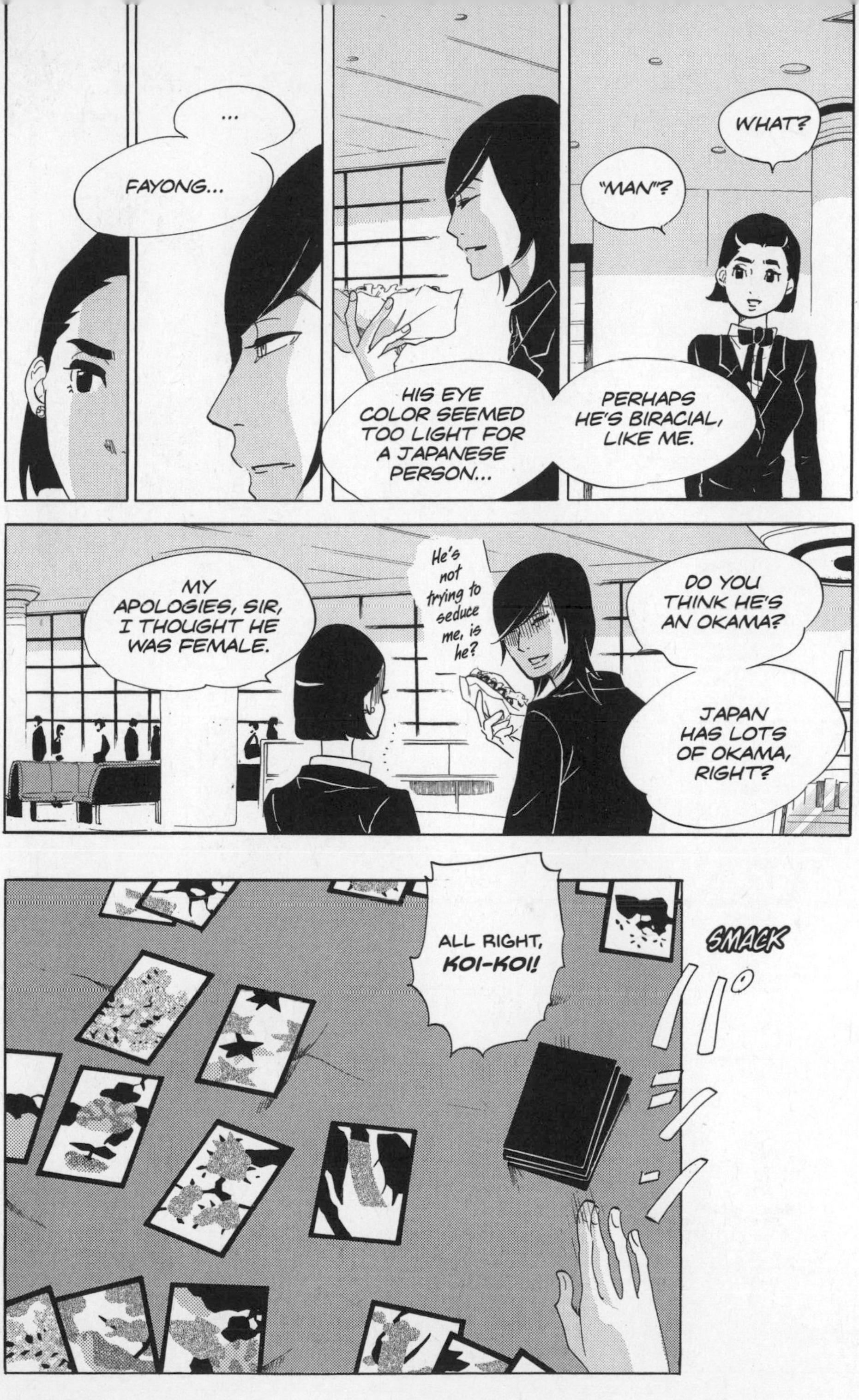
WHAT?
"MAN"?
PERHAPS HE'S BIRACIAL, LIKE ME.
HIS EYE COLOR SEEMED TOO LIGHT FOR A JAPANESE PERSON...
...
FAYONG...
DO YOU THINK HE'S AN OKAMA?
JAPAN HAS LOTS OF OKAMA, RIGHT?
He's not trying to seduce me, is he?
MY APOLOGIES, SIR, I THOUGHT HE WAS FEMALE.
SMACK
ALL RIGHT, KOI-KOI!

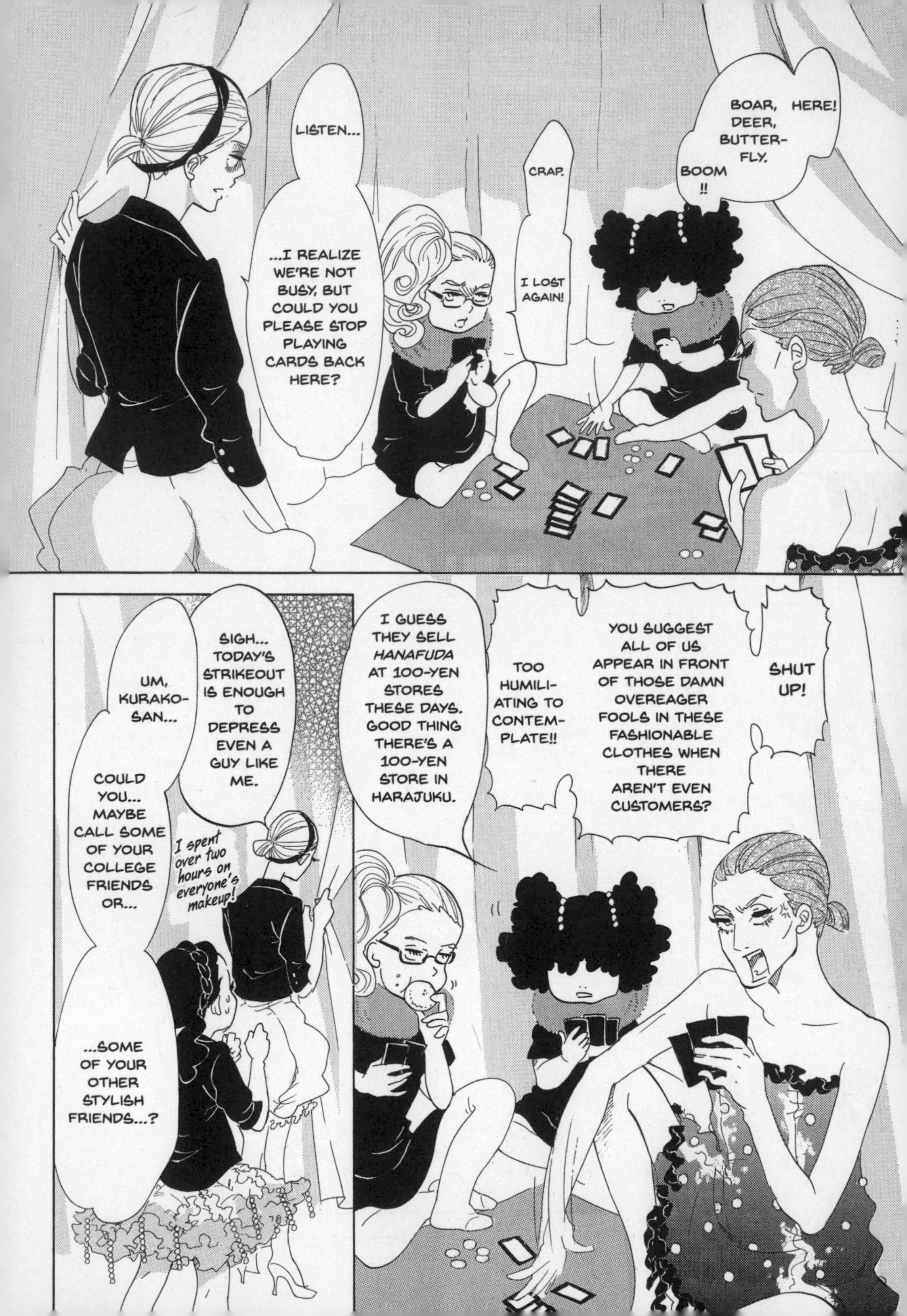
HERE!
BOAR, DEER, BUTTERFLY.
BOOM!!
CRAP.
I LOST AGAIN!
LISTEN...
...I REALIZE WE'RE NOT BUSY, BUT COULD YOU PLEASE STOP PLAYING CARDS BACK HERE?
SHUT UP!
YOU SUGGEST ALL OF US APPEAR IN FRONT OF THOSE DAMN OVEREAGER FOOLS IN THESE FASHIONABLE CLOTHES WHEN THERE AREN'T EVEN CUSTOMERS?
TOO HUMILIATING TO CONTEMPLATE!!
I GUESS THEY SELL *HANAFUDA* AT 100-YEN STORES THESE DAYS. GOOD THING THERE'S A 100-YEN STORE IN HARAJUKU.
SIGH... TODAY'S STRIKEOUT IS ENOUGH TO DEPRESS EVEN A GUY LIKE ME.
UM, KURAKO-SAN...
I spent over two hours on everyone's makeup!
COULD YOU... MAYBE CALL SOME OF YOUR COLLEGE FRIENDS OR...
...SOME OF YOUR OTHER STYLISH FRIENDS...?

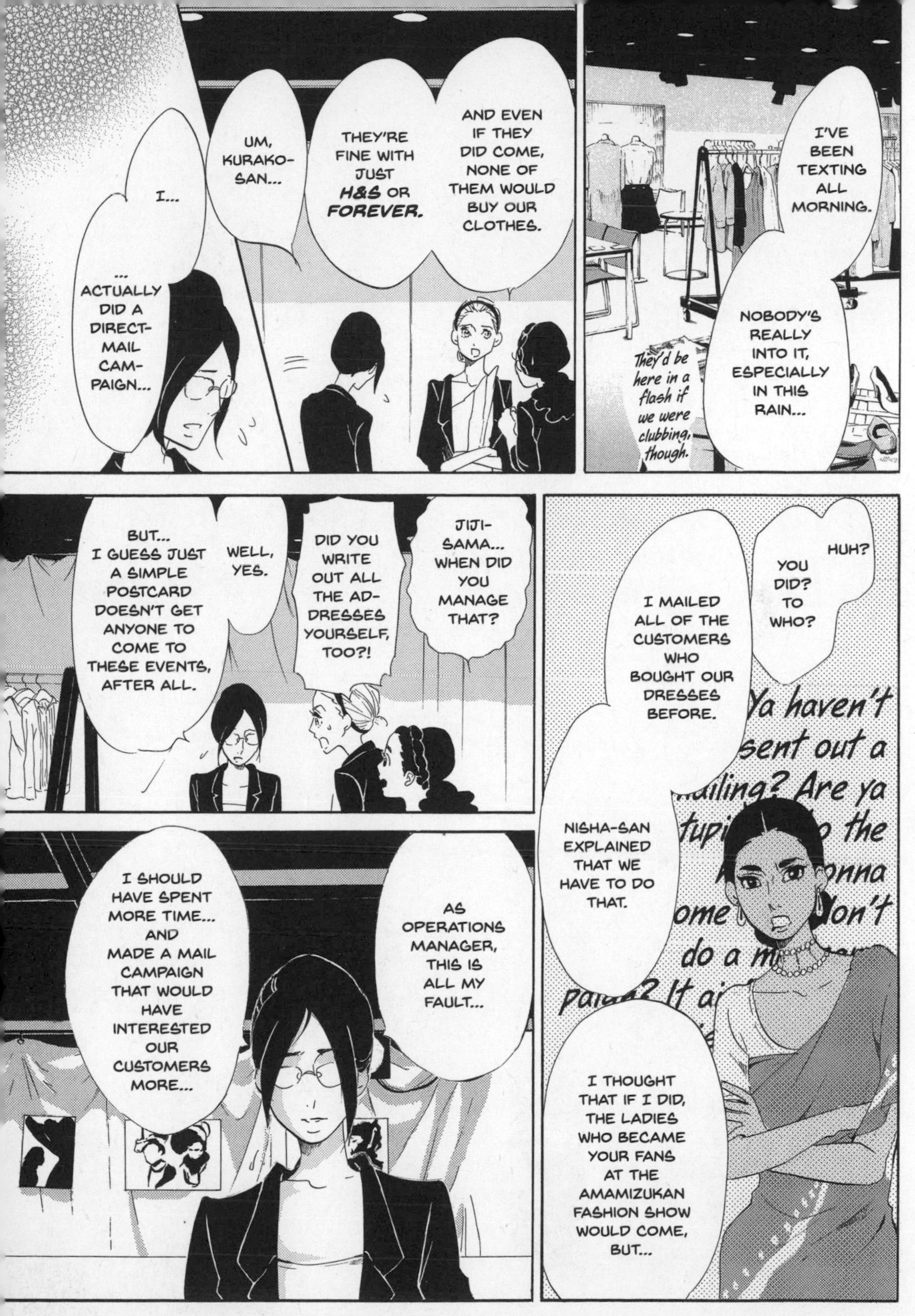

I'VE BEEN TEXTING ALL MORNING.
NOBODY'S REALLY INTO IT, ESPECIALLY IN THIS RAIN...
They'd be here in a flash if we were clubbing, though.
AND EVEN IF THEY DID COME, NONE OF THEM WOULD BUY OUR CLOTHES.
THEY'RE FINE WITH JUST H&S OR FOREVER.
UM, KURAKO-SAN...
I...
... ACTUALLY DID A DIRECT-MAIL CAMPAIGN...
HUH?
YOU DID? TO WHO?
I MAILED ALL OF THE CUSTOMERS WHO BOUGHT OUR DRESSES BEFORE.
Ya haven't
sent out a
NISHA-SAN EXPLAINED THAT WE HAVE TO DO THAT.
I THOUGHT THAT IF I DID, THE LADIES WHO BECAME YOUR FANS AT THE AMAMIZUKAN FASHION SHOW WOULD COME, BUT...
JIJI-SAMA... WHEN DID YOU MANAGE THAT?
DID YOU WRITE OUT ALL THE ADDRESSES YOURSELF, TOO?!
WELL, YES.
BUT... I GUESS JUST A SIMPLE POSTCARD DOESN'T GET ANYONE TO COME TO THESE EVENTS, AFTER ALL.
AS OPERATIONS MANAGER, THIS IS ALL MY FAULT...
I SHOULD HAVE SPENT MORE TIME... AND MADE A MAIL CAMPAIGN THAT WOULD HAVE INTERESTED OUR CUSTOMERS MORE...

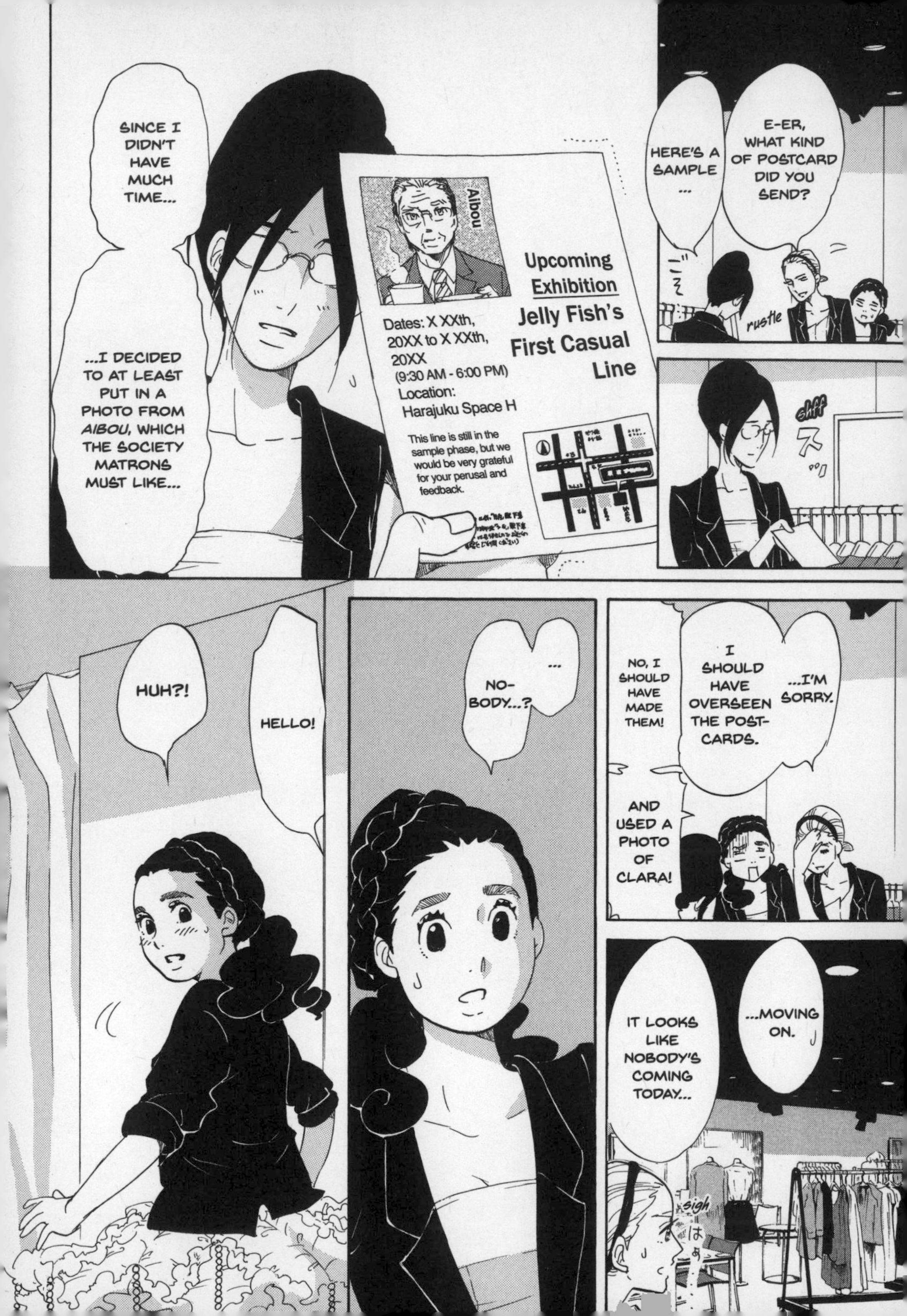
E-ER, WHAT KIND OF POSTCARD DID YOU SEND?
HERE'S A SAMPLE ...
rustle
shff
SINCE I DIDN'T HAVE MUCH TIME...
Aibou
Upcoming Exhibition
Jelly Fish's First Casual Line
Dates: X XXth, 20XX to X XXth, 20XX (9:30 AM - 6:00 PM)
Location: Harajuku Space H
This line is still in the sample phase, but we would be very grateful for your perusal and feedback.
...I DECIDED TO AT LEAST PUT IN A PHOTO FROM *AIBOU*, WHICH THE SOCIETY MATRONS MUST LIKE...
...I'M SORRY.
I SHOULD HAVE OVERSEEN THE POST-CARDS.
NO, I SHOULD HAVE MADE THEM!
AND USED A PHOTO OF CLARA!
...MOVING ON.
IT LOOKS LIKE NOBODY'S COMING TODAY...
sigh
...
NO-BODY...?
HELLO!
HUH?!

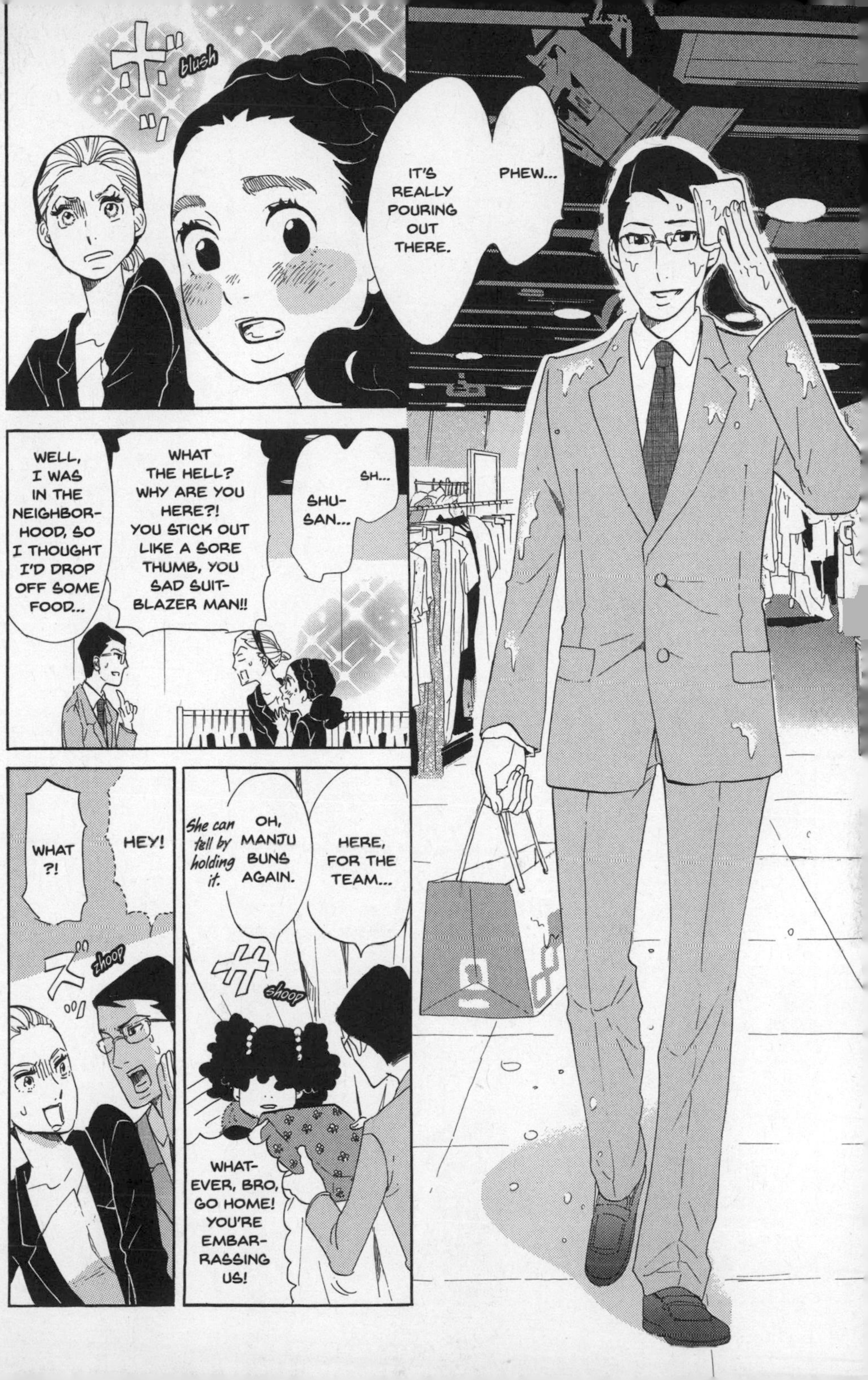
PHEW...
IT'S REALLY POURING OUT THERE.
blush
SH... SHU-SAN...
WHAT THE HELL? WHY ARE YOU HERE?! YOU STICK OUT LIKE A SORE THUMB, YOU SAD SUIT-BLAZER MAN!!
WELL, I WAS IN THE NEIGHBORHOOD, SO I THOUGHT I'D DROP OFF SOME FOOD...
HERE, FOR THE TEAM...
OH, MANJU BUNS AGAIN.
She can tell by holding it.
shoop
WHATEVER, BRO, GO HOME! YOU'RE EMBARRASSING US!
HEY!
WHAT?!
zhoop

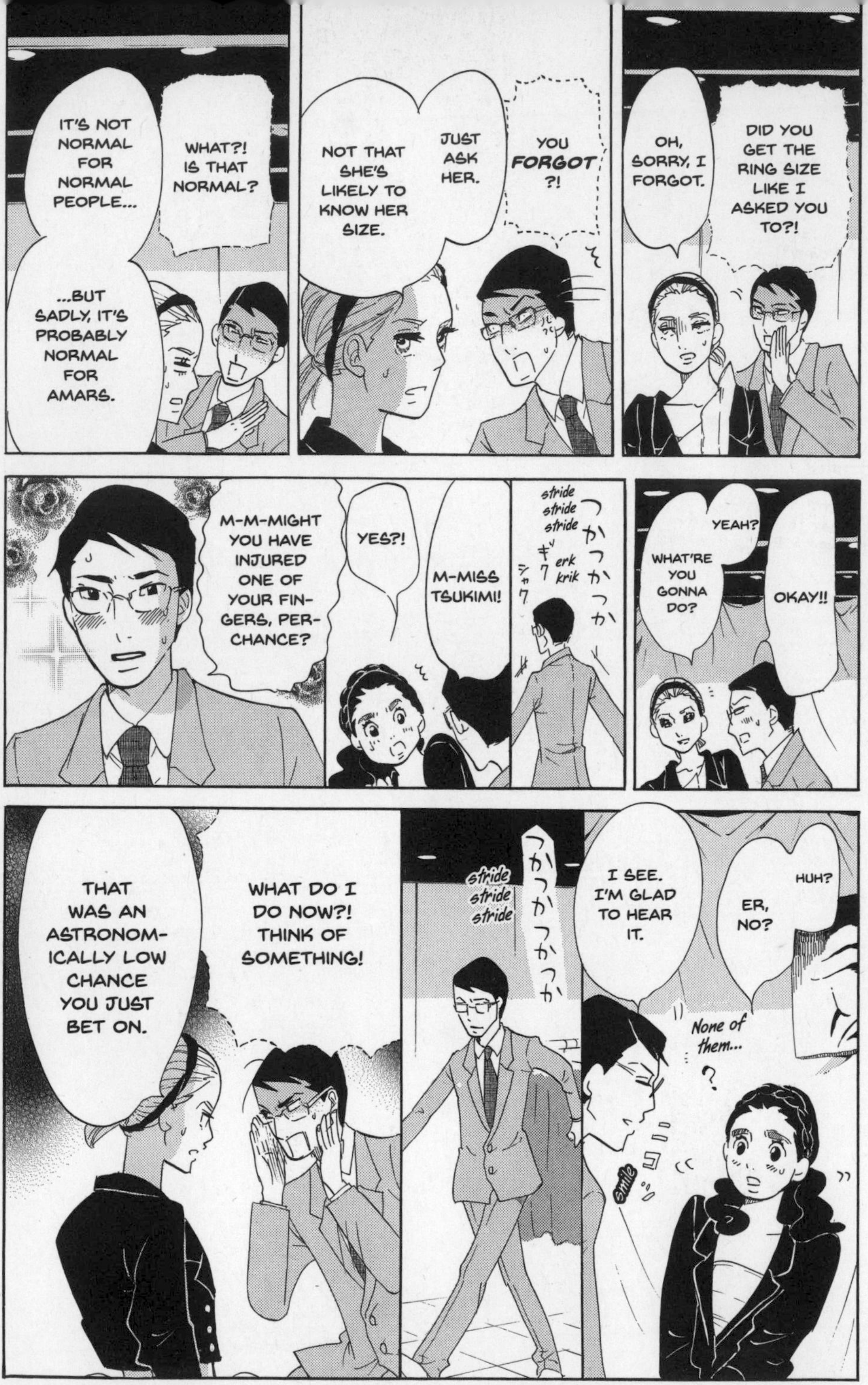
DID YOU GET THE RING SIZE LIKE I ASKED YOU TO?!
OH, SORRY, I FORGOT.
YOU FORGOT?!
JUST ASK HER.
NOT THAT SHE'S LIKELY TO KNOW HER SIZE.
WHAT?! IS THAT NORMAL?
IT'S NOT NORMAL FOR NORMAL PEOPLE...
...BUT SADLY, IT'S PROBABLY NORMAL FOR AMARS.
OKAY!!
YEAH?
WHAT'RE YOU GONNA DO?
stride stride stride
つかつかつか
ギシャク
erk krik
M-MISS TSUKIMI!
YES?!
M-M-MIGHT YOU HAVE INJURED ONE OF YOUR FINGERS, PERCHANCE?
HUH?
ER, NO?
I SEE. I'M GLAD TO HEAR IT.
None of them...
smile
つかつかつか
stride stride stride
WHAT DO I DO NOW?! THINK OF SOMETHING!
THAT WAS AN ASTRONOMICALLY LOW CHANCE YOU JUST BET ON.

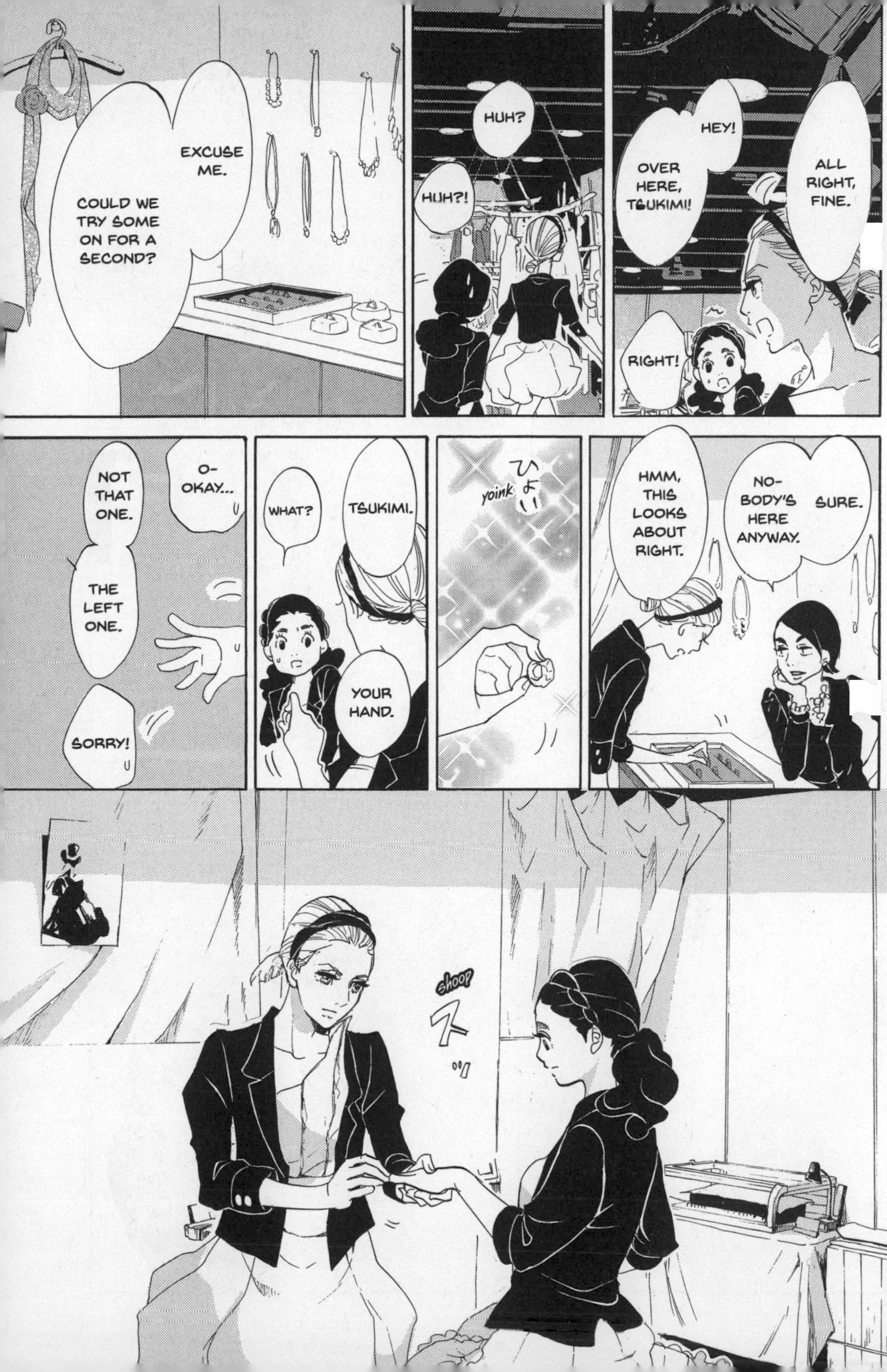
ALL RIGHT, FINE.
HEY!
OVER HERE, TSUKIMI!
RIGHT!
HUH?
HUH?!
EXCUSE ME.
COULD WE TRY SOME ON FOR A SECOND?
SURE.
NO-BODY'S HERE ANYWAY.
HMM, THIS LOOKS ABOUT RIGHT.
ひょい
yoink
TSUKIMI.
WHAT?
YOUR HAND.
O-OKAY...
NOT THAT ONE.
THE LEFT ONE.
SORRY!
shoop
ス

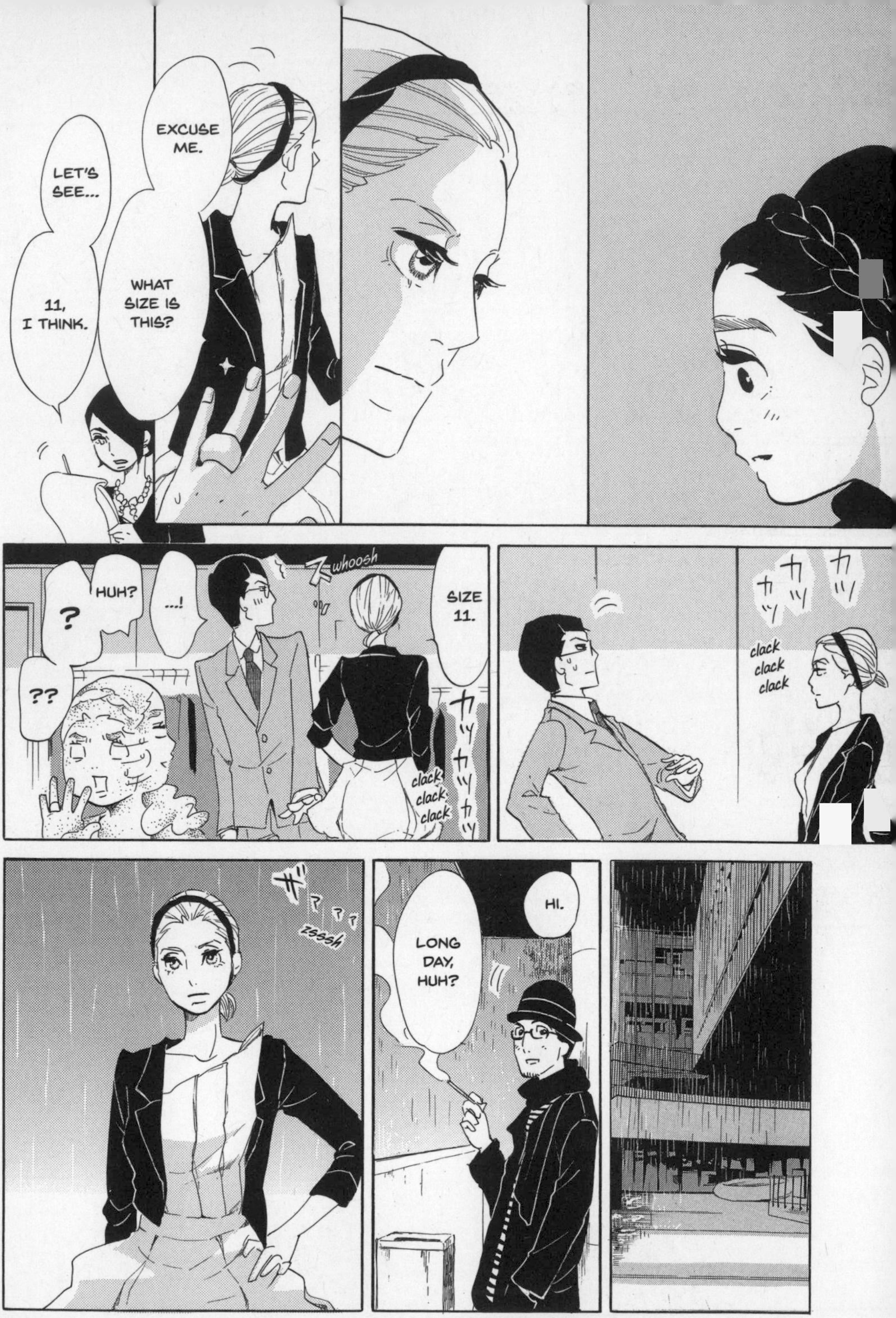
EXCUSE ME.
LET'S SEE...
WHAT SIZE IS THIS?
11, I THINK.
カッカッカッ
clack clack clack
SIZE 11.
whoosh
...!
HUH?
?
??
カッカッカッ
clack clack clack
HI.
LONG DAY, HUH?
zsssh

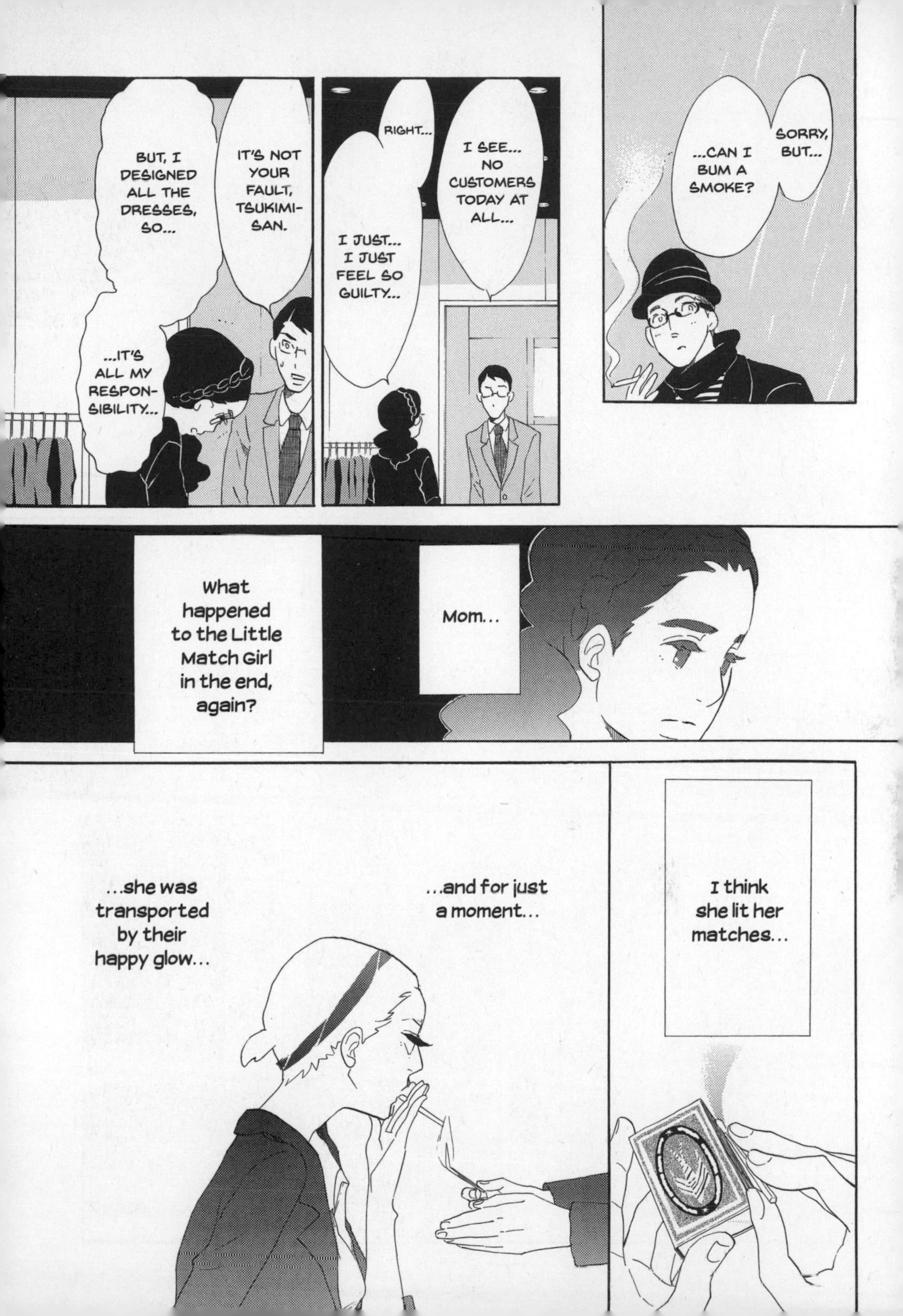
SORRY, BUT...
...CAN I BUM A SMOKE?
I SEE... NO CUSTOMERS TODAY AT ALL...
RIGHT...
I JUST... I JUST FEEL SO GUILTY...
IT'S NOT YOUR FAULT, TSUKIMI-SAN.
BUT, I DESIGNED ALL THE DRESSES, SO...
...IT'S ALL MY RESPONSIBILITY...
Mom...
What happened to the Little Match Girl in the end, again?
I think she lit her matches...
...and for just a moment...
...she was transported by their happy glow...

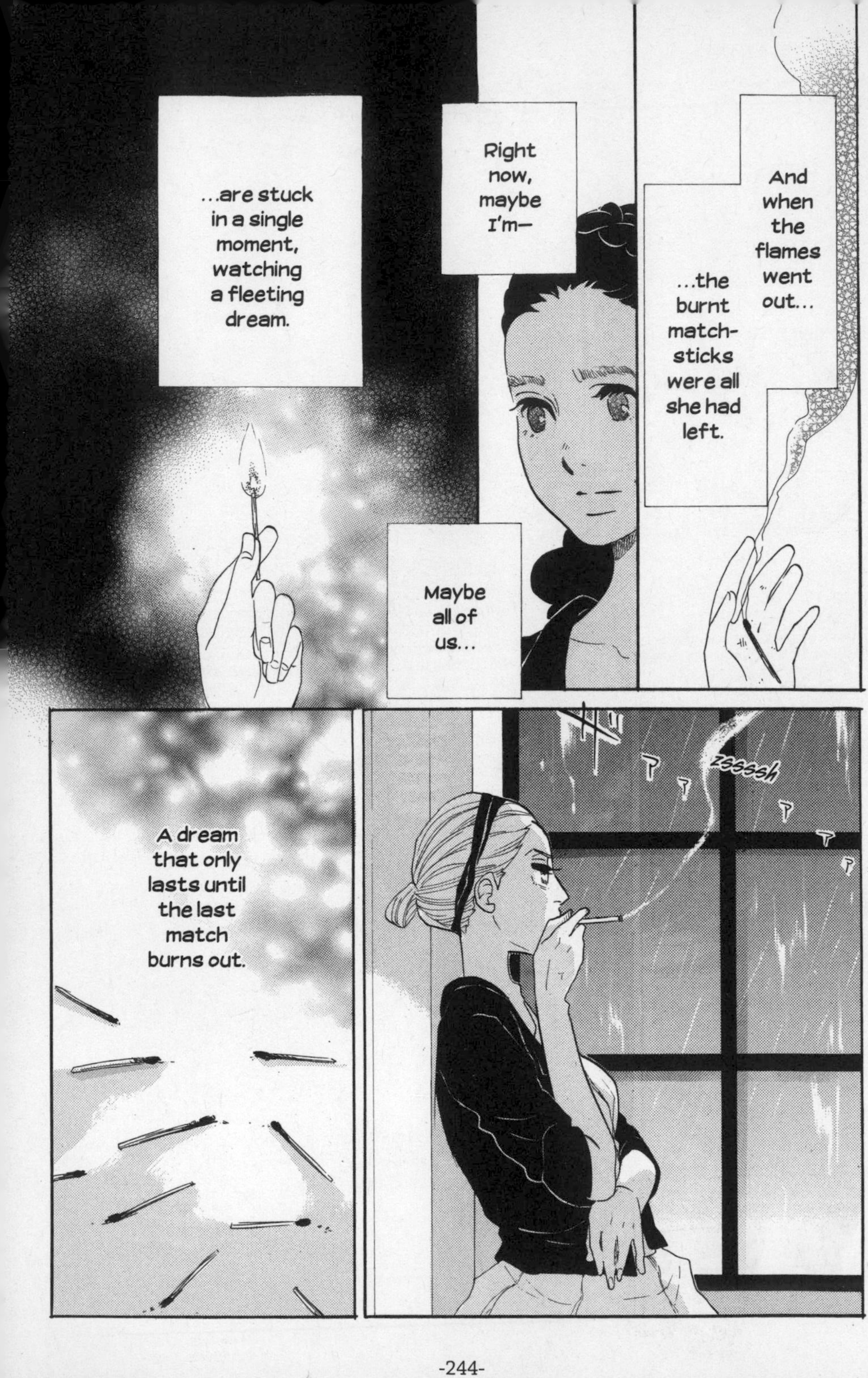
And when the flames went out…
…the burnt match-sticks were all she had left.
Right now, maybe I'm—
Maybe all of us…
…are stuck in a single moment, watching a fleeting dream.
zsssh
A dream that only lasts until the last match burns out.

Episode 62
Call Me Anytime

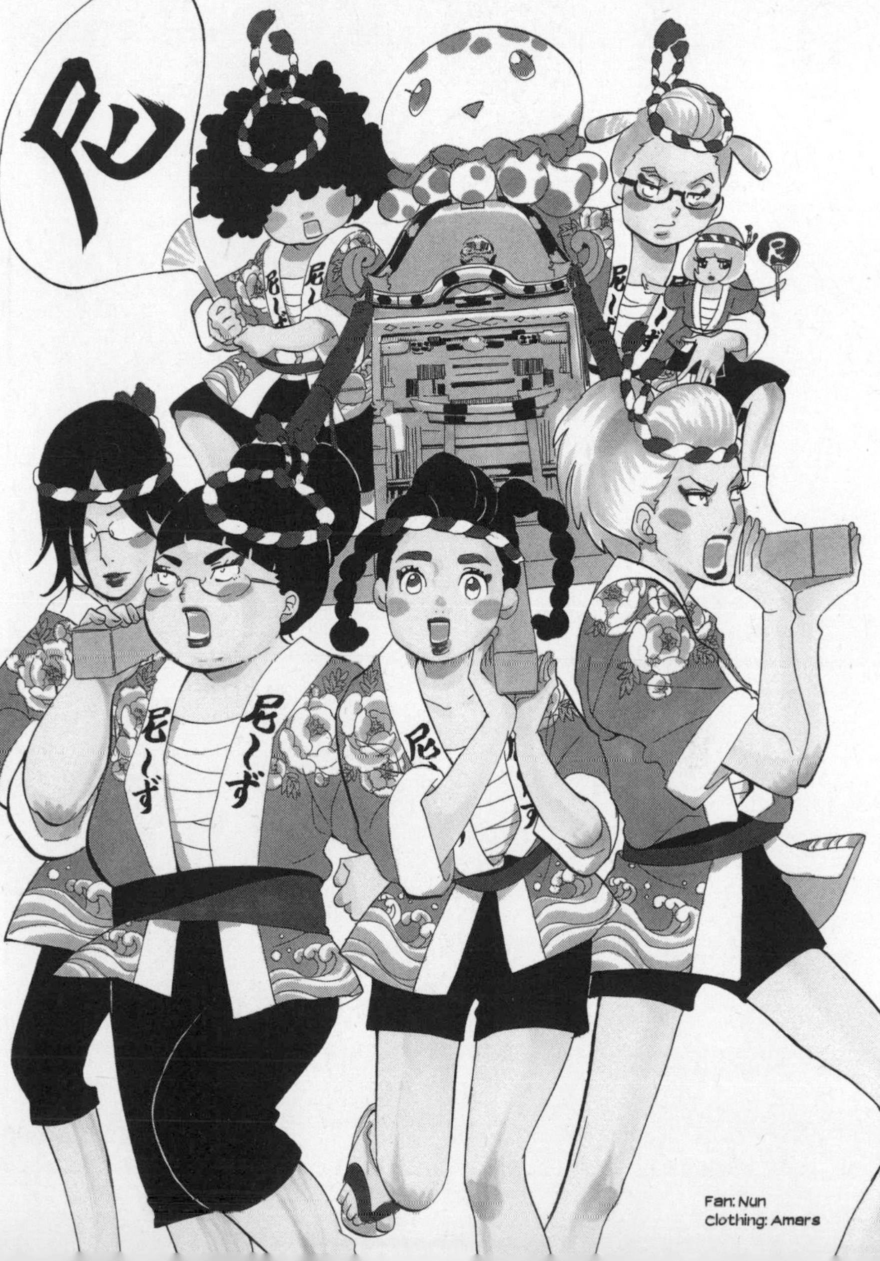
尼〜ず

Fan: Nun
Clothing: Amars

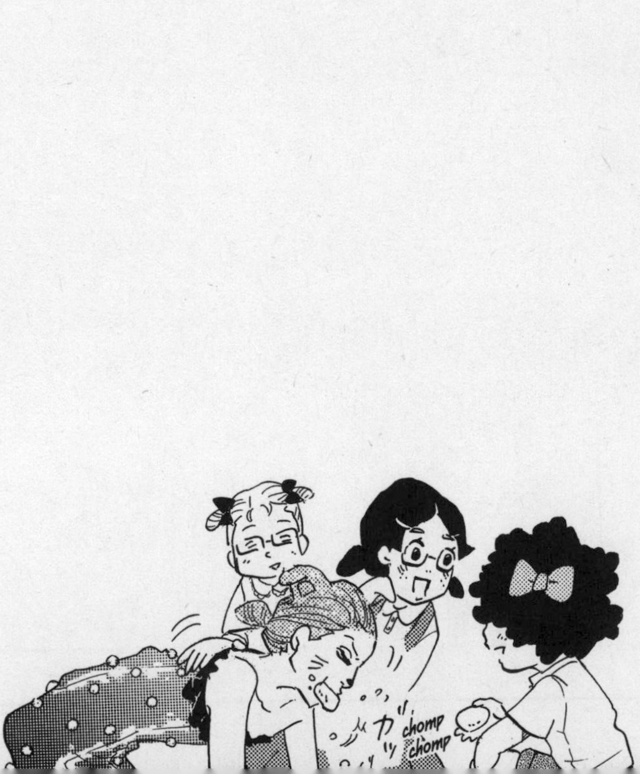
ガツ
chomp
chomp

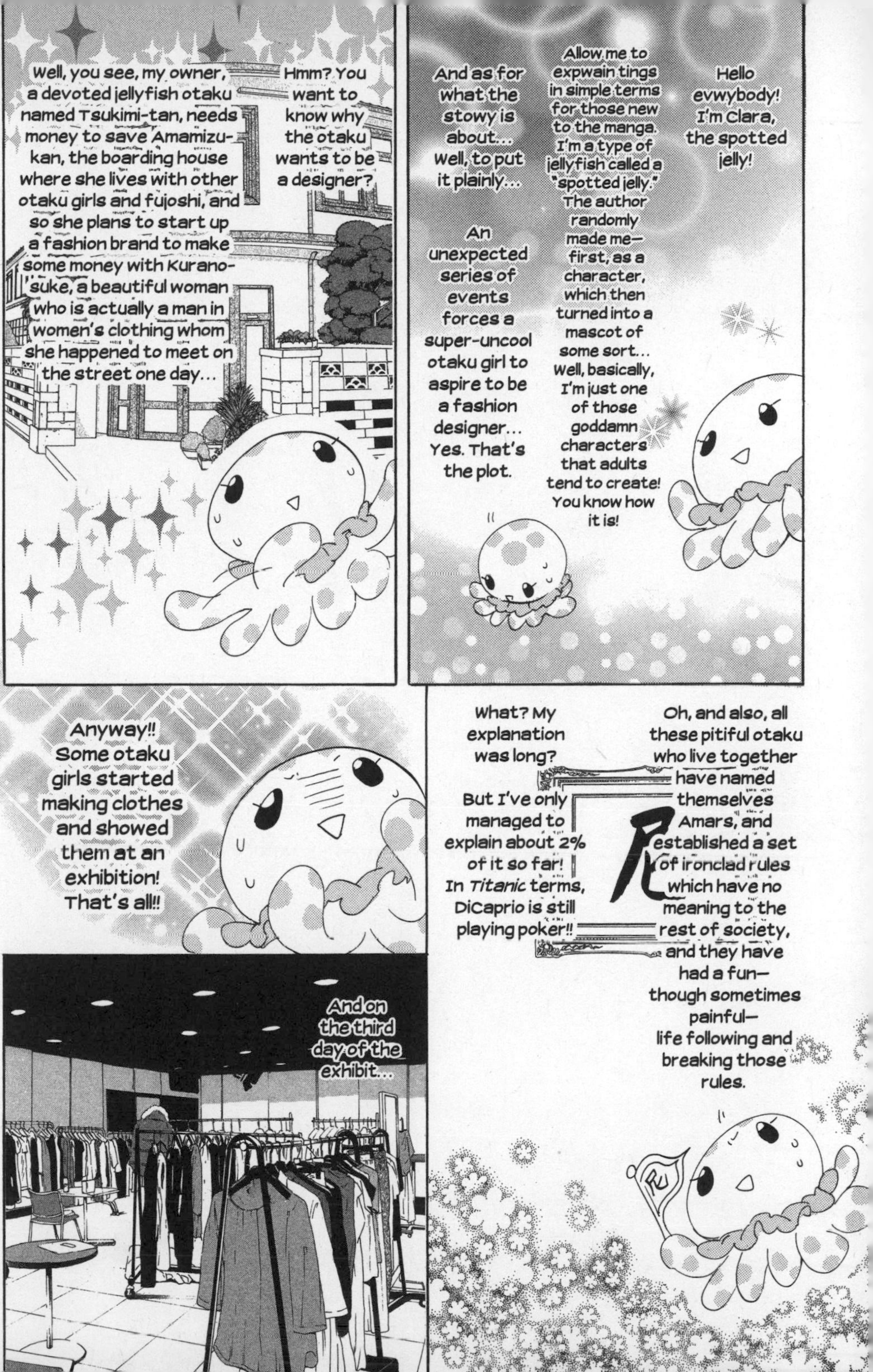
Hello evwybody! I'm Clara, the spotted jelly!
Allow me to expwain tings in simple terms for those new to the manga. I'm a type of jellyfish called a "spotted jelly." The author randomly made me—first, as a character, which then turned into a mascot of some sort... Well, basically, I'm just one of those goddamn characters that adults tend to create! You know how it is!
And as for what the stowy is about... Well, to put it plainly...
An unexpected series of events forces a super-uncool otaku girl to aspire to be a fashion designer... Yes. That's the plot.
Hmm? You want to know why the otaku wants to be a designer?
Well, you see, my owner, a devoted jellyfish otaku named Tsukimi-tan, needs money to save Amamizukan, the boarding house where she lives with other otaku girls and fujoshi, and so she plans to start up a fashion brand to make some money with Kuranosuke, a beautiful woman who is actually a man in women's clothing whom she happened to meet on the street one day...
Oh, and also, all these pitiful otaku who live together have named themselves Amars, and established a set of ironclad rules which have no meaning to the rest of society, and they have had a fun—though sometimes painful—life following and breaking those rules.
What? My explanation was long?
But I've only managed to explain about 2% of it so far! In *Titanic* terms, DiCaprio is still playing poker!!
Anyway!! Some otaku girls started making clothes and showed them at an exhibition! That's all!!
And on the third day of the exhibit...

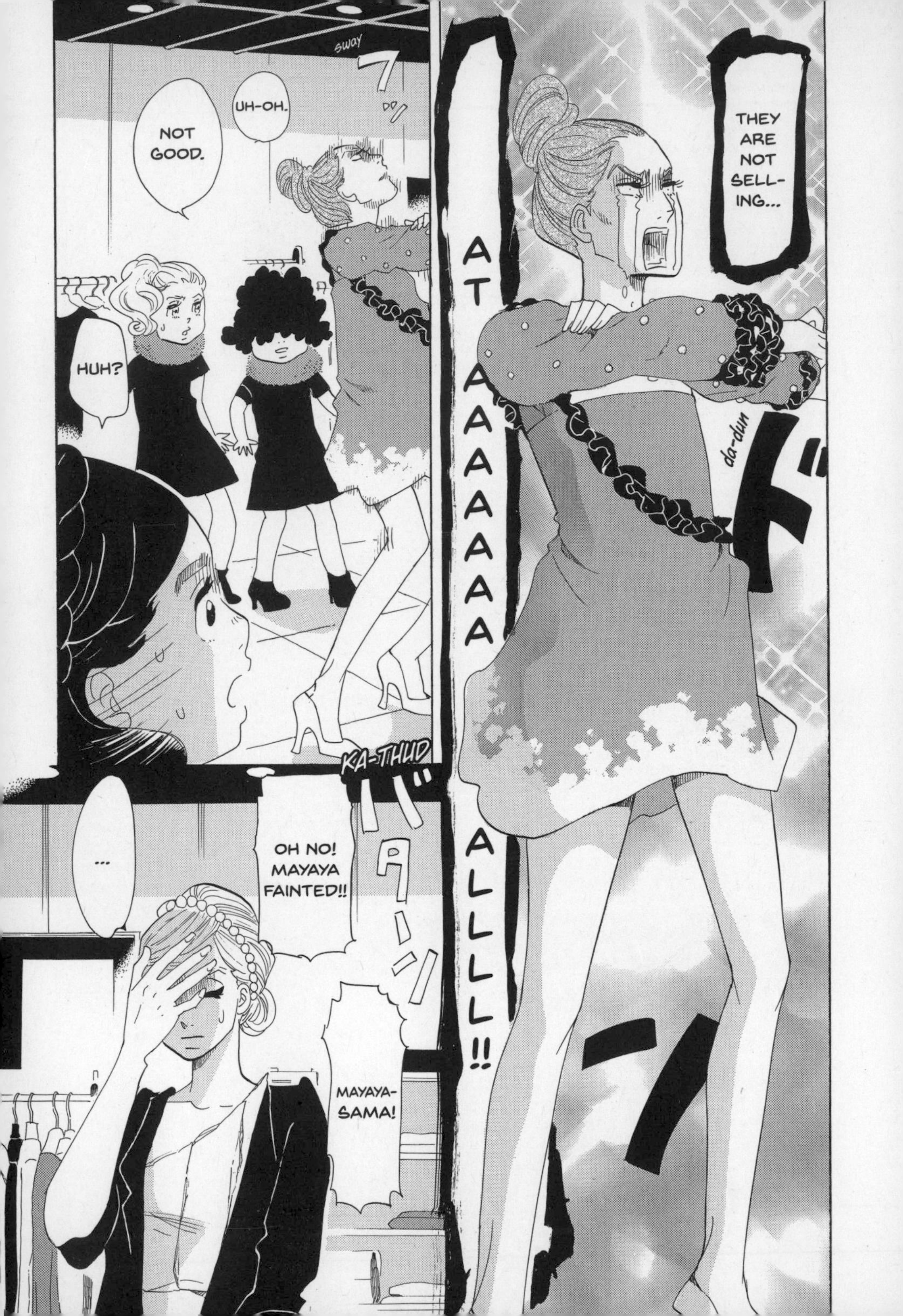
THEY ARE NOT SELLING...
AT AAAAAAAAA ALLLLL!!
da-dun
sway
UH-OH.
NOT GOOD.
HUH?
KA-THUD
OH NO! MAYAYA FAINTED!!
MAYAYA-SAMA!
...

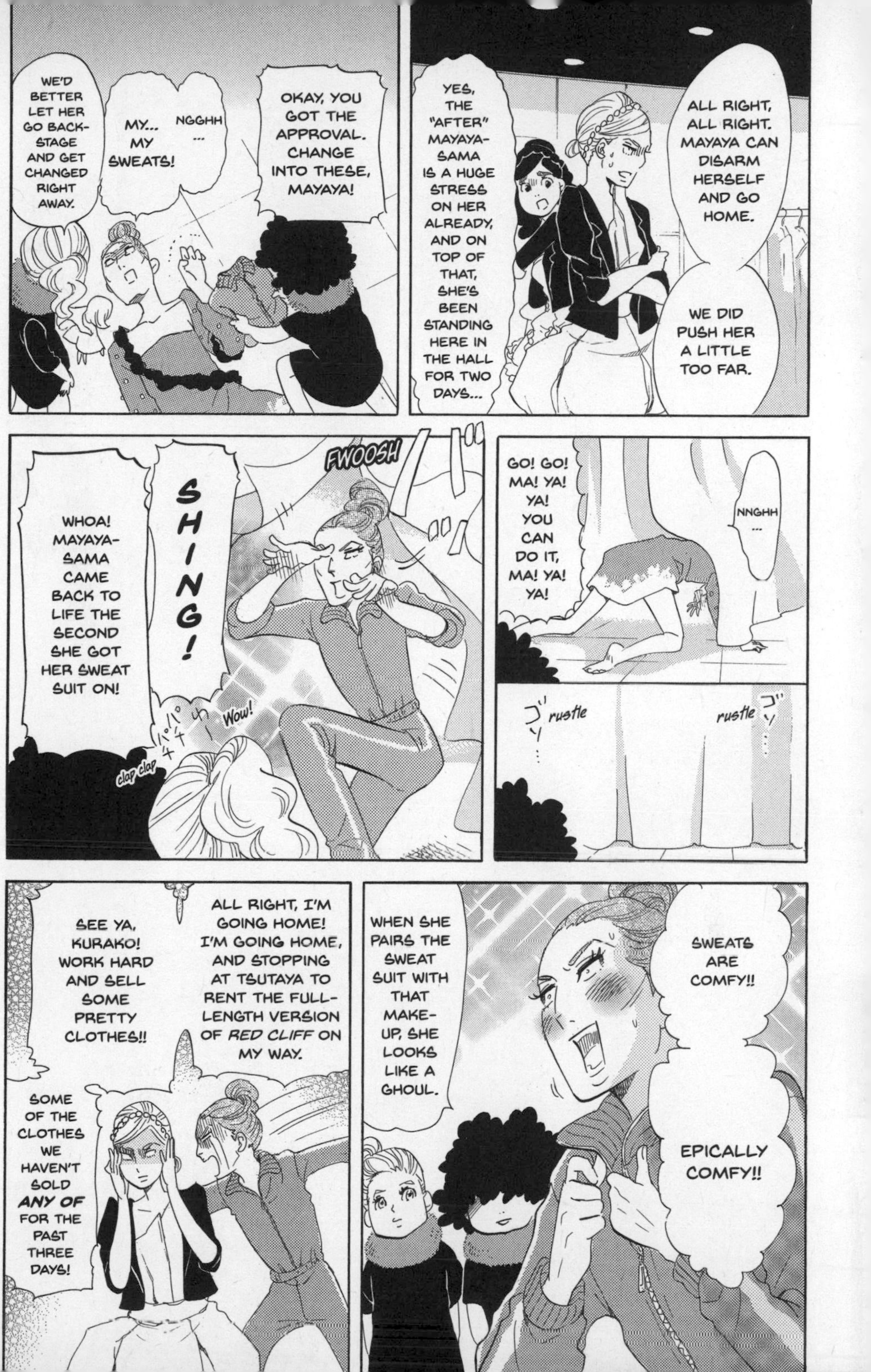
ALL RIGHT, ALL RIGHT. MAYAYA CAN DISARM HERSELF AND GO HOME.
WE DID PUSH HER A LITTLE TOO FAR.
YES, THE "AFTER" MAYAYA-SAMA IS A HUGE STRESS ON HER ALREADY, AND ON TOP OF THAT, SHE'S BEEN STANDING HERE IN THE HALL FOR TWO DAYS...
OKAY, YOU GOT THE APPROVAL. CHANGE INTO THESE, MAYAYA!
NGGHH...
MY... MY SWEATS!
WE'D BETTER LET HER GO BACKSTAGE AND GET CHANGED RIGHT AWAY.
NNGHH...
GO! GO! MA! YA! YA! YOU CAN DO IT, MA! YA! YA!
rustle
rustle
FWOOSH
SHING!
WHOA! MAYAYA-SAMA CAME BACK TO LIFE THE SECOND SHE GOT HER SWEAT SUIT ON!
Wow!
clap clap
SWEATS ARE COMFY!!
EPICALLY COMFY!!
WHEN SHE PAIRS THE SWEAT SUIT WITH THAT MAKE-UP, SHE LOOKS LIKE A GHOUL.
ALL RIGHT, I'M GOING HOME! I'M GOING HOME, AND STOPPING AT TSUTAYA TO RENT THE FULL-LENGTH VERSION OF *RED CLIFF* ON MY WAY.
SEE YA, KURAKO! WORK HARD AND SELL SOME PRETTY CLOTHES!!
SOME OF THE CLOTHES WE HAVEN'T SOLD **ANY OF** FOR THE PAST THREE DAYS!

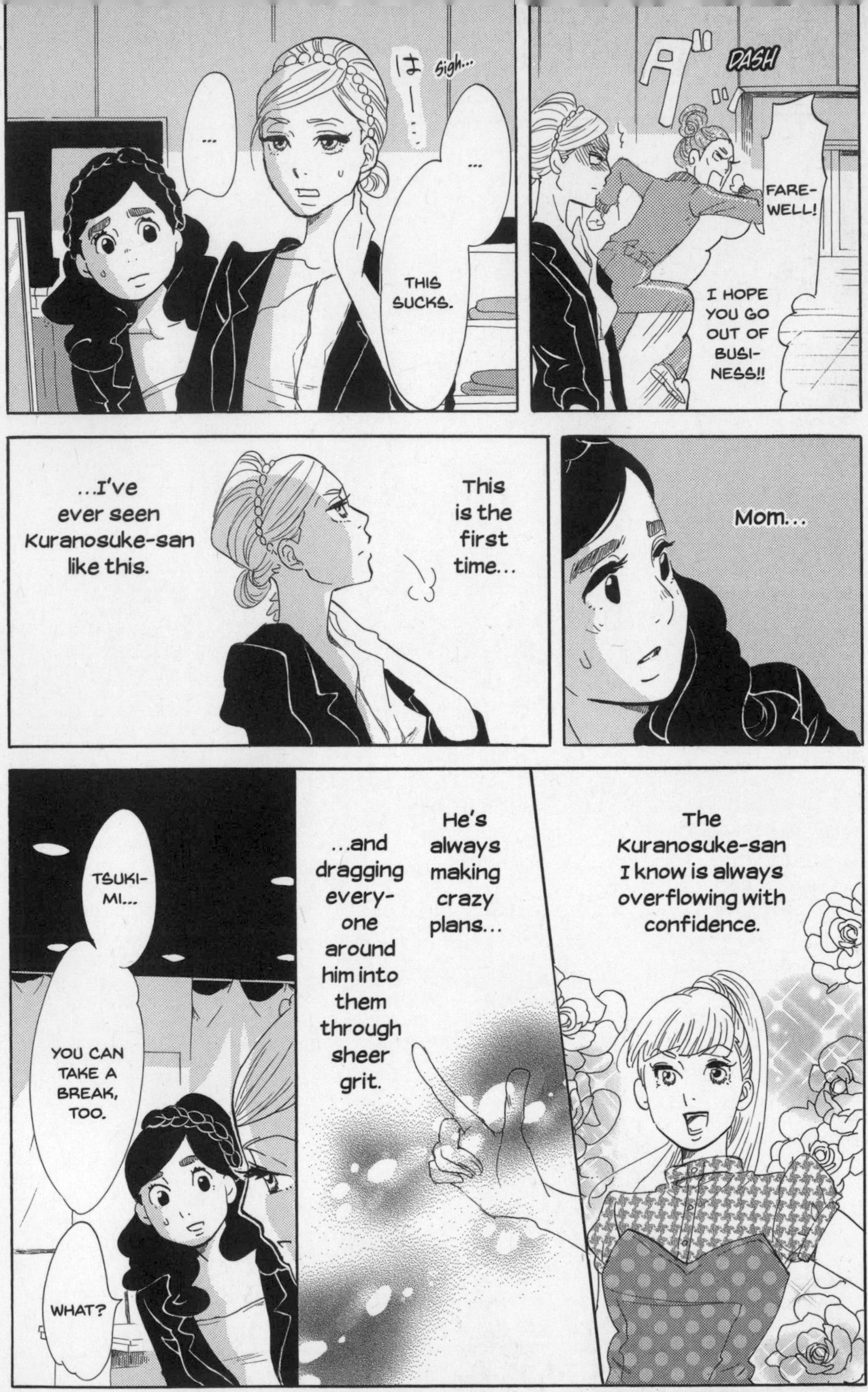

DASH
FARE-WELL!
I HOPE YOU GO OUT OF BUSI-NESS!!
Sigh...
...
THIS SUCKS.
...
Mom...
This is the first time...
...I've ever seen Kuranosuke-san like this.
The Kuranosuke-san I know is always overflowing with confidence.
He's always making crazy plans...
...and dragging every-one around him into them through sheer grit.
TSUKI-MI...
YOU CAN TAKE A BREAK, TOO.
WHAT?

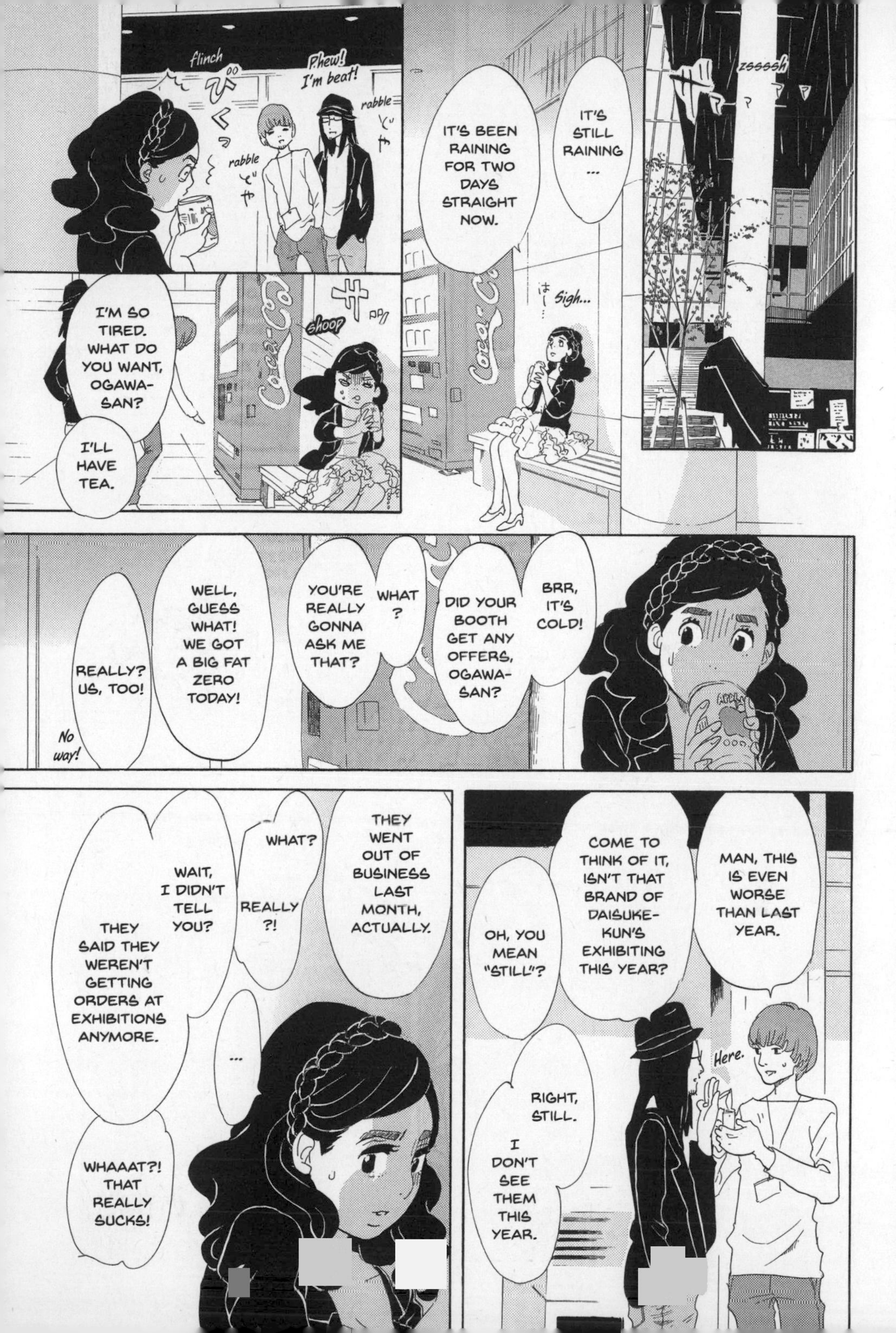
zssssh
IT'S STILL RAINING ...
IT'S BEEN RAINING FOR TWO DAYS STRAIGHT NOW.
Sigh...
flinch
Phew! I'm beat!
rabble
rabble
shoop
I'M SO TIRED. WHAT DO YOU WANT, OGAWA-SAN?
I'LL HAVE TEA.
BRR, IT'S COLD!
DID YOUR BOOTH GET ANY OFFERS, OGAWA-SAN?
WHAT?
YOU'RE REALLY GONNA ASK ME THAT?
WELL, GUESS WHAT! WE GOT A BIG FAT ZERO TODAY!
REALLY? US, TOO!
No way!
MAN, THIS IS EVEN WORSE THAN LAST YEAR.
COME TO THINK OF IT, ISN'T THAT BRAND OF DAISUKE-KUN'S EXHIBITING THIS YEAR?
OH, YOU MEAN "STILL"?
Here.
RIGHT, STILL.
I DON'T SEE THEM THIS YEAR.
THEY WENT OUT OF BUSINESS LAST MONTH, ACTUALLY.
WHAT?
REALLY ?!
WAIT, I DIDN'T TELL YOU?
THEY SAID THEY WEREN'T GETTING ORDERS AT EXHIBITIONS ANYMORE.
...
WHAAAT?! THAT REALLY SUCKS!

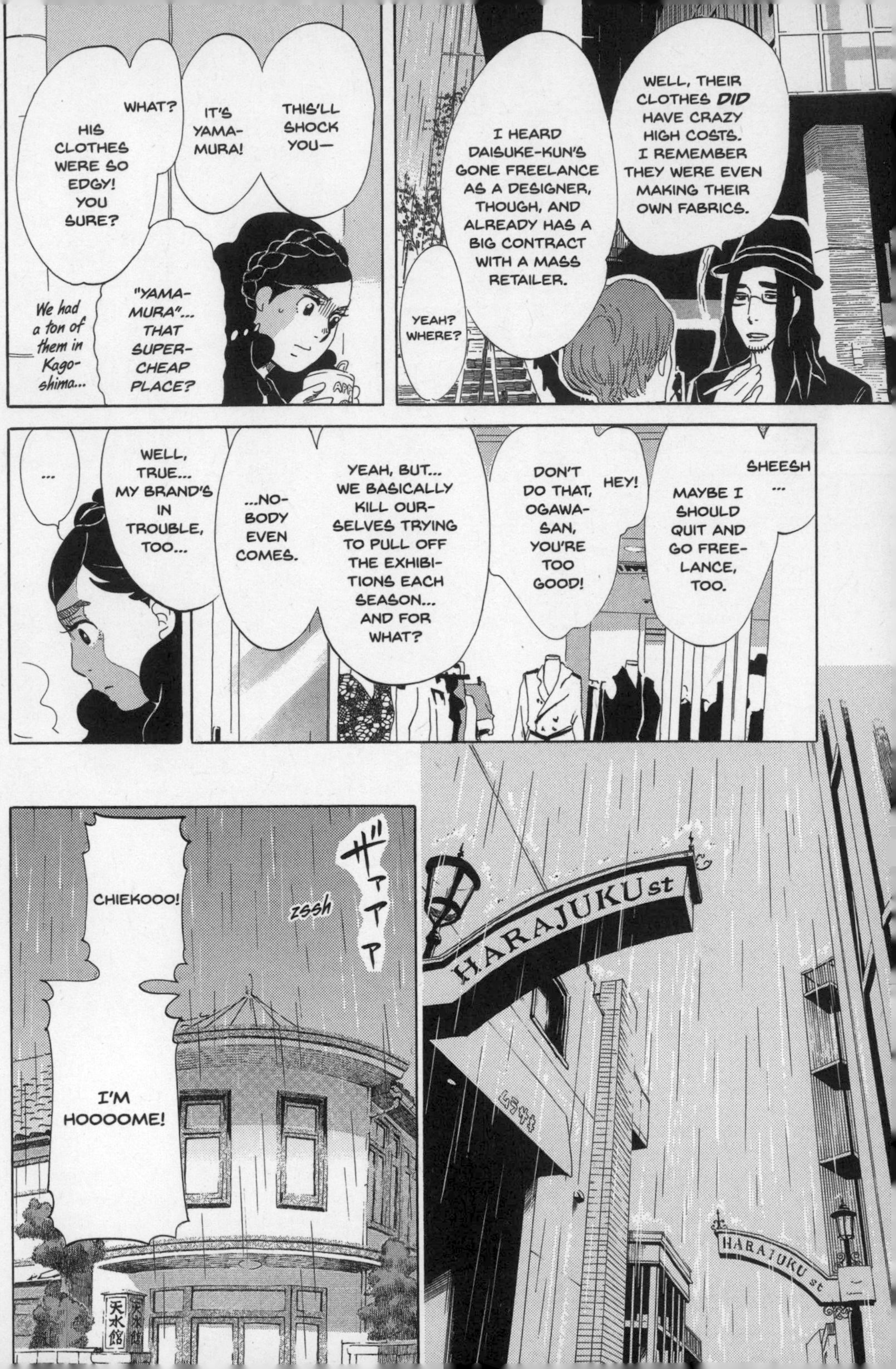
WELL, THEIR CLOTHES DID HAVE CRAZY HIGH COSTS. I REMEMBER THEY WERE EVEN MAKING THEIR OWN FABRICS.
I HEARD DAISUKE-KUN'S GONE FREELANCE AS A DESIGNER, THOUGH, AND ALREADY HAS A BIG CONTRACT WITH A MASS RETAILER.
YEAH? WHERE?
THIS'LL SHOCK YOU—
IT'S YAMAMURA!
WHAT? HIS CLOTHES WERE SO EDGY! YOU SURE?
"YAMAMURA"... THAT SUPER-CHEAP PLACE?
We had a ton of them in Kagoshima...
SHEESH...
MAYBE I SHOULD QUIT AND GO FREELANCE, TOO.
HEY!
DON'T DO THAT, OGAWA-SAN, YOU'RE TOO GOOD!
YEAH, BUT... WE BASICALLY KILL OURSELVES TRYING TO PULL OFF THE EXHIBITIONS EACH SEASON... AND FOR WHAT?
...NOBODY EVEN COMES.
WELL, TRUE... MY BRAND'S IN TROUBLE, TOO...
...
HARAJUKU st
HARAJUKU st
ザァァァ
zssh
CHIEKOOO!
I'M HOOOOME!
天水館

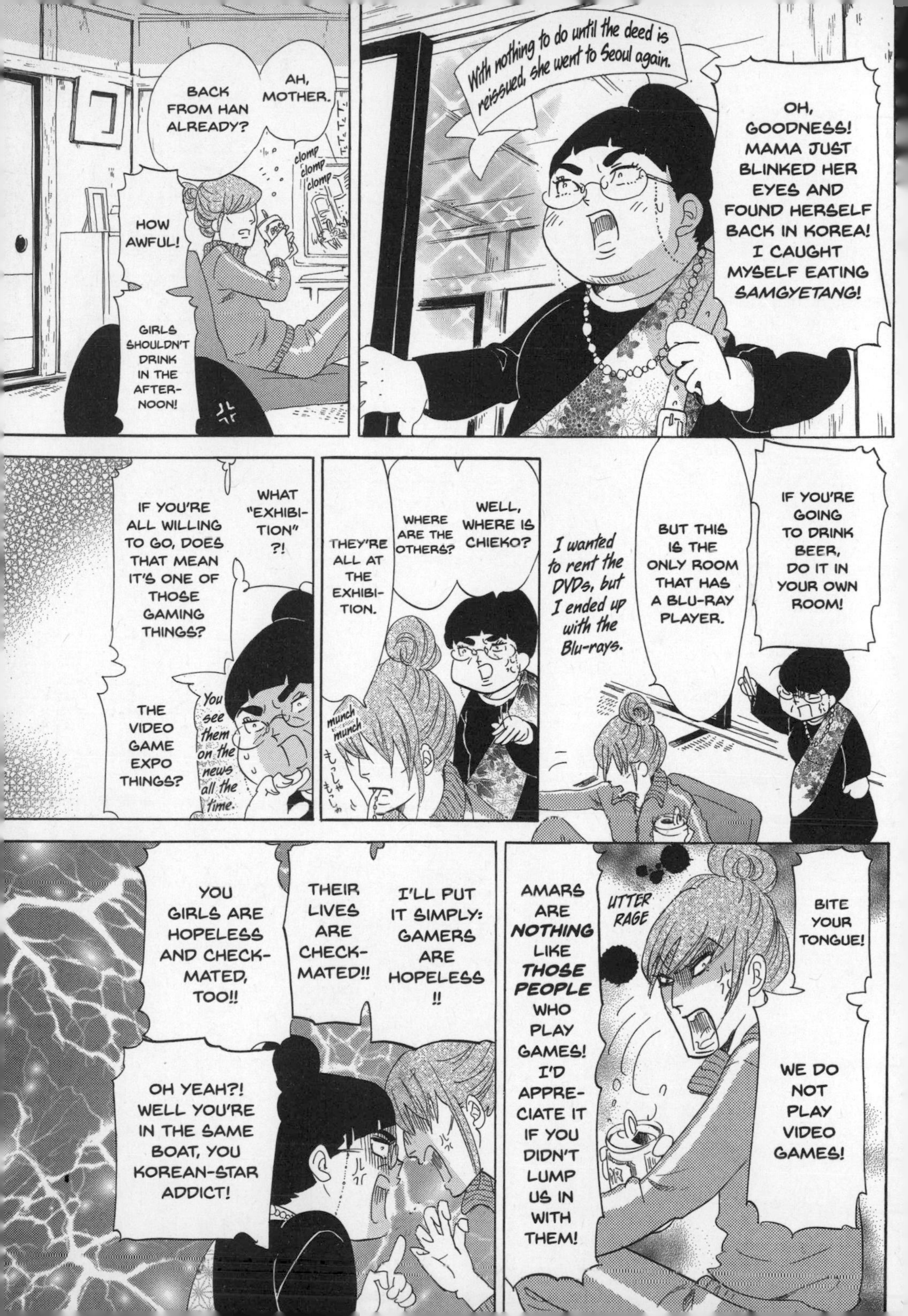
With nothing to do until the deed is reissued, she went to Seoul again.
OH, GOODNESS! MAMA JUST BLINKED HER EYES AND FOUND HERSELF BACK IN KOREA! I CAUGHT MYSELF EATING *SAMGYETANG*!
AH, MOTHER.
BACK FROM HAN ALREADY?
clomp clomp clomp
HOW AWFUL!
GIRLS SHOULDN'T DRINK IN THE AFTER-NOON!
IF YOU'RE GOING TO DRINK BEER, DO IT IN YOUR OWN ROOM!
BUT THIS IS THE ONLY ROOM THAT HAS A BLU-RAY PLAYER.
I wanted to rent the DVDs, but I ended up with the Blu-rays.
WELL, WHERE IS CHIEKO?
WHERE ARE THE OTHERS?
THEY'RE ALL AT THE EXHIBI-TION.
munch munch
もっしゃもっしゃ
WHAT "EXHIBI-TION"?!
IF YOU'RE ALL WILLING TO GO, DOES THAT MEAN IT'S ONE OF THOSE GAMING THINGS?
You see them on the news all the time.
THE VIDEO GAME EXPO THINGS?
BITE YOUR TONGUE!
UTTER RAGE
AMARS ARE **NOTHING** LIKE ***THOSE PEOPLE*** WHO PLAY GAMES! I'D APPRE-CIATE IT IF YOU DIDN'T LUMP US IN WITH THEM!
WE DO NOT PLAY VIDEO GAMES!
I'LL PUT IT SIMPLY: GAMERS ARE HOPELESS!!
THEIR LIVES ARE CHECK-MATED!!
YOU GIRLS ARE HOPELESS AND CHECK-MATED, TOO!!
OH YEAH?! WELL YOU'RE IN THE SAME BOAT, YOU KOREAN-STAR ADDICT!

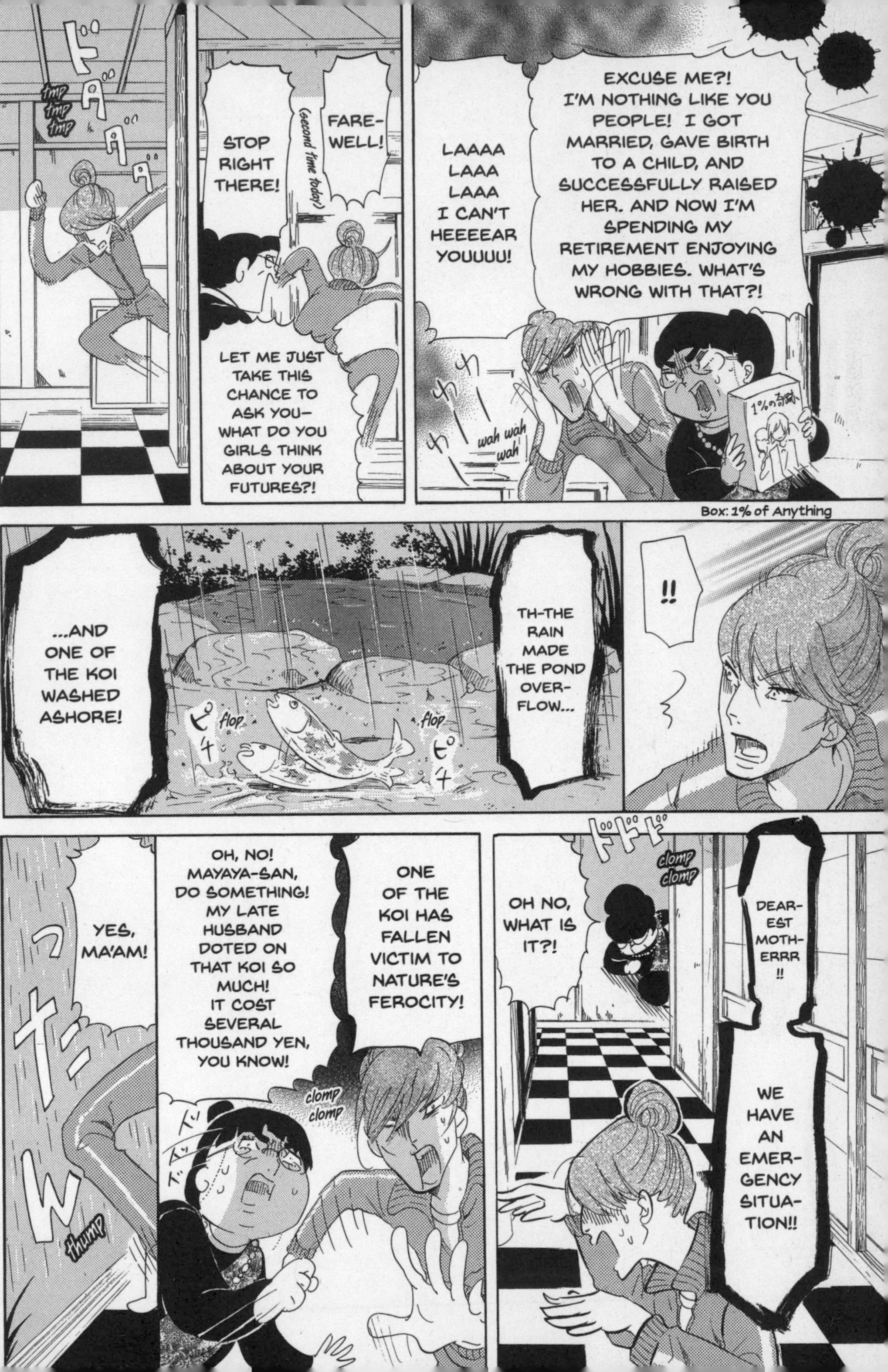
EXCUSE ME?! I'M NOTHING LIKE YOU PEOPLE! I GOT MARRIED, GAVE BIRTH TO A CHILD, AND SUCCESSFULLY RAISED HER. AND NOW I'M SPENDING MY RETIREMENT ENJOYING MY HOBBIES. WHAT'S WRONG WITH THAT?!
LAAAA LAAA LAAA I CAN'T HEEEEAR YOUUUU!
wah wah wah
Box: 1% of Anything
FARE-WELL!
(second time today)
STOP RIGHT THERE!
LET ME JUST TAKE THIS CHANCE TO ASK YOU—WHAT DO YOU GIRLS THINK ABOUT YOUR FUTURES?!
tmp tmp tmp
!!
TH-THE RAIN MADE THE POND OVER-FLOW...
flop
flop
...AND ONE OF THE KOI WASHED ASHORE!
DEAR-EST MOTH-ERRR !!
WE HAVE AN EMER-GENCY SITUA-TION!!
clomp clomp
OH NO, WHAT IS IT?!
ONE OF THE KOI HAS FALLEN VICTIM TO NATURE'S FEROCITY!
OH, NO! MAYAYA-SAN, DO SOMETHING! MY LATE HUSBAND DOTED ON THAT KOI SO MUCH! IT COST SEVERAL THOUSAND YEN, YOU KNOW!
clomp clomp
YES, MA'AM!
thump

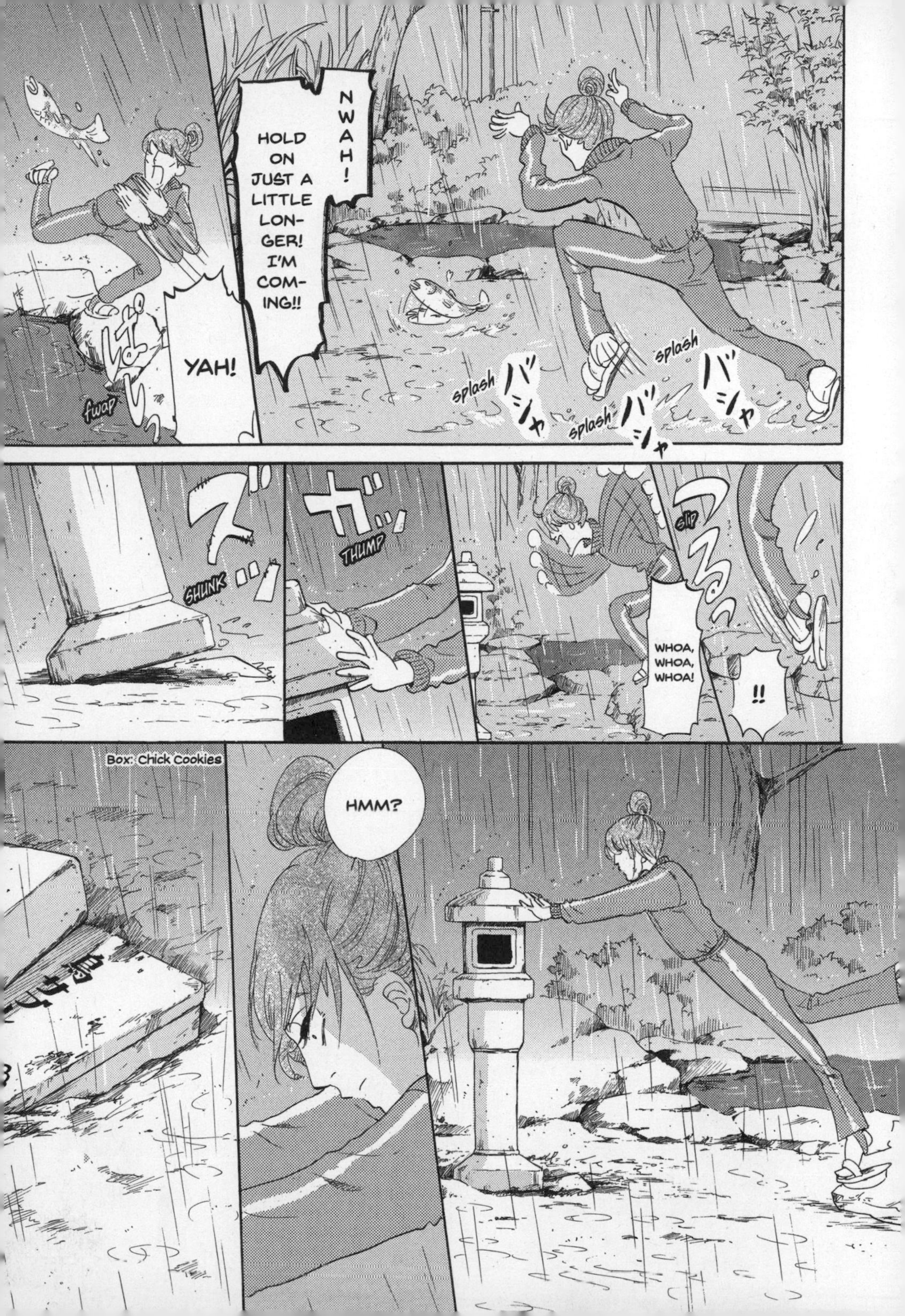
NWAH!
HOLD ON JUST A LITTLE LONGER! I'M COMING!!
splash
splash
splash
YAH!
fwap
!!
slip
WHOA, WHOA, WHOA!
THUMP
SHUNK
HMM?
Box: Chick Cookies

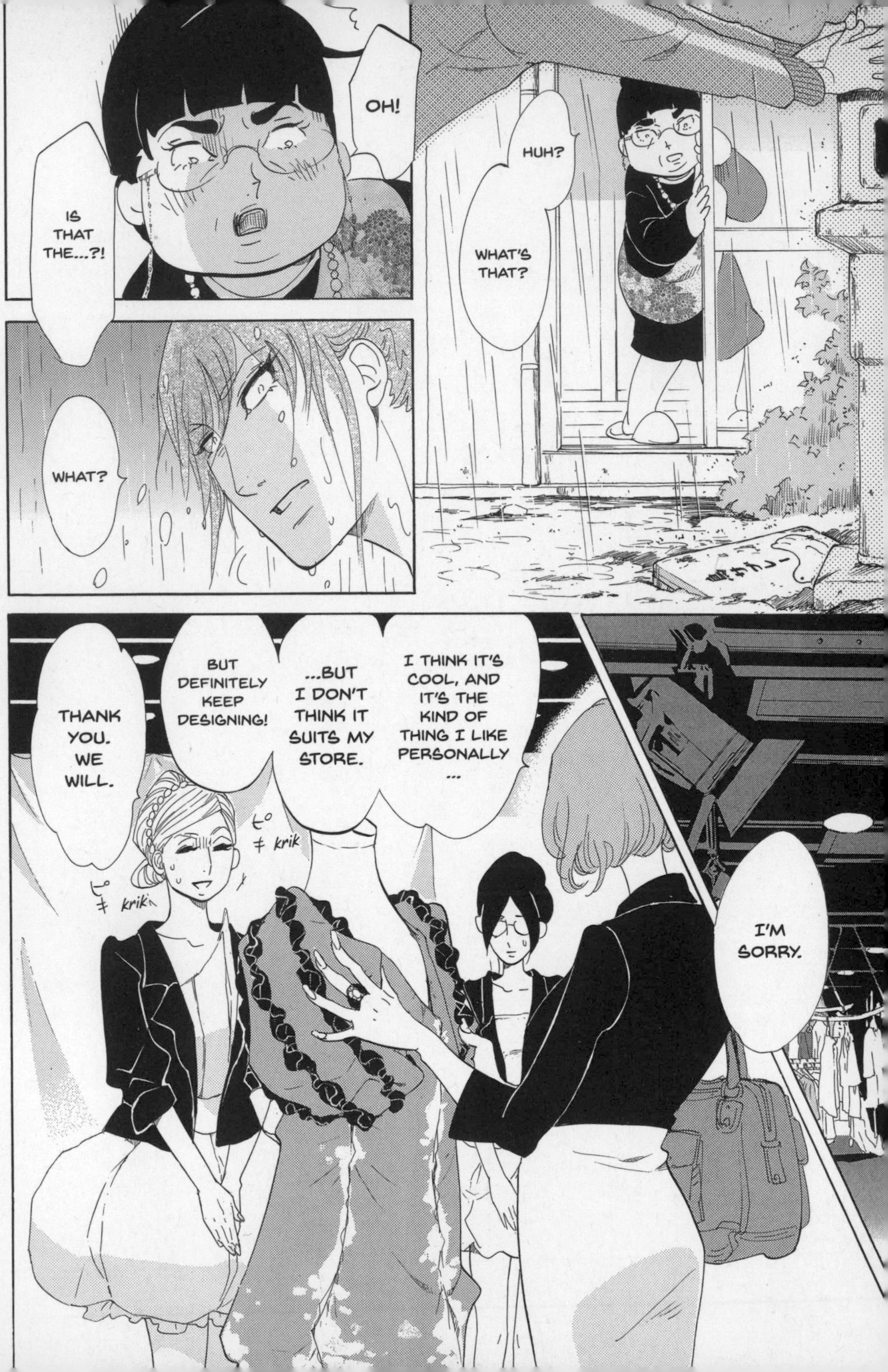
HUH?
WHAT'S THAT?
OH!
IS THAT THE...?!
WHAT?
I'M SORRY.
I THINK IT'S COOL, AND IT'S THE KIND OF THING I LIKE PERSONALLY ...
...BUT I DON'T THINK IT SUITS MY STORE.
BUT DEFINITELY KEEP DESIGNING!
THANK YOU. WE WILL.
ピキ krik
ピキ krik

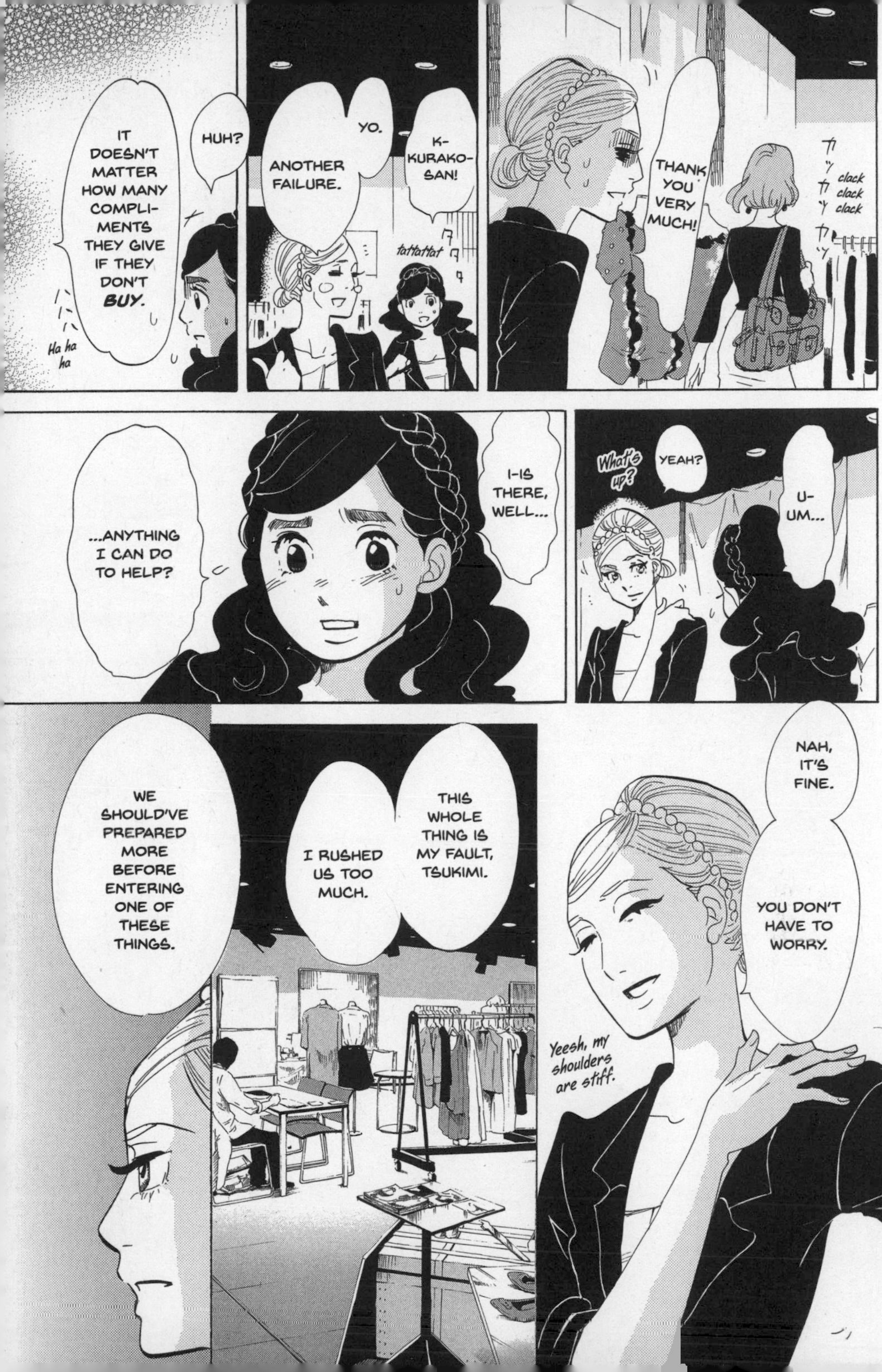
THANK YOU VERY MUCH!
clack clack clack
K-KURAKO-SAN!
tattattat
YO.
ANOTHER FAILURE.
HUH?
IT DOESN'T MATTER HOW MANY COMPLIMENTS THEY GIVE IF THEY DON'T BUY.
Ha ha ha
U-UM...
YEAH?
What's up?
I-IS THERE, WELL...
...ANYTHING I CAN DO TO HELP?
NAH, IT'S FINE.
YOU DON'T HAVE TO WORRY.
Yeesh, my shoulders are stiff.
THIS WHOLE THING IS MY FAULT, TSUKIMI.
I RUSHED US TOO MUCH.
WE SHOULD'VE PREPARED MORE BEFORE ENTERING ONE OF THESE THINGS.

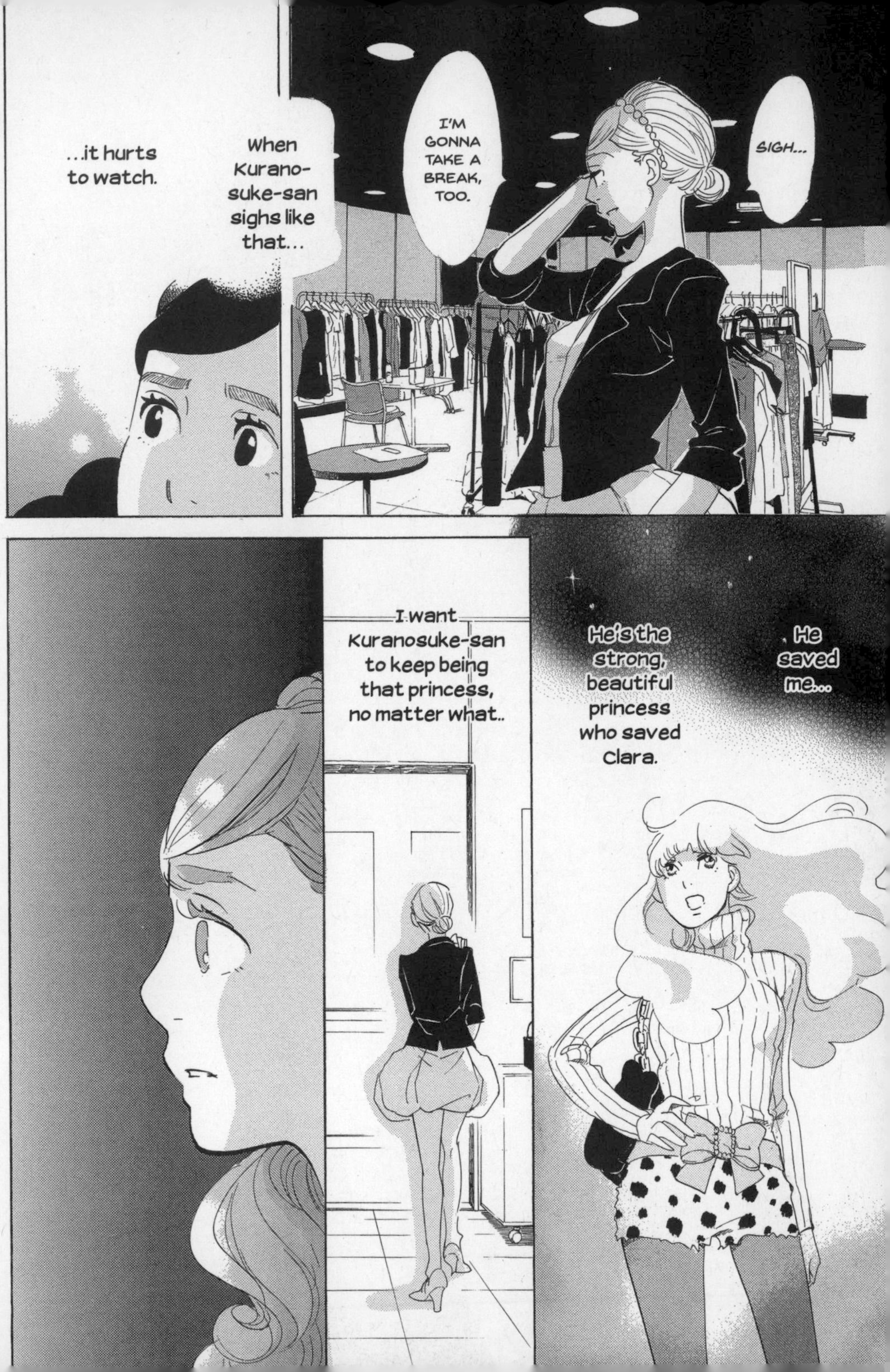
SIGH...
I'M GONNA TAKE A BREAK, TOO.
When Kuranosuke-san sighs like that...
...it hurts to watch.
He saved me...
He's the strong, beautiful princess who saved Clara.
I want Kuranosuke-san to keep being that princess, no matter what..

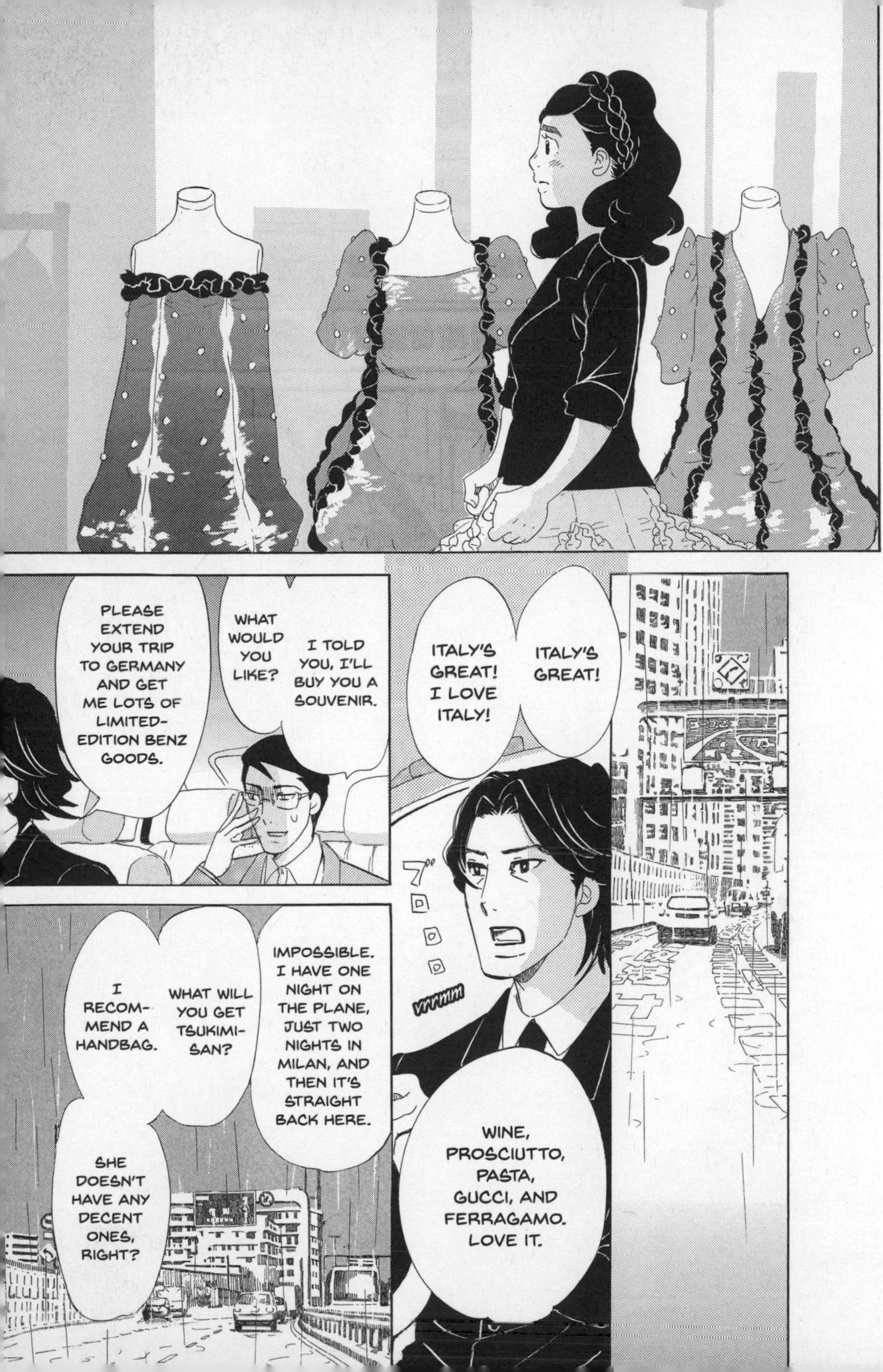
ITALY'S GREAT!
ITALY'S GREAT! I LOVE ITALY!
vrrmm
WINE, PROSCIUTTO, PASTA, GUCCI, AND FERRAGAMO. LOVE IT.
I TOLD YOU, I'LL BUY YOU A SOUVENIR.
WHAT WOULD YOU LIKE?
PLEASE EXTEND YOUR TRIP TO GERMANY AND GET ME LOTS OF LIMITED-EDITION BENZ GOODS.
IMPOSSIBLE. I HAVE ONE NIGHT ON THE PLANE, JUST TWO NIGHTS IN MILAN, AND THEN IT'S STRAIGHT BACK HERE.
WHAT WILL YOU GET TSUKIMI-SAN?
I RECOMMEND A HANDBAG.
SHE DOESN'T HAVE ANY DECENT ONES, RIGHT?

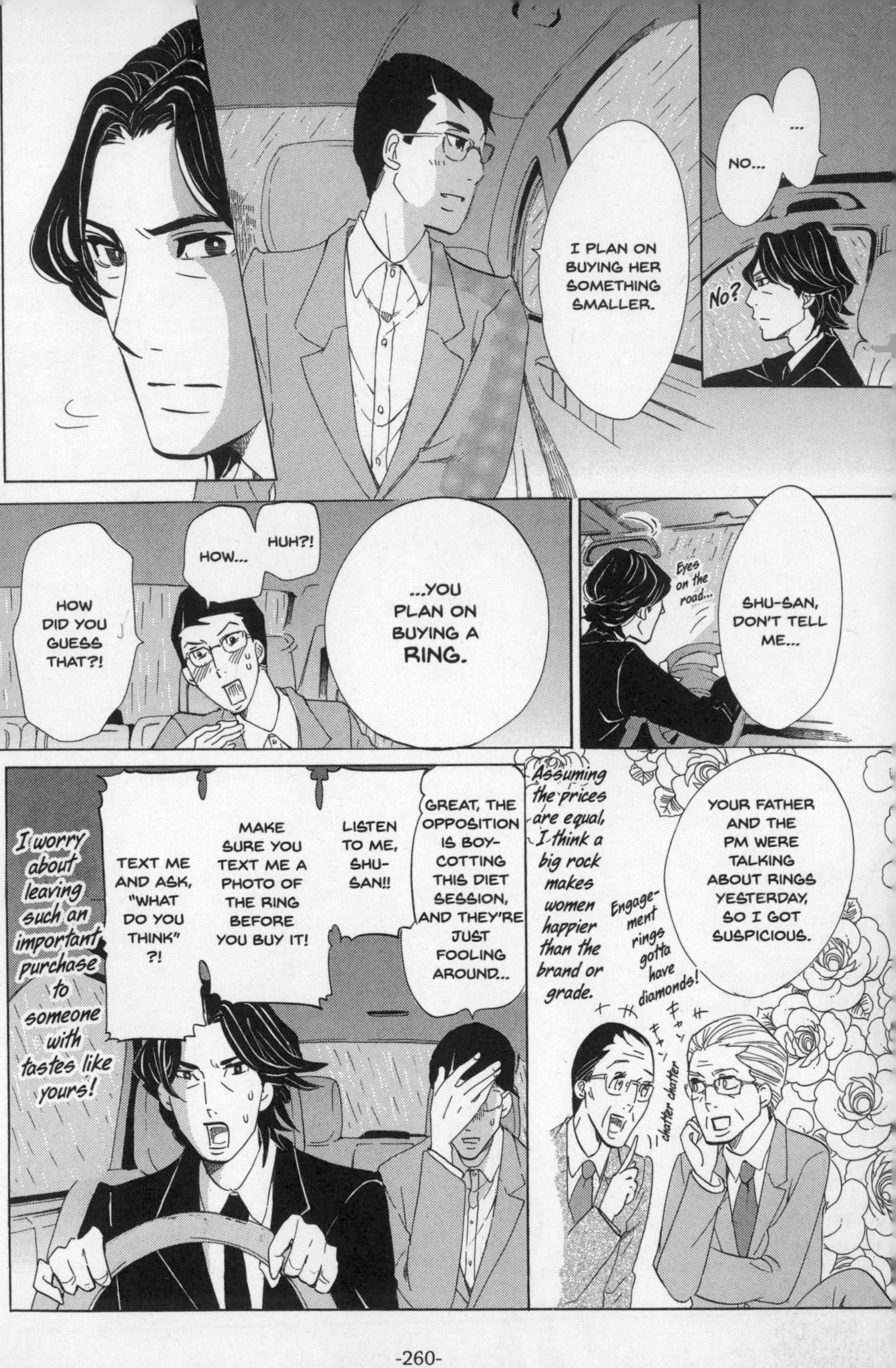
...
NO...
No?
I PLAN ON BUYING HER SOMETHING SMALLER.
SHU-SAN, DON'T TELL ME...
Eyes on the road...
...YOU PLAN ON BUYING A RING.
HUH?!
HOW...
HOW DID YOU GUESS THAT?!
YOUR FATHER AND THE PM WERE TALKING ABOUT RINGS YESTERDAY, SO I GOT SUSPICIOUS.
Assuming the prices are equal, I think a big rock makes women happier than the brand or grade.
Engage-ment rings gotta have diamonds!
chatter chatter
GREAT, THE OPPOSITION IS BOY-COTTING THIS DIET SESSION, AND THEY'RE JUST FOOLING AROUND...
LISTEN TO ME, SHU-SAN!!
MAKE SURE YOU TEXT ME A PHOTO OF THE RING BEFORE YOU BUY IT!
TEXT ME AND ASK, "WHAT DO YOU THINK"?!
I worry about leaving such an important purchase to someone with tastes like yours!

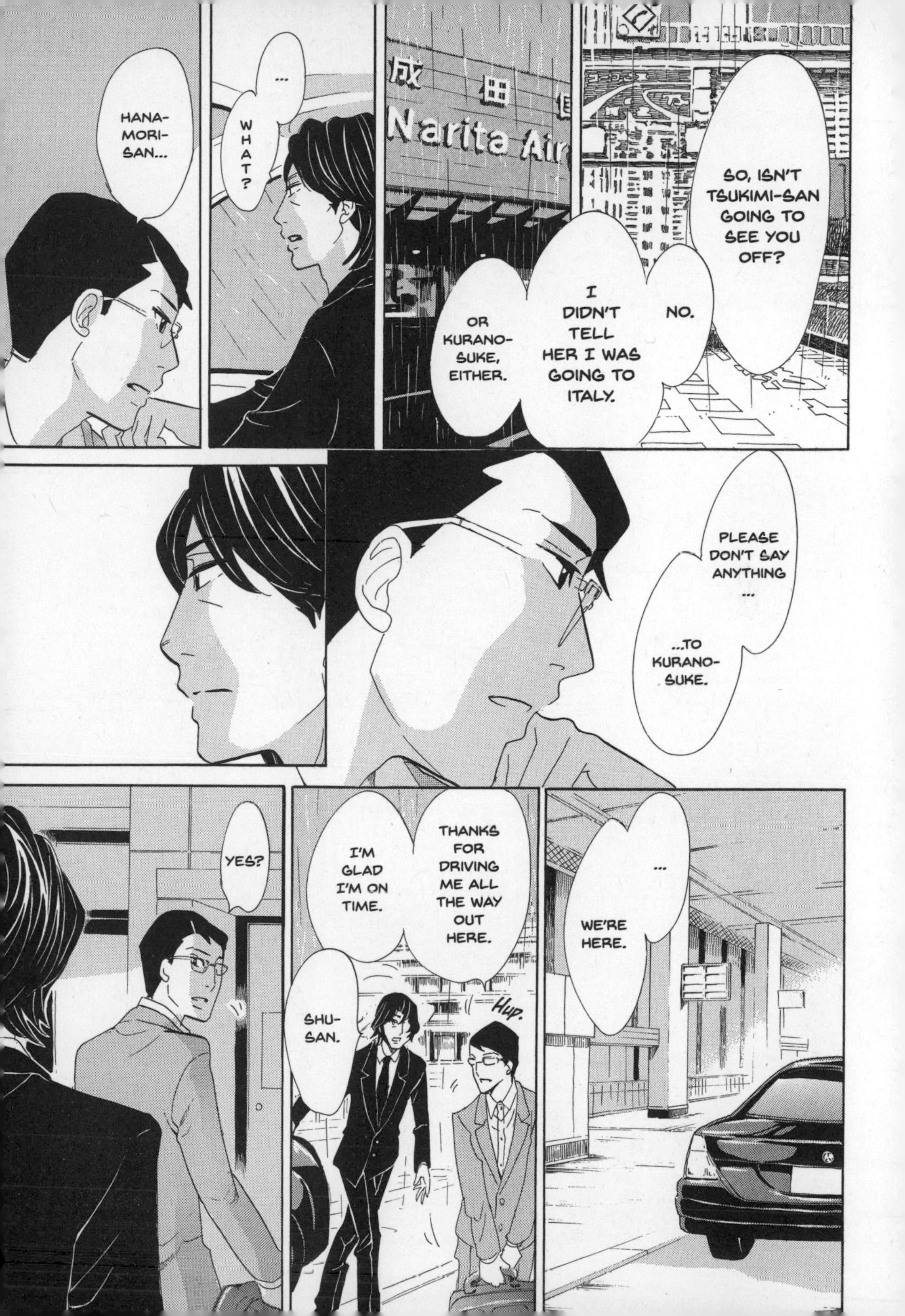
SO, ISN'T TSUKIMI-SAN GOING TO SEE YOU OFF?
NO.
I DIDN'T TELL HER I WAS GOING TO ITALY.
OR KURANO-SUKE, EITHER.
...
WHAT?
HANA-MORI-SAN...
PLEASE DON'T SAY ANYTHING ...
...TO KURANO-SUKE.
...
WE'RE HERE.
THANKS FOR DRIVING ME ALL THE WAY OUT HERE.
I'M GLAD I'M ON TIME.
HUP.
SHU-SAN.
YES?

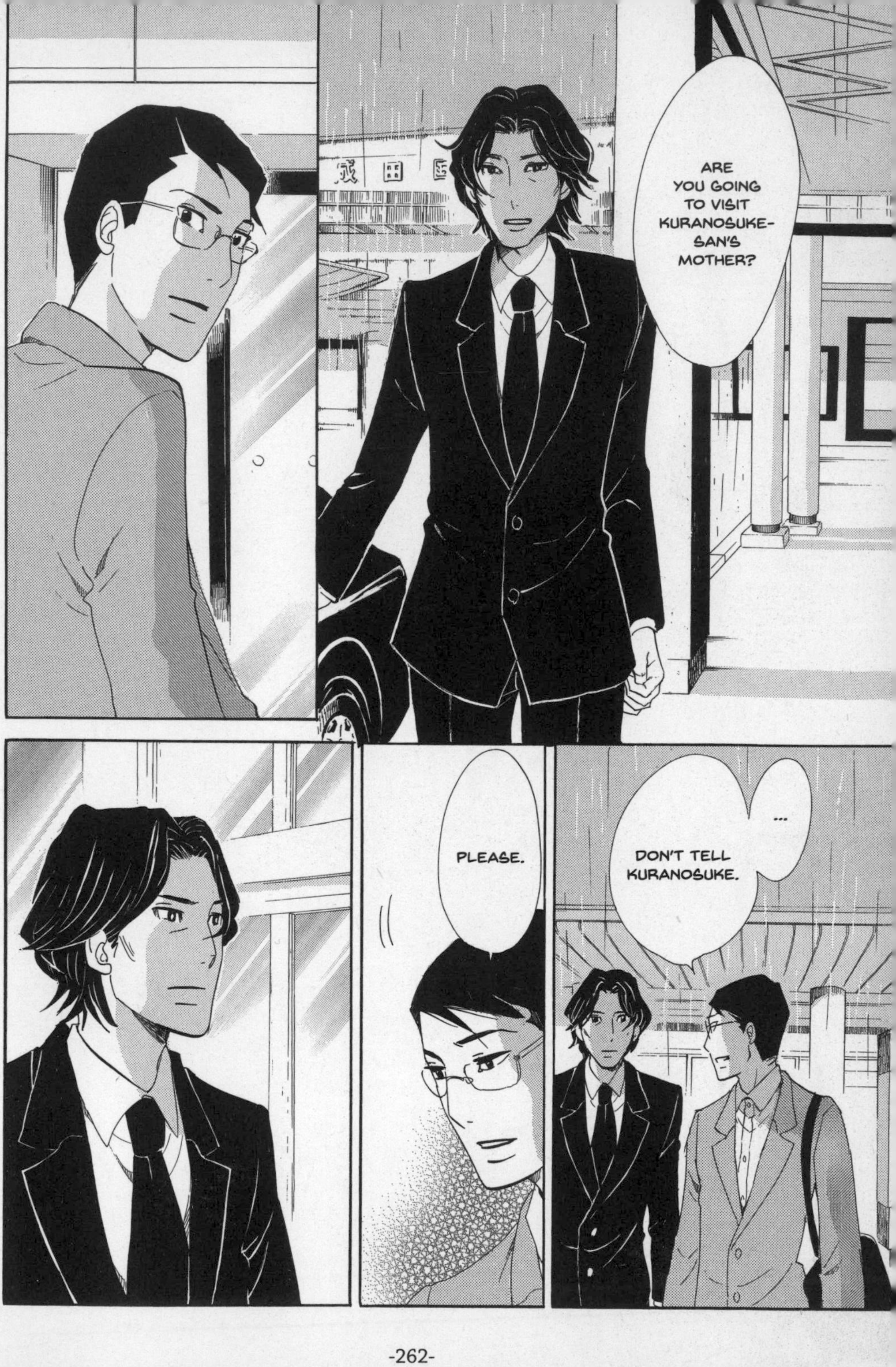
ARE YOU GOING TO VISIT KURANOSUKE-SAN'S MOTHER?
...
DON'T TELL KURANOSUKE.
PLEASE.

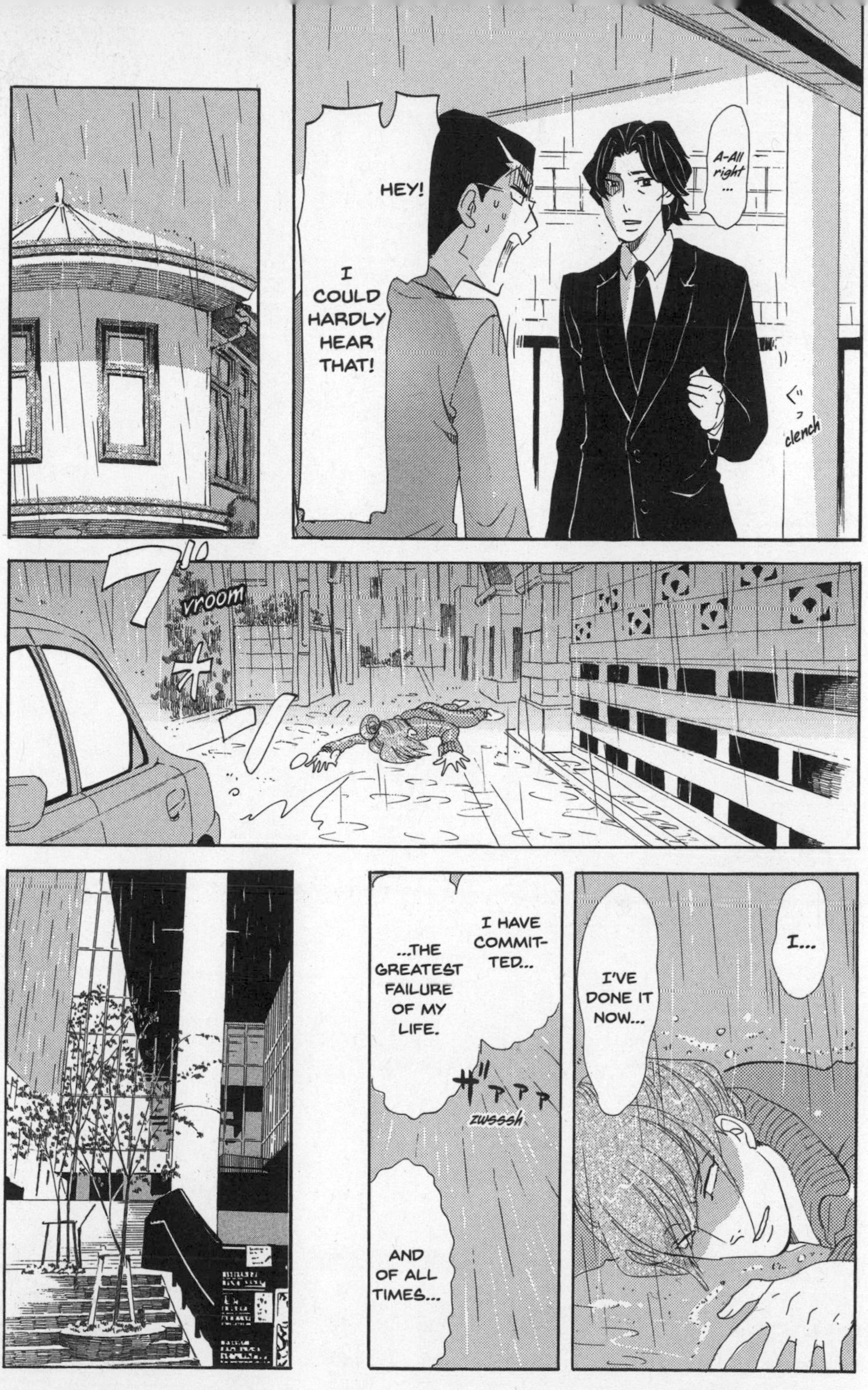
A-All right ...
HEY!
I COULD HARDLY HEAR THAT!
clench
vroom
I...
I'VE DONE IT NOW...
I HAVE COMMIT-TED...
...THE GREATEST FAILURE OF MY LIFE.
zwsssh
AND OF ALL TIMES...

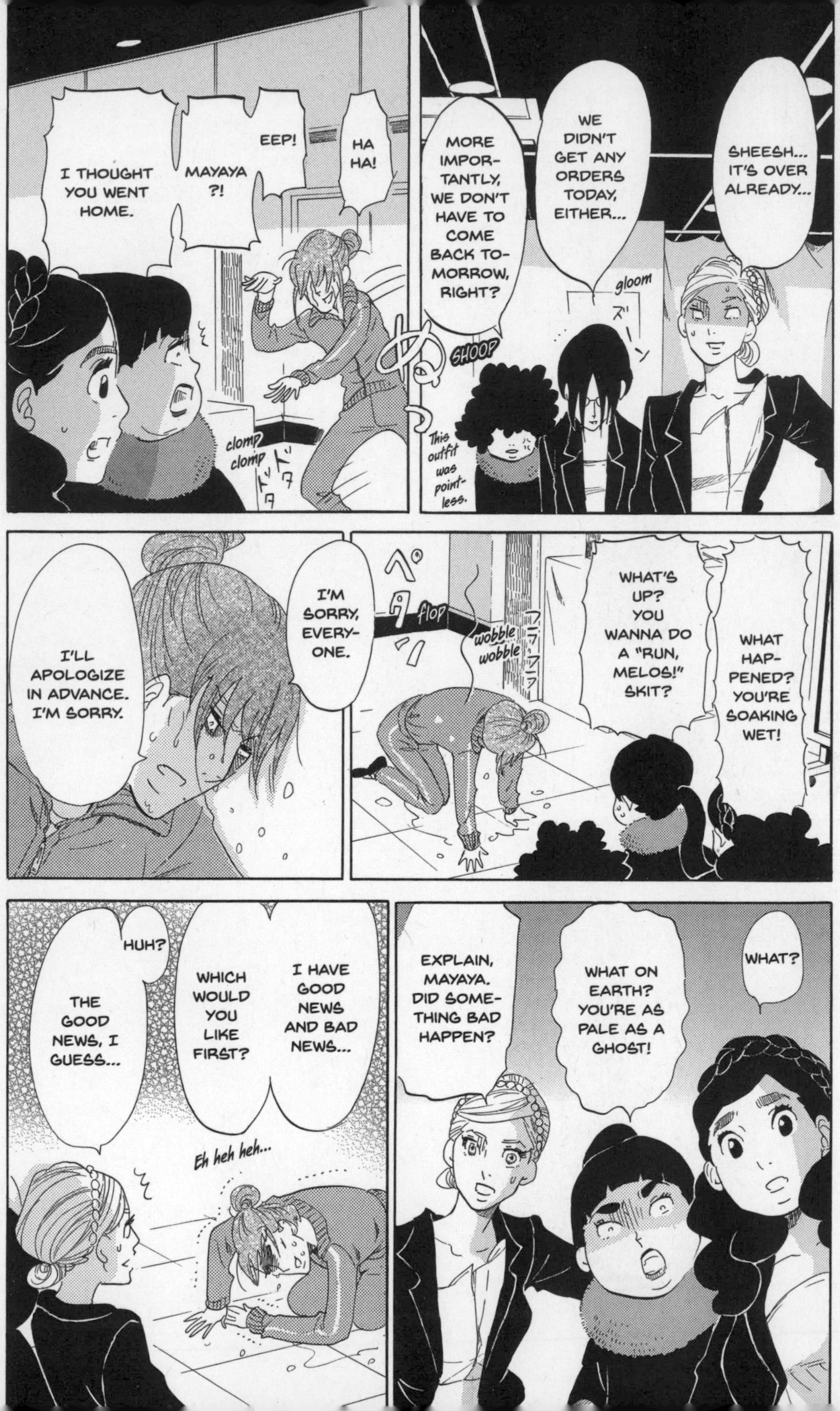
SHEESH... IT'S OVER ALREADY...
WE DIDN'T GET ANY ORDERS TODAY, EITHER...
gloom
MORE IMPORTANTLY, WE DON'T HAVE TO COME BACK TOMORROW, RIGHT?
SHOOP
This outfit was pointless.
HA HA!
EEP!
MAYAYA?!
I THOUGHT YOU WENT HOME.
clomp clomp
WHAT HAPPENED? YOU'RE SOAKING WET!
WHAT'S UP? YOU WANNA DO A "RUN, MELOS!" SKIT?
wobble wobble
flop
I'M SORRY, EVERYONE.
I'LL APOLOGIZE IN ADVANCE. I'M SORRY.
WHAT?
WHAT ON EARTH? YOU'RE AS PALE AS A GHOST!
EXPLAIN, MAYAYA. DID SOMETHING BAD HAPPEN?
I HAVE GOOD NEWS AND BAD NEWS...
WHICH WOULD YOU LIKE FIRST?
HUH?
THE GOOD NEWS, I GUESS...
Eh heh heh...

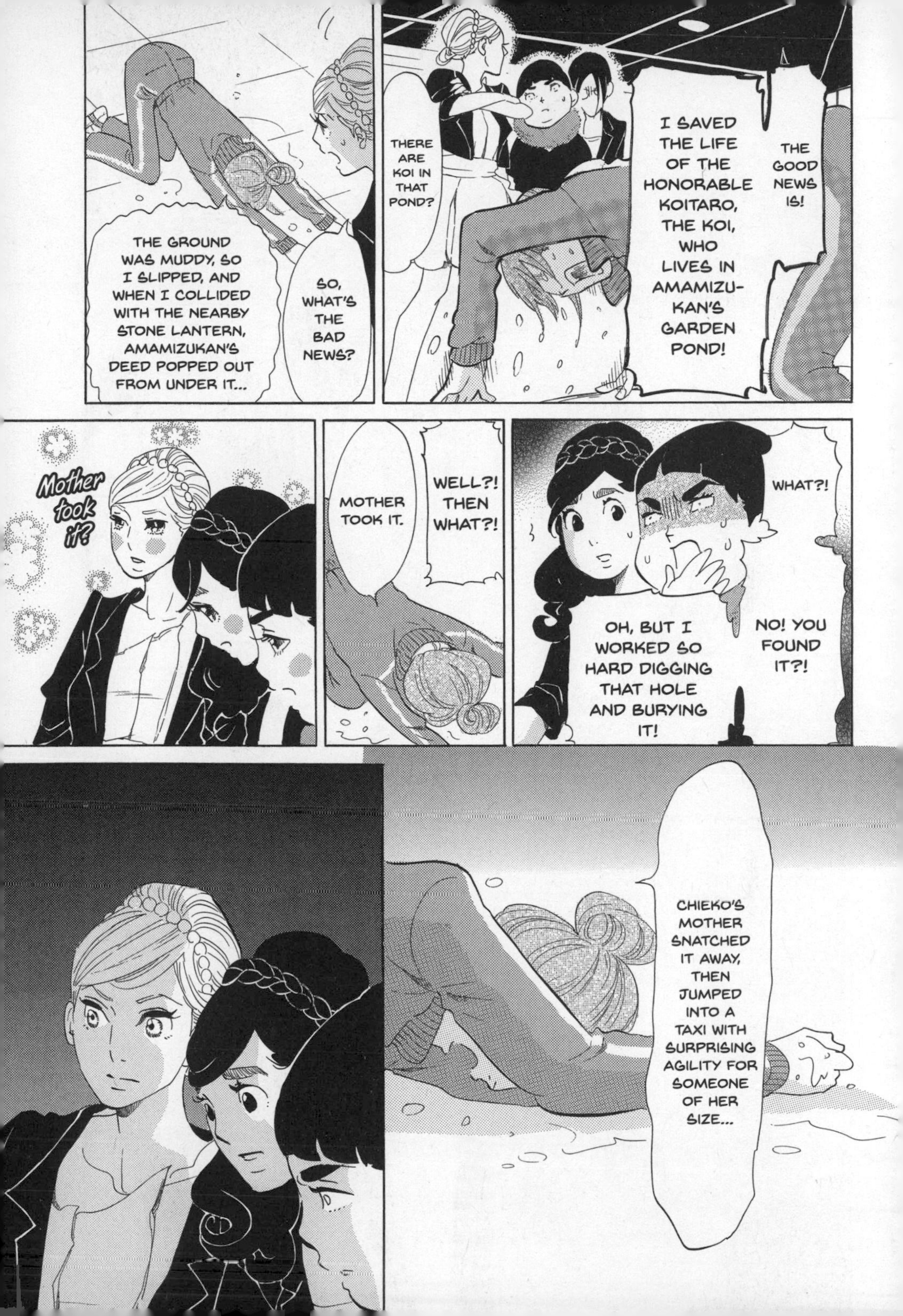
THE GOOD NEWS IS!
I SAVED THE LIFE OF THE HONORABLE KOITARO, THE KOI, WHO LIVES IN AMAMIZUKAN'S GARDEN POND!
THERE ARE KOI IN THAT POND?
SO, WHAT'S THE BAD NEWS?
THE GROUND WAS MUDDY, SO I SLIPPED, AND WHEN I COLLIDED WITH THE NEARBY STONE LANTERN, AMAMIZUKAN'S DEED POPPED OUT FROM UNDER IT...
WHAT?!
NO! YOU FOUND IT?!
OH, BUT I WORKED SO HARD DIGGING THAT HOLE AND BURYING IT!
WELL?! THEN WHAT?!
MOTHER TOOK IT.
Mother took it?
CHIEKO'S MOTHER SNATCHED IT AWAY, THEN JUMPED INTO A TAXI WITH SURPRISING AGILITY FOR SOMEONE OF HER SIZE...

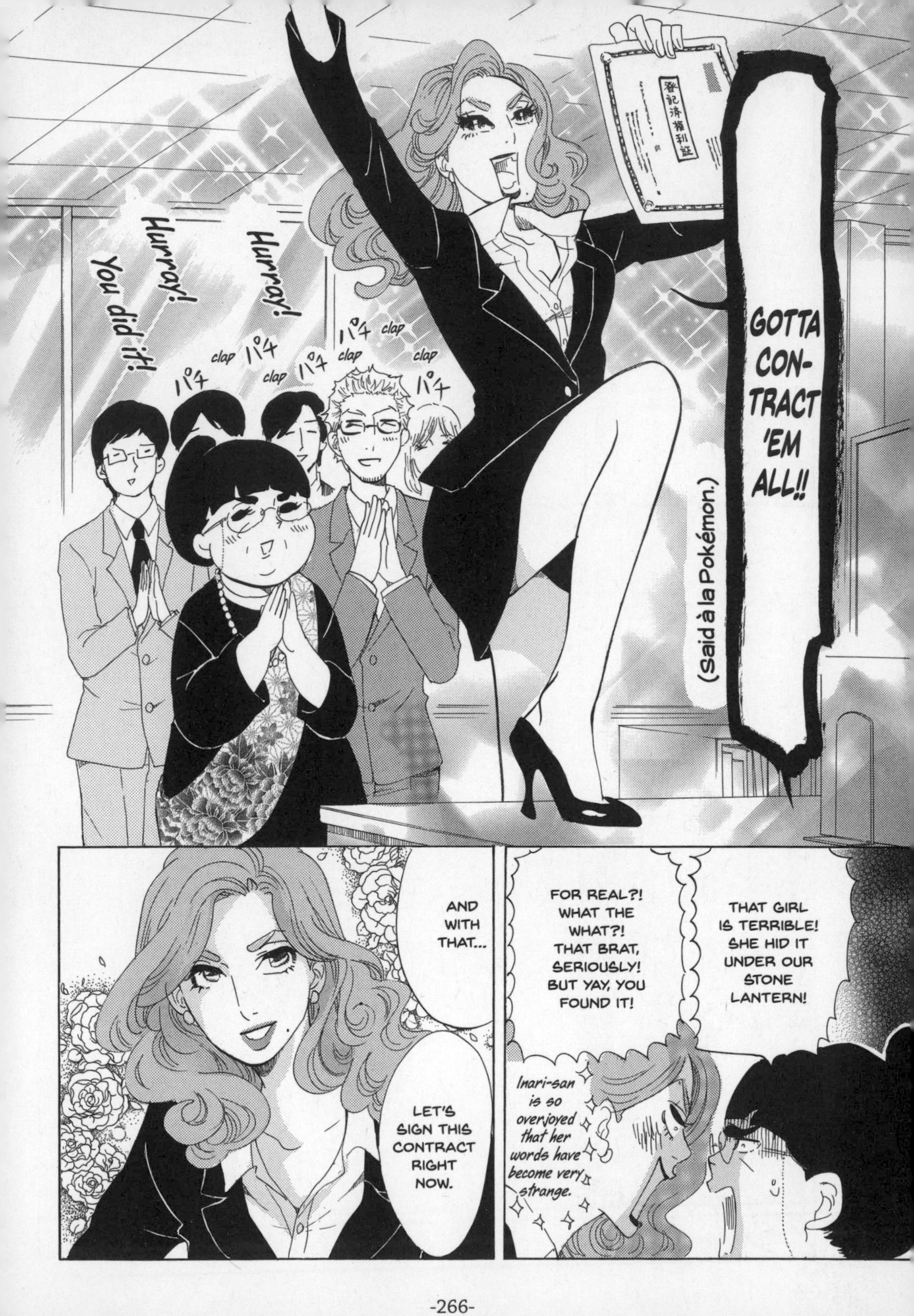
登記済権利証
GOTTA CON-TRACT 'EM ALL!!
(Said à la Pokémon.)
Hurray!
Hurray! You did it!
パチ clap パチ clap パチ clap パチ clap パチ clap
THAT GIRL IS TERRIBLE! SHE HID IT UNDER OUR STONE LANTERN!
FOR REAL?! WHAT THE WHAT?! THAT BRAT, SERIOUSLY! BUT YAY, YOU FOUND IT!
Inari-san is so overjoyed that her words have become very strange.
AND WITH THAT...
LET'S SIGN THIS CONTRACT RIGHT NOW.

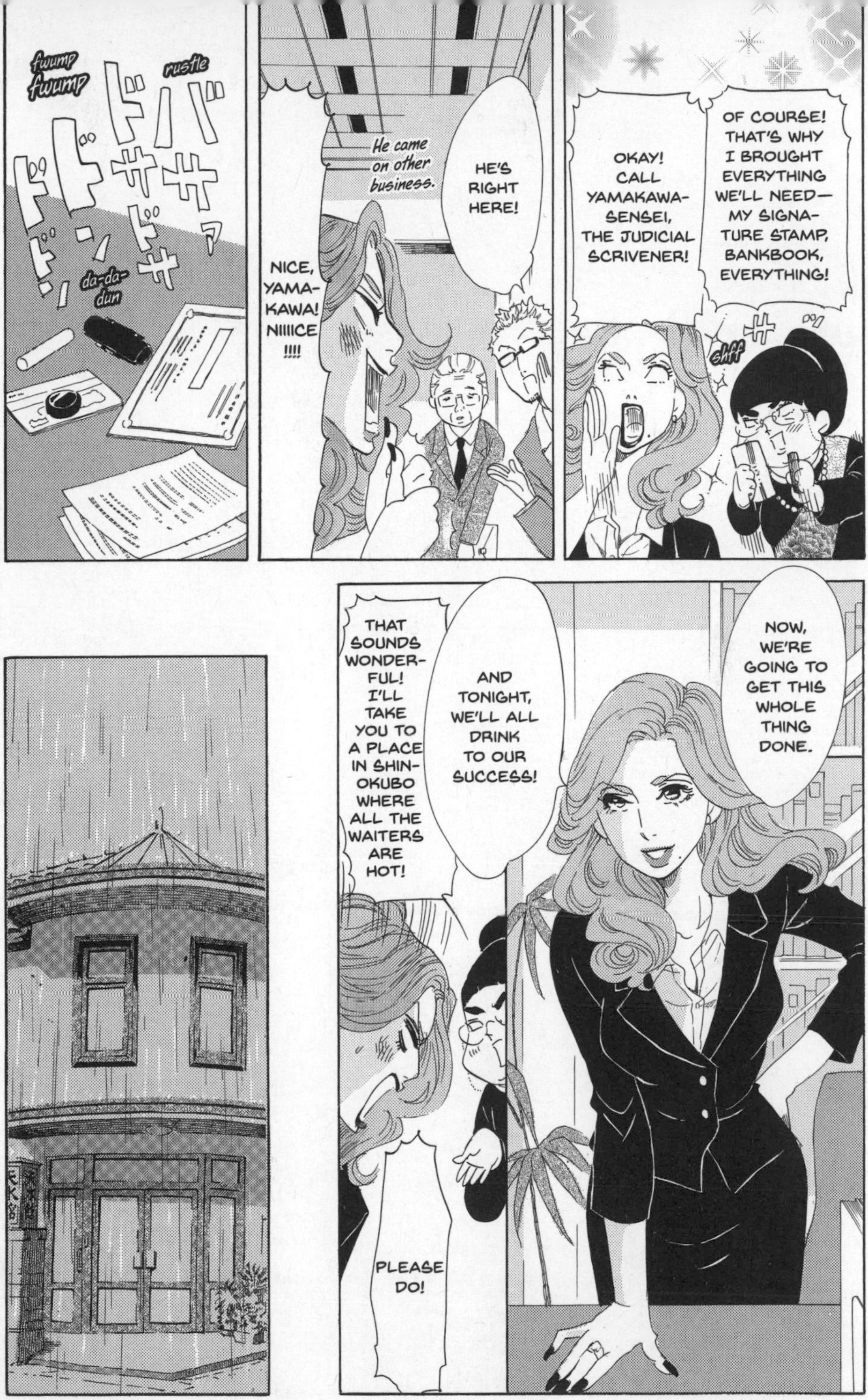
OF COURSE! THAT'S WHY I BROUGHT EVERYTHING WE'LL NEED—MY SIGNATURE STAMP, BANKBOOK, EVERYTHING!
OKAY! CALL YAMAKAWA-SENSEI, THE JUDICIAL SCRIVENER!
shff
HE'S RIGHT HERE!
He came on other business.
NICE, YAMAKAWA! NIIIICE !!!!
rustle
fwuump fwuump
da-da-dun
NOW, WE'RE GOING TO GET THIS WHOLE THING DONE.
AND TONIGHT, WE'LL ALL DRINK TO OUR SUCCESS!
THAT SOUNDS WONDERFUL! I'LL TAKE YOU TO A PLACE IN SHIN-OKUBO WHERE ALL THE WAITERS ARE HOT!
PLEASE DO!

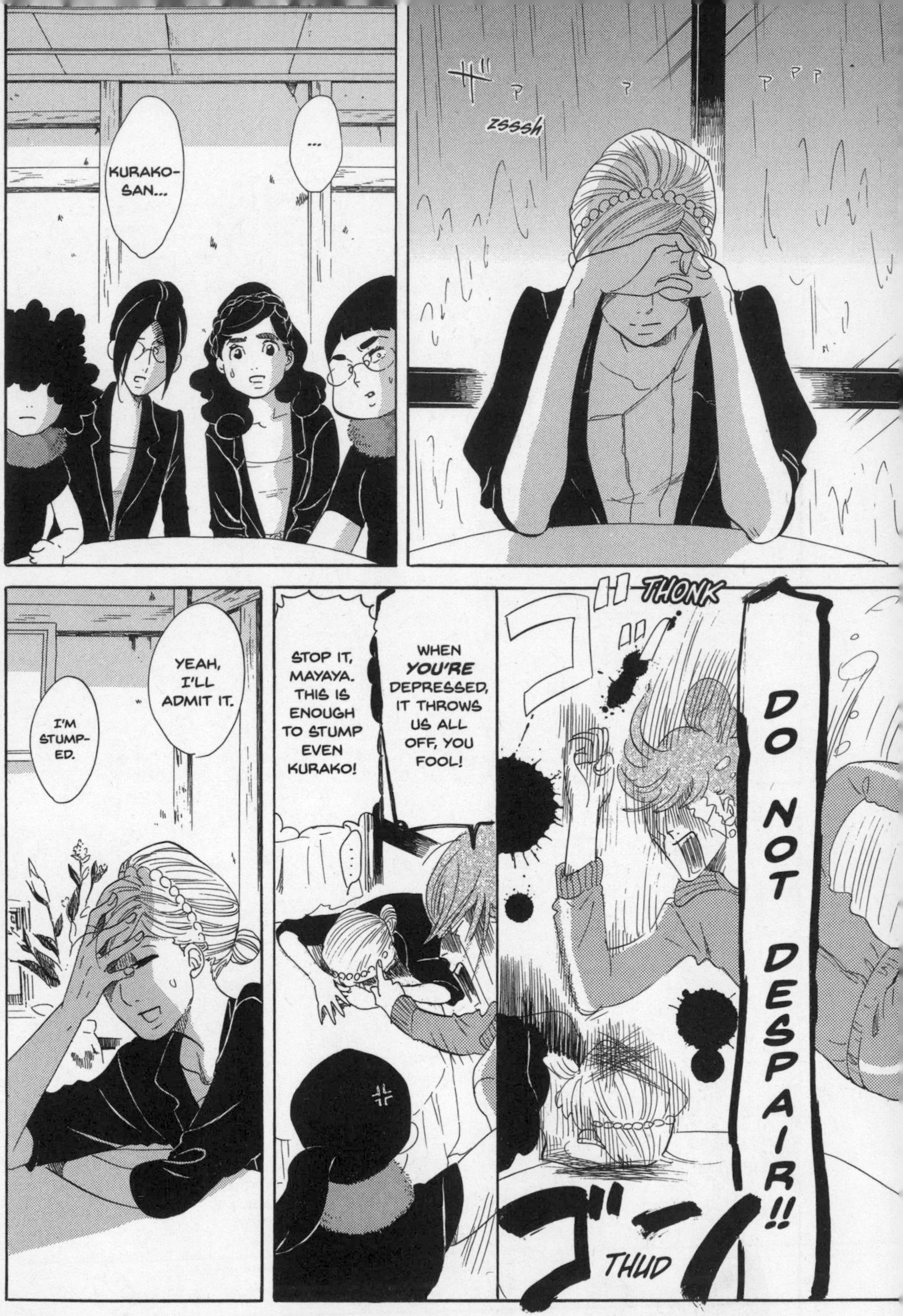

ZSSSH
...
KURAKO-SAN...
THONK
DO NOT DESPAIR!!
THUD
WHEN *YOU'RE* DEPRESSED, IT THROWS US ALL OFF, YOU FOOL!
STOP IT, MAYAYA. THIS IS ENOUGH TO STUMP EVEN KURAKO!
YEAH, I'LL ADMIT IT.
I'M STUMP-ED.

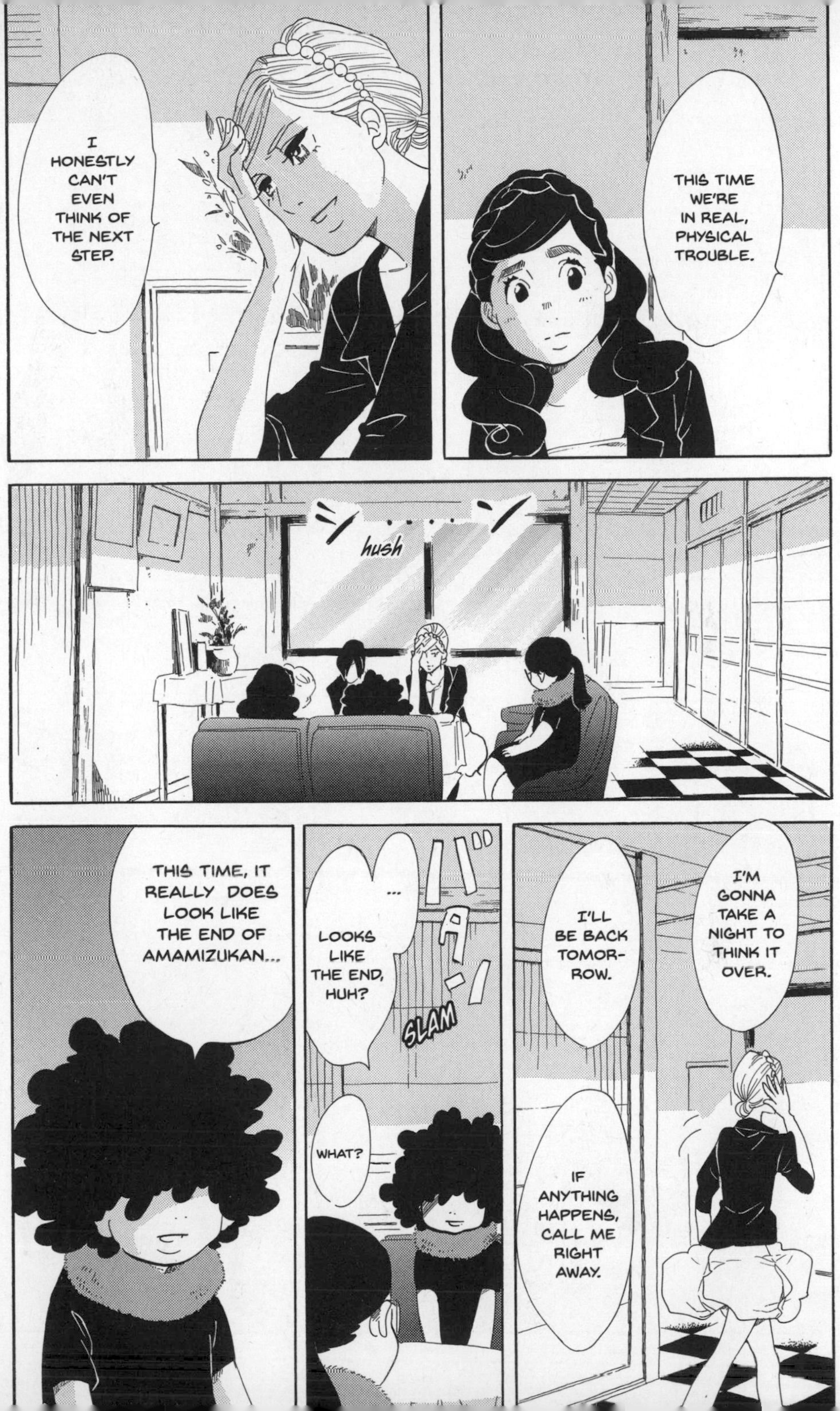
THIS TIME WE'RE IN REAL, PHYSICAL TROUBLE.
I HONESTLY CAN'T EVEN THINK OF THE NEXT STEP.
hush
I'M GONNA TAKE A NIGHT TO THINK IT OVER.
I'LL BE BACK TOMORROW.
IF ANYTHING HAPPENS, CALL ME RIGHT AWAY.
... LOOKS LIKE THE END, HUH?
SLAM
WHAT?
THIS TIME, IT REALLY DOES LOOK LIKE THE END OF AMAMIZUKAN...

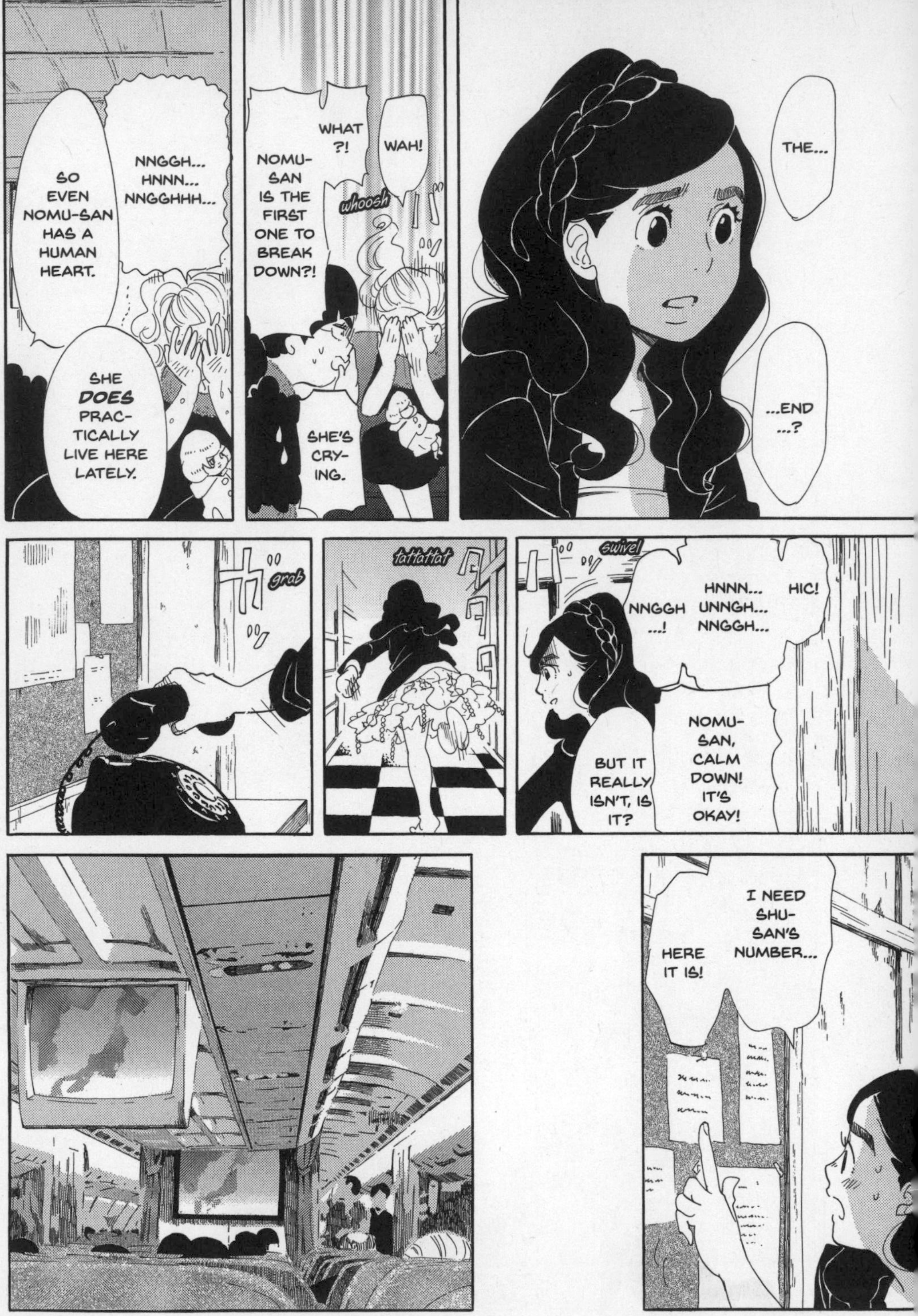
THE...
...END ...?
WAH!
WHAT ?!
whoosh
NOMU-SAN IS THE FIRST ONE TO BREAK DOWN?!
SHE'S CRY-ING.
NNGGH... HNNN... NNGGHHH...
SO EVEN NOMU-SAN HAS A HUMAN HEART.
SHE **DOES** PRACTICALLY LIVE HERE LATELY.
swivel
HIC!
HNNN... UNNGH... NNGGH...
NNGGH ...!
NOMU-SAN, CALM DOWN! IT'S OKAY!
BUT IT REALLY ISN'T, IS IT?
tattattat
grab
I NEED SHU-SAN'S NUMBER...
HERE IT IS!

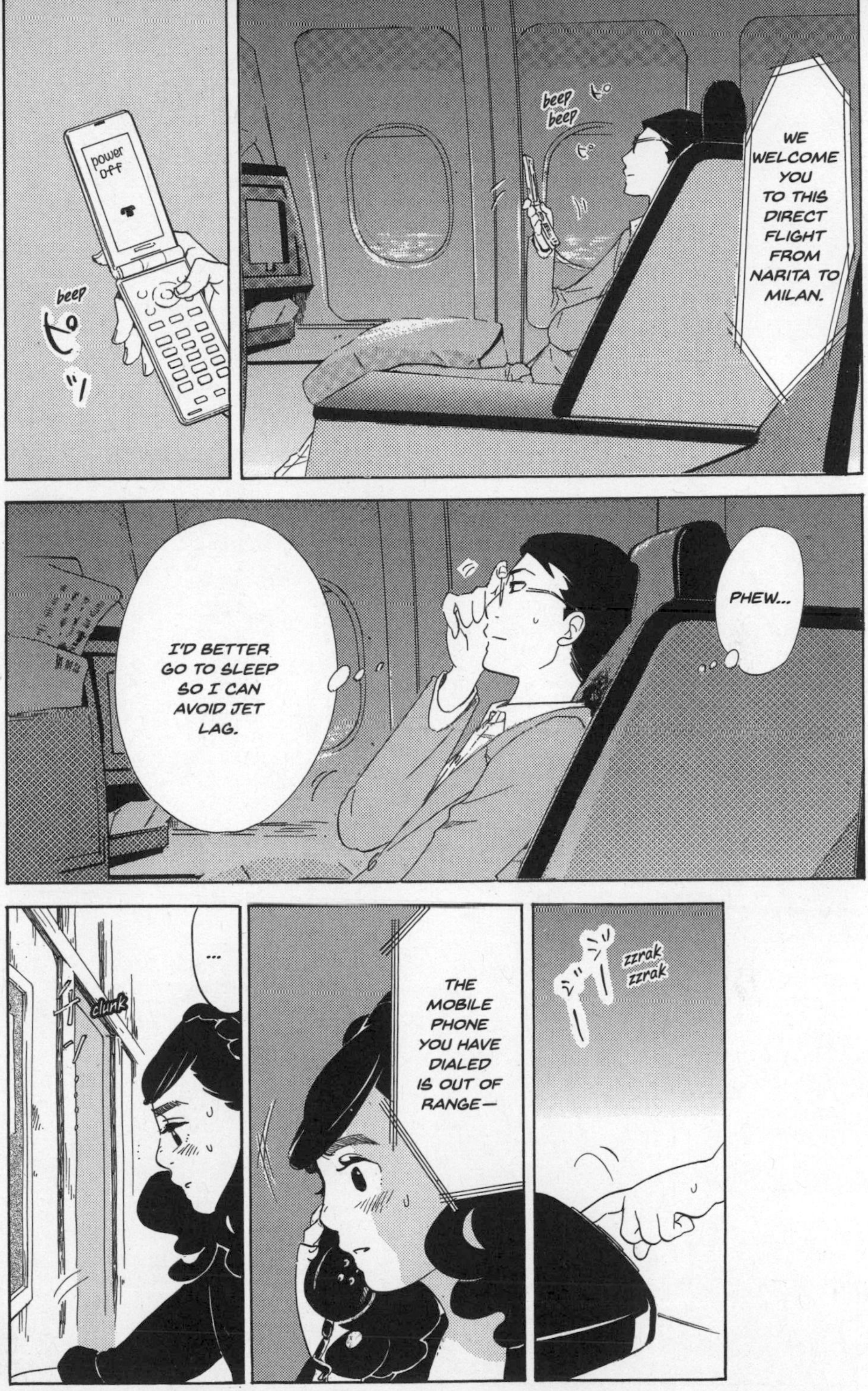
WE WELCOME YOU TO THIS DIRECT FLIGHT FROM NARITA TO MILAN.
beep beep
power off
beep
PHEW...
I'D BETTER GO TO SLEEP SO I CAN AVOID JET LAG.
zzrak zzrak
THE MOBILE PHONE YOU HAVE DIALED IS OUT OF RANGE—
...
clunk

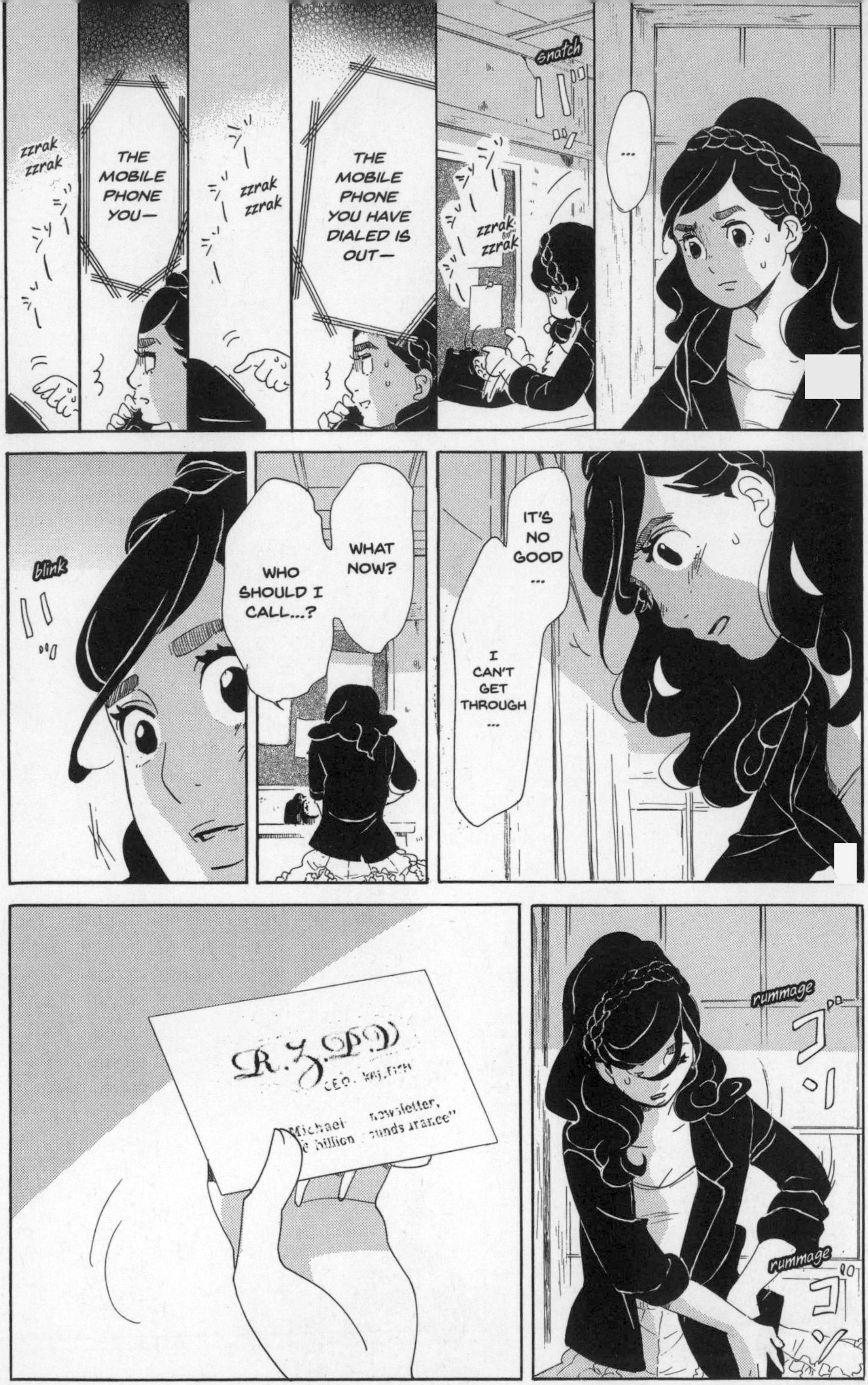
...
snatch
zzrak zzrak
THE MOBILE PHONE YOU HAVE DIALED IS OUT—
zzrak zzrak
THE MOBILE PHONE YOU—
zzrak zzrak
IT'S NO GOOD ...
I CAN'T GET THROUGH ...
WHAT NOW?
WHO SHOULD I CALL...?
blink
rummage
rummage

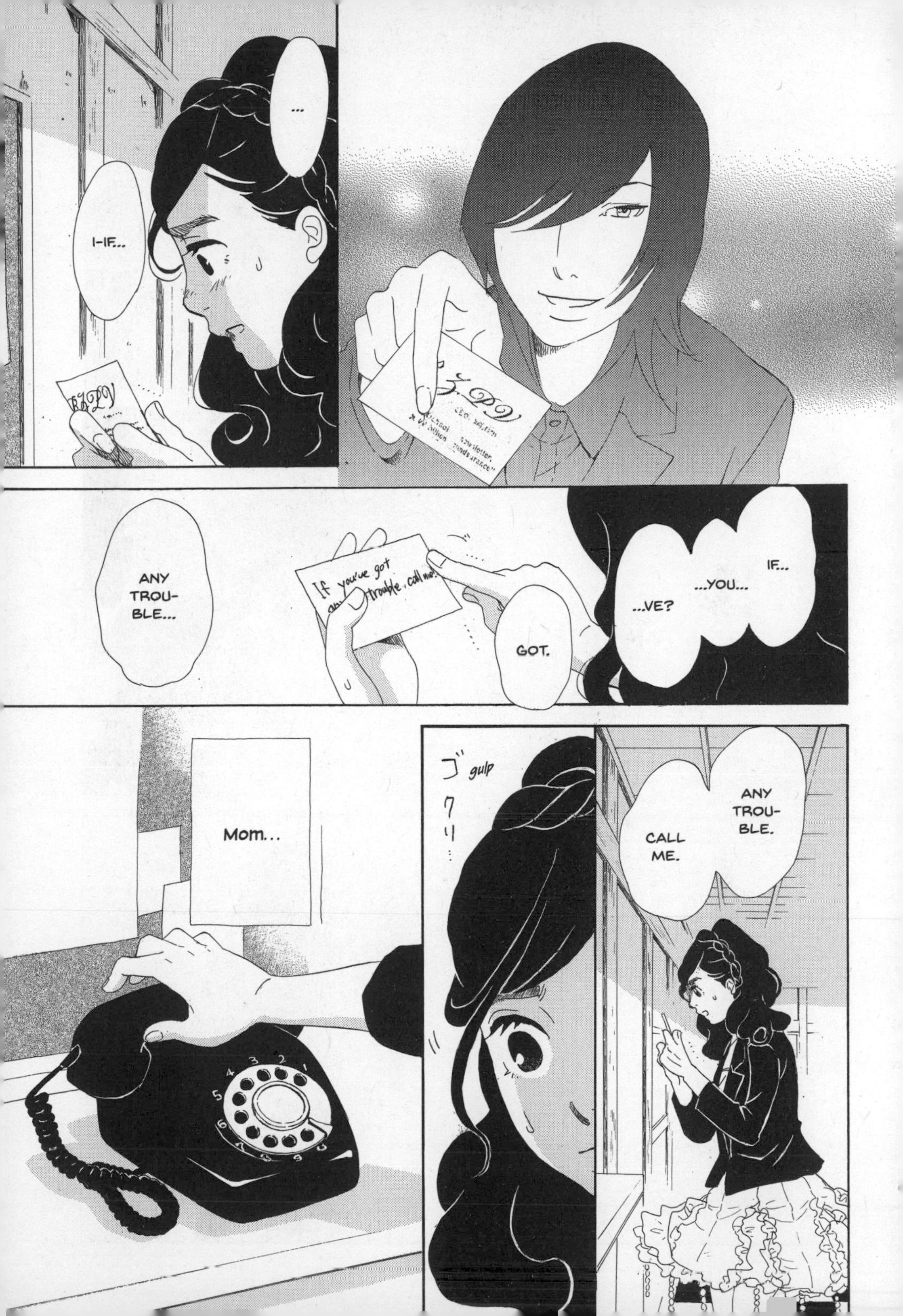
...
I-IF...
IF...
...YOU...
...VE?
GOT.
If you've got
trouble, call me!
ANY TROU-BLE...
ANY TROU-BLE.
CALL ME.
ゴクリ
gulp
Mom...

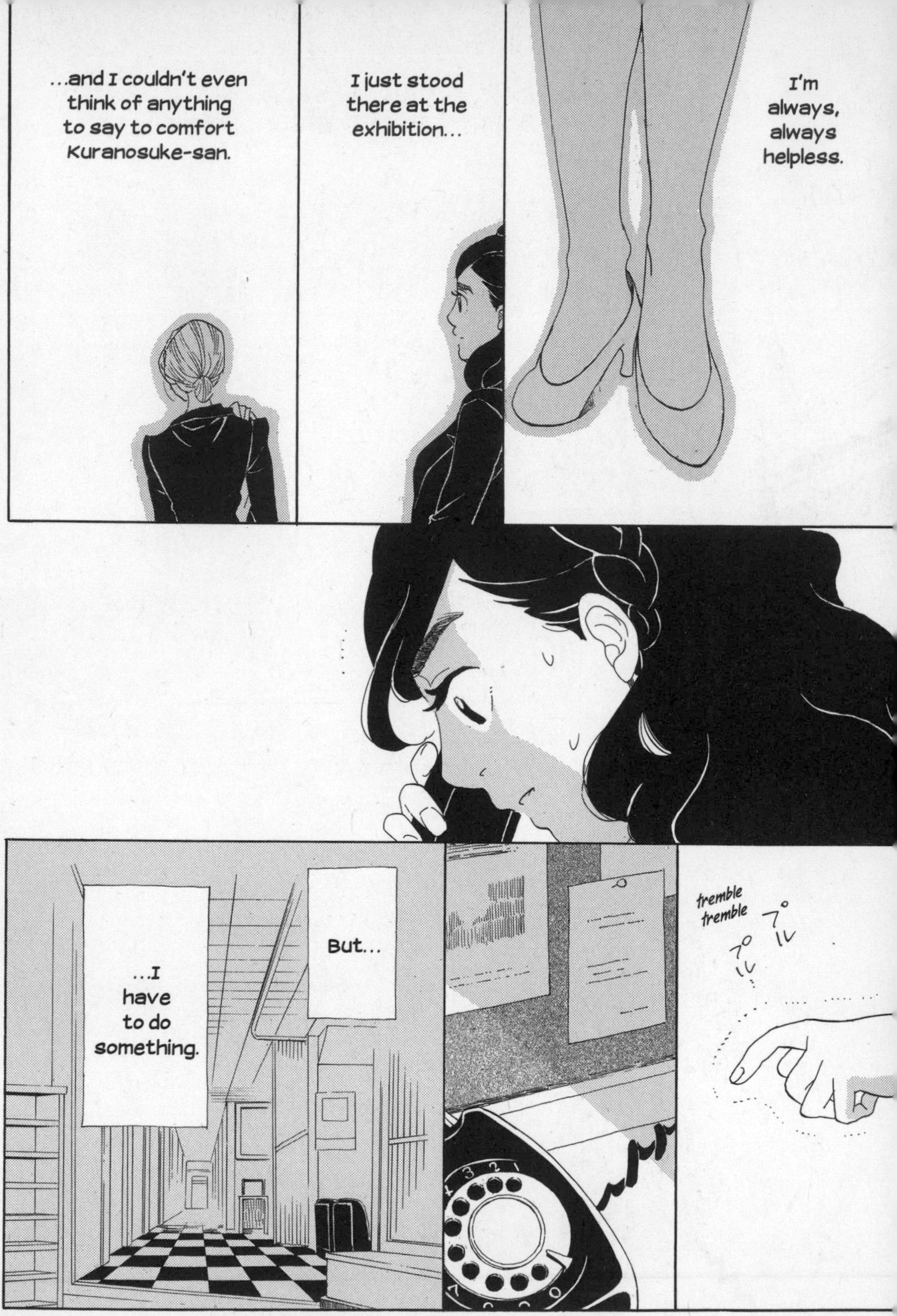
I'm always, always helpless.
I just stood there at the exhibition...
...and I couldn't even think of anything to say to comfort Kuranosuke-san.
tremble tremble
プル
プル
But...
...I have to do something.

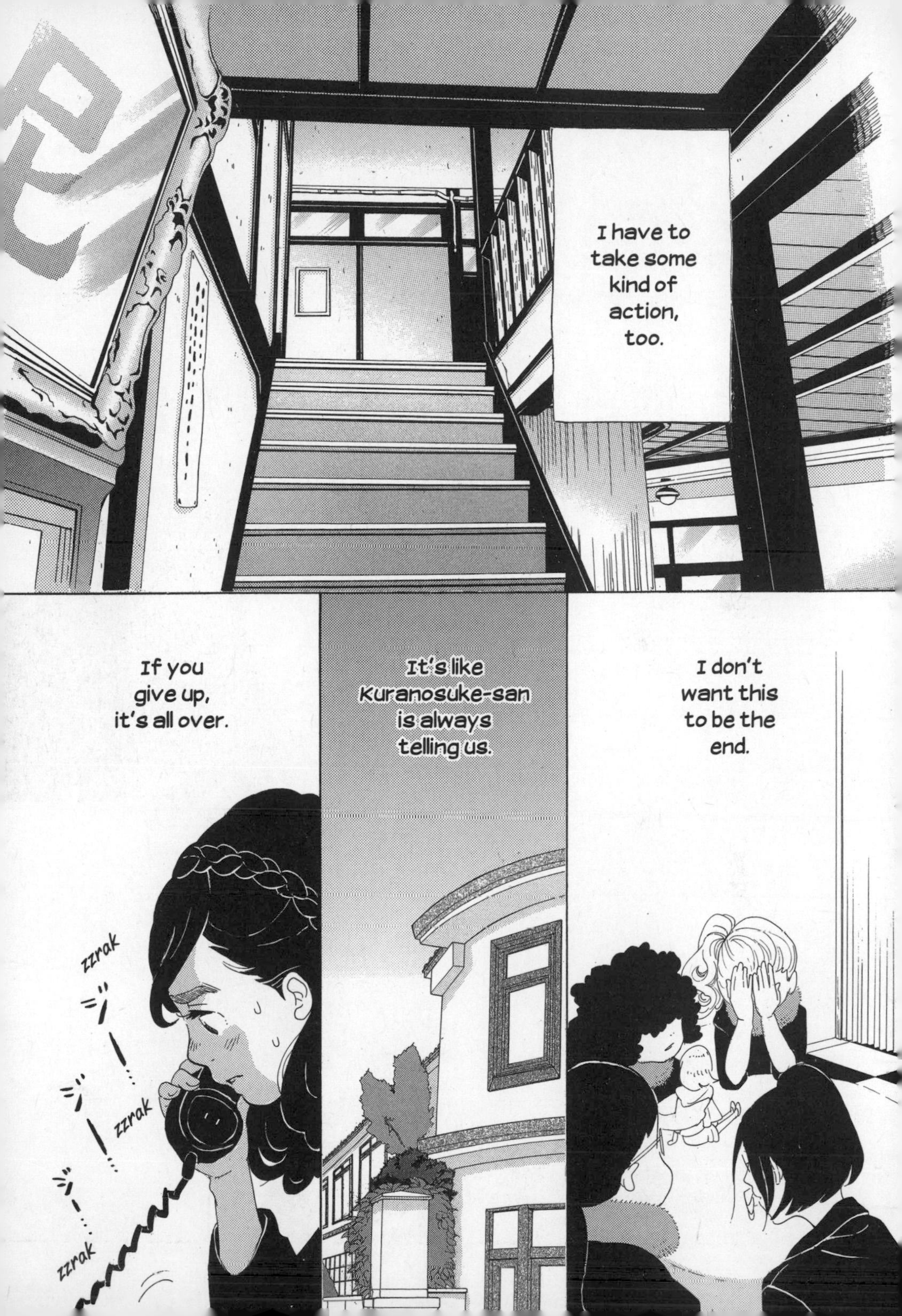
I have to take some kind of action, too.
I don't want this to be the end.
It's like Kuranosuke-san is always telling us.
If you give up, it's all over.
zzrak
zzrak
zzrak

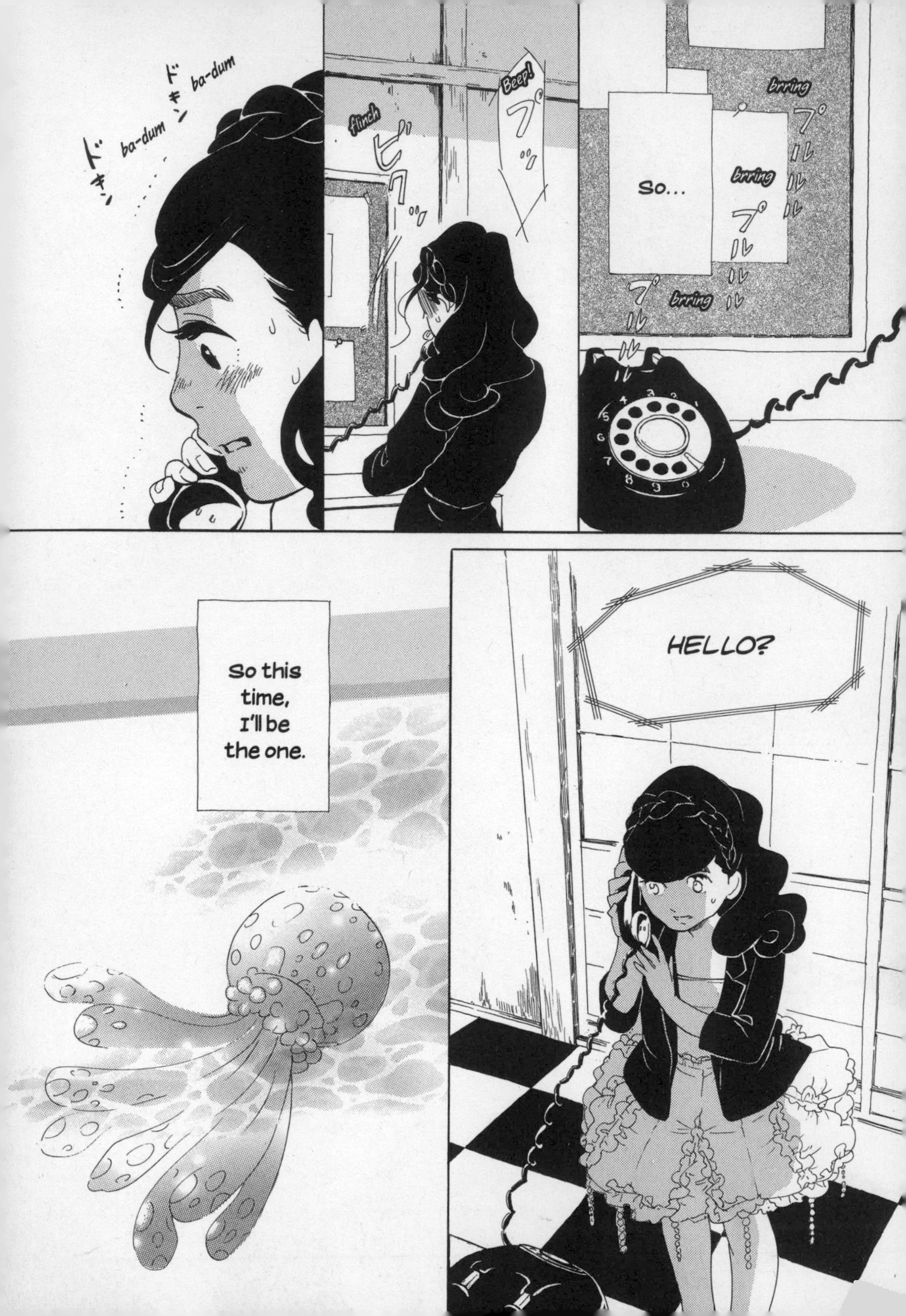
brrring
プルルル
So...
brrring
プルルル
brrring
プルル
Beep!
プツッ
flinch
ビクッ
ba-dum
ドキン
ba-dum
ドキン
HELLO?
So this time, I'll be the one.

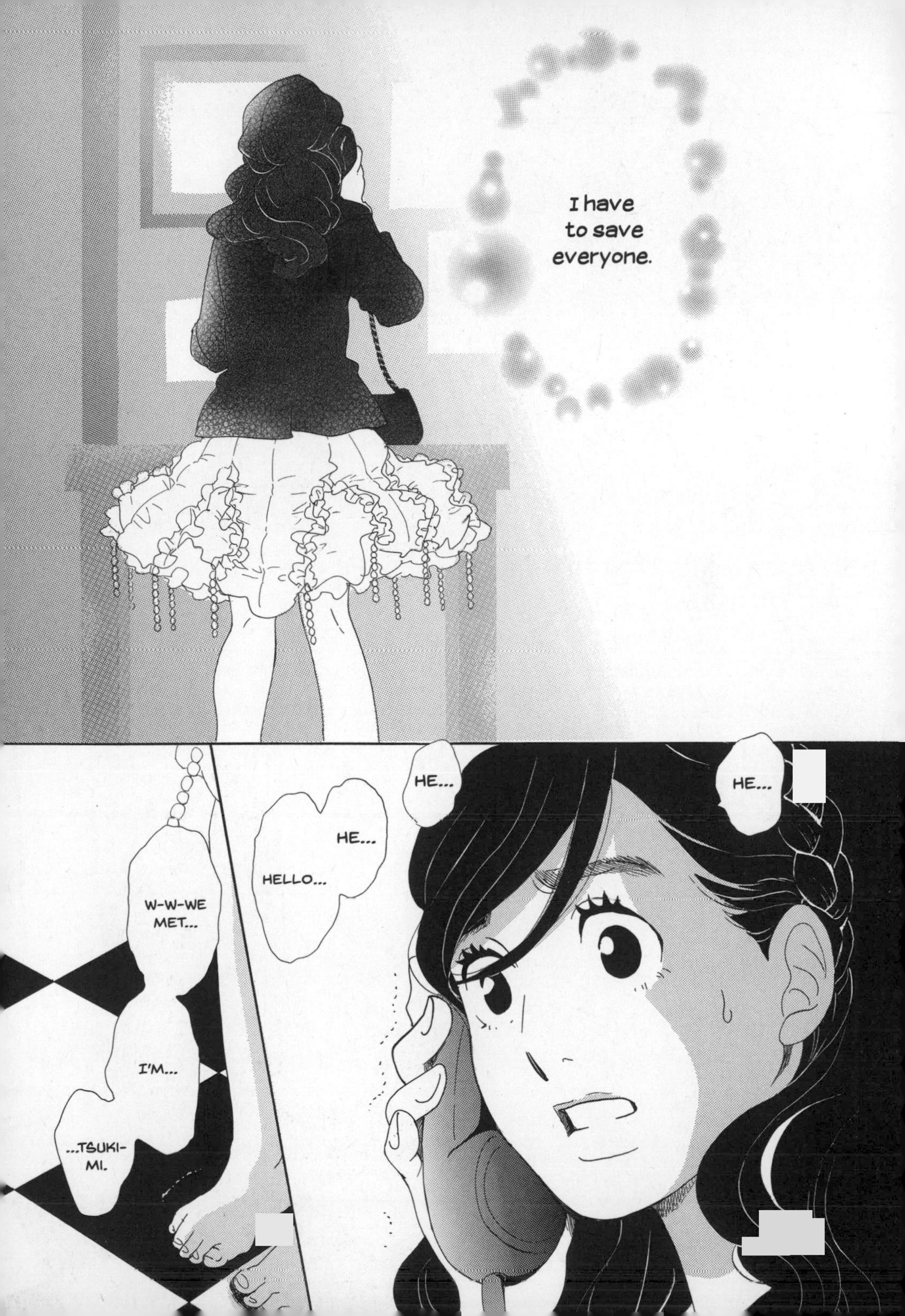
I have to save everyone.
HE...
HE...
HE... HELLO...
W-W-WE MET...
I'M...
...TSUKI-MI.

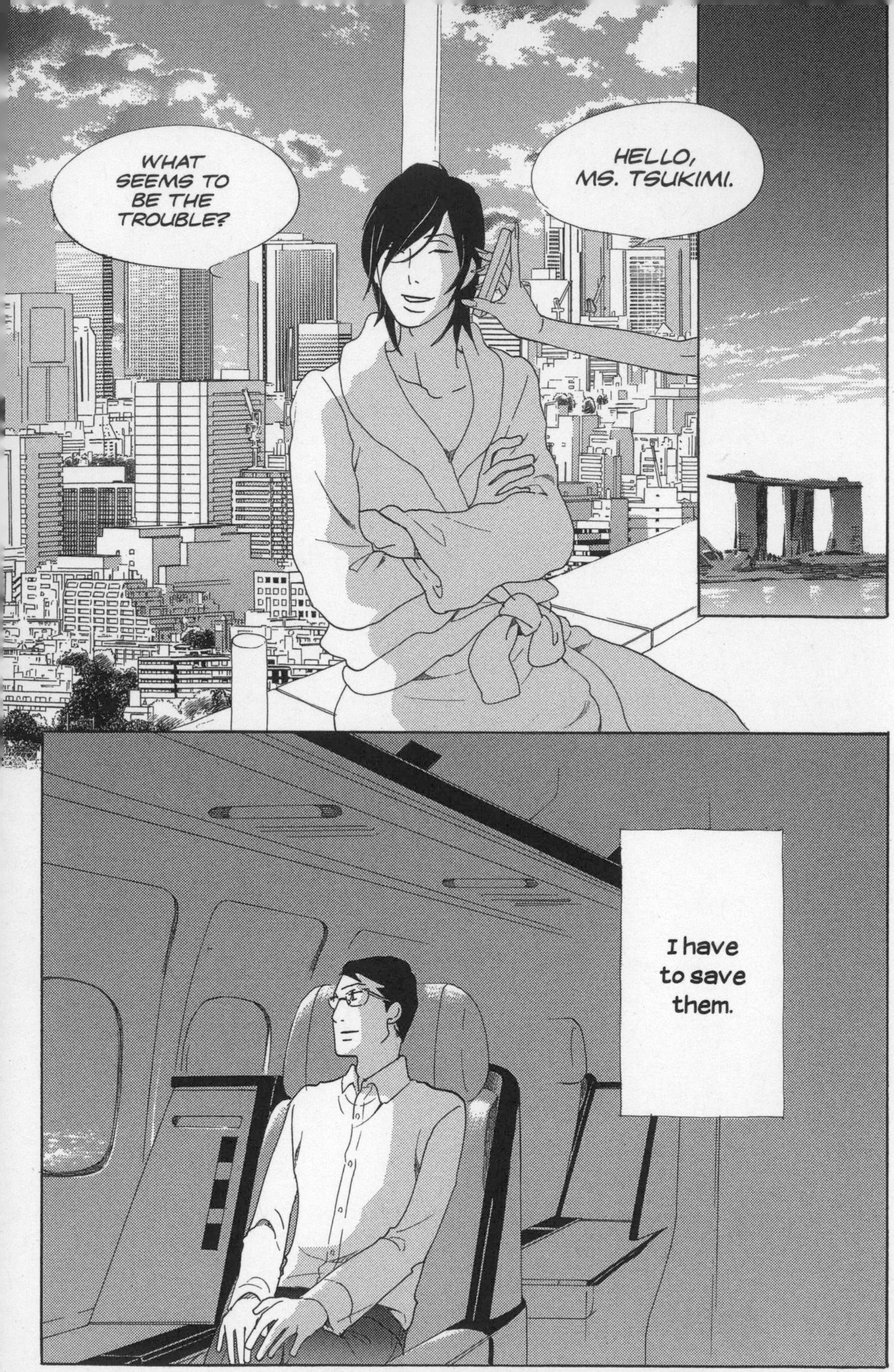
HELLO, MS. TSUKIMI.
WHAT SEEMS TO BE THE TROUBLE?
I have to save them.

Episode 63

Midnight Flight

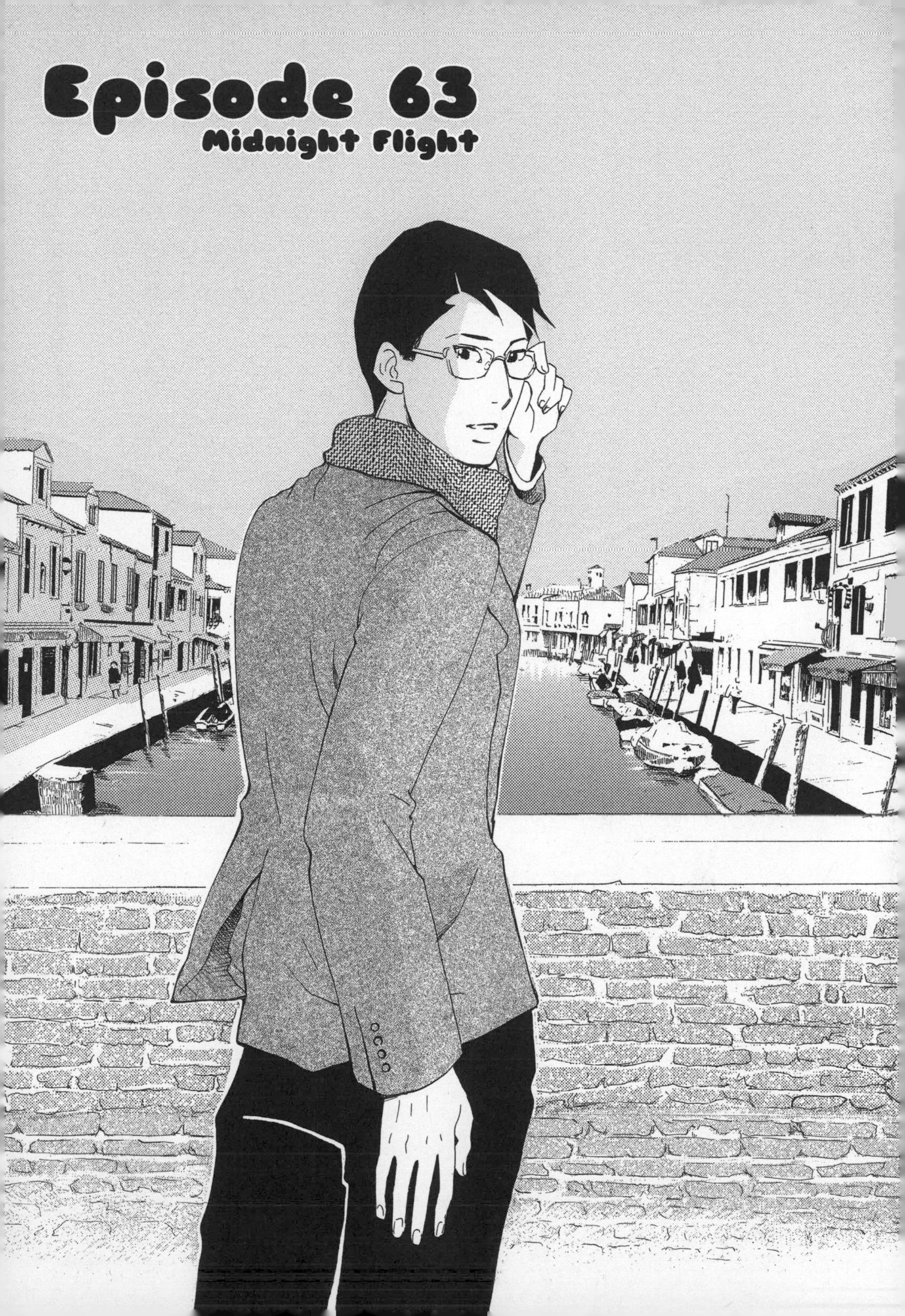

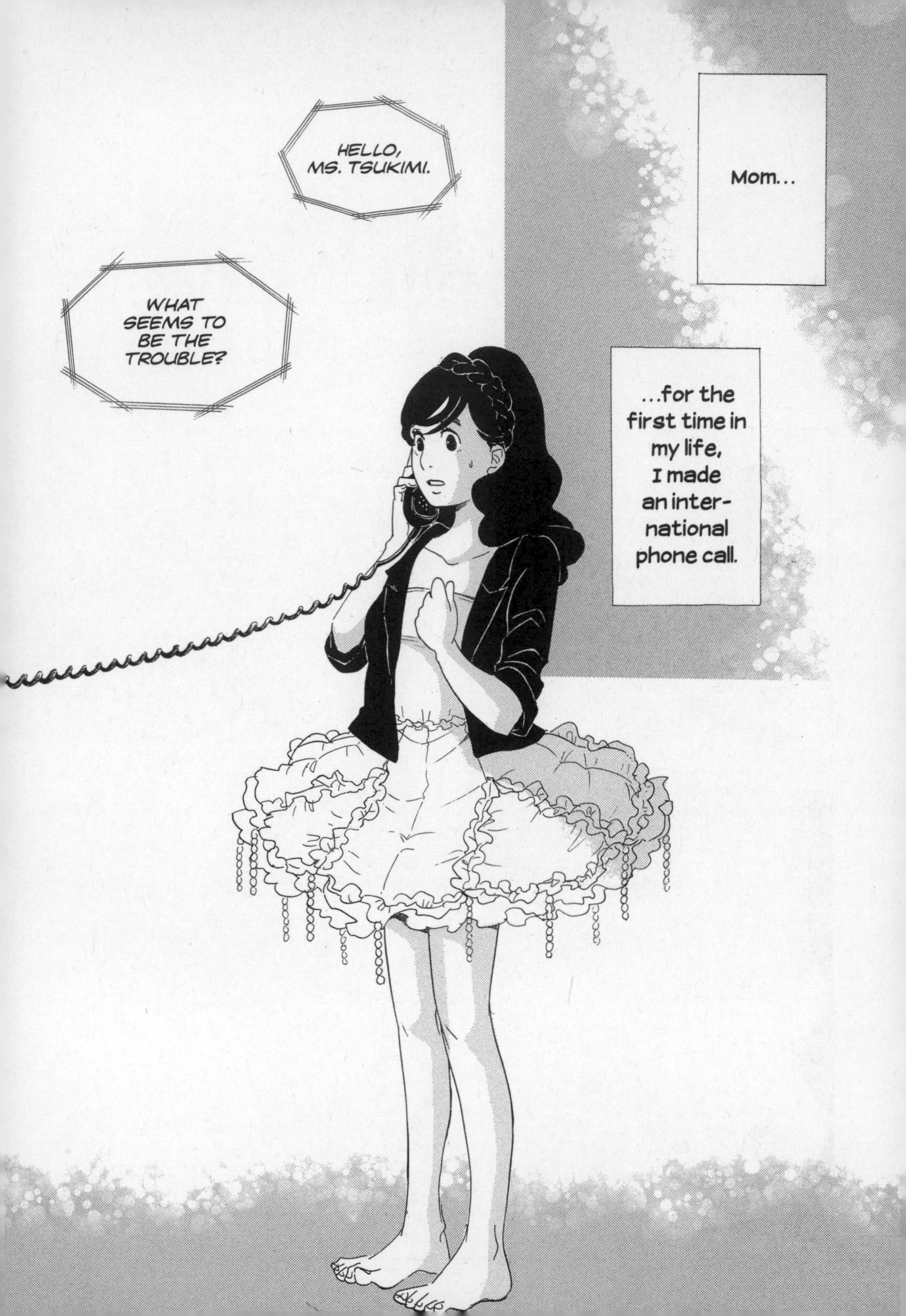
Mom...
...for the first time in my life, I made an inter-national phone call.
HELLO, MS. TSUKIMI.
WHAT SEEMS TO BE THE TROUBLE?

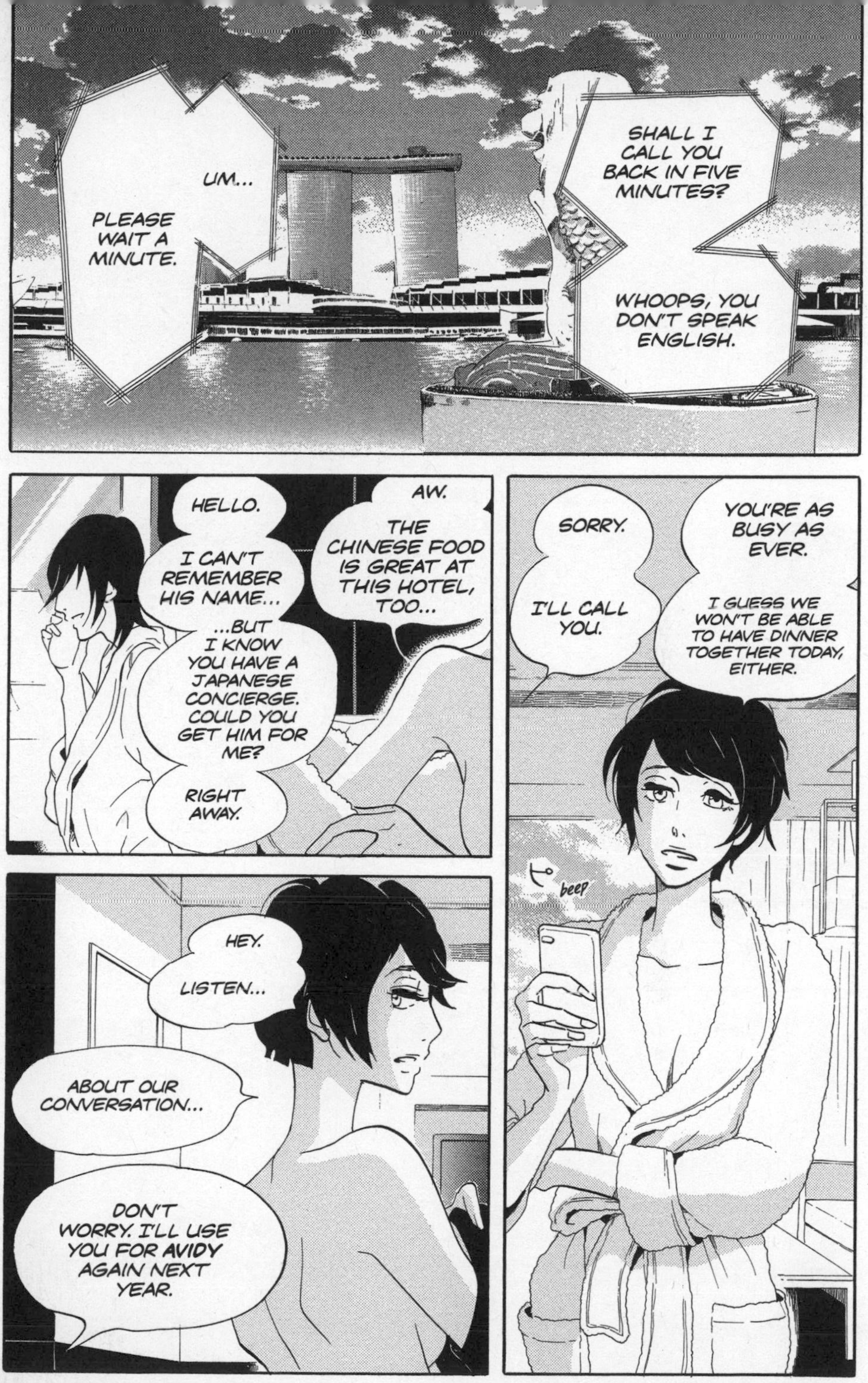
SHALL I CALL YOU BACK IN FIVE MINUTES?
WHOOPS, YOU DON'T SPEAK ENGLISH.
UM...
PLEASE WAIT A MINUTE.
YOU'RE AS BUSY AS EVER.
I GUESS WE WON'T BE ABLE TO HAVE DINNER TOGETHER TODAY, EITHER.
SORRY.
I'LL CALL YOU.
beep
AW.
THE CHINESE FOOD IS GREAT AT THIS HOTEL, TOO...
HELLO.
I CAN'T REMEMBER HIS NAME...
...BUT I KNOW YOU HAVE A JAPANESE CONCIERGE. COULD YOU GET HIM FOR ME?
RIGHT AWAY.
HEY.
LISTEN...
ABOUT OUR CONVERSATION...
DON'T WORRY. I'LL USE YOU FOR AVIDY AGAIN NEXT YEAR.

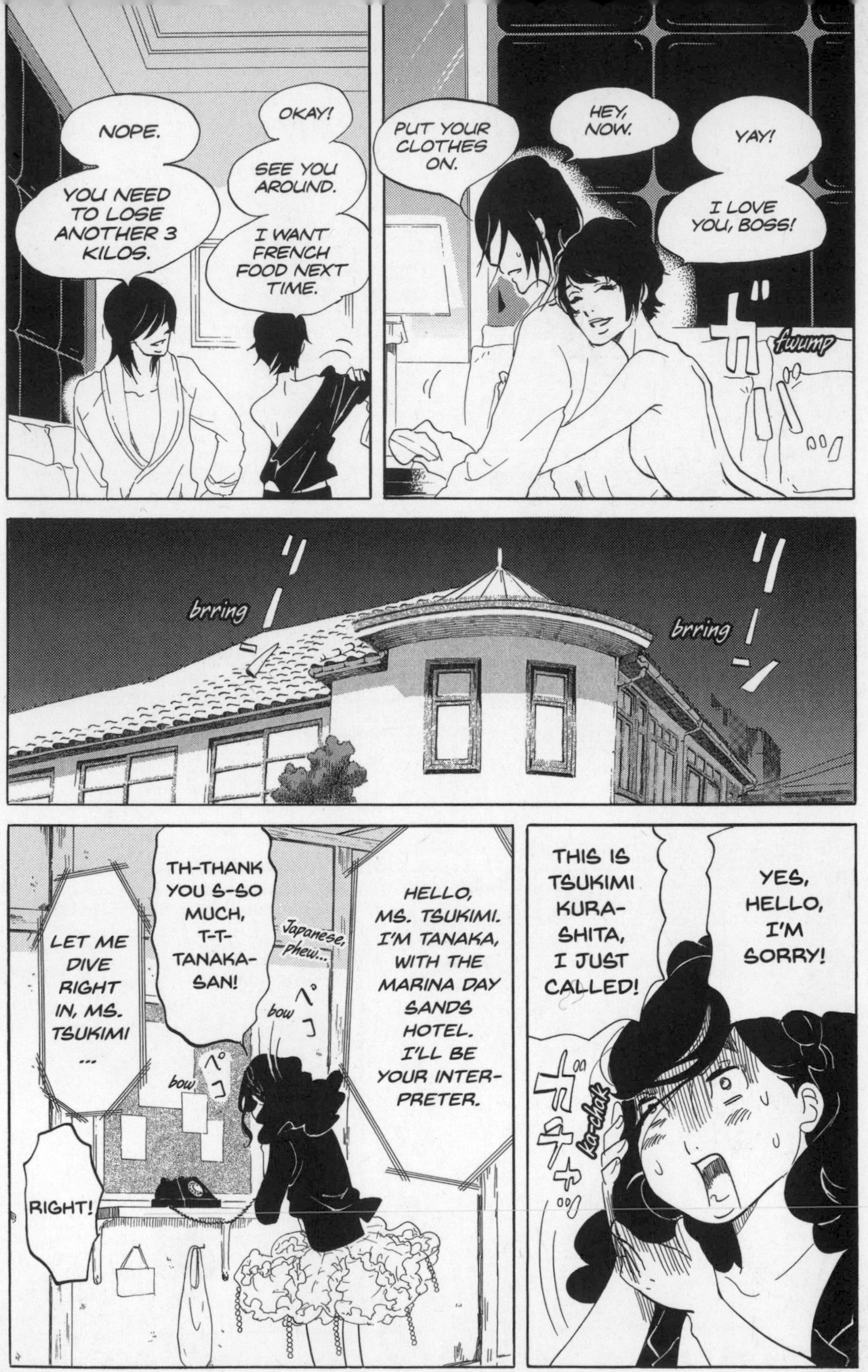
YAY!
I LOVE YOU, BOSS!
HEY, NOW.
PUT YOUR CLOTHES ON.
fwump
OKAY!
SEE YOU AROUND.
I WANT FRENCH FOOD NEXT TIME.
NOPE.
YOU NEED TO LOSE ANOTHER 3 KILOS.
brrring
brrring
YES, HELLO, I'M SORRY!
THIS IS TSUKIMI KURA-SHITA, I JUST CALLED!
ka-chak
HELLO, MS. TSUKIMI. I'M TANAKA, WITH THE MARINA DAY SANDS HOTEL. I'LL BE YOUR INTER-PRETER.
Japanese, phew...
TH-THANK YOU S-SO MUCH, T-T-TANAKA-SAN!
bow
bow
LET ME DIVE RIGHT IN, MS. TSUKIMI ...
RIGHT!

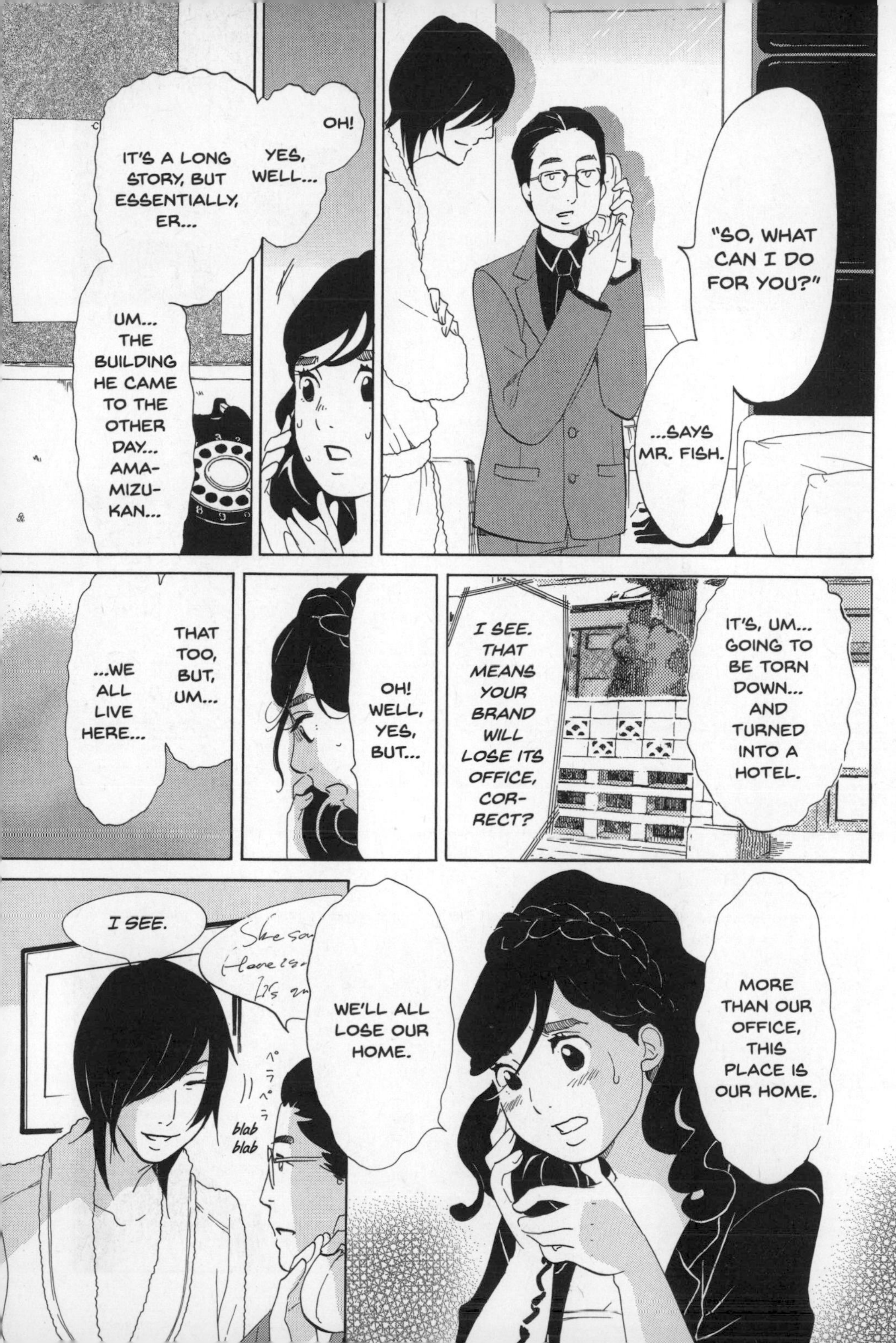
"SO, WHAT CAN I DO FOR YOU?"
...SAYS MR. FISH.
OH!
YES, WELL...
IT'S A LONG STORY, BUT ESSENTIALLY, ER...
UM... THE BUILDING HE CAME TO THE OTHER DAY... AMA-MIZU-KAN...
IT'S, UM... GOING TO BE TORN DOWN... AND TURNED INTO A HOTEL.
I SEE. THAT MEANS YOUR BRAND WILL LOSE ITS OFFICE, COR-RECT?
OH! WELL, YES, BUT...
THAT TOO, BUT, UM...
...WE ALL LIVE HERE...
MORE THAN OUR OFFICE, THIS PLACE IS OUR HOME.
WE'LL ALL LOSE OUR HOME.
I SEE.
ペラペラ
blab blab

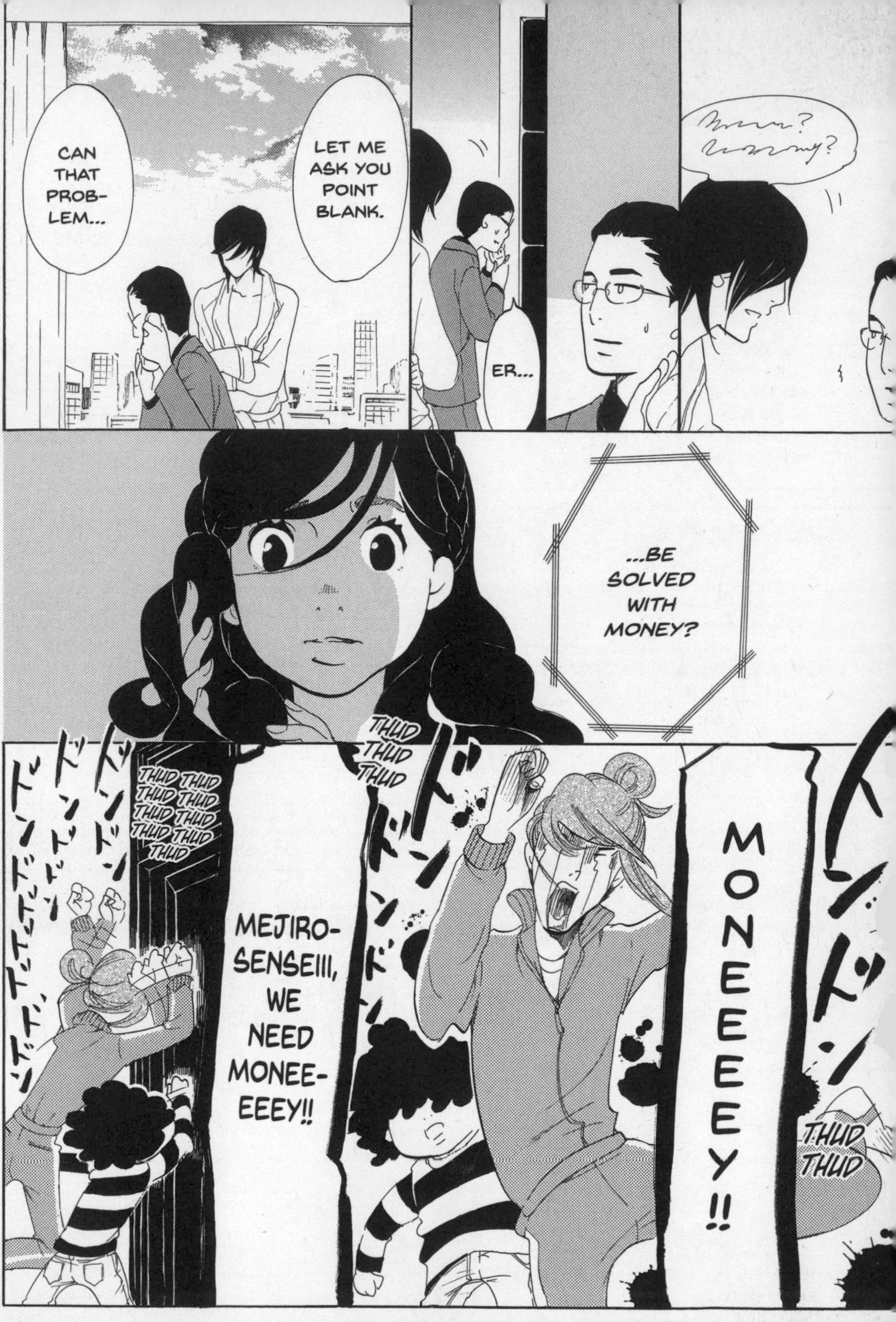
ER...
LET ME ASK YOU POINT BLANK.
CAN THAT PROB-LEM...
...BE SOLVED WITH MONEY?
MONEEEEY!!
THUD THUD
THUD THUD THUD
MEJIRO-SENSEIII, WE NEED MONEE-EEEY!!
THUD THUD THUD THUD THUD THUD THUD THUD THUD

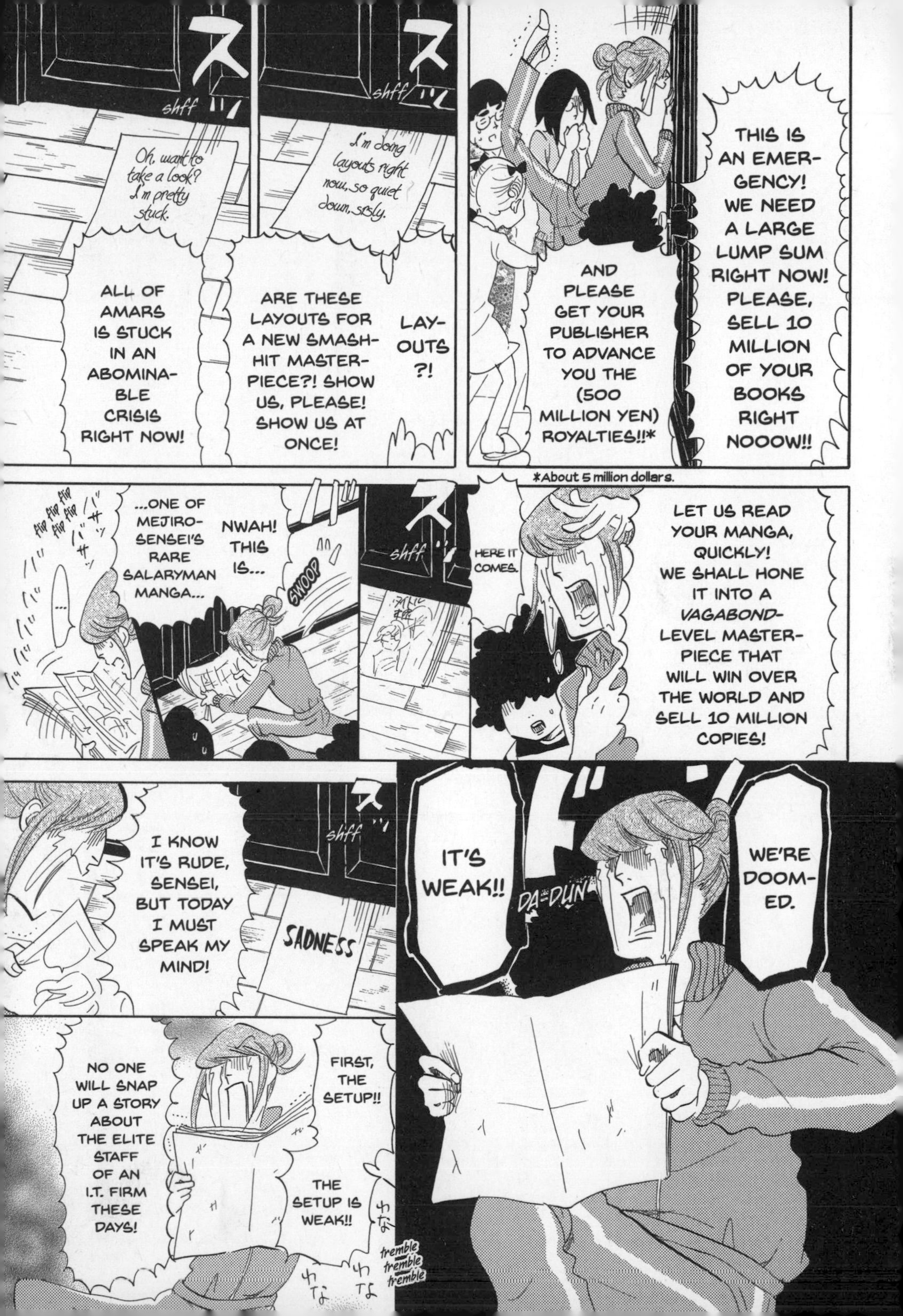

THIS IS AN EMERGENCY! WE NEED A LARGE LUMP SUM RIGHT NOW! PLEASE, SELL 10 MILLION OF YOUR BOOKS RIGHT NOOOW!!
AND PLEASE GET YOUR PUBLISHER TO ADVANCE YOU THE (500 MILLION YEN) ROYALTIES!!*
shff
I'm doing layouts right now, so quiet down, srsly.
LAYOUTS?!
ARE THESE LAYOUTS FOR A NEW SMASH-HIT MASTERPIECE?! SHOW US, PLEASE! SHOW US AT ONCE!
shff
Oh, want to take a look? I'm pretty stuck.
ALL OF AMARS IS STUCK IN AN ABOMINABLE CRISIS RIGHT NOW!
LET US READ YOUR MANGA, QUICKLY! WE SHALL HONE IT INTO A VAGABOND-LEVEL MASTERPIECE THAT WILL WIN OVER THE WORLD AND SELL 10 MILLION COPIES!
HERE IT COMES.
shff
SWOOP
NWAH! THIS IS...
...ONE OF MEJIRO-SENSEI'S RARE SALARYMAN MANGA...
flip flip flip flip
...
WE'RE DOOMED.
IT'S WEAK!!
DA-DUN
shff
I KNOW IT'S RUDE, SENSEI, BUT TODAY I MUST SPEAK MY MIND!
SADNESS
FIRST, THE SETUP!!
NO ONE WILL SNAP UP A STORY ABOUT THE ELITE STAFF OF AN I.T. FIRM THESE DAYS!
THE SETUP IS WEAK!!
tremble tremble tremble

*About 5 million dollars.

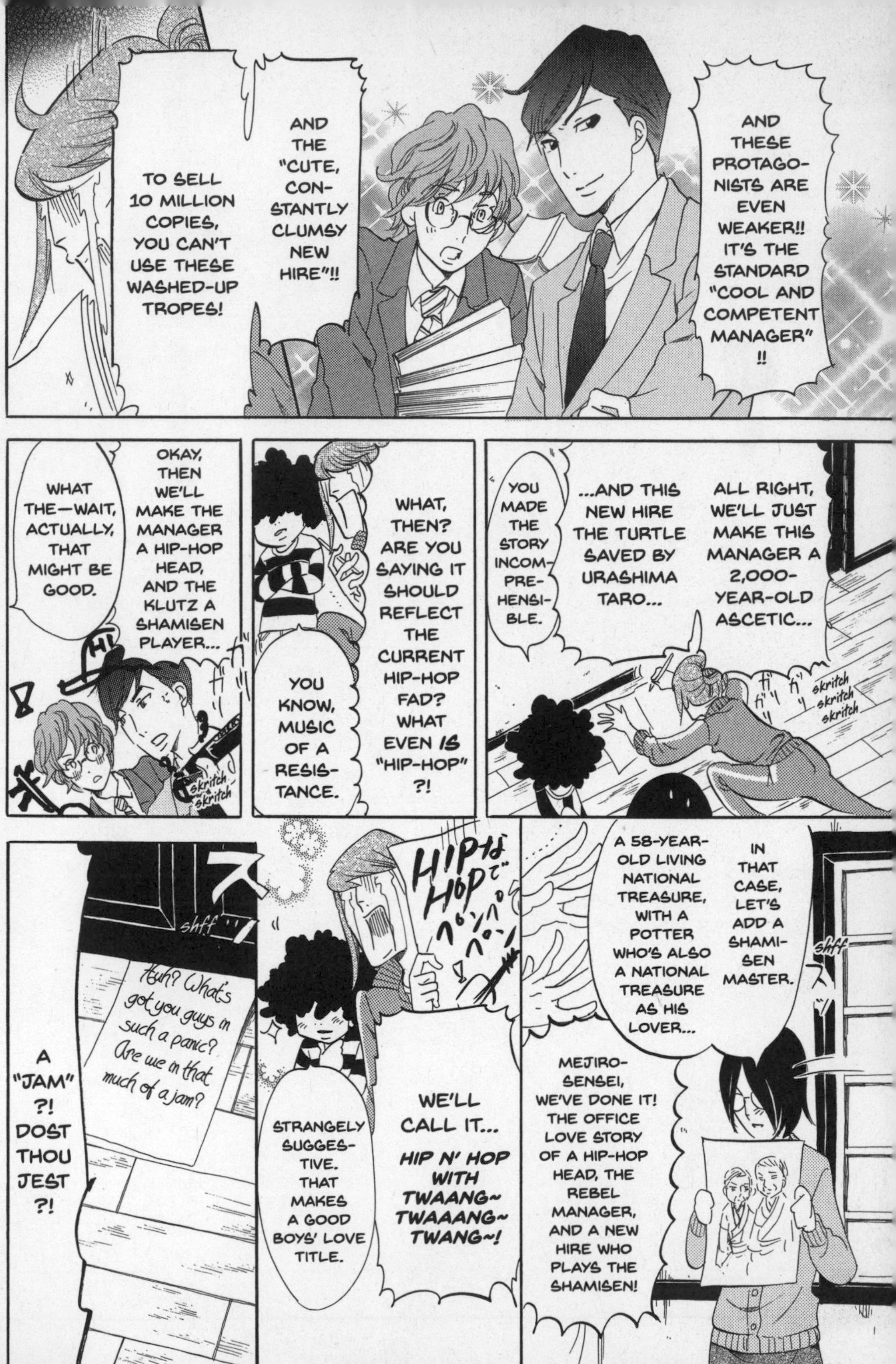
AND THESE PROTAGONISTS ARE EVEN WEAKER!! IT'S THE STANDARD "COOL AND COMPETENT MANAGER" !!
AND THE "CUTE, CONSTANTLY CLUMSY NEW HIRE"!!
TO SELL 10 MILLION COPIES, YOU CAN'T USE THESE WASHED-UP TROPES!
ALL RIGHT, WE'LL JUST MAKE THIS MANAGER A 2,000-YEAR-OLD ASCETIC...
...AND THIS NEW HIRE THE TURTLE SAVED BY URASHIMA TARO...
YOU MADE THE STORY INCOMPREHENSIBLE.
skritch skritch skritch
WHAT, THEN? ARE YOU SAYING IT SHOULD REFLECT THE CURRENT HIP-HOP FAD? WHAT EVEN IS "HIP-HOP" ?!
YOU KNOW, MUSIC OF A RESISTANCE.
OKAY, THEN WE'LL MAKE THE MANAGER A HIP-HOP HEAD, AND THE KLUTZ A SHAMISEN PLAYER...
WHAT THE—WAIT, ACTUALLY, THAT MIGHT BE GOOD.
skritch skritch
IN THAT CASE, LET'S ADD A SHAMISEN MASTER.
shff
A 58-YEAR-OLD LIVING NATIONAL TREASURE, WITH A POTTER WHO'S ALSO A NATIONAL TREASURE AS HIS LOVER...
MEJIRO-SENSEI, WE'VE DONE IT! THE OFFICE LOVE STORY OF A HIP-HOP HEAD, THE REBEL MANAGER, AND A NEW HIRE WHO PLAYS THE SHAMISEN!
WE'LL CALL IT... HIP N' HOP WITH TWAANG~ TWAAANG~ TWANG~!
STRANGELY SUGGESTIVE. THAT MAKES A GOOD BOYS' LOVE TITLE.
shff
Huh? What's got you guys in such a panic? Are we in that much of a jam?
A "JAM" ?! DOST THOU JEST ?!

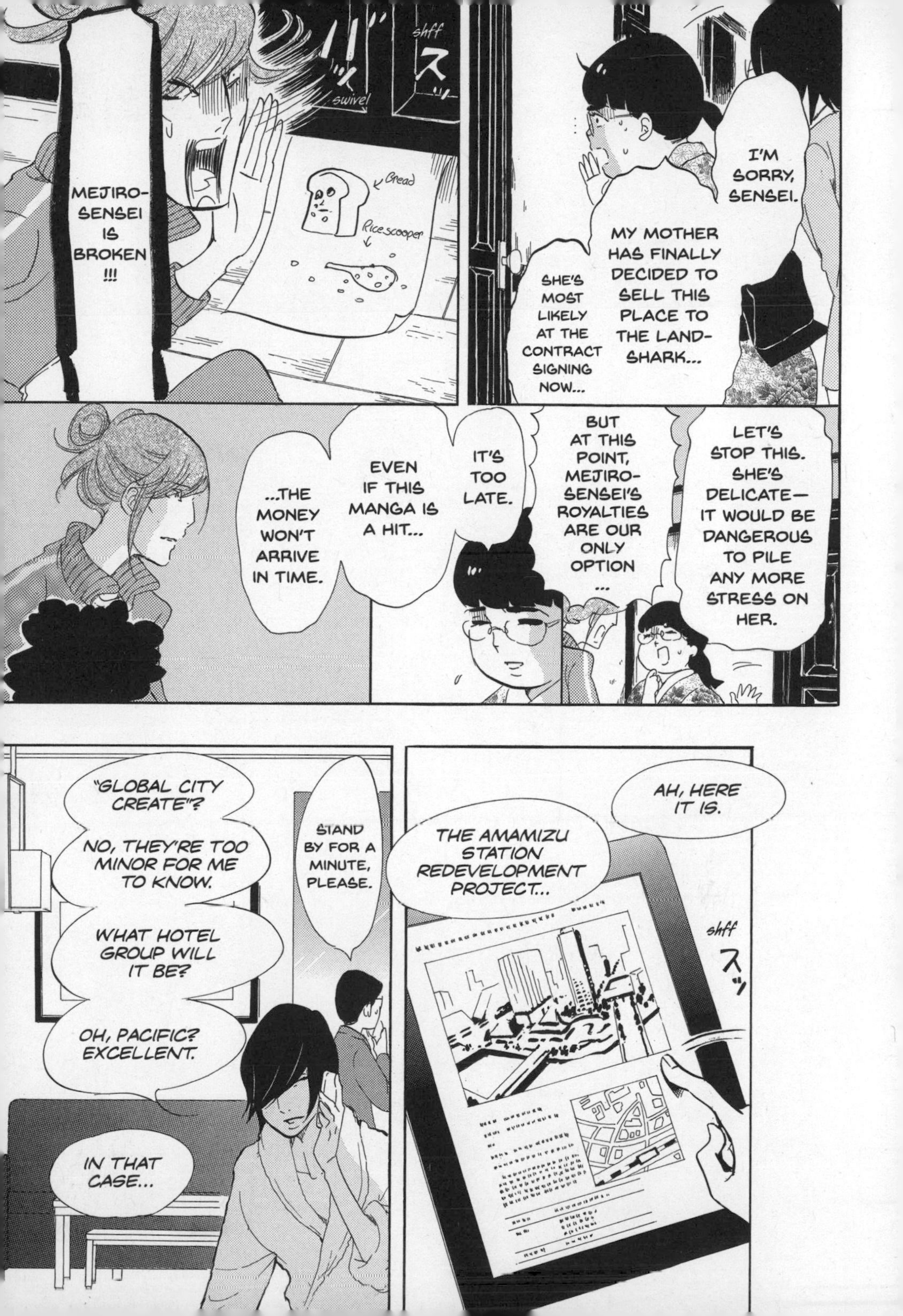
I'M SORRY, SENSEI.
MY MOTHER HAS FINALLY DECIDED TO SELL THIS PLACE TO THE LAND-SHARK...
SHE'S MOST LIKELY AT THE CONTRACT SIGNING NOW...
shff
swivel
Bread
Ricescooper
MEJIRO-SENSEI IS BROKEN!!!
LET'S STOP THIS. SHE'S DELICATE—IT WOULD BE DANGEROUS TO PILE ANY MORE STRESS ON HER.
BUT AT THIS POINT, MEJIRO-SENSEI'S ROYALTIES ARE OUR ONLY OPTION...
IT'S TOO LATE.
EVEN IF THIS MANGA IS A HIT...
...THE MONEY WON'T ARRIVE IN TIME.
AH, HERE IT IS.
THE AMAMIZU STATION REDEVELOPMENT PROJECT...
shff
"GLOBAL CITY CREATE"?
NO, THEY'RE TOO MINOR FOR ME TO KNOW.
STAND BY FOR A MINUTE, PLEASE.
WHAT HOTEL GROUP WILL IT BE?
OH, PACIFIC? EXCELLENT.
IN THAT CASE...

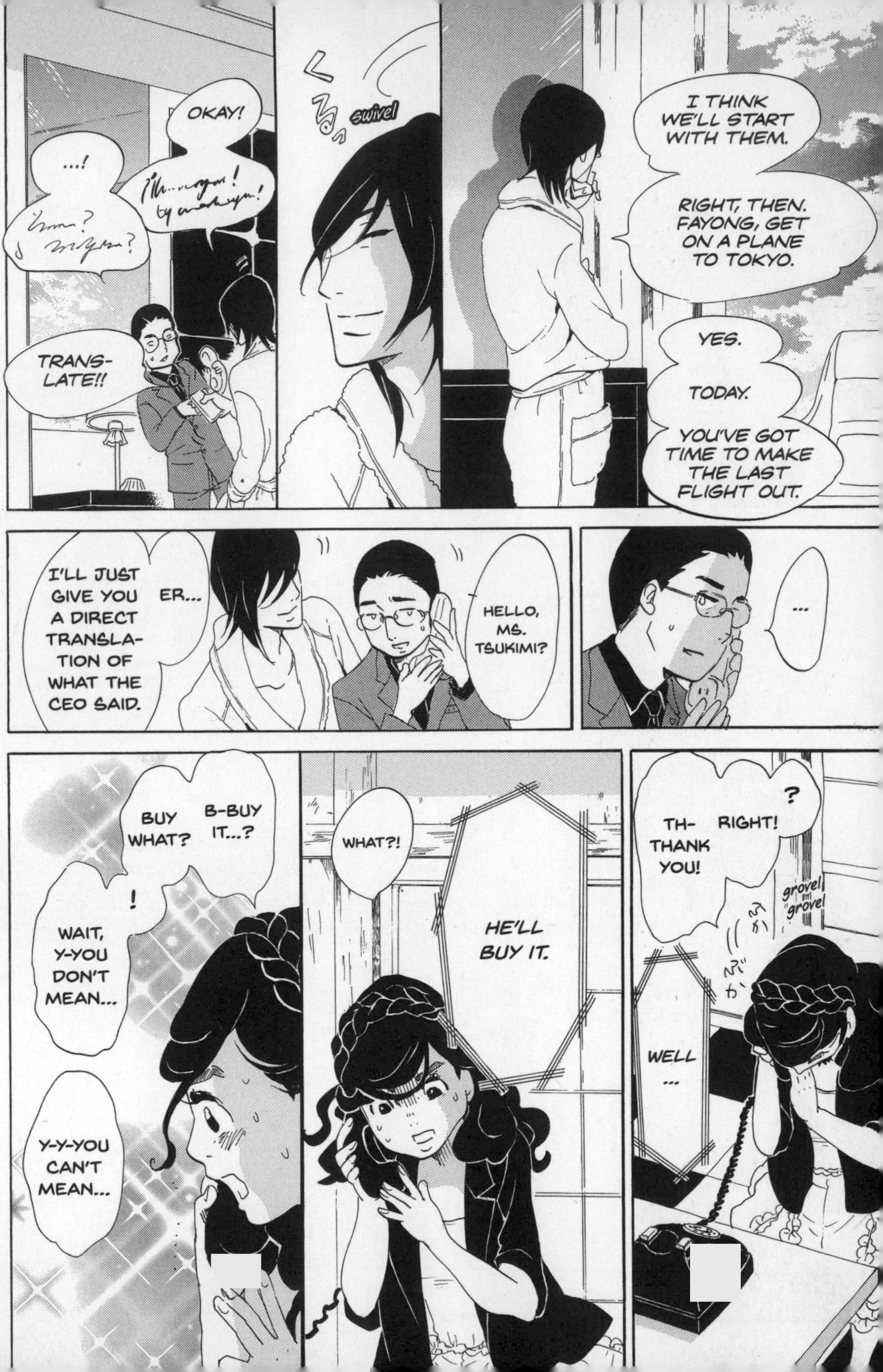
I THINK WE'LL START WITH THEM.
RIGHT, THEN. FAYONG, GET ON A PLANE TO TOKYO.
YES.
TODAY.
YOU'VE GOT TIME TO MAKE THE LAST FLIGHT OUT.
swivel
OKAY!
...!
TRANS-LATE!!
...
HELLO, MS. TSUKIMI?
ER...
I'LL JUST GIVE YOU A DIRECT TRANSLATION OF WHAT THE CEO SAID.
?
RIGHT!
TH- THANK YOU!
grovel grovel
WELL ...
WHAT?!
HE'LL BUY IT.
B-BUY IT...?
BUY WHAT?
!
WAIT, Y-YOU DON'T MEAN...
Y-Y-YOU CAN'T MEAN...

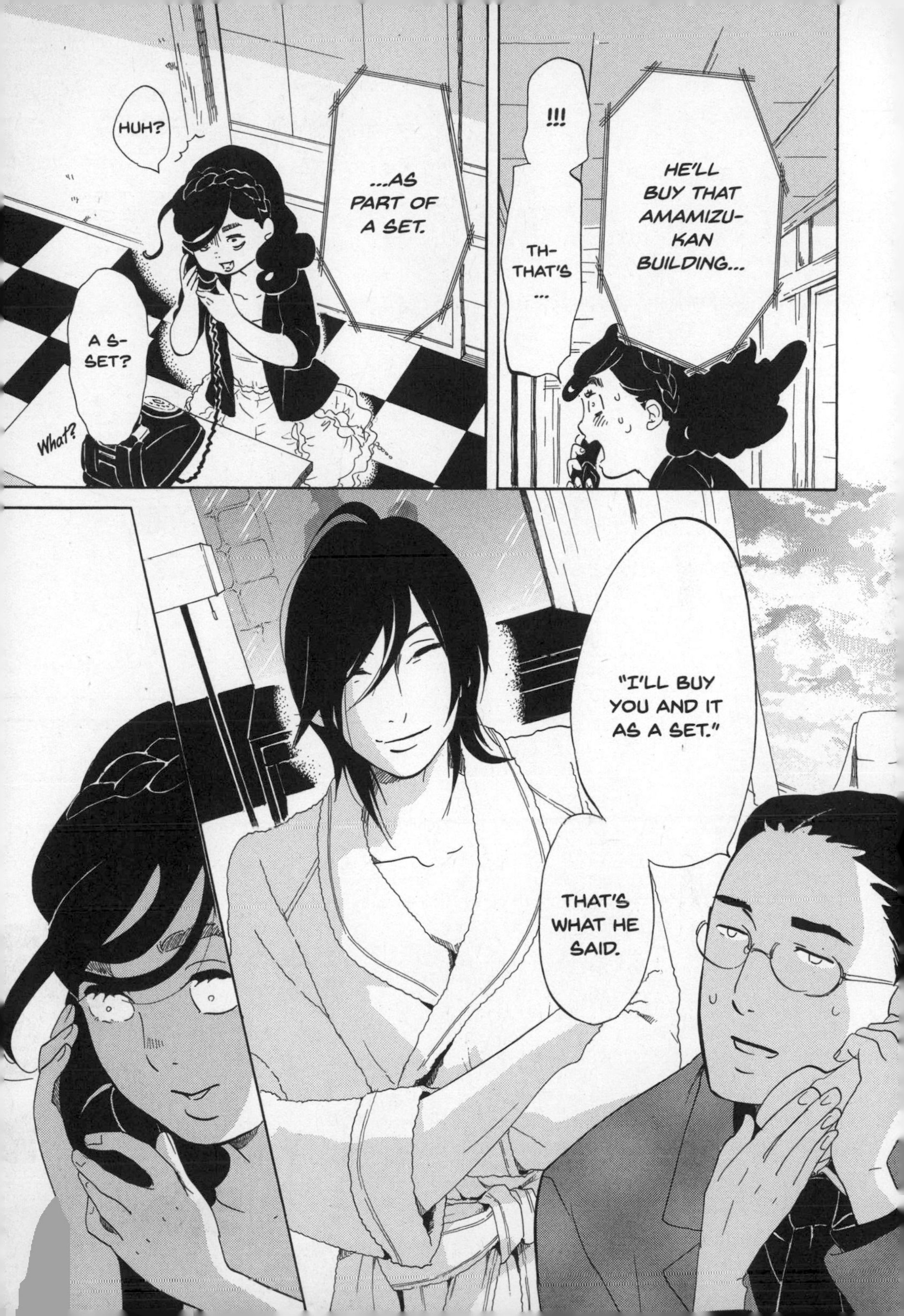
HE'LL BUY THAT AMAMIZU-KAN BUILDING...
!!!
TH-THAT'S ...
...AS PART OF A SET.
HUH?
A S-SET?
What?
"I'LL BUY YOU AND IT AS A SET."
THAT'S WHAT HE SAID.

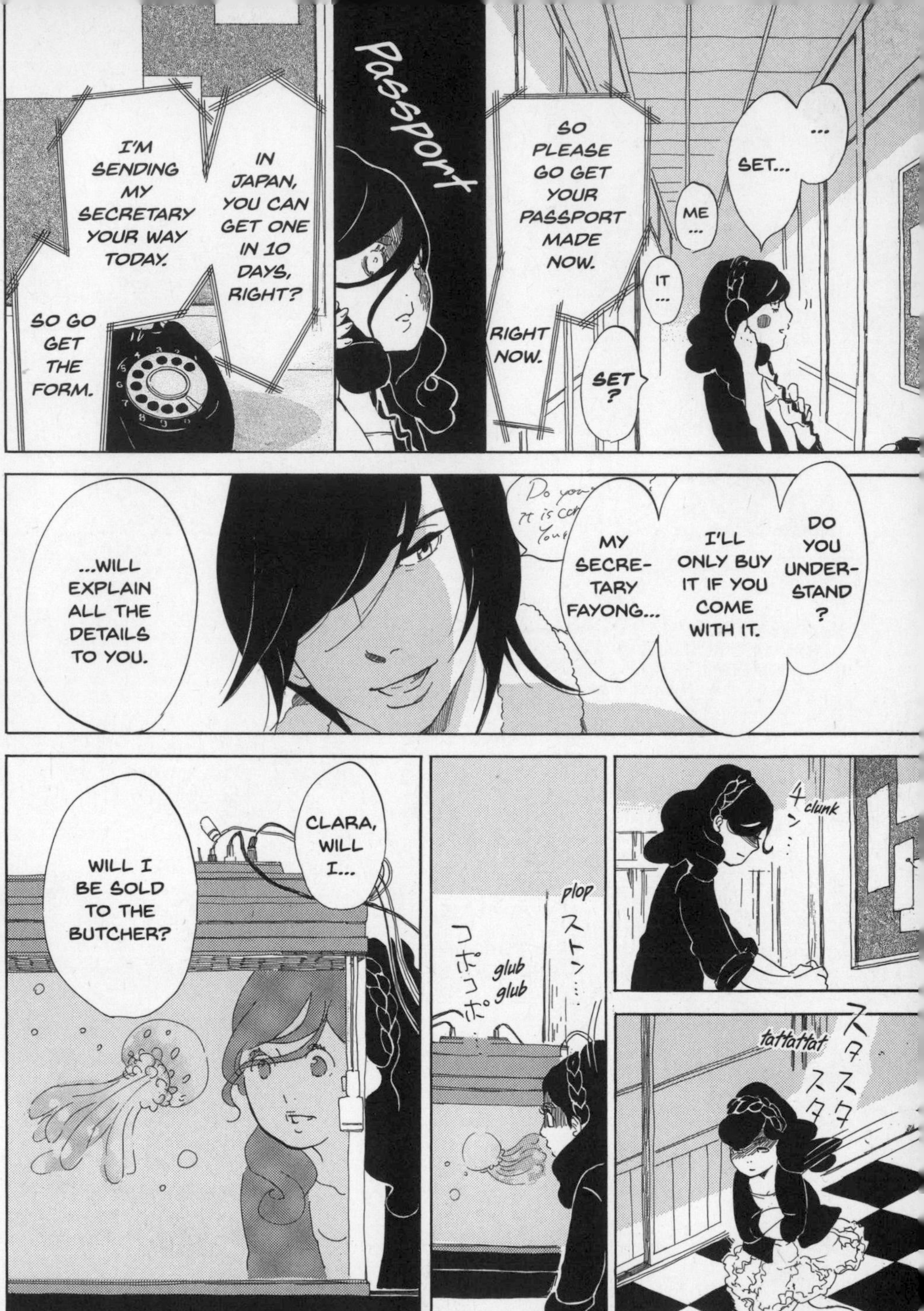
...
SET...
SO PLEASE GO GET YOUR PASSPORT MADE NOW.
ME...
IT...
RIGHT NOW.
SET?
Passport
IN JAPAN, YOU CAN GET ONE IN 10 DAYS, RIGHT?
I'M SENDING MY SECRETARY YOUR WAY TODAY.
SO GO GET THE FORM.
DO YOU UNDER-STAND?
I'LL ONLY BUY IT IF YOU COME WITH IT.
MY SECRE-TARY FAYONG...
...WILL EXPLAIN ALL THE DETAILS TO YOU.
clunk
スタスタスタ
tattattat
ストン...
plop
コポコポ
glub glub
CLARA, WILL I...
WILL I BE SOLD TO THE BUTCHER?

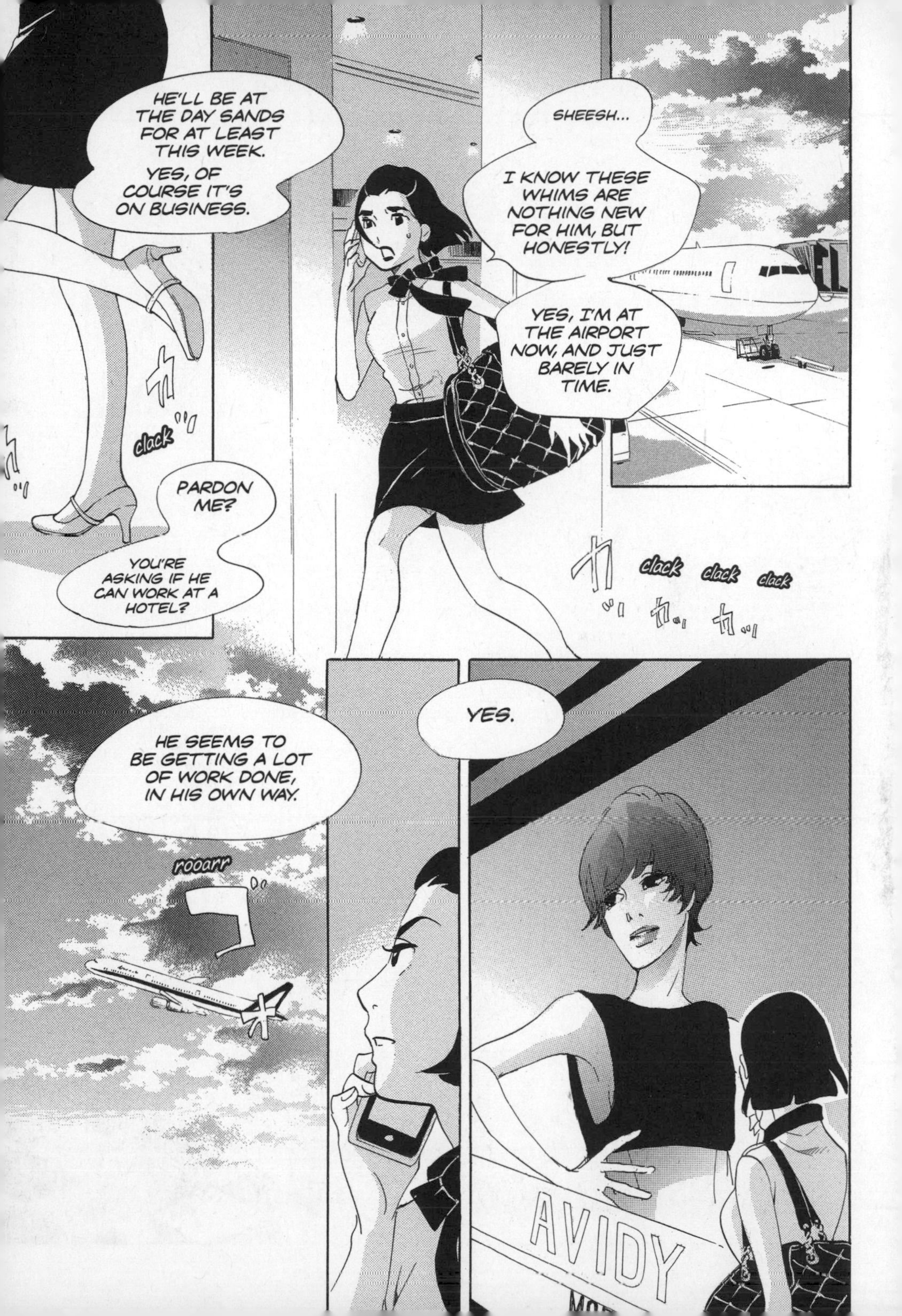
SHEESH...
I KNOW THESE WHIMS ARE NOTHING NEW FOR HIM, BUT HONESTLY!
YES, I'M AT THE AIRPORT NOW, AND JUST BARELY IN TIME.
clack clack clack
HE'LL BE AT THE DAY SANDS FOR AT LEAST THIS WEEK.
YES, OF COURSE IT'S ON BUSINESS.
clack
PARDON ME?
YOU'RE ASKING IF HE CAN WORK AT A HOTEL?
YES.
AVIDY
HE SEEMS TO BE GETTING A LOT OF WORK DONE, IN HIS OWN WAY.
rooarr

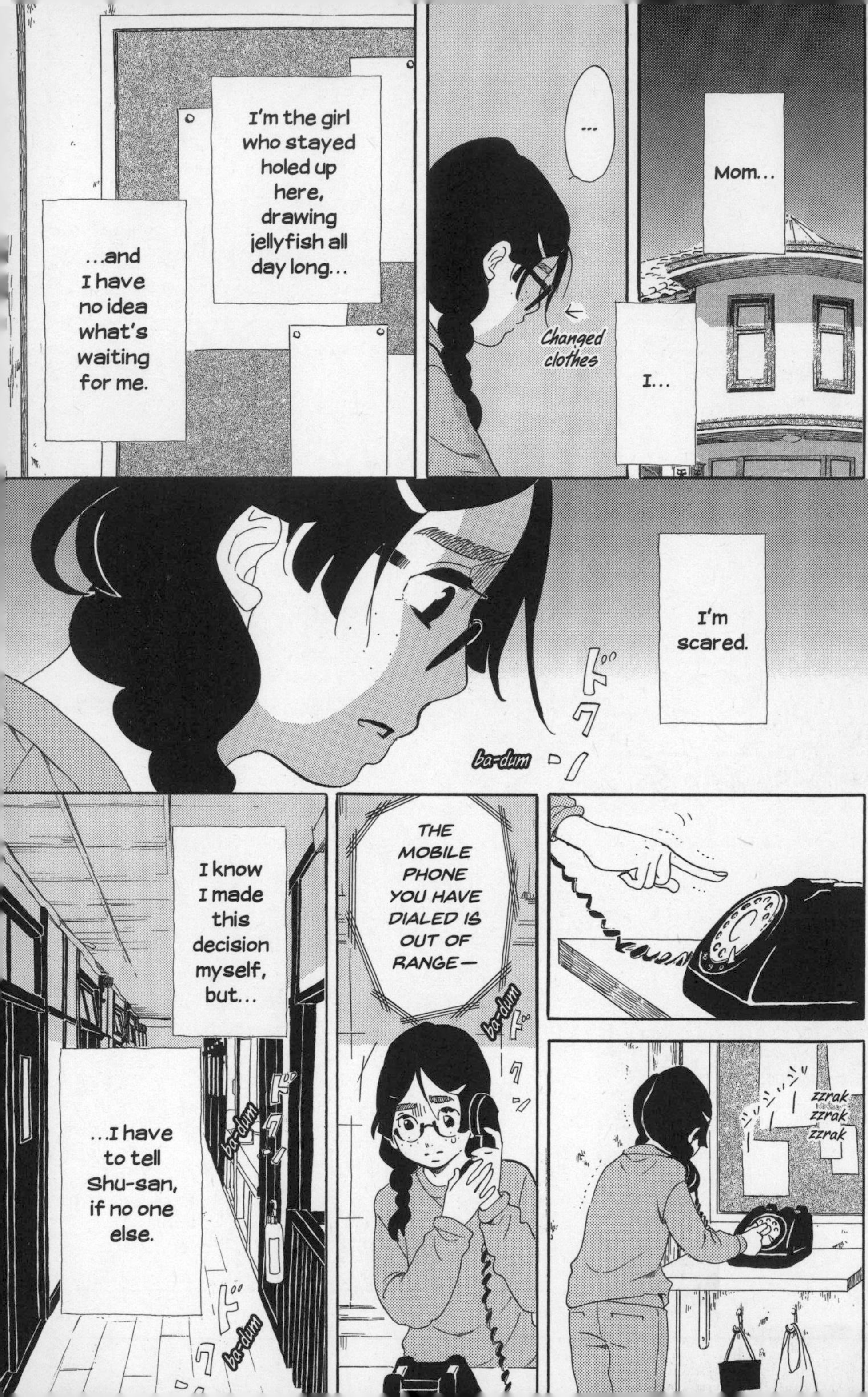

Mom...
I...
...
Changed clothes
I'm the girl who stayed holed up here, drawing jellyfish all day long...
...and I have no idea what's waiting for me.
I'm scared.
ba-dum
zzrak zzrak zzrak
THE MOBILE PHONE YOU HAVE DIALED IS OUT OF RANGE—
ba-dum
I know I made this decision myself, but...
...I have to tell Shu-san, if no one else.
ba-dum
ba-dum

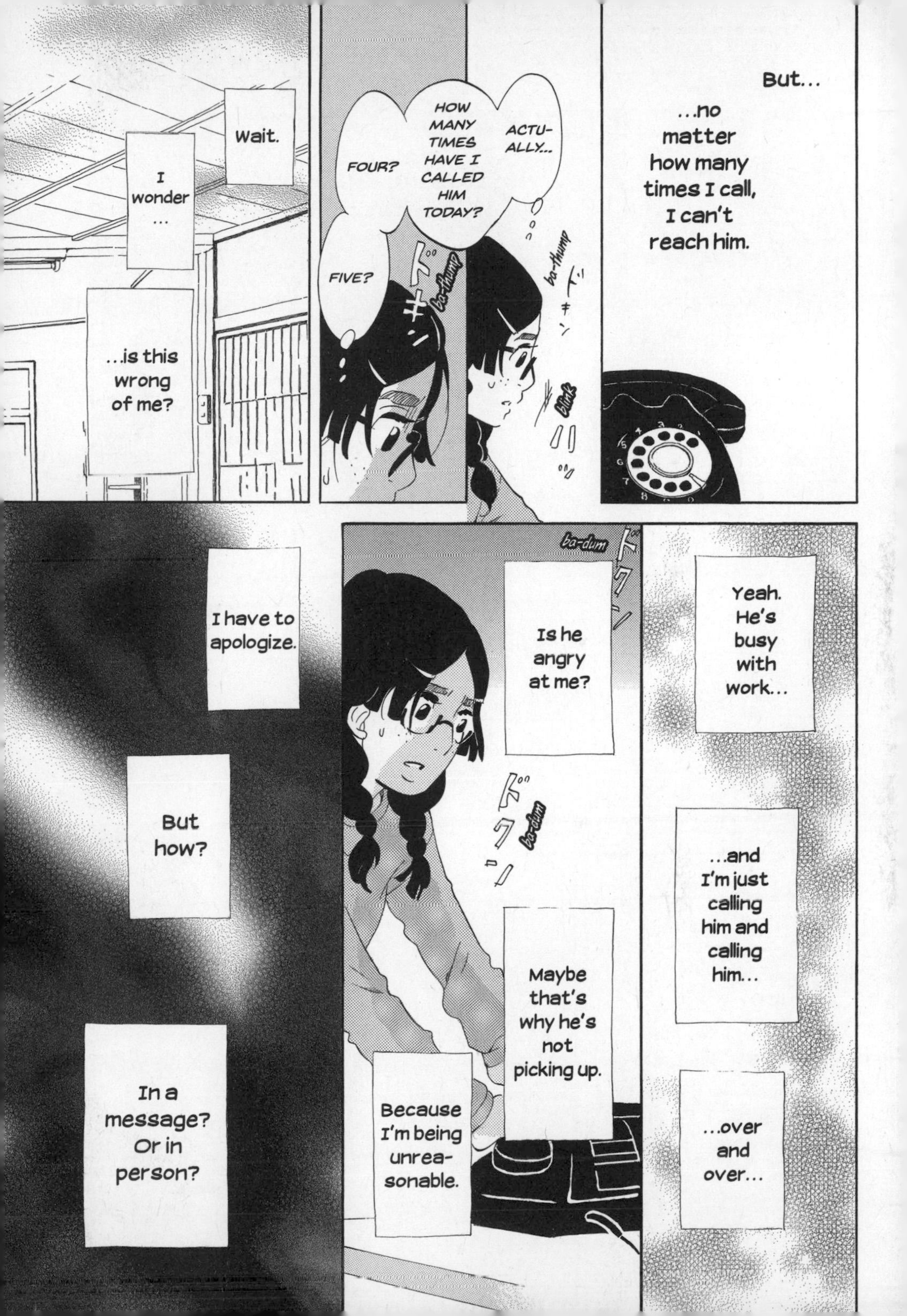
But...
...no matter how many times I call, I can't reach him.
ACTU-ALLY...
HOW MANY TIMES HAVE I CALLED HIM TODAY?
FOUR?
ba-thump
FIVE?
ba-thump
blink
Wait.
I wonder...
...is this wrong of me?
Yeah. He's busy with work...
...and I'm just calling him and calling him...
...over and over...
ba-dum
Is he angry at me?
ba-dum
Maybe that's why he's not picking up.
Because I'm being unrea-sonable.
I have to apologize.
But how?
In a message? Or in person?

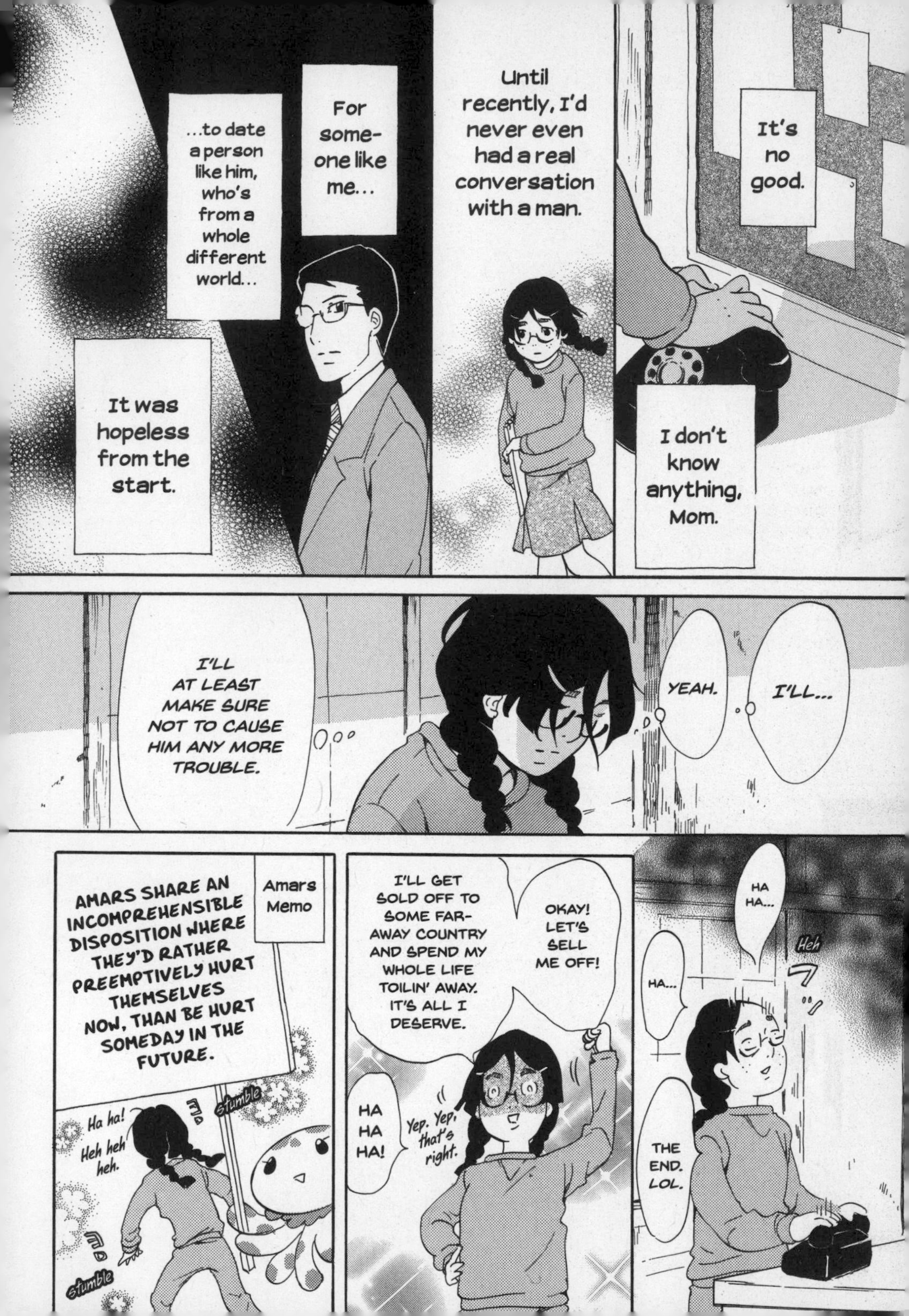
It's no good.
I don't know anything, Mom.
Until recently, I'd never even had a real conversation with a man.
For someone like me...
...to date a person like him, who's from a whole different world...
It was hopeless from the start.
I'LL...
YEAH.
I'LL AT LEAST MAKE SURE NOT TO CAUSE HIM ANY MORE TROUBLE.
HA HA...
Heh
HA...
THE END. LOL.
OKAY! LET'S SELL ME OFF!
I'LL GET SOLD OFF TO SOME FAR-AWAY COUNTRY AND SPEND MY WHOLE LIFE TOILIN' AWAY. IT'S ALL I DESERVE.
Yep. Yep, that's right.
HA HA HA!
Amars Memo
AMARS SHARE AN INCOMPREHENSIBLE DISPOSITION WHERE THEY'D RATHER PREEMPTIVELY HURT THEMSELVES NOW, THAN BE HURT SOMEDAY IN THE FUTURE.
stumble
Ha ha!
Heh heh heh.
stumble

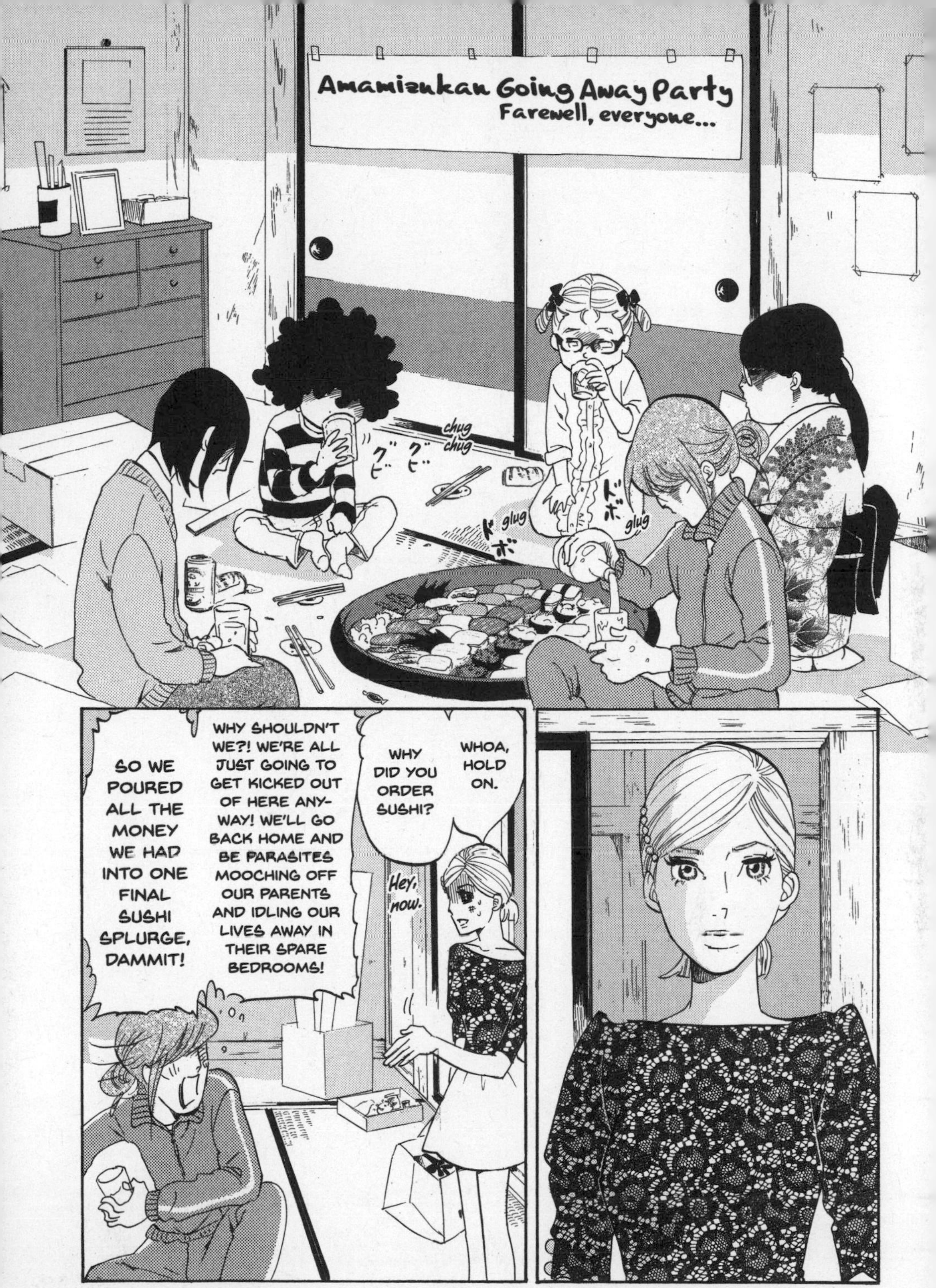
Amamizukan Going Away Party
Farewell, everyone...
chug chug
glug glug
WHOA, HOLD ON.
WHY DID YOU ORDER SUSHI?
Hey, now.
WHY SHOULDN'T WE?! WE'RE ALL JUST GOING TO GET KICKED OUT OF HERE ANY-WAY! WE'LL GO BACK HOME AND BE PARASITES MOOCHING OFF OUR PARENTS AND IDLING OUR LIVES AWAY IN THEIR SPARE BEDROOMS!
SO WE POURED ALL THE MONEY WE HAD INTO ONE FINAL SUSHI SPLURGE, DAMMIT!

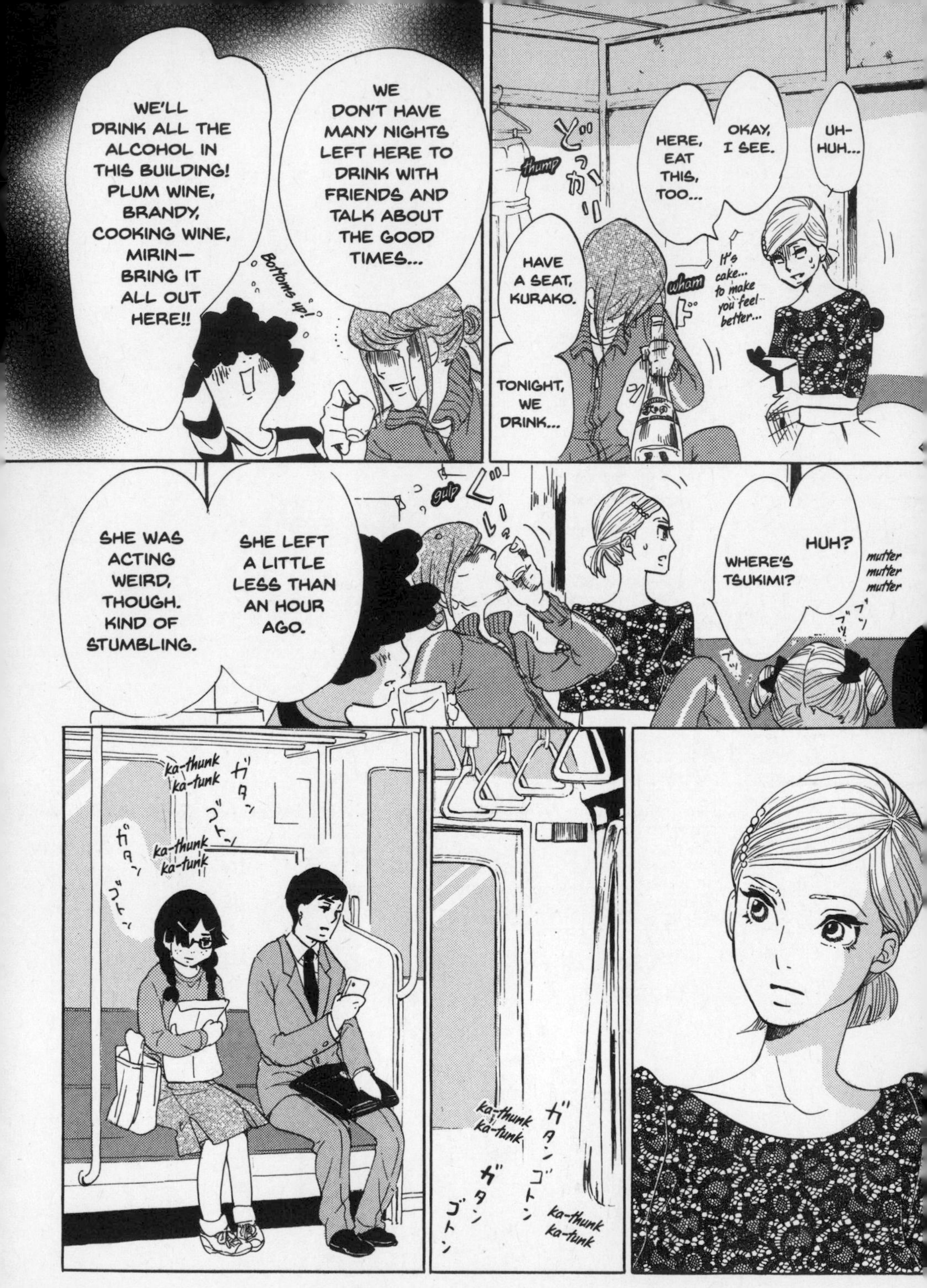
UH-HUH...
OKAY, I SEE.
HERE, EAT THIS, TOO...
It's cake... to make you feel better...
wham
thump
HAVE A SEAT, KURAKO.
TONIGHT, WE DRINK...
WE DON'T HAVE MANY NIGHTS LEFT HERE TO DRINK WITH FRIENDS AND TALK ABOUT THE GOOD TIMES...
Bottoms up!
WE'LL DRINK ALL THE ALCOHOL IN THIS BUILDING! PLUM WINE, BRANDY, COOKING WINE, MIRIN—BRING IT ALL OUT HERE!!
mutter mutter mutter
HUH?
WHERE'S TSUKIMI?
gulp
SHE LEFT A LITTLE LESS THAN AN HOUR AGO.
SHE WAS ACTING WEIRD, THOUGH. KIND OF STUMBLING.
ka-thunk ka-tunk
ka-thunk ka-tunk
ka-thunk ka-tunk
ka-thunk ka-tunk

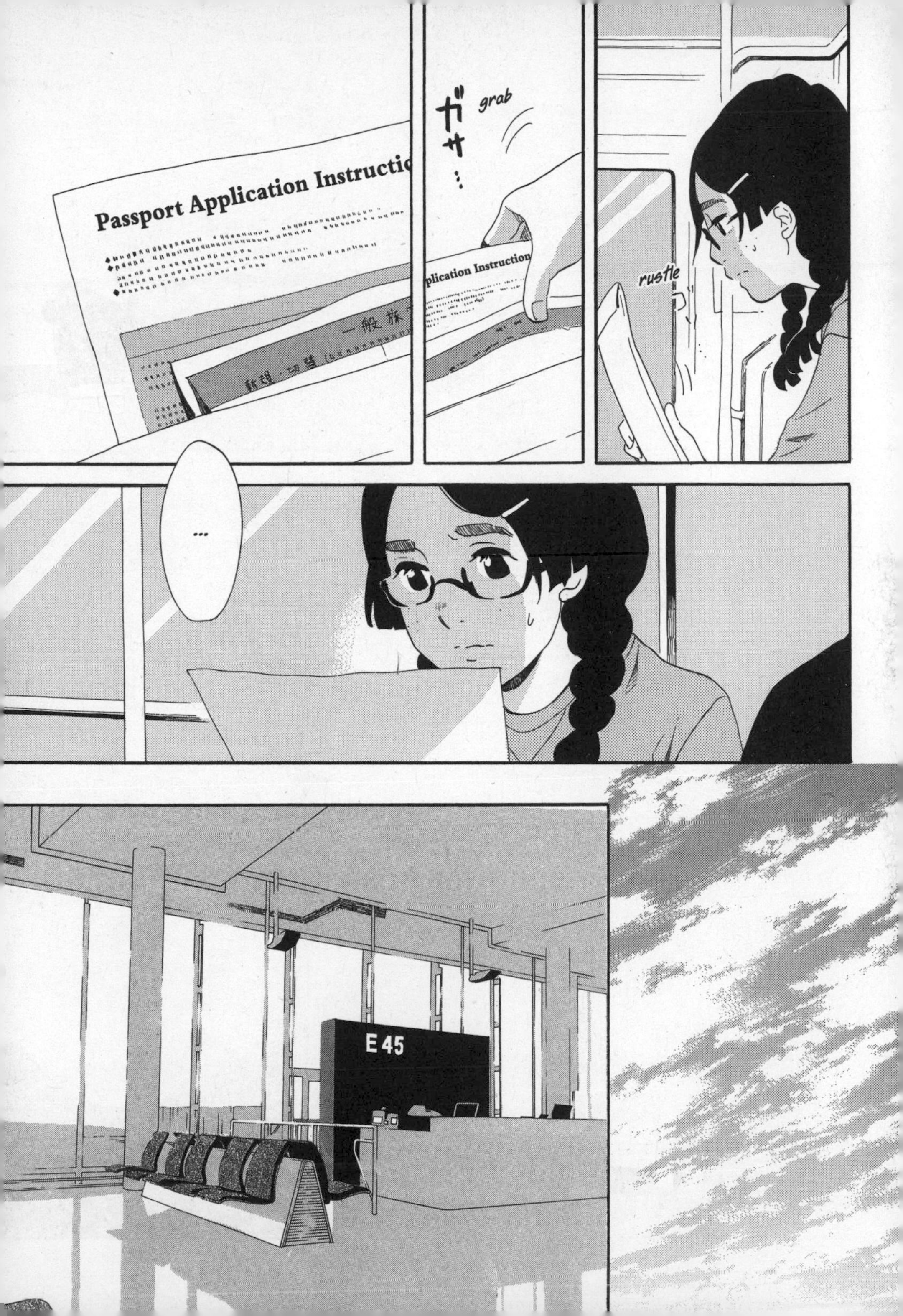
rustle
ガサ…
grab
Application Instruction
Passport Application Instructio
一般旅
新規・切替
...
E 45

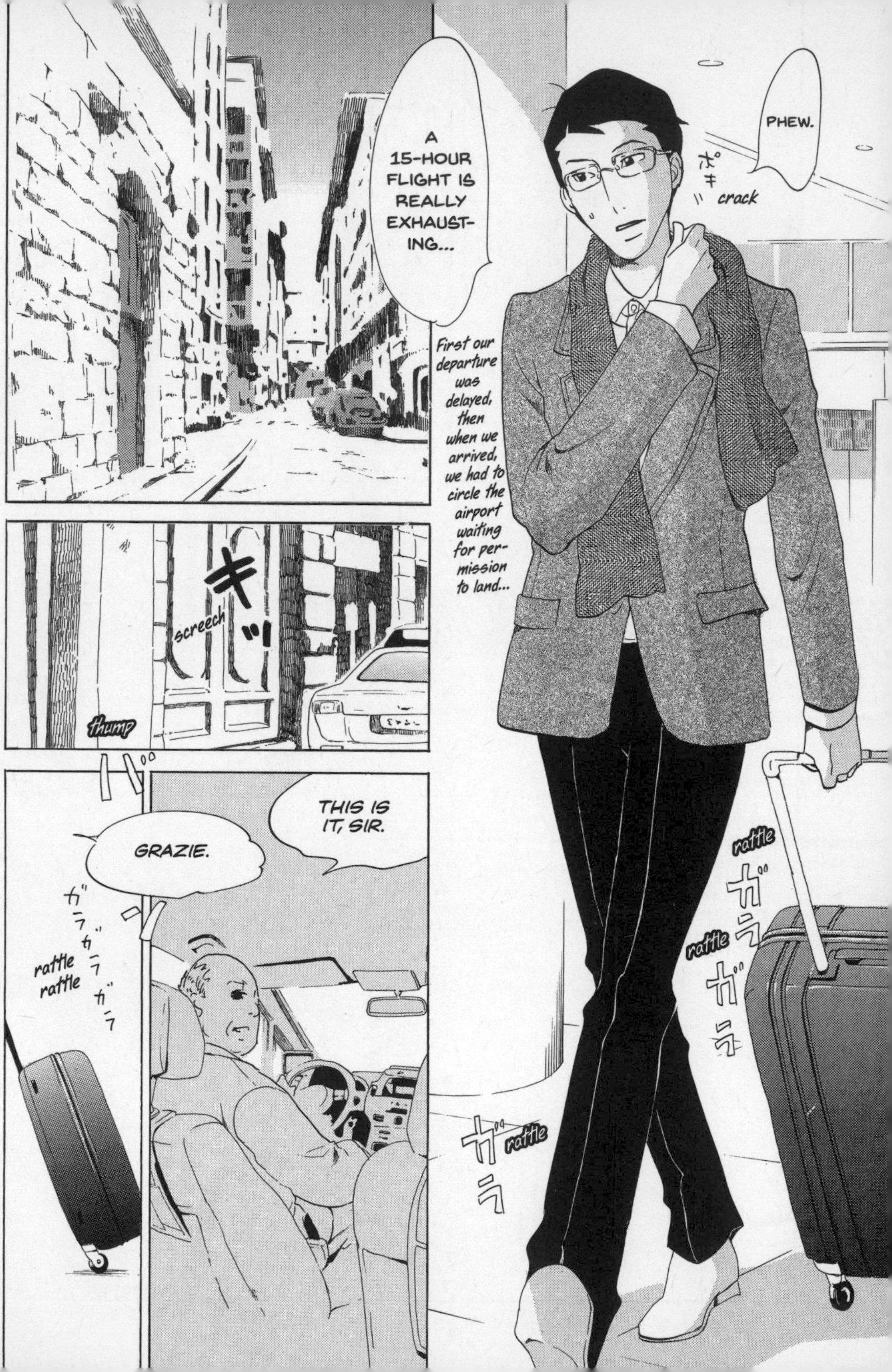
PHEW.
ポキ
crack
A 15-HOUR FLIGHT IS REALLY EXHAUSTING...
First our departure was delayed, then when we arrived, we had to circle the airport waiting for permission to land...
rattle
ガラ
rattle
ガラ
ガラ
rattle
キッ
screech
thump
THIS IS IT, SIR.
GRAZIE.
ガラガラガラガラ
rattle rattle

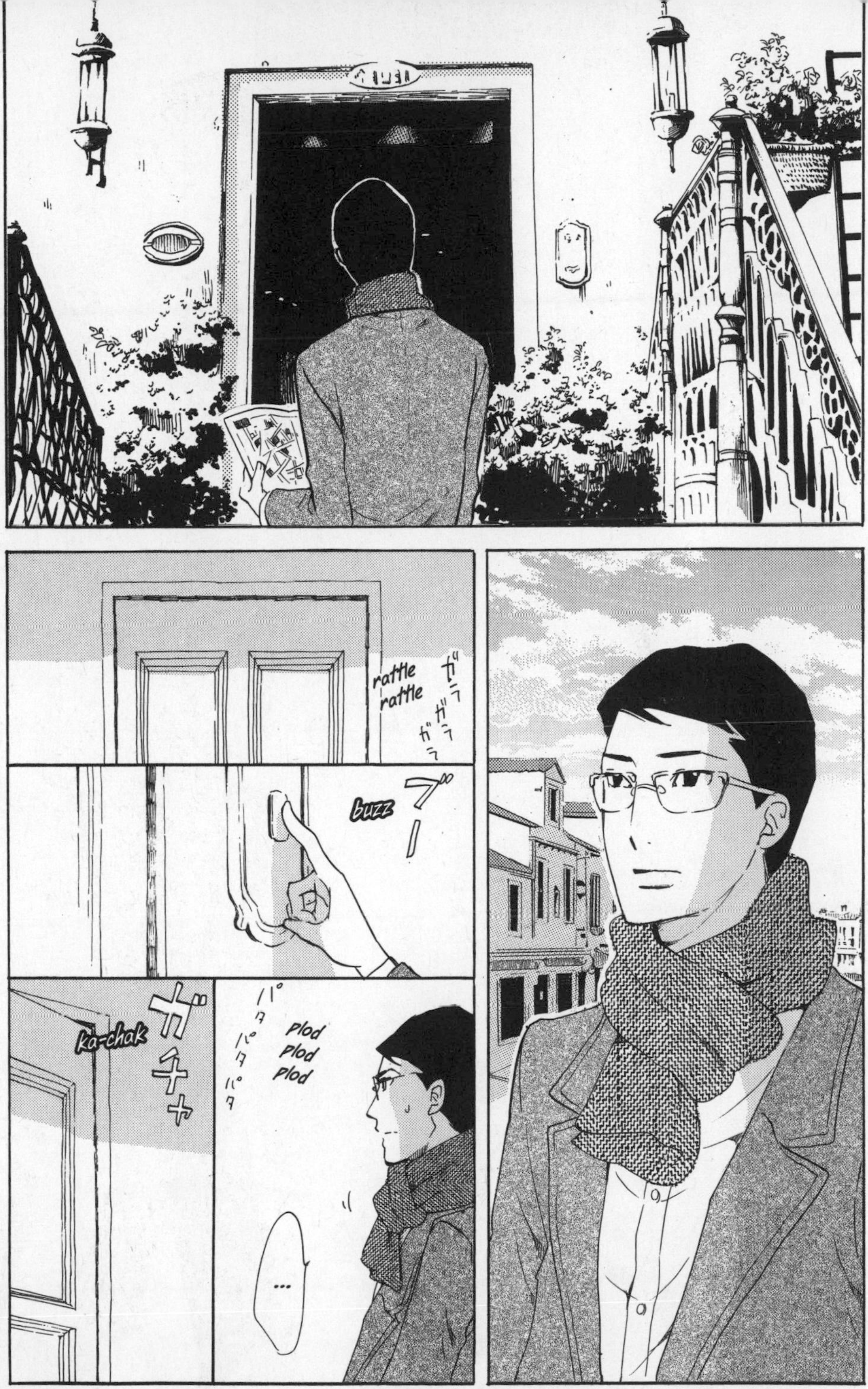
rattle rattle
ガラガラガラ
buzz
ブー
パタパタパタ
plod plod plod
...
ガチャ
ka-chak

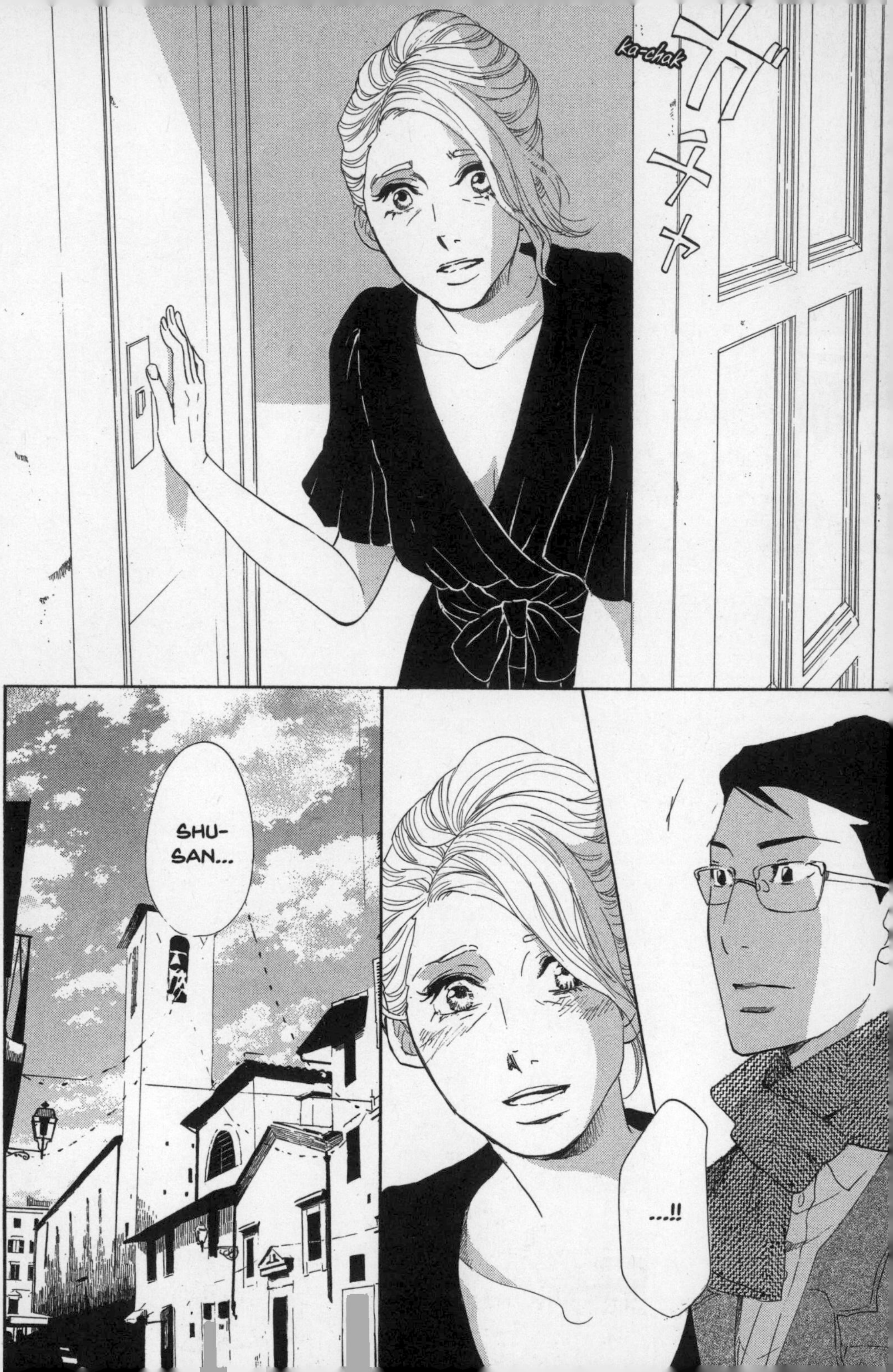
ka-chak
ガチャ
...!!
SHU-SAN...

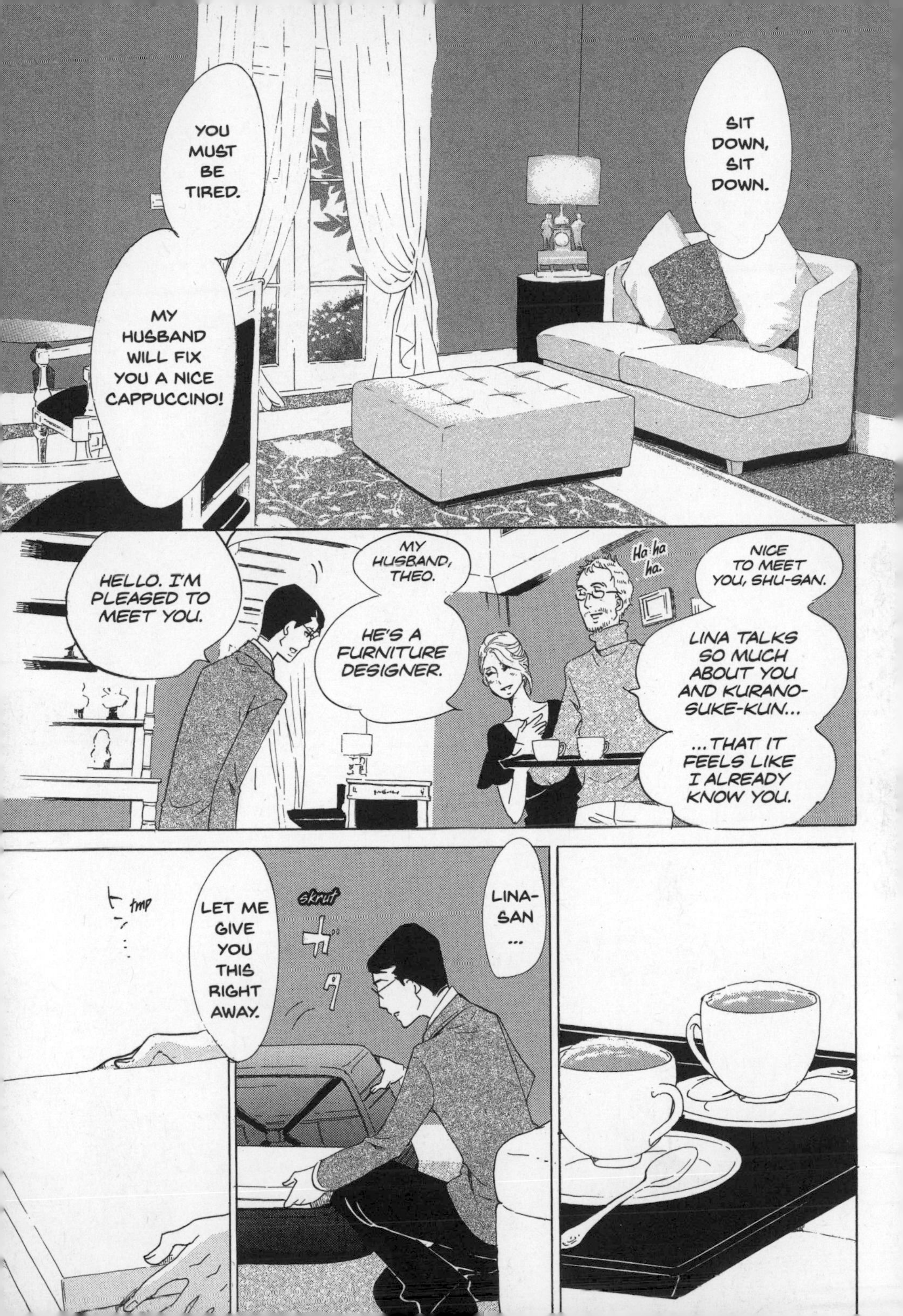
SIT DOWN, SIT DOWN.
YOU MUST BE TIRED.
MY HUSBAND WILL FIX YOU A NICE CAPPUCCINO!
NICE TO MEET YOU, SHU-SAN.
LINA TALKS SO MUCH ABOUT YOU AND KURANO-SUKE-KUN...
...THAT IT FEELS LIKE I ALREADY KNOW YOU.
Ha ha ha.
MY HUSBAND, THEO.
HE'S A FURNITURE DESIGNER.
HELLO. I'M PLEASED TO MEET YOU.
LINA-SAN...
skrut
LET ME GIVE YOU THIS RIGHT AWAY.
tmp

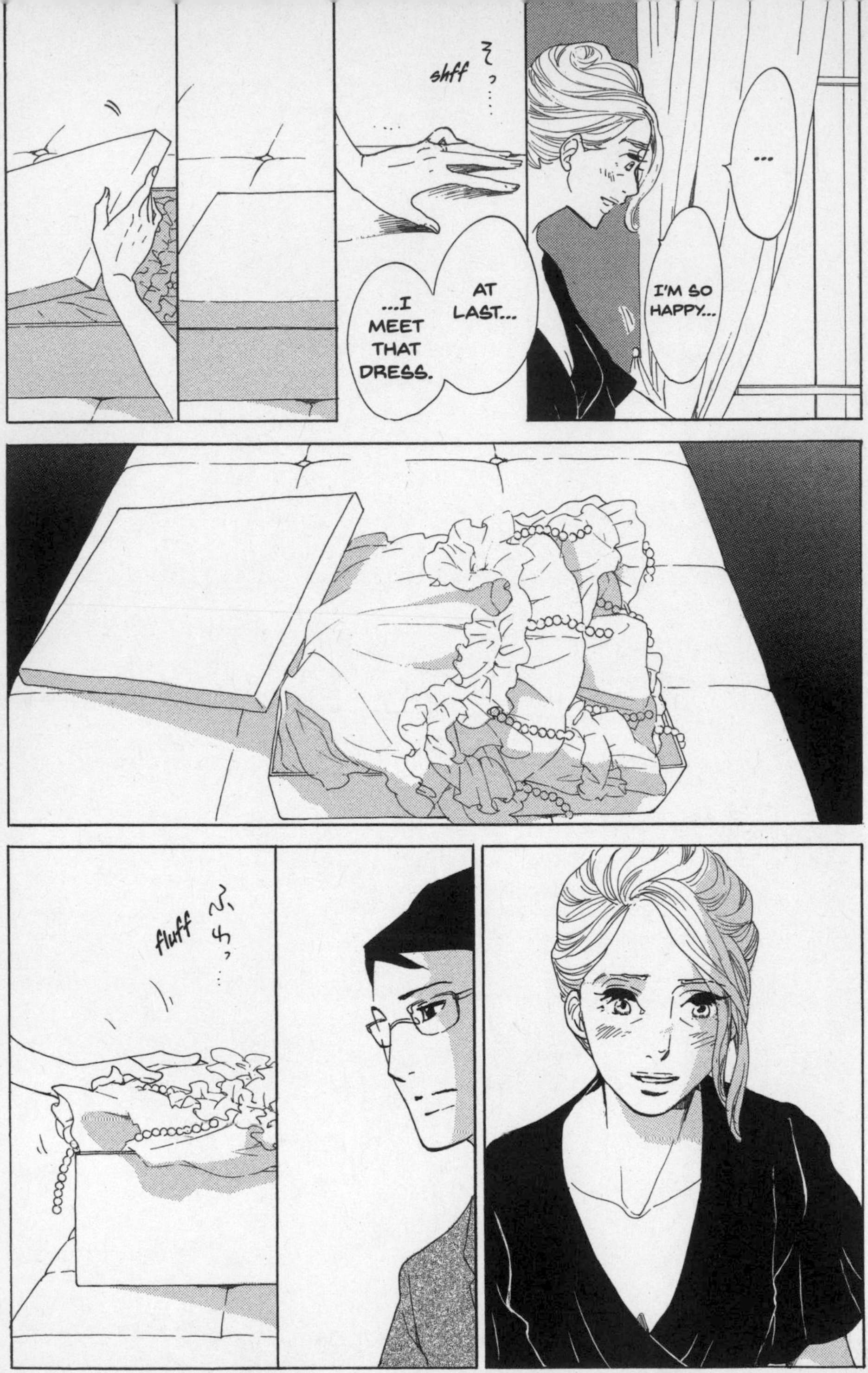
...
I'M SO HAPPY...
shff
AT LAST...
...I MEET THAT DRESS.
fluff

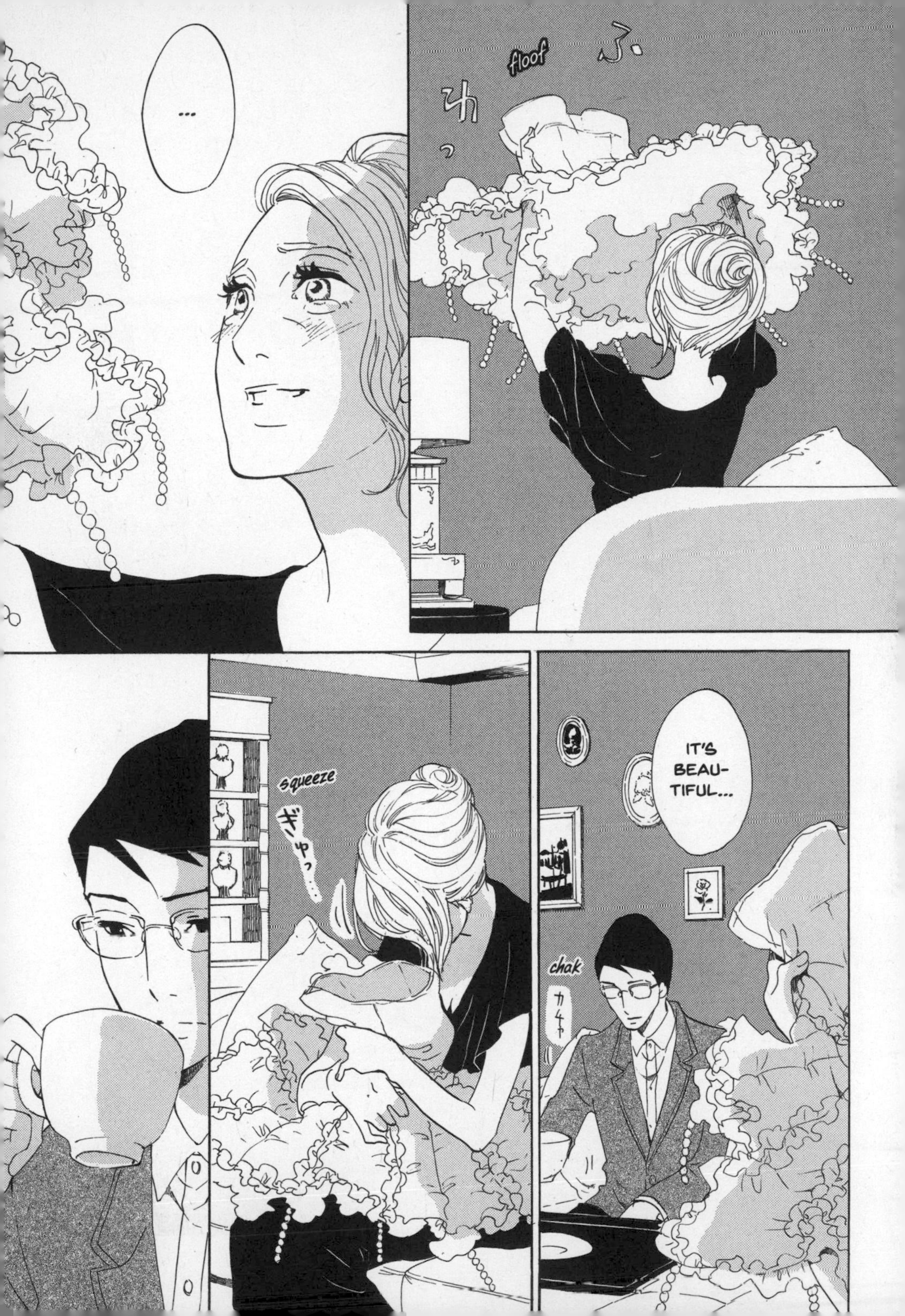
floof
ふわっ
...
IT'S BEAU-TIFUL...
chak
カチャ
squeeze
ぎゅっ…

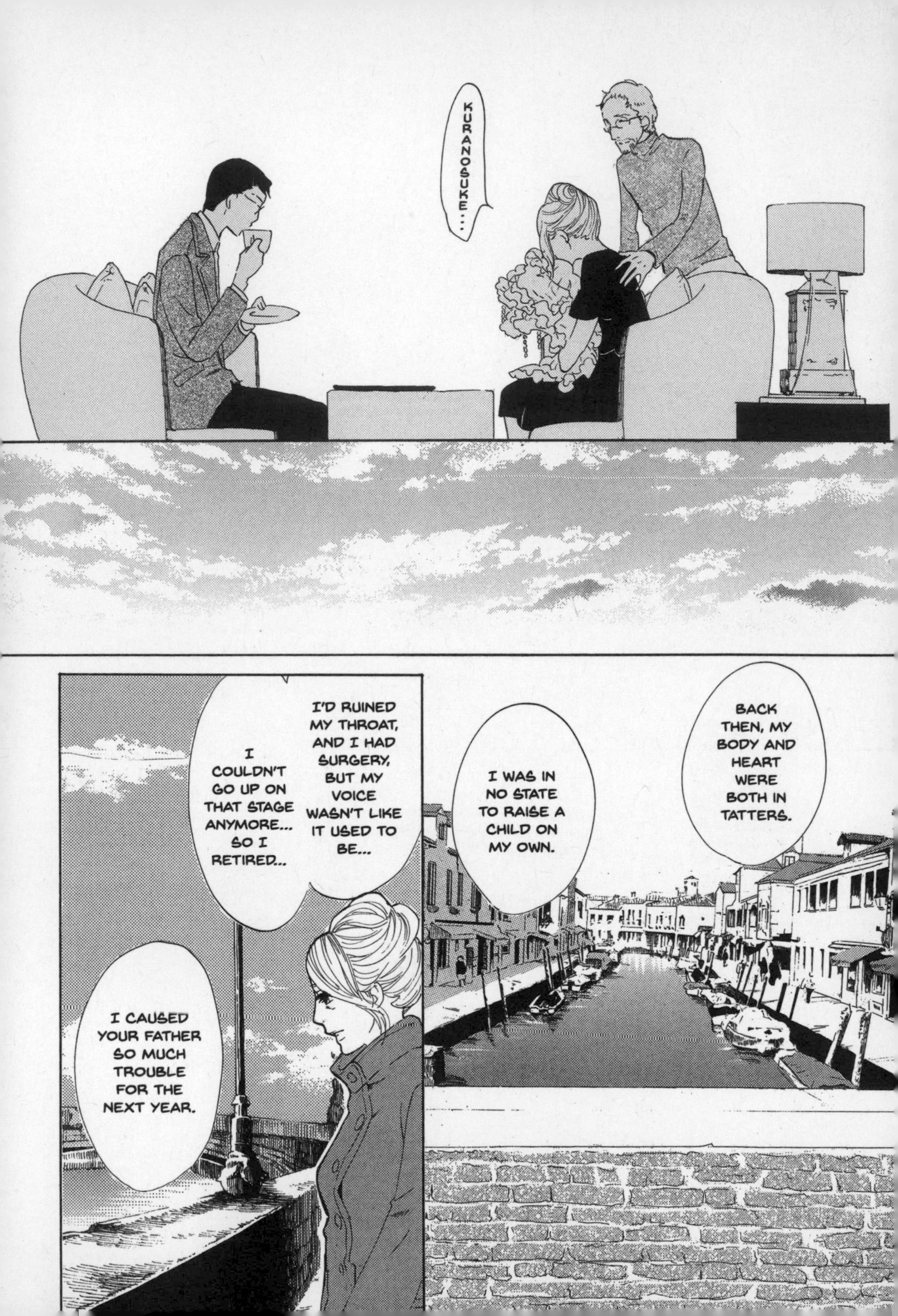
KURANOSUKE...
BACK THEN, MY BODY AND HEART WERE BOTH IN TATTERS.
I WAS IN NO STATE TO RAISE A CHILD ON MY OWN.
I'D RUINED MY THROAT, AND I HAD SURGERY, BUT MY VOICE WASN'T LIKE IT USED TO BE...
I COULDN'T GO UP ON THAT STAGE ANYMORE... SO I RETIRED...
I CAUSED YOUR FATHER SO MUCH TROUBLE FOR THE NEXT YEAR.

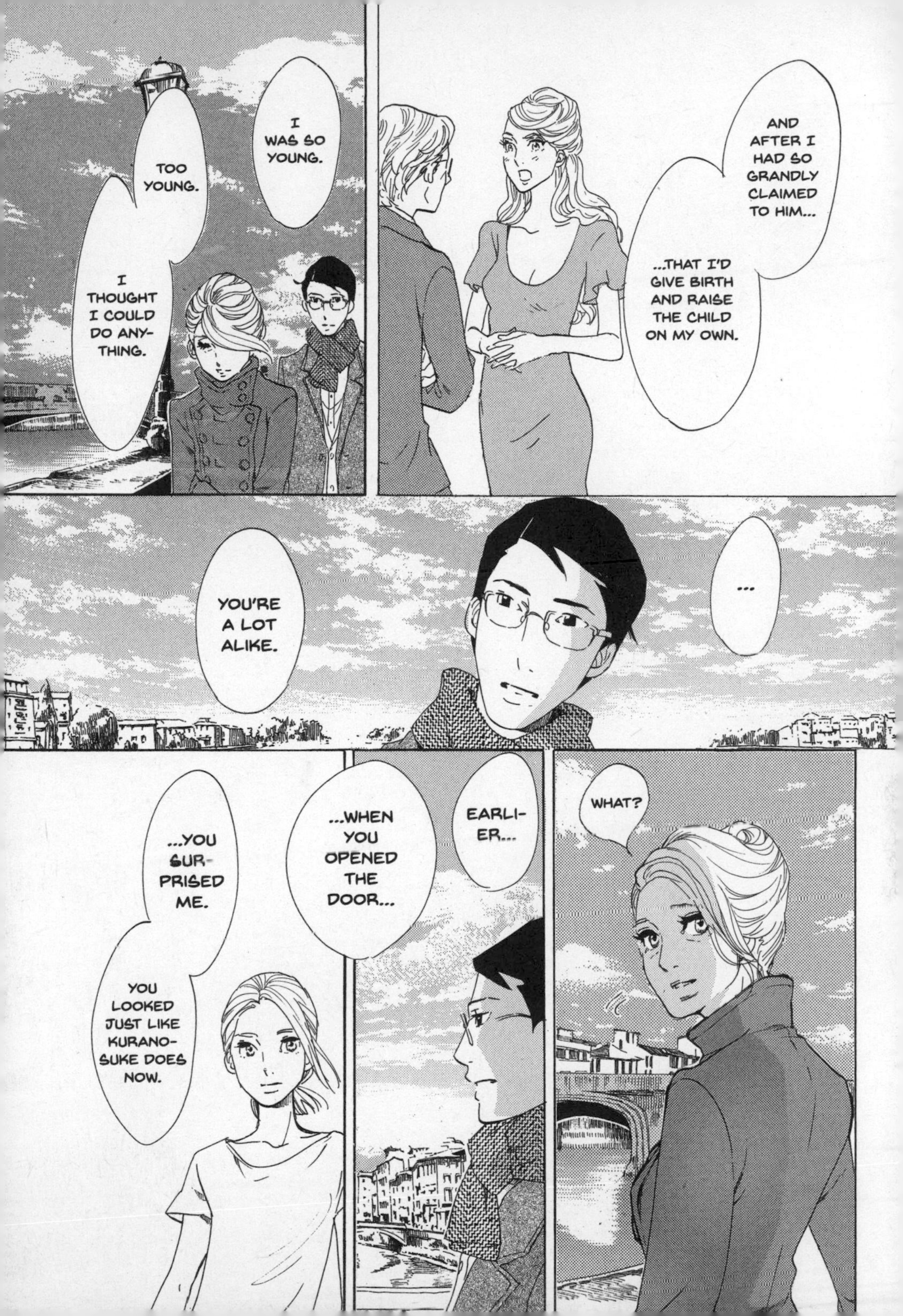
AND AFTER I HAD SO GRANDLY CLAIMED TO HIM...
...THAT I'D GIVE BIRTH AND RAISE THE CHILD ON MY OWN.
I WAS SO YOUNG.
TOO YOUNG.
I THOUGHT I COULD DO ANY-THING.
...
YOU'RE A LOT ALIKE.
WHAT?
EARLI-ER...
...WHEN YOU OPENED THE DOOR...
...YOU SUR-PRISED ME.
YOU LOOKED JUST LIKE KURANO-SUKE DOES NOW.

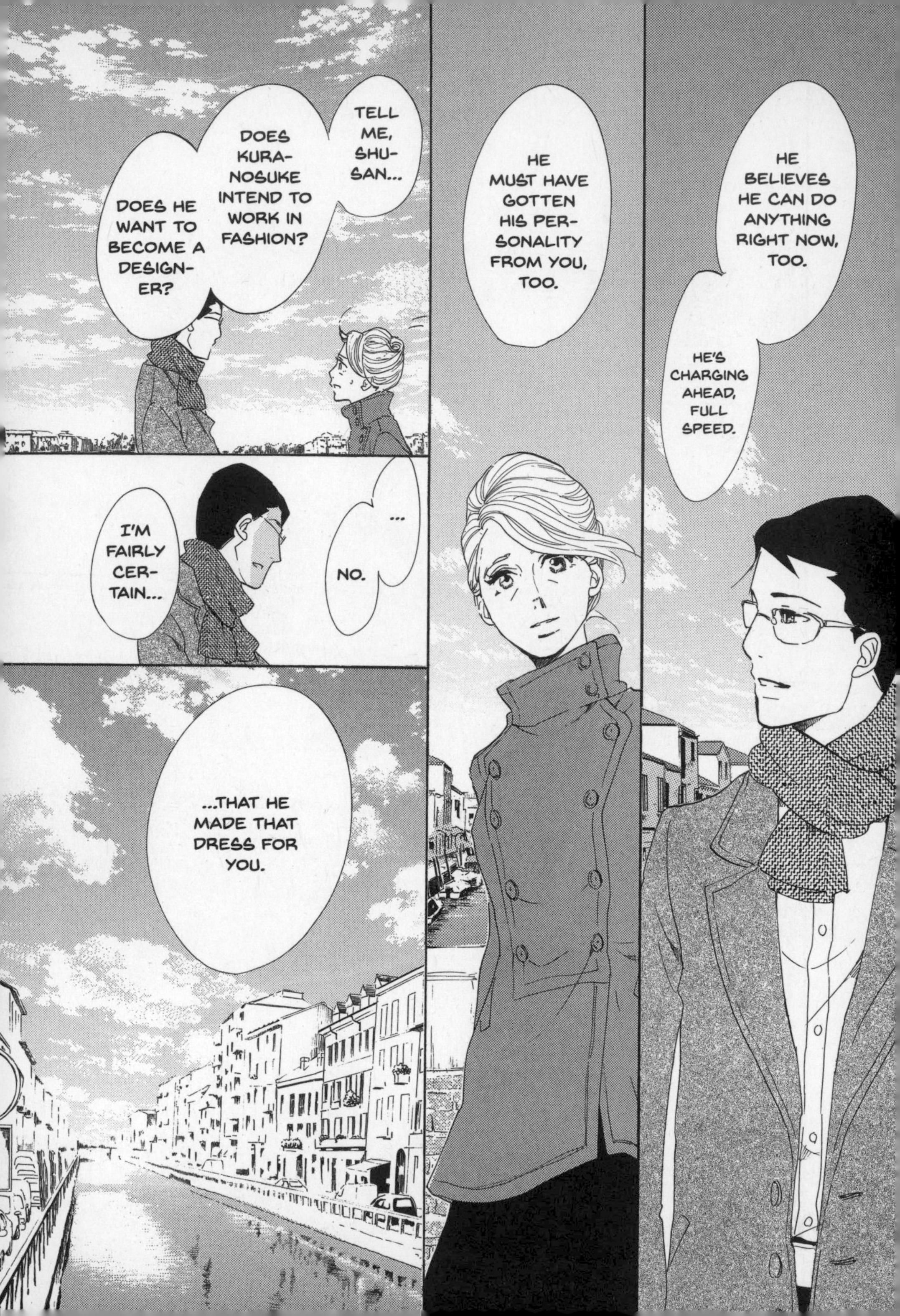
HE BELIEVES HE CAN DO ANYTHING RIGHT NOW, TOO.
HE'S CHARGING AHEAD, FULL SPEED.
HE MUST HAVE GOTTEN HIS PERSONALITY FROM YOU, TOO.
TELL ME, SHU-SAN...
DOES KURANOSUKE INTEND TO WORK IN FASHION?
DOES HE WANT TO BECOME A DESIGNER?
... NO.
I'M FAIRLY CERTAIN...
...THAT HE MADE THAT DRESS FOR YOU.

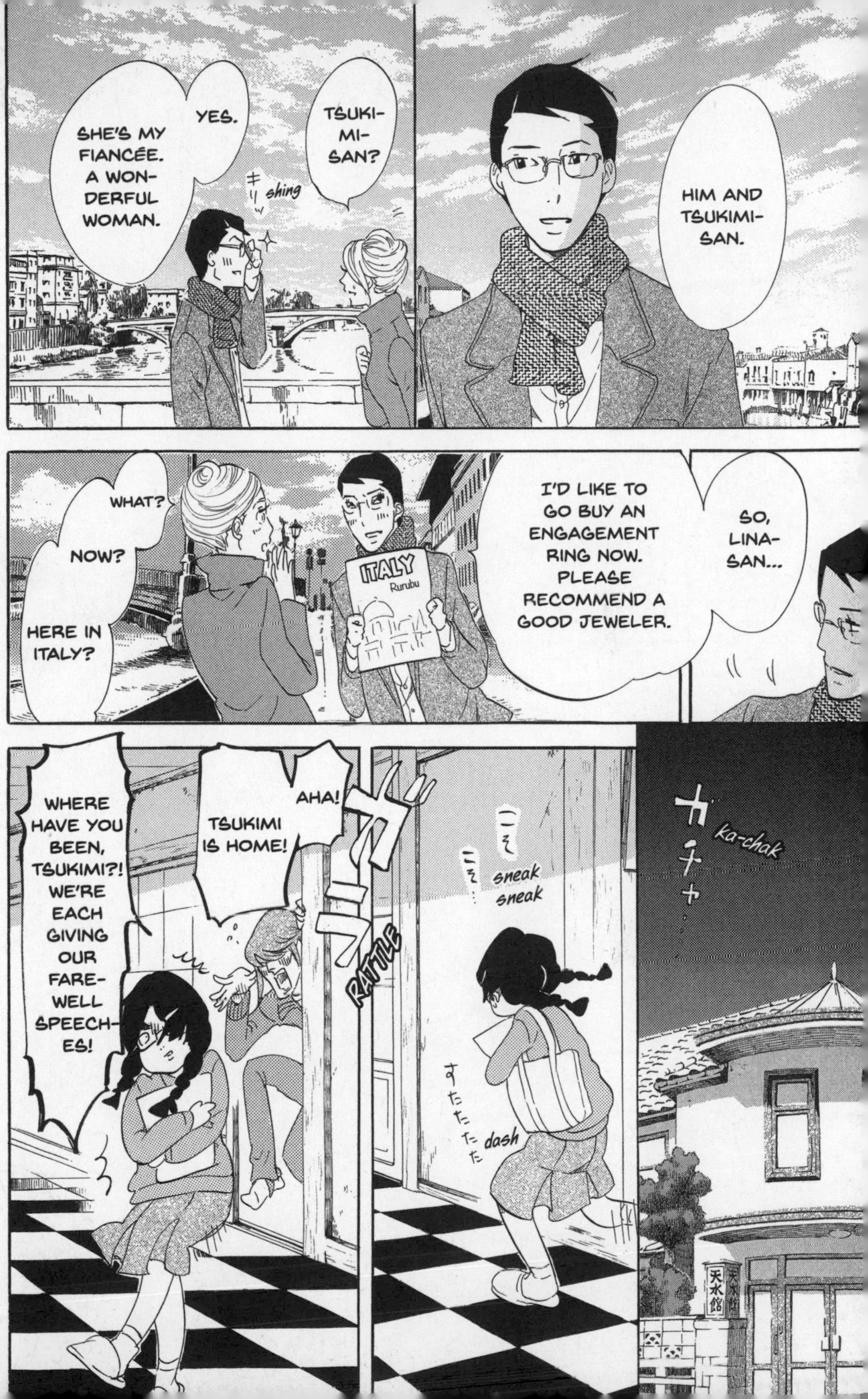
HIM AND TSUKIMI-SAN.
TSUKIMI-SAN?
YES.
SHE'S MY FIANCÉE. A WONDERFUL WOMAN.
キリッ shing
SO, LINA-SAN...
I'D LIKE TO GO BUY AN ENGAGEMENT RING NOW. PLEASE RECOMMEND A GOOD JEWELER.
ITALY Rurubu
WHAT?
NOW?
HERE IN ITALY?
ガチャ ka-chak
天水館
こそこそ sneak sneak
すたたた dash
AHA! TSUKIMI IS HOME!
RATTLE
WHERE HAVE YOU BEEN, TSUKIMI?! WE'RE EACH GIVING OUR FAREWELL SPEECHES!

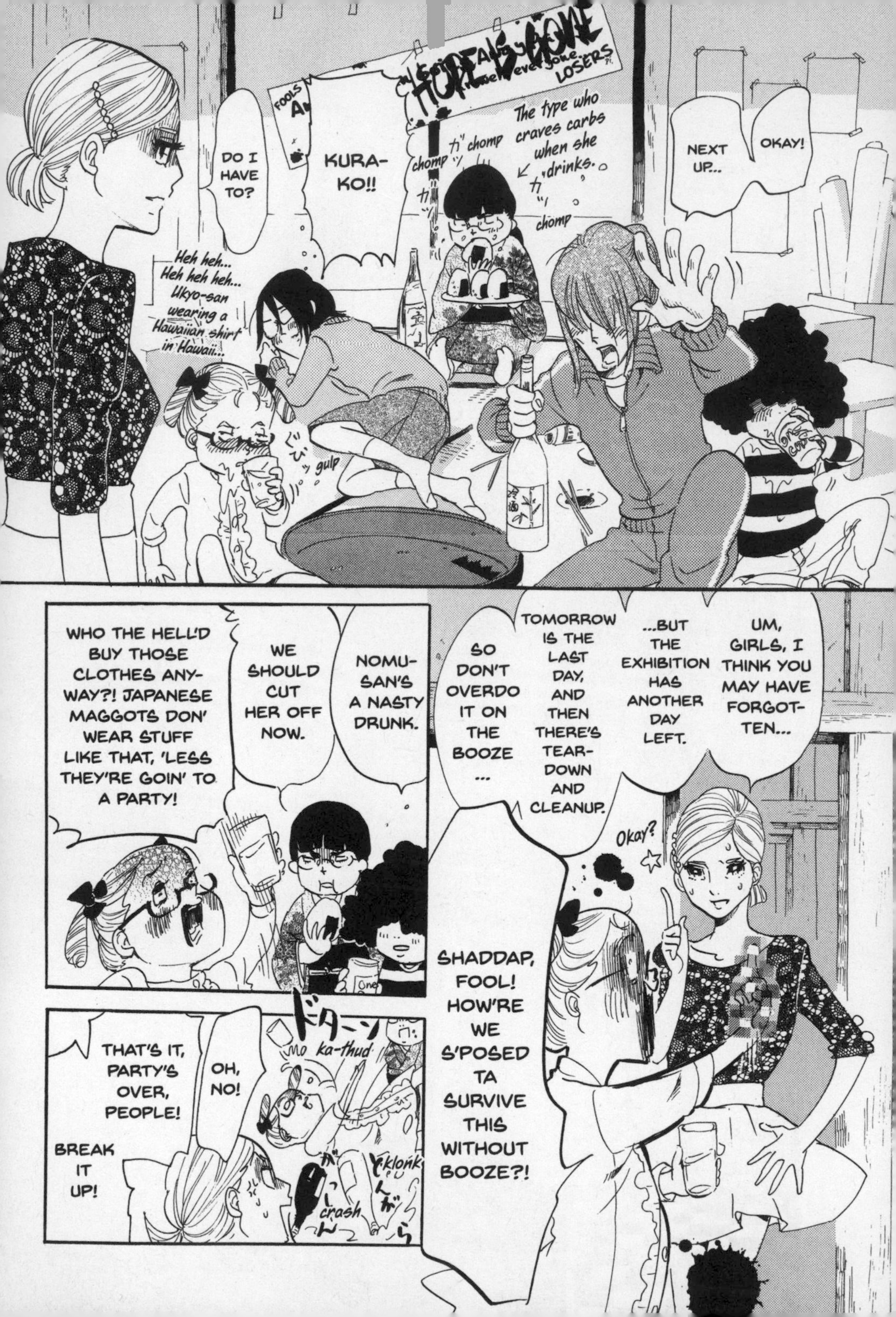
HOPE IS GONE
LOSERS
OKAY!
NEXT UP...
The type who craves carbs when she drinks.
chomp
chomp
chomp
KURA-KO!!
DO I HAVE TO?
Heh heh... Heh heh heh... Ukyo-san wearing a Hawaiian shirt in Hawaii...
gulp
UM, GIRLS, I THINK YOU MAY HAVE FORGOT-TEN...
...BUT THE EXHIBITION HAS ANOTHER DAY LEFT.
TOMORROW IS THE LAST DAY, AND THEN THERE'S TEAR-DOWN AND CLEANUP.
SO DON'T OVERDO IT ON THE BOOZE...
Okay?
SHADDAP, FOOL! HOW'RE WE S'POSED TA SURVIVE THIS WITHOUT BOOZE?!
NOMU-SAN'S A NASTY DRUNK.
WE SHOULD CUT HER OFF NOW.
WHO THE HELL'D BUY THOSE CLOTHES ANY-WAY?! JAPANESE MAGGOTS DON' WEAR STUFF LIKE THAT, 'LESS THEY'RE GOIN' TO A PARTY!
ka-thud
OH, NO!
THAT'S IT, PARTY'S OVER, PEOPLE!
BREAK IT UP!
klonk
crash

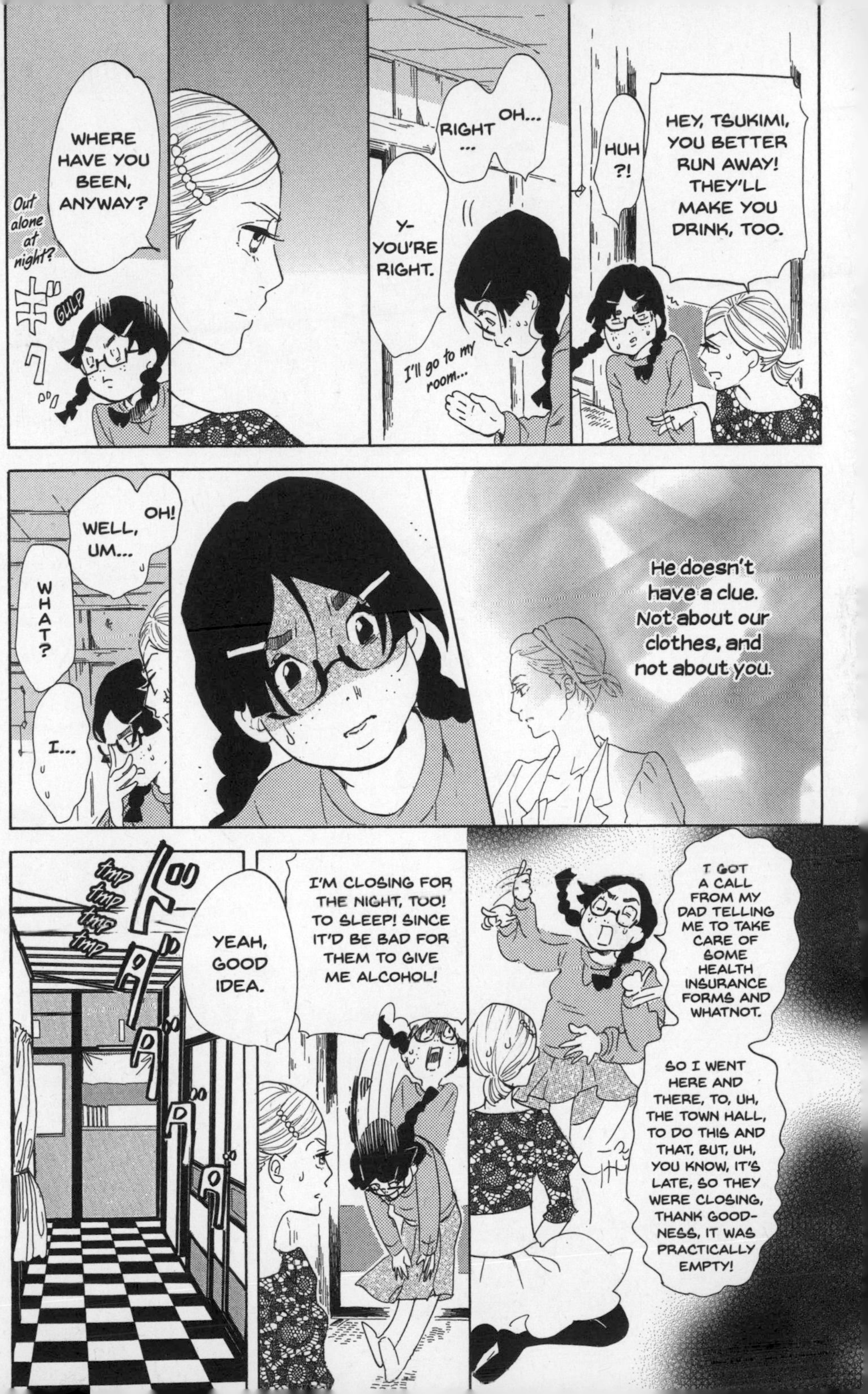
HEY, TSUKIMI, YOU BETTER RUN AWAY! THEY'LL MAKE YOU DRINK, TOO.
HUH ?!
OH... RIGHT...
Y- YOU'RE RIGHT.
I'll go to my room...
WHERE HAVE YOU BEEN, ANYWAY?
Out alone at night?
GULP
He doesn't have a clue. Not about our clothes, and not about you.
OH! WELL, UM...
WHAT?
I...
I GOT A CALL FROM MY DAD TELLING ME TO TAKE CARE OF SOME HEALTH INSURANCE FORMS AND WHATNOT.
SO I WENT HERE AND THERE, TO, UH, THE TOWN HALL, TO DO THIS AND THAT, BUT, UH, YOU KNOW, IT'S LATE, SO THEY WERE CLOSING, THANK GOODNESS, IT WAS PRACTICALLY EMPTY!
I'M CLOSING FOR THE NIGHT, TOO! TO SLEEP! SINCE IT'D BE BAD FOR THEM TO GIVE ME ALCOHOL!
YEAH, GOOD IDEA.
tmp tmp tmp tmp

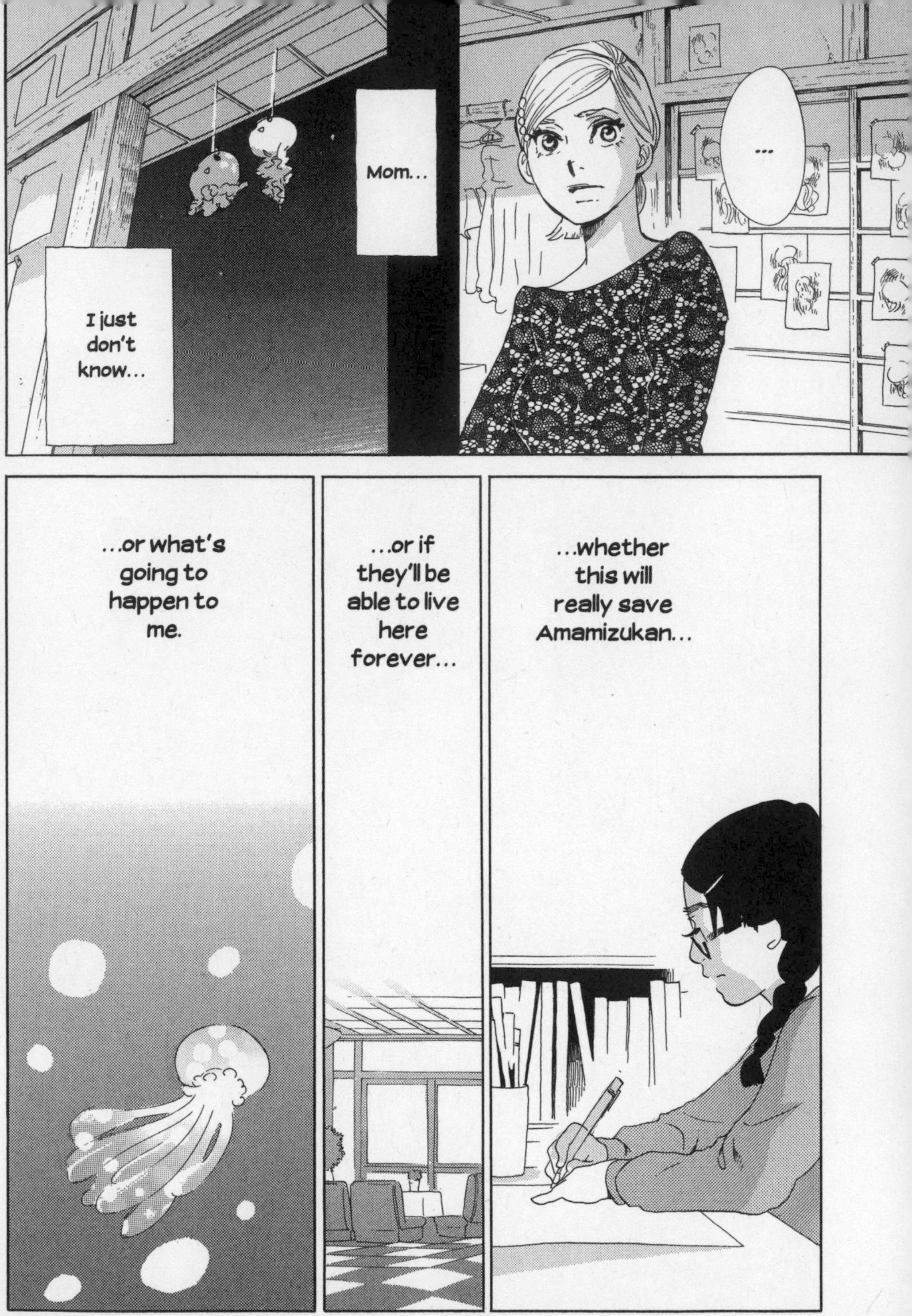
...
Mom...
I just don't know...
...whether this will really save Amamizukan...
...or if they'll be able to live here forever...
...or what's going to happen to me.

Episode 64
Far Away, So Close

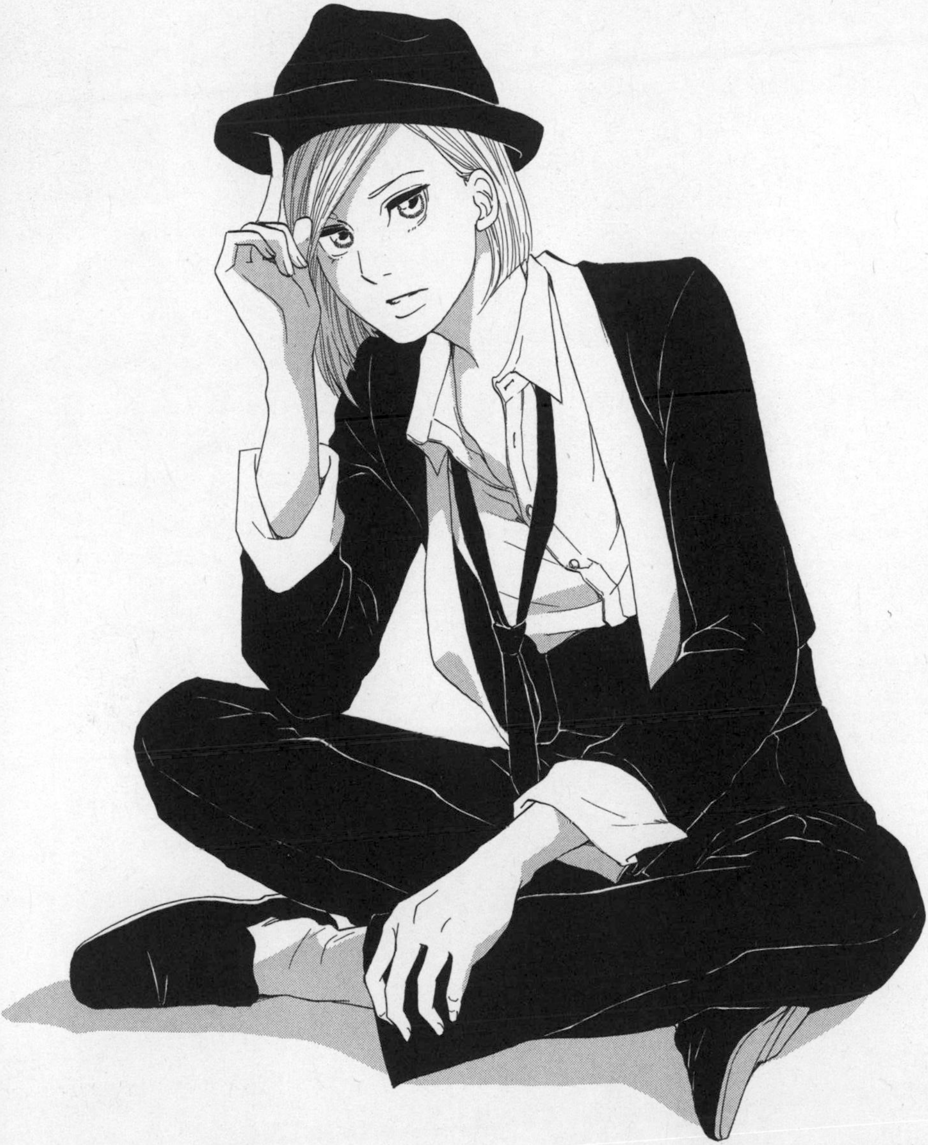

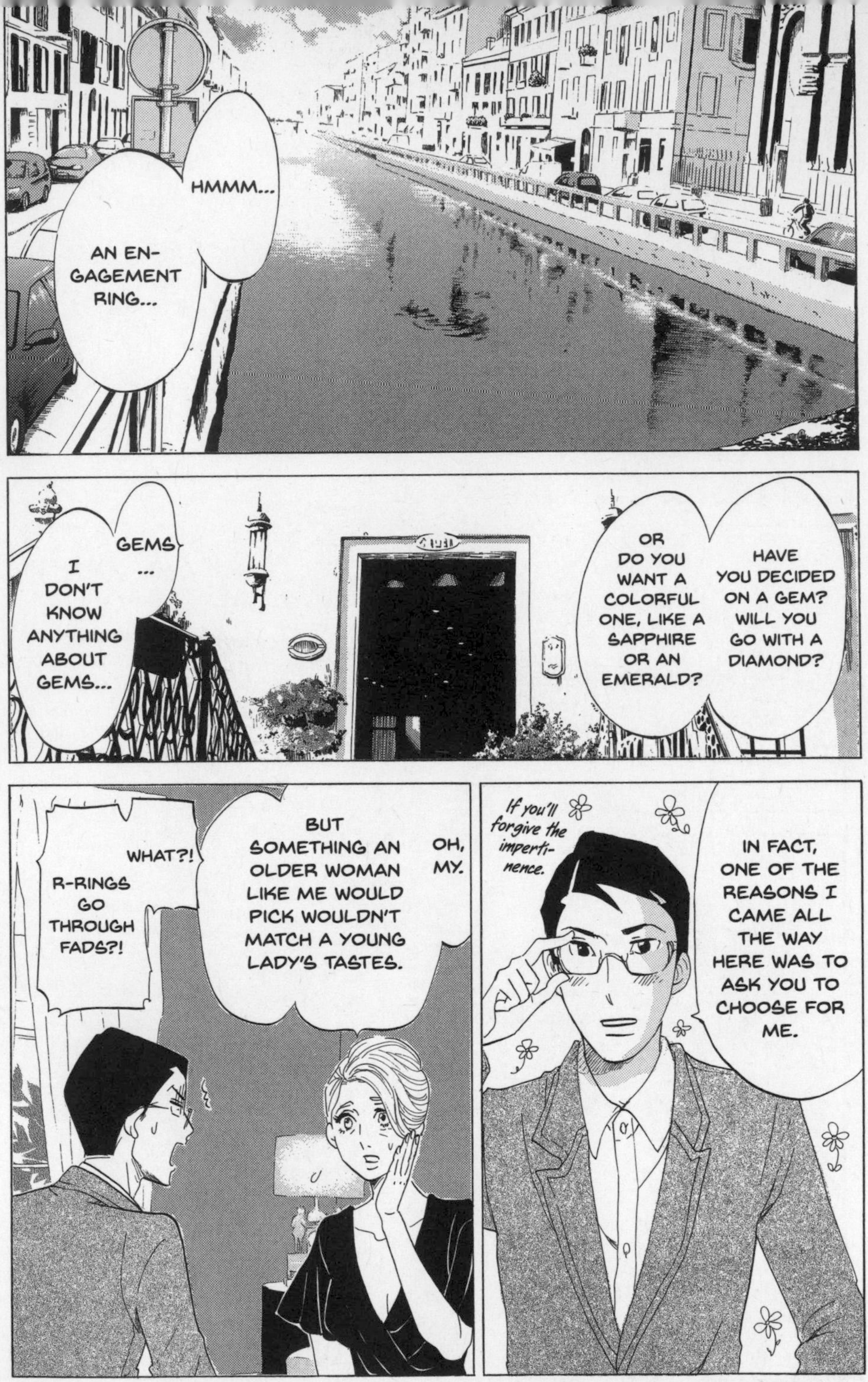
HMMM...
AN EN-GAGEMENT RING...
HAVE YOU DECIDED ON A GEM? WILL YOU GO WITH A DIAMOND?
OR DO YOU WANT A COLORFUL ONE, LIKE A SAPPHIRE OR AN EMERALD?
GEMS...
I DON'T KNOW ANYTHING ABOUT GEMS...
IN FACT, ONE OF THE REASONS I CAME ALL THE WAY HERE WAS TO ASK YOU TO CHOOSE FOR ME.
If you'll forgive the imperti-nence.
OH, MY.
BUT SOMETHING AN OLDER WOMAN LIKE ME WOULD PICK WOULDN'T MATCH A YOUNG LADY'S TASTES.
WHAT?!
R-RINGS GO THROUGH FADS?!

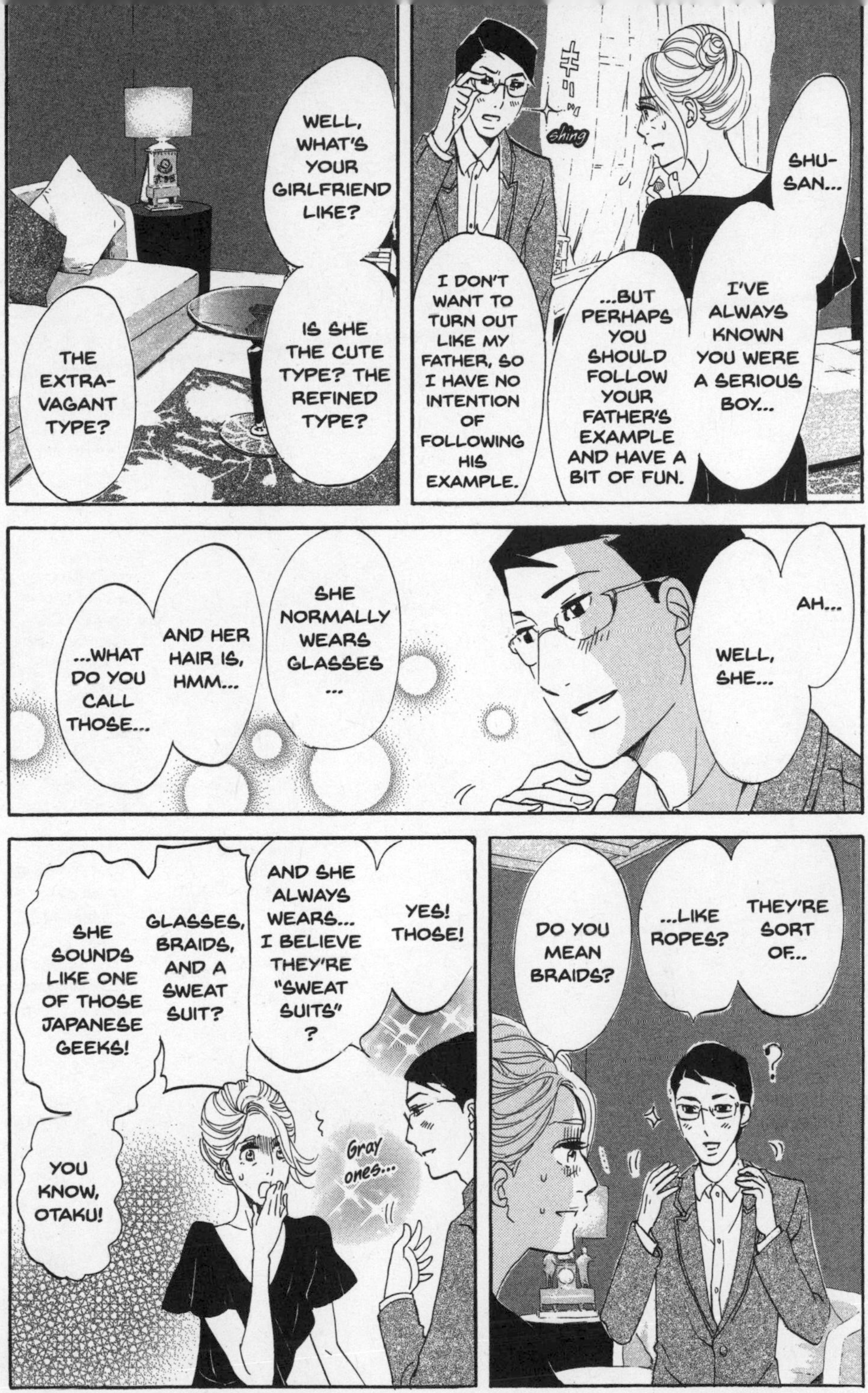
SHU-SAN...
I'VE ALWAYS KNOWN YOU WERE A SERIOUS BOY...
...BUT PERHAPS YOU SHOULD FOLLOW YOUR FATHER'S EXAMPLE AND HAVE A BIT OF FUN.
shing
I DON'T WANT TO TURN OUT LIKE MY FATHER, SO I HAVE NO INTENTION OF FOLLOWING HIS EXAMPLE.
WELL, WHAT'S YOUR GIRLFRIEND LIKE?
IS SHE THE CUTE TYPE? THE REFINED TYPE?
THE EXTRA-VAGANT TYPE?
AH...
WELL, SHE...
SHE NORMALLY WEARS GLASSES ...
AND HER HAIR IS, HMM...
...WHAT DO YOU CALL THOSE...
THEY'RE SORT OF...
...LIKE ROPES?
DO YOU MEAN BRAIDS?
YES! THOSE!
AND SHE ALWAYS WEARS... I BELIEVE THEY'RE "SWEAT SUITS" ?
Gray ones...
GLASSES, BRAIDS, AND A SWEAT SUIT?
SHE SOUNDS LIKE ONE OF THOSE JAPANESE GEEKS!
YOU KNOW, OTAKU!

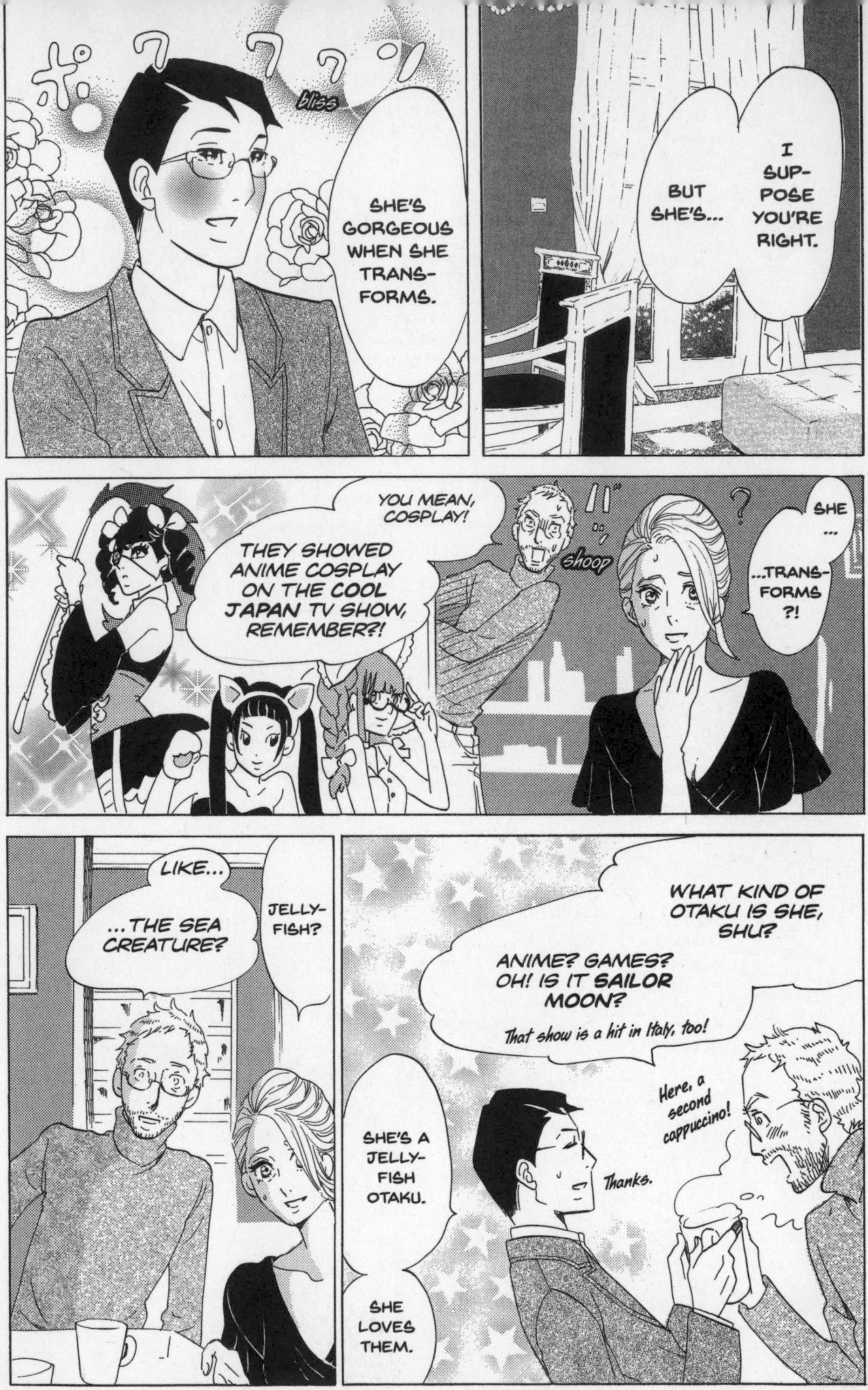
I SUPPOSE YOU'RE RIGHT.
BUT SHE'S...
ポワワワ
bliss
SHE'S GORGEOUS WHEN SHE TRANSFORMS.
SHE ... ...TRANSFORMS ?!
shoop
YOU MEAN, COSPLAY!
THEY SHOWED ANIME COSPLAY ON THE COOL JAPAN TV SHOW, REMEMBER?!
WHAT KIND OF OTAKU IS SHE, SHU?
ANIME? GAMES? OH! IS IT SAILOR MOON?
That show is a hit in Italy, too!
Here, a second cappuccino!
Thanks.
SHE'S A JELLYFISH OTAKU.
SHE LOVES THEM.
JELLYFISH?
LIKE...
...THE SEA CREATURE?

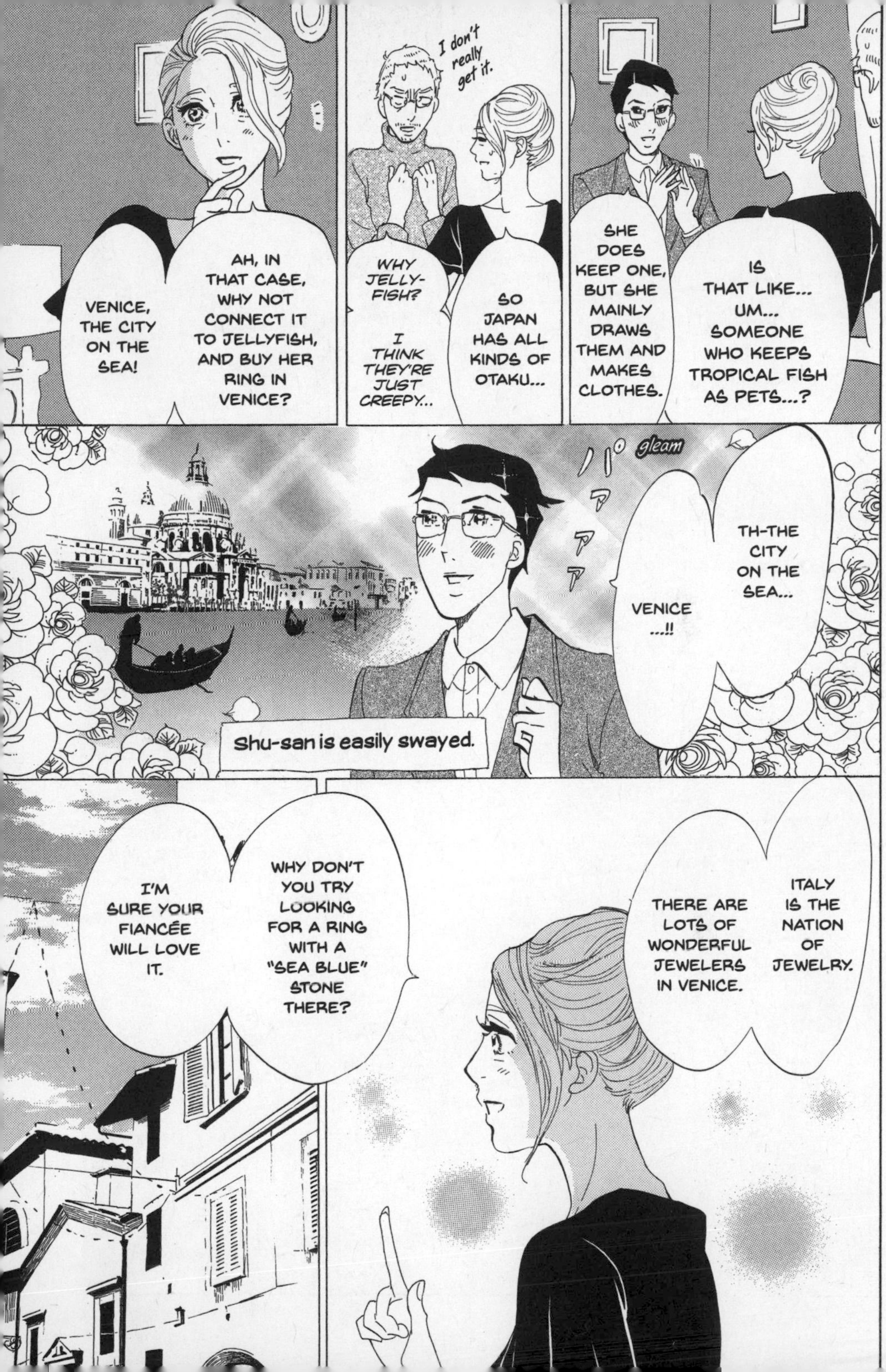
IS THAT LIKE... UM... SOMEONE WHO KEEPS TROPICAL FISH AS PETS...?
SHE DOES KEEP ONE, BUT SHE MAINLY DRAWS THEM AND MAKES CLOTHES.
I don't really get it.
SO JAPAN HAS ALL KINDS OF OTAKU...
WHY JELLYFISH? I THINK THEY'RE JUST CREEPY...
AH, IN THAT CASE, WHY NOT CONNECT IT TO JELLYFISH, AND BUY HER RING IN VENICE?
VENICE, THE CITY ON THE SEA!
gleam
TH-THE CITY ON THE SEA...
VENICE ...!!
Shu-san is easily swayed.
ITALY IS THE NATION OF JEWELRY.
THERE ARE LOTS OF WONDERFUL JEWELERS IN VENICE.
WHY DON'T YOU TRY LOOKING FOR A RING WITH A "SEA BLUE" STONE THERE?
I'M SURE YOUR FIANCÉE WILL LOVE IT.

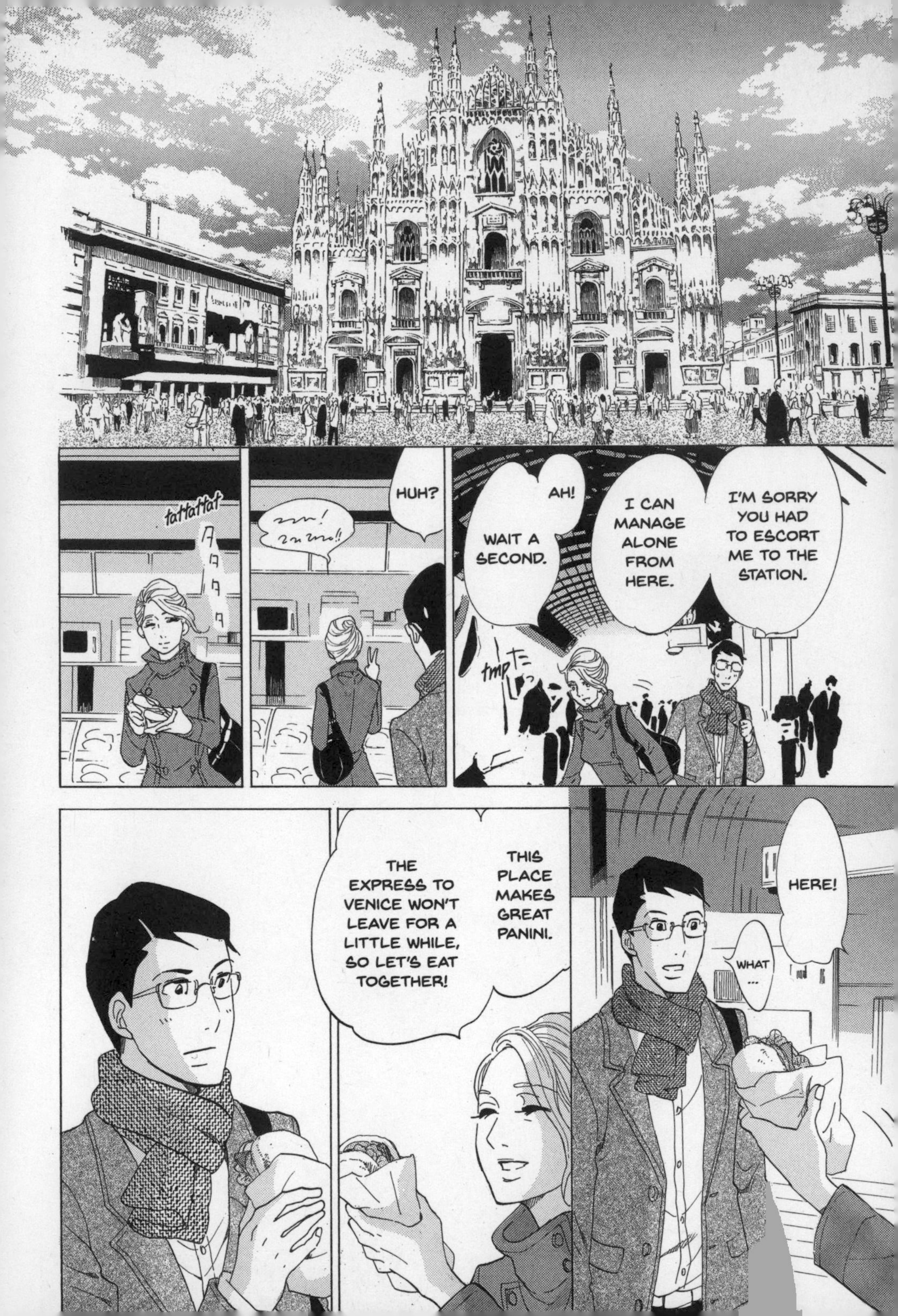
I'M SORRY YOU HAD TO ESCORT ME TO THE STATION.
I CAN MANAGE ALONE FROM HERE.
AH!
WAIT A SECOND.
tmp
HUH?
tattattat
HERE!
WHAT ...
THIS PLACE MAKES GREAT PANINI.
THE EXPRESS TO VENICE WON'T LEAVE FOR A LITTLE WHILE, SO LET'S EAT TOGETHER!

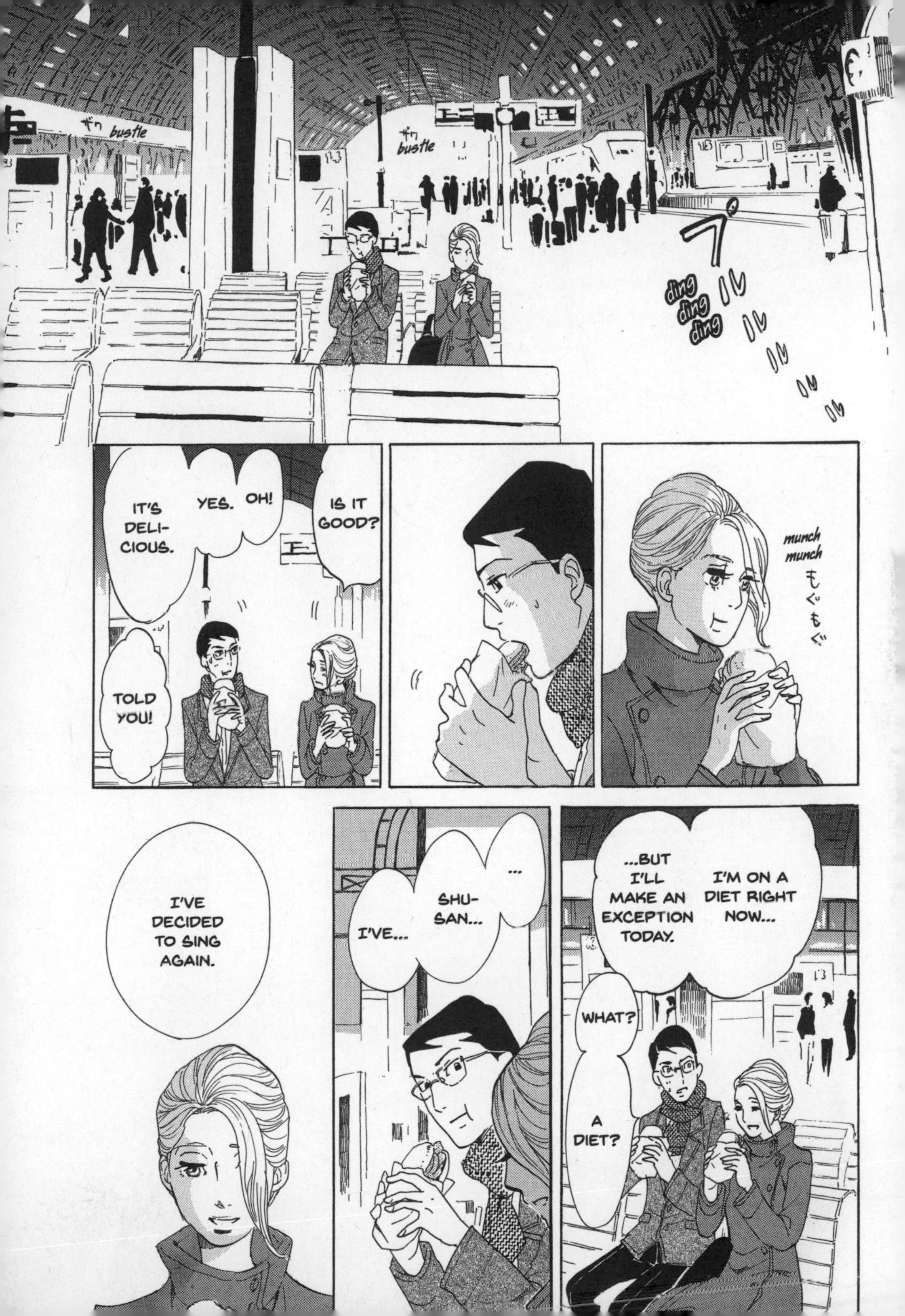
bustle
bustle
ding ding ding
munch munch
IS IT GOOD?
OH!
YES.
IT'S DELICIOUS.
TOLD YOU!
I'M ON A DIET RIGHT NOW...
...BUT I'LL MAKE AN EXCEPTION TODAY.
WHAT?
A DIET?
...
SHU-SAN...
I'VE...
I'VE DECIDED TO SING AGAIN.

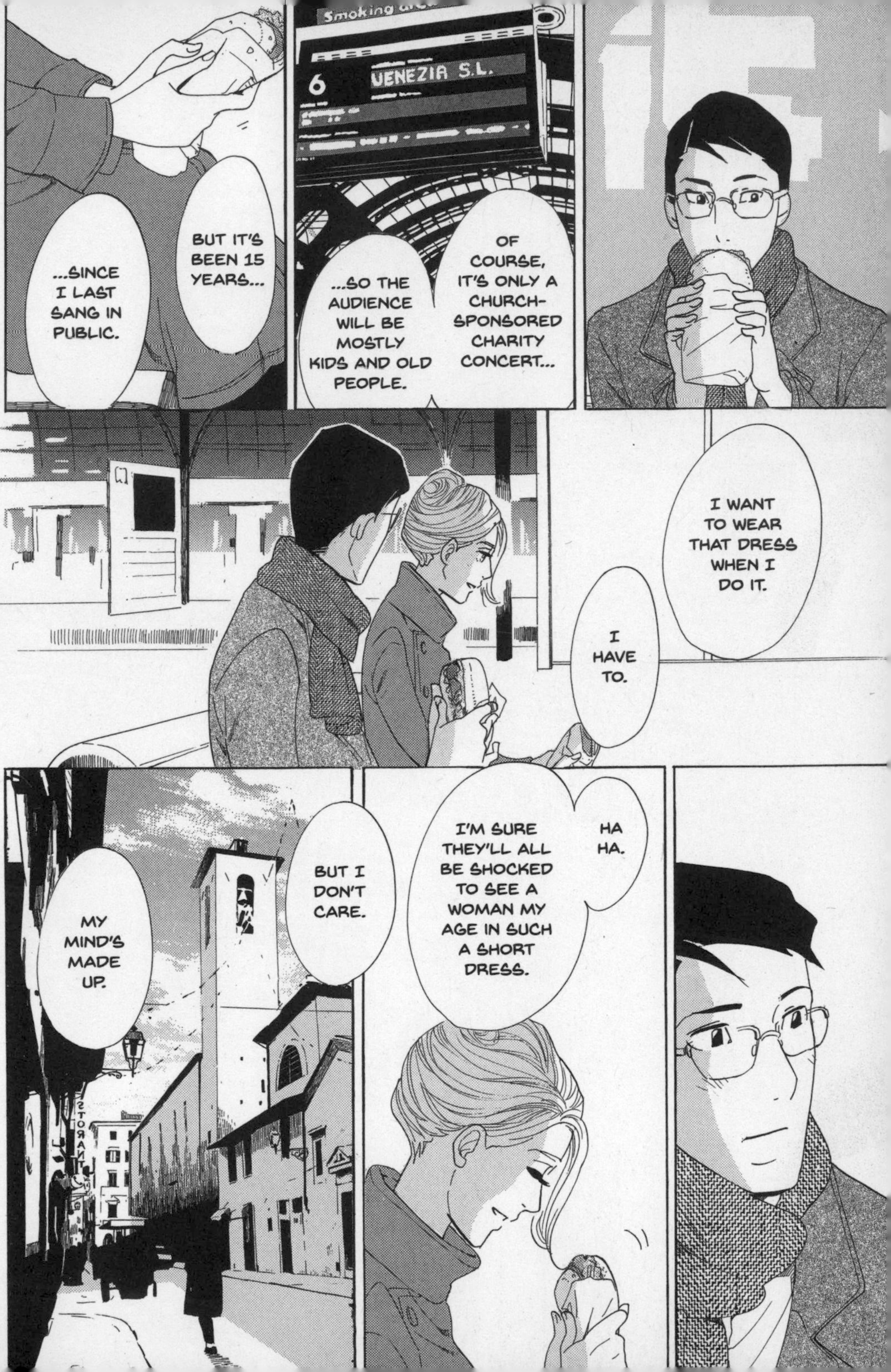
6
VENEZIA S.L.
OF COURSE, IT'S ONLY A CHURCH-SPONSORED CHARITY CONCERT...
...SO THE AUDIENCE WILL BE MOSTLY KIDS AND OLD PEOPLE.
BUT IT'S BEEN 15 YEARS...
...SINCE I LAST SANG IN PUBLIC.
I WANT TO WEAR THAT DRESS WHEN I DO IT.
I HAVE TO.
HA HA.
I'M SURE THEY'LL ALL BE SHOCKED TO SEE A WOMAN MY AGE IN SUCH A SHORT DRESS.
BUT I DON'T CARE.
MY MIND'S MADE UP.

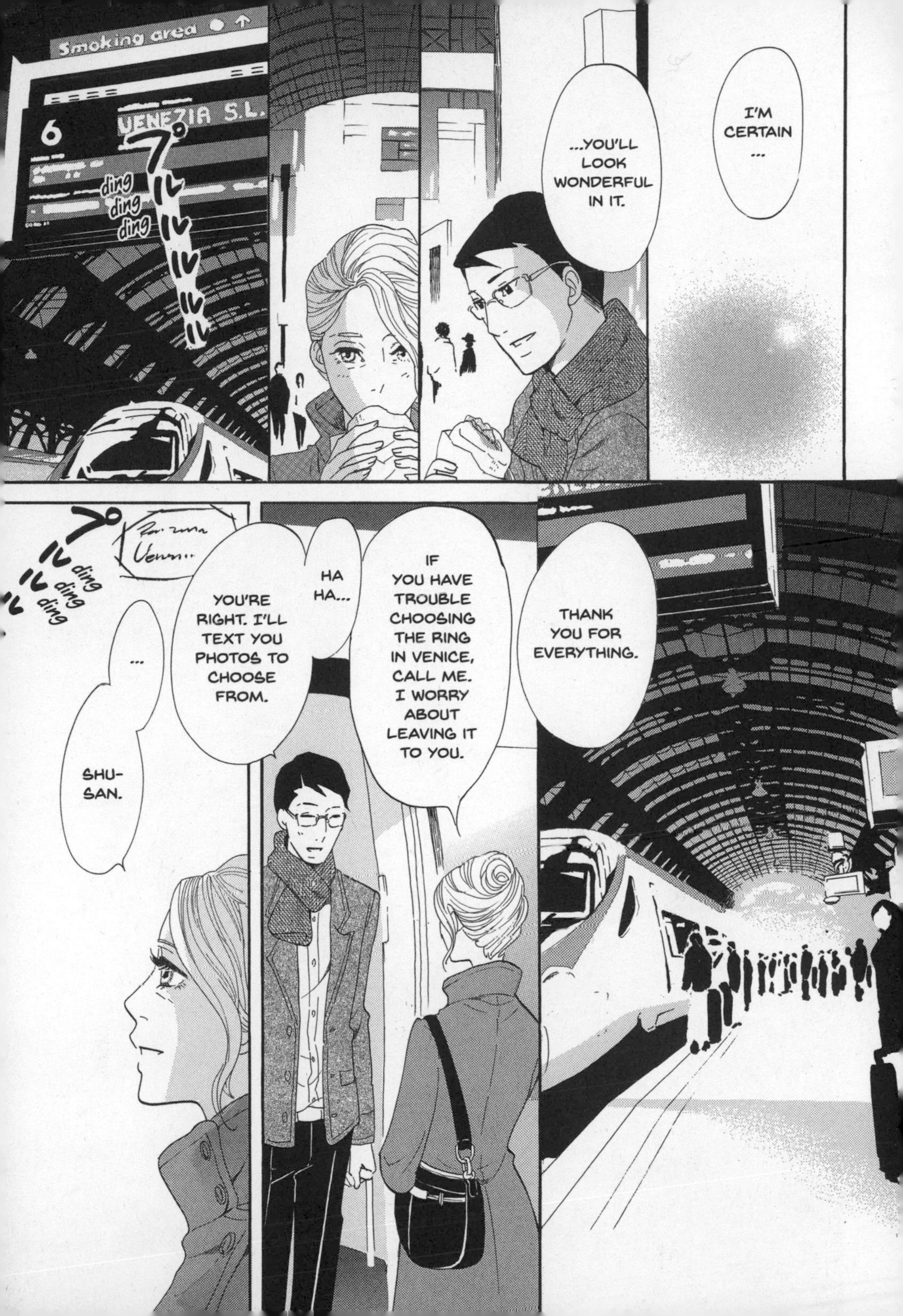
I'M CERTAIN ...
...YOU'LL LOOK WONDERFUL IN IT.
Smoking area
6
VENEZIA S.L.
プルルルルル
ding ding ding
THANK YOU FOR EVERYTHING.
IF YOU HAVE TROUBLE CHOOSING THE RING IN VENICE, CALL ME. I WORRY ABOUT LEAVING IT TO YOU.
HA HA...
YOU'RE RIGHT. I'LL TEXT YOU PHOTOS TO CHOOSE FROM.
プルルル
ding ding ding
...
SHU-SAN.

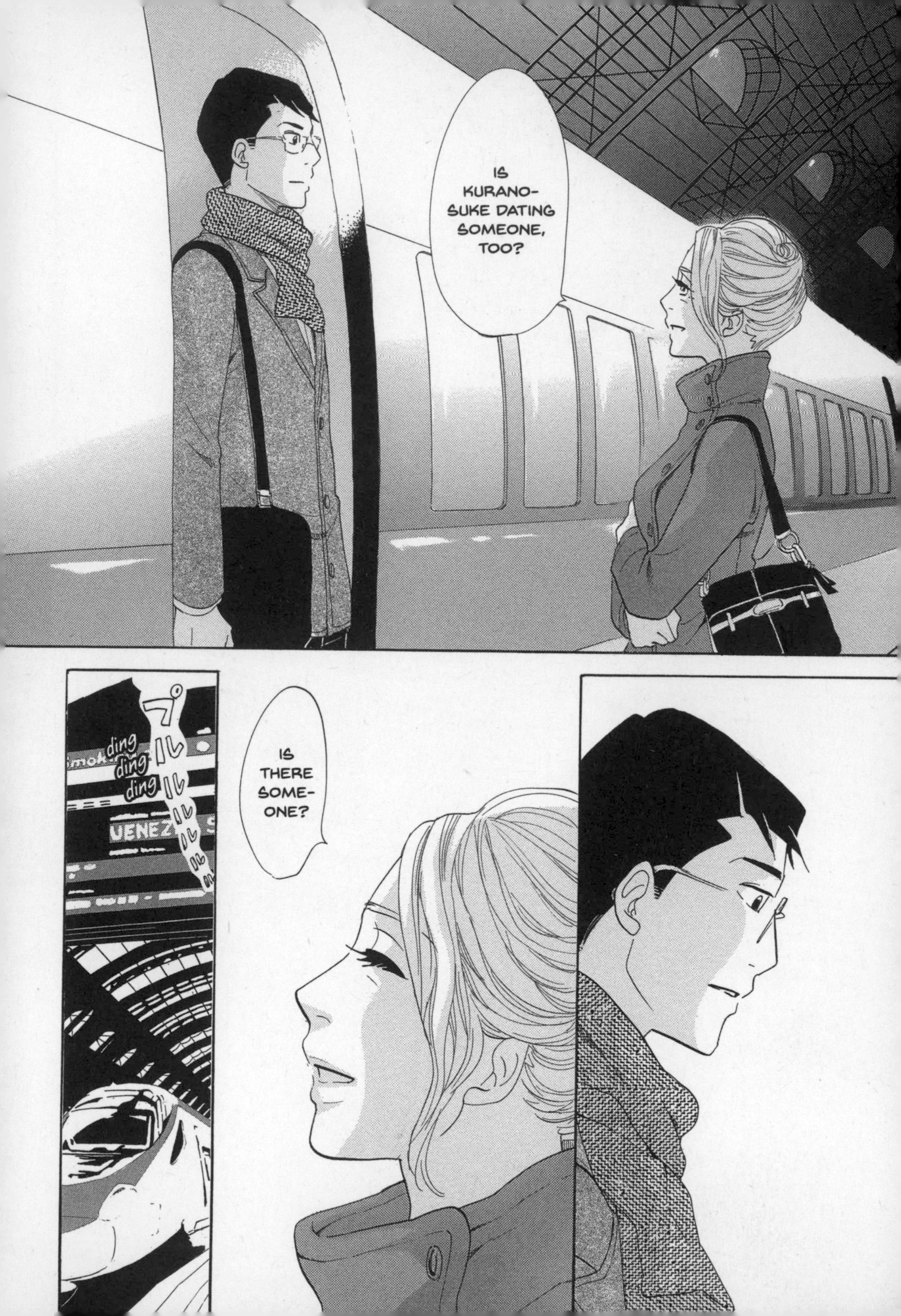
IS KURANOSUKE DATING SOMEONE, TOO?
IS THERE SOMEONE?
ding ding ding

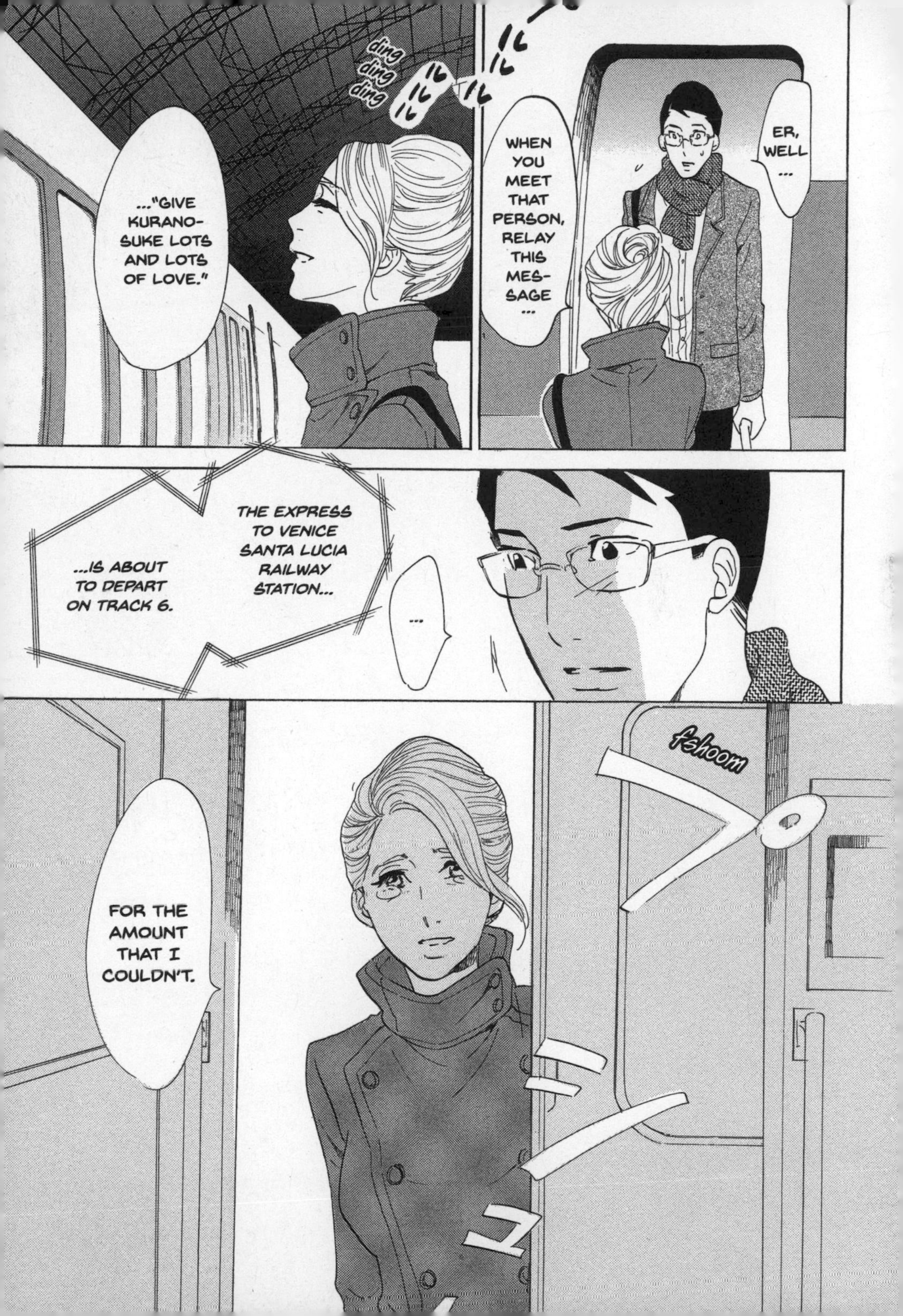
ER, WELL ...
WHEN YOU MEET THAT PERSON, RELAY THIS MESSAGE ...
ding ding ding
..."GIVE KURANOSUKE LOTS AND LOTS OF LOVE."
...
THE EXPRESS TO VENICE SANTA LUCIA RAILWAY STATION...
...IS ABOUT TO DEPART ON TRACK 6.
fshoom
FOR THE AMOUNT THAT I COULDN'T.

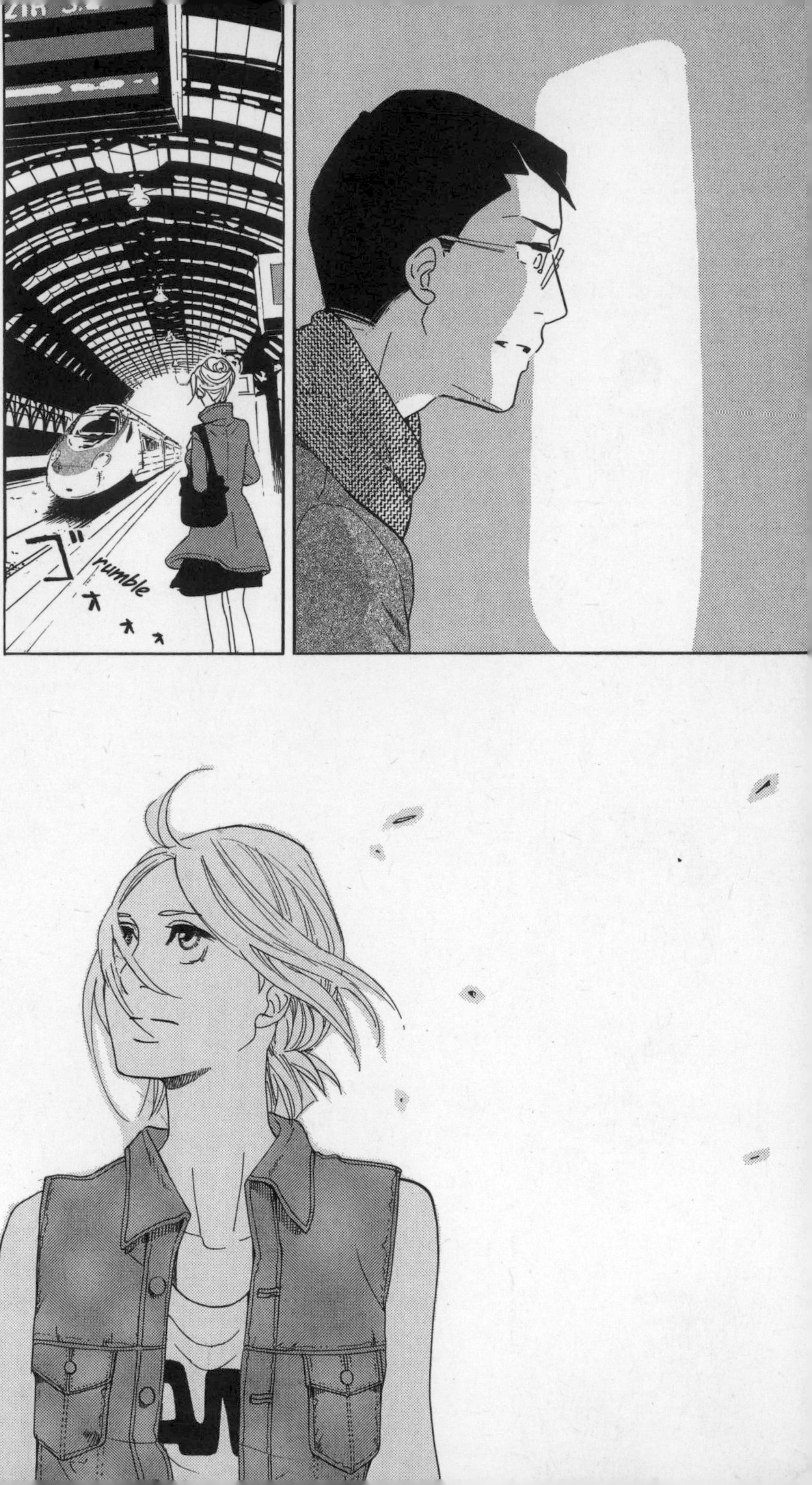
rumble

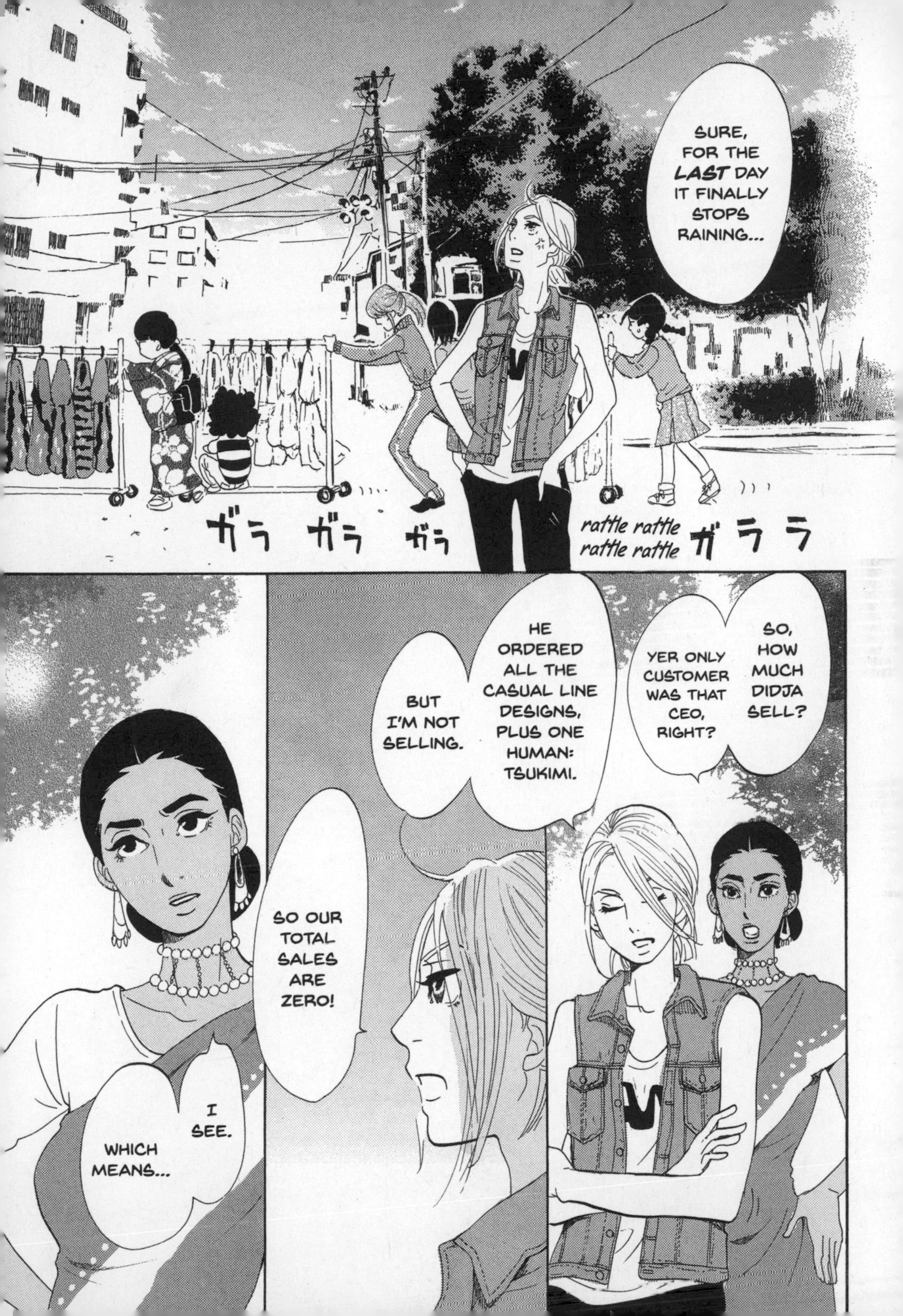
SURE, FOR THE LAST DAY IT FINALLY STOPS RAINING...
rattle rattle rattle rattle
ガララ
ガラ ガラ ガラ
SO, HOW MUCH DIDJA SELL?
YER ONLY CUSTOMER WAS THAT CEO, RIGHT?
HE ORDERED ALL THE CASUAL LINE DESIGNS, PLUS ONE HUMAN: TSUKIMI.
BUT I'M NOT SELLING.
SO OUR TOTAL SALES ARE ZERO!
I SEE.
WHICH MEANS...

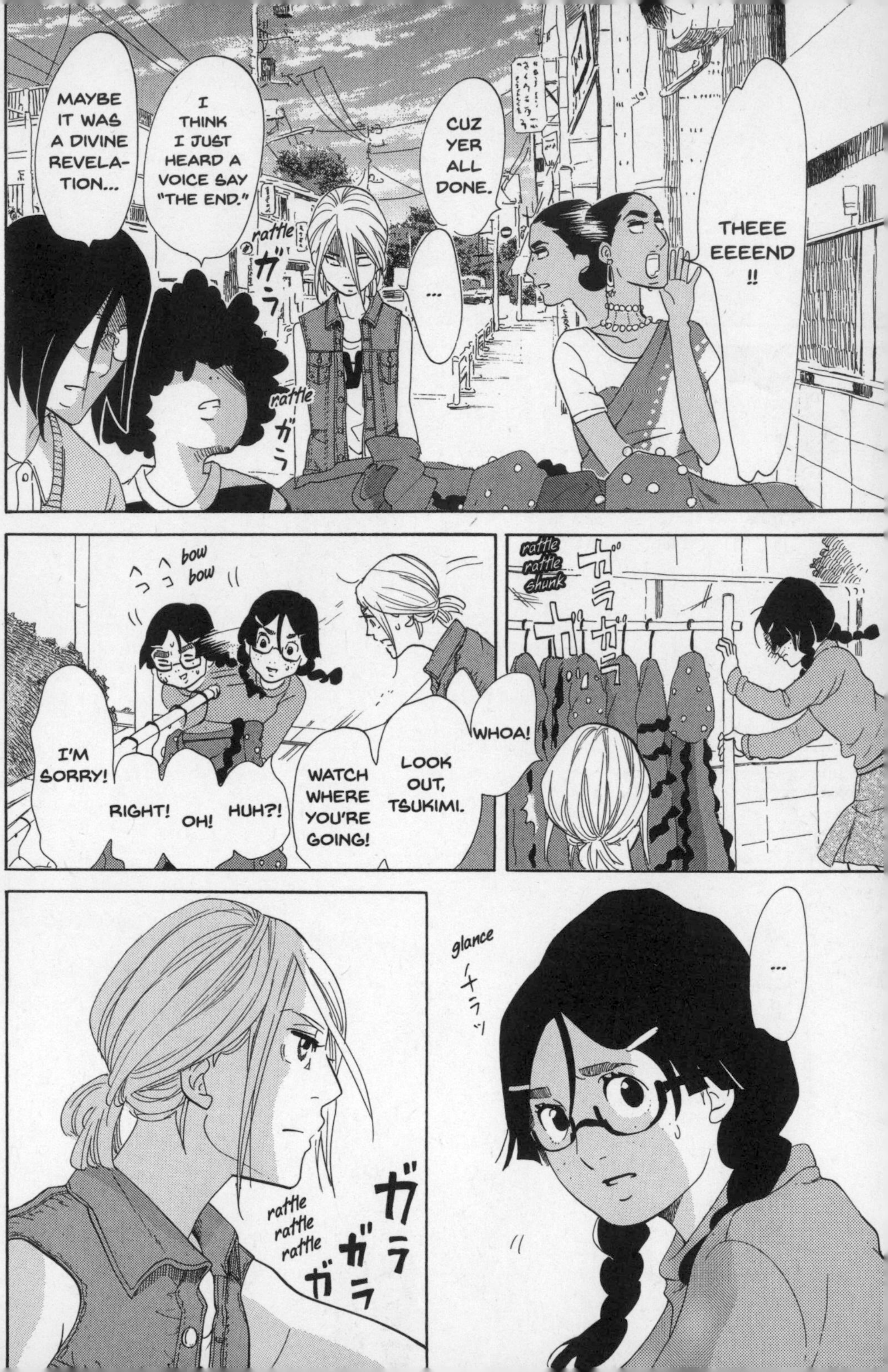
THEEE EEEEND !!
CUZ YER ALL DONE.
...
rattle
rattle
I THINK I JUST HEARD A VOICE SAY "THE END."
MAYBE IT WAS A DIVINE REVELATION...
rattle rattle shunk
WHOA!
LOOK OUT, TSUKIMI.
WATCH WHERE YOU'RE GOING!
HUH?!
OH!
bow bow
RIGHT!
I'M SORRY!
...
glance
rattle rattle rattle

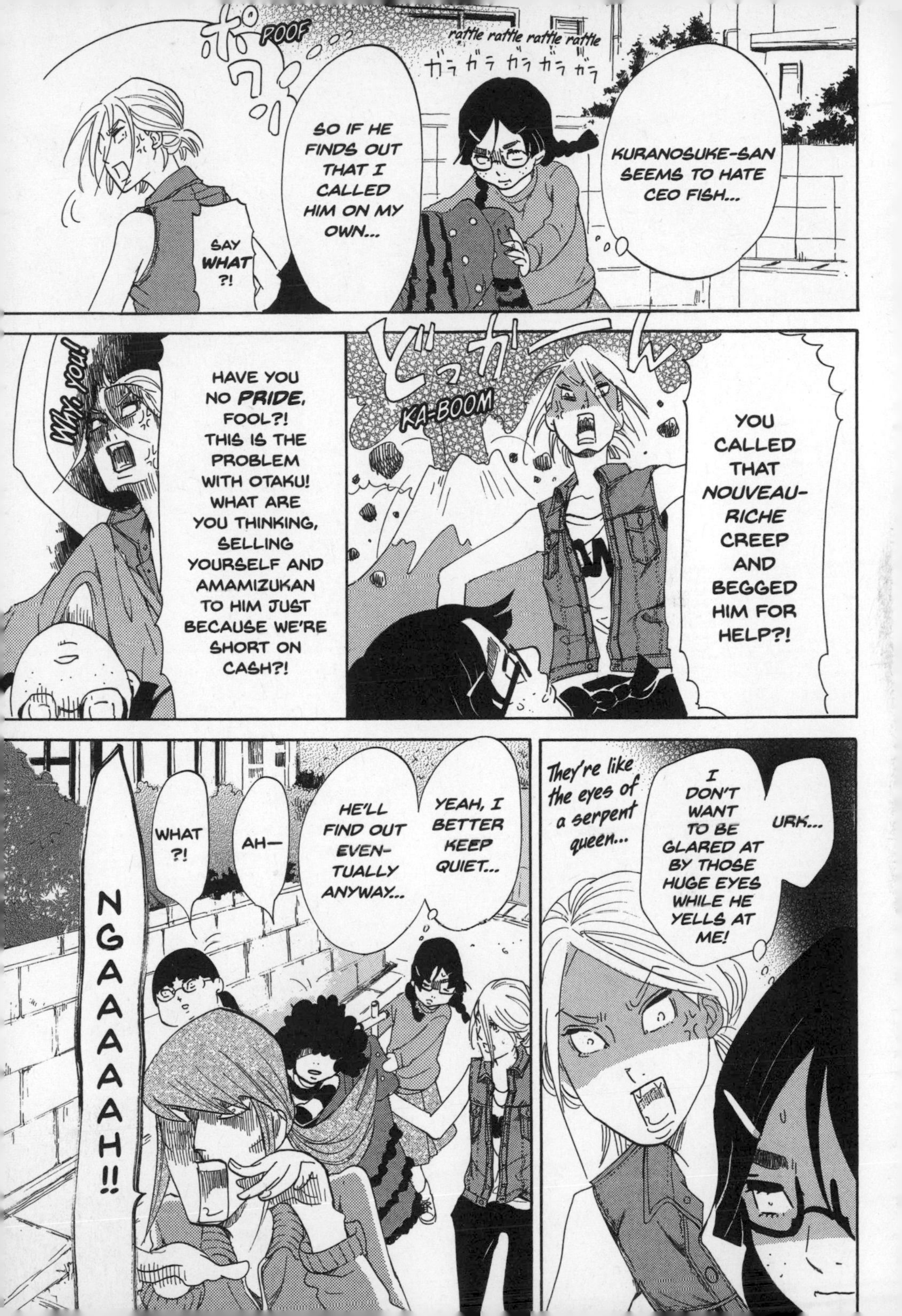
rattle rattle rattle rattle
ガラガラガラガラガラ
KURANOSUKE-SAN SEEMS TO HATE CEO FISH...
SO IF HE FINDS OUT THAT I CALLED HIM ON MY OWN...
ポワ
POOF
SAY WHAT ?!
どっかーん
KA-BOOM
YOU CALLED THAT NOUVEAU-RICHE CREEP AND BEGGED HIM FOR HELP?!
HAVE YOU NO PRIDE, FOOL?! THIS IS THE PROBLEM WITH OTAKU! WHAT ARE YOU THINKING, SELLING YOURSELF AND AMAMIZUKAN TO HIM JUST BECAUSE WE'RE SHORT ON CASH?!
Why you!
URK...
I DON'T WANT TO BE GLARED AT BY THOSE HUGE EYES WHILE HE YELLS AT ME!
They're like the eyes of a serpent queen...
YEAH, I BETTER KEEP QUIET...
HE'LL FIND OUT EVENTUALLY ANYWAY...
AH—
WHAT ?!
NGAAAAAAH!!

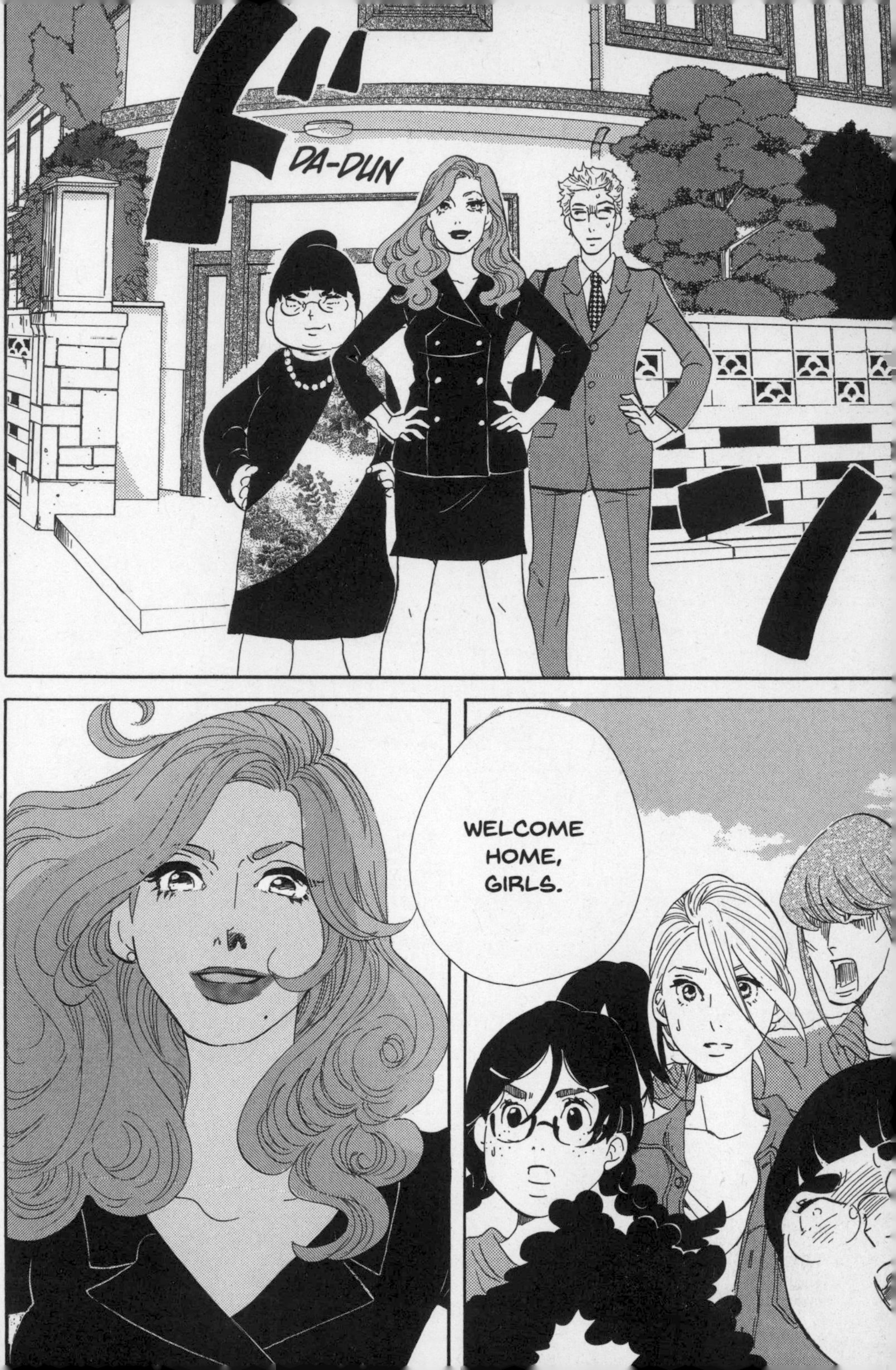
DA-DUN
WELCOME HOME, GIRLS.

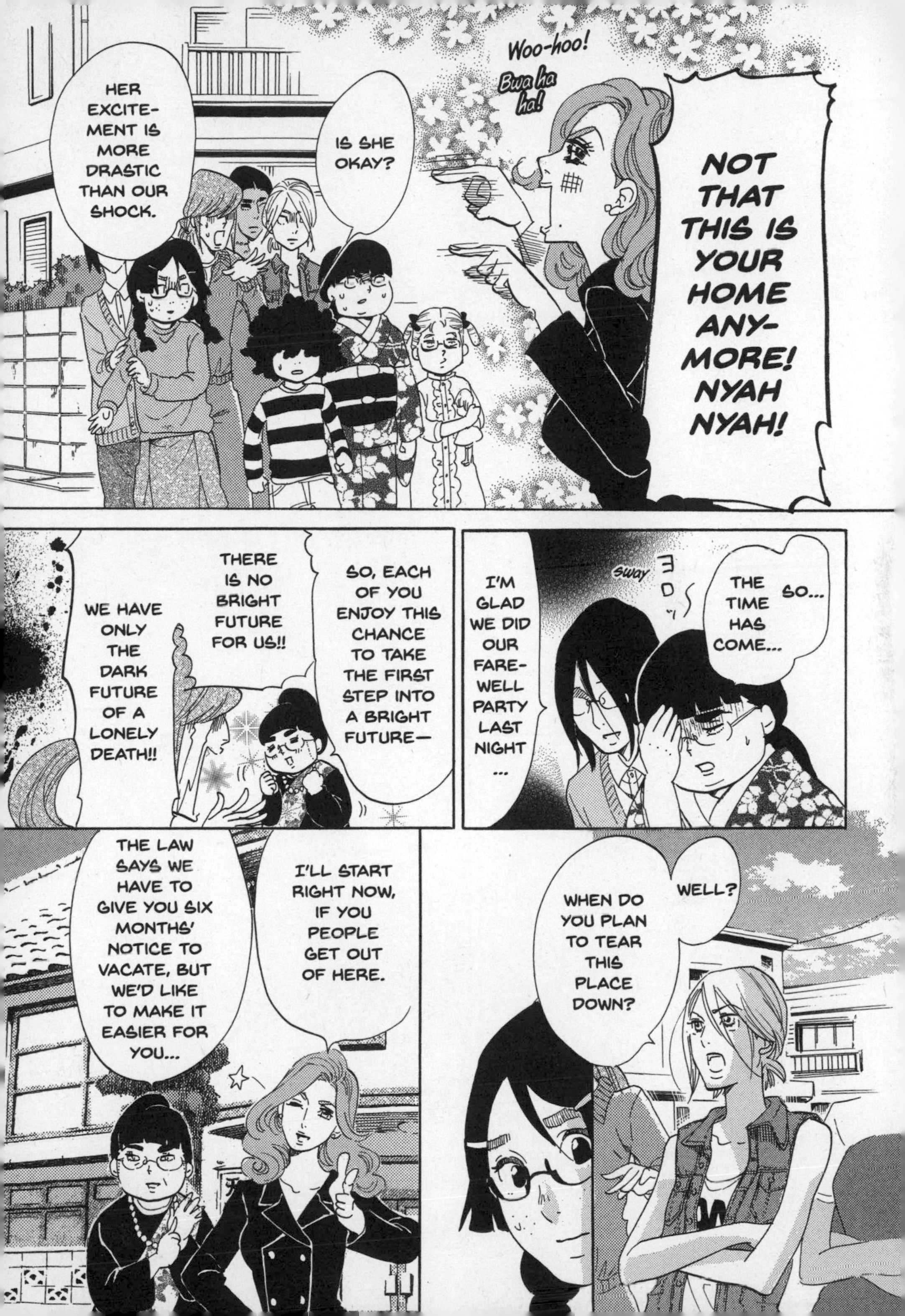
Woo-hoo!
Bwa ha ha!
NOT THAT THIS IS YOUR HOME ANYMORE! NYAH NYAH!
IS SHE OKAY?
HER EXCITEMENT IS MORE DRASTIC THAN OUR SHOCK.
SO... THE TIME HAS COME...
sway
I'M GLAD WE DID OUR FAREWELL PARTY LAST NIGHT ...
SO, EACH OF YOU ENJOY THIS CHANCE TO TAKE THE FIRST STEP INTO A BRIGHT FUTURE—
THERE IS NO BRIGHT FUTURE FOR US!!
WE HAVE ONLY THE DARK FUTURE OF A LONELY DEATH!!
WELL?
WHEN DO YOU PLAN TO TEAR THIS PLACE DOWN?
I'LL START RIGHT NOW, IF YOU PEOPLE GET OUT OF HERE.
THE LAW SAYS WE HAVE TO GIVE YOU SIX MONTHS' NOTICE TO VACATE, BUT WE'D LIKE TO MAKE IT EASIER FOR YOU...

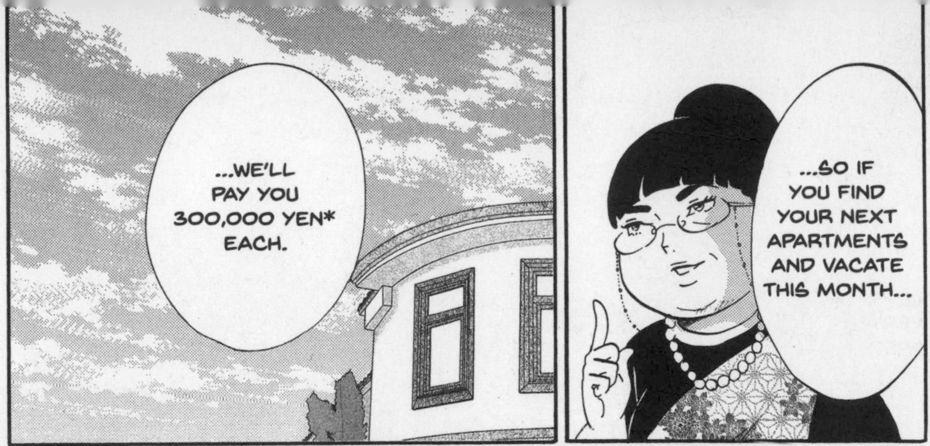
...SO IF YOU FIND YOUR NEXT APARTMENTS AND VACATE THIS MONTH...
...WE'LL PAY YOU 300,000 YEN* EACH.

*About $3,000 USD.

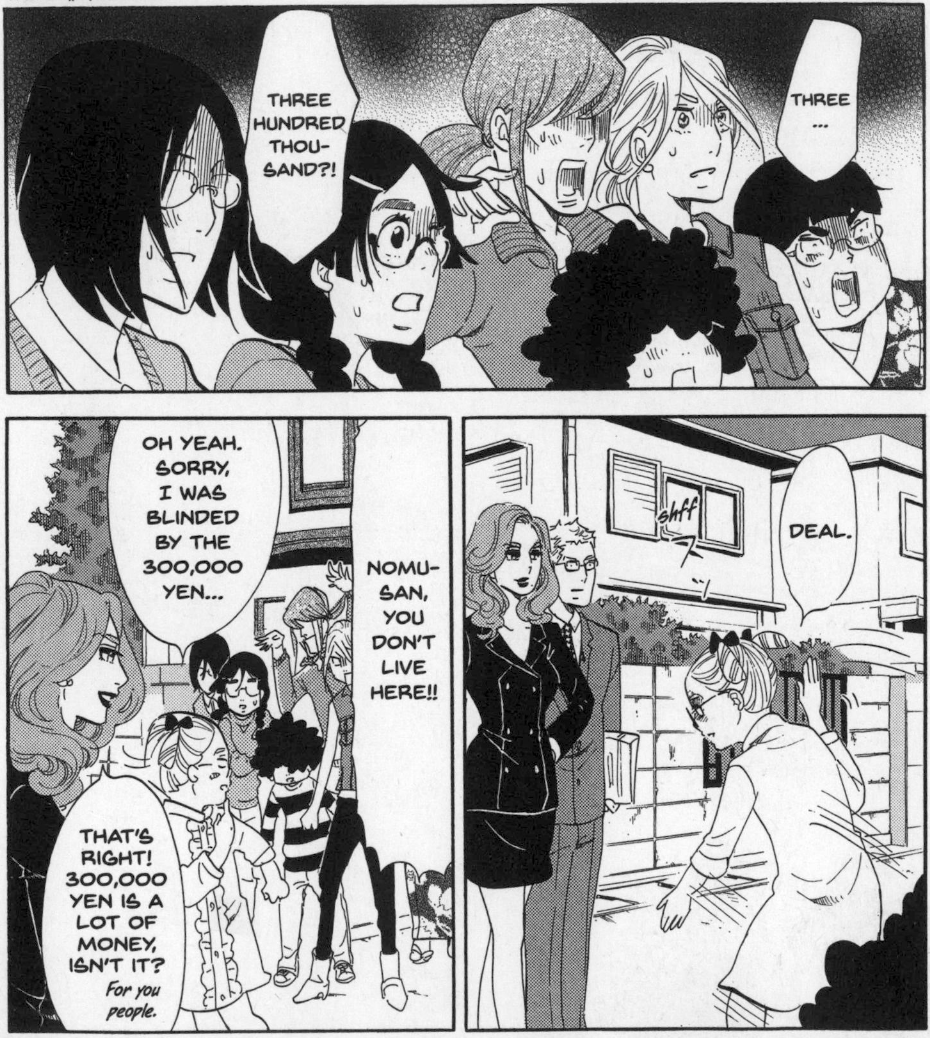
THREE ...
THREE HUNDRED THOU-SAND?!
shff
DEAL.
NOMU-SAN, YOU DON'T LIVE HERE!!
OH YEAH. SORRY, I WAS BLINDED BY THE 300,000 YEN...
THAT'S RIGHT! 300,000 YEN IS A LOT OF MONEY, ISN'T IT?
For you people.

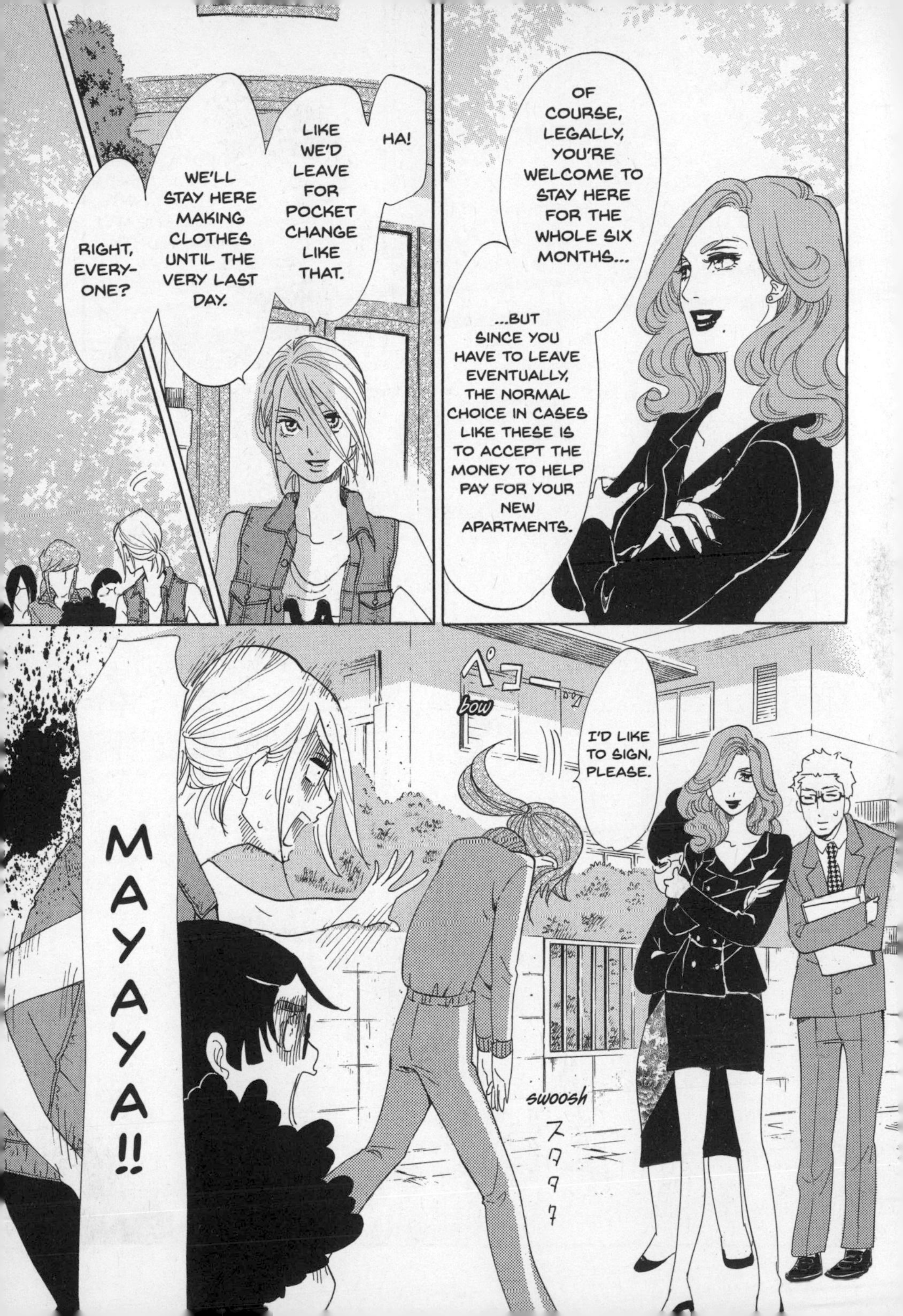
OF COURSE, LEGALLY, YOU'RE WELCOME TO STAY HERE FOR THE WHOLE SIX MONTHS...
...BUT SINCE YOU HAVE TO LEAVE EVENTUALLY, THE NORMAL CHOICE IN CASES LIKE THESE IS TO ACCEPT THE MONEY TO HELP PAY FOR YOUR NEW APARTMENTS.
HA!
LIKE WE'D LEAVE FOR POCKET CHANGE LIKE THAT.
WE'LL STAY HERE MAKING CLOTHES UNTIL THE VERY LAST DAY.
RIGHT, EVERY-ONE?
bow
I'D LIKE TO SIGN, PLEASE.
swoosh
MAYAYA!!

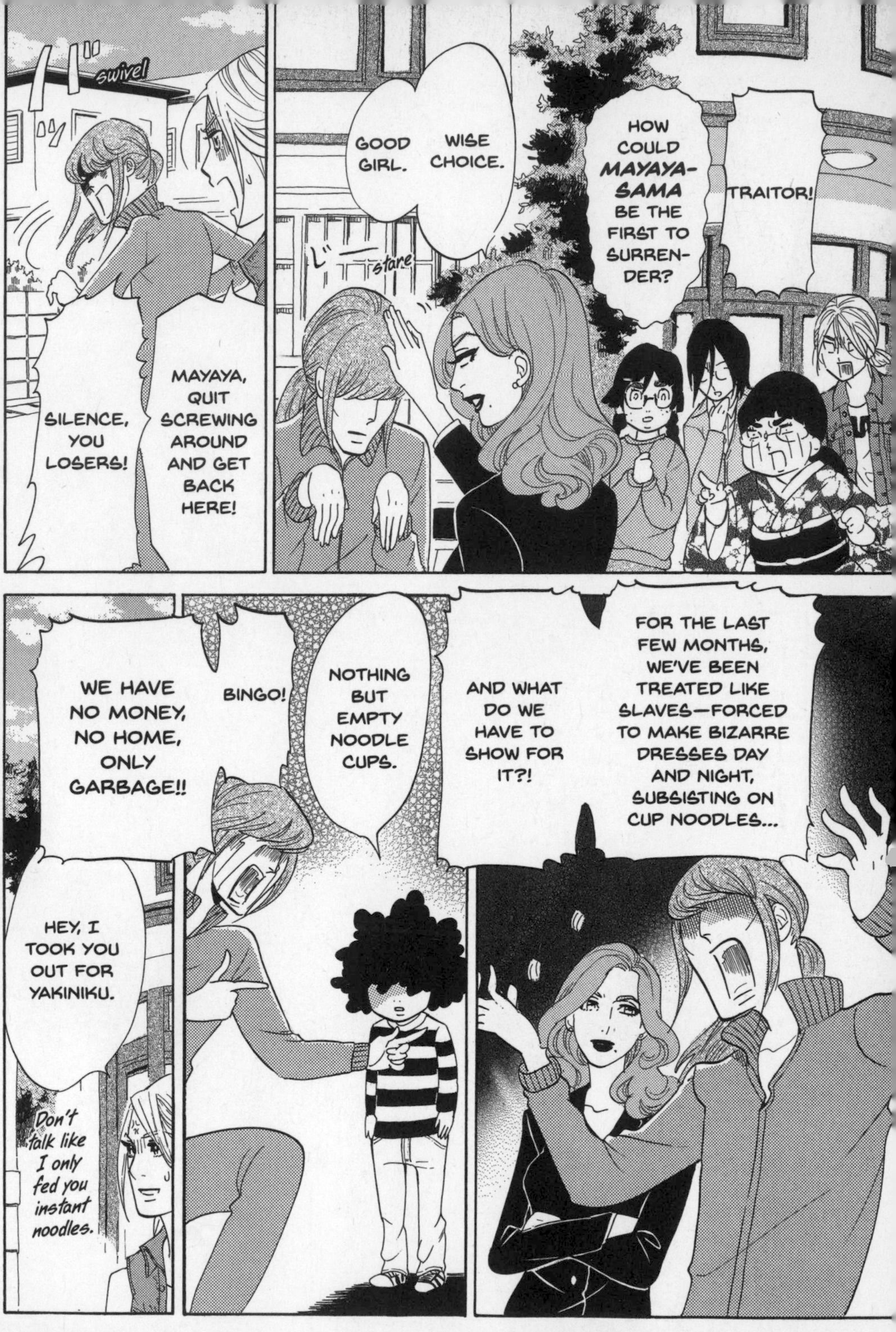
TRAITOR!
HOW COULD MAYAYA-SAMA BE THE FIRST TO SURRENDER?
GOOD GIRL. WISE CHOICE.
stare
swivel
MAYAYA, QUIT SCREWING AROUND AND GET BACK HERE!
SILENCE, YOU LOSERS!
FOR THE LAST FEW MONTHS, WE'VE BEEN TREATED LIKE SLAVES—FORCED TO MAKE BIZARRE DRESSES DAY AND NIGHT, SUBSISTING ON CUP NOODLES...
AND WHAT DO WE HAVE TO SHOW FOR IT?!
NOTHING BUT EMPTY NOODLE CUPS.
BINGO!
WE HAVE NO MONEY, NO HOME, ONLY GARBAGE!!
HEY, I TOOK YOU OUT FOR YAKINIKU.
Don't talk like I only fed you instant noodles.

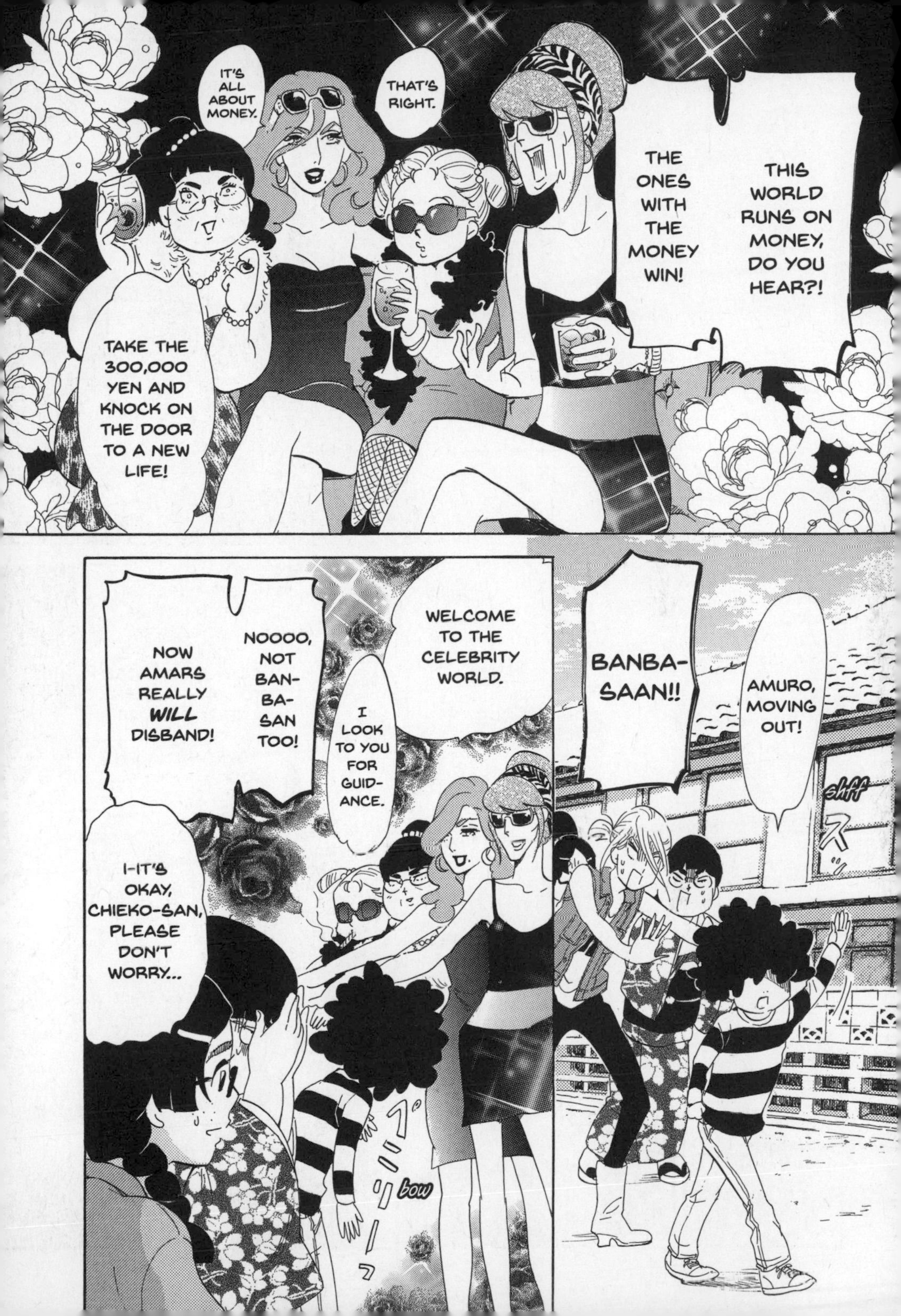
THIS WORLD RUNS ON MONEY, DO YOU HEAR?!
THE ONES WITH THE MONEY WIN!
THAT'S RIGHT.
IT'S ALL ABOUT MONEY.
TAKE THE 300,000 YEN AND KNOCK ON THE DOOR TO A NEW LIFE!
AMURO, MOVING OUT!
BANBA-SAAN!!
shff
WELCOME TO THE CELEBRITY WORLD.
NOOOO, NOT BAN-BA-SAN TOO!
NOW AMARS REALLY WILL DISBAND!
I LOOK TO YOU FOR GUIDANCE.
I-IT'S OKAY, CHIEKO-SAN, PLEASE DON'T WORRY...
bow

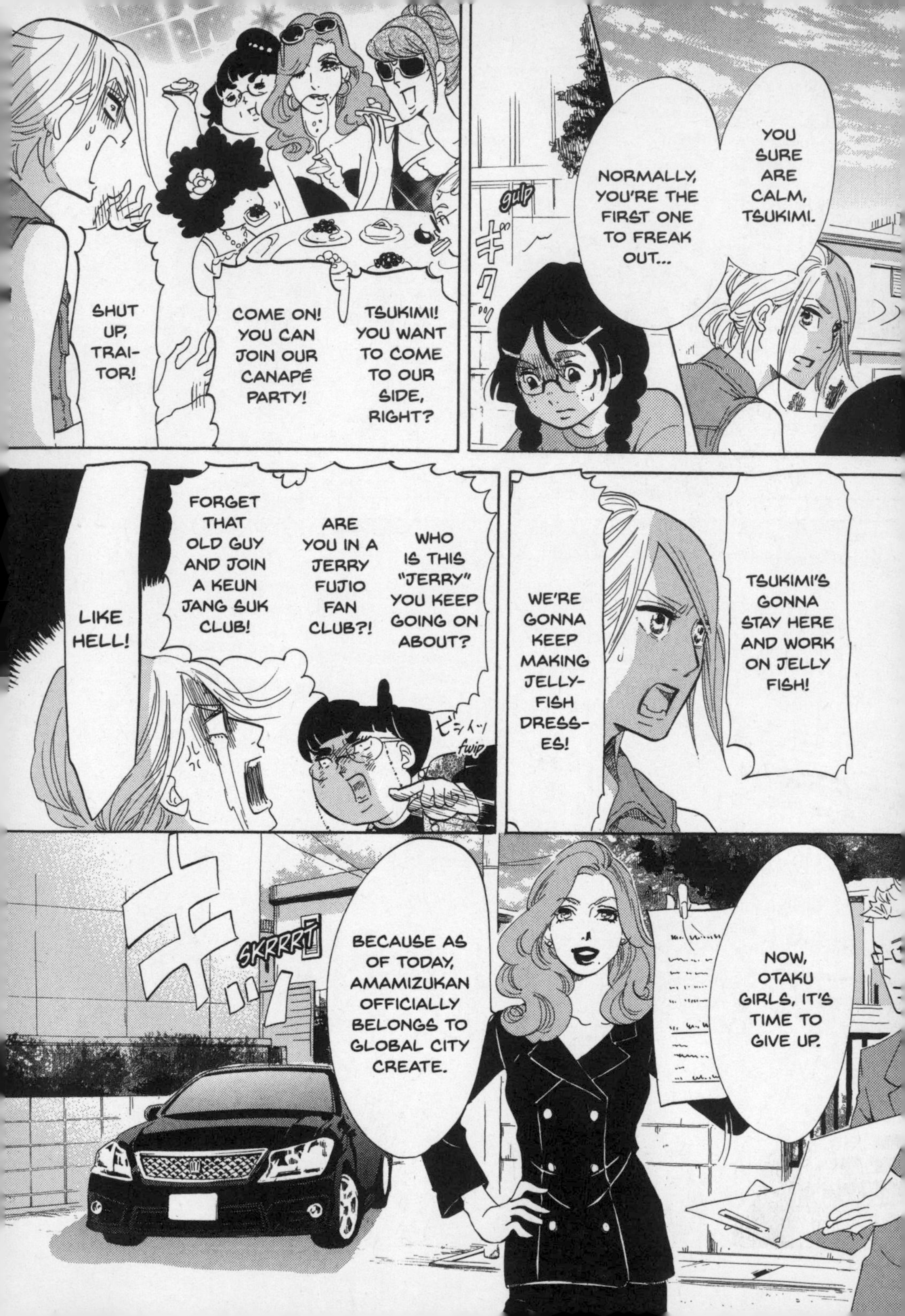
YOU SURE ARE CALM, TSUKIMI.
NORMALLY, YOU'RE THE FIRST ONE TO FREAK OUT...
gulp
TSUKIMI! YOU WANT TO COME TO OUR SIDE, RIGHT?
COME ON! YOU CAN JOIN OUR CANAPÉ PARTY!
SHUT UP, TRAI-TOR!
TSUKIMI'S GONNA STAY HERE AND WORK ON JELLY FISH!
WE'RE GONNA KEEP MAKING JELLY-FISH DRESS-ES!
WHO IS THIS "JERRY" YOU KEEP GOING ON ABOUT?
ARE YOU IN A JERRY FUJIO FAN CLUB?!
FORGET THAT OLD GUY AND JOIN A KEUN JANG SUK CLUB!
LIKE HELL!
fwip
NOW, OTAKU GIRLS, IT'S TIME TO GIVE UP.
BECAUSE AS OF TODAY, AMAMIZUKAN OFFICIALLY BELONGS TO GLOBAL CITY CREATE.
SKRRRT

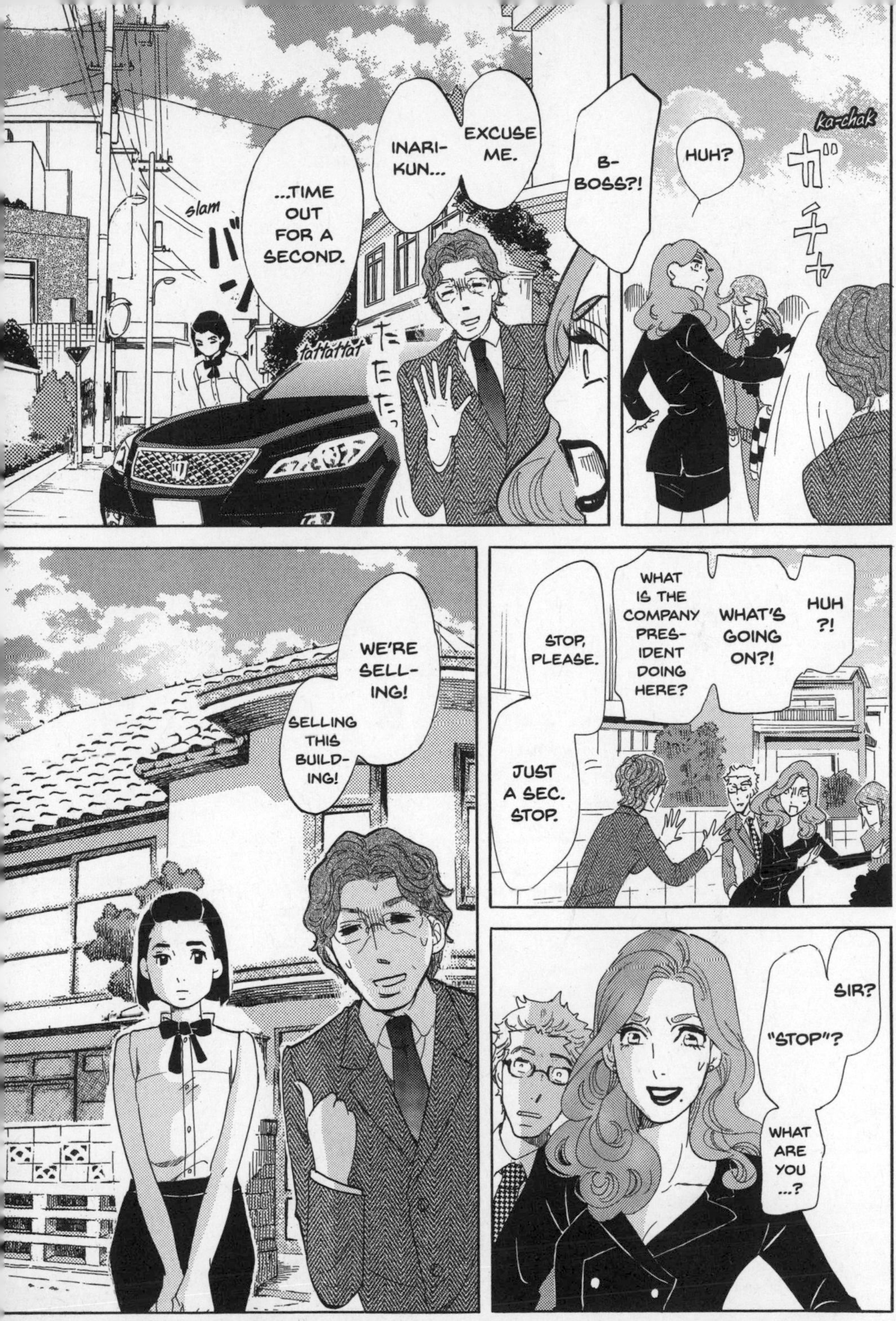
ka-chak
ガチャ
HUH?
B-BOSS?!
EXCUSE ME.
INARI-KUN...
...TIME OUT FOR A SECOND.
slam
バン
tattattat
たたたっ
HUH?!
WHAT'S GOING ON?!
WHAT IS THE COMPANY PRESIDENT DOING HERE?
STOP, PLEASE.
JUST A SEC. STOP.
SIR?
"STOP"?
WHAT ARE YOU ...?
WE'RE SELLING!
SELLING THIS BUILDING!

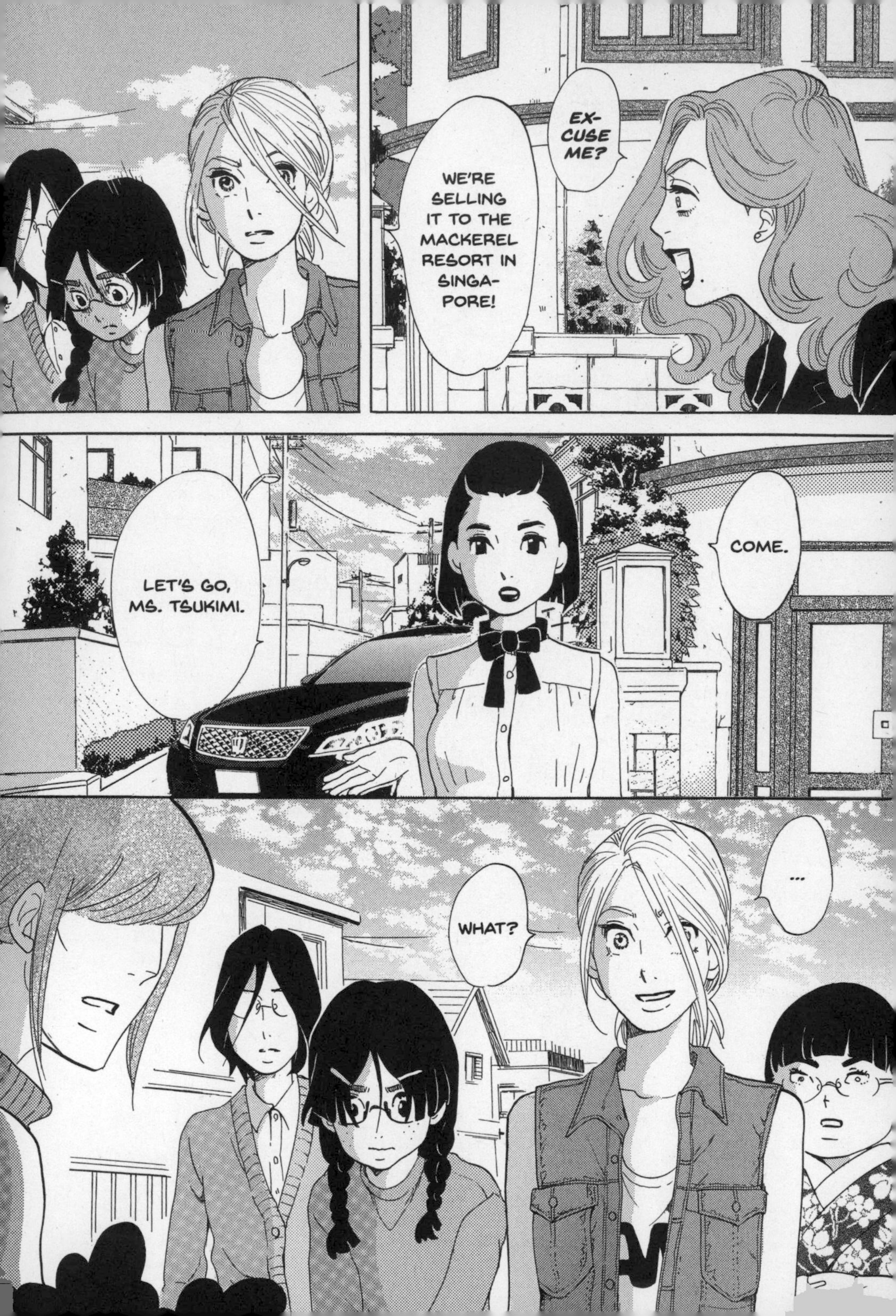
EX-CUSE ME?
WE'RE SELLING IT TO THE MACKEREL RESORT IN SINGA-PORE!
COME.
LET'S GO, MS. TSUKIMI.
...
WHAT?

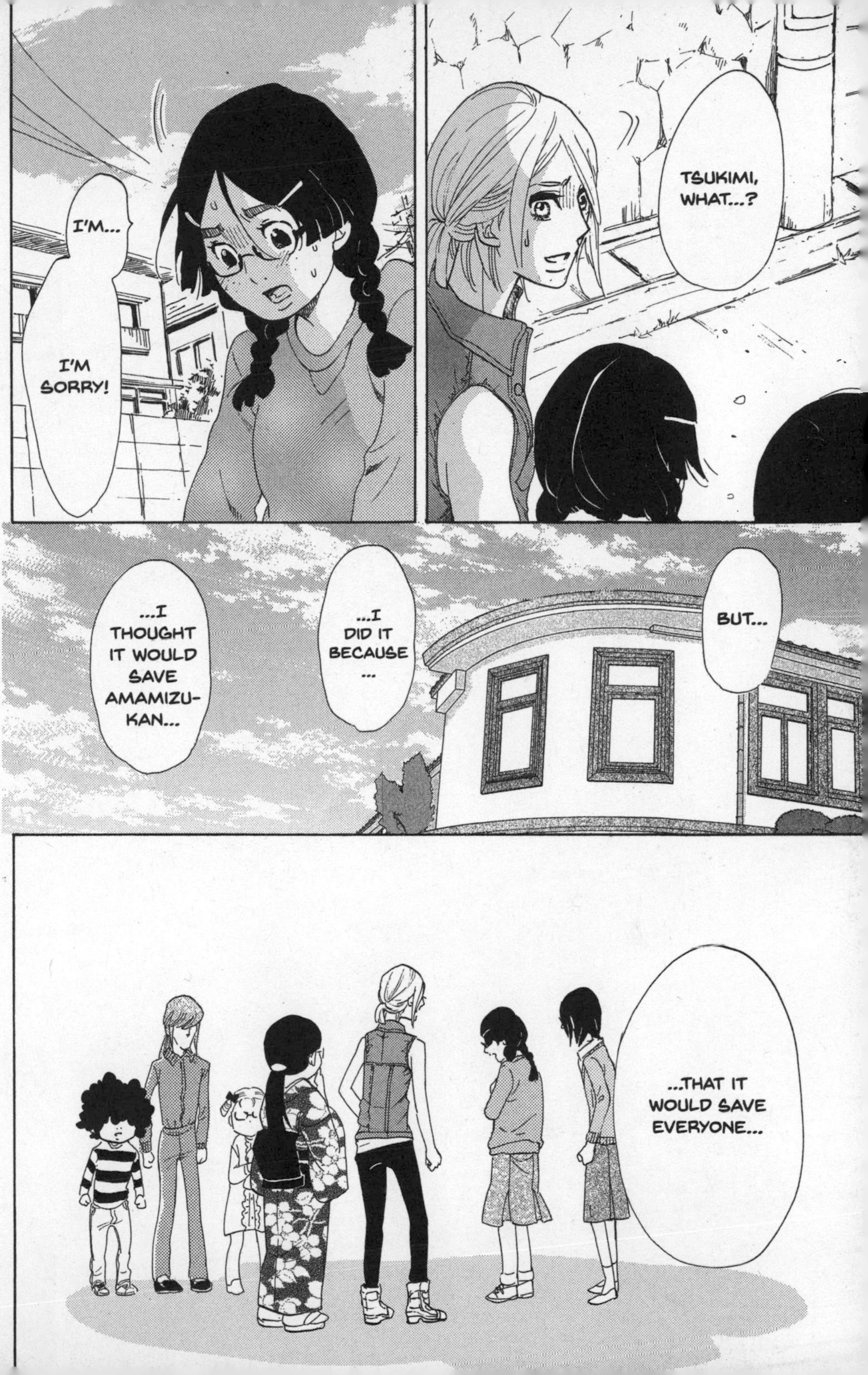
TSUKIMI, WHAT...?
I'M...
I'M SORRY!
BUT...
...I DID IT BECAUSE ...
...I THOUGHT IT WOULD SAVE AMAMIZU-KAN...
...THAT IT WOULD SAVE EVERYONE...

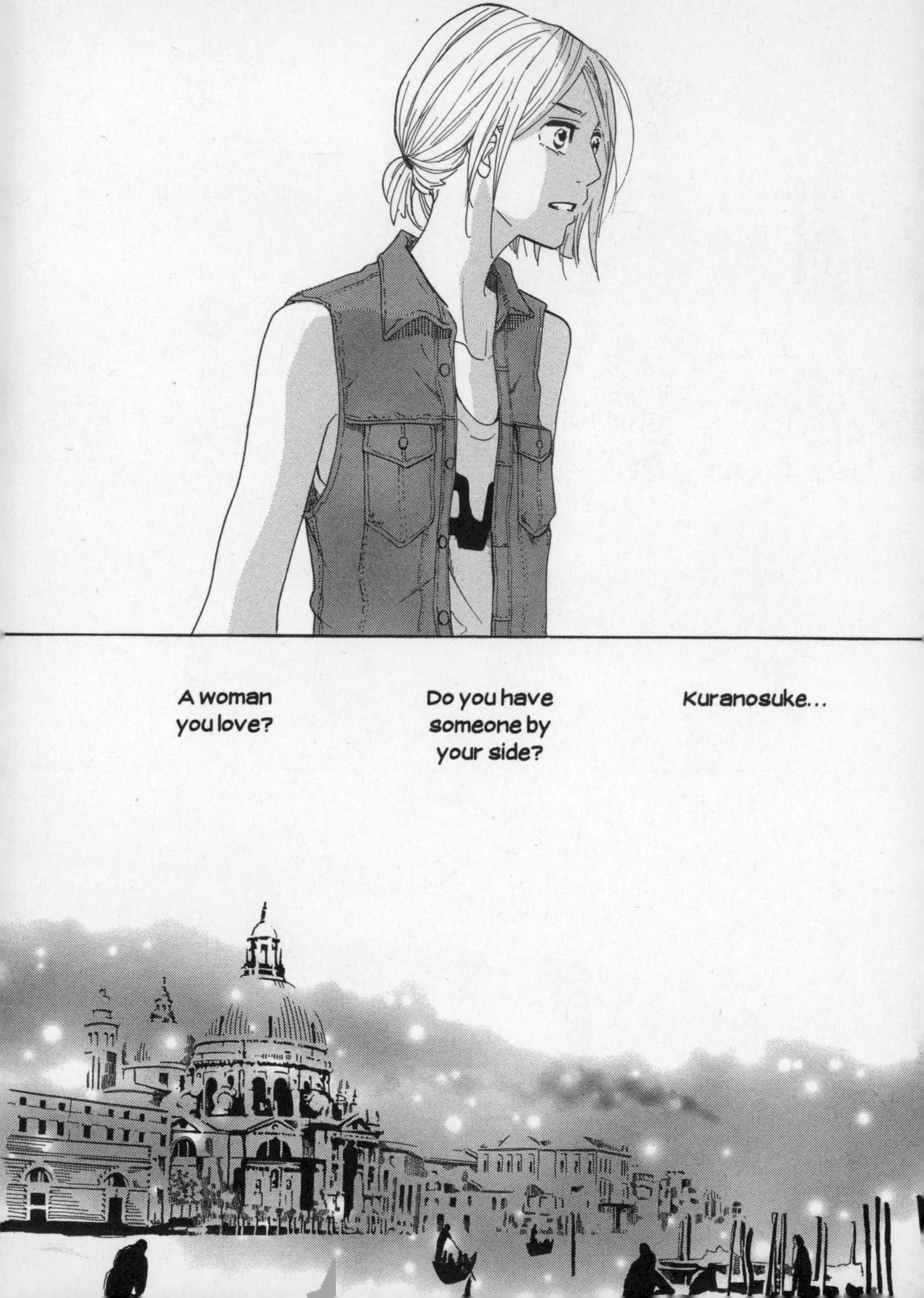
Kuranosuke...
Do you have someone by your side?
A woman you love?

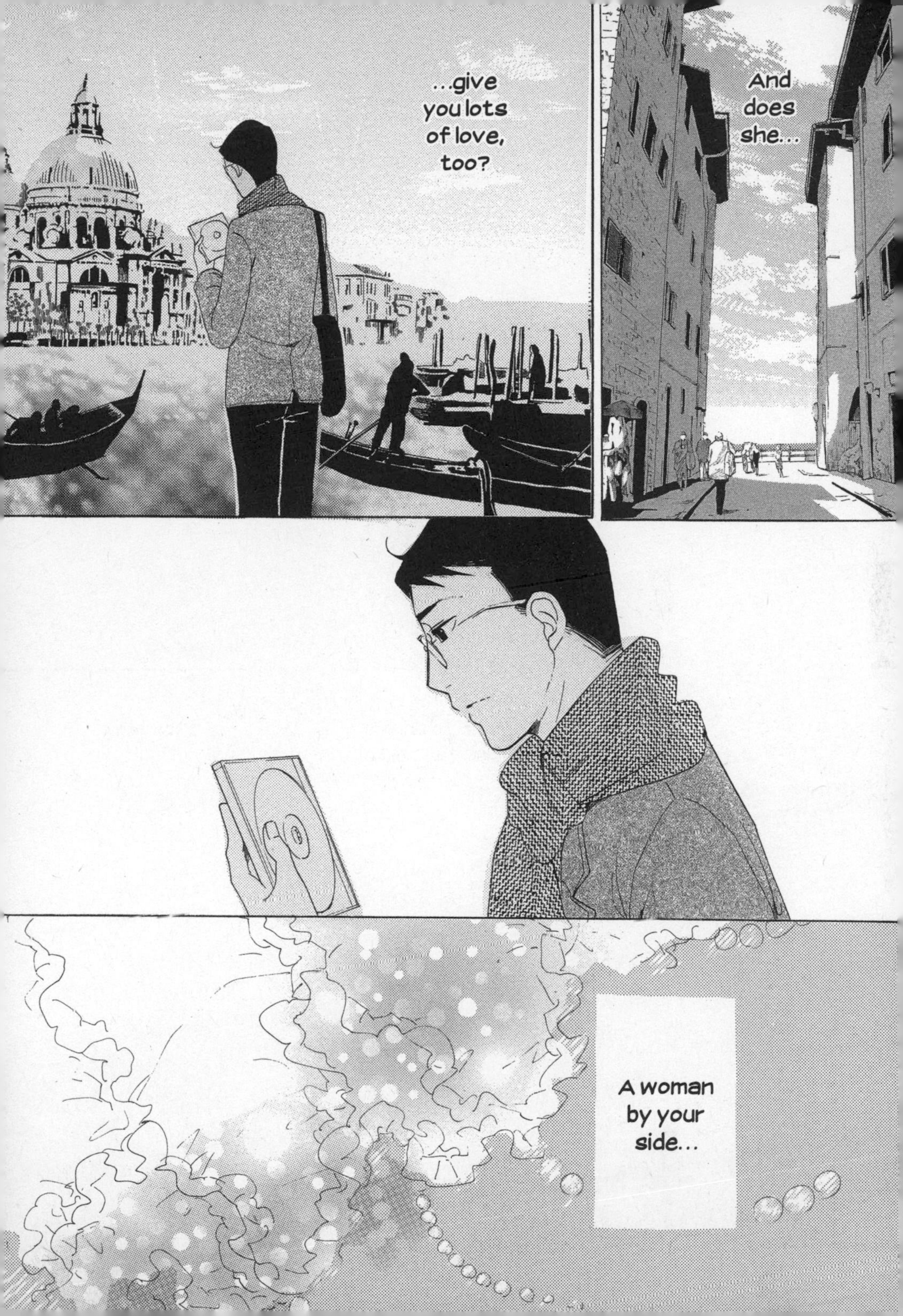
And does she...
...give you lots of love, too?
A woman by your side...

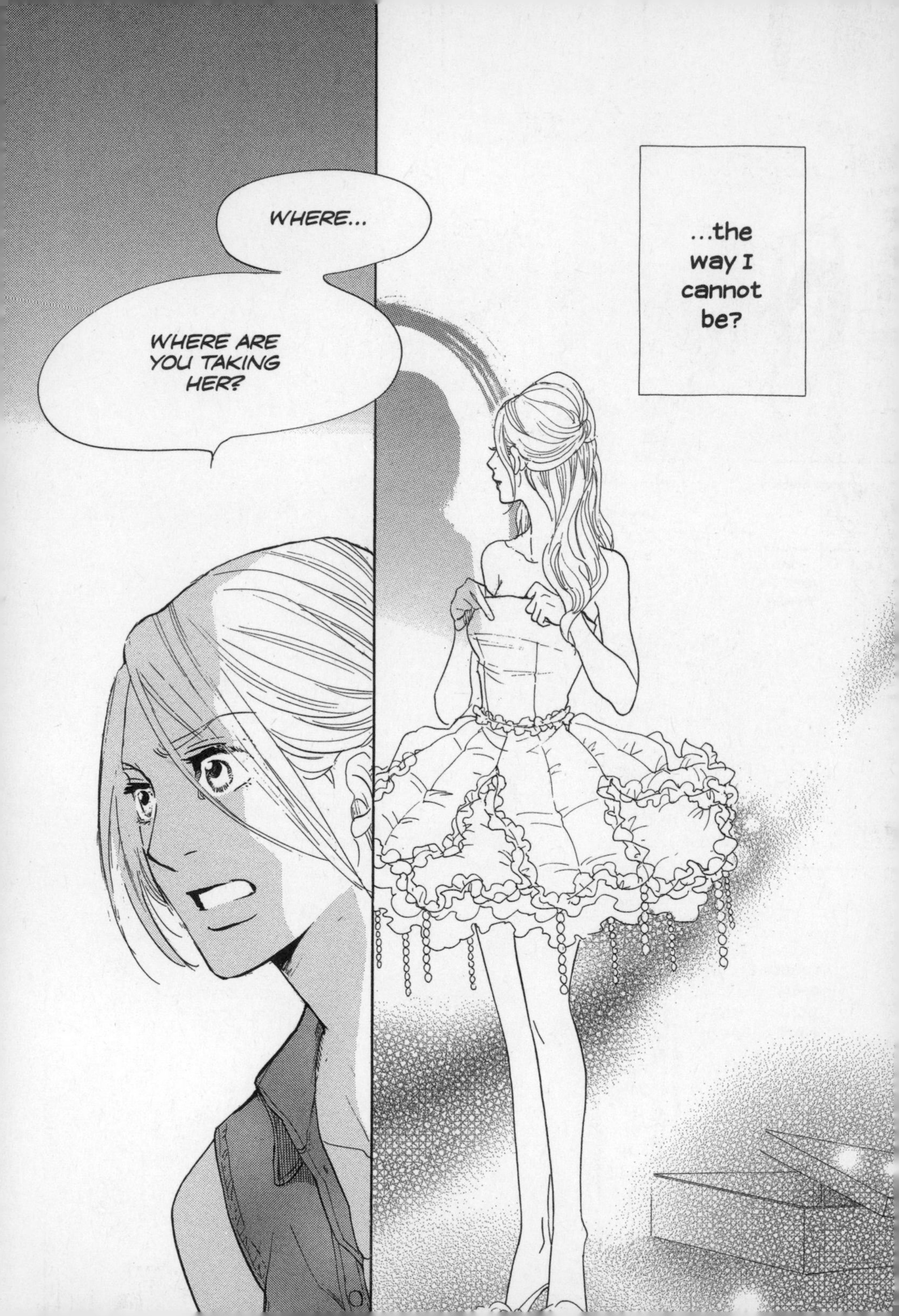
...the way I cannot be?
WHERE...
WHERE ARE YOU TAKING HER?

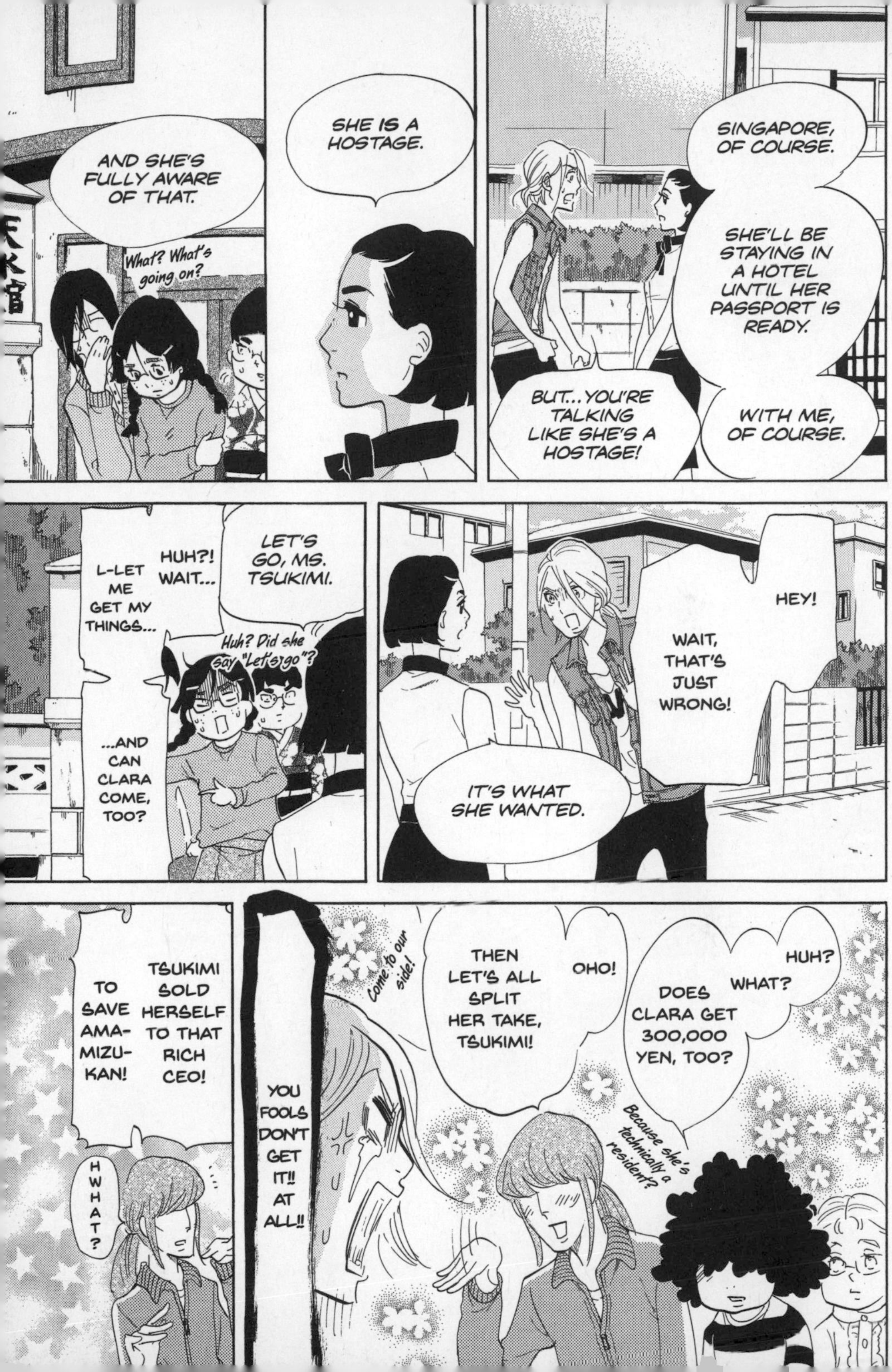
SINGAPORE, OF COURSE.
SHE'LL BE STAYING IN A HOTEL UNTIL HER PASSPORT IS READY.
WITH ME, OF COURSE.
BUT...YOU'RE TALKING LIKE SHE'S A HOSTAGE!
SHE IS A HOSTAGE.
AND SHE'S FULLY AWARE OF THAT.
What? What's going on?
HEY!
WAIT, THAT'S JUST WRONG!
IT'S WHAT SHE WANTED.
LET'S GO, MS. TSUKIMI.
HUH?! WAIT...
L-LET ME GET MY THINGS...
Huh? Did she say "Let's go"?
...AND CAN CLARA COME, TOO?
HUH? WHAT?
DOES CLARA GET 300,000 YEN, TOO?
Because she's technically a resident?
OHO!
THEN LET'S ALL SPLIT HER TAKE, TSUKIMI!
Come to our side!
YOU FOOLS DON'T GET IT!! AT ALL!!
TSUKIMI SOLD HERSELF TO THAT RICH CEO!
TO SAVE AMAMIZUKAN!
HWHAT?

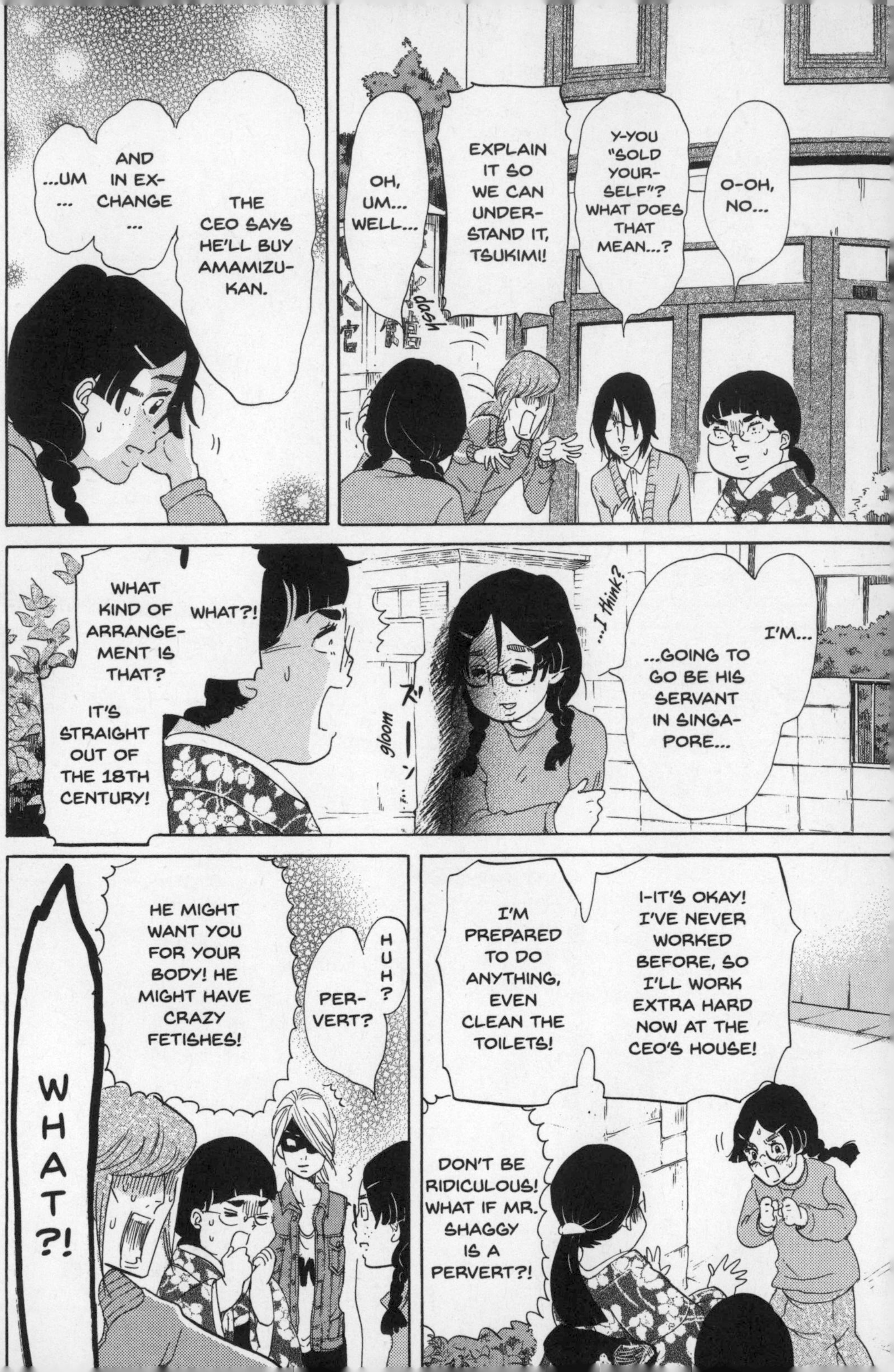
O-OH, NO...
Y-YOU "SOLD YOURSELF"? WHAT DOES THAT MEAN...?
EXPLAIN IT SO WE CAN UNDERSTAND IT, TSUKIMI!
dash
OH, UM... WELL...
THE CEO SAYS HE'LL BUY AMAMIZUKAN.
AND IN EXCHANGE ...
...UM ...
I'M...
...GOING TO GO BE HIS SERVANT IN SINGAPORE...
...I think?
gloom
WHAT?!
WHAT KIND OF ARRANGEMENT IS THAT?
IT'S STRAIGHT OUT OF THE 18TH CENTURY!
I-IT'S OKAY! I'VE NEVER WORKED BEFORE, SO I'LL WORK EXTRA HARD NOW AT THE CEO'S HOUSE!
I'M PREPARED TO DO ANYTHING, EVEN CLEAN THE TOILETS!
DON'T BE RIDICULOUS! WHAT IF MR. SHAGGY IS A PERVERT?!
HUH?
PERVERT?
HE MIGHT WANT YOU FOR YOUR BODY! HE MIGHT HAVE CRAZY FETISHES!
WHAT?!

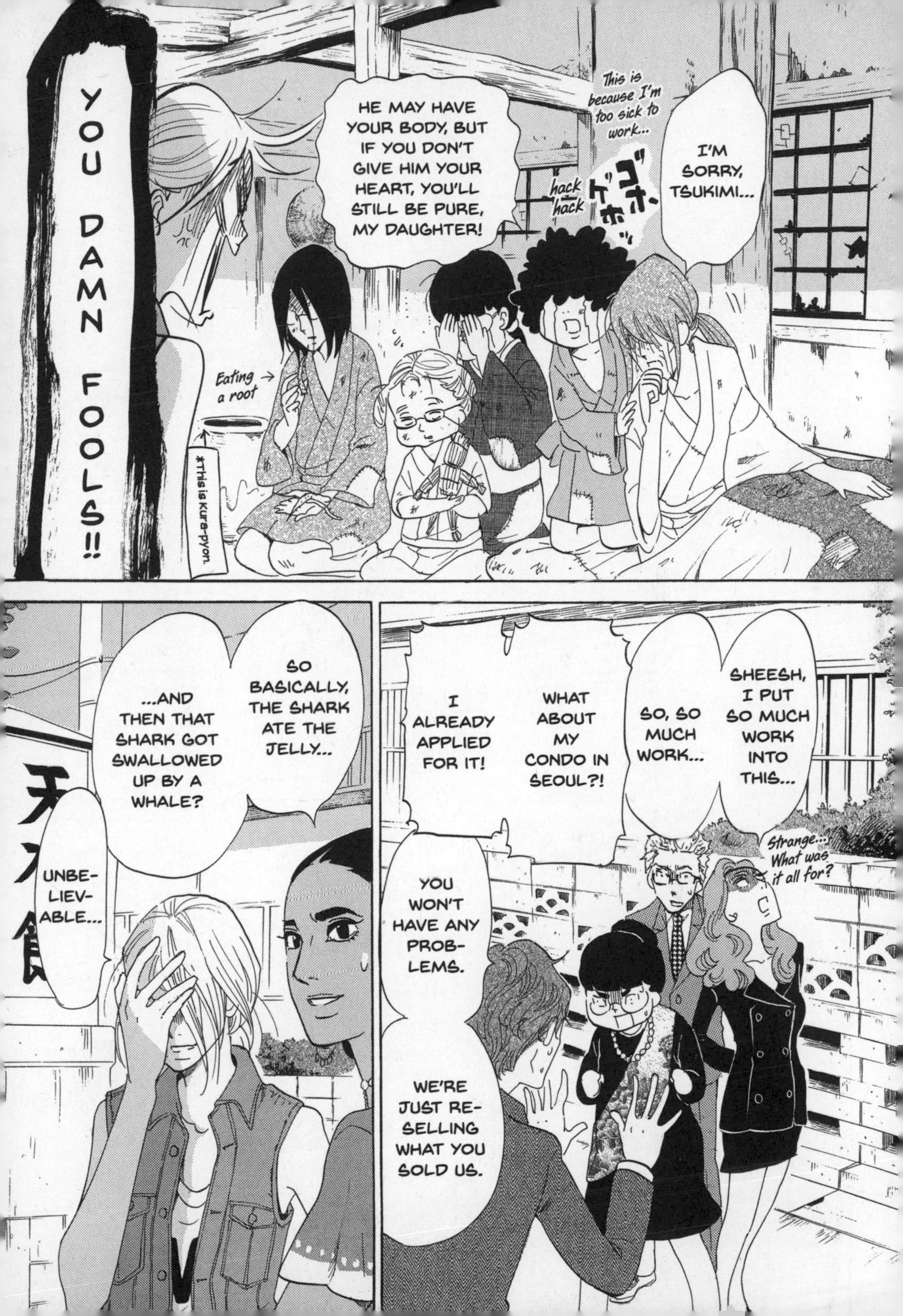

I'M SORRY, TSUKIMI...
This is because I'm too sick to work...
hack hack
ゲホゴホッ
HE MAY HAVE YOUR BODY, BUT IF YOU DON'T GIVE HIM YOUR HEART, YOU'LL STILL BE PURE, MY DAUGHTER!
YOU DAMN FOOLS!!
Eating a root
*This is Kura-pyon.
SHEESH, I PUT SO MUCH WORK INTO THIS...
SO, SO MUCH WORK...
WHAT ABOUT MY CONDO IN SEOUL?!
I ALREADY APPLIED FOR IT!
Strange... What was it all for?
YOU WON'T HAVE ANY PROBLEMS.
WE'RE JUST RE-SELLING WHAT YOU SOLD US.
SO BASICALLY, THE SHARK ATE THE JELLY...
...AND THEN THAT SHARK GOT SWALLOWED UP BY A WHALE?
UNBELIEVABLE...

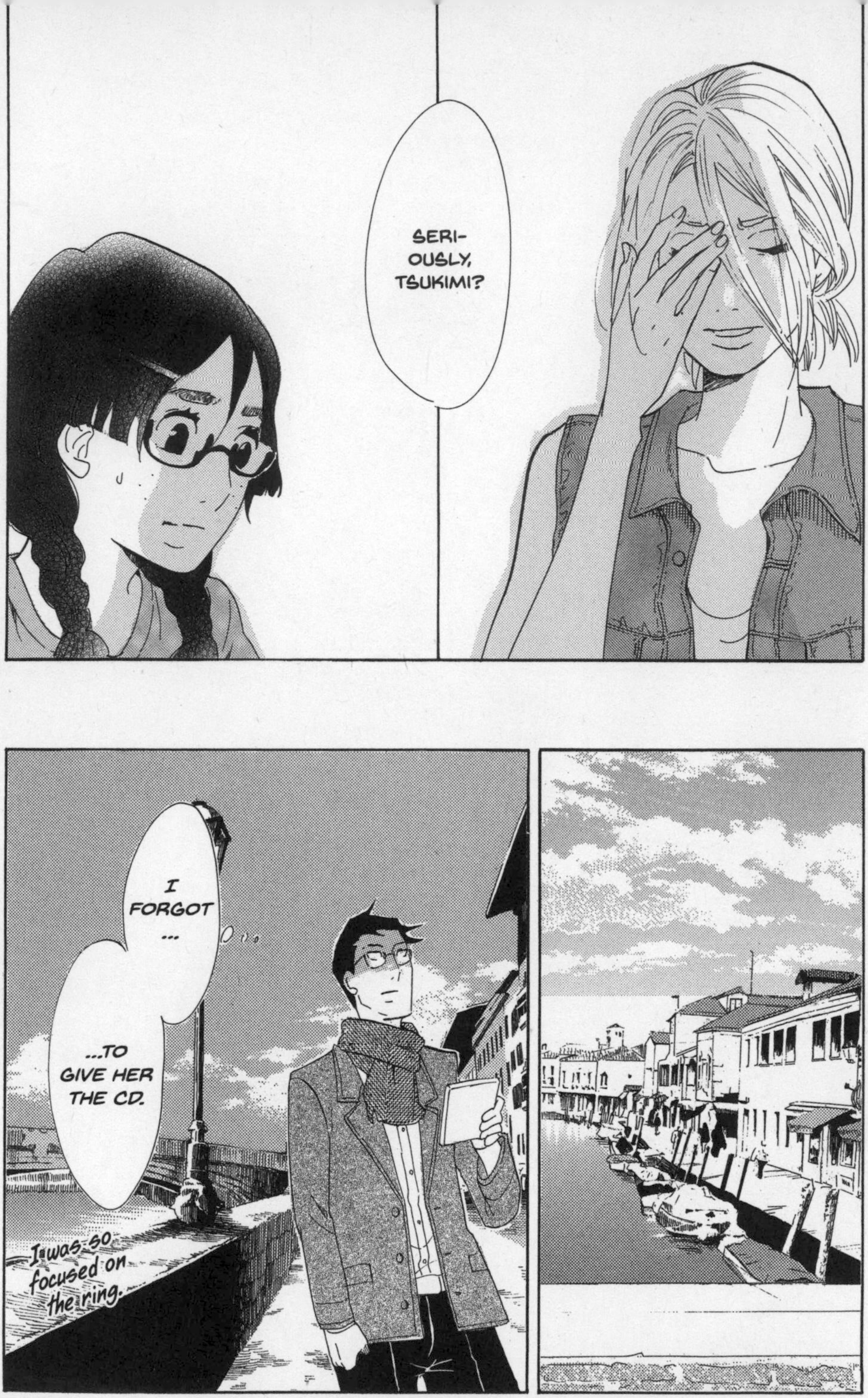
SERI-OUSLY, TSUKIMI?
I FORGOT ...
...TO GIVE HER THE CD.
I was so focused on the ring.

Princess Jellyfish Vol. 6/End

Latest Entry!!
Higashimura Productions Crime Blotter

"A Traitor of Few Words"

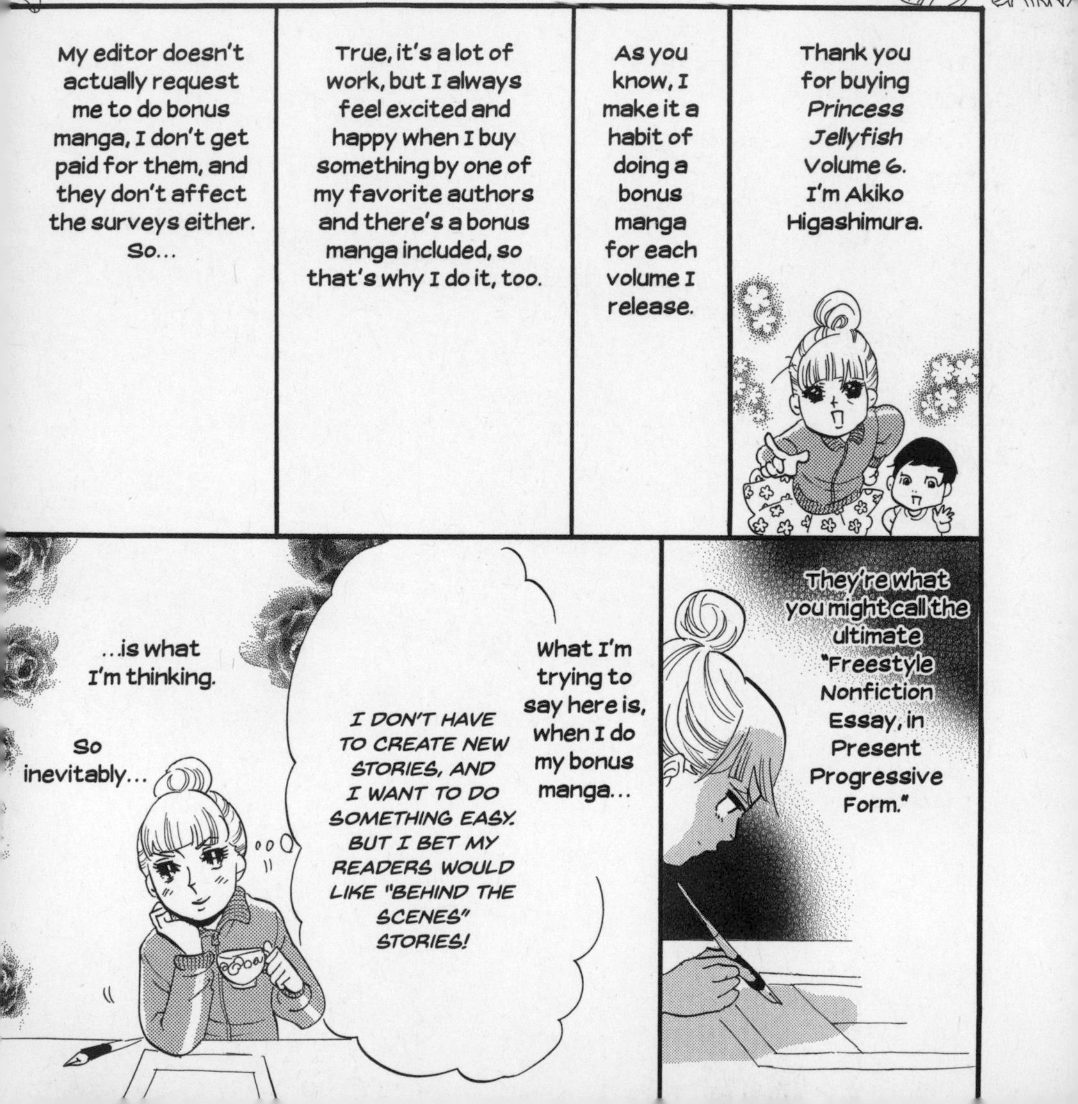

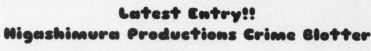

Thank you for buying *Princess Jellyfish* Volume 6. I'm Akiko Higashimura.
As you know, I make it a habit of doing a bonus manga for each volume I release.
True, it's a lot of work, but I always feel excited and happy when I buy something by one of my favorite authors and there's a bonus manga included, so that's why I do it, too.
My editor doesn't actually request me to do bonus manga, I don't get paid for them, and they don't affect the surveys either. So...
They're what you might call the ultimate "Freestyle Nonfiction Essay, in Present Progressive Form."
What I'm trying to say here is, when I do my bonus manga...
I DON'T HAVE TO CREATE NEW STORIES, AND I WANT TO DO SOMETHING EASY. BUT I BET MY READERS WOULD LIKE "BEHIND THE SCENES" STORIES!
...is what I'm thinking.
So inevitably...

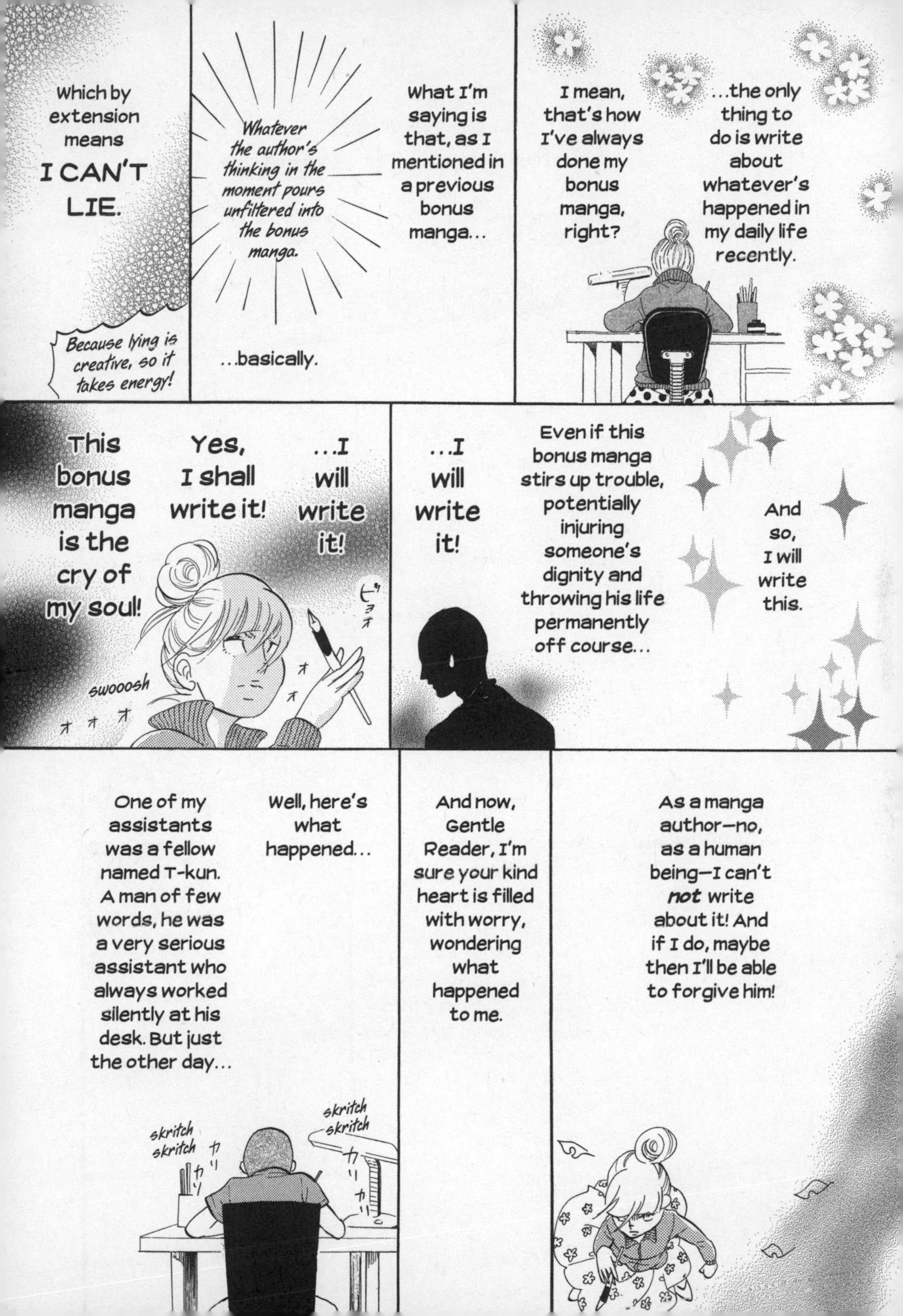

...the only thing to do is write about whatever's happened in my daily life recently.
I mean, that's how I've always done my bonus manga, right?
What I'm saying is that, as I mentioned in a previous bonus manga...
Whatever the author's thinking in the moment pours unfiltered into the bonus manga.
...basically.
Which by extension means I CAN'T LIE.
Because lying is creative, so it takes energy!
And so, I will write this.
Even if this bonus manga stirs up trouble, potentially injuring someone's dignity and throwing his life permanently off course...
...I will write it!
...I will write it!
Yes, I shall write it!
This bonus manga is the cry of my soul!
swooosh
As a manga author—no, as a human being—I can't *not* write about it! And if I do, maybe then I'll be able to forgive him!
And now, Gentle Reader, I'm sure your kind heart is filled with worry, wondering what happened to me.
Well, here's what happened...
One of my assistants was a fellow named T-kun. A man of few words, he was a very serious assistant who always worked silently at his desk. But just the other day...
skritch skritch
skritch skritch

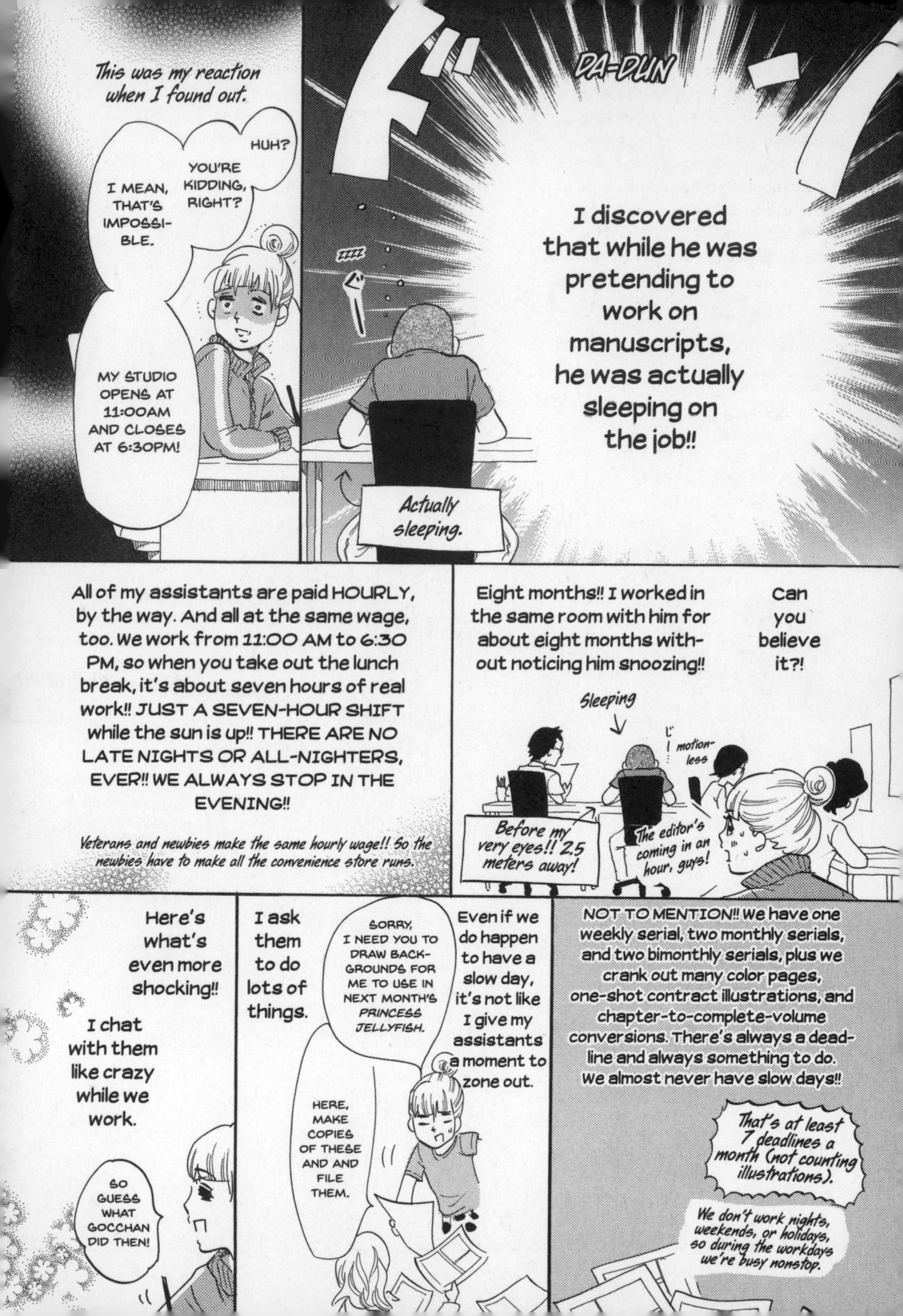
DA-DUN
I discovered that while he was pretending to work on manuscripts, he was actually sleeping on the job!!
ZZZZ
Actually sleeping.
This was my reaction when I found out.
HUH?
YOU'RE KIDDING, RIGHT?
I MEAN, THAT'S IMPOSSI-BLE.
MY STUDIO OPENS AT 11:00AM AND CLOSES AT 6:30PM!
Can you believe it?!
Eight months!! I worked in the same room with him for about eight months with-out noticing him snoozing!!
Sleeping
motion-less
Before my very eyes!! 2.5 meters away!
The editor's coming in an hour, guys!
All of my assistants are paid HOURLY, by the way. And all at the same wage, too. We work from 11:00 AM to 6:30 PM, so when you take out the lunch break, it's about seven hours of real work!! JUST A SEVEN-HOUR SHIFT while the sun is up!! THERE ARE NO LATE NIGHTS OR ALL-NIGHTERS, EVER!! WE ALWAYS STOP IN THE EVENING!!
Veterans and newbies make the same hourly wage!! So the newbies have to make all the convenience store runs.
NOT TO MENTION!! We have one weekly serial, two monthly serials, and two bimonthly serials, plus we crank out many color pages, one-shot contract illustrations, and chapter-to-complete-volume conversions. There's always a dead-line and always something to do. We almost never have slow days!!
That's at least 7 deadlines a month (not counting illustrations).
We don't work nights, weekends, or holidays, so during the workdays we're busy nonstop.
Even if we do happen to have a slow day, it's not like I give my assistants a moment to zone out.
I ask them to do lots of things.
SORRY, I NEED YOU TO DRAW BACK-GROUNDS FOR ME TO USE IN NEXT MONTH'S PRINCESS JELLYFISH.
HERE, MAKE COPIES OF THESE AND AND FILE THEM.
Here's what's even more shocking!!
I chat with them like crazy while we work.
SO GUESS WHAT GOCCHAN DID THEN!

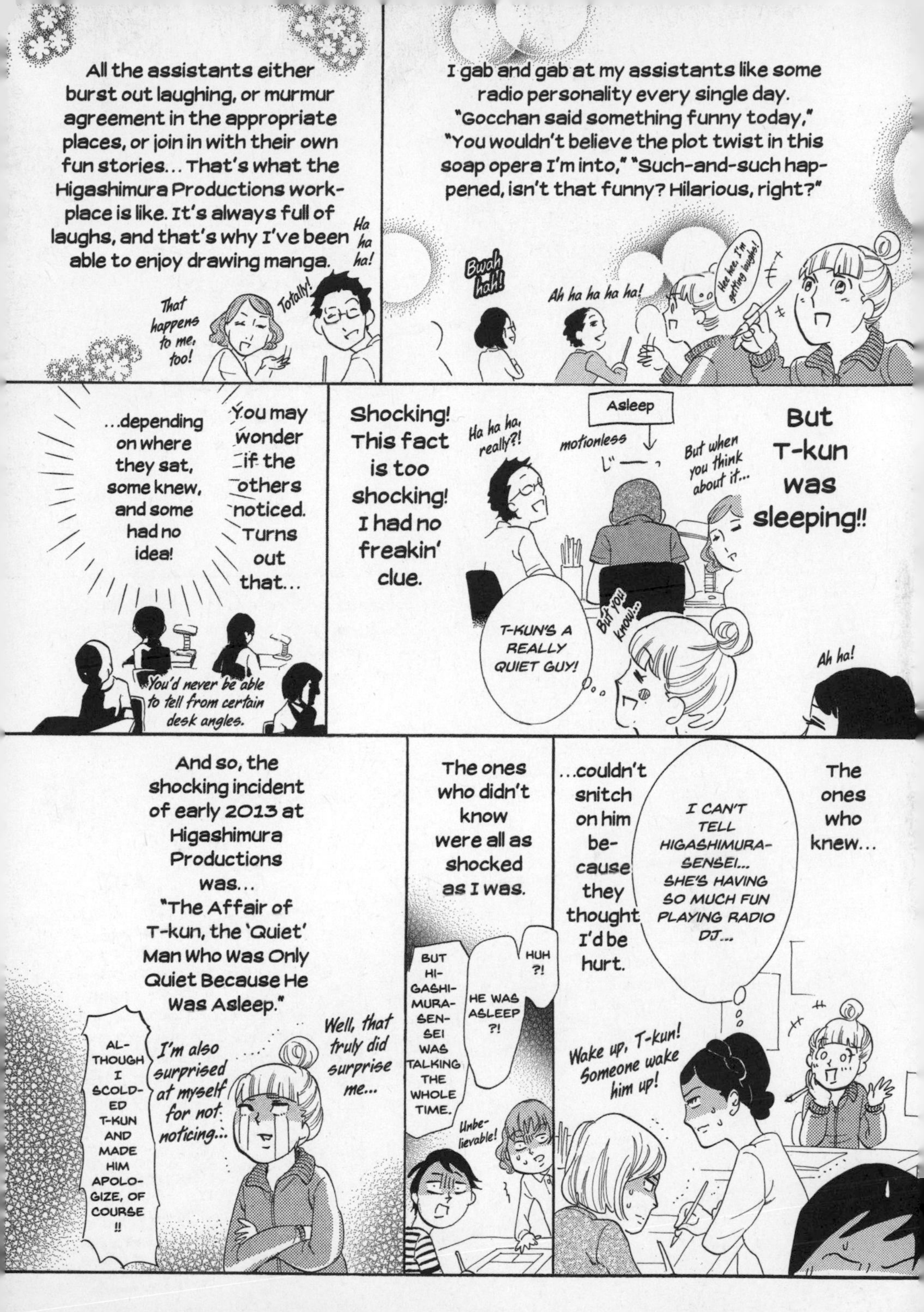
I gab and gab at my assistants like some radio personality every single day. "Gocchan said something funny today," "You wouldn't believe the plot twist in this soap opera I'm into," "Such-and-such happened, isn't that funny? Hilarious, right?"
Hee hee, I'm getting laughs!
Ah ha ha ha ha!
Bwah hah!
All the assistants either burst out laughing, or murmur agreement in the appropriate places, or join in with their own fun stories... That's what the Higashimura Productions workplace is like. It's always full of laughs, and that's why I've been able to enjoy drawing manga.
Ha ha ha!
Totally!
That happens to me, too!
But T-kun was sleeping!!
Asleep
But when you think about it...
motionless
Ha ha ha, really?!
Shocking! This fact is too shocking! I had no freakin' clue.
But you know...
T-KUN'S A REALLY QUIET GUY!
Ah ha!
You may wonder if the others noticed. Turns out that...
...depending on where they sat, some knew, and some had no idea!
You'd never be able to tell from certain desk angles.
The ones who knew...
...couldn't snitch on him because they thought I'd be hurt.
I CAN'T TELL HIGASHIMURA-SENSEI... SHE'S HAVING SO MUCH FUN PLAYING RADIO DJ...
Wake up, T-kun! Someone wake him up!
The ones who didn't know were all as shocked as I was.
HUH?!
HE WAS ASLEEP?!
BUT HIGASHIMURA-SENSEI WAS TALKING THE WHOLE TIME.
Unbelievable!
And so, the shocking incident of early 2013 at Higashimura Productions was... "The Affair of T-kun, the 'Quiet' Man Who Was Only Quiet Because He Was Asleep."
Well, that truly did surprise me...
I'm also surprised at myself for not noticing...
ALTHOUGH I SCOLDED T-KUN AND MADE HIM APOLOGIZE, OF COURSE!!

Translation Notes

Teru-teru-bozu, page 177
A *teru-teru-bozu* is a doll hung in a window frame, or from the eaves, as a good-weather charm, to keep the rain away. For more information, see Volume 2 translation notes.

Interpret him, Natsuko Toda style!, page 183
Natsuko Toda is a Japanese interpreter and film subtitle translator.

An extra from the "Hone Hone Rock" video, with Fune's hairdo, page 219
"Hone Hone Rock" is a song featuring rock-dancing skeletons in the music video. Fune is Sazae's mother in the manga and anime *Sazae-san*. She does indeed have the hairstyle Mayaya is sporting here.

Hanafuda and Koi-Koi, page 236
Hanafuda, or "flower cards," are a type of Japanese playing card that comes in decks of 48. The particular hanafuda game they're playing here is called Koi-Koi, and Ban-ba just called the name of the game to keep going for another *yaku* card combination beyond whatever *yaku* she already formed. Her new *yaku* "boar, deer, butterfly" is a three-of-a-kind hand.

Aibou, which the society matrons must like, page 238
Aibou, which translates to "Partners," is a Japanese police procedural. The detective duo referred to in the title are considered outsiders even within the police force, and generally fall into a Sherlock Holmes and John Watson sort of relationship as they take the liberty of involving themselves in cases other departments can't solve. It has been on-air since 2000, and is currently on Season 14.

Ring size 11, page 242
Ring size measurements vary from region to region. The Japanese ring size 11 is equivalent to an American ring size 6.

Back from Han already?, page 253
Mayaya is pronouncing the name of South Korea in the Chinese way, which is actually also closer to the Korean pronunciation.

1% of Anything, page 254
1% of Anything is a 2003 K-drama starring Gang Dong Won, whom you may remember from Higashimura's previous bonus manga. He's the "boy she likes."

You wanna do a "Run, Melos!" skit?, page 264
"Run, Melos!", sometimes called "Run, Moerus!", is a short story by Osamu Dazai. It's been adapted multiple times into animated films.

A Vagabond-level masterpiece, page 285
Vagabond is a hit manga by Takehiko Inoue, who is also the author of *Slam Dunk*.

Salaryman, page 285
Comparable to the term "businessmen," salaryman refers to men who have a salaried job. It is common for a salaryman to enter the workforce right after high school or college. Many stay at the same company for the majority, or the entirety, of their lives, and often suffer from overworking. Because of this, "salaryman" can be used to negatively refer to a man who is not unique, and who can only define his identity through monotonous work.

Urashima Taro, page 286
Amars and company sure do love Urashima Taro! As you may remember from Volume 3, this is the fairy tale boy who rode to the Dragon King's Palace on the back of a turtle. Their undersea journey was the turtle's thank-you gift after Urashima Taro saved it from a group of bullies.

Ukyo-san wearing a Hawaiian shirt in Hawaii, page 308
Ukyo Sugishita is Yutaka Mizutani's "Sherlock" character on *Aibou* and a known Jiji favorite. In her hazy state here, she's referring to him familiarly by his first name!

Far Away, So Close, page 311
This is the English title of Masahiko Nagasawa's 2013 film *Tooku de Zutto Soba ni Iru*, based on Kyoko Inukai's novel about a 27-year-old woman who loses a decade of her memories in a fateful accident.

Cool Japan TV Show, page 314
Cool Japan is a weekly TV series that has been airing since 2005, both internationally and in Japan, through NHK. It is a show featuring discussions, panels, and interviews with non-native Japanese individuals who are fans of Japanese culture. Topics of discussion change from episode to episode. The term "cool Japan" is based on the concept that Japan's culture is "cool" to outsiders, and has the soft power to indirectly influence aspects of the Japanese economy, politics, global status, and more.

Amuro moving out!, page 331
Banba is playing Amuro Ray, the famous protagonist of the original *Mobile Suit Gundam* series, shouting just before he flies off to battle.

Jerry Fujio vs. Keun Jang Suk, page 332
Jerry Fujio is an actor known for movies such as *A Colt Is My Passport*; Keun Jang Suk is a fictional scrambling of the name Jang Keun Suk, a trilingual singer and actor whose credits include the K-drama *Beethoven Virus*.

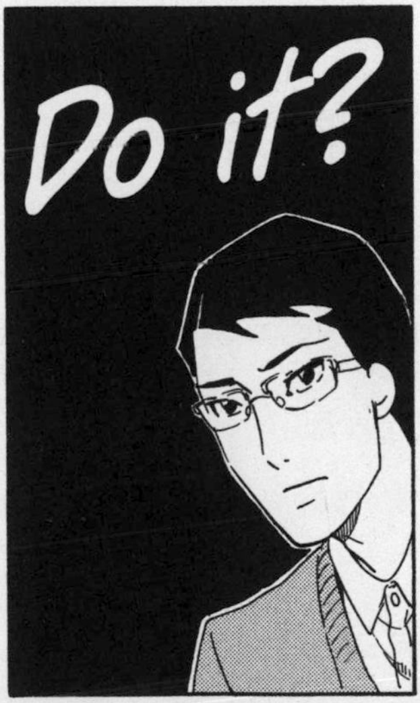
Do it?

The prince in his dark days

By **Hico Yamanaka**

A drunkard for a father, a household of poverty... For 17-year-old Atsuko, misfortune is all she knows and believes in. Until one day, a chance encounter with Itaru–the wealthy heir of a huge corporation–changes everything. The two look identical, uncannily so. When Itaru curiously goes missing, Atsuko is roped into being his stand-in. There, in his shoes, Atsuko must parade like a prince in a palace. She encounters many new experiences, but at what cost...?

THE SPACE OPERA
MASTERPIECE FROM
MANGA LEGEND
LEIJI MATSUMOTO
AVAILABLE FOR THE
FIRST TIME IN
ENGLISH!

LEIJI MATSUMOTO'S
Queen
Emeraldas

KC
KODANSHA
COMICS

AKIRA

THE TIMELESS SCI-FI EPIC RETURNS LIKE NEVER BEFORE!

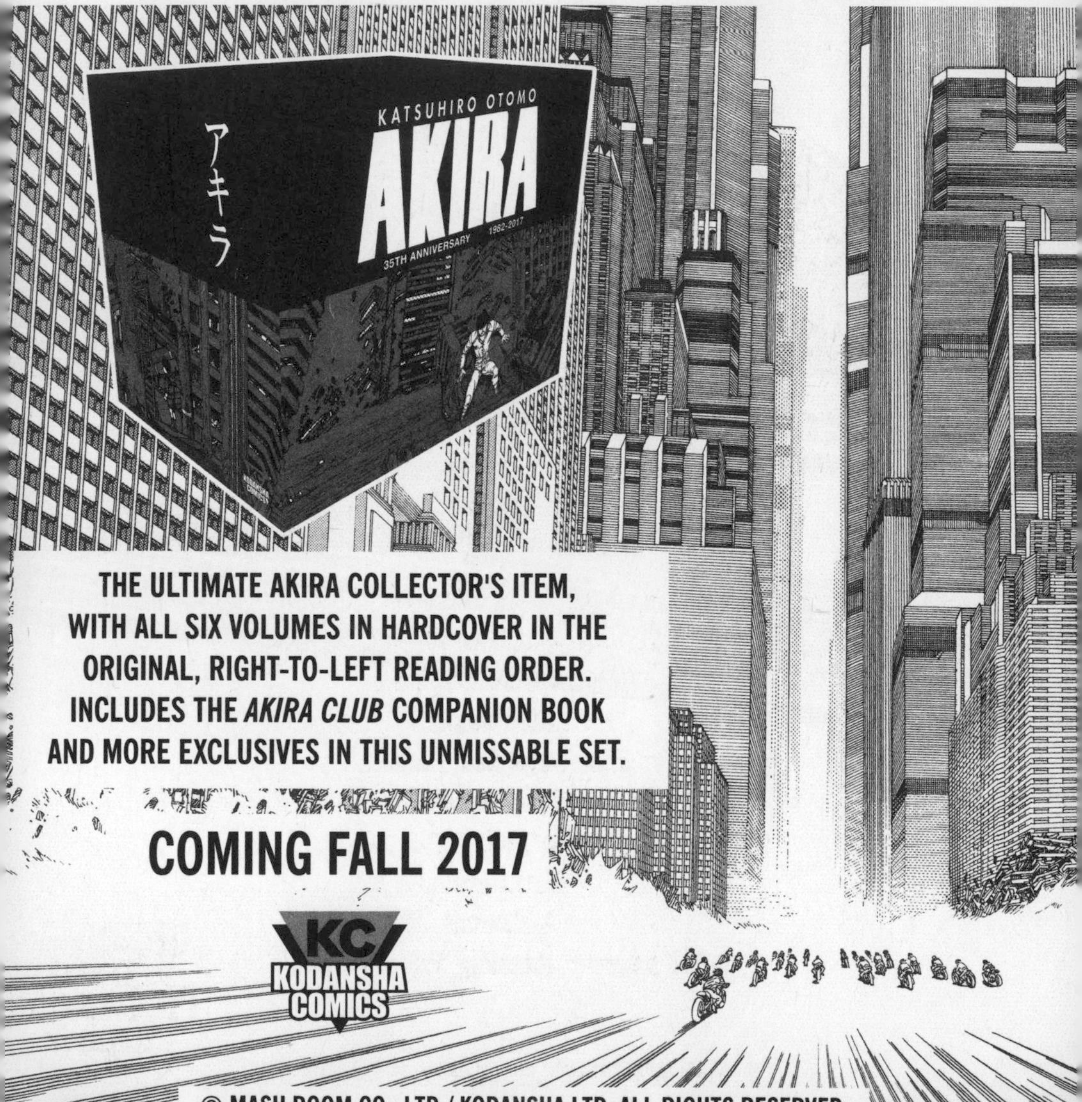
KATSUHIRO OTOMO
アキラ
AKIRA
35TH ANNIVERSARY
1982-2017
THE ULTIMATE AKIRA COLLECTOR'S ITEM, WITH ALL SIX VOLUMES IN HARDCOVER IN THE ORIGINAL, RIGHT-TO-LEFT READING ORDER. INCLUDES THE *AKIRA CLUB* COMPANION BOOK AND MORE EXCLUSIVES IN THIS UNMISSABLE SET.
COMING FALL 2017
KC
KODANSHA COMICS

OTOMO

A GLOBAL TRIBUTE TO
THE MIND BEHIND AKIRA

A celebration of manga legend Katsuhiro Otomo from more than 80
world-renowned fine artists and comics legends
With contributions from:
- Stan Sakai
- Tomer and Asaf Hanuka
- Sara Pichelli
- Range Murata
- Aleksi Briclot
And more!
168 pages of stunning, full-color art

KC
KODANSHA
COMICS

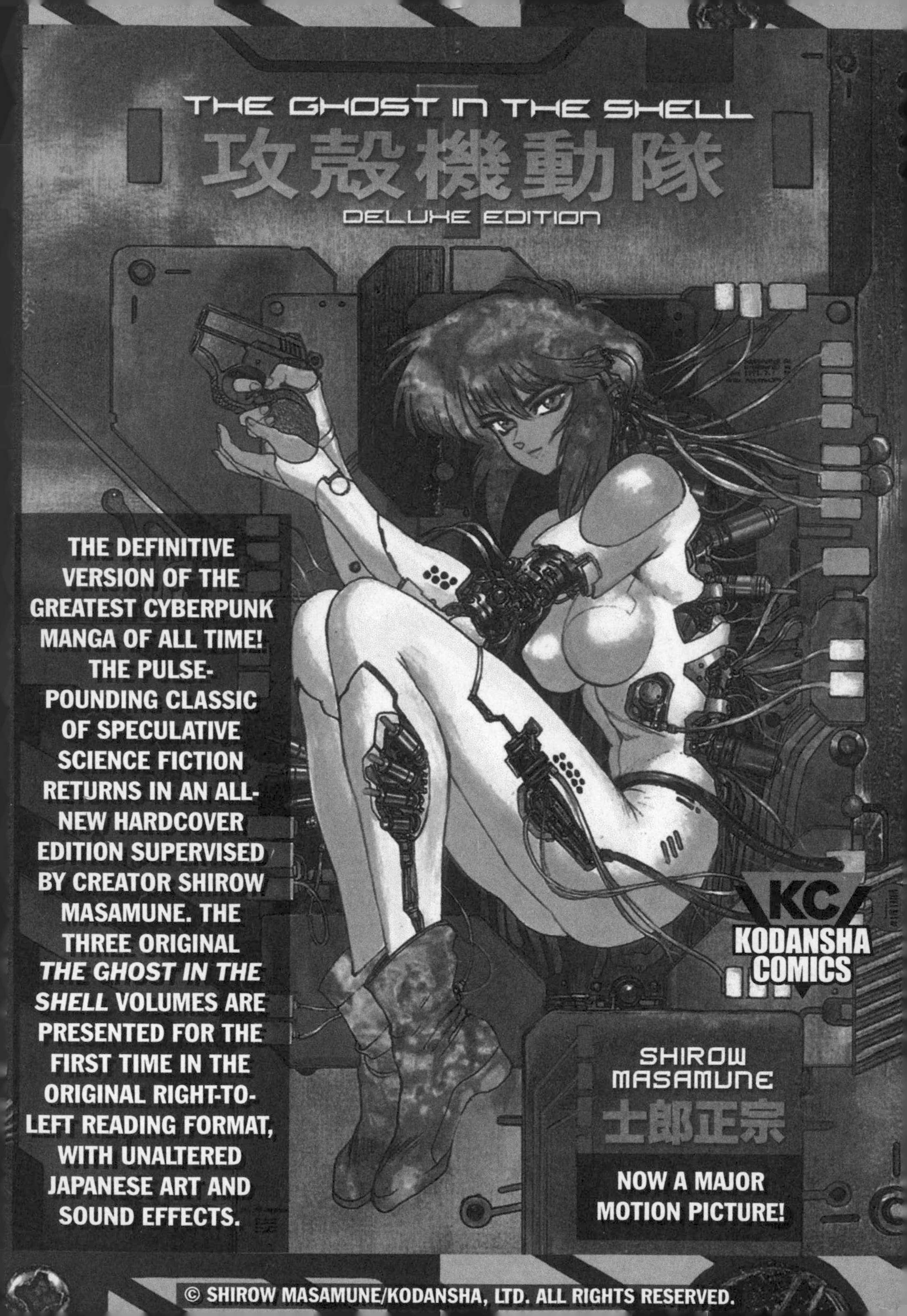

THE GHOST IN THE SHELL
攻殻機動隊
DELUXE EDITION
THE DEFINITIVE VERSION OF THE GREATEST CYBERPUNK MANGA OF ALL TIME! THE PULSE-POUNDING CLASSIC OF SPECULATIVE SCIENCE FICTION RETURNS IN AN ALL-NEW HARDCOVER EDITION SUPERVISED BY CREATOR SHIROW MASAMUNE. THE THREE ORIGINAL *THE GHOST IN THE SHELL* VOLUMES ARE PRESENTED FOR THE FIRST TIME IN THE ORIGINAL RIGHT-TO-LEFT READING FORMAT, WITH UNALTERED JAPANESE ART AND SOUND EFFECTS.
KC
KODANSHA COMICS
SHIROW MASAMUNE
士郎正宗
NOW A MAJOR MOTION PICTURE!
© SHIROW MASAMUNE/KODANSHA, LTD. ALL RIGHTS RESERVED.

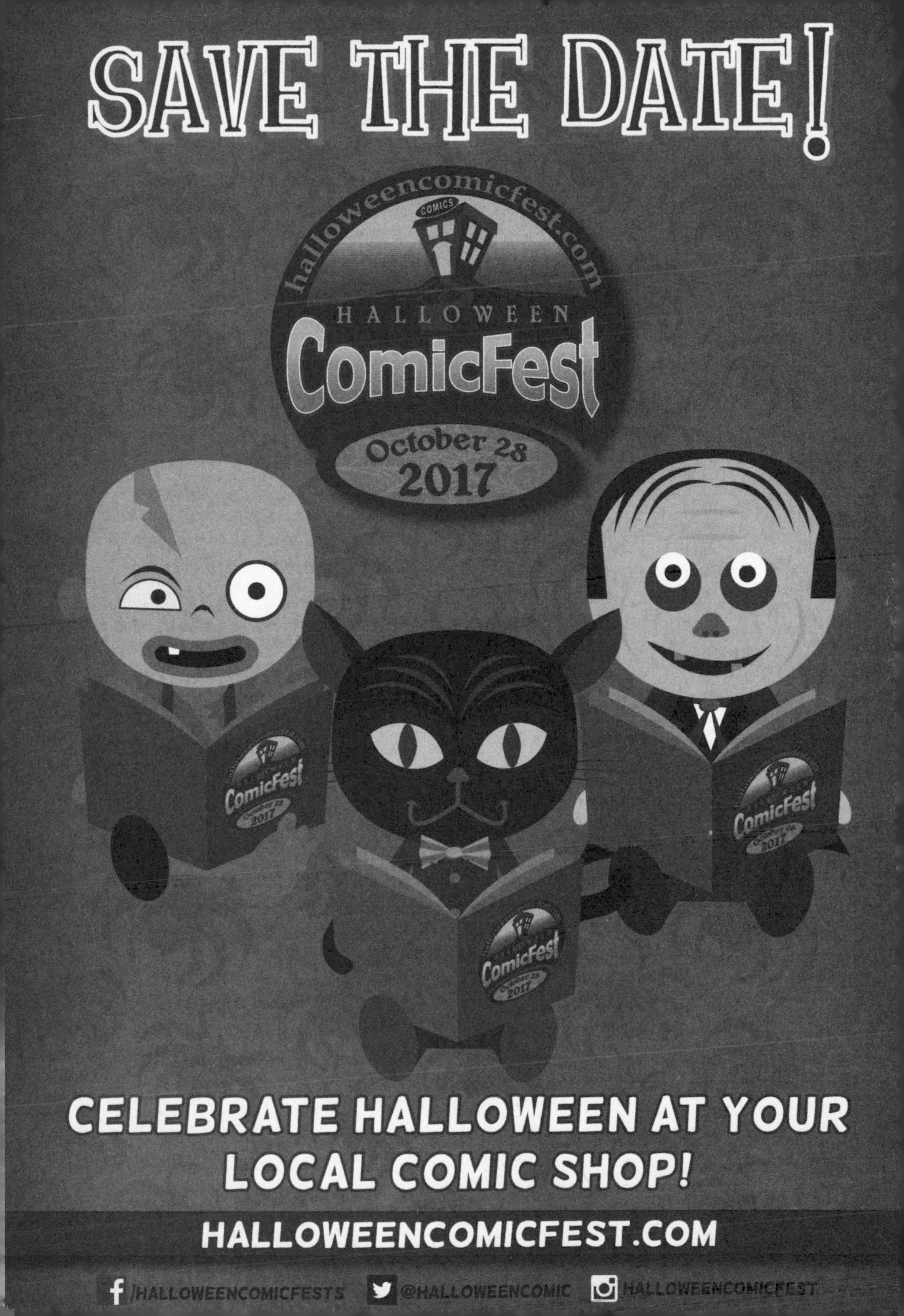
SAVE THE DATE!
halloweencomicfest.com
COMICS
HALLOWEEN
ComicFest
October 28
2017
CELEBRATE HALLOWEEN AT YOUR
LOCAL COMIC SHOP!
HALLOWEENCOMICFEST.COM
/HALLOWEENCOMICFESTS
@HALLOWEENCOMIC
HALLOWEENCOMICFEST

A Kodansha Comics Trade Paperback Original.

Princess Jellyfish volume 6 copyright © 2013 Akiko Higashimura
English translation copyright © 2017 Akiko Higashimura

Published in the United States by Kodansha Comics,
an imprint of Kodansha USA Publishing, LLC, New York.

Publication rights for this English edition arranged through Kodansha Ltd., Tokyo.

First published in Japan in 2013 by Kodansha Ltd., Tokyo,
as *Kuragehime* volumes 11 & 12.

ISBN 978-1-63236-232-2

Icon design by UCHIKOGA tomoyuki & RAITA ryoko (CHProduction Inc.)

Printed in the United States of America.

www.kodanshacomics.com

9 8 7 6 5 4 3 2 1

Translation: Sarah Alys Lindholm
Lettering: Carl Vanstiphout
Additional Layout: Belynda Ungurath
Editing: Haruko Hashimoto
Kodansha Comics Edition Cover Design: Phil Balsman